The Divine Politician

Samuel Cooper
and the American Revolution
in Boston

Samuel Cooper by John S. Copley

Courtesy of the Williams College Museum of Art

The Divine Politician

Samuel Cooper
and the American Revolution
in Boston

CHARLES W. AKERS

Northeastern University Press   Boston   1982

Book and jacket design, Leon Steinmetz

Northeastern University Press
Copyright © 1982 Charles W. Akers

Library of Congress Cataloging in Publication Data

Akers, Charles W.
    The divine politician.

    Includes bibliographical references and index.
    1. Cooper, Samuel, 1725-1783. 2. Boston (Mass.)
—Politics and government—Revolution, 1775-1783.
3. Politicians—Massachusetts—Boston—Biography.
4. Congregational churches—Clergy—Biography.
5. Clergy—Massachusetts—Boston—Biography.
I. Title.
F73.44.C7A38   973.3'092'4 [B]   81-18917
ISBN 0-930350-19-7   AACR2

ISBN 0-930350-19-7

87 86 85 84 83 82   8 7 6 5 4 3 2 1

Printed in the United States of America

To Robert Earle Moody

Contents

Illustrations

Acknowledgments

I undertook this study at the urging of the late Clifford K. Shipton, who was the first modern historian to recognize the importance of Samuel Cooper in Revolutionary Boston. The staff of the Henry E. Huntington Library facilitated my research by preparing a microfilm of the Cooper manuscripts, without which a close study of his sermons and personal papers would have been much more difficult. Research grants from the American Philosophical Society and Oakland University made possible the copying of hundreds of documents in this country and in Europe. In addition, the following institutions have generously assisted my research: Massachusetts Historical Society, Harvard University Library, American Philosophical Society, New York Public Library, British Museum, Archives du Ministère des Affaires étrangères (Paris), Papers of Benjamin Franklin, Yale University Library, Library of Congress, Princeton University Library, American Antiquarian Society, New-York Historical Society, University of Bristol Library (England), Boston Athenaeum, William L. Clements Library, and Boston Public Library.

I am indebted to my former colleague J.G. Blair for tracking down the La Luzerne Letterbooks in France when they were still in private hands. Howard C. Rice, Jr., made helpful suggestions on the sections of the manuscript that deal with Cooper and the French. I have profited from critiques of the manuscript by Oscar Handlin and Gerald C. Heberle.

In more ways than I can ever properly acknowledge, the late Marian Wilson of Oakland University contributed to this study during the fourteen years that I was privileged to work with her. For expert typing I am indebted to Bonita Sayre, Marcie A. Copenhaver, and Patricia A. Tucker. The final draft benefited from the consummate editorial skill of Anne Lalas of Oakland University. The entire staff of the Kresge Library of Oakland University, and particularly Jennie B. Cross and Elizabeth Titus, have rendered unfailing assistance over many years.

The Divine Politician *is dedicated to Robert Earle Moody, Professor of History Emeritus of Boston University, who awakened my interest in colonial America and has stimulated it ever since.*

Prologue

The foremost Massachusetts loyalists made no secret of their belief that an unthinking populace had been blindly led into the American Revolution by a treasonous faction of Boston politicians, whose principal leaders were Samuel and John Adams, John Hancock, and Samuel Cooper. This judgment spread until Jonathan Odell, the major loyalist poet of the Revolution, wrote of those "United comrades, quadruple allies,"

> Bostonian Cooper, with his Hancock join'd,
> Adams with Adams, one in heart and mind;
> . . . .
> Whilst in mid-heav'n shines forth the golden flame,
> Hancock and Adams shall be words of shame;
> Whilst silver beams the face of night adorn,
> Cooper of Boston shall be held in scorn.[1]

Given such a reputation, it is not surprising that British intelligence agents placed these four first on their list of the leading men of Massachusetts or that all grew in prestige among their contemporaries as a result of the successful struggle against the mother country.[2] What jars the modern mind is the disappearance of Cooper's fame, while the other three have been forever enshrined in the pages of American history.

There is no mystery. Hancock and the Adamses were politicians, always conspicuous to the public eye. Cooper was a preacher, pastor of Boston's affluent Brattle Street Church, and consequently his political activity could seldom be publicly acknowledged. Although he stood united with the Boston leaders of rebellion and participated as a peer in their planning and propagandizing, his public role was limited to the proper functions of a minister. Strategy settled upon in his study had to be played out on the public stage by others.

Yet Benjamin Franklin well understood Cooper's importance and made him his chief confidant in New England. Likewise, when the French allies reached Boston they hastened to use the services of le Docteur Cooper, the man they recognized as "one of the principal instigators of independence in New England."[3] Eventually the French foreign minister opened his purse to this preacher whose influence he considered vital to the preservation of the alliance. But most of these activities remained hidden behind the curtain of clerical dignity and immunity that preserved Cooper's public image as the devoted pastor of the town's wealthiest and politically most important church.

His personal talents alone would have made him a notable figure. But Cooper's significance cannot be separated from that of his congregation, in which sat not only the Hancocks and the Bowdoins but also a quarter of Boston's merchants. His parishioners held at least a fourth of the town's wealth and exercised a political influence out of proportion to their numbers. In his eloquent sermons and prayers, he both blessed wealth and spread freely the adhesive of a Christian folk culture that bound rich and poor together in the social order. His message held particular appeal for the wealthy, but ordinary Bostonians responded to it as well. Cooper was the prophet and many in his congregation the disciples of a religion that sanctified the pursuit of self-interest. Given the authority of Holy Writ, the doctrine of self-interest infused resistance to British economic coercion with a radicalism that swept Boston into leadership of the movement for independence.

Much of the evidence for the covert political activity of the "Divine Politician," as Cooper was dubbed, was oral and thus irrecoverable. But what can be discovered concerning this preacher and his church adds a new dimension to the history of Revolutionary Boston, the town where the struggle for independence began. To bring his major political role out of the shadows requires considerable attention to the more conspicuous leaders and to that large segment of the Boston elite that joined ordinary citizens in resisting British efforts to confine American development within the limits of colonialism. Thus, a biography of Cooper becomes almost as much a study of his church and town as one of the man. Only when viewed in this broad perspective does he appear to deserve the importance contemporaries ascribed to him.

The recovery after two centuries of Samuel Cooper's lost reputation helps to balance one-sided interpretations of the Boston chapter of the American Revolution. Of all the town's major leaders, he stood nearest the center of the local Revolutionary movement. Consequently, his life draws us closer to the core elements of Boston society that moved a sizable majority of townsmen from resistance to revolution and sustained them through seven years of wartime hardships.

1

Godly Seed

*J*udge Samuel Sewall of Boston regarded the birth of Judith, his fourteenth child, as a near miracle that transformed his fiftieth year, 1702, into a golden jubilee. Judith grew up as the special object of her father's affection. When she turned eighteen, he proudly gave her in marriage to William Cooper, a dynamic Boston minister. On her father's seventy-third birthday, Sunday, 28 March 1725, Judith bore a son and named him Samuel. Cherishing the knowledge that his own birth had also been on the Sabbath, Judge Sewall believed this line from his loins to be truly blessed. He presented his namesake with a solid silver spoon engraved with the infant's birth and baptismal dates. The gift was perfectly appropriate to commemorate the birth of the "silver-tongued" preacher-politician of Revolutionary Boston. As a sign of his affluence, this silver spoon also symbolized the tensions between the material and the spiritual in the judge's complex personality—tensions that this grandson would teach a later generation of Bostonians to balance with an ease foreign to the Puritan soul of his grandfather.[1]

Sewall's diary shows his adult life to have been torn by a struggle between God and mammon. After marriage to Hannah Hull, a plump heiress who brought him a dowry that according to legend equalled her weight in pine-tree shillings, he attempted to silence his call to the ministry while managing the business of his deceased father-in-law. At first fearful that he would be "stricken dead" for unworthily approaching the communion table, in time he became more hopeful that his prosperity and health were a testimony to God's blessing. Even so, Sewall eventually found public service more conscionable than trade. On the bench of the Superior Court and in the Governor's Council he sought to apply the Puritan ethic with its countervailing incentives to economic gain and holiness. Of all the judges who condemned the Salem witches, Sewall alone later acknowledged his error; and he raised one of the age's few strong voices against the evil of slavery. Still, he saw the chastening hand of God upon him in the deaths of his wife and ten of their fourteen children. There remained for his old age the chief consolation that his son Joseph now preached the gospel from the pulpit of Boston's Old South Church and his son-in-law Cooper from the Brattle Street Church.[2]

Unlike Sewall, Samuel Cooper's paternal grandfather left no diary detailing his inner thoughts. Thomas Cooper came to Boston as an apprentice in the early 1670s and within a decade emerged as a successful merchant. He assured his place in Massachusetts society by marrying Mehetable Minot, related to several of the colony's most prestigious families. By 1693 Cooper paid some of the highest taxes in Boston and moved in the leading social and political circles. He died in 1705 on a voyage to London, leaving his young widow with two children.[3]

William, the older child, was thrust into an early maturity by his father's untimely death. His course was set toward the ministry "as the Needle to its Pole, . . . without a Tremor or Variation." At fourteen he entered Harvard College, where he was placed second in his class under the system of ranking undergraduates according to the status of their families. A serious, diligent student, his warm, outgoing manner won him friendship as well as respect. After graduation in 1712, he remained at Harvard to prepare for the ministry. Those who heard his first sermons in churches of the area were amazed to discover that he was already nearly a "perfect Preacher." The Brattle Street Church hastened to secure his talents for its pulpit.[4]

The Church in Brattle Square, usually called the Brattle Street Church, was the fourth Boston Congregational meeting and the first to be formed since the Old South thirty years before. Unlike the typical New England town with its single meetinghouse, Boston required more and more churches to serve its growing population. But since a new congregation came partially from existing ones, there was usually initial resistance to the erection of another meetinghouse. Brattle Street's genesis proved unusually rancorous

because its founders introduced significant departures from
previous practices. Broadminded men, most of substantial wealth
and social standing like Thomas Cooper, they had little concern for
the preservation of New England's unique religious traditions.
Although they sought the aura of piety and legitimacy that accompanied church membership, they were uncomfortable with the
seventeenth-century Congregationalism now dominated by the
town's father-and-son clerical giants, Increase and Cotton Mather.
In 1699 the Brattle Street leaders erected a meetinghouse, secured a
pastor, and issued a *Manifesto* that promised adherence to orthodoxy but provided less restrictive requirements for baptism and
membership and a more graceful worship service. After a year of
ecclesiastical warfare, peace came gradually, in large measure the
result of the amicable spirit of Brattle Street's first pastor.[5]

A native Bostonian and Harvard graduate, Benjamin Colman
had preached in England for three years before being called to Brattle Street. By accepting the offer from Boston, he gave up his prospects for an important dissenting pulpit in the mother country and
marriage to a literary-minded Englishwoman. But it was a fortunate choice for both pastor and congregation. For the next forty-
seven years Colman proved to be an ideal minister to this congregation of enterprising men and their families. Orthodox but not over-
concerned with theology, genteel in manners and dress, moving
and clear if not brilliant or profound in the pulpit, he offered a
fashionable Congregationalism free of the turgid style and strident
militancy of the Mathers. Under Colman's ministry, Brattle Street
continued to attract men from the mold of its founders.[6]

The success of the new church created the need for a co-pastor.
Young William Cooper was exactly what Colman's congregation
wanted. In addition to his precocious pulpit talents, they were
drawn to him because his life exemplified perfectly the ideal that
godly parents held up to their children, a life in great contrast to
that of the impious Franklin brothers, James and Benjamin, and
many others among the increasing percentage of youth in the
town's population. After his ordination in 1716, Cooper undertook
a vigorous ministry. He nicely balanced Colman's urbane sentimen-
talism by his ability to make evangelical truths starkly clear, particularly to the young. While Cooper hewed to the Calvinistic theological line more closely than Colman, the two pastors nonetheless
labored together harmoniously. Between them they made Brattle
Street the most prosperous and one of the largest of Boston's
religious societies.[7]

Unmarried and devoted to his pastoral duties, Cooper lived with his mother for four years after his ordination. It required some matchmaking by relatives to bring him and Judith Sewall together. At seventeen she had several notable suitors, but her father's respect for the young minister and his mother seems to have counted heavily. The judge officiated at their wedding in 1720 with all the ecstasy the reins on his nature would permit. The Brattle Street congregation responded by raising Cooper's salary and providing him a house which Sewall helped to furnish by a rush order for luxurious English goods. Judith gave birth to a son in the following year, then a daughter, and then Samuel in 1725. As Sewall listened to the "Lisping Language" of these grandchildren, he reflected that they "do plainly tell me that I had need provide to remove to a better Country." He died in 1730, three months before his seventy-eighth and Samuel Cooper's fifth birthday, hoping that he had sown an abundance of "godly seed."[8]

Since Samuel Cooper's passion for religious truth seldom matched his father's, he may have more resembled his mother, but after the last entry in her father's diary little more is known of Judith Sewall Cooper until her death on 23 December 1740. She had borne three sons—William, Samuel, and Thomas—and four daughters, three of whom died in infancy. Only after the shock of losing her first girl had Judith entered the fold of the church. This shred of evidence suggests that she did not share easily the intensive piety of her father and husband. Whatever the mother's influence on her children, they paid her the silent tribute of naming three of her granddaughters for her.[9]

At his mother's death, Samuel, now fifteen, was already in his second year at Harvard. He had prepared for college by enduring the Boston Latin School (then the South Grammar School) from 1732 to 1739, where Headmaster John Lovell terrorized Boston's brightest boys into mastering the classics. Unlike his older brother William, who had dropped out of Boston Latin to go into trade, Sam stuck out the seven-year ordeal. A good memory and a natural facility with language enabled him to excel in the classics under the repression of Master Lovell, the "Old Gaffer" who became the symbol of tyranny for two generations of Boston men.[10]

William Cooper's third son, Thomas, had failed to display any academic capacity; so Sam entered Harvard in the summer of 1739 as the only claimant to his father's mantle. He took with him the Sewall-Cooper prestige. The members of each class were placed according to the reputed social status of their fathers, with public of-

fice given the greatest weight in the calculation. Since in this order
students participated in most functions of the college, placing was
no light matter. Sam placed third among the thirty-nine members of
the class of 1743.[11]

A boy from Barnstable placed thirteenth. Born two months
before Sam, James Otis, Jr., was the son of a rising local politician
ambitious to extend his influence. Jemmy Otis had entered Harvard
to improve his and the family's prospects and, in the father's view,
to benefit the world as well. These paternal hopes were not entirely
unfounded, for the nervous and erratic brilliance of the younger
Otis soon became apparent to his classmates.[12]

During the freshman year of Sam Cooper and Jemmy Otis,
Samuel Adams enjoyed the dignity and prerogatives of a senior. He
lived well at college through the largess of his father, Deacon
Adams, maltster and Boston politician. Upon graduation he was
expected to make the ministry his calling. Three years later, at the
commencement when Cooper and Otis received their bachelor's
degrees, Sam Adams returned to Cambridge for his master's. Required to defend a thesis if called upon, he stood ready to maintain
the proposition "that it is lawful to resist the supreme magistrate if
the commonwealth cannot otherwise be preserved." Shaken by his
father's recent political reverses, he had given up all thought of
preaching, and now nothing could keep him out of politics.[13]

With the classes of 1744 and 1745 there came to Harvard
others who would leave their marks on the movement for American
independence. Scion of the feudal lords of Martha's Vineyard,
Jonathan Mayhew was older and more outspoken than most
undergraduates. Tommy Cushing, who had been baptized at Brattle Street the Sunday before Sam Cooper, sprang from a family of
prosperous Boston merchants. The Huguenot father of James Bowdoin had amassed the largest fortune of New England and won acceptance in Boston society. His son's course—baptism at Brattle
Street, Boston Latin School, and now Harvard—completed the
process of alienation from the Bowdoins' French origins. And from
Plymouth arrived James Warren, whose family occupied a position
in Plymouth County much like that of the Otises in Barnstable
County.[14]

Also at Harvard with these future American patriots were
some who would choose loyalism and exile, including Foster
Hutchinson, placed first in Sam's class because of his father's importance in the Massachusetts government. During his six years'
residence in Cambridge, young Cooper associated closely with boys

from all but the lowest segments of New England life.[15] The college was cosmopolitan in student body if not in faculty. But President Edward Holyoke and the two professors, Edward Wigglesworth in theology and John Winthrop in mathematics, were tolerant gentlemen and capable scholars who encouraged students to expand their horizons. The professors gave occasional lectures, while a tutor supervised the day-by-day work of each class. The entire system was sufficiently flexible that an undergraduate who avoided pronounced heresy and flagrant misconduct found considerable freedom to pursue his own interests.[16]

Sam Cooper took Harvard in stride. One of the few students not fined for repeated violations of college rules, he offended only by failing once to return on time from a summer vacation.[17] Though quick and bright enough to do the required work easily, he gave no indication that he felt the intellectual stimulation a few others received at Harvard in these years. Rather, he developed a reputation for eloquence in both poetry and prose. His friend Jonathan Mayhew concluded a letter to Sam in 1743 with a plea for a reply in verse because "a little Jingle of yours would make my Soul all ear and all Harmony."[18] From Samuel Cooper's college years only one manuscript by him has survived, a poem of thirty-three stanzas entitled "Mr. Pope's *Messiah* imitated." Though roughly imitative, these verses were sufficiently good to impress classmates who had never heard a first-rate poet read his work. The eloquence which became his main stock in trade for life was already conspicuous during college days.[19]

At the beginning of Cooper's sophomore year at Harvard, George Whitefield made his first appearance in New England. After months of eagerly reading about the revivals elsewhere under the preaching of this "Son of Thunder," the Brattle Street ministers jubilantly welcomed the English evangelist in September 1740. He preached his extemporaneous, hellfire sermons to the largest crowds the town had ever seen and left after a month. Wilder itinerant evangelists came after him. William Cooper was overjoyed at the renewed concern for religion and seized leadership of the town's New Lights, the party supporting the revival as an authentic work of God against those who saw in it only a runaway enthusiasm. After Charles Chauncy, the young co-pastor of the First Church, stepped to the head of the antirevival forces, the Old Lights, he and Cooper hardly spoke to each other. The Great Awakening touched off by Whitefield and his followers brought bitterness and division, not the new apostolic age Cooper had expected. When Colman faced the threat to ecclesiastical peace, he prudently retreated halfway from his earlier position as a sponsor of the revival. Yet their love and respect for each other prevented an open break between the Brattle Street pastors.[20]

Ministers might quarrel and congregations split over the revival, but masses of young people experienced its emotional contagion as a joyful release from the burden of guilt for sin and spiritual discipline heaped on them by ministers and parents. From infancy they had been regularly told they were godly seed and urged to early piety as the way to come into their spiritual heritage. Though the ministers had held up example after example of early piety, their models were almost always sickly, melancholic personalities, with the result that, after three generations of preaching early piety to their offspring, Congregationalists still had little success in adapting their standards of holiness to youthful spirits. Benjamin Colman, for all his urbanity, felt the need to lecture "the young Gentlemen of Boston" on the control and proper use of mirth because "it may be there never was more Mirth, nor under less Regulation, than in this Age, and among too many in this Place."[21] Particularly in cosmopolitan Boston, where it was impossible to shield children from other styles of life, Congregationalists fought a losing battle to socialize their youth in an acceptable fashion. Such behavior as "Riotous young Men" singing "filthy Songs" under a minister's window intensified the fears of devout parents that their children could not be protected from evil influences in this town.

By enabling the children of the elect to be both holy and spontaneously joyous, the Great Awakening seemed for a few months to meet this crisis of socialization. Now a young person could shout, jump, cry, or stay up all night with his friends to sing and pray, while parents and pastors praised God for his conduct. He could speak out with religious sanction against the authority of unconverted adults. Pent-up emotions were vented freely, for repression had suddenly given way to expression as the method of holiness. Some only cried through a Whitefield sermon. Others, most often in outdoor services, found more demonstrative outlets for their emotions. And for those young men whose physical needs overpowered their conviction of sin, maidens in a like state mingled with the thronging crowds that followed the succession of evangelists.

Whatever behavior it produced, the contagion of the Awakening seemed almost universal among the young. Colman was "struck with Wonder" at what had taken place "among the young People" of his church. "Here with us," rejoiced William Cooper, "it has lain mostly amongst the Young. Sprightly Youth have been made to bow like Willows to the Redeemer's Sceptre, and willingly to subscribe with their own Hands to the Lord."[22]

William Cooper had reason to rejoice: his son Samuel was among these "Sprightly Youth." In one day's preaching at Cambridge, Whitefield shook the Harvard community by calling the college to return to its pristine spirituality. A handful of students were awakened that day, and they nourished the revival that continued under the college pastor, who became "more close and affecting in preaching." Three months later, Gilbert Tennent, a New Jersey evangelist, produced the "great shock" at the college when he preached during an extended stay in the Boston area. Tutor Henry Flynt, no admirer of Whitefield, noticed that many young men "appeared to be in great concern as to their souls and Eternal State." Some thirty students—among them Sam Cooper, Jemmy Otis, and Jonathan Mayhew—formed a society to sing psalms, fast, pray, read evangelical books, and engage in spiritual discourse. Given a few hours' notice, undergraduates could pour into Boston to hear a visiting preacher. Some followed evangelists into other sections, while a few rushed to remote villages in response to reports that revivalistic fires burned more furiously in the country than in the metropolis. In the words of one student, "religion seemed for some time to get the upper hand, and to bear all before it."[23]

Even for those students most affected, the heat of the Awakening dissipated in time, and they reached what one described as "a more even state." While the spell of the revival lasted, decisions had been made and directions altered. Jonathan Mayhew vowed to enter the ministry, Jemmy Otis turned his genius to serious study, and Sam Cooper sought church membership.[24] On 6 September 1741, still only sixteen, he became a communicant of Brattle Street. At this time, perhaps, he composed these opening stanzas of his imitation of Pope's *Messiah*:

> Tho' Songs profane have long employ'd
> In pleasing Strains my Ear and Voice:
> They now delight no more, nor more
> Shall be the Object of my Choice.

A nobler Theme inspires the muse
To which sublimer Strains belong:
O thou! who touch'd with Sacred Fire
The Prophet's Lips, inspire the Song.[25]

With all of this, Samuel Cooper's participation in the Awakening appears to have been marked by public rather than personal piety. Tutor Flynt best remembered him for once interrupting daily college prayers with an outburst of laughter that frightened another student into fleeing the room for fear of the devil. No, confessed Sam, not the devil but a friend's joke had made him laugh.[26]

When Samuel Cooper decided to make the ministry his calling is uncertain. He may never have considered another course, or the final decision may have been a product of the Awakening. In any case, after graduation in the summer of 1743, he returned to Cambridge in August to pursue ministerial studies. Harvard bestowed the master of arts degree after three years on graduates of good reputation who returned prepared to defend a thesis. Ministerial candidates customarily studied theology in this interval at the college or in a minister's home. With no financial worries, Sam could look forward to three years of relaxed study and congenial association with Harvard friends, while the social amenities of Boston remained only an hour away.[27]

Four months later, the death of his father shattered these comfortable prospects. On 26 December Colman opened the church book and began to write: "It is awful to me to enter on this Leaf the sudden Death of the Reverend Mr. Cooper, who has been with me in the Pastoral Office twenty seven Years, and a Pastor after God's own Heart unto this Church."[28] For twenty years past, William Cooper had predicted he would die before fifty, "as the House of his Father generally had done before him." Dead in the prime of life, just as his "Fame for Piety and Learning, Zeal for God and Care for Souls, was spreading abroad," he was laid in the Hull-Sewall tomb four months before his fiftieth birthday.[29]

The following Sunday Colman preached the most masterful of his many funeral sermons. There was no doubt of the climax, which came in these words: "In a special Manner may that Son of the Family, who has devoted himself to the Work of the Ministry by the Will of God, and is pursuing his Evangelical Studies for that End, be graciously accepted of God, and assisted in them; . . . May he ever have the Example of his Father before his Eyes day and night. . . . May he improve the singular Advantages he has above others, to come eminently furnished for Service to the Church of Christ."[30]

In three years Sam Cooper had lost both parents and had lived through the trauma of the Great Awakening. He was still only eighteen, but he was not too young to understand how much would now be expected of him.

2

One Chosen of God

*T*he death of William Cooper came at the most critical moment in the history of the Brattle Street Church since its founding. Its merchants had for three decades divided over proposals to ease credit in Massachusetts. The latest credit crisis, brought on by the formation of the Land Bank—a scheme to issue paper money secured by mortgages on land—had produced a nearly even split among merchants in the congregation. Both pastors had been caught in the middle of these economic struggles and had welcomed the revival as a means of restoring harmony.[1]

Their hopes were disappointed. Although the majority of the congregation had followed Colman's hesitant retreat from the excesses of the Great Awakening, the New Lights among his parishioners, many of them Land Bank supporters, cherished the memory of their deceased pastor's leadership of the Boston revival. Futhermore, the Awakening had unloosed democratic forces in this congregation hitherto dominated by a mercantile elite. William Cooper's sermons reveal that even this aristocratic minister could be caught up in the democratic surge of revivalistic Calvinism as he preached that God is no respecter of persons, that the most humble man might be saved, while the wealthiest might be eternally damned.[2] Such doctrine held the potential for social disruption in Boston, where workingmen were beginning to suffer from the town's economic stagnation.[3] Colman's forty-five-year quest for a genteel but godly upper class, to whom ordinary persons naturally and gladly deferred in spiritual as well as in temporal matters, seemed near failure. In theory, if not in past practice, the New England pattern of church government gave every man in the congregation a voice in church affairs. Thus the calling of a new associate for Colman could easily occasion a contest with economic, social, and theological issues that would leave the church permanently split.

Colman, seventy and infirm at Cooper's death, struggled through the year of mourning customary before the installation of a successor. In September 1744 four young men received invitations to become candidates, each to preach for one month in turn. Three had been nominated by vote of the congregation, but from the beginning Colman had reserved "the Liberty of asking Mr. Samuel Cooper to preach also, if he finds himself inclined to begin his Evangelical Services." The youngest of the four, Sam accepted and took his turn in December after the others.[4]

The sight of this tall, good-looking youth of nineteen standing in his father's pulpit must have thrilled those who had shed tears at the funeral a year before and now displayed in their parlors the "effigy" of their deceased pastor that a newspaper advertised for sale. As he began to read from his sermon booklet, it soon became apparent that Samuel Cooper's candidacy need not rest solely on emotional ties to the past. He spoke clearly, with a pleasing mixture of his father's earnestness and the Colman charm. The one sermon of his trial preserved in manuscript reveals a remarkable ability to appeal to all segments of his audience in a single discourse. Preaching on the parable of Lazarus and the rich man, he first explained that "our Lord did not blame this man for being rich, nor for dressing well, and faring deliciously. These things being proportioned to his Rank and Fortune, there was no Sin in all this." The blame lay rather in "forgetting that God had placed him in such Circumstances" so that he might "do good" for others. The same parable provided an opportunity to please New Lights by mentioning the "Torments of the damned in Hell" and concluding from the case of Lazarus that "a poor and mean Condition in this Life, is often the Lot of those who are yet the Favourites of Heaven."[5]

This sermon contained more diplomacy than divinity. The newspapers had been spreading controversy over George Whitefield's recent return to Boston; and Colman, still straddling the fence, had been publicly criticized for again opening his pulpit to the evangelist.[6] Two of the candidates leaned too far toward the New Lights to be acceptable to Colman and his leading parishioners. The third, though eminently qualified, was apparently passed over because he came from an artisan family and thus might lack sympathy for the wealthy. As Colman had thought from the beginning, only young Cooper could unite a majority in his favor. When the congregation met to vote on the last day of 1744, the aged pastor first prayed, "Show Lord which thou hast chosen!" His prayer was answered with 116 of 138 votes for the son of his late colleague. A committee of distinguished members informed Cooper of his election, but he did not give a formal acceptance until 7 March, when he requested that, in view of his age and "great Want of Study and Experience," his ordination be postponed for a year, during which he would preach only on alternate Sundays.[7]

Though Colman and the congregation agreed to this arrangement, 1745 was not to be a year of quiet study and sermon preparation while the minister-elect continued in residence at Harvard. Poor health kept Whitefield in the vicinity through June, giving him ample time to counter the charges against him, including the Harvard faculty's *Testimony* describing him as a "Deluder of the People." New Lights now gave more credence than ever to rumors of widespread heresy among Harvard students and insisted that every ordination be preceded by an examination of the candidate's theology and state of grace. Not even the glorious news that the French stronghold at Louisbourg had fallen to a New England expeditionary force could entirely crowd religious controversy from the newspapers.[8] Colman remained calm but his strength ebbed. When in the winter of 1745–1746 a wave of sickness passed through the town, he had to call his new colleague from Cambridge to visit the sick, a task the young man performed with sufficient grace to please the congregation and to convince himself that he had chosen the right vocation. When the date for Cooper's ordination was finally set for 21 May 1746, he was requested to make a public confession of faith two or three Sundays before this day. Not only would a satisfactory confession follow the example of his father, it would also clear the air of any suspicion of guilt by association with reputed religious liberals at Harvard.[9]

Accordingly, on 6 April, "Mr. Cooper gave in a Sermon, a Confession of his Faith to the general Satisfaction of the Audience." It was a masterful performance that moved smoothly and with forensic perfection over the points currently disputed. He first took his stand on scripture as the only basis of religious authority. By avoiding "speculative Points, which have been controverted between the greatest Divines, and upon which the best of Men have differed among themselves," he vowed to "keep as close to the Infallible Oracles of Truth" as possible. As he outlined his theology from "the Being and Perfection of God" to a final judgment with rewards and punishments, nothing was omitted but, more important, nothing was emphasized except the sufficiency of revelation. He stressed that for him Christianity was much more than doctrine: "The End of all Knowledge is Practice"—"An Orthodox Head, will be of little Advantage to us if we have an unsound Heart." Rest assured that "if any Man will do the Will of God, says our Saviour, . . . he shall not fall into any fatal Error; but shall understand all that is necessary for him to know in Order to his obtaining Eternal Life."[10]

His confession of faith set the pattern for Cooper's ministry. He would remain a moderate Calvinist who sought to cool polemical passions with biblical preaching that emphasized practical, heartfelt religion.[11] It was a safe faith. No suspicion of heresy would trouble his career. He had built a temporary bridge between the evangelical Calvinism of William Cooper and the rational Christianity of his friend Jonathan Mayhew and other liberal ministers of the area.

The solemnity of 21 May was carried out with endless nostalgia. Colman summoned all his strength to deliver the ordination sermon from the text "One chosen of God," in which he reviewed the forty-seven years of the Brattle Street Church and repeatedly called on the son to follow in the footsteps of his father. Uncle Joseph Sewall gave the charge to the candidate, and another of the father's intimates among the clergy extended the "Right Hand of Fellowship" or official welcome into the sacred clerical order. Last came the feast for congregation and visitors which traditionally followed Congregational ordinations. A lavish array of choice foods and expensive beverages ensured that the day would end in a high state of "spiritual joy." An expenditure of up to £300—more than a year's income for an average family and nearly twice the church's last annual collection for the poor—had been authorized to make this festivity unforgettable.[12]

At twenty-one he was the Reverend Mr. Samuel Cooper, co-pastor with the noted Dr. Colman of one of the great churches of the British Empire. In an age when Harvard still sent the majority of its best scholars into the ministry, when able clergymen continued to influence society as much as merchant princes and public officials, when most people felt uncomfortable without religious sanctions supporting their life goals and patterns, he had won an enviable position. At the Harvard Commencement in July, where most of the class of 1743 reassembled to be awarded master's degrees, he heard no success story to match his.[13]

Later that year he received substantial evidence of his good fortune in the form of a gift of £1,472 to enable him to go to "house keeping." It came from 105 individuals, mostly heads of church families. The wealthiest, such great merchants as Thomas Hancock, Edmund Quincy, and James Bowdoin, Sr., had given £50 each to set the standard of contributions, which ranged down to the widow's mite of £2. Wartime inflation and the depreciated Massachusetts currency drastically reduced the actual value of this gift; that it was nevertheless a handsome sum is indicated by the action of the church this year fixing the pastors' salaries in the same currency at £10 a week plus £80 a year for house rent.[14] William Cooper had lived well and acquired a splendid library, but his inheritances had become hopelessly tangled in the probate courts and he had so suffered from inflation, currency manipulation, and credit schemes that he had died insolvent.[15] The gift from the good people of Brattle Street enabled his son not only to survive until Massachusetts stabilized its currency in 1750 but also to take a wife without delay.

On 11 September 1746 Colman married his colleague to Judith Bulfinch, a bride with all the proper religious and social credentials. Her family, descended from an ambitious sailmaker who had arrived in New England shortly after Thomas Cooper, had attended Brattle Street from the beginning. She had been baptized there the Sunday before her future husband and, like him, had been prompted to church membership by the heat of the great revival. Her father, Dr. Thomas Bulfinch, Boston physician, had completed his medical education in England and France before returning to Boston in 1722 to prosper in medical practice and marriage. He built a large house on land provided by his father-in-law and became known more for the sumptuousness of his table than for his piety. As befitted his background and social standing as minister of Brattle Street, Sam Cooper had married into an important Boston family.[16]

In August 1747 Colman baptized their first child, a daughter christened Judith.[17] It was Colman's nearly last baptism. Although very conscious of his "gradual Decay," he continued to preach regularly, not missing the Sunday before Saturday, 29 August, when he died quickly and peacefully. The surviving minister fulfilled his sad duty on Monday by preceding the hearse to the grave as Boston ceremoniously buried "one of the most shining Lights and greatest Honours of this Town and Land." In a sermon the following Sunday, Cooper eulogized Colman, though encomiums proved difficult because Colman's greatest accomplishments had been in spirit and style more than in deeds. In a town remarkable for its scholarly clergy and aggressive merchants, he had best adapted the traditional religion to the needs and aspirations of the men responsible for Boston's preeminent place among American urban centers.[18]

Breaking with custom, Cooper did not publish this sermon, apparently from a desire to avoid provoking further religious disputation. No literary monument appeared until 1749 when Colman's son-in-law published a long *Life and Character*. It went on the study shelves along with ninety titles by Colman and twenty-five by William Cooper to remind Sam often in whose shoes he stood.[19]

For thirty-six years following Colman's death, Cooper ministered alone to his large flock with no recorded thought of taking a colleague. To do so might lighten his pastoral load but also perhaps open a Pandora's box. He could best keep the church united by avoiding division over the choice of candidates, their theology, and degree of "New-Lightness." Perhaps, too, unconsciously he sought relief from the scrutiny of his own work which even the most congenial co-pastor would inadvertently exercise. Though not lazy, he was careless of detail and impatient with petty routine. During a long pastorate he made a total of five short entries in the church records, hitherto faithfully kept.[20] He recorded the vital statistics of membership, baptism, and marriage only in his personal diaries. In contrast to his predecessors, Cooper published only nine titles, not because his writing was inferior but because he was preoccupied with personal relations, preaching, and attention to the spiritual needs of his flock. They were well satisfied, and not merely because one minister cost less than two. Jokes made during the Revolution concerning his neglect of duty for politics reflected even then the envy of detractors more than fact. For twenty years after his induction into holy orders, Congregationalism could point to no more devoted or successful pastor.

Laboring without an associate meant a steady and heavy workload. There were weddings, funerals, endless rounds of visits to the sick, and semigovernmental functions such as the Harvard Board of Overseers and inspections of the Boston schools. Most burdensome and inescapable of all was sermon preparation. The

Congregational service consisted mainly of an hour-long sermon preceded by a pastoral prayer, a reading from scripture, and a psalm or two. In addition to the morning and afternoon services every Sunday, sermons were required at lectures, fasts, and other special occasions, so that a minister without a colleague might have to deliver one hundred or more sermons a year. In the two pre-Revolutionary years from which his diary has been preserved, Cooper preached 101 times in 1753 and 98 in 1764. The burden was eased in part by the practice of exchanging pulpits with other pastors, which meant that an old sermon could be repeated. During these two years he exchanged for one service on half the Sundays.[21] He also drew on the manuscripts he had inherited from his father, and in time could repeat his own sermons by carefully noting when and where each had been given—more than a dozen times in some cases. Using all the tricks of the trade, he might get by with one new sermon a week—still a demanding assignment.[22]

As he had demonstrated in his trial sermon, Cooper's would be a ministry of reconciliation. He recognized that "a bold and burning Spirit, untempered with the Meekness and Gentleness of Christ, has shed Torrents of Blood in the pretended Cause of God; and torn and devoured the Flock of Jesus under the Title of a Pastor." The heir of the irenic Colman could not hide his impatience with the "reverend Fathers and Brethren in the Ministry" who regularly flayed each other in print.[23] On the question of doctrine he left room for individual differences of interpretation and consequently could welcome into the Brattle Street pulpit champions of liberal theology, while retaining full fellowship with Calvinists of all shades.[24]

As year after year he proclaimed his pragmatic version of the faith of the fathers, that faith became increasingly clear and simple. The "Principles of Religion are fixt," Cooper believed; "they will not bend to you," you must bend to them. The task of the minister, then, was to strengthen faith by demonstrating "how agreeable to Reason the main Principles of Religion are" and that, notwithstanding minor disagreements, "they have gained the Assent of all wise and sober Men in all Ages." But reason must have emotional support, for, "though the Gospel carried with it Evidence sufficient to convince the Understanding, yet unless the Affections closed with it, it would be heard in vain."[25]

Foreshadowing the twentieth-century preachers of positive-thinking Christianity, Cooper interwove throughout his sermons the twin themes of the reasonableness of Christianity and the rewards of a religious life. "The Service of Christ requires Nothing of Us but What is reasonable." Furthermore, "It very much adds to the Easiness of Christ's Yoke, that his Commands are all plain and easy to be understood: simple and direct, without any windings, and Perplexitys." Religion brings "the truest and most substantial Happiness" and its practice is "commonly attended with a sweet Peace and Satisfaction of Mind: which pays us well for our Labor." Those who have accepted Christ's invitation know that "his Service is Sweet and delightful, . . . that his Ways are Ways of Pleasantness and that his Yoke is easy."[26] In one of his most typical sermons, given fourteen times between 1750 and 1783, Cooper used all of his eloquence and rhetoric to contrast "the Folly and Unhappyness of wicked Men" with "the Wisdom and Happyness of Good Men" who "have made a wise Estimate of Things, and act accordingly."[27]

As he had promised in his confession of faith, Cooper stuck to the Bible. His references to uninspired writers were few and judicious. By using biblical rather than theological language, he could be protectively vague on heated issues. Though preaching that God's goodness does not exclude the punishment of "impenitent Sinners," Cooper could not put his heart into hellfire preaching and treated the topic matter-of-factly.[28] As a nominal Calvinist, he taught that eternal life cannot be secured "in a Way of Debt or Wages: it must be conveyed to us as a Free Gift: and through the abounding Grace of God."[29] But he preached more enthusiastically on the possibility of obtaining an "Assurance of Hope" that removed most doubts of one's election to salvation.[30] His sermons skirted the question of *how* to be saved. If you have the will to salvation, he implied to his audience, God will handle the mechanics.[31] Salvation was a simple matter at Brattle Street: "As we dread the Wrath of Almighty God, and Value the Favour of the Author of our Being, Let us be perswaded to acquaint Ourselves now with Him and be at peace." Others might heatedly debate the intricacies of conversion; Samuel Cooper had more practical matters on his mind.[32]

Rejecting the attempt of Jonathan Edwards to lift the concept of true virtue from the foundation of self-love on which it commonly rested in the eighteenth century and ground it on the broader base of general benevolence, Cooper argued against downgrading self-love. "That a due Regard to our own Happiness is consistent with Piety, no one, who but slightly considers the Frame and Texture of our holy religion can doubt. The Gospel condemns only an

ill-proportioned and vicious Self-Love." Cooper saw no reason to
mistrust self-love when guided by "true Piety and Vertue."[33]

From his biblical platform Cooper could ignore controversy
and sidestep the intellectual currents that disturbed contemporary
Christian scholars such as Edwards. Whatever the topic and text of
a Cooper sermon, it offered solace to the individual and
urged him to persist in the Christian way as the certain means of
achieving all the best in life. Yet, to sustain the faith of a people
faced with epidemics, natural disasters, wars, and revolution, he
tempered the optimism of his preaching with a strong emphasis on
the acknowledgment and acceptance of divine providence. The
recognition that whatever men think "of their own Influence and
Importance, it is God that governs the World" had large social utility, as the following chapters will show.[34]

The effectiveness of a Cooper sermon came as much from its
delivery as from its ideas. His eloquence soon became the standard
by which New England pulpit orators were measured. Attending
one's first service in Brattle Street could be a memorable experience.
As a younger contemporary rhapsodized, "In Brattle street men
were charmed into the ways of wisdom by the eloquent, the
graceful Doctor Samuel Cooper. With a voice melodious in the
tones of a delicate flute, with an elegant address, in Attic diction, he
allured his hearers to virtue, with soothing tenderness he poured
the oil and the wine into the wounded bosom, and in persuasive
language he recalled the vicious from the paths which lead to
Death."[35] The black poet Phillis Wheatley struck the same note:

> The Sons of Learning on thy lessons hung,
> While soft persuasion mov'd th' illit'rate throng.
> . . . .
> Thy every sentence was with grace inspir'd,
> And every period with devotion fir'd; . . .[36]

When Jane Mecom, the impoverished sister of Benjamin Franklin,
returned to church after an extended period of bereavement, she
went away consoled from hearing Cooper preach a sermon she
described as a "master Peec."[37]

While living in Boston, John and Abigail Adams attended Brattle Street. Abigail discerned intuitively the source of Cooper's pulpit
success: he had "feeling and sensibility"; he could "take one up with
him." Her husband refused to fall under Cooper's spell, but when
John Adams wanted to make clear to his wife the dynamic effect of
a prayer opening a session of the First Continental Congress, there

was only one way to convey his meaning: "Dr. Cooper himself never prayed with such fervour, such Ardor, such Earnestness and Pathos, and in Language so elegant and sublime."[38] Abigail understood perfectly, for Bostonians regarded Cooper's prayers as even more moving than his sermons. During the Revolution he was often invited to open critical public meetings with prayer, not so much because of his politics—patriot preachers were in inexhaustible supply—as because of his ability to unite the crowd and render them more susceptible to the leadership of Whig politicians. It was a skill he had perfected from long weekly practice. Had Sam Cooper made no contribution to American independence other than praying in public, he would have done his share in the common cause.[39]

Like prayer, the monthly administration of the communion sacrament fully utilized Cooper's ability to empathize. As one parishioner expressed it, "When celebrating the peculiar mysteries of our holy religion—how was he carried even beyond himself, with such a flow and fulness of expression as often bore away the intelligent and spiritual worshipper as on angels wings towards heaven!"[40] Cooper was equally successful in arousing appropriate feelings during the almost weekly baptisms of children together with an occasional adult. The combined effect of prayer, sacrament, and sermon at Brattle Street was supplemented by an effort to make the most of the limited possibilities for church music in Congregational worship. In 1753 Cooper persuaded the congregation to adopt the popular Tate and Brady psalter augmented by an appendix of hymns compiled by a committee from the works of Watts and others. This change became possible after the demise of Colman, who had expressed opposition to all "Hymns of meer human Composure, . . . even those of Dr. Watts himself." Later the church developed what amounted to a choir of worshipers sitting in the "singing seats." During the Revolution and perhaps for some time before, these singers were led by Daniel Rea, "the celebrated Vocal performer" who was said to have "the greatest compass of voice ever known."[41]

For all his later political importance, the reputation of "silver-tongued" Samuel Cooper can be understood only in the context of the complete worship service, where he appeared a man perfectly designed and trained for the role in which he had been cast. He had mastered all the formulas for success in the Congregational pastorate. As the occasion demanded he could draw tears for the departed, create hope of recovery in the ill, offer solace to the distressed, ease the conscience of the merchant, convince the troubled soul of its election, or unite his people in a common cause. Distinguished visitors to Boston were often drawn to the Brattle Street meetinghouse on Sunday to witness "all those graces which so eminently distinguish his public performances."[42]

Because he had so easily achieved complete success in the ministry, Cooper's sincerity and dedication to his calling would always be suspect, and the more so because the gravity of his pulpit deportment contrasted sharply with his jovial behavior in social relations. Even in a eulogy a friend spoke of him as "the entertaining companion" whose "most engaging politeness, . . . rendered him so agreeable in every private circle." As one writer long remembered, Cooper was "singularly neat in his dress. He wore a white bushy wig, a cocked hat, and a gold-headed cane. He was tall, well formed, and had an uncommonly handsome, intelligent, and amiable face. One could not fail to remember him well who had ever seen him."[43]

It was difficult to forget—or trust completely—a preacher who appeared to shine even more brilliantly in private than in public. Sometimes he seemed to believe the old proverb he once quoted in a circle of intimates: "An Ounce of Mother Wit, is worth a Pound of Clergy."[44]

As the Revolution drew near, Tories made the most of this vulnerability. Among other inventions, they insisted that some ladies of Boston found such a charming man irresistible despite his clerical collar. Later, in domestic political struggles, foes struck hard at the professional insincerity evidenced in his preoccupation with politics. But to those who had no ulterior motive to impugn his conduct, "his whole life was worthy the imitation of all who wish to live admired, or die lamented."[45] There was never any tangible evidence to suggest that Samuel Sewall would have been disappointed in his namesake.

3

This British Israel

*D*uring the first seventeen years of his ministry, Samuel Cooper masterfully fused the traditional New England religion with the commercial ethos of the port town in which his church stood. Such a faith helped to sustain his congregation through war and natural disasters and increased their confidence that the American colonies enjoyed a glorious future in the British Empire.

Cooper's Boston, one of the leading seaports of the empire, was a worldly metropolis, not a provincial Puritan community. Yet appearances could be deceiving, for church buildings—meeting-houses, as the Congregationalists called them—dominated the town. Built on a small, irregular peninsula approximately two miles long and a mile wide, Boston was completely surrounded by water except for a narrow neck connecting with the mainland on the southwest. With few exceptions the churches were the largest buildings on this peninsula. Their roofs peaked at twice the height of most other structures and their steeples rose much higher, as if they were spiritual lightning rods seeking to attract bolts of divine grace from the heavens. Seamen sighted on the steeples as they entered the bay. On land, directions were given in reference to the meetinghouses, and merchants advertised that their shops were located near a particular minister's meeting. Clocks in the church towers performed such a vital function that they were often maintained at public expense. Church bells served as alarms for fire and other emergencies. And the largest meetinghouses could be pressed into service for public assemblies. Had Boston been a medieval town with a bishop to force its ecclesiastical energies into a single channel, it would have built a cathedral to match those of Western Europe. Instead, it erected substantial edifices all over town, so that as the sun moved across the sky in the course of a day, few locations escaped the shadow of a steeple. But no one who walked its streets, stood on its fifty wharves, traded in its countless shops, drank in its dozens of taverns, observed its riotous lower classes, or dined in one of its many fine homes could for long believe Boston to be a refuge for otherworldly saints.[1]

The Brattle Street Church stood as the most conspicuous illustration of this fusion of religion and commercial enterprise. Altogether the church spent £2,672, a fortune in the eyes of most townsmen, to bury William Cooper and settle his son.[2] Under Samuel Cooper, Brattle Street's affluence increased until a significant proportion of the town's wealth was concentrated in his congregation. When a great fire devastated a section of Boston in 1760, Brattle Street contributed a quarter of the sum raised by all seventeen churches for relief of the victims.[3] One-third of those Bostonians sufficiently wealthy and vain to commission a portrait by John Singleton Copley attended this one church.[4] By 1763 one-fourth of the town's merchants sat under Cooper's preaching.[5]

Later evidence can be found in the Boston tax valuation list for 1771. Of the one hundred Bostonians with the highest assessments on the rental value of the homes in which they lived, twenty-seven attended Brattle Street, as did twenty-four of the one hundred merchants with the highest assessments on their trading stocks. Twenty of the eighty taxed on shipping tonnage were Brattle Streeters, whose collective assessment was 49 percent of the total. The tax list shows about £104,000 loaned at interest by eighty-seven lenders, twenty from this one congregation. These twenty held nearly £50,000 of this debt.[6]

John Adams tersely summarized the significance of what he once referred to as "Dr. Cooper's tasty Society" when he advised a young lawyer to attend this church in order to be seen by people of "more Weight and Consequence."[7]

The gospel preached at Brattle Street appealed not only to the few men of large fortunes but equally to those who hoped to flourish in Boston's precarious economic climate. At the beginning of Cooper's ministry, the town's population had leveled off near 16,000. Still, there were many transients: artisans moving in and out as employment opportunities changed, sailors waiting for a ship, indigents seeking charity, apprentices escaping masters, and runaway slaves. In good times, some workingmen could save enough in a few years to purchase a humble dwelling, and a few of the ambitious and fortunate artisans did much better. But during the frequent depressions the lower income groups often faced hunger and cold because of the necessity to import food and firewood at high prices. As merchants and shipowners attempted to cope with changing markets, hurricanes, wars, bursting credit bubbles, and other perils to trade, they might strike it rich one year and go bankrupt the next, taking down with them those to whom they were indebted. The instability of economic life in Boston was a constant reminder that commercial man needed the blessings of providence on his enterprise.[8]

Commercial man also sought the freedom to pursue his self-interest. He was convinced that the free market economy promoted the general welfare because it motivated individuals to greater effort and ingenuity, that people improved society as they improved themselves. This social philosophy seemed self-evident in the American colonies that enjoyed the highest standard of living in the Western world as part of an empire that placed few effective restrictions on the natural flow of trade. The conspicuous display of wealth by the elite kept alive the hope of many average men to become wealthy themselves. Enterprising men united in the belief that the pursuit of one's material welfare served the good of society as a whole, and they craved a divine sanction for this modern economic philosophy.

A child of commercial Boston who had mastered the tools of his ministerial trade without being consumed by otherworldliness, Samuel Cooper readily adapted his ministry to the needs and aspirations of those he served. It was not enough to use his pulpit to bless wealth. To be effective he had to create a sense of religious legitimacy for the modern society in which his parishioners lived. He had no patience with Jonathan Edwards, who, in western Massachusetts, employed his towering intellect in a plea for the restoration of the ordered Christian society governed by disinterested benevolence. By contrast, in Brattle Street Cooper justified the pursuit of self-interest and denied the scriptural basis of the Puritan theory of a society that held the common welfare always paramount to the interest of the individual. "We see," he said in one oft-preached sermon, "that the Glory of God and our own Happiness ought never to be set in opposition to one another; that we can never be called to renounce the one for the sake of the other; that they are both so strongly enjoyned that if we attain one we infallibly secure the other." He carefully hedged such teaching with the warning that "true Piety and Virtue are the proper Guides to Self-Love," and his language and doctrine remained traditional. Yet more than other Boston clergymen, Samuel Cooper sensed the significance of the culture around him and adjusted his ministry to it. With the message that God is "calling upon us to pursue our own Welfare in that Path which he himself has marked out to us," Samuel Sewall's grandson taught Brattle Street merchants that they had to make no hard choice between profits and holiness.[9]

Religion was made to serve another—if less acknowledged—purpose at Brattle Street by Cooper's emphasis on the interrelationship of all orders of society. Boston's economic instability was particularly threatening in light of the potential for social disruption on this small peninsula. One half of the sixteen thousand inhabitants were under sixteen, and nearly a thousand were free or enslaved blacks.[10] Unruly youth and victims of racial injustice, together with unemployed sailors and laboring men, provided ample tinder for the fires of social unrest. A town without a police force, Boston had to rely on other means of social control. Society held together in part out of a recognition of the economic interdependence of all classes. Religion also provided a strong cohesive force, particularly in the Congregational folk culture shared by most Bostonians, with its emphasis on the providential control of human affairs and the obligations of Christian stewardship.

As Cooper ministered simultaneously to rich and poor, he stressed the mutual obligations the gospel imposed on them. He taught that the wealthy Christian should be a "Man of christian Benevolence" who, in seeking his own happiness, remembers that "Charity is the very Temper of Happiness." Such a man knows the true value of riches, that "there is no Good in them, but for a Man to rejoice and to do Good in his Life." Accordingly, "he can chearfully retrench the Expences of Vanity and Luxury, that his Opportunities of doing Good may be the greater: he can gladly deny himself the Delicacies of Life, that others may be furnished with the Means of Subsistence: and were his Power equal to his Will, Pain and Poverty would be wholly unknown in the World." There are dangers, of course, in dispensing charity, so "the Man of christian Benevolence" will take care that "these Bounties do not become the Wages of Idleness: being well aware, that then they would be worse than lost; and that nothing but Industry, and a full Employment of such as have Ability for Work, can make Plenty and Happiness circulate through a whole Community."[11]

To the poor, "the Bulk of Mankind," Cooper's preaching offered no great hope for relief in this world. Theoretically, he put little stock in social distinctions: "May we all remember that we are now upon a short State of Tryal; and the Distinctions that may now subsist between us will soon cease." He advised the lower classes in the meantime to accept God's providence in placing them where they were, to avoid degenerating vices, and to follow diligently their callings as the "most likely means" of improving their circumstances. Do not waste time envying the rich, he preached: "this is odious to God and contrary to Gospel" which "teaches you to be cautious, humble and modest, to those whom God has placed above you."[12] In a town where the road up, though steep and treacherous, was still open, such an admonition was more practical than otherworldly.

There were, of course, other popular preachers and flourishing churches in Boston. At the New North Church, Andrew Eliot attracted lower middle class families until he had the town's largest congregation. Jonathan Mayhew's repeated attacks on creeds, bishops, and clerical opponents from his West Church pulpit made him one of the most controversial Bostonians. Although Charles Chauncy's solid, prosaic, weak-voiced sermons at the First Church did not pack in listeners, he enjoyed prestige as an intellectual leader and in time as the town's senior pastor. Chauncy seemed dull indeed after one had heard Samuel Stillman of the First Baptist Church. An entertainer as much as a moralizer, he created an immediate sensation and preached to a full house for forty years. So many were the offerings and so intense the competition that a dreary bore like Samuel Mather, son of the famous Cotton, gradually lost his congregation. Yet none of Boston's other churches could match Brattle Street's wealth and political influence, and Cooper relished the knowledge.[13]

The young Brattle Street pastor's position among Boston's elite was evident from the beginning of his ministry. In 1750 he made an extensive trip as far south as Pennsylvania with a few companions, including his college friends James Bowdoin, who had just come into a share of his father's fortune, and Thomas Cushing. At New Haven the college president awarded master's degrees to Cooper and others of the party who paid a fee to be admitted at Yale to the same degree held from Harvard. In New Jersey they were welcomed by Governor Jonathan Belcher, who had formerly held the same office in Massachusetts. The governor persuaded Cooper to preach twice in his church and recorded his great satisfaction in hearing such a "sweet" preacher. The climax of this journey came in Philadelphia where the young men were welcomed by ex-Bostonian Benjamin Franklin, already retired at forty-five from a highly successful printing business. Franklin introduced them to his electrical experiments, soon to be published in a book that would spread his fame throughout the Western world. For Cooper, this visit marked the beginning of a lifelong friendship with the sage of Philadelphia.[14]

Having seen Philadelphia and New York, both beginning to surpass Boston in population, Cooper was better able to appreciate the benefits enjoyed by British-Americans at mid-century. During the six-year interval of peace (1748–1754) between the last two Anglo-French wars, colonials were generally happy with their place in an empire in which bills of sale seemed to carry more weight than orders from Whitehall. Some New Englanders still cried foul at the restoration of Louisbourg to France by the treaty of 1748, a move which appeared to discount their sacrifices in the capture of that fortress. Britain's generous reimbursement of military expenses had helped to take the sting out of the return of Louisbourg, although the specie received had been used to put Massachusetts on a hard-money basis and trade had suffered during the readjustment. Yet Boston merchants with ships temporarily idle were well aware of the economic, political, and religious freedoms under which they lived and prospered. Even Jonathan Mayhew's famous sermon of 1750, repudiating the Anglican doctrine of unlimited submission and non-resistance to the higher powers, began with a tribute to British freedom.[15]

Still, over the prosperity and freedom of mid-century colonial America hung a large dark cloud. Most colonial leaders sensed that the present peace with France was only a lull before the severest storm of all, that French power in North America must now check British expansion or abandon its scattered, underpopulated possessions to aggressive English colonists. While diplomats vainly conferred in Europe, each side stepped up its hostile activity in America. A final war for possession of the continent seemed inevitable.

Cooper saw at firsthand some of the implications of the approaching war, while inspecting in person one section of the long border where France and Great Britain vied for Indian support. In September 1753 he sailed on the province sloop with the commissioners appointed to pacify the Maine Indians. Three of the five commissioners were Cooper's parishioners, who had invited him to accompany them in a semiofficial capacity as chaplain of the House of Representatives, a position to which he had been elected a few months before. As he dined at the Maine home of the most distinguished member of the commission, Sir William Pepperrell, leader of the 1745 Louisbourg expedition, the stakes of the contest seemed starkly clear.[16]

Events of the next six years subjected Americans—and particularly Bostonians—to a prolonged emotional ordeal. The American conflict, breaking out in 1754, two years before war was declared in Europe, went disastrously until the summer of 1758. French successes everywhere prepared the colonial mind to anticipate a shameful peace purchased by surrender of British territory and claims.[17] Then, as if Boston must be completely humbled at one of the darkest moments of the struggle, an early morning earthquake in November 1755 brought thousands of terrified citizens into the streets to see substantial brick buildings crumbling.[18]

Beginning with the British capture of Louisbourg in July 1758, the fortunes of war changed suddenly. By the time Quebec fell in September 1759, colonial emotions had run the gamut from nearly complete despair to unbounded joy. But in victory Boston felt chastisement when in March 1760 a fire burned from the center of the town eastward to the water and then fanned out among the docks. When the smoke cleared, more than three hundred buildings lay in ashes.[19] Still, not even a disaster of this magnitude could dampen spirits for long in the wonderful year during which all Canada surrendered to British arms. While the war continued in remote theaters and negotiations progressed toward the peace treaty of 1763, it became evident that New England had undergone a profound transformation. The removal of the French threat had lessened dependence on military protection by the mother country at the same time that the emotional ordeal of 1754–1760 had hardened those attitudes that most sharply differentiated the majority of New Englanders from their countrymen in England.

War, earthquake, and fire had stimulated in Boston an orgy of preaching. Influenced by the example of ancient Israel, the Puritan leaders who came to New England had founded their wilderness communities on the theoretical base of a social covenant. It took in everyone, sinners as well as saints, since under its terms the entire community was held collectively responsible to the Almighty for its actions. A covenanted nation stood in a special relationship to God: if righteous, thus fulfilling the covenant, it could be assured of steady success; but conversely, unlike uncovenanted nations, it must be prepared to accept collective punishment for the sins of the land. Thus depression, war, plague, or other calamity required a close scrutiny of society to discover the source of God's anger. Only after the offending sins were acknowledged and pardon obtained would secondary corrective measures prove effective.

Over the century after 1630, the Congregational ministry gave increased attention to the social covenant until it became a major focus of their preaching. The concept of a national covenant offered a wide range of practical benefits. By linking morality and success the clergy blessed temporal gain and simultaneously sharpened the social consciousness of those who prospered most. By holding up rulers before the community as answerable to God for the adoption of policies promoting the righteousness that brought peace and prosperity, the preachers underlined the fiduciary nature of political office and demonstrated that political and religious liberties must be defended together. By offering ceremonial rites of confession and pardon, the minister could renew and strengthen the believer's conviction that he served God in his daily calling. And in hours of crisis the theory of a national covenant enabled the churches to rally the community behind whatever action the present peril demanded.

The instrument by which the theory of the social covenant became utilitarian was the jeremiad, a sermon rigidly following the proven formula of acknowledging the hand of divine providence in the present affliction, cataloging the sins of the time which accounted for God's just action against his covenanted people, calling for confession, and offering assurance that pardon is available and, when accompanied by vigorous exertion, will bring relief.[20] In the first years of his ministry Samuel Cooper made only casual use of the jeremiad. Unlike many preachers he took no delight in detailing the supposed sins of his congregation. And he surely knew that some of the events typically regarded in the jeremiad as the punishing hand of God brought economic gain to those prepared to profit from human misery. While he halfheartedly followed the formula of the jeremiad during a New England drought in the summer of 1749, his parishioner Thomas Hancock rushed ten thousand bushels of wheat from England to sell at famine prices. The shipment arrived too late, and Hancock frantically shipped the wheat to another market in the hope of avoiding a complete loss.[21] Hancock's great fortune, like most others made in Cooper's day, resulted from taking advantage of wartime economic opportunities.

Yet Cooper could not reject the covenant theory without repudiating the Congregational ecclesiastical structure on which his church rested; even to slight it meant denying his ministry the dominant mode of moralizing practiced by his clerical colleagues. So he set about adapting the jeremiad to his buoyant spirit and fashioned it into an instrument for encouraging confidence in the future rather than a plaint of declension from the pristine saintliness of the New England fathers. A sermon preached in April 1754 marked his perfection of the form. He told his congregation, most of whom lived by trade, what they wanted to hear: from Scripture we learn that the prosperity of God's covenanted people is his "passionate Wish." He wants to see them "flourishing and happy." But God's "Honour as a moral Governor" requires obedience to him as the price of such blessings. Therefore, "Obedience to the Commands of God, is the sure and only Method for a People, to obtain public Prosperity and Happiness."[22]

He stressed the rewards of obedience. "When Religion prevails, Industry will also Flourish"—industry which "procures an Abundance of the Necessaries and Conveniences of human Life" and "wonderfully enlarges the Wealth and Power of a State." If a people "remarkable for their Religion and Vertue, should be invaded by a foreign Enemy, their Vertue would prove a natural Means of their Security and Success." To summarize, "thus does pure and undefiled Religion, carry along with it, public Security and Prosperity: It defends, it cherishes, it enlarges Nations; and rewards them with an Abundance of the good Things of Life."[23]

Cooper explained temporary economic depression and other light strokes of God's reproving hand as necessary and beneficial chastisement because "great and uninterrupted prosperity hardens the heart."[24] Presumably, a little punishment today conditioned one to receive greater blessings tomorrow. But the string of defeats in the early years of the war with France could only be interpreted in covenant theory to mean that God's anger with New England was great, and justly so. Shortly after Cooper had declared from the pulpit that military success depended on prior "Supplication to the Almighty," the town was stunned by the news that General Braddock had been ambushed and crushed in Pennsylvania by an inferior force of French and Indians.[25] Cooper recovered quickly and rose to the occasion with a militant jeremiad. Such a "Rebuke ought to humble but not discourage us." The time had come to repent and then fight: "Tamely to give up our civil and religious rights to every Invader, is not Christian Meekness, but base Cowardice."[26] A month later he reiterated that New Englanders could not "sit still and expect to see miraculous Salvation as God sometimes afforded to his antient People."[27] Though God is the "sole Monarch" of the world, including the ocean, "where even the *British* Navy cannot triumph, without the Aid of His Providence," victory still requires man's best endeavor in addition to the divine blessing.[28]

As battlefield reverses continued and as Boston was shaken by earthquake, Cooper reverted more toward the customary jeremiad with its emphasis on the sins of the people and God's resulting anger.[29] But by the end of 1757 he had regained his confidence: "While the British Nation has been united with some tokens of the divine Displeasure, which call us to Humility and Repentence, it yet enjoys many great and distinguishing Blessings, which demand our warmest Gratitude and sincerest Praise. The visible Kingdom of God still abides with us: our happy Constitution of Government, our civil and religious Rights, still remain; and we have yet in our Hands the means of defending ourselves, and humbling our Enemies, if God please to add his Blessing to them."[30]

Jeremiad by jeremiad, Samuel Cooper had taken his people through the darkest years of their lives. With the changing tide of war he faced a different task, for the jeremiad was more effective in depression and defeat than in prosperity and victory. Ecstatic over their delivery from the hands of France, Bostonians were in no mood to regard their sins as heinous. In September 1758 General Jeffrey Amherst encamped his victorious troops briefly on Boston Common in observance of the town's thanksgiving day for the capture of Louisbourg. Thousands of townspeople, drinking heavily themselves, plied the soldiers with such quantities of rum that military operations were temporarily delayed. In vain Amherst sent out military patrols to protect his veterans against God's chosen people.[31] Yet in covenant theory God smiled again on New England, a sure sign of public morality.

Cooper's thanksgiving sermon on the reduction of Quebec carefully and fully acknowledged the hand of providence in the success of British arms. Still, the magnitude of victory made unavoidable the implication that God smiled in proportion to the righteousness he found among his covenanted people who had "received a Salvation from Heaven, greater perhaps than any since

the Foundation of the Country."[32] The clergy seemed unconsciously relieved when the Boston fire of 1760 enabled them to
decry from the pulpit a sign of renewed heavenly displeasure. On
this occasion even Cooper listed the specific sins he suspected of being responsible for "this signal Chastisement."[33] Then the town's,
and particularly his church's, magnanimous aid to fire victims appeared to convince him that the local supply of virtue was ample.
When Spain belatedly entered the war in 1762, he confidently
preached that the God who had defended "this British Israel"
against Spain at the peak of its glory would not fail now when such
an implacable foe of "true Religion" and liberty had degenerated
into a second-rate power.[34]

By the time of the official proclamation of peace in 1763,
Bostonians had enjoyed nearly five years of victory and three of
distance from the main theaters of conflict. Though worried concerning the restoration of their trade, they looked to the future with
optimism. Cooper's sermon in August at the thanksgiving for peace
affords a clear window into the mind of Boston's affluent Congregationalists as they reviewed their war experiences. After dwelling at length on the horrors of war and blessings of peace, he
reached his climax in an eloquent summation of the meaning of the
late struggle according to covenant theory:

> Perhaps our Annals cannot furnish a Treaty of
> Peace attended with so many truly national Advan-
> tages. . . . What Enlargement of the British Empire do
> we now behold! What a security to these Colonies!
> What Room to expand themselves: what a Fund of
> Wealth and Commerce to the Mother Kingdom! . . .
> How remarkably has divine Providence appeared in our
> Favor; what great Things has God done for us! Even
> Canada, in all its Extent, is but a small Part of that Ter-
> ritory that is now added to our Sovereign's Dominions
> upon this Continent. . . .
>
> We must religiously regard the Works of the Lord
> and the operation of his Hand; and give him the glory
> that is due unto his Name. We must perceive and
> acknowledge ourselves to be the People of his Care and
> the Sheep of his Hand, who has guided and defended us
> like a tender Shepherd; who has led us into green
> Pastures and beside the still Waters, and has made our
> Peace as a River. May our Righteousness be answerable

to his Goodness, and become like the Waters of the Sea.[35]

Who had a better right than Samuel Cooper, heir to the legacy of Samuel Sewall, Benjamin Colman, and William Cooper, to tell the spiritual descendants of the Puritan founders that they had triumphed over France because they had heeded the call to repentance? And that continued obedience to God ensured the constant outpouring of blessings on the order of the conquest of Canada? The millennial hope of the Great Awakening was to be fulfilled after all, but through the power of the British Empire under God rather than by the preaching of the evangelists. Convinced of their righteousness and thus assured a glorious future, and with the French and Indian knife no longer at their backs, American Calvinists could be expected to insist that the empire remain on the path of virtue as they defined the term.[36]

As compared with Catholic France and Spain, the British Empire seemed indeed the main defender of Protestantism and political freedom. During the war the clergy had repeatedly claimed the Whig interpretation of history as the inheritance of "British Israel" and had transformed the House of Hanover into guardians of this goodly portion. In his fast-day sermon following Braddock's defeat, Cooper explained tersely the lessons of history for New England in the present conflict:

> . . . The European Nations were once free; Their Gothic Ancestors . . . brought with them that most happy Constitution of civil Government that Britain now enjoys. But how few of these Nations have preserved the Inheritance left them by their Fathers! How many have sold their Birth right and sunk into an Abject State of Slavery. . . .
>
> The invaluable Rights both civil and religious which the British Nation and its Dependencies have so long injoyed, call for our most grateful Acknowledgments to the great Governor of the world, whose Providence has so happily distinguished us. God has treated us as Children and not as Slaves: He has called us unto Liberty; and mercifully preserved us from those Chains under which many Nations who once were free, are now groaning. Our Nation has been so wise as to set a high Value upon their Liberties, and to watch over them

with a jealous Eye; . . . These priviledges were peculiarly dear to our Fathers the Founders of this Country, who when they thought them in Danger of being diminished if not lost, in Europe, transplanted them into these western Regions, where by the Favor of divine Providence, they have taken Root, and begun to flourish.[37]

During the war Bostonians had looked upon the lethargic and uninspiring George II as the defender of human freedom and the protector of colonial rights. Cooper hailed him as a "monarch who wanted no other Power than that of doing good."[38] When the king died in 1760, New England churches rang with his praises, and to him were attributed the many achievements of British civilization. Young George III's accession generated expectations of even greater days ahead. In Cooper's words, "Who does not anticipate the Blessings which seem ready to descend upon the Nation in his Government; and the Gratitude that must fill the Hearts of those who enjoy them?"[39]

New England's desire to remake the British monarchy in its own image comes clearly through *Pietas et Gratulatio,* Harvard College's memorial volume marking the transition on the throne. George III received a specially bound copy of this work, then considered a masterpiece of typography. Its thirty-one poems in Latin, Greek, and English gush over the two kings to the point of nausea. Although contributions were anonymous, most authors have been identified.[40] The two compositions attributed to Cooper cloy the reader with adulation of the monarch. After eulogizing the late king as that "godlike man," he celebrated the immature George III as "the Heaven-Inspir'd youth."

> See him begin his royal race!
> 　　Stretching each nerve to freedom's goal,
> A Briton's name his highest joy:
> 　　The prize, he sees securely lodg'd
> Within the center of his subject's heart.
>
> Virtue, bright goddess! guards his throne,
> 　　Her sacred volume opening wide,
> And points him to the page of kings:
> 　　Fame spreads his glory all around,
> And distant realms the chearful chorus join.[41]

As much as New England men might in print fawn before the throne, no reading between the lines is necessary to understand their message. The king-worship in *Pietas et Gratulatio* followed a preface which lectured George III on liberty. He was advised to note "the miserable effects of despotic power" in Europe and to found his empire "upon the maintenance of the Freedom of the people, the security of their Possessions and the Encrease of their numbers."[42] Similarly, Cooper preached his sermon on the death of George II from the text, "Put not your trust in princes." Good, god-fearing princes deserve the trust and confidence of their subjects, he asserted; "but this Trust ought never to be absolute and unlimited. There is one Being, and only one, who claims our unbounded Confidence." Princes are mortal and the "cruel Monarch, the impious Tyrant" returns to dust along with his humblest subjects. By praising English kings for what they were not or were assumed to be, Cooper and his countrymen also established what monarchs must be.[43]

Bostonians were not ungrateful for blessings derived from their place in the empire. They recognized, as Cooper said in 1759, "how chearfully has our Mother Country employed her Riches and Strength for the Preservation of her tender and exposed Offspring! . . . An Obligation which ought ever to be remembered with filial Respect, and the warmest Gratitude."[44] All was well—if the empire continued as in the past.

In the ecstasy of victory over France, Cooper could make room in his "British Israel" for the mother country. But if the future should reveal that George III was not the champion of Protestant liberty, that the homeland had sunk into a degeneracy past hope of restoration of virtue, or that evil-minded ministers of state and crypto-Catholic Anglican bishops plotted to reshape the empire to crush colonial freedom, then the covenant theory could operate against the mother country as it had been used recently in the conflict with France. In that case, the concept of a just war, a favorite theme of sermons preached in New England from 1754 to 1763, could be used to support matricide, for as Cooper explained in 1756, "Nothing can be more plain than that War in certain Cases is just, and that there may be some Circumstances that not only allow, but oblige even the Disciples of the Prince of Peace to take up Arms."[45]

Fourteen years after the glorious defeat of France in 1763, Cooper climbed into his pulpit to preach a fast-day sermon. With General Burgoyne marching south from Canada to crush the rebellious colonies, the American outlook had never seemed darker. In such an hour the preacher's words struck home: "In Time of profound Peace, and without the least Provocation given on our Part, our Territories have been treacherously invaded, by our inveterate and powerful Enemies; . . . who seem to aim at Nothing less than dispossessing us of the fair Inheritance left us by our Fathers. This unjust and perfidious Conduct of theirs, has obliged us to oppose Force to Force; and to exert ourselves in the Defence of our Priviledges and just Possessions. And blessed be God we have not yet been dismayed at the Approach of the Enemy. . . . An uncommon Ardor has appeared among us, early to oppose the Incroachments of our Anti-Christian Enemies."[46]

The sermon containing this passage had been written in 1755. It could be repeated unaltered except for an occasional oral substitution, usually only England for France when naming the foe. During the War for Independence Cooper repeated many sermons first written and preached two decades earlier to arouse his hearers against the Gallic peril. At most he added a few pages of adaptation to the new war.[47] In part the repetition reflects his reluctance to prepare new sermons while concerned with the war effort. But even more, it provides evidence that for Samuel Cooper, as for many of his countrymen, the Great War for Empire of 1754–1763 had been intellectually, emotionally, and spiritually a rehearsal for the American Revolution.

Some men grow intensely spiritual in the hour of trial because they crave moral sanction for whatever action is necessary to meet the crisis. These are the individuals most influenced by preaching, and they respond more to an ostensibly spiritual message than to sermons patently political in motivation and content. During the contest with France, the large segment of Boston's elite worshiping at Brattle Street had seen new meaning in the struggle of the Old Testament fathers to obey Jehovah's command to preserve their wealth and gain the Promised Land. As Abraham, Isaac, and Jacob had demonstrated, the people of God could be practical men of affairs and means.[48] Thus those Bostonians schooled by Samuel Cooper could pursue their secular interests in full confidence that they served the Lord of this modern "British Israel."

4

Tom Pewman

Samuel Cooper's ministerial office officially excluded him from participation in politics except for the few ritualistic, nonpartisan civil functions of the Congregational clergy. But his clerical robe could never completely conceal a passion for involvement in the political hurly-burly of Massachusetts. There is no evidence that he ever admitted to himself that he had chosen the wrong profession, though his detractors believed that he had soon become bored with the ministry and had then turned to covert political activity as a first love. Yet his clandestine activities reveal how clearly he recognized that politicians were replacing clergymen as the leaders of the colony.

The politics of self-interest was nothing new to Massachusetts. Almost from the beginning, its unique system of town and colony government had bred litters of politicians. Early in the eighteenth century, sporadic political struggles between the House of Representatives and royal governors gave off flashes of heat hardly surpassed in the decade before the final break with the mother country. As the House exploited every opportunity to enlarge its powers at the expense of the governor's, the central consideration of Massachusetts government became clear: to be successful, a governor must simultaneously retain the favor of his English patrons while developing a broad base of power in the colony by constructing a coalition of leading families with their opposing economic, regional, and religious interests. It was nearly an impossible task, for in normal times the governor lacked sufficient patronage with which to bind men to him.[1]

William Shirley proved to be the first governor with the political acumen and energy required to make the office effective. During his long term from 1741 to 1757, he taught Massachusetts the essentials of party government he had learned from his patron, the Duke of Newcastle, master spoilsman of the century. Through his power of appointment, limited though it was, Shirley created henchmen in all sections of the province. Unlike most other governors, he held military as well as civil office and thus had fat war contracts at his disposal. These he awarded to loyal merchants, among them James Bowdoin, Thomas Hutchinson, and Thomas Hancock. Even in remote Barnstable the Otises profited as suppliers of small boats. To the unabashed use of power Shirley added remarkable talents of personal diplomacy.[2]

In Shirley's school of politics the Boston merchants learned a major political lesson. The House of Representatives, dominated by a rural majority, passed a bill in 1754 that closed loopholes in the excise laws through which the coastal merchants and distillers had hitherto largely escaped paying liquor taxes. With the blessing of Shirley's friendly neutrality, Hancock led a fight to kill the measure but failed to muster enough votes. Finally, to preserve his relations with the House, the governor reluctantly signed a revised bill into law.[3]

The Crisis, one of the anonymous pamphlets called forth by this controversy, has usually been attributed to Samuel Cooper, though his brother took public responsibility for it. Direct proof of authorship is lacking, but the style of *The Crisis,* including a stanza of verse, resembles the minister's known writings. This short pamphlet provides striking evidence of his complete identification with the cause of Boston merchants. He, of course, shared their general outlook and might be expected to enlist his pen in the cause of Hancock, Bowdoin, and other merchants of his church. Since Cooper had been chaplain of the House of Representatives for two years before the excise controversy but was not reelected in the spring of 1755, it can be assumed that the rural majority dispensed with his services because they knew he had written *The Crisis.*[4]

The author lectured agrarian Massachusetts on the need to treat trading interests with tender care: "Many a Country has grown rich and affluent by Trade alone, no Country without it. 'Tis as easy to lose Trade, as to lose Reputation, and 'tis equally hard to recover either." The majority of the House scorned such warnings, for they viewed the mercantile community as profiteers at the expense of the poor and the farmer. The lesson was unforgettable: if the merchants wanted to protect their vital interests, they must associate themselves with a party capable of controlling the legislature.[5]

His talents and drive notwithstanding, Shirley's successful administration would have been impossible in peacetime. Even with the unanimity behind the war effort and the allure of British military gold, his shifting political alliances left an outspoken opposition in their wake. As he found it more difficult to hold his followers together, he leaned increasingly on the advice and services of Thomas Hutchinson, who had distinguished himself in the last decade as a public servant of unusual dedication and integrity. The Hutchinson family, living in Boston and nearby towns, appeared to receive the choice patronage plums, while the Otises and others picked up only a few crumbs that fell from the table. When Shirley was removed from office in 1757, his supporters began a new scramble for power.[6]

Thomas Pownall, Shirley's successor, occupied the governor's chair for less than three years. Afterwards, for nearly a quarter century, he would continue to influence Massachusetts affairs, often through his friend Samuel Cooper. Of the many figures standing in the shadows where the preacher carried on his political activities, Governor Pownall ranks first in genius and high in importance, notwithstanding the quirks of personality and temperament that hampered his career and denied him the wide following among contemporaries that would have made him conspicuous to historians.

Pownall had come to America in 1753 to fulfill an ambition whetted by a Cambridge education but unsatisfied by a family position among the lower gentry. Through travel, observation, and writing he made himself known as an expert on the colonies and in 1755 was appointed the lieutenant governor of New Jersey. A year later, coached by his good friend Benjamin Franklin, he self-assuredly refused the governorship of Pennsylvania because the Penns would not give him a free hand in that unruly proprietary colony. His intrigues with enemies of Governor Shirley helped to create the vacancy in the Massachusetts government to which Pownall was elevated in 1757. That August, before his thirty-fifth birthday, he arrived in Boston to take up the reins of government.[7]

Pownall's views of history and constitutional theory nearly matched those of American Whigs.[8] Aware of a governor's lack of real power, he proposed to lead rather than drive the people of his province. He usually accepted the Massachusetts General Court for what it claimed to be—the supreme *legislature for the colony's internal concerns—and defended the compromises of imperial authority he was forced to accept in order to secure passage of vital war measures. As he rode the crest of the wave of total victory over France, Pownall in practice confirmed interpretations held by the majority in Massachusetts of their institutions and place in the British Empire.[9]

At first the new governor seemed determined to keep himself above factionalism and backed Thomas Hutchinson's appointment as lieutenant governor. But shortly, as the divided loyalties and lingering enmity of Shirley's friends came to the surface, Pownall accepted the support of the former governor's political foes and charted a course independent of Hutchinson. James Otis, Jr., became the governor's trusted intimate and brought the elder Otis into the new alignment. In return, the son received a comfortable position as deputy advocate-general of the vice-admiralty court and the father a promise of political preferment. Pownall came to rely heavily on the counsel of Thomas Hancock, now the leading merchant of Boston, thanks to four years of supplying the armed forces and the death of his associate in this enterprise. In 1758 Hancock was elected to the Council, a body that served as both the upper house of the General Court and executive advisers to the governor. Perhaps more significant in their relationship, Pownall entrusted Hancock to invest for him the handsome sum of almost £5,000. James Bowdoin, who had been promoted from the House to the Council in 1757, developed a close friendship with the governor. Obviously Boston merchants had little fear that this governor would encourage customs officials to be overzealous in detecting and prosecuting illegal trade. Hutchinson complained that he had "intirely lost Mr. Pownall's Friendship," and set about strengthening his own political following.[10]

Those opposed to Pownall found him an easy mark for ridicule. Short, vain, and hot-tempered, he made more than his share of enemies. His contradictory behavior sometimes baffled citizens. He might insist on the last bit of pompous ceremony due his station, or he might transact business so casually as to demean the office. Hutchinson's partisans relished the tale that their governor had boxed the ears of a gentleman who, failing to recognize whom he was passing on the council chamber steps, had not removed his hat.[11] Twenty years later Samuel Adams still recalled

---

*General Court and legislature are used interchangeably hereafter.

with disgust the "Riots & Routs" the bachelor governor reportedly gave in the Province House for the town's younger social elite.[12] Otis, Bowdoin, and Cooper—all close to him in years—likely were included in this circle, as may have been John Hancock, recently come of age. Thoroughly pragmatic in religion, Pownall seemed more at home with Congregationalists than with Anglicans of his own communion, who despised any governor not a zealous defender of the king's church.[13] Also conspicuous among Pownall's foibles were an awkwardness and a roughness in speaking and writing that led one observer to notice that "he now and then broke the Rules of Grammar in his public Speeches."[14]

A major public attempt to ridicule Pownall came off the press at the end of his term. Samuel Waterhouse, a customs officer who took his family to the Brattle Street Church, is credited with writing *Proposals for Printing by Subscription, the History of the public Life and distinguished Actions of Vice-Admiral Sir Thomas Brazen, Commander of an American Squadron in the last Age. Together with his slighter Adventures and more entertaining Anecdotes.*[15] Among Brazen's (or Pownall's) petty acts, he had "run down the poor chaplain, who could not get out of his way."[16] The reference is apparently to Ebenezer Pemberton, minister of the New Brick Church in Boston and Hutchinson's "near friend," who had replaced the Brattle Street pastor as chaplain of the House. Cooper had been reelected in 1758 at the first election after Pownall's arrival.[17]

Among the "most forward" of Admiral Brazen's "pick'd forecastle hands" was "Tom Pewman," who could hardly be anyone but the Brattle Street minister:

> [Tom Pewman] . . . was as well known as any one hand in the fleet, for the Jacks [sailors] were often very merry with him; and soon from his prodigious affection for prate and harangue in a somewhat fanatical tone, they dubb'd him Parson; for which character he discovered (forsooth) very great contempt, and immediately chang'd manner, and mightily affected the military stile and character, upon which he was dubb'd col'nel, which tickled him not a little; but some unlucky Jacks in a very short time settled it the preaching colonel; (than which character nothing in the present age inspires stronger contempt.) And one or other of them was always girding at him; sometimes with great solemnity

of phrase & face, addressing him, would begin, "Reverend Colonel": at other times, and most frequently, would deal somewhat plainly, telling him of his unfaithfulness in his master's vineyard, that it now produced only the degenerate plant of a strange vine, that the grapes were those of Sodom and the clusters of Gomorrah; all which most intimately mortified him, for he could as little bear any quotations in his presence from scripture, as could the poor fellow who had stood in the pillory, the sight of a pudding or custard, or even the bare mention of eggs.[18]

Assuming that "Tom Pewman" was Cooper, the meaning of this passage is clear. "Colonel" in its Hudibrastic sense meant someone playing the part of an officer raising a regiment or, in a political setting, beating the bushes for votes.[19] Thus a "Reverend Colonel" was a clerical politician who inspired contempt by neglecting the care of souls to mingle in politics.

The specific charge was that Cooper had joined two Boston members of the House in steering through the legislature a resolution authorizing the only armed ship maintained by the province to leave off guarding the coast long enough to ferry the governor to England. Early in 1760 Pownall had received notice that he was being transferred to the governorship of South Carolina, but he had obtained permission to visit England on business before taking the new post. His close friends sponsored the resolution, thereby being able to offer him as a farewell present assurance of a safe passage across the war-infested north Atlantic. Much as they liked Pownall's support of trade, coastal merchants were aghast at this proposal, which would leave their shipping unprotected for several months. A petition of 114 merchants failed to change the Council's vote, but Pownall diplomatically arranged for passage on a private vessel.[20]

Cooper may have been embarrassed by being included in this attack on Pownall written by a member of his own parish. A considerable number of the petitioners sat in Brattle Street pews on Sundays. Irked by their pastor's behavior in this case, they might come to believe oft-repeated charges of politicizing. Whether through more circumspect conduct or better covering of his tracks, he escaped most public criticism for the next fifteen years. Yet, at this early date, the pattern of future jibes at him was established:

social gaiety, political machinations, neglect of pastoral duty, a jaded view of his sacred office, insincerity in the pulpit, and betrayal of his family heritage.

Pownall embarked from Boston in June.[21] He had not been loved by the people, perhaps not even by such intimates as Hancock, Bowdoin, Cooper, and the Otises, who found him so useful and interesting. The Hutchinson circle rejoiced at the transfer.[22] Unmistakably, nevertheless, Pownall had given the province a brief glimpse of a quality of colonial government that could preserve the loyalty of the colonies to the British Empire.[23] And he left behind men who expected more of the same. Hutchinson, of course, was now acting governor, but one of Pownall's last official acts was to approve the election of the elder Otis as Speaker of the House.[24] The battle lines were drawn. By and large, men close to Pownall from 1757 to 1760 would stand firm in the next decade against economic encroachments by the mother country, while Hutchinson's followers would tolerate innovation in the interest of preserving royal authority. Both groups had learned the role that political action was to play in the contest.

On board with Pownall and in his care, John Hancock sailed for England to explore the London business community before becoming a partner in his uncle's firm. Young Hancock would return, but Pownall would not. He turned down the South Carolina appointment to remain home and become the sharpest critic of colonial administration, first in print and later on the floor of the House of Commons.[25]

Pownall had understood what Boston's great merchants, smaller traders, petty shopkeepers, ship captains, sailors, shipbuilders, distillers, and artisans all knew: the town lived by trade and the prosperity of all classes was linked to the general level of commerce. To them Pownall's constitutional views and political alliances had seemed of less importance than the encouragement and protection he had afforded their trade. The farewell address of the Boston merchants praised him for attempting to "soften and alleviate the Inconveniences and Hardships to which Trade is exposed in a Time of War."[26] During his first year in office he had written to Pitt of his surprise "to see the Alteration in the Trade of Boston from what it was when I was here three Years Ago."[27] He did not exaggerate, for commerce had suffered a serious decline from the peaks reached during the last prewar years, though some fortunate merchants had more than recouped their losses through contracts to supply the armed forces. The war had played havoc with the fishery, and scores of merchant ships had been sunk or captured by the French. Bankruptcies reached a record high in 1758. Economic collapse had been averted only because the mother country subsidized the wholesale importation of military materiel and the transport of troops.[28] With the surrender of all Canada in the fall of 1760, the artificially sustained economy must soon be replaced by peacetime competition for markets. Could Boston regain and increase its share of the empire's trade? The ecstasy of the victory celebration momentarily drove out all doubts.[29]

Even had the British ministry permitted imperial administration to relapse into its prewar laxity, Boston's economic outlook would have lacked promise. For a century after its founding, the town's prosperity had rested on a steady increase of population and its relative importance in the entire colonial economy. But growth halted in the 1740s and the population remained stable until the Revolution. In that same period (1740–1775) the population of Massachusetts nearly doubled, and New England as a whole and the other colonies grew even faster. No longer could Bostonians boast of living in the greatest urban center of North America. Both New York and Philadelphia were larger than Boston in 1760 and expanding rapidly. Each year their merchants made new inroads into Boston's trade. Closer to home, a half-dozen New England towns now competed with the capital in manufacturing and commerce.

In the two decades after 1740 Bostonians had suffered through runaway inflation followed by steady deflation, ten years of the unusual physical and human sacrifices demanded by war, the normal run of epidemics plus an outbreak of smallpox in 1752 that brought life to a standstill during the summer months, a terrifying earthquake in 1755, and finally, in 1760, the most disastrous fire in their history. Food prices continued high and uncertain as compared with those in the countryside. As a result of the town's peninsular location, winter firewood sold at what seemed a prohibitive figure to those of moderate or low income. Too often, skilled workers migrated to nearby towns, leaving the poor behind. The large seagoing population meant a constant oversupply of widows, now augmented by the wives of men killed in recent battles. To care for the poor and support the war, tax rates were raised above other areas.[30]

Hoping that these difficult times were behind them, Boston's aggressive merchants looked forward in 1760 to a new era of peace and prosperity in an expanded empire where commercial rivalries might be fiercer but profits all the greater. They confidently assumed that the home government had permanently conceded in practice, at least, that the series of acts regulating the trade of the empire—the navigation laws—were for the purpose of giving general guidance to commerce without strangling it. Thus where the laws threatened to curtail New England's basic trade, as in the cases of regulations concerning molasses and tea, unofficial nonenforcement constituted a pragmatic concession to reality. What clearer expression of this attitude did Boston need than the presence of Thomas Lechmere, surveyor general of customs for the northern district, who for several years had been too aged, infirm, and perhaps too intoxicated to perform his duties? His friends estimated that he had consumed while in office sufficient Madeira wine to float a 74-gun man-of-war. Since the navigation acts permitted direct trade with Madeira, ship captains whose cargoes would not bear full inspection found this legally imported wine an excellent gift for the surveyor general.[31]

In their petition of 1760 Boston merchants acknowledged the obvious—that a "great Part of our Trade is to the West-Indies."[32] During the present war, Great Britain forbade entirely the substantial portion of this commerce conducted legally in peacetime—except for molasses and sugar—with the French sugar islands. In Whitehall trade with the enemy constituted treason, in Boston economic necessity. Losing a major source of revenue to the neutral Dutch could hardly serve the national interest. Given the difficulty of enforcing the boycott and the intensity of intercolonial commercial competition, Boston merchants had no faith that their rivals in New York and Philadelphia would put patriotism above profits. And how could war taxes be paid from diminishing incomes? The issue of supplying the plantations of enemy islands represented a legitimate conflict of interest between Americans and the mother country, backed by planters in the English West Indies. Even so, New England traders seem to have heeded the boycott more than merchants to the south.[33]

If in 1760 Boston's great merchants and shipowners were sometimes technically smugglers and disloyal traffickers with the enemy, at home they were patriots, church members, and ardent admirers of William Pitt. The first inkling that rosy expectations of their future in the British Empire might prove illusory came the month after the celebration of the fall of Quebec, when they heard that Pitt had ordered American governors "to put the most speedy and effectual Stop" to the "illegal and most pernicious Trade" carried on by the king's subjects with the French "in open Contempt of the Authority of the Mother Country."[34] In the last two years of conflict, 1761–1763, while the fighting went on far from New England, the Royal Navy waged war on colonial shipping in the West Indies as well as on the fleets of France and Spain.[35] Seen in retrospect, these events amounted to a declaration of war against Boston's trade, a war that would be fought for fourteen years and would in the end close the port to all trade.

The final peace with France and Spain in 1763 touched off another round of celebration; but no amount of joy over the removal of the French at their backs could disguise the severe postwar problems faced by the trading community.[36] The merchant might well feel that he had been taken to the mountaintop, shown the promised land, and then cast down on the rocks below.

Samuel Cooper preached to a quarter of Boston's merchants and major shipowners.[37] Far from being revolutionaries, they wanted nothing more than for the empire to resume its former course. Without a threat to their common interest in the pursuit of profits, they would have remained a loose group, jealous of each other's successes and concerned primarily with the improvement of family fortunes and social prestige. They preferred trade to politics but had become aware that they must at times preserve the one with the other. In 1761 they stood ready to use whatever political, economic, or ideological weapons might be available and necessary. And their pastor stood with them.

5

The Characters...
Most Conspicuous...
Ardent and Influential

*D*uring the early 1760s Samuel Cooper drew increasingly closer to the men caught up in the struggle to defend Boston's commercial interests. Of these, no one was more vital to his clandestine activities than his brother, William.

When the Boston town meeting elected William Cooper town clerk in March 1761, no one took notice. He died in 1809, still town clerk and just as inconspicuous. During nearly a half century of service his moments of fame came only when epithets were hurled at him by political foes temporarily out of range of more significant targets. But anyone who reads the Boston press of the period soon discovers that William Cooper was not so obscure as he at first seems. In almost every issue of the newspapers one sees his name in connection with the dozens of necessary but routine tasks assigned his office. Standing one step behind the leaders at every juncture from 1760 to 1783, he appears more omnipresent in the Boston Revolutionary movement than any other man, even Samuel Adams.

Slightly older than his brother Samuel, William Cooper had turned to public service after unenthusiastically trying his hand at trade. Holding some minor offices at first, he settled down in the 1760s as town clerk and register of probate for Suffolk County.[1] His social and perhaps economic position had been assured in 1745 by marriage to Katherine, daughter of Jacob Wendell, Boston merchant, colonel of militia, and member of the province Council. From a poor Dutch family of Albany, Wendell was another of those self-made Boston men who had gravitated toward the Brattle Street Church.[2] Katherine bore seventeen children to her husband, who was apparently too occupied with weightier matters to make an official record of their births. The town records he kept for a half century still drive the genealogist to despair.[3]

The relationship between the brothers is scantly documented. Living together in the same town, on intimate terms, and often engaged in backstairs political enterprises, they had little need to express on paper their attachment to each other. Samuel summarized the whole story in three lines of a letter written in 1769 to Will, then on a summer vacation trip: "As to News, what shall I say? Your absence is no small Disadvantage both to my collecting and relishing it."[4] It is misleading to suggest, as some loyalists later did, that the town clerk served merely as a front, an errand boy, or a collector of information for the preacher. They were partners, each working in his respective sphere. No surer evidence of their friendship and mutual respect is necessary than knowledge that Will faithfully sat under his brother's ministry for thirty-eight years and regularly presented his children for baptism, including one christened Samuel. When that infant died, the name was given again to the next boy.[5]

John Adams knew the Cooper brothers intimately. A decade after William's death, the aged former president let his fading memory wander back over the rise of colonial resistance to British measures. He wrote that "the characters the most conspicuous, the most ardent and influential in this revival ["of American principles and feelings"], from 1760 to 1766, were, first and foremost, before all and above all, James Otis; next to him was Oxenbridge Thacher; next to him, Samuel Adams; next to him, John Hancock; then Dr. Mayhew; then Dr. Cooper and his brother."[6]

The presence of the two Coopers has blurred the historical identity of each. When referring in writing to one of them, townsmen knew which was intended and often omitted the first name; the modern reader can seldom be certain. A few minutes spent scanning indexes and annotations of documentary collections on Revolutionary Boston reveal some of the tricks the Cooper brothers inadvertently played on historians.

Another man of major importance in Samuel Cooper's life entered the Boston scene in 1761. John Temple became a citizen of two countries and, as a result, found a place in the history of neither.[7] In overlooking him, American historians have denied their narratives an intriguing character who runs like a bright thread through Boston's Revolutionary history. As the following chapters will demonstrate, Temple's enigmatic career was of crucial importance to Cooper's circle of political leaders.

Temple came from a Scotch-Irish family that had migrated in the 1720s to the Boston area and now enjoyed considerable social prestige, in part the result of influential family connections in the mother country. He spent much time in England preserving these ties with important relatives, among them Earl Temple (Richard Grenville) and his brother George Grenville, both political allies of their brother-in-law William Pitt. George Grenville had taken a special interest in his young kinsman from America but had been unable to secure a suitable political preferment for him until 1760. That summer Temple crossed to London from New York and saw Pitt shortly after his arrival. The following year, not yet thirty, he returned home as surveyor-general of customs for the northern colonies and lieutenant governor of New Hampshire. The latter office, merely honorary, made the surveyor-generalship more prestigious.[8]

Temple was charged with revitalizing the enforcement of the navigation acts. In October he landed at New York and made his way northward, discovering ample evidence of laxity, inefficiency, and fraud en route. When he reached Boston on 23 November a far different situation greeted him. Charles Paxton, customs surveyor and searcher for the port of Boston, had begun a campaign to locate smugglers through the use of paid informers. Among others he caught John Erving, member of the Council, father-in-law of James Bowdoin, and parishioner of Cooper. It was a profitable enterprise for Paxton, who received one-third of the proceeds from the sale of forfeited goods. In August the new governor, Francis Bernard, entered Boston bringing firm instructions to require compliance with the navigation acts. Since the governor also received a one-third share of confiscations, he could help supply the needs of his large family by carrying out his orders, and thus gladly gave full support to Paxton. Temple at once took a more conciliatory attitude toward the merchants' cause. While awaiting advice from his superiors in England, he endeavored to remain on good terms with those he had been sent to watch.[9]

Though Temple sought fair and uniform administration of the customs regulations, he indulged in no dreams of perfect enforcement, particularly of the act of 1733, which placed a prohibitive duty on sugar and molasses from the foreign West Indies. He seemed to share the fear of Boston's merchants that Paxton's activity would put them at a disadvantage with competitors from other colonies where the laws were not so rigorously executed. Merchants respected him because, not sharing in forfeitures prosecuted by lower officers, he appeared to exert a moderating influence on the rapacity of Paxton and Bernard and to afford some protection against the greater threat of arbitrary and unlawful seizures by naval captains whose wartime authority to apprehend smugglers Parliament extended into peacetime. Typical of the eighteenth-century English official, his personal objectives reached no higher than building a customs service loyal to him and thus a source of political strength for himself and the faction in England to which he was related.[10]

The contest of 1760–1762 over customs enforcement propelled James Otis into political leadership in Massachusetts for the entire decade. After graduation from Harvard, he had yielded to the pressure of a domineering father to transfer his genius from classical literature to the more practical study of law. Following a short period of practice in the country, he opened an office in Boston, where he found Hancock and other economic leaders ready to employ his dazzling legal talents. His cherubic appearance and earlier reputation as a recluse notwithstanding, he had married a merchant's daughter, both beautiful and rich. In Boston social and business circles of the 1750s, no one seemed more at home and flourishing than James Otis, who gave few signs of the mental illness that would plague his later years. Pownall's appointment to the vice-admiralty court of one so closely tied to the mercantile community had proved a source of comfort for the merchants as well as of regular income to Otis.[11]

Governor Bernard's small measure of political insight was sufficient to make him wary of siding with either the Hutchinson or Otis factions, but within two months of his taking office the death of the chief justice of the Superior Court had removed all possibility of neutrality. The senior Otis believed his long legal experience and political service entitled him to the next vacancy on the bench, and Pownall had promised as much. Instead, Bernard appointed Hutchinson, a man of no legal training who already held office as lieutenant governor, member of the Council, county probate judge, and commander of the harbor fort. While attempting to win this judicial post for his father, Otis had seen evidence of Charles Paxton's strong hand in the appointment of Hutchinson. Convinced of a plot to swing the Superior Court behind rigorous enforcement of the navigation acts, Otis had resigned his post in the vice-admiralty court to join the legal maneuvers of the merchants.[12]

With Hutchinson and his supporters forming a solid majority on the Superior Court bench, suits to restrain customs officers were doomed. Nevertheless, Otis executed a series of legal stratagems that reduced the financial incentives for informers and threw the odium of enforcement on the chief justice and governor. The presence of the new surveyor-general and Otis's successes cooled the ardor for seizures.[13]

Boston rewarded the brilliant young advocate of its mercantile interests by electing him to the *assembly in 1761. In that body, Otis united the country followers of his father with delegates from the trading communities and used their combined strength to challenge Bernard and Hutchinson.[14] The *Boston Gazette* enlivened its otherwise dull weekly edition by becoming the organ of the antiadministration forces. Its publishers, Benjamin Edes and John Gill, had excellent advertising support from the great merchants most opposed to customs enforcement. With a broader advertising clientele, the *Boston Evening-Post* could safely open its pages to both sides and, as a result, published major attacks on Otis.[15] If we can believe his enemies, Otis also made effective use of the caucus organized by Thomas Dawes to control town-meeting politics through bloc voting, brought about in part, it seems, through economic pressure exerted by merchants.[16]

Otis himself had become so indifferent to religion that his father thought him hardly a Christian.[17] Still, he sought to make political allies of the "black Regiment" of Congregational clergy by implicating Bernard in an intrigue to force an Anglican bishop on New England. Though some of the clergy mistrusted Otis and his methods, he could always count on his blustery college friend Jonathan Mayhew and on the older Charles Chauncy of the First Church to contribute enough martial zeal for an entire regiment. In sharp contrast, Samuel Cooper attempted to maintain the public fiction that the Brattle Street pulpit was above politics even while he was suspected of being privy to every move of his Harvard classmate Otis.[18]

Such suspicions are difficult to verify. In February 1763 John Adams learned that a Cooper belonged to the "Caucus Clubb" meeting in the garret of Tom Dawes. This may have been William and not Samuel; however, a few weeks later Jonathan Sewall, a young Boston lawyer supporting the crown, issued a newspaper

---

*Assembly and House of Representatives are used interchangeably hereafter.

blast against the "Reverend Chaplain to the Junto" and threatened to disclose him by name if he did not cease associating with the "[type]setters, pimps, bullies, and incendiaries" stirring up opposition to royal government. At the time he wrote, Sewall may have been more incensed at Mayhew's inflammatory sermons than Cooper's politicizing, yet he took aim more directly at the "Chaplain," who could hardly have been anyone but the Brattle Street pastor. John Adams thought that he meant Cooper, and three years later in a newspaper contest with Sewall reminded Bostonians that his opponent had once "falsely and maliciously slandered" one of the ablest divines of North America. As much as Cooper covered his tracks, it became a matter of faith among friends of Bernard and Hutchinson that this preacher presided at the "Night Garret Meetings" of dangerous radicals.[19]

Otis won a notable series of victories in the legislative session of 1761–1762, but the coalition he had assembled proved too weak to survive his inordinate attacks on Hutchinson that disgusted many belonging to neither faction. Though still firmly in control of Boston, his party suffered an overwhelming defeat in the May legislative election of 1763. When the House assembled, Hutchinson's supporters were in full control. The publishers of the *Gazette* lost their printing contract with the province and Cooper his honorary position as chaplain of the House. Shattered by their defeat, the Otises achieved a reconciliation with the governor which won more offices for the father and brought a temporary lull in the son's abuse of Hutchinson.[20]

In August the entire British Empire observed a day of thanksgiving for the treaty that officially and so victoriously concluded the war. Cooper's optimistic and deeply spiritual sermon on this occasion gave no hint of the political struggles of the last three years resulting from fusion of the merchants' cause with efforts of the Otis family to wrest power from the Hutchinsons. He spoke of "Our gracious King, whose Counsels and Endeavors for the Restitution of Tranquility to his Dominions, and for the Security and Happiness of these Colonies, we now behold crowned with such Success." But his references to the anticipated economic fruits of victory—increased commerce with Africa and the West Indies, new sources of trade in the East Indies, enlargement of the New England fishery, and territorial expansion on the North American continent—suggest clearly the thoughts resting most heavily on the minds of the Brattle Street merchants this Thursday in August 1763 as they listened to the pious friend of the irreligious Mr. Otis.[21]

While Cooper preached in celebration of peace, the *Wolfe* sailed the high seas returning to Boston with the first illicit cargo imported directly from Russia. This vessel belonged to Nicholas Boylston, whose brother Thomas Boylston of the Brattle Street congregation would soon join him in opening the lucrative but illegal Baltic trade.[22] Boston merchants faced the new challenges of the postwar era with their customary aggressiveness and stamina. Already they had organized formally into "The Society for encouraging Trade and Commerce within the Province of the Massachusetts Bay." With 147 members, mostly from Boston, the society's rolls contained the names of nearly all the major merchants of the town. Not all had supported Otis in the legislature, and thus the bylaws ruled out "as much as possible, all Party disputes"; but they were ready to unite against "any Thing which may be judged prejudicial" to trade.[23]

Boston's gentlemen of trade had more to fear than they knew. For the last quarter century, an accumulation of reports in Whitehall had documented American violations of the navigation acts. Deliberately choosing to take the path of least resistance, earlier ministers of state had ignored evidence of colonial commercial independence. At the end of the conflict in 1763, George Grenville and the men around him concluded that the colonial system had never really worked at all and must be reformed now, if ever, while the British army in the colonies remained strong and the navy sailed American waters temporarily free of rival men-of-war. When Grenville became head of the ministry in 1763, an investigation disclosed that the colonial customs service collected far less than it spent. Facing a staggering war debt at home and believing it desirable to maintain a large army in newly captured American territories, the Grenville ministry determined to reform the customs administration and to seek other means of raising revenue in the colonies. Acting both from principle and expediency, Grenville in effect sought a fundamental change in the constitutional relationship of mother country and colonies established by tacit agreement over the previous century.[24]

Already in April 1763, as Grenville took office, Parliament had authorized the navy to inspect merchant vessels hovering off colonial coasts and to seize those suspected of violating regulations. Later in the year American customs officials received a new set of instructions mandating full enforcement and promising immediate dismissal of anyone failing to do so. Temple called public attention to his new orders by a series of newspaper advertisements warning shipmasters of the law.[25]

The Boston merchants had failed to anticipate the new emphasis on adherence to the so-called sugar or molasses act of 1733, due to expire in 1764. This measure, placing a prohibitive duty on the importation of rum, sugar, and molasses from the foreign West Indies, had been aimed chiefly at the New England rum industry, dependent on a plentiful supply of inexpensive molasses, a by-product of sugar refining which had domestic as well as industrial uses. It constituted the one major exportable commodity from the foreign islands and thus appeared indispensable to the West Indian trade on which much of New England's commercial prosperity rested. Never rigorously enforced, the act of 1733 had proved to be more a nuisance than a deterrent to illegal trade.[26]

Boston merchants hoped to see this act lapse without renewal, or at least the duty lowered from six pence a gallon to one or two pence. Instead, the ministry secured passage of a comprehensive bill —the Sugar Act of 1764—fixing the duty at three pence, a figure still considered prohibitive by the merchants. But this provision was only the beginning. The act went on to strike crippling blows at American trade with changes in enforcement procedures. Most serious of all in colonial eyes, prosecutions under any of the navigation laws might now be commenced in admiralty courts, which meant in effect removing such cases once and for all from colonial courts where juries of fellow citizens seldom convicted smugglers. Furthermore, prosecutors now had the option of taking customs cases for trial to a new vice-admiralty court established at Halifax, Nova Scotia, where no local pressures could possibly prevent judges from carrying out the royal will.[27]

Massachusetts had failed to make effective protest against renewal of the duty on molasses, in part because of a drawn-out controversy over whether Thomas Hutchinson should be sent to England to deliver a remonstrance in person.[28] But both before and after he knew the terms of Grenville's bill, much of the merchant's difficulty in defending himself lay in the ambivalence he felt when pleading his case. Fiercely loyal to his sovereign, grateful for the blessings of British liberty, dependent on an ordered society and its civil authority for the security of his property, he nevertheless had to admit that he was sometimes forced to break the law in order to prosper. Yet the naked question of whether it was right to violate

an unjust law, even one restraining trade, so disturbed the merchant that he turned to those advocates who could dress the issue in
broad constitutional, legal, and economic theory.

Samuel Adams made his debut as a propagandist in May 1764
when he drafted the instructions of the Boston town meeting to its
newly elected assemblymen. Though a little older than Otis and
Cooper, until now Adams had distinguished himself only by
failure. Elected a tax collector in 1756, his collections were currently in such arrears as to suggest defalcation. As sanctimonious as
Otis was blasphemous, Adams excelled in raising all arguments to
the level of principle. Written just before it became certain that a
new sugar act had passed Parliament, the instructions moved rapidly through the economic case to the higher ground of "our
Charter Right to Govern and Tax ourselves" and concluded with
the question, "If Taxes are laid upon us in any shape without ever
having a Legal Representation where they are laid, are we not
reduced from the Character of Free Subjects to the miserable state
of tributary Slaves?"[29]

Adams had reached for the ultimate issue too quickly. After
word came confirming passage of the "Black Act," two of the
lawyers closest to the mercantile community published pamphlets
which struggled with the points Adams had swept aside. Less flam-
boyant than Otis, Oxenbridge Thacher reminded Britain that much
of her prosperity resulted from trade with the colonies, that royal
officials were about to kill the hen that laid golden eggs for the
mother country.[30] In four pamphlets of 1764 and 1765, James Otis
thrashed about wildly in a frantic attempt to relate the "supreme
absolute power" of Parliament to the inequity of taxing America.[31]
In the process, he so thoroughly confused his townsmen that they
charged him with disloyalty and nearly repudiated his political
leadership. In one short year Otis underwent the agony of mind and
soul that many Boston merchants with less intellectual sensitivity
but greater emotional stability would endure more slowly as they
watched opposition to English economic policies mature into
rebellion against the monarch.[32] Despite the evidence of mental
strain that marked his constitutional tergiversations, Otis never
wavered from his role as advocate for the merchants. He remained
lucid on the question central to his clients: "Can any one tell me
why trade, commerce, arts, sciences and manufactures, should not
be as free for an American as for an European?" He also attempted
to transfer the guilt of illicit trade from the majority of merchants to

corrupt royal officials who shared profits with a few importers they permitted to smuggle, a position remarkably identical with John Temple's.[33]

The need to support his patron's policy of raising a revenue from the colonies complicated the surveyor-general's plans to use the customs organization as a means of enhancing his political power and reputation as an administrator. But Temple determined to maintain firm control of his district and to tolerate no usurpation of power by governors, naval captains, or subordinates in the customs service. He seems to have settled on a policy of collecting as much revenue as possible while avoiding the punitive seizures so notoriously frequent since 1760. Who could object to a surveyor-general who merely collected legal duties from a shipper detected in smuggling?[34]

In September 1764, on the day before the "Black Act" took effect, Temple suspended from office James Cockle, collector of the ports of Salem and Marblehead. The merchants of Salem welcomed the news by firing guns, lighting bonfires, and giving "Entertainments." In Boston "our worthy surveyor-general" was "much applauded by the merchants . . . for his Good and Spirited Behaviour."[35] Well might they rejoice, for Temple had exposed Cockle and Governor Bernard in the act of plotting to enrich themselves through prosecution in cases where Temple required merely postpayment of the duty that should have been paid at the time of entry. Cockle as much as admitted his complicity and attempted to bribe the surveyor-general to overlook the affair. Bernard's connections in England protected him but could not get Cockle reinstated. In Massachusetts it became clear that mercantile interests could expect no favors from a governor forced to give primary attention to the financial needs of his ten children. Bernard's reputation as a moneygrubber contributed to the esteem in which Temple was held as a reasonable and uncorruptible public official who favored local interests wherever possible.[36]

Boston's greatest merchant did not see the Sugar Act become law. On 1 August 1764 Samuel Cooper noted in his line-a-day diary: "My dear and Honored Friend Mr. Hancock died of an apoplectic Disorder—in a few Hours. bequeathed me 200£ Lawful Money and a Suit of Mourning." The tensions of amassing a fortune and the physical toll of rich living ended Thomas Hancock's life suddenly at age sixty-one. An obituary in the *Boston Gazette* reviewed his rapid rise from birth in a country parsonage to acquisition of "a plentiful Fortune"; it pointed also to the "Seat of Hospitality" which he had made of his mansion on Beacon Hill and to "His constant and devout Attendance upon the Duties of Religion."[37] Cooper's funeral sermon held up Hancock as a rich man who was not "high minded" and did not trust in "uncertain riches" as the path to eternal life. The year before his death Thomas Hancock had added to a business letter a postscript sending the compliments of his pastor and wife, two of the persons nearest him. A bequest of £200—nearly a year's salary—was no token remembrance. The will of the senior James Bowdoin had similarly remembered the Brattle Street minister, who had served so well the two wealthiest families of his parish.[38]

Management of the Hancock business and most of the fortune passed to a slim bachelor of twenty-seven. Childless, Thomas and Lydia Hancock had adopted their nephew, John Hancock, after the death of his father, minister of Braintree, Massachusetts. The removal of a seven-year-old boy from rural parsonage to Boston mansion was hardly the drastic move biographers have imagined, and young John adapted easily to his new life. Boston Latin School, Harvard College, a year in London, and eight years' faithful service to his uncle's firm had prepared him well for the partnership to which he had been admitted at the end of 1761. Now in 1764 he was marked as the richest man—or nearly so—in New England. But he was not a self-made man; consequently, for the remainder of his life, friends as well as enemies scrutinized him daily for evidence that he did not deserve the fortune thrust upon him. Samuel Cooper understood perfectly that no man could win such a contest, for he too suffered from comparison with the giants in his past.[39]

More than they could have dreamed in 1764, events of the next two decades would intertwine the lives of the Cooper brothers with John Temple, James Otis, Samuel Adams, James Bowdoin, and John Hancock. Another man, younger even than Hancock, must be added. The year before, Dr. Joseph Warren had opened his medical office in Boston. Having peddled milk from his father's farm in Roxbury through the streets of Boston a dozen years before proved no barrier to success now, for his practice grew rapidly. In September 1764 Cooper solemnized Warren's wedding to the fair and well-to-do daughter of a deceased merchant. The handsome couple took a pew at Brattle Street and began to present babies for baptism.[40]

6

The Lord Reigneth

The year in which he turned forty brought the first major test of Samuel Cooper's determination to keep his pulpit free of controversy as he ministered to the spiritual needs of his people. But on his birthday (28 March 1765) he had no inkling of what this year would hold.

For twenty years he had faithfully pastored Boston's wealthiest congregation. He had preached 2,000 sermons, administered the sacrament 240 times, solemnized 200 marriages, baptized 600 babies, and buried perhaps 750 parishioners.[1] In a town noted for its preachers, his reputation as the foremost pulpiteer had grown throughout the two decades. Unlike Jonathan Mayhew at the West Church, who owed an international notoriety to radical preaching and public disputes, Cooper had preached his sweet gospel while remaining unperturbed by the polemical battles around him. Even the suspicion that he engaged in covert political activity had not marred the public image he so carefully preserved.

After a sermon in 1760 on the death of George II, Cooper published nothing more for thirteen years. Such a lapse in scholarly production, inexcusable in a great Boston minister of the past, did not mean that he was jaded with the ministry but that, above all, he hoped to keep his pulpit free from controversy. To take a public stand on almost any religious issue of the day exposed the moderate Calvinist to simultaneous attack by rationalistic Arminians, who had abandoned some of the most cherished doctrines of the traditional theology, and by zealous followers of Edwards, who de-

nounced as unconverted liberals those orthodox Congregational
clergy not sharing their enthusiasm for the reinvigorated Calvinism
of Edwardian theology. Likewise, to preach on any political topic
was certain to affront a segment of his congregation.

Remaining above controversy enabled Cooper to hold the
Brattle Street congregation together while he enjoyed the prestige of
his clerical office and channeled his surplus energy into informal
political associations. As a group, the merchants agreed on little
but clear-cut questions of their own economic interest. With its
blessing on the doctrine of self-interest, Cooper's bland Christianity
provided a safe common ground where men of like tradition could
unite spiritually, however divided and vexed they might be in the
temporal world. In these troubled times he had no intention of
abandoning the proven formula of a worship service that relaxed
the believer and sent him home buoyed in mind and spirit.

As proud as they were of their pastor, many Brattle Street
parishioners must have wondered why such a giant in the pulpit
could not be greeted as "Doctor." The Scottish universities had
proved willing to grant honorary doctorates to distinguished Congregational ministers in what amounted to a sheepskin war against
local Anglican clergy who occasionally received similar honors
from Oxford. Mayhew had been rewarded with an Aberdeen
degree for his first volume of sermons, Chauncy had been recognized by Edinburgh during the Great Awakening, and a few other
Boston clergy, all with congregations inferior to Brattle Street in
size and wealth, were doctors. In an age without earned doctorates,
the title carried considerable distinction.[2]

As early as 1757 Dr. Thomas Bulfinch had unsuccessfully
sought an honorary degree for his son-in-law Cooper. Ten years
later the Boylstons of his congregation used their London connections to bring results. After a recommendation from Benjamin
Franklin, Cooper received a diploma from the University of Edinburgh, whose faculty repeated the favor a few weeks later for
Andrew Eliot. Now in London as an agent for the Pennsylvania
Assembly, Franklin had spent nearly four months visiting Boston in
1763, during which time he renewed his ties to acquaintances in
that town, including Cooper. In thanking him for his recommendation, Cooper began a correspondence with Franklin that would in
time ripen into a close friendship of kindred minds.[3]

A schoolgirl who saw the pulpit gown Cooper now put on as
befitting his new dignity wondered whether one sleeve would not
"make a full trimm'd negligee as the fashion is at present."[4] Simi-

larly, a London newspaper commented sarcastically that Boston would have to erect a cathedral for such an ecclesiastical dignity as *Doctor* Cooper. But in the eyes of his leading parishioners, the honor bestowed on their pulpit luminary was well deserved and belated.[5]

As always, the Brattle Street minister was as much involved in the temporal as in the spiritual concerns of his parishioners. By 1765 Bostonians believed themselves to be in a severe depression. A difficult postwar commercial readjustment, new British trade policies, and the Sugar Act had combined to produce a crisis of confidence in the mercantile mind that made economic ruin seem imminent. In Boston a few conspicuous business firms failed in 1764, and others seemed to totter on the brink of bankruptcy. John Hancock wrote in January 1765 that "times are very bad and precarious here," and he predicted worse to follow.[6] Six months later, the *Boston Post-Boy* bewailed the plight of the town: "Our Trade is in a most deplorable Situation, not one fifth Part of the Vessels now employed in the West-India Trade, as was before the late Regulations. Our Cash almost gone; . . . Bankruptcies multiplied, our Fears increased, and the Friends of Liberty under the greatest Despondency: What these Things will end in, Time only can discover!"[7] Prices had dropped to one-half of their wartime high, and profits were consequently lower, even when the volume of trade increased. The new enterprises through which merchants sought to compensate for losses elsewhere often proved risky. As always, the laboring men and the poor bore the brunt of economic dislocations. By the early months of 1765 Boston's mood had come full cycle from the great expectations of the peace celebrations to an apprehension concerning the future that nearly matched the gloom of those first war years when a French triumph seemed near.[8]

From Boston's perspective, Great Britain could hardly have chosen a less propitious moment to impose on the colonies a stamp tax that irritated almost everyone. Passed in March 1765 to take effect on 1 November, the Stamp Act taxed most documents an American would use in his lifetime, including those numerous papers required by the acts of trade, already a major annoyance to merchants. Each newspaper, almanac, and pamphlet—even the sermons of the clergy—must be printed on stamped paper. Newspaper advertisements, the means by which the merchant offered his goods for sale, carried an additional duty. College diplomas were to be taxed along with playing cards, dice, bail bonds, and licenses to retail liquor.

The Stamp Act was a monstrous piece of stupidity in that it threatened the vital interests of the colonists while relying only on their sense of lawfulness for enforcement, a strain of fidelity out of all proportion to the revenue anticipated even with full compliance. Its passage raised the long-deferred constitutional issue of whether Parliament could lay on Americans a direct tax no longer disguised as a duty to regulate trade, or whether only the colonial assemblies could tax their constituents. By giving jurisdiction, either original or appellate, in cases arising under the Stamp Act to vice-admiralty courts, Parliament violated further the Englishman's cherished right to be tried by his peers. If admiralty judges and customs officials did their duty, those provisions requiring stamps on commercial documents would be enforced entirely by men beyond the political or judicial control of the merchants. But the merchant did not have to stand alone in this case. Everywhere colonists faced up to the difficult truth that they no longer believed that Parliament had the right to tax them.[9]

Though they had known for many months of Grenville's intention to propose a stamp tax and had made some ineffective attempts to stave it off, Bostonians did not grasp the full significance of the act until a copy arrived at the end of May.[10] In the middle of that month, amid endless rumors concerning what the British government had in store for America, the Boston town meeting convened to select its representatives to the Massachusetts House of Representatives for the coming year. The reelection of James Otis seemed doubtful at best. His political machinations in behalf of family interests and his uncertain pronouncements on the question of parliamentary authority had destroyed confidence that he would place the town's goals above personal concerns. On the eve of the election he appealed to the voters in the *Gazette* and requested an opportunity to speak at the meeting before the vote was taken.[11] That same day in the *Evening-Post*, Samuel Waterhouse—Cooper's antagonist, now no longer attending Brattle Street—sought to deliver the *coup de grace* with the "Jemmibullero," a full column of scurrilous verse calling Otis such names as "lying dog," "thief," "clown," "poltroon," "stupid fellow," and "filthy scunk." He was also labeled "a Cooper's vessel," which apparently meant that he thought Otis to be a tool of the preacher.[12]

As a result of the "Jemmibullero," Otis received a more sympathetic hearing from the voters, for anyone who drew such fire from the Bernard-Hutchinson forces must be very obnoxious to them. He narrowly avoided defeat by winning the last of four

Boston seats. Reelected with the most votes was Thomas Gray, a Brattle Street merchant of moderate political views. The town meeting also returned Oxenbridge Thacher and Thomas Cushing to the legislature. Boston chose representatives who stood solidly behind her vital economic interests, who contested for a cause more important than the personal popularity of James Otis.[13]

When the legislature convened on 29 May, firm knowledge of the Stamp Act's terms heightened tensions. Andrew Eliot delivered the election sermon customarily heard by governor and legislature before voting for members of the new Council. If any preacher could find the right message for such a day it would be this popular apostle of good will. He knew thoroughly the New England intellectual and religious heritage, and he knew equally well the attitudes of the mechanics and other ordinary people who formed the bulk of his congregation. His long sermon rebuked men who "stir up factions and seditions against" rulers who are "wise and good," denied that Americans craved independence, and refused to "impeach the justice of the British Parliament." Nonetheless, after stressing the biblical injunctions to obey good rulers, he acknowledged the right and duty of the Christian to withdraw support from rulers who "endeavour to subvert the constitution, and to enslave a free people," for submission to tyranny is a "crime" against man and God. The Stamp Act had swept even the gentle Eliot into preaching the right of revolution.[14]

Enforcement of the Sugar Act and other trade regulations made the impending Stamp Act loom more tyrannical. At the beginning of June, Temple served notice that the new forms required for coastal shipping were available and hereafter mandatory —likely a greater blow to most merchants than the threat of stamp duties.[15] Since the passage of the Sugar Act, Boston had seen efforts to discourage the use of unnecessary British manufactures, particularly articles of clothing available in cruder forms of colonial origin. A new demand for spurning all luxuries from England arose in the summer of 1765.[16] By then the nature of the contest had become clear. Colonial Americans as a whole stood ready to defend their conviction that they should be taxed only by their local assemblies, which understood the disadvantages resulting from colonial status. But Boston's commercial leaders had as yet no inkling of the popular fury to be unloosed by this new threat to the town's prosperity.

On 14 August citizens in the south part of the town awakened to see hanging from a large tree an effigy of Andrew Oliver, the secretary of the province who had been recently designated as stamp distributor for Massachusetts. After being viewed throughout the day by throngs of people, Oliver's image was taken down at nightfall, placed in a coffin, paraded through the town by a sizable crowd, and finally beheaded and burned before Oliver's door. As an act of defiance the coffin had been carried through the first floor of the Town House, where the governor and Council were meeting on the second floor to consider means of controlling the mob. According to one contemporary account, these gentlemen—the highest governmental authority of the province—"thought it prudent to extinguish their Lights and take to their Heals as fast as they could." Hutchinson demonstrated his bravery by facing the mob at Oliver's residence, but he could not stop them from capturing and severely damaging the house before calling off the evening's "entertainment." Earlier that same night the mob had leveled an office building Oliver was erecting, reputedly as a stamp office. The following day, to save his house from complete destruction, he resigned the office of stamp distributor even before his commission had arrived from England.[17]

Long accustomed to riots against British press gangs and to the annual mock battles of Pope's Day, most Bostonians saw the crowd action of 14 August as necessary and proper resistance to the Stamp Act. In September the great royal elm on which the effigy of Oliver had hung was formally dedicated as "The Tree of Liberty." "The Glorious and never-to-be-forgotten 14th. of August 1765" would be celebrated in Boston until after the Revolution. It became the first holiday of the Revolutionary movement, to be observed, of course, by drinking fourteen toasts, the last of which contained such a sentiment as, "May the 14th of August be the annual Jubilee of Americans, till Time shall be no more."[18]

The events of 14 August had not originated spontaneously. Until the final plundering of Oliver's mansion, activities had been directed by substantial citizens spearheaded by the Loyal Nine, the nucleus of what would become the Sons of Liberty. Mostly mechanics and shopkeepers, the Loyal Nine included one publisher of the *Boston Gazette* and John Avery, Harvard graduate and future son-in-law of Thomas Cushing. Avery wrote of his work on 14 August, "What will be the Consequence I know Not, neither do I Care but Hope that all these Provinces will follow this laudible Example."[19]

On the evening of 26 August, a Boston mob followed and improved on "this laudible Example." At sunset a crowd gathered to intimidate local customs officials who, as rumor had it, sent to England a steady stream of documentation on the smuggling activities of Boston merchants. The mob attacked the house and office and burned the papers of a deputy register of the vice-admiralty court and looted the splendid home of Benjamin Hallowell, comptroller of customs. Then, emboldened by the contents of Hallowell's wine cellar, the rioters moved on to the mansion of Thomas Hutchinson. By daybreak one of the finest dwellings of colonial America lay gutted, its owner's valuable possessions stolen or scattered. For eight hours the mob had vented its hostility on the lieutenant governor, while hundreds of solid citizens looked on, trying to convince themselves that the victim deserved his fate.[20]

Some could not. Hutchinson had vigorously opposed passage of the Stamp Act, but after it became law he felt bound to observe it and had attempted unsuccessfully to halt the activities of 14 August. But his long-standing unpopularity lent credence to the report that he and Bernard had been instigators of the revenue acts. What was happening to the minds of Boston intellectuals and merchants was well illustrated by Jonathan Mayhew's sermon on civil liberty preached the day before the destruction of Hutchinson's house. Knowing full well the lieutenant governor's work against passage of the Stamp Act, Mayhew nevertheless mentioned in his sermon "the suspicions of many, that persons in the colonies had encouraged, and been instrumental of bringing upon us, so great a burden and grievance, for the sake of present gain"; but he added, "This I would charitably hope is not true." Mayhew then undercut any ground for such a hope by discussing the "mere hypothetical" case of "men who could be so mercenary as to ruin their country, for the sake of posts and profits."[21]

After hearing this sermon, Richard Clarke, a Hutchinson ally and leading Boston tea merchant, angrily withdrew from the West Church and took a pew for his large family at Brattle Street, where he felt certain his children would not be corrupted by such libertarian ideas. As a result, Samuel Cooper would be called on in 1769 to unite in marriage Clarke's daughter Sukey to John Singleton Copley, the preeminent portrait painter of colonial America. While Mayhew made profuse apologies to Hutchinson and Clarke for being "too far carried away with the common current," Cooper could reflect with satisfaction on the wisdom of keeping his pulpit free from political preaching.[22] But Clarke had missed the point that the truly radical message of this hour was the gospel of self-interest, a doctrine that freed laboring men as well as merchants to employ the necessary means for their own advancement. However instructive they might find the political theory of Locke and Sidney or even the lessons that the Congregational clergy drew from the history of the ancient Hebrew commonwealth, opposition by Bostonians to British revenue measures sprang from the belief that it was right and just to pursue self-interest. In the face of new restrictions on American economic growth, the belief that the Christian should be "on the gaining hand" had become a radical doctrine. No one excelled Cooper in mustering the power of the Christian religion behind the acquisitive society.[23]

Most respectable Bostonians professed to be horrified at the outrage against Hutchinson, though they were not sufficiently remorseful to prosecute those responsible or to support measures for speedy indemnification of the victim. Hatred of the Stamp Act had politicized the town's workingmen, on whose natural leaders now rested the burden of preserving order.[24] As Governor Bernard wrote home, two days after the attack on the Hutchinson mansion, "The Mob was so general and so supported, that all civil Power ceased in an instant, and I had not the least authority to oppose or quiet the Mob." The chief lesson of August 1765 was clearly that British authority had crumbled before united colonial resistance.[25]

In this frame of mind, Boston together with the other American port towns proceeded to nullify the Stamp Act entirely. No authority dared order the unloading of ships carrying stamps to the harbor. Consequently, when the "long-dreaded" November first arrived, stamps were unavailable. Gradually, though with great uncertainty, normal activities resumed in defiance of Parliament. Informal organizations at the various levels of society cooperated to prevent further violence while coercing civil officials and the few reputed supporters of the Stamp Act. In December Andrew Oliver was brought to the Liberty Tree to resign formally his commission as stamp distributor which had arrived from England since his earlier resignation. Also in December, the Boston merchants joined their counterparts in other trading towns in agreeing to cut off imports of nonessential English goods until repeal of the Stamp Act.[26]

During the crisis of 1765–1766 Samuel Cooper seems never to have gone on record. No extant letter, sermon, or diary entry records his views or reports his actions. Ten years later he explicitly denounced the Stamp Act as the first great example of "a restless Desire in the British Administration to establish a Revenue in America, at their own Disposal" and of "an equal Eagerness in some Men of no small Influence here, to have a Share in this Revenue." He then rejoiced over the memory that "America took the Alarm, and instantly opposed [it]."[27] But Clarke's move from West Church to Brattle Street suggests how publicly restrained Cooper must have appeared in 1765. Was he as irresolute as his friend Otis, who feared parliamentary retaliation for American riots and who, at the intercolonial Stamp Act Congress he had helped initiate, hesitated until the last minute before signing the resolution denying Parliament's right to tax the colonies?[28] Certainly not. Cooper appears a thoroughly political man, as cool as Otis was disturbed. Even lacking more evidence, we can be certain that he stood firm with Hancock, Bowdoin, Cushing, and other prudent men dedicated to repeal. In contrast to Otis and Mayhew, men of this cut worked to force repeal of the revenue acts with as little rhetoric as need be. As William Cooper noted in his diary, one did not have to become a rioter to join the "opposition to the unconstitutional Stamp Act."[29]

At the close of the Revolution, when he sought to prove his loyalty to the American cause, John Temple asserted that, beginning with the time of the "accursed stamp act," Cooper had enjoyed "a great share of Mr. Temple's confidence and was privy to almost the whole of his conduct."[30] Cooper appears to have been instrumental in the surveyor-general's drawing closer to the mercantile community in 1765 and 1766. Alone among the chief royal servants in New England, Temple had demonstrated that colonial policy could be executed by an official who understood and valued local interests. By example he made his colleagues seem inimical to Boston's commercial pursuits. Conversely, Temple's popularity was cherished by New Englanders as evidence that they were completely loyal to those few royal officials who could rise above the pettiness and venality of the eighteenth-century English political system.[31]

When news reached Boston in September that the Grenville ministry had fallen, Temple's position became precarious. He must renew his defenses at home against the hostile representations of Bernard, and, though opposed to the Stamp Act, he would have to enforce those sections applying to shipping. Thus his support in England had weakened at the time his popularity in America faced its severest test.

Temple's difficulties increased when the first of November arrived and no stamps were to be had. Pressed to open the ports for business as usual, he refused to instruct local customs officers until he received orders from England. Boston merchants then issued an unmistakable warning to the surveyor-general: "We Really are afraid of what may happen Should You persist in Still keeping the Office Shut up—don't imagine that we are Stirring up the People, 'tis our Pleasure and Happiness to keep them in Good order—but We Really are afraid it will be Out of Our power to prevent Mischief." This threat led to the opening of the port on 17 December, the day of Oliver's second resignation as stamp distributor. Temple's irresolution while trying to serve two masters brought him no accolades from either, but his reputation remained untarnished in Boston.[32]

A cadre of rising political leaders took full advantage of the political potency of nearly unanimous and successful opposition to the Stamp Act. As a reward for unwavering opposition to the revenue measures, Samuel Adams had been elected to the House in September 1765 in place of the deceased Oxenbridge Thacher. At once the tempo of the legislative session increased. In the May election of 1766 Adams led all other candidates with 691 of 746 votes. Cushing did nearly as well, and Otis recovered sufficient popularity to run a strong third. John Hancock, not yet thirty, won the fourth seat after Thomas Gray conspicuously withdrew from the race in what had all the earmarks of a prearranged move.[33]

In Boston a new alliance of merchants and politicians had been forged by the heat of resistance to parliamentary measures. Adams, Cushing, and Hancock would continue as representatives until the Revolution. After his sanity waned in the early 1770s, Otis would be replaced by another member of the alliance, William Phillips, Old South deacon and very successful merchant. James Bowdoin, a member of the Council since 1757, though otherwise inactive in politics until now, was bestirring himself to begin exercising in that body the influence exerted by Boston delegates in the House. Hancock, Bowdoin, Cushing, and Phillips spoke for those commercial interests that had been driven to full recognition of their need for political power to ward off future attempts of Parliament to tax Americans or strangle their commerce and to draw into a common cause the forces of popular unrest unleashed in Boston by the Stamp Act. Otis had always been the servant of trade, and he would remain useful for a while despite his many vagaries. Now to Otis's flighty brilliance Samuel Adams joined his steady politicizing. Hereafter he would be so conspicuous on the center stage of the resistance movement that historians and biographers have naturally cast him in the role of master revolutionary who raised attempts to redress economic grievances into open rebellion. Bernard and Hutchinson blamed most of their troubles first on Otis and later on Adams, thus further obscuring the truth that both these political leaders served the trading interests forming the upper-class base of resistance to Britain.

The alliance remained too informal to name itself. Bernard referred to it as "the Popular party," but the term "Whigs" became more common. As Hutchinson explained, "Officers of the crown, and such as were for keeping up their authority, were branded with the name of tories, always the term of reproach; their opposers assuming the name of whiggs, because the common people, as far as they had been acquainted with the parties in England, all supposed the whiggs to have been in the right, and the tories in the wrong."[34]

Instructions of the Boston town meeting to its representatives in 1766 constituted a Whig manifesto. Drafted by a committee of traders, the instructions called for a far-reaching program designed to broaden support for the merchants' cause.[35] In the spring election of 1766, influence of the Boston Whigs reached across the province as they contributed to the defeat of two-thirds of the representatives they identified in Boston newspapers as supporters of the Stamp Act.[36] But before the assembly met at the end of May, one of Hancock's ships made port on Friday, the sixteenth, with "the Glorious News of the total Repeal of the Stamp Act." On Sunday the Brattle Street congregation heard Cooper preach from the text, "The Lord reigneth; let the earth rejoice." The town did just that on Monday in an official day of celebration that spontaneously turned into twenty-three hours of continuous ecstasy. No one celebrated more enthusiastically or conspicuously than John Hancock, "who gave a grand and elegant Entertainment to the genteel Part of the Town, and treated the Populace with a Pipe of Madeira Wine." He "erected at the Front of his House, which was magnificently illuminated, a Stage for the Exhibition of his Fireworks," with which he answered the pyrotechnics set off by the Sons of Liberty across the Commons.[37]

Soon after this greatest celebration in the town's history, the hollow nature of their victory became apparent to Boston merchants. They could overlook as merely theoretical the Declaratory Act accompanying repeal of the Stamp Act, which asserted that Parliament had "full power and authority . . . to bind the colonies and people of America, . . . in all cases whatsoever." But they could not afford to disregard the new acts of Parliament favoring

British and West Indian over northern merchants and increasing the restrictions under which colonial trade must operate. By the fall of 1766 Hancock had abandoned his expectation that Britain would grant the colonies a "free and extensive trade," a hope he had expressed in a letter to Thomas Pownall the preceding March.[38]

Even before learning of these changes in commercial policy, the Boston Whigs had refused to relax their guard. They used their slight majority in the House of Representatives to elect Otis speaker and Adams clerk. As chaplain, Samuel Cooper replaced Andrew Eliot, whose "discreet" conduct during the Stamp Act crisis had pleased Bernard more than the Whigs. Anticipating their moves, the governor sought to play a strong hand by exercising his charter right to negative the choice of a speaker. Unfazed, the Whigs proceeded as planned to deny reelection to Hutchinson and other members of the Council who held offices from the crown. Bernard, in retaliation, vetoed the election of six councillors friendly to the Whigs, but he accepted Cushing as speaker in place of Otis.[39]

Incapable of standing on the sidelines, Mayhew recovered quickly from the shock of accusations that he had incited a mob. Late in May he rushed into print with a widely read sermon on repeal of the Stamp Act. In June, during the legislative session, he warned Otis that "it is not safe for the colonies to sleep, since they will probably always have some wakeful enemies in Britain." A month later he died suddenly of a nervous disorder. The untimely death of his college friend and clerical colleague of twenty years saddened Samuel Cooper and put him in a reflective mood. Though their friendship had never wavered even when most other Boston clergy ostracized Mayhew, their personalities, ministerial style, and theology had been radically different. Bostonians remembered for the next two generations that Cooper had leaned over Mayhew's deathbed to inquire whether he clung in death to the heretical gospel he had preached in life. The answer, "My integrity I hold fast, and will not let it go," was vintage Mayhew.[40]

Like Cooper, Mayhew had owed some of his rapid rise in the ministry to important family connections. In eighteenth-century Boston the road to success as often as not lay through a suitable marriage. Family connections weighed heavily in politics and trade; often the simple desire to aid one's children and in-laws was a more primary motivation than some ideological bent or religious affiliation.[41] Their political rivalry has brought the Hutchinsons and Otises to historical prominence, but others have gone largely unnoticed. Measured by a combination of wealth, social prestige, and political power, Boston had no more important family group on the eve of the Revolution than that formed by the intermarriages of the Bowdoins, Pitts, and Ervings—all associated with the Brattle Street congregation. During January 1767 Samuel Cooper officiated at two wedding ceremonies at which daughters of this family alliance married customs officials.

Nancy Erving, the sister of James Bowdoin's wife, married Duncan Stewart, collector of customs at New London. The bride's father, Captain John Erving, had amassed one of the town's largest fortunes solely through shrewdness in trading and gained a prestige that brought regular election to the Council along with his son-in-law James Bowdoin. Cooper took particular satisfaction in having led the captain late in life into full church membership. One son had married a daughter of Governor Shirley. Now the marriage of the youngest child brought an important customs officer into the family of a merchant who had once been caught in Charles Paxton's net for smugglers. Stewart, like Temple, had proved amenable to the demands of merchants for sympathetic enforcement of the acts of trade.[42]

Two weeks later John Temple carried off the most desirable bride in New England. James Bowdoin's only daughter, Elizabeth, had reached a precocious seventeen. So striking in appearance that for the next quarter century men debated the nature of her beauty, "Betsey" Bowdoin would have been attractive even had she been as ugly as sin, for she was related to three of the wealthiest and most powerful mercantile families. The fortune of her uncle, James Pitts, was on a par with that of her father and Grandfather Erving. Beginning in 1766 all three sat together in the Council as they did in church.[43]

Thirty-five, married once before, perhaps already suffering from the deafness that became serious a few years later, and with an inadequate and uncertain income, Temple nevertheless had successfully pressed his suit. Betsey joined the Anglican communion of her husband, and they moved at the center of Boston's highest social circle where *joie de vivre* seemed to count for more than the political and religious issues discussed in the newspapers. Here Cooper's brother-in-law, Dr. Thomas Bulfinch, also circulated with ease.[44]

The marriages of Stewart and Temple into the Bowdoin-Pitts-Erving family oligarchy did not, of course, constitute an open alliance between the customs service and the mercantile community but rather revealed the vulnerability of customs officials to the influence of the society in which they had been placed to guard royal interests. As Dr. Cooper put on his doctoral robe and climbed into his pulpit each Sunday, he remained confident that this society of which he was so intimate a part could meet any challenge to its prosperity.

7

At the End of Their Tether

*E*vents of the three years after repeal of the Stamp Act forced Samuel Cooper to change the basis of his optimism. In 1766 he still believed that the British sense of justice would ultimately prevail to restore the former happy relationship of colonies to mother country. By 1769 he could only hope that the British ministry would eventually grow weary of its futile attempts to coerce Americans.

At first, enough of the euphoria stimulated by Britain's retreat on the Stamp Act remained to keep alive the expectation that continued colonial resistance would bring about a modification of the objectionable features of the acts of trade. The Boston preacher knew exactly what he and the other Whig leaders wanted: Parliament must return to "the old Ground" when it "evidently intended nothing more than a simple regulation of Trade for the Benefit of the whole" empire.[1] But Parliament was in no mood to turn a sympathetic ear toward the trading centers of her mainland colonies. Worried lest repeal of the Stamp Act be construed as a reward for violent opposition to it, British legislators looked for American gratitude to put them at ease. Instead, the New York assembly willfully evaded the Quartering Act, and the Massachusetts assembly refused to compensate victims of the Stamp Act riots until December 1766, when it voted both compensation and a full pardon for the rioters. English officials believed that smuggling continued as rampantly as ever and that it was essential to suppress the practice.[2]

Only a strong ministry could have restrained a Parliament so inclined, but at the moment England was virtually leaderless. Charles Townshend, the self-directed chancellor of the exchequer, gave the Commons and Lords what they wanted in a new revenue measure, an act creating an American board of customs commissioners, and another bill suspending the New York assembly until it complied with the Quartering Act. All three passed easily in June without noticeable opposition, even from the reputed friends of America. By the Townshend Acts, Parliament declared to Americans that the Declaratory Act of the previous year, far from being a face-saving gesture, represented the truth of their relationship: the British legislature could and would pass laws binding on colonists "in all cases whatsoever." The revenue act established the principle of taxation by placing token duties, payable in scarce sterling, on several commodities commonly imported from England, including a tax of three pence a pound on tea. Though this list might be expanded later, other provisions of the act loomed more ominous at the moment. Receipts could be expended in the colonies to pay the salaries of judges and royal officials, a stipulation that raised in Boston the spectre of a Bernard or a Hutchinson freed from financial dependence on the assembly. Equally threatening to the merchant, the act settled the long controversy over writs of assistance in favor of the customs service. To John Rowe, one of the most active members of the Boston merchants' organization, the new revenue act was "an Imposition on America in my opinion as Dangerous as the Stamp Act." James Bowdoin reacted in Calvinistic language: "To slavery we think ourselves now damned."[3]

Another act turned the management of continental American customs over to a five-man board of commissioners resident in Boston. The board included Charles Paxton, the most obnoxious of local customs officers. Temple's connections in England, too powerful to be ignored, assured him of a place on the new board but not as the first-ranking member. His salary had been reduced slightly, and he was surrounded by commissioners unsympathetic to local interests.[4]

After a summer of rumors based on the latest letters and newspapers from London, in October Bostonians learned the full details of the new measures. The Whigs realized that they now required a different tactic from that used against the Stamp Act. There would be no popular uprising, no nearly universal protest against the Townsend Acts. In the May election of 1767 Hancock had been returned to the assembly with an unprecedented unanimous vote of the town meeting; and Cushing, Adams, and Otis also had received strong votes. Nevertheless, in a protracted economic struggle with Britain this solid support could be quickly dissipated. For most merchants the constitutional issue was second-ary to the question of how the economic weapons used affected in-dividual businesses. Likewise, new violence would alienate mer-chants who feared the consequences of a continued mobocracy and the resultant likelihood of British troops being sent to pacify Boston, already a subject of lively rumors. Early in November the *Boston Gazette* made the point clearly. Though it pointed out that "swarms of new officers are flying over to us, to fatten themselves on the spoils of trade, and Governor Bernard and his junto are ex-ulting at the news of new appointments and encreased salaries," the *Gazette* advised, "No Mobs and Tumults, let the Person and Prop-erties of our most inveterate Enemies be safe." Hancock and the other Boston selectmen, all good Whigs, issued a public statement deploring mobs and urging coolness and moderation in the face of "incitements artfully thrown out to beguile you into illegal measures."[5]

For the time being the Whigs contented themselves with a voluntary agreement not to buy, after the first of the year, a long list of articles imported from England. "Save your Money, and you Save your Country!" became their slogan. At the same time, domestic manufactures received the official blessing of the town meeting. Still, there remained grave doubts that this program could accomplish more than arousing the opposition of those whose habits of consumption or livelihoods would be most affected.[6]

The bitter opponents of the Whigs continued to hammer away at Otis, whose erratic behavior and talk made him the easiest target. No public figure in Boston, not even Bernard, had suffered from as much personal abuse.[7] That inveterate scribbler Samuel Waterhouse threw a little light on Otis's sphere of influence with another attempt at verse. The "Jemmiwilliad," published in the *Evening~Post* at the end of November 1767, maintained that William Cooper was the alter ego of Otis:

> Dear, virtuous friendship's sacred bands
> Unite these Peers,—their force, their skill:—
> One heart, one head, one pair of hands
> Have Jemmy Split and Cooper Will![8]

We know too little concerning the relationship of the two men to understand the full significance of these lines. They were published at a time when Otis was the butt of jokes contrasting his past belligerency with his current demand for moderation.[9] At the town meeting of 20 November, he delivered an "animated address" urging townsmen not to take out on the commissioners their dislike of the new duties; rather, "behave like men and use the proper and legal measures to obtain redress." Led by Otis, the meeting unanimously voted to suppress "all Disorders that may arise." Even the *Evening-Post* commented that the conduct of Otis and the selectmen on this occasion was "greatly applauded." Some few radicals may have wanted more, but the Whig merchants like Hancock, Cushing, and Rowe, with their political henchmen such as Otis and Town Clerk Cooper, held the reins of power.[10]

The Boston Whigs received unexpected and dramatic support at the end of 1767 with John Dickinson's "Letters from a Farmer in Pennsylvania," published in newspapers throughout the colonies. Though he accepted Parliament's right to regulate trade in the common interest of harmonious imperial relations, Dickinson denied totally the power of the mother country "to lay upon these colonies any 'tax' whatever," including those taxes disguised as duties to control trade. Like the Boston town meeting, Dickinson recommended moderate action and expressed optimism that petitions and resolves against the Townshend measures "will have the same success now, that they had in the time of the Stamp Act."[11]

In this spirit the Whigs set to work in the legislature. Their master stroke was a letter to the assemblies of other colonies informing them "of the Measures which this House have taken with regard to the Difficulties they are apprehensive will arise from the operation of several Acts of Parliament for levying Duties and Taxes on the American Colonies." This circular letter briefly reiterated the constitutional arguments against parliamentary taxation, the Quartering Act, and the powers granted the customs commissioners, and issued a faint call for common action by the assemblies.[12]

In January, at the beginning of this legislative session, Bernard had thought he was winning the battle to quiet the province; two months later he had changed his opinion so far as to write home that "a total Repeal of the Laws of Trade imposing Duties and nothing less" would appease the merchants, who, until such repeal took place, "propose to suspend Execution of the Laws."[13] Nothing had been more instrumental in his change of mind than Joseph Warren's pseudonymous letter in the *Gazette* which labeled the governor a man "totally abandoned to Wickedness," who "can never merit our regard." Bernard's unsuccessful efforts to punish the printers of this slanderous letter backfired by subjecting him to the additional charge of attempting to restrict freedom of the press. He was now willing to believe anything concerning such a people; and the *Gazette*, free from the threat of prosecution, became even less cautious in attacking royal government in Massachusetts.[14]

Bernard's despair resulted from more than personal pique. He knew that the Whig merchants were attempting to organize a colonial boycott of most British goods, but he considered the greatest threat to be the growing antagonism of the town toward the customs commissioners.[15]

When Otis at first advocated restraint toward the commissioners, he may have clung to the hope that Temple could dominate the board and thus continue a benevolent pattern of enforcement. Instead, the former surveyor-general quickly became a minority of one opposing the other four. Early in March they broke openly with their colleague. Temple now considered his situation "truely disagreeable." Not only had he lost all influence with the commissioners, but they began sending to the home government a series of memorials which he believed contained "Wicked and Injurious Falsehoods" concerning American affairs. By marshalling evidence against the town in the hope of securing military and naval protection, the other members of the board placed Temple in a difficult position. To sign their memorials meant the loss of his standing among townsmen; not to do so would suggest to English officials that he condoned illegal activities. He emerged from this strait in a fashion typical of his career in the customs service. As long as possible he remained publicly on good terms with the other commissioners, signed most of their memorials, and then communicated the contents of these documents to Samuel Cooper and other Whig leaders.[16]

Once it became clear that they intended to enforce the acts of trade as far as possible, the commissioners, Temple excepted, became "objects of the public odium"—fair game for harassment by gangs of boys and Negroes. Bernard could offer no protection and refused to take responsibility for formally requesting troops, though he resigned himself to the inevitability of their coming. Thoroughly frightened, the commissioners renewed more vigorously their own appeals for support. They are, wrote someone in the *Boston Gazette*, "a set of harpies, who are sent to suck the blood of the industrious part of the community."[17]

In the town meeting at the beginning of May, Boston reelected its four representatives—Otis, Adams, Cushing, and Hancock— with little opposition. The provincial election at the end of the month saw Hancock elevated to the Council for the first time. Hutchinson again failed to gain a seat in the Council because, so he believed, of the revelation that he had been authorized to draw part of his salary from customs revenue. In retaliation, Bernard nega- tived the election of Hancock and five other Whigs. Under the leadership of Bowdoin the Whigs were transforming the Council into an instrument of their own, thus depriving the governor of his main source of strength in the civil government. Bernard preferred to keep the Council below its normal size rather than see it have a large Whig majority.[18]

As Hutchinson explained, Hancock was kept from the Council because he had been "so officious in opposing the Commissioners of the Customs and encouraging illicit trade that the Governor sup- posed he should be censured by the Ministry if he accepted him." Smugglers leave no records, so the question of how much illegal trade was carried on by Boston merchants will never be settled. Certainly Hancock, like others, had no scruples against smuggling when he thought it convenient or necessary; but such an attitude toward the commercial regulations seems typical of all those en- gaged in the trade of the British Empire, even the London suppliers. Opposition to the customs service in 1768 represented more than a desire to evade duties, for that organization had come to symbolize the efforts of postwar ministries to change the nature of imperial relations, to depart from "the old Ground." John Hancock, just entering his thirties, emerged as the human symbol of this opposi- tion. One of New England's richest men and the employer on whom many waterfront families depended for their living, he had already established a reputation for public service and philan- thropy. According to the commissioners, he had declared on the floor of the assembly that customs officers would not be permitted on his London ships. Early in April there had been a near riot when a tidesman was discovered illegally inspecting the hold of Hancock's *Lydia*.[19]

With that flair for the dramatic which contributed to his popularity, Hancock gave the name *Liberty* to one of his sloops employed in the European trade. This vessel docked at Hancock's wharf on 9 May after a voyage from Madeira. In the middle of the month, the *Romney*, a fifty-gun man of war, sailed into Boston Harbor in response to the entreaties of the commissioners. On a

charge of smuggling, the *Liberty* was seized at sunset on 10 June
and anchored for safekeeping under the guns of the *Romney*. As
they took control of the *Liberty*, the marines had to fight off
townsmen gathered on the wharf, who then stoned and beat the
customs officials responsible for executing the seizure. That evening a mob—two or three thousand, "chiefly sturdy boys and
negroes," according to Hutchinson—made such an uproar that no
member of the customs service felt safe in Boston. The commissioners and most of their officers fled to the *Romney* and then to
Castle William, the island fortress in the harbor.[20]

During this same month the Boston newspapers gave many of
their columns to reports from London of the triumphal return from
exile of John Wilkes. In Boston, wrote a victim of the *Liberty* riot,
Hancock is "the Idol of the Mob, just as Mr. Wilkes is in England.
Hancock and Liberty being the cry here, as Wilkes and Liberty is in
London!" By attempting to make an example of Hancock, the
customs organization had struck at the one Bostonian capable of
uniting the strength of the mercantile community with those Sons
of Liberty—Samuel Adams, Joseph Warren, and now others—who
were just beginning to find personal fulfillment in permanent opposition to the mother country.[21] In the end Hancock lost his
sloop, which was condemned and sold to the commissioners as a
revenue cutter, with Bernard receiving his third of the proceeds. But
the compensations were more than adequate. The government's
personal prosecution in the admiralty court against Hancock was
dropped after a long trial that publicized throughout the colonies
Hancock's struggle against the customs service, and the Whig
leaders made capital propaganda out of the seizure.[22]

After the other commissioners had fled in fear to Castle
William, John Temple walked the streets as living proof that Bostonians did not abuse royal officials.[23] On 16 June the commissioners dispatched to the Treasury their account of the *Liberty* incident together with a memorial submitting their opinion "that
nothing but the immediate exertion of military power will prevent
an open revolt of this town, which may probably spread
throughout the provinces." Temple signed this memorial but
dissented from its comments in a formal disclaimer which explained that he had signed only as a matter of form. Fourteen years
later, when his loyalty to the American cause came under attack, he
revealed his subsequent action:

> After Mr. Temple had signed the memorial, . . .
> he carried a copy of the same with three others he had

also signed to the Rev. Dr. Cooper, in Boston, and communicated their contents to him, that the friends of his country might know what was going forward against it, . . .

When Mr. Temple went with these memorials to Dr. Cooper, the doctor told him that Mr. Otis, Mr. Hancock, and Mr. S. Adams were in the further room of his house, and requested that he might be permitted to shew the said memorials to those gentlemen, to which Mr. Temple consented, and remained until the doctor returned with them, . . .

Moreover, during the whole time that Mr. Temple was a commissioner in this country he communicated to Dr. Cooper, and in several instances to Mr. Otis and to Mr. Adams every act or deed of the commissioners (and of their infamous advisers, Bernard and Hutchinson) that came within his knowledge, that was injurious to the peace and happiness of his country; . . .[24]

Since Cooper did not deny this statement published in the *Boston Gazette*, it can be presumed to contain a measure of truth and thus provides a rare glimpse into his covert political activity. A few years later Commissioner Henry Hulton wrote that "when the Board arrived at Boston in November 1767, Mr. Otis's popularity and influence were on the decline; and Mr. Adams together with Dr. Cooper, a smooth, artful, civil, Jesuitical Priest, with Mr. James Bowdoin, one of the Council, were the Leaders of the Faction." Hulton's statement lends credence to Temple's account.[25]

Before the tensions of the *Liberty* crisis could ease, Bernard confronted the House of Representatives with the demand to rescind the circular letter of February. Lord Hillsborough, who held the newly created post of colonial secretary, had so ordered. If the House refused, it was to be dissolved. Hillsborough's order came at the moment that favorable responses to the circular letter from other assemblies began to arrive. After a week of delay, the representatives voted 92-17 not to rescind. As Bernard dissolved the House, its members prepared a petition imploring the king to send them a governor more "worthy to represent the greatest and best Monarch on Earth." "The glorious 92 is the reigning toast," wrote a moderate Whig with amazement. Hutchinson gloomily reported that "our Demagogues" are in high spirits: William Cooper and Samuel Adams "say it is the most glorious day they ever saw."[26] By late summer 1768 the Boston Whigs seemed confident of victory as they drank to "A speedy repeal of unconstitutional Acts of Parliament, and a final Removal of illegal and oppressive Officers" and raised their voices in the chorus of the new "Liberty Song."[27]

How far the Whig leaders were prepared to go in pressing their advantage over a demoralized governor became apparent at the town meeting of 12–13 September. Dr. Cooper opened with prayer, then moderator Otis presided over a two-day session that verbally approached the edge of revolution. A call went out for a convention of Massachusetts towns to meet in ten days, so that the people might exercise their charter and natural rights in the present crisis; and the town meeting issued a blunt reminder of the provincial law requiring adult males to possess a musket and ammunition. Finally, the ministers were requested to "set apart" Tuesday, 20 September, "as a Day of Fasting and Prayer" on which "to Address the Supreme Ruler of the World."[28]

Thus, two days before they opened an extralegal convention with revolutionary implications, the Whigs sat in church to attend the traditional Calvinist rite of the public fast. They knew they could depend on most of the Congregational clergy to do their duty on this occasion. How could any man of God, exclaimed one newspaper writer, hold his peace when "the cause of God" was threatened![29] Another voice cried for a new Mayhew to speak out in this critical hour. But Samuel Cooper found conciliatory words for his congregation on 20 September:

> The Interest of Great Britain and these Colonies is really one; God grant, that all on both the Sides the Atlantic, may clearly discern, may warmly regard, and unitedly promote, this one Interest, and that no Weapon formed to divide and to destroy it may prosper!
>
> We all I trust are disposed to cultivate this Union. We esteem it our Honor and Felicity, to be a Part of the greatest and freest Nation upon Earth. We only wish and pray that our Brethren separated from us by the Ocean would cherish a Fellow feeling for us: and allow us to enjoy those Rights, of which they justly boast, and for the Preservation of which the Nation has made such great and successful Efforts; and which if we did not prefer to our chief temporal [blessings?], we should be unworthy to be called their Brethren. Rights, which are not constituted by human Compact, but by the im-

mutable Rule of Equity, and the eternal Laws of the
God of Nature. In every Step we take for the Preservation of these Rights, may we be calm, prudent, steady,
and united; Loyal to our Sovereign; obedient to our
God; observant of his Will; and confiding in his Care
and Protection. Then we may upon the best Ground
commit our Cause to Heaven.[30]

In the fall of 1768 Cooper could still give thanks for "the
Benefits of a Commerce already diffused beyond the Examples of
former Ages, and which promises, if not checked and controled, to
stretch itself far beyond its present limits." Neither the Brattle Street
merchants nor their pastor were rebels against their king in 1768,
and not all would embrace rebellion even in 1776. Most, however,
had come to countenance public words and private acts that
smacked of disloyalty because they considered their economic prospects threatened by changes in imperial policy. Cooper made this
point very clear in his thanksgiving sermon of December 1768:

> With Hearts truly loyal, and affections entirely
> British, we have the Task to preserve ourselves at pres-
> ent, under the Frown of our gracious Sovereign, and the
> ruling Part of the Nation. I do not mean to inquire into
> the Causes of this, let every Man search his own Heart,
> and consider his own Ways. The Fact however is in-
> disputable, and ought to be religiously regarded by us; it
> is upon this Account I mention it upon such an Occa-
> sion; and if we love our Sovereign, if we love our Parent
> Country, as I am thoroughly persuaded we sincerely do,
> this Frown is enough to chastise our Joys, and abate the
> Relish of those outward Blessings we still possess. From
> our local Circumstances, and our Distance from the
> Body of the Nation, there are certain Points, which we
> account of the greatest Importance to our civil Hap-
> piness, and which from not having been touched till
> very lately, we were ready to imagine had been con-
> ceded to us [but] are now become involved in Perplex-
> ity; and we cannot be so insensible as not to be anxious
> for the Decision. . . .
>
> There is one Thing, I think, that looks not un-
> favorable to us, and that is, Our Affairs are now re-
> garded with deep Attention, through the whole Nation.
> Britain sensible of its own Interest in these Affairs, will

carefully examine them in all their Circumstances; and through the Wisdom and Goodness of our Sovereign, and the British Parliament, we may hope, the Issue of all will be a thorough Discernment of the true Interest of the whole Empire, amidst all the Clouds in which it has been involved, and a Reestablishment of our Tranquility and Happiness upon a just and firm Basis.[31]

This mild statement was typical of Samuel Cooper's public pronouncements. His deep personal involvement in Boston's struggle against innovations in British policy had resulted from a natural identification with the economic interests of his leading parishioners and from a personal need to find nonclerical outlets for his talents. He supported this cause from the pulpit to whatever extent was possible without dividing his congregation. He sensed that the prime radicalism of the day arose from unfulfilled economic expectations of all those who depended on trade for a livelihood, workingmen as well as merchants and shipowners. Publicly he went no further than to give an aura of high moral purpose to the struggle and to unite his hearers behind spiritual principles which could form a proper guide to self-interest. Privately he worked the political engines with Hancock, Bowdoin, Otis, Adams, and brother William. Both roles contributed to the Boston resistance movement, and he harmonized them so well as to remain virtually free from public criticism before 1775.

In 1769 Samuel Cooper's correspondence with Franklin and Thomas Pownall begins to reveal more precisely his position in Boston's political affairs. At first Pownall's friendship seemed more important than Franklin's.[32] After returning to England the former governor of Massachusetts had written the first edition of an essay, The Administration of the Colonies, and secured a place for himself in London society through marriage to a wealthy and socially prominent widow. Thereafter, he devoted his energies to enlarging the Administration into a lengthy treatise and serving in the House of Commons, to which he was first elected in 1767.[33]

Pownall's evolving theories of imperial government emphasized concepts compatible with American desires, especially the importance of commerce and "the necessity of a general British union" founded on the political liberty of all sections of the empire.[34] More important, he persistently defended colonial interests in Parliament from 1767 to 1773, a period when the great men reputed to be America's friends were conspicuously silent or noncommittal. Attached to no political faction, forensically inferior to the great legislative orators of his day, and compelled to oppose the strong sentiments of his colleagues, he was "very ill-heard," as Franklin phrased it. Consequently, American schoolboys of the nineteenth century would declaim selections from Burke's speeches, not Pownall's. But the record stands: the little ex-governor spoke the plain truth as he saw it in nearly every parliamentary debate on America between 1767 and 1780, correctly predicted the results of an intransigent British policy toward the colonies, and at the end of 1777 courageously advocated saving the empire by recognition of complete American autonomy.[35]

Cooper welcomed the opportunity to communicate the Whig point of view to a sympathetic member of Parliament. As he explained to Pownall, "The People of this Town and Province, are under this great Disadvantage, that living so distant from the great Fountain of Government, they Know not what has been alledged against them, nor in what Light their Conduct has been placed, and consequently it is out of their Power to vindicate themselves till the Misrepresentation has had its Effect."[36] Since he believed that royal officials in the colonies regularly sent home distorted accounts of illicit trade, rioting, and disloyalty, Cooper viewed Pownall as the most important channel through which to counter these falsehoods.

No event of this decade proved more susceptible to conflicting interpretations than the Massachusetts Convention of Towns of September 1768. In the end the delegates did nothing more radical than profess their loyalty to the king and "Government as by Law established," call for "constitutional and prudent Methods" of redressing their grievances, and ratify the petitions which the House of Representatives had sent to the home government last February. The convention demonstrated, nevertheless, that the majority of Massachusetts towns supported the moderate Whig leaders even to the point of defying the governor's order for this illegal assembly to disband.[37]

Massachusetts Tories jumped to the conclusion that Boston had called the convention to organize armed resistance to the landing of British troops and that the mildness of its pronouncements could be attributed to a loss of nerve in the face of military might. In England news of the convention shocked Parliament into passing a series of resolutions condemning the Massachusetts legislature and the town of Boston for their "subversive" activities of the past year, and approving an address to the king urging him to transport to England for trial any Massachusetts citizen against whom evidence of treason could be gathered.[38]

In a letter to Pownall, Cooper ably summarized the contrasting Whig view of the convention:

> I find it has been received among you, as an undoubted Fact, that the Convention was called by the Town of Boston, upon the Precedent of 1688—on Supposition of the Dissolution of Government, and with Intention to erect a new one. Had this been true, I should not wonder at the Resentment expressed against the Town of Boston, . . . But this is far from the Truth. I never heard that they intended to proceed upon such a Ground, till it came from your Side of the Water, suggested I believe from hence. . . . It was, I am persuaded, far from the Intention of those who proposed and carried that measure. . . . The Design of it was, to calm the People, to prevent Tumults, to recognize the Authority of Government by humble Remonstrances and Petitions, and to lead the People to seek Redress only in a Constitutional Way. The discerning [men?] who promoted this Measure, saw that it must have this Effect. Had any Thing been intended in Opposition to Government, common Sense would have forbid the calling the Members to assemble in this Capital, where all they said and did must be Known, and would have left them to act more secretly, and effectually in the several Districts where they had influence. The Publicity of the Meeting, was considered as the surest Pledg of the Prudence and good Temper of their Proceedings. Candor would have thus represented it to the Administration.[39]

Pownall did not disappoint Cooper and his other American friends. In the parliamentary debates over the Massachusetts Convention he warned that "where the whole spirit and bent of a people, who have the powers of government within themselves, is fixed and determined against a tax—experience and common sense will convince you, that no civil power, no civil coercion, will ever assess or collect it." Furthermore, armed force used against New Englanders will raise in them a spirit "superior to all force." If they believe they are persecuted, these sons of Puritans will revive "that spirit of enthusiasm" which drove their fathers to forsake England for the wilderness. "And if the ministers once fall in with this spirit, if the people once call upon them, they must take the lead. And if they do, the people (to use their own phrase) will be led by Moses and Aaron, by the civil and religious, under a bond of unity that no factions will divide, no force can break. The spirit of their religion—or if you please so to call it of fanaticism—will, like Moses' serpent, devour every other passion and affection; their love for the mother country, changing its nature, will turn to the bitterest hate; their affectation of our modes and fashions, (the present source of great part of our commerce) will become an abomination in their sight."

Pownall offered a pragmatic compromise on the question of Parliament's authority over the colonies: "Let the matter of right rest upon the declaratory law, and say no more about it." Thereafter avoid the issue of rights and act with restraint. "Go into no innovations in practice, and suffer no encroachments on government." Lay no internal taxes on the colonies, and levy the various forms of external taxes as before 1760 "with prudence and moderation, and directed by the spirit of commercial wisdom."[40]

Pownall's speeches of January and February 1769 received wide circulation in the colonies through publication as a single speech in newspapers and a pamphlet. The *Virginia Gazette* gave a front page to an ingenious condensation.[41] Cooper wrote him that "the Gentlemen of the convention and particularly the Selectmen of Boston are greatly obliged to you for your Candid and accurate Vindication of them, from these artful and cruel Misrepresentations which aimed at nothing Short of involving them in the Penalties of Treason."[42]

On 19 April 1769, Pownall moved for repeal of the Townshend duties. The House of Commons appeared to favor the motion until the ministry urged postponement. A propitious moment for improving relations with the colonies had slipped away.[43] "You Americans will not want to be told at this time that everything here is Party," Pownall wrote despondently to the Boston preacher. He added in a later letter, "You are destined to be the sport of parties, as Ireland is. You will, I see it clearly, be turned over from one faction to another, and will ever lose as much as you can get by every turn."[44] Parliament's refusal to heed this moderate and realistic man only hardened the attitudes of Whig leaders such as Cooper, Hancock, and Bowdoin. A few Whigs, among them Samuel Adams, remained adamant in their distrust of Pownall as "an ambitious, crafty, designing man" who "would only carry us to market and make the best bargain he could for himself." Even so, on the king's birthday in 1769, the House of Representatives toasted "the late Governor Pownal" among other outstanding English friends of America.[45]

While their former governor defended them in Parliament, Bostonians struggled with the problems of living under military occupation. As the convention met, Bernard released official information that two regiments would land soon and two more were to follow. On 1 October 1768 a thousand soldiers disembarked and marched into town; then in November new arrivals filled the barracks on Castle William. More than a dozen vessels of war rode at anchor in the harbor. After a verbal battle over quartering the troops, the town seemed for a moment to accept its fate. Thomas Hutchinson began to sleep better than he had in years. General Thomas Gage, British military commander in North America, reported to Hillsborough his optimism that it might now be possible "to curb effectually the Licentious and Seditious Spirit, which has so long prevailed in this Place."[46]

Bostonians reacted variously to the presence of British redcoats. Dr. Mather Byles, the punning, practical-joking minister of the Hollis Street Congregational Church, laughed that the Sons of Liberty "might now behold American grievances red-dressed."[47] Others—among them at least one Whig merchant—scurried to grab their share of military gold. Most simply gawked at the unfamiliar army routine. More important for the literate Whigs, military occupation afforded a real life test of the libertarian theory which taught that standing armies had been the chief instrument of the destruction of freedom among free peoples. *Cato's Letters*, the handbook of radical English whiggery in the eighteenth century, had made the point starkly clear: "It is absolutely impossible, that any Nation which keeps them [standing armies] amongst themselves can long preserve their Liberties; nor can any Nation perfectly lose their Liberties who are without such Guests." For those who understood, 1 October marked Massachusetts's entrance into "one of the classic stages in the process of destroying free constitutions of government." From the Whigs' point of view Boston's chapter of the continued story of the suppression of freedom by standing armies had to be written for compelling reasons: to convince fellow citizens less sensitive to tyranny, to show Parliament the folly of its innovations, to inform other colonies of what likely lay in store for them one after another, and finally—in case all was lost—to record the sad tale as a warning for posterity.[48]

Almost at once the Boston Whigs hit upon the perfect vehicle. On 13 October 1768 the *New York Journal* published a daily "Journal of Transactions in Boston," detailing events of the first week of military occupation. In Philadelphia the *Pennsylvania Chronicle* printed the same "Journal" on 17 October. Both newspapers continued to carry the "Journal" weekly for the next ten months. The *Boston Evening-Post*, hitherto chief source of anti-Whig writing, succumbed to local pressure and ran a slightly edited version of the "Journal" two months behind the events it described. At least eleven other American and three English newspapers copied it in whole or in part. Thus the English-speaking world read of the horrors of British militarism and conspiratorial officialdom at Boston in America's first syndicated newspaper column.[49]

The "Journal of the Times," as the *Evening-Post* entitled it, bears the marks of a group effort. Before he knew it would also be published in Boston, Hutchinson wrote, "I think sometimes we have ½ dozen of the most wicked fellows among us of any upon the Globe. They stick at nothing. For some 5 or 6 weeks past they have been sending a Diurnall to be printed at York. They knew such infamous falshoods could obtain no credit here but at that distance there is no body to contradict them and they are inflaming the Gov[ernments] of New York and Pennsilvania which for some time past seem to have been cool."[50]

What little evidence exists concerning authorship of the "Journal" reveals that William Cooper served as its editor and compiler. He may even have done a large part of the writing himself, incorporating whatever materials his colleagues furnished him. Most identifications of authorship of pseudonymous or anonymous newspaper writing in Boston from 1765 to 1776 are made from the annotated newspaper file of shopkeeper Harbottle Dorr, who consistently maintained that "these Journals were done by Mr. William Cooper, Town Clerk of Boston."[51] In the light of Dorr's attribution, a sentence in a letter of Samuel Cooper to his brother, written during the period of publication, takes on new significance: "You will see by the Papers that the Pacquet is arrived at N. York."[52] Apparently the weekly copy, after preparation in Boston, was dispatched to New York by a swift coastal packet. Here also is the suggestion that Samuel Cooper had more than a casual interest in the endeavor. The closeness of the brothers and the confusion of their identities makes it difficult to know in this case, as a Tory writer had queried concerning an earlier Whig piece, "What Cooper has hoop'd up this barrel?"[53]

Unlike most later historians, Hutchinson and Bernard knew better than to dismiss William Cooper as a minor functionary. The lieutenant governor had heard that he was one of a small group, including Otis and Adams, who gathered on Saturday to prepare Monday's *Gazette*. As the "Journal" neared its end, the governor had concluded that the town clerk was "unfit to bear any Commission under the King"; indeed, in the "faction" which had set the country "in Opposition to the King and Parliament," Bernard believed William Cooper "to bear a principal Part." Such a contemporary reputation was in keeping with the modern evaluation of the "Journal of the Times" as "the most ambitious venture in systematic and sustained propaganda by the press that the patriots ever attempted anywhere." Nothing in Will Cooper's long career affords any ground for doubting Dorr's identification of him as the principal author.[54]

Read in its entirety, the "Journal of the Times" must be accounted one of the major documents of the American Revolution because of its success in fusing ideas and events. Day by day for ten months Boston's unhappy experiences were made to confirm radical Whig theory in a here-and-now sense which no discourse on past history could match. After selecting events that could be reported to partisan advantage, the "Journal" often editorialized in a few italicized sentences, tersely reiterating Whig maxims.

The authors exhibited no hesitation on the one pervasive issue felt by all colonies: "It is certain that the right of taxation is the cause of the present controversy." Boston had been singled out to be treated with "particular severity" as a result of an "absurd opinion that if the spirit of liberty was once thoroughly quelled in this capital, it must not only be extinguished through the province, but in all the colonies. Vain imagination! One spirit animates all America; and both the justice and importance of the cause is so plain, that to quench the spirit, all the colonies must be absolutely destroyed."[55]

The "Journal" appealed to the Calvinistic heritage of the majority of colonists by a regular emphasis on the degeneracy of the troops. Nearly every daily entry presented examples to support the charge "that our enemies are waging war with the morals as well as the rights and privileges of the poor inhabitants." Since the arrival of troops, "the air is contaminated with oaths, and blasphemies; violences are in the midst of us; and the sun as well as the moon and stars, witnesseth to the shameful prostitutions, that are daily committed in our streets and commons." Some soldiers openly pursued married as well as single women through the streets. Public executions and savagely brutal whippings of deserters jolted the sensibilities of townsmen, who naturally sympathized with the desire of men from corrupt and decaying old England to desert and settle in New England's "Canaan, a land not indeed, abounding with silver and gold, but a land flowing with milk and honey." Military watches set to catch deserters restricted the free movement of citizens more than they halted runaways. Not only had soldiers personally no respect for the Sabbath, but military operations continued as on weekdays, sometimes disturbing divine services.[56]

The "Journal" also lost no opportunity to support its contention that Britain, in effect, had made "a formal declaration of war against the trade and navigation of this continent." But all to no avail, for Britain must "soon fully perceive that they cannot have our monies in the way of a revenue, and trade both; that what the merchants and manufacturers receive, serves to increase the wealth and opulence of the nation, while the other only tends to destroy trade and increase ministerial dependence."[57]

During its period of publication the authors of the "Journal" could report some notable successes. At last the commissioners abandoned their prosecution of Hancock. Two of the regiments left for other bases. Best of all, the final number, under a dateline of 1 August 1769, could comment on the sailing for England this day of that "infamous pimp to a Secretary of State," Governor Bernard: "Upon his departure every demonstration of joy was to be seen in his government, in which all America partook."[58]

These victories apparently convinced the Boston Whigs that the "Journal" had done its work and could now be safely discontinued. Harbottle Dorr noted in the margin of his *Boston Evening-Post* of 18 December 1769, "Thus ends the Famous Journal of the Times; in the opinion of all unprejudiced Persons, it is a True candid narration of Facts."[59]

Samuel Cooper articulated the confidence of his comrades when he wrote Pownall in September 1769: "Many among us are of opinion that it would be best for the Colonies to . . . concern ourselves no more about Remonstrances and Petitions, which have had hitherto so little effect, and to leave the Ministry to procure their own measures till they find themselves like Governor Bernard at the end of their Tether, to which if I mistake not they are by this Time very near if not quite arrived."[60] And to Franklin Cooper wrote of his doubt whether there remained "Wisdom and Moderation enough in the British Councils" to adopt measures removing "the Ground of our Uneasiness" and reducing "Things to their old Channel."[61]

However mild and conciliatory his pulpit utterances, the Brattle Street minister in private stood at the center of those openly defiant Bostonians who believed in the fall of 1769 that they had nearly won their decade-long economic and political struggle against a corrupt Parliament and its succession of blundering ministries.

8

The Serpent Lies Hidden

*T*hroughout nearly a decade of political turmoil and uncertain profits most Boston merchants had remained adamantly opposed to all British attempts to raise a revenue in America by taxes or customs duties. The local mercantile community did not clearly perceive that a changing English economy had ushered in a new age of interest politics, a competition for which the colonies were ill-equipped by reason of their geographical remoteness and their consequent incapacity in English politics.[1] But the increasing threat to Boston's material growth had been sufficiently evident to generate open resistance to any change in the lax economic and political system under which the town had prospered in the past. Innovations resulting from administrative decree or parliamentary statute had raised constitutional questions which, though intrinsically important, might have remained unresolved in the absence of economic frustration. As Samuel Cooper explained to Pownall on the first day of 1770, a colonial government which had always adequately safeguarded the interests and power of the mother country could not be drastically altered at this late date without encouraging Americans to reexamine their place in that empire: ". . . the Body of the People are for recurring to first Principles—the old establishment upon which they have grown and Flourished. . . . It is extremely dangerous to touch Foundations."[2]

This implied threat did not mean that in 1769 Boston Whigs entertained thoughts of revolution and independence; they fought only to protect and enlarge their place in the empire. If Britain wants to see peace and order restored in America, declared Bowdoin, she must give up the right of taxation, institute a trade policy fair to American commercial interests, and remove from office those obnoxious persons "in whom all confidence is lost."[3] Cooper listed four specific grievances: the board of customs commissioners, the revenue laws, the "Unconstitutional Powers of the Admiralty Courts, and the Standing Army in Time of Peace." Any one of these remaining "will prove a root of Bitterness." In Cooper's view, Governor Bernard had "essentially though undesignedly" served the Whig cause by governing so foolishly that the province united against the changes in policy attempted by the mother country during his administration.[4]

In the year before Bernard's departure Bowdoin had led a majority of the Council into open opposition. That body had hastened the governor's recall by publishing his incriminating letters to a British official and by otherwise confronting him at each turn.[5] Yet during their final confrontation with Bernard, the Whig leaders seized every opportunity to demonstrate loyalty to their sovereign. When Governor Wentworth of New Hampshire visited the Boston area in June, the Council and House received him and his lieutenant governor, John Temple, with conspicuous warmth. As the *Evening-Post* made clear, a governor who was a "worthy Representative of his Majesty, and a favorite of the People," had nothing to fear in this province, however strong the dislike of its citizens for those officials "whose Deportment is unworthy the Royal Favour."[6] Similarly, General Alexander Mackay, commander of the Boston garrison for a few months in 1769, won the praise of the *Gazette* for his "unexceptionable" conduct. Regarding enforcement of the revenue acts as impracticable, Mackay had attempted to lessen tensions between citizens and soldiers through frequent communication with leaders of the opposition. For example, he had listened appreciatively as Samuel Cooper read the text of the amended mutiny act from the only copy in the town, which had been rushed to the preacher by Thomas Pownall, who had been partially responsible for softening its terms.[7]

On 14 August 1769, two weeks after Bernard had sailed, the Sons of Liberty transformed their annual festival into a seven-hour celebration of his removal, the preservation of colonial liberty, and their loyalty to the monarch. After fourteen toasts around the Liberty Tree, more than three hundred Sons repaired to the "Liberty-Tree Tavern" in Dorchester for an afternoon of entertain-

ment and forty-five more bumpers (according to individual capacity) in symbolic tribute to John Wilkes. Climaxing the return trip to
Boston, John Hancock led a triumphal procession of 139 vehicles
into the town and around the state house. On this day, four years
after the riot of 1765, the Sons of Liberty believed that they had
successfully maintained their "Constitutional opposition to illegal,
oppressive and arbitrary Measures, at home and from abroad." If
ever Samuel Cooper regretted his choice of career, it must have
been on an occasion such as this. Brother Will was there, and so
were friends Otis, Adams, Hancock, Cushing, and Bowdoin. But
the appearance of the clergy on so partisan a political scene violated
the cherished concept of their sacred calling and destroyed the
public image that the Brattle Street pastor worked hard to
preserve.[8]

In October Cooper presided at the marriage of Josiah Quincy,
Jr., to the daughter of William Phillips, one of the most politically
active Whig merchants. An impetuous and impressionable young
lawyer, Quincy's rhetorical radicalism would soon earn him the
sobriquets of "Wilkes Quincy" and the "Boston Cicero." But like
many Whigs—perhaps the majority—he remained more radical in
word than in deed.[9]

Quite the opposite, the acting governor to whom Bernard had
delivered the province seal advocated yielding in theory while seeking concessions in practice. Nearing sixty when he took the government, Thomas Hutchinson stood inflexibly committed to parliamentary supremacy as he faced the younger Whig leaders: William
Cooper was forty-eight; Samuel Adams, forty-seven; Cushing,
Otis, and Samuel Cooper, forty-four; Bowdoin, forty-three; Hancock, thirty-two; while Warren and Quincy were only in their
twenties. Privately, Hutchinson longed for an act of Parliament dis-
qualifying from any public office a Massachusetts citizen who persisted in a conspiracy against the crown. Such an act, he believed,
"would make a number of those people and among the rest Will
Cooper, Adams, &c. tremble, though I don't think this half enough
for so atrocious a crime, and for any persons who hereafter should
be concerned no penalty is too great." Publicly, nevertheless,
Hutchinson undertook his new role with far more political skill
than Bernard had ever displayed. Though admitting the acting
governor's initial success in improving relations with the Council,
Samuel Cooper questioned whether Hutchinson could dissociate
himself from the odium cast on his predecessor without a "change
of Measures at home."[10]

The preacher received contradictory advice on how best to bring about such a change of measures. Though Franklin retained confidence in the king, he advised his Boston friend in a long letter against placing hope in a "wiser and juster" Parliament of the future.[11] As much as he might agree with this view, Cooper remained reluctant to encourage the open repudiation of parliamentary authority over the colonies. To do so, he feared, would alienate more merchants from the nonimportation agreements by which the Whigs hoped to force repeal of the Townshend duties. Thus he deleted references to Parliament in the excerpt from Franklin's letter he had inserted in three Boston newspapers. The published section made a fervent plea for perseverance in nonimportation to confound the British ministers and merchants who believed that Americans "cannot long subsist without their manufactures"—that the colonies will "quietly one after the other submit to their Yoke, and return to the Use of British fineries."[12]

Pownall offered different counsel. As a member of Commons he could not dispense so easily with total parliamentary authority over the colonies. Nor did he think the revenue question could be more than compromised. Rather, he urged Americans to stand firm on basic questions of rights, such as taxation without representation, independence of colonial courts, and civil control of the military. He wrote Cooper that "if these points be once avowedly brought forward in claim, they must be decided—and they cannot be decided against you." Pownall warned against further petty disputes with royal officials, and deplored "compulsive measures" to enforce nonimportation agreements.[13]

As with Franklin's, Cooper made selective use of Pownall's correspondence as he saw best "for the Good of my Country." Only a "trusty few" read the original letters. But extracts he thought useful to the Whig cause appeared in the local press with attributions indicating the importance of the writer without revealing his name.[14]

Whig strategy against the Townshend acts had been shaped by the apparent success of the boycott of English manufactures in forcing repeal of the Stamp Act. But a second nonimportation movement proved to be much more difficult to organize and maintain. Present grievances, largely commercial, elicited less spontaneous support. A sustained effort would be required this time, for English manufacturers were opening up new markets and would thus not feel the pinch so quickly. Problems of cooperation among American ports would be more troublesome over a longer period.

Most unpromising of all, a lengthy boycott would bring genuine distress to smaller and less affluent importers of European goods whose stocks were depleted at the time the ban took effect. Hancock and Bowdoin, who lived on inherited wealth and took a casual approach to their business affairs, could more enthusiastically support nonimportation than the retailer whose livelihood depended on each quarter's sales. So great were the difficulties that the nonimportation movement achieved little success until after the British ministry demonstrated in Boston that it meant to back its commercial policies with military force. Then, by the summer of 1769, nonimportation agreements in the colonial port towns covered sufficient American trade to constitute a strong economic weapon if they were religiously observed.[15]

No sermons have survived to reveal whether the Brattle Street congregation now listened to homilies on the evils of foreign luxuries and the spiritual efficacy of homespun garments. Though such were often heard in country churches, these would be strange doctrines emanating from this edifice. In his correspondence, however, Cooper boasted of the success of native manufactures, praised the firmness of Boston merchants in holding to the nonimportation agreement, and sanctioned the blacklisting of violators.[16]

The overwhelming majority of politically active citizens in Boston stood squarely behind efforts to alter Britain's commercial policies. On bedrock issues concerning the town's economic future, few failed to sense the necessity of opposing restrictive innovations, even though they might detest partisan politics and mobbishness. Despite its past attacks on Whig politicians, the *Evening-Post* now often seemed as radical as the *Gazette*.[17] On the private advice of the commissioners of customs, whose printing they did, the owners of the *Boston Post-Boy* had resisted Whig pressure to carry the "Farmer's Letters." The result, they maintained, was the loss of the "largest part" of their subscribers.[18] Even the *News-Letter*, normally the most conservative and lifeless of the town press, gave some reluctant and timid support to the merchant's cause for two years after arrival of the troops.[19] In such a climate of opinion, those who were "building themselves up upon the Ruin of their Fellow Citizens" could expect to have various forms of compulsion directed against them.

More than ever the customs commissioners became objects of public detestation. His popularity at its peak, John Temple no longer concealed his connections with the Whigs, and he continued to furnish evidence to use against the other commissioners.[20] The commissioners struck back by purging the customs organization of

Temple's appointees, by renewing their efforts to enforce the acts of trade, and by enlisting the services of John Mein.[21] A fiery Scotsman who had moved to Boston in 1764, Mein had quickly enlarged his business concerns from bookselling to printing and to publishing a newspaper, the *Boston Chronicle*. After some unprofitable attempts at neutrality, he turned to the commissioners for support and began publishing in the *Chronicle* ship manifests supplied by them to prove that Hancock and other leading Whig merchants imported regularly in violation of their own agreement. The commissioners made certain that these numbers of the *Chronicle* circulated widely in other colonial ports.[22] Samuel Adams publicly warned Mein "not to set himself in Opposition to an awakened, and enlightened and a Determined Continent, lest he be found to kick against the Pricks."[23]

Meanwhile, James Otis's troubled psyche neared eruption. In September he and Commissioner John Robinson came to blows at the British Coffeehouse, where Otis received a severe cut on the head from the commissioner's walking stick. Since most witnesses had been army officers and other crown servants, Otis could with plausibility soon speak of "the premeditated, cowardly and villainous attempt last week to assassinate me." Whatever the truth, the act was symbolically perfect: after nine years of struggle against British trade regulations, the Boston Whigs could report to the world that "our chairman," as one called him, had been struck down by a royal official.[24]

Public agitation increased as Mein, braving minor harassments, continued publishing cargo manifests during September and October, together with charges and insinuations designed to destroy public confidence in the nonimportation agreement. At the end of October the *Chronicle* published an attack on the leading Whigs that provoked a mob to threaten Mein. In making his escape he fired a shot, whereupon a warrant was issued for his arrest. Not wanting to trust his fate to a Boston jury, he went into hiding. Hutchinson believed it folly to use troops in an attempt to guarantee Mein's safety in Boston; so the Scotsman sailed for England leaving his partner to continue the *Chronicle*. Boston's mood had been made clear when the mob pursuing Mein ended its rampage by tarring and feathering an alleged customs informer. Troops or no troops, the forces of resistance effectively controlled the town.[25]

At this point the Boston Whigs widened their goals to include repeal not only of the Townshend duties but of all the trade restrictions imposed, beginning with the Molasses Act of 1733. When the

New York and Philadelphia merchants evinced less enthusiasm for so sweeping a demand, Boston acquiesced "for the sake of Preserving Union," as Cooper explained. Nevertheless, in December a committee of merchants stated the case for the stronger position in a pamphlet entitled *Observations on Several Acts of Parliament*, which summarized clearly and convincingly the effects of the restrictions imposed by England on colonial trade and emphasized that "the whole trade of America lies at the mercy of the officers of the customs" and vice-admiralty courts who gain financially from the sale of vessels they seize and condemn.[26]

The original Boston nonimportation agreement lasted throughout 1769. With the beginning of 1770 some of the reluctant subscribers refused to enter the new agreement under which orders might be placed with English suppliers to be shipped only when the Townshend duties should be "totally repealed, and not otherways." Along with others the two older sons of Thomas Hutchinson had been able to remove their names from the Whig blacklist by storing in their warehouse the goods that they had imported in 1769, contrary to the agreement, and giving the key to a committee of merchants. After 1 January the Hutchinson boys demanded the release of their property. When this was refused, they broke into the warehouse and began the clandestine sale of tea, a product in great demand among a colony of tea drinkers whose supply had been curtailed by the nonimportation movement.[27] Their father attempted unsuccessfully to break up a meeting of Whigs—the "Body"—called to protest the actions of his sons, and he was finally forced to agree that the boys return the tea to the warehouse and pay for that already sold.

Cooper saw in this affair the first major test of Hutchinson's mettle as acting governor. He described Hutchinson's failure to Pownall:

> He was greatly embarrassed, sensible that He and his Sons were considered as the chief Bulwark of those who wished to see the Merchants Agreement annihilated. He was blamed for appearing below his Dignity, as a Negotiator in the Business. His Sons were blamed, even by his own Friends, for their inconsistent and Dishonorable Conduct with the Merchants. The Commissioners were offended with what they called his Weakness in this Instance, declaring that He had now given the Reins of Government into the Hands of the

People, and that he could never recover them. His unpopularity is increased by this Step, He being considered as the first Governor upon the Continent, who has publicly and directly opposed Himself to the Meeting of the Merchants as illegal. He told Mr. Phillips He was ruined.[28]

Hutchinson's resolution quickly revived, and he ordered the merchants to cease their "unlawful Assemblies" and coercive activities. Led by William Molineux, an unsuccessful Irish retailer who blamed England for his failures, the "Body" defied the acting governor and on 23 January voted the complete outlawry of importers. During January and February 1770 the Boston newspapers constantly fed the flames of controversy over nonimportation. Outside Boston the *Chronicle*'s accusations did serious damage to intercolonial unity on nonimportation. In January Hancock felt compelled to make a public declaration, in response to an inquiry by New York merchants concerning the accuracy of Mein's manifests, that he had "not in one single Instance, directly or indirectly," violated the nonimportation agreement.[29]

Benjamin Edes and John Gill, owners of the *Gazette*, encapsulated a decade of Whig propaganda in their *Almanack* for 1770 published during February. It included three different liberty songs. A stanza of one struck at royal officials:

Ye insolent Tyrants! who wish to enthrall,
Ye Minions, ye Placemen, Pimps, Pensioners all;
How short is your Triumph, how feeble your Trust,
Your Honors must wither, and nod to the Dust.

In this spirit, the resistance movement seemed to peak toward the end of February when the town staged a massive funeral for a boy shot while harassing a customs informer.[30] Soon the Whig cause found more martyrs. Renewed clashes between soldiers and townsmen at the beginning of March set the stage for what Cooper described as the "Horrors of the Bloody Massacre" of Monday, 5 March. That evening rumors of anticipated trouble brought more than the usual number into the streets despite snow and cold. A single sentry standing guard at the customhouse on King Street became the center of attention after he struck a badgering apprentice with his musket. Someone gave the alarm by ringing bells at the Brattle Street Church and another meetinghouse near the scene. More men rushed into King Street to surround the sentry. The

watch officer, Captain Thomas Preston, marched a relief guard of
seven men to the customhouse, where the crowd quickly pressed
them against the building. Fearful and confused, the soldiers eventually discharged their weapons. Of several hit, three fell dead and
two more received fatal wounds. Hutchinson prevented a general
battle with assurances that justice would be done. By Tuesday noon
Captain Preston and the eight soldiers were in prison charged with
murder.[31]

The Whigs now had the incident they needed to support their
demand for the withdrawal of troops. Tuesday morning Hancock
and the other Boston selectmen met with Hutchinson and the
Council to insist that the soldiers leave. While these deliberations
continued, a crowded town meeting convened in Faneuil Hall at
11 A.M. It voted to have a constable "wait upon the Rev. Dr.
Cooper, and acquaint him that the Inhabitants desire him to open
the Meeting with Prayer." Another vote sent a large committee to
the lieutenant governor with the message that only the "immediate
removal of the Troops" could prevent "blood and Carnage."

At 3 P.M. the town meeting assembled to hear Hutchinson's
reply. Faneuil Hall could not accommodate the masses pressing in,
and so they adjourned to the Old South Church, the largest
auditorium in town, which soon overflowed with a crowd reminiscent of Whitefield's first visit. They were told that Hutchinson dis-
claimed any power over the troops. The local commanding officer
had agreed to transfer one of the two regiments to the harbor fort
where it had been originally assigned, but the other had to remain
in town pending orders from General Gage. Unanimously rejecting
this position, the town appointed a smaller committee—Hancock,
Samuel Adams, Molineux, Warren, Phillips, and two other staunch
Whigs—to inform the governor that they would be satisfied with
nothing less "than a total and immediate removal of the Troops."[32]

According to Dr. Cooper, Hutchinson now stood alone
against the vote of the town meeting, advice of the Council, and
even the inclination of the commanding colonel, who "signified his
readiness, and even appeared to desire it." Finally, toward evening,
Hutchinson "gave way with reluctance." Both regiments would go
to the island fort until Gage issued new orders. When William
Cooper read the committee's report to the throng of citizens still
waiting in the Old South at twilight, they "could not but express the
high satisfaction, which it afforded them"; thus Town Clerk
Cooper recorded the historic moment in his usual dispassionate
style.[33]

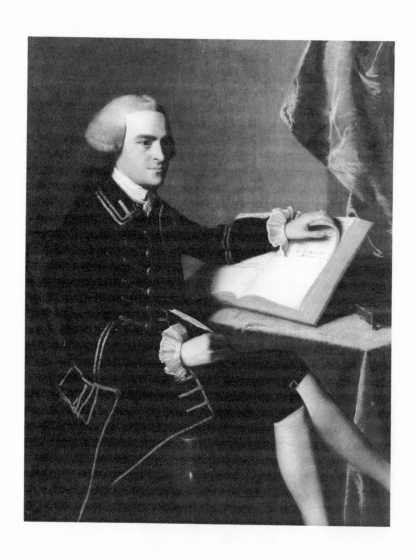

John Hancock by John S. Copley

Courtesy of Museum of Fine Arts, Boston

James Bowdoin II
by Robert Feke
Courtesy
of Bowdoin College
Museum of Art

A leading Whig in the
Brattle Street Church
Portrait of James Pitts
by Joseph Blackburn
Courtesy
of The Detroit
Institute of Arts

William Cooper
father of Samuel Cooper
Mezzotint by Peter Pelham
*Courtesy
of the Worcester
Art Museum*

Samuel Sewall
grandfather of Samuel
Cooper
by John Smibert

*Courtesy,
Museum of Fine Arts,
Boston*

The Brattle Street Church
from a Photograph
taken in 1857 by J.J. Hawes

*Courtesy of the Society
for the Preservation
of New England Antiquities*

"A View of the Town of Boston
with Several Ships of War in the Harbour,"
engraving by Paul Revere, 1774

Courtesy of the American Antiquarian Society

The pulpit supplied by John Hancock
for the Brattle Street Church building
erected in 1773

*From Records of the Church in Brattle Square (Boston, 1902),
courtesy of the Massachusetts Historical Society*

Samuel Adams by John S. Copley

Courtesy, Museum of Fine Arts, Boston

Within five days Boston was cleared of soldiers, except for the officers who sometimes came ashore in the daytime. The Whigs had never been so flushed with victory since repeal of the Stamp Act. The last week in March Samuel Cooper wrote to Pownall that "we cannot suppose that Troops will ever again be quartered in the Body of the Town" and that the commissioners were reported to be "so sensible of the public Odium, and so tired of their Employment, as to wish for a Removal."[34]

The minority of townsmen who regarded the troops as guardians of law and order felt betrayed. Of these, Dr. Henry Caner, rector of King's Chapel, appeared one of the most despondent. A native American, he had labored tirelessly to strengthen his parish and to make Anglicanism a political and social force in New England. But long dependence on the patronage of royal government and its national church had foreclosed the possibility of his assuming even a neutral position in the present troubles with Britain. The month after the Boston Massacre, Caner wrote that "Sam Adams, W. Cooper, W. Mollineux and such Scoundrels rule the Town Meetings and the Town Meetings rule all." He added, "The peevish Dr. Chauncy and the insidious Dr. Cooper retain their Old Influence with the Mobb and rioters and are more Intimate than ever with . . . Temple."[35]

Notwithstanding his intimacy with the leading Whigs, John Adams quickly consented to serve as legal counsel for Captain Preston and the eight soldiers accused of the Massacre deaths. In an equally startling move, "Wilkes" Quincy joined Adams in the defense. The two had agreed to take the cases even while a public outcry for vengeance could be heard. In explaining why they entered these cases, both lawyers referred to the right of any accused to counsel; and Quincy revealed that he had been "advised and urged to undertake it, by an Adams, a Hancock, a Pemberton, a Warren, a Cooper, and a Phillips." The Whig leaders understood that the strongest defense of the soldiers required the amassing of evidence against the town. As irresistible as was the propaganda to be gained from convicting Preston and his men of shooting down unarmed civilians, it would not pay to achieve this result at the price of irrevocable damage to the town's reputation in British public opinion.[36]

Cooper became concerned when Commissioner John Robinson quietly sailed for London on 16 March. The minister alerted Pownall that the commissioner carried "Depositions secretly taken, relating to the firing upon the Inhabitants" with which he "hopes

for the advantage of making the first Impression." Even before
Robinson's departure the town had appointed a committee to draft
the Whig view of the Massacre. Now its members, including Bowdoin and Warren, quickly collected nearly a hundred depositions
favorable to the town. These, prefaced by Bowdoin's commentary,
were printed in *A Short Narrative of the horrid Massacre in Boston*
and rushed to influential persons across the Atlantic on a packet
ship hired for the purpose. Cooper explained to Pownall that this
pamphlet disproved Tory reports that "a great Mob in King Street"
attacking the customhouse had provoked Preston's men to fire.[37]

In another tract on the Massacre, this one designed for local
consumption, Bowdoin gave the blessing of his wealth and prestige
to the past five years of extralegal opposition to British policies and
illustrated the cutting edge of mercantile radicalism: The action of
the troops on the evening of 5 March was so "outrageous" and
"contrary to law" as to render them "traitors" to the king. "If there
had been no other means of getting rid of them, the inhabitants
would have had a right by that law of nature, which superceeds all
other laws, when they come in competition with it—the law of self-
preservation—to have compelled them to quit the town." While
maintaining that nothing remained more alien to his countrymen
"than a disposition to rebellion," Bowdoin also warned that Great
Britain's hope of becoming a "mighty empire" could be destroyed
by her conduct toward her colonies.[38]

Meanwhile the Whig leaders pressed for early trials, hoping, it
seems, for a speedy conviction to force the ministry to save those
condemned with a royal pardon that would amount to assumption
of responsibility for the Massacre. With skillful management of the
trials, the British government could be brought to the bar of justice
in a Boston courtroom.[39]

Hutchinson displayed his improving political dexterity in taking advantage of every excuse to delay the opening of the trials for
seven months. During this period he complained to Bernard of the
pressure put on the judges. Years later when he had become an embittered exile, one of the judges suggested that Cooper and Temple
had concerned themselves in this harassment of the judiciary: "The
Leaders of the Faction met at the House of Mr. Temple, . . . and
from thence a Party came into the Court, and insolently insisted on
an immediate Trial of Capt. Preston and his Soldiers. Two of the
Heads of this Faction . . . appeared in the Front, John Hancock
and Samuel Adams, who had just parted from that pious Divine
Dr. Cooper."[40]

In the end, the delay served well the cause of justice and also of the town, though in a way the Whigs had not foreseen. By summer they realized that Boston's best defense against the allegations of its enemies lay in an impeccable observance of the principle of justice toward the defendants. In July Cooper boasted to Pownall of the "Tenderness" shown Preston and commented that "People seem universally to wish him a fair Trial," even though "a Tendency prevails that from Court Favor the Law will be eluded."[41] This suspicion rested on fact. Before Preston's trial in October, Hutchinson received instructions to "reprieve any, who might be convicted, until the King's pleasure could be known." But royal intervention proved unnecessary because, by the end of the trials in December, the captain and six of his men had been acquitted and the other two soldiers, convicted on the lesser count of manslaughter, had been branded on the thumb and released. Likewise, a jury quickly freed the four civilian customhouse employees who also had been indicted for the Massacre.[42]

Cooper made certain that Franklin appreciated the implications of what had taken place: "These Trials must, one would think, wipe off the Imputation of our being so violent and blood thirsty a People as not to permit Law and Justice to take place on the Side of unpopular Men! and I hope our Friends will make this kind Improvement of them." At the same time, Cooper wanted Franklin to understand that the outcome of the trials had not noticeably "at all altered the Opinion of the People in General of that tragical Scene" on the evening of 5 March that had taught a classic lesson in the evils of a standing army.[43]

During the nine months required to free the soldiers, Hutchinson's political fortitude had been tested with equal severity in the legislature. As a last desperate measure in the summer of 1769, Bernard had moved the assembly from the Boston Town House to Harvard College in Cambridge. He had hoped in vain that the representatives would prove more tractable when gathered a few miles away from the troops and the foul political air of the capital. Hutchinson intended to return the winter session of 1770 to Boston until he received instructions from Hillsborough, coached by Bernard, to delay until March the opening of this term and to keep it in Cambridge unless there should be overriding reasons for meeting in Boston. The lieutenant governor hid his discretionary authority behind the ministry's earlier order that instructions to royal governors must not be made public. Sensing clearly that the Whig course led inevitably to open repudiation of parliamentary authority over the province, Hutchinson seemed eager for a showdown on this issue. By keeping the General Court out of Boston for the next two years, he forced Massachusetts Whigs to face the difficult theoretical questions they had hitherto avoided in their campaign to secure redress of immediate grievances.[44]

Cooper and Hutchinson met in a face-to-face clash at the 1 May meeting of the Harvard Board of Overseers. One of the two governing bodies of the college, the Board of Overseers included the governor, Council, and representatives of the clergy. On this occasion Chauncy and Cooper pushed for passage of a resolution declaring that the General Court's use of college buildings constituted an "Infringement" of the "rights of this Corporation" and a great inconvenience to students and faculty. "After a large Debate," the Overseers divided evenly, and the lieutenant governor then cast the deciding negative vote. In reporting this meeting to Bernard, Hutchinson explained that Chauncy had been "warm and rather boisterous." In contrast, Cooper, "with a very sanctified air," had "declared he was not in the least moved by any party views"; but, Hutchinson added, "I dare say no body present believed him." Like other Tories, he had come to consider the minister a hypocrite. Or, as he put it a few months later in commenting on the Whig clergy in general, Dr. Cooper "has the greatest government of his temper and is more upon his guard but *latet anguis* [the serpent lies hidden]."[45]

Two days later Harvard's other governing board, the Corporation, voted unanimously to do what the overseers had narrowly declined doing: to express its "deep concern" over the General Court's continued use of college buildings. Having been elected a Fellow of Harvard College in 1767, Cooper was also a member of this board, composed of the president and fellows who were usually professors or tutors.[46]

As the spring election of 1770 approached, the political temperature of the province rose. Several outlying towns voiced their support of Boston and the provincial legislature. Abington led the way with a widely printed set of resolves declaring that no act of Parliament for raising a revenue was binding on colonists and that any official attempting to enforce such duties "ought to be deemed no better than a highwayman." Though likely the work of an Abington printer, Tories believed the resolves to have been written in Boston and, according to one report, by Dr. Cooper.[47]

In the May election Boston returned Hancock, Cushing, and Samuel Adams to the House with nearly unanimous votes. For the first time in nine years Otis was left out. In the polite language of the town records, he had "retired into the Country for the recovery of his Health." Among other features of his erratic behavior, he was wont to fire his guns wildly until his family took them away from him. John Adams replaced him. As usual, the town instructed its representatives. This year Josiah Quincy, Jr., prepared instructions that accounted the lieutenant governor's holding the Court in Cambridge as additional proof that "a Deep laid and desperate plan of Imperial despotism has been laid, and partly executed, for the extinction of all civil liberty." While they acted as counsel for Captain Preston and his men, John Adams received a seat in the House and Quincy penned Whig propaganda that in Hutchinson's judgment reached the limits of infamy.[48]

Though the General Court opened at Cambridge on 30 May, Boston refused to be denied its annual election day festivity. A parade with music, firing of the town's batteries of cannon, and roasting an ox on the common all contributed toward making this a memorable election day. In his unofficial election sermon, Dr. Chauncy reviewed the events leading to this "day of darkness." After service, several hundred dignitaries and Sons of Liberty attended "an elegant Entertainment" at Faneuil Hall, where toasts rang out to, among others, the Harvard Corporation and "Our suffering Brethren at Cambridge, whose Hearts are with us while their Bodies are unconstitutionally torn from us."[49] Across the Charles River that same day, the General Court listened to the most unusual official election sermon preached since the practice began in 1634. Discarding much of the traditional formula, the Reverend Samuel Cooke of Cambridge, Hancock's uncle, reviewed the full range of Whig political principles in an aphoristic style of remarkable clarity and terseness.[50]

While he struggled with the legislature, Hutchinson harbored fears that his correspondence to England might fall into Whig hands and be exposed to the public. He had heard that a considerable number of letters from American Tories, including at least one of his, had recently arrived in Boston and now could be seen spread out on a large table in Dr. Cooper's study. Bernard received an earnest entreaty to prevent future purloining, because if his reports to the ministry, though accurate, were made public he would have "no security against the rage of the People."[51]

Since early spring Bostonians had known that Parliament was considering repeal of the Townshend duties. In January Lord North had taken control of the ministry with a firm majority in Commons and the warm approval of George III, who exerted increasing influence in policy making. On the day of the Boston Massacre, North proposed in Commons the removal of all the Townshend duties except on tea. By partial repeal he hoped to break up the nonimportation agreements without appearing to abandon the mother country's right to tax the colonies. Pownall moved to extend North's motion to repeal the entire Townshend Act. He rested his argument for a total repeal on the grounds of English economic self-interest rather than on leniency for the colonies. Distilling the contents of Cooper's letters, he argued that only a complete repeal could restore the "old boundaries" behind which Americans believed their liberties to be secure. Commons struck down the amendment by a vote of 142 to 204 and unanimously passed North's motion. Supporters of total repeal failed in an attempt to reopen the question in April just before the bill received the king's signature. When a copy of Pownall's 5 March speech reached Cooper, he rushed it to Speaker Cushing, who "admired it, and carried it to Cambridge the same Day, and read it to the House. It was heard with great Avidity and Pleasure" because, as Cooper explained, "we have seen Nothing like it from any Member of Parliament." A Boston reprint made the speech available to the public.[52]

As news of the impending repeal crossed the Atlantic, enforcement of the nonimportation agreements became more difficult; and with official word of Parliament's action, to take effect 1 December 1770, the movement began to collapse despite the best efforts of the Sons of Liberty in the various port towns. Throughout the summer numerous attempts to continue some semblance of a common nonimportation policy demonstrated the inherent difficulties of intercolonial cooperation. Slow communications, mutual distrust and recrimination, unequal sharing of economic hardships, and differences in regional outlook all contributed to the confusion. Above all, laboring men had made nonimportation more a political than an economic issue. As Cooper explained, "It is got in a great Measure under the controul of the Body of the People through the Continent." The Boston leaders resolved to stand firm and hold importers in line, but before the summer had ended even the Whig merchant John Rowe pointed with alarm to the sight of Dr. Thomas Young, controversial physician and imported political agitator, leading a parade of the "Body" through the streets to its meeting with "Three Flags Flying, Drums Beating and a french Horn."[53]

But the threat of the mob could not hold the line in Boston after the merchants of New York and Philadelphia began importing British goods with the exception of tea. In October the *Gazette* announced as inconspicuously as possible the news that Boston would follow suit. The town's Whigs displayed little open discouragement at the end of the "grand Tryal," as Samuel Adams styled the nonimportation movement. Cooper's interpretation, addressed to Pownall, pointed to its lasting effects: "The Measure is exhausted, but its effect may long remain. The true spirit of it has been a good deal diffused through the Country and there, according to an observation of yours, it flourishes in its native soil."[54]

As the nonimportation movement neared its end, Hutchinson raised afresh the prerogative issue by suddenly transferring command of Castle William, the provincial fort in Boston Harbor, from Massachusetts to royal officers. The order had come from the home government, and he executed it quickly and decisively before the opposition could organize. Cooper saw it as a foreboding move inspired by the commissioners, who purposely remained at the Castle to bolster their charge that Boston continued unsafe for all of them except Temple.[55]

Hutchinson's instruction to make the Castle into a British garrison seemed to confirm the central theme of Pownall's letters to his Boston friends during the past six months. Even before learning of the tragedy of 5 March, he attempted to prove that the British military establishment in America constituted an unlawful violation of the principle that the king commanded the army in his civilian capacity; and thus that in Massachusetts, for example, only the governor could rightfully exercise command of royal troops. In May Pownall unsuccessfully pressed this point in a major debate on the floor of Commons and privately with Lord North. Two months later Pownall warned Bowdoin and Cooper of the ministry's military and naval plans and urged cautious behavior by the town lest some rash action prejudice the case for civil control of the military. When the Council met a few days after the change of command at the Castle, Bowdoin read aloud Pownall's letter as a commentary and protest. The lieutenant governor now acknowledged Bowdoin to be "at the head of the opposition both in the Council and in the Town of Boston."[56]

Hutchinson called the legislature into session again in September. Now he had to defend his action concerning the Castle as well as his holding the Court in Cambridge. When both branches

joined in a fast to seek divine guidance, he scoffed privately that
they made religion into a "stalking horse" behind which to advance
"bad measures"—that they sought not the Lord but an excuse for
employing the language of 1641. The House finally consented to
proceed to essential public business while maintaining its protest
against government by royal instructions. But the Council intensified the struggle by unanimously voting a resolution of censure
against Andrew Oliver, secretary of the province, for false reporting of the Council's deliberations following the Boston Massacre. It
was partially a personal slap at the lieutenant governor, for he and
Oliver had married sisters, and two weeks before the censure their
families had been joined again by the marriage of Thomas Hutchinson, Jr., to Oliver's daughter.[57]

In this disputatious legislative session of two months' duration,
the House took one step of major consequence by selecting a
replacement for its deceased London agent. Though seldom officially recognized by the ministry, the agents lobbied for colonial
interests and occasionally proved to be of great service. Pownall
had advanced his own availability for the agency. By combining
this position with membership in Commons, he hoped to
strengthen his individualistic labors to improve relations between
mother country and colonies. What he really desired was perhaps
best revealed in his suggestion to Cooper that instead of agents the
colonies needed an English "patron" who would exercise a paternal
watchfulness over their interests. In the fall of 1770 Bowdoin and
Cooper wrote Pownall that a strong agency was needed and could
best be obtained by joining him and Franklin in that office. Since
the two in England currently stood on good terms, they might have
welcomed such an arrangement. Yet both Bowdoin and Cooper
must have understood that the ex-governor's enemies in the House
would block his selection; so their proposal may have been merely a
way of soothing his feelings. Despite his signal defense of the province in Parliament, Pownall had not overcome a reputation as an
untrustworthy "thorough modern politician," and his recent
counsel of moderation had increased the long-standing animosity
Samuel Adams felt toward him.[58]

Furthermore, recent events had moved Boston's Whig leaders
closer to Franklin's view of imperial relations. In a letter of 8 June
1770 to the Brattle Street pastor, Franklin came quickly to the
point: a standing army stationed in a colony during peacetime
without the consent of its assembly is an unconstitutional act
because each colony is a "distinct and separate" state having the

same sovereign as the mother country and therefore must give its consent before military forces may be employed within its boundaries. He advised Americans to avoid "such Expressions as, *The Supreme Authority of Parliament; The Subordinacy of our Assemblies to the Parliament,* and the like, (which in Reality mean nothing, if our Assemblies with the King have a true Legislative Authority)." If they stood firm against Parliament, Franklin believed the colonies could reestablish their correct constitutional relationship with the king.[59]

With this letter to Cooper Franklin enclosed a reply he had written the previous November to several queries of a prominent London printer friendly to colonial interests. Without explicitly repudiating parliamentary authority over the colonies, Franklin's reply skillfully defended the American Whig position and prophesied dire consequences, even to "Separation," should the ministry continue to act on its misconceptions of colonial resistance to British trade policies.[60]

Franklin's letter and its enclosure reached Cooper "most seasonably" a few weeks before the House chose an agent. "With great caution, knowing the delicacy the times require," the minister showed them to "some of the leading Members of the House," who expressed the "highest satisfaction" with their contents. The result was decisive, Cooper informed Franklin: "A Majority readily confided the Affairs of the Province at this critical Season to your Care."[61] The House *Journal* made it clear that Franklin had been chosen "to support the constitutional Rights of this House and the Province." Hutchinson informed Pownall that he believed the choice to have resulted from the recommendation of Cooper and Bowdoin. As if he knew what the lieutenant governor had written, the preacher hastened to reassure Pownall: "I did all in my Power for the sake of my Country to bring you into a share of that Trouble."[62]

It was poetic justice that Massachusetts enlisted in its defense the services of the most famous colonial American, one of the world's greatest living natural philosophers, forty-seven years after, as a runaway apprentice, he had shaken the dust of Boston off his shoes. More important, the Whig leaders now could share his doctrine of empire. In the short session of the General Court at the end of July, Hutchinson had heard from the representatives, "This House has the same inherent rights in this province, as the House of Commons has in Great Britain." At the time of Franklin's appointment, the House contended with the lieutenant governor over whether the General Court should imitate Parliament in the language it used to indicate that a bill had been enacted into law.[63]

After explaining the position of the representatives on this question of form, Hutchinson apologized to Bernard for troubling him with such a "trifling argument." It was obviously no trifle to Samuel Cooper, who now began to refer to the Massachusetts assembly as "our House of Commons."[64]

9

Plain and Simple

"There seems now to be a Pause in Politics," Cooper wrote Franklin on the first day of 1771.[1] Repeal of the Townshend duties except on tea, collapse of the nonimportation movement, and acquittal of Captain Preston and his men all contributed to the onset of an extended period of reduced political agitation.

The removal of John Temple's inflammatory presence also eased tensions. Thoroughly unhappy with his situation, he had unsuccessfully sought leave to present his case before his superiors at Whitehall. At last he sailed without leave at the end of November 1771. But before his ship cleared port, word arrived that he had been dismissed unheard and replaced as a commissioner. Though he carried recommendations from Cooper and other Boston Whigs, his hopes to reestablish himself in London rested on family connections rather than on the damning praise of American friends.[2]

Other influences made for tranquillity. George Whitefield renewed his inexplicable power over the mass psyche by returning to town on 14 August 1770, the day on which the Sons of Liberty held their annual festival. It was his first visit since before the Stamp Act crisis. For three weeks he preached daily in the Boston area to crowds nearly as large as those of the 1740s. General Gage welcomed the evangelist's reportedly preaching "Obedience to Government and Laws," while Whig organs reported from his sermons whatever they could interpret as favorable to their cause. Some of the old controversy flared anew, perhaps explaining why

Cooper did not invite Whitefield to preach once more in the Brattle Street pulpit. At the end of September he died suddenly at Newburyport and was buried under the meetinghouse there. His tomb became at once a shrine to the Anglican priest who had used the force of revivalistic Calvinism to spur the American colonies to righteousness because he found there the largest remnant of the children of God. The emotional catharsis induced by Whitefield's return and dramatic death tranquillized his thousands of devotees, and at the same time renewed their confidence in the rectitude of their conduct toward a mother country they believed to be increasingly enervated by political corruption and moral degeneracy.[3]

Another calming influence came with the arrival in October of James Gambier to replace Commodore Hood as commander of the British fleet based at Boston. Some of the Whigs, especially Bowdoin, had enjoyed cordial social relations with Hood, who, like General Mackay, did not relish being cast as an "oppressor" and tried to carry out his orders with as much good will as possible. Commodore Gambier proved even more conciliatory. He came recommended to Cooper and Bowdoin by Pownall as one who "wishes to render his command (as it ought to be) a benefit and advantage to trade and commerce, and not a distress to and oppression of it." For the next ten months he gave general satisfaction to the mercantile community only to be transferred unexpectedly, and in Boston eyes suspiciously. Cooper characterized Gambier's command as having favored "Trade in every Point consistent with his Duty as a Commander." But why, "after putting himself to great Trouble and Expence in providing for this Station," had the commodore "not been allowed to remain upon it above one Third of the usual Time"?[4]

The illusion of returning prosperity also contributed to tranquillity. At Gambier's departure in August 1771, Boston approached the peak of a trading boom. Since 1769 the entire empire had felt the effects of credit expansion produced by the phenomenal advance of the British economy in the first stages of industrial growth. Once the nonimportation movement collapsed, English firms gladly raised the limits of credit granted American merchants attempting to profit from the backlog of demand. New England as a whole imported in 1771 goods from Britain valued at three times the imports of 1768. This rush of trading activity continued into 1772 before the credit bubble burst.[5]

The available figures indicate roughly that every fifth family in Boston involved itself directly in merchandising, but two-thirds of these only at the shopkeeper level.[6] There were also the sailors, sea captains, artisans, and laborers necessary to build, sail, service, and maintain the merchant fleet and those workers in the small industries producing a few exportable commodities. Thus the susceptibility of Boston's economic health to fluctuations in trade becomes clearly visible. Though families with accumulations of liquid capital might survive temporary disruptions of trade and sometimes even profit from the hardships of others, in the long run their fate rested on the welfare of the entire community. Shipping was inextricably connected with trade and was of vital concern to Cooper's leading parishioners. In 1771 at least 35 percent of Boston's mercantile tonnage was held by twenty members of this church.[7] Since shipping services, particularly to the West Indies, constituted the largest single source of earnings with which to pay the steady deficit resulting from the unfavorable balance of trade with the mother country, Boston's economic welfare depended far more than has been realized on the successes of three dozen or so of the largest shipowners.[8]

A half century later, John Adams remembered hearing that before the Revolution "not less than a thousand families were, every day in the year, dependent on Mr. Hancock for their daily bread."[9] Though an exaggeration, this statement pointed to the essential truth of a citizenry economically reliant on the activities of its wealthiest 1 or 2 percent, who consequently formed also a political elite. The fame of Hancock in time came to blot out the memory of other members of this elite with somewhat less wealth and political ambition—forgotten individuals such as Isaac Smith, John Webb, John Brown, John Erving, James Pitts, or Timothy Fitch.[10] Samuel Cooper knew these men well because he preached to them. At least moderately Whiggish in outlook, they and the perhaps two hundred others who dominated Boston's economy had for the past four years almost to a man supported resistance to the Townshend duties and to the commissioners sent to collect them; and the majority had been in opposition since 1761, when the first changes in imperial relationships became apparent. Once their vital interests had been threatened, they looked to fundamental constitutional rights. But in 1771, after partial repeal of the duties and the opening of what at first appeared to be a boom period, they regained some of their optimism of 1760 and 1766. Even while the customs service collected the remaining duties more rigorously in Boston than in other ports, these merchants and shipowners appeared willing to give the mother country one more chance to restore New England to an acceptable place in the British Empire. As long as prosperity continued, most others in this trading town would share their outlook.[11]

As usual, Cooper sensed the mood of his leading parishioners. At the beginning of 1771, he explained to Franklin that the "Pause in Politics" offered the ministry "a fair Opportunity of adopting the mildest and most prudent Measures respecting the Colonies without the Appearance of being threatened or drove"—a chance "of securing the Affections as well as the Submission of the Colonies." Should the English government "be so temperate and just as to place us on the old Ground on which we stood before the Stamp Act, there is no Danger of our rising in our Demands." Six weeks earlier Cooper had written Franklin of the power enjoyed by the crown in Massachusetts stemming from the charter and the natural affection of colonial Englishmen for their monarch. Consequently, he added, "whoever takes a View of these Advantages collectively and in all their Extent, as they have in Fact been found to operate, must be convinced that had Things been left exactly as they stood before the Stamp Act Britain would have been far from having any just reason to complain of the Independence of our Constitution. We had indeed scarce any Thing left on the Side of Privilige but the Granting of our own Monies for the Support of Government and the furnishing necessary military Aids to the Crown. This Palladium seems about to leave us; for after all the Complaints made of our Obstinacy and Ungovernableness we are daily paying Taxes not granted by us, but exacted from us for both these Purposes."[12]

Here, then, Boston rested its case in 1771: the provincial assembly must control the purse and exercise a check on the disposition of military force within its boundaries in order to offset the natural advantages of royal prerogative in colonial administration. Equally important, whatever legislative authority remained to Parliament in the gray area of regulation of imperial trade must not be used to restrict the commerce of one section of the empire in favor of another beyond the broad outlines of past operation of the vague mercantile system. If Britain would in practice make these concessions, the town's economic elite would not raise the abstract question of right posed by the Declaratory Act.

Of course, not everyone engaged in or dependent upon commerce saw his interest to lie in firmness toward England. Tea importers and those serving as factors or commission agents for English firms seemed the most reluctant to support resistance.[13] Nor had anyone forgotten that, until the uniting force of the

Townshend program, a strong minority of Boston's mercantile community had vented its detestation of radical Whig politicians through the *Evening-Post*. Now the expansion of economic activity in 1771 raised the question of how long the resistance movement could survive both prosperity and the absence of further provocation from Whitehall.

Cooper understood the situation better than his colleagues among the clergy. His lack of concern with theological or political absolutes helped, as did his intimacy with the economic elite and ear for political reality. Despite its pastor's decade of behind-doors involvement in the resistance movement, the Brattle Street Church remained a neutral sanctuary. Though Hutchinson might think him a hypocrite, Cooper gave no credence to this private opinion by letting it outwardly disturb him or change the nature of his public ministrations. A ballad on the Boston clergy circulating in manuscript in 1770 identified four of the most prominent ministers— Samuel Mather, Charles Chauncy, Ebenezer Pemberton, and Andrew Eliot—as being unable to disguise their political leanings, but not so with the most active of the divine politicians:

> In Brattle Street we seldom meet,
> With silver-tongued Sam,
> Who gently glides between both sides,
> And thus escapes a jam.[14]

The allusion to Cooper's frequent absences from his pulpit was not a sneer, as has sometimes been suggested, but rather an indication of the demand for him as a guest preacher in other churches, a popularity explained by a reluctance to enter public controversy as much as by the "silver-tongued" quality of his clerical oratory.

Like the Whig elite, Cooper held himself to be "an enemy to all Disorders" and wished "they could be prevented." The entire colony, he insisted, should not be judged by the violent actions of "a few obscure Persons in it." Even so, some disorder was to be expected and perhaps excused in a time when the power of civil authority had been weakened by an attempt to "enforce Measures that People of all orders apprehend to be unconstitutional." Knowing full well that the present constitutional crisis had issued from a commercial contest, Samuel Cooper appeared content with the turn of events in 1771 and 1772.[15]

A few zealous Whigs could not so calmly accept the "Pause in Politics." Of these, Samuel Adams overshadows all others. A brilliant propagandist and an indefatigable ward politician, since

1764 he had repeatedly demonstrated his usefulness to the Whig merchants. Sometimes troubled by his intense need for moral absolutes and for enemies to attack, they did not, nevertheless, oppose his taking center stage. He served their purpose by writing, organizing, and drawing the fire of Tories, who took comfort in blaming the province's disturbances more on the lunacy of Otis and the fiendishness of Adams than on the deliberate efforts of commercial leaders who were struggling to protect and enlarge their interests. In this camouflage lay the source of the persistent myth that Samuel Adams almost singlehandedly led Massachusetts down the road to the Revolution. His role would enlarge in years to come, but until now he had been a tool of the disaffected elite more than a prime mover of resistance to Britain. But already Tories had begun the practice adopted later by historians of attributing to his "serpentine Cunning" all revolutionary activity not otherwise explainable by solid evidence.[16]

Not until the spring of 1770 did Adams escape the threat of prosecution for the shortages in his accounts while tax collector from 1756 to 1764. Answers to two critical questions concerning this case have never been documented. Did he fall into arrears as a result of using tax favors to build a political base? And did Hancock, as was widely believed, put up the money that enabled Adams to meet the terms of a reduced settlement finally offered him in 1770? Whatever the facts, Adams clearly could not have survived politically without the steady support of his elitist patrons.[17]

Belittling John Hancock during the Revolution and afterwards, loyalists and political foes made it an article of faith that in the decade before 1775 Adams controlled this rich young man like a puppet on a string. To balance this distortion one should recall a contemporary description of Adams in 1767 as a little barking dog called "Jet," who, when he sees any of his masters, "runs to them, fawns, licks their hands, and leaps upon them with so much cunning and good humour, that they forget all about the Money, spit in his mouth, clap him on the side; then away goes Jet, wagging his tail, and glad enough you may be assured."[18] The truth of their relationship lay somewhere between puppetry and sycophancy, and perhaps at first displayed a little of each extreme. But after a few years Adams was to know better than any other man alive that no one controlled the willful and inscrutable John Hancock.

Since the name of Samuel Adams appears on the church records, historians naturally jumped to the conclusion that the archrevolutionary sat under Cooper's preaching, together with Hancock, Bowdoin, and Warren. As interesting as this portrait in revolution first appears, it contains an incongruity; for the contracted soul of Adams would have worshiped its maker uneasily in the midst of the Brattle Street congregation's conspicuous display of wealth and social position. Thus it comes as a relief to discover the Samuel Adams of the church records to be another man of the same name.[19] The famous Sam seems always to have attended the New South Church, a society his father had helped to found and his father-in-law had served as pastor. Cooper's intimacy with Adams sprang from political and not religious association; both had been privy to the same Whig caucuses for the past half-dozen years. Preacher Sam appreciated the talents and contributions of politician Sam but could never understand nor fully excuse a series of excesses, particularly Adams's long-standing grudge against Pownall, his joining Arthur Lee in opposition to Franklin, and his persistent refusal to recognize the worthiness of Commodore Gambier. Cooper acknowledged in 1771 that on these and perhaps a few other issues he too had received "unkind Treatment" from Adams and his closest disciples. But to Pownall he dismissed the matter lightly: "I would pride myself however in any thing of that kind that may occur to me from a Regard to the cause of Justice, Candor, and Friendship. I should tire you were I to enter into a Detail."[20]

Adams and other radical Whigs groaned in distress when they observed in the first half of 1771 a series of assemblies (or balls) given to bring together socially "a large number of the principal Gentlemen of the town who have been of very different sentiments in the late party disputes," in the hope that "Harmony Peace and Friendship will once more be Established in Boston." John Rowe, a leading Whig merchant who delighted in these assemblies, reported that the first featured "Very Good Dancing and Good Musick but very Bad Wine and Punch." In the *Gazette* "Sidney" warned Rowe and those like him that they danced in their chains with the very ones bent on "enslaving America." Commodore and Lady Gambier made these assemblies their special concern—one reason for Adams's dislike of the naval commander. While thus disgruntled, Samuel Adams discovered the limitations of his political power when in April he was soundly defeated for the office of Suffolk County register of deeds by a well-to-do townsman with a long record of faithful public service.[21]

Samuel Adams's discomfort in the quiet years of 1771–1772 was in part a personal reaction to the obvious polarization of political power between Hancock and Hutchinson, graphically illustrated in a news item printed by the *Gazette* in February 1771:

> Some Days ago was brought to this Market and sold by Mr. Joseph Vose of Milton, an extraordinary Fat Sheep raised by Capt. John Pierce of Dighton, which weighed Thirty Pounds a Quarter, the Tallow weighed Twenty Two Pounds, and judged by all who saw it to be the fattest that ever was brought to this Market, or any other. Lt. Gov. Hutchinson purchased one Side, and the Hon. John Hancock, Esq; the other.[22]

Thirty-four in 1771, Hancock had lost interest in the daily struggle to cope with the perplexities of trade. He found politics far more to his liking. Wealth tempered by conspicuous philanthropy gave him immediate access to political power. In March 1765, by accepting election as a Boston selectman, he had launched the public career of the most popular leader in Massachusetts history.

The seven selectmen exercised the authority of voters between town meetings. Forced to meet frequently, sometimes several days a week, they formed the one body that gave municipal government a measure of stability and continuity. Through the selectmen the economic elite kept much of the town's business in its hands. They were always men of property and means, though few of the wealthiest could for long give the time demanded by the position. It is all the more striking, consequently, that for ten years before the Revolution Boston's richest merchant and shipowner labored faithfully as a selectman, when during that period no one else held the office for more than eight years, and most sought to be excused after much shorter terms. The eighteen men who served with Hancock in these ten years display remarkably similar characteristics. All came from or had ties to the economic elite and supported the Whig cause. In the last three years before the Revolution, the same six staunch Whigs remained in office with him, five of the seven selectmen being members of the Brattle Street congregation. Most noticeable, perhaps, no radical Whig ever won election as a selectman; yet no one who held that office after 1765 became a loyalist.[23]

Elected to the Assembly in 1766 and later frequently chosen moderator of the town meeting, Hancock appeared on these public stages in the shadow of the three dynamic and articulate leaders:

Otis, Adams, and Warren. The realities of political power, nevertheless, began to surface as Otis lost his effectiveness in the later 1760s. Never able alone to win the full confidence of any segment of the economic elite, Samuel Adams could retain and enlarge his influence only by contributing to the developments which left Hancock the effective center as well as symbolic head of the Whig movement.

Hancock consciously sought popularity and power. He neglected his business to perform diligently the duties of selectman and representative. Minutes of the selectmen and journals of the House contain ample evidence of the fulfillment he found in political activity. People were bound to him through economic dependence and also out of gratitude for his largess. But above all Hancock possessed a flair for the dramatic that raised him above other politicians. A notable example of the public pageantry with which he surrounded himself took place in the summer of 1769 when his new brigantine, *Rising Liberty*, obviously a replacement in name for the confiscated *Liberty*, made its trial run in a day-long pageant that included several gentlemen "of Distinction from the Southern Colonies."[24]

In 1770 a parody on the "Liberty Song" dubbed him "King Hancock." His friends and followers replied to such loyalist slurs by portraying the patriot who in seeking the welfare of his country had been "dignified with the Reprobation of base Ministers and dirty Minions." As one reads the *Gazette* from 1770 to 1775 it becomes plain how much the Whig movement seems intertwined with the "Fortune, Abilities, and Integrity of that Gentleman." A letter from Portsmouth, New Hampshire, in 1770 blamed on a lack of leadership the hesitation of that town's merchants to sign a nonimportation agreement: "Happy should [we] be, had we a generous Hancock here to lead the Way! Such a Blessing is reserved for Boston."[25]

As the only leader of Boston's economic elite who both craved an extensive political career and enjoyed the popularity to make one possible, he had become indispensable to the Whig cause—and everyone knew it. On occasion Hancock found the radicals useful, but they required his constant support. John Hancock had neither the temperament nor the desire to become a political boss, but while he was on the scene no one else could ever completely assume that role. Until his death he would remain the central figure in Massachusetts public life and the focus of political power. Close behind him stood the Cooper brothers. Samuel became Hancock's closest adviser, and as town clerk the ubiquitous William spent more time with the selectmen than with any other officials. For both brothers an association with Hancock would help to distinguish their participation in the American Revolution.

Hutchinson's commission as "Captain-General and Governor in Chief" of Massachusetts reached Boston two weeks after he and Hancock had split between them the record-size sheep. With it came other commissions appointing his kinsman Andrew Oliver, lieutenant governor, and Bowdoin's Tory brother-in-law, Thomas Flucker, secretary of the province.

Hutchinson was sixty. A year before receiving his commission he had written Lord Hillsborough that he lacked the "strength of constitution" to be governor in these difficult times and requested the early appointment of a chief executive possessing "superior powers of body and mind." In the fall of 1770 his mood had begun to change, and by the new year he took much of the credit for having reversed the province's drift toward rebellion. Confident that "our Demagogues" could not revive a spirit of opposition to parliamentary authority, Governor Hutchinson sent to England for a coach, plain and as inexpensive as possible, but still "more in fashion" than his old one. His doctrinaire position on parliamentary supremacy remained impervious to all assaults. You might as well attempt to reason "with an Enthusiast, who holds an absurd Tenet in Religion" as with an American who believes his provincial assembly to be the supreme legislature for the colony—so he wrote Hillsborough. A self-assured Hutchinson refused to consider returning the legislature to Boston until the House acknowledged his right to convene it wherever he deemed advisable. But his admission that the governor had been freed from dependence on the legislature for his salary by an income from customs revenue strengthened the resistance of the House, with the result that little legislative business could be concluded throughout 1771.[26]

Samuel Cooper related to Franklin the new fears aroused by Hutchinson's firm stand. "The Project for making Governors independent for their Salaries upon the Grants of the People they govern gives great Uneasiness to the most considerate Friends of the Constitution." In the governor's insistence in carrying out his instruction from Whitehall to exempt the customs commissioners from local taxation, Cooper saw a broader threat: those same instructions can just as well exempt "all Friends to Government, as Men of slavish Principles affect to be called, and have the whole Burden of Taxes upon these who wish well to the Rights of their

Country." Such a threat " is bold and open, and strikes every Size of Men. It is not a Point confined to Trade," but will particularly touch the farmer who is always sensitive in the pocket. Thus Cooper could believe—or hope—that "Good may rise from this."27

In November 1771 he summarized the Massachusetts political outlook for Pownall:

> It is not true as you have been informed that the Spirit of the Assembly and of the People is totally altered, and that they would now gladly receive as a Favor, and ask and hold upon that Tenure what they before claimed as a Right. Such Representations tend only to deceive, and mislead Government. The Tone of the House, on every Point of Privilege is as firm as ever; and though an high Ferment cannot be expected to continue long among the People, and the irritation into which they were thrown has abated, yet their inward Sentiments are not altered but by far the greater Part have a settled Persuasion, that we are in a State of Oppression, that our most important Privileges are violated, that our Parliaments here ought to come between the Sovereign and the American Subject, just in the same Manner that the British Parliament does with respect to the British Subject.28

Seeking to impress a member of Parliament, the Boston preacher naturally exaggerated the solidarity of Bostonians in the face of Hutchinson's constitutional principles. Yet no one could better speak for Hancock, Bowdoin, and others at the center of the Whig circle. Their apparent hesitation, resulting from the tactical difficulty of standing fast in opposition to British policies without intensifying the contest, could be interpreted as weakness. Governor Hutchinson had made that error of judgment.

Cooper understood, far better than the governor, that social tensions in Boston added force to the constitutional arguments used by Whigs to justify resistance to Britain. During the winter of 1771–1772, notwithstanding the relaxation of politics, those tensions were plainly evident in the newspapers. The Whig elite welcomed the quiet period as an opportunity to test and consolidate the social base required to support continued opposition to British measures.

Nearly one Bostonian in fifteen was black, and more than half of these remained in slavery.29 Fifty Brattle Street families had at least one house slave.30 Samuel Cooper had grown up in a household with one slave, and now he was served by "Glasgow," a Negro whose African fables the Doctor delighted in retelling.[31] In August 1771 he had baptized the town's most famous slave, Phillis Wheatley, whose volume of poetry would soon be published in England.[32] House slaves could hope for no better lot than Cato, the favorite servant of John Hancock. Cato received his freedom at thirty, married, and baptized his children at Brattle Street, while remaining in service.[33] Most slaves were less fortunate. While Boston newspapers attacked the tyranny of the British ministry, they also announced slave auctions and advertised for sale scores of skilled and well-behaved slaves, who were being uprooted and subjected once more to the inhumanity of the market for no fault but "want of Employ." Unlike the plantation South, in urban Boston the children of slaves were often regarded as an unjustified expense. As a result, advertisement after advertisement contained such words as, "A Likely Negro Child of a good Breed to be given away. Inquire of the Printers."[34] The newspapers also carried frequent notices of rewards for the return of runaways, particularly for young male slaves who had sought to escape by going to sea.

Some Whigs had recognized the contradiction between their libertarian principles and the presence of chattel slavery, and a few had contributed to the growing attack on that institution, an attack joined by several free blacks and literate slaves. Yet most Whigs remained psychologically unprepared to grant actual freedom to anyone of African descent. Seeming to mirror the attitude of those he served, Cooper appeared unmoved by the black quest for freedom, even though his grandfather had raised one of the earliest colonial voices against slavery.[35] Whig ambivalence toward both slave and free blacks had surfaced with the arrival of British troops in 1768, who, it was charged, promised freedom to slaves who cut the throats or burned the dwellings of their masters. As a result the selectmen restricted the freedom of all blacks, and the fear of a slave rebellion increased the elite's concern over the sources of social unrest.[36]

Free Negroes and slaves formed a permanent lower class, as did those common seamen or Jack tars not bound to society by the cement of home and family. Fiercely independent and accustomed to riot against British naval press gangs, Boston seamen welcomed the opportunity to harass customs officers and other royal officials with the tacit approval of the shipowners and merchants on whom their livelihood depended.[37] In addition, Boston had significant numbers of poor widows, periodically unemployed mechanics, unhappy apprentices, and other propertyless individuals. Scores of poor young women who could boast "a fine Breast of Milk" earned their keep only by going into "a Gentleman's Family to suckle a Child." Though in the past the social controls of family, congregation, economic dependence, and municipal government had held this society together even without a police force, it could easily break apart in a political revolution not supported by a large cross section of the population.[38]

The increase of foreign-born royal officeholders, such as the customs commissioners and their appointees, strengthened the only rival system of social control. For example, much of John Temple's significance lay in his attempt to administer British policy from inside the local social structure rather than imposing such policy on it. Then, with their appeals to Negroes, disregard for local mores, and contempt for the authority of selectmen and magistrates, the redcoats and their officers who came in 1768 posed a threat to the established pattern of control in the name of preserving order, as the *Journal of the Times* emphasized on nearly every page. By closing ranks against the mother country after 1767, and by calling on all classes to defend their common cause, Boston's Whig elite maintained its grip on society.

Through all the turmoil of the past decade the town meeting had followed an even course since 1761. A Whig ticket of representatives, headed by Thomas Cushing, was returned to the House each May, and the election of selectmen displayed equal consistency. Boston politics wore a democratic mien because the majority of white adult males of fixed residence and settled occupation met the property qualifications for voting in both town and provincial elections. Hutchinson declared the Boston town meeting to be merely the mob assembled in legal session—at best a corruption of the democratic process from which "men of weight and value" withdrew "for fear not only of being out voted but affronted and insulted." He made such statements in hope of invoking parliamentary authority to curb the power of an institution he could not control. His words have tended to disguise the truth that for all its democratic trappings, the Boston town meeting had become the agency through which a caucus of Whig leaders, operating in a pattern still not fully understood, placed the force of community sanction behind their policies.[39]

The Whig movement could produce an almost complete consensus on such issues as the need for general opposition to the Townshend system where the economic leaders stood united, but it achieved less success on specific questions such as nonimportation that divided them according to each man's assessment of his personal interests. Yet, despite these differences, from 1767 until the Revolution the Boston Whigs elected their representatives to the House with near-unanimous votes of those attending election meetings. In the elections of 1767 through 1774, out of 4,167 possible votes, Hancock received 4,101, Cushing 4,053, and Adams 3,875.[40] That never more than a half, and usually closer to a third, of the eligible voters exercised their franchise constituted a tribute both to the power of the Whig caucus and to the strength of the consensus it produced for the program of the economic elite. With Hancock as representative and leading selectman, with Cushing in the speaker's chair of the assembly, with Bowdoin dominating the Council, and, beginning in 1771, with William Phillips as a replacement for Otis in the House, Whig leadership in Boston remained unassailable.

Recognizing that the Whig movement would crumble if serious cracks developed in its interclass base, the Tories advanced the fundamental misconception that the actual Whig leaders were irresponsible and fanatical men bent on destroying a society in which they had no stake. At the same time, Tory propagandists attacked the wealthy Whigs for raising the expectations of the lower classes in order to secure their temporary support in the struggle against Britain.[41] It is difficult to analyze the manifestation of repressed social unrest as open and sometimes violent hostility toward British measures and officials. Pressures from the lower classes cannot be dismissed lightly from accounts of mob violence or explanations of the determination of the Whig elite to keep town government firmly under their control. Hancock, Bowdoin, and other wealthy Whigs obviously understood to some small degree the need to rechannel social discontent. But to whatever extent such rechanneling took place, it remained for most Bostonians an unconscious and natural —and thus more effective—process by which emotional tensions were relieved.

Cooper saw no mystery in Boston's mass resistance, for he believed that the British hand in the colonial pocketbook could be felt by all orders of society except those placemen and pensioners who stood to profit from the scheme to raise a revenue in America:

> It is plain and Simple; it lies level to every Understanding and comes home to every Bosom. The Peasant may as well decide it as the Philosopher. The honest Tiller of the Ground, knows and feels equally with the greatest

Scholar, that the Fruits of his Industry are his own ex-
clusively; that Government was appointed for the Protection of Property, not violently to wrest it from the innocent Owner; and that Self-Preservation is the first
Law of Nature, and consequently of the God of Nature.
These Propositions strike the plainest Mind with Conviction at the first Glance. And to this it is owing that
the Measures of the British Government respecting
America have been regarded with such universal Indignation and Abhorrence, and so strenuously opposed
by the whole Body of the People in these Colonies.[42]

As Dr. Cooper had proclaimed so often from his pulpit, God
wanted every Christian to pursue his self-interest.

10

An Uncommon Degree of Harmony

*I*n the four years after the Boston Massacre, Samuel Cooper's skill in avoiding public controversy helped to minimize the social and religious tensions so evident in Boston. He wanted more than to hold his congregation together; he fully understood that Whig solidarity was essential to the continued success of the resistance movement. On Sundays he preached harmony; on the other six days he practiced what he preached.

In an expression of the unity in the Brattle Street congregation and as a pledge of confidence in Boston's future, Cooper moved his parishioners to erect a sumptuous new meetinghouse in 1772. In one conspicuous respect the Brattle Street Church had not lived up to its reputation as the town's most prosperous religious society. Its plain, unpainted wooden meetinghouse, after nearly three-quarters of a century of regular use and exposure to the rigors of New England weather, would have done no credit to a country village, let alone a metropolis that boasted such notable examples of American church architecture as the Old South Church (1729) and King's Chapel (1749). Following years of talk concerning the need for a new building, John Hancock forced the issue in February 1772 by pledging a generous contribution if the membership would vote to build. They accepted his offer without delay and in one week obtained a subscription of £3,200 with £1,000 of it pledged by Hancock, who, as one townsman commented, "suffers no body to outdoe him in acts of public utility." It was understood in Boston that Dr. Cooper's parishioners planned to erect "as grand a house as our native materials will admit of."[1]

The old site in Brattle Square seemed too cramped for an enlarged edifice without the purchase of adjacent land. In lieu of his contribution of £200, James Bowdoin offered to donate a spacious and well-situated corner plot on Tremont Street, together with some building materials already on the property. He must have realized the emotional shock of asking pious Christians to desert grounds hallowed by their fathers, for he conditioned his offer on its acceptance "with the utmost unanimity." Tradition has it that Hancock favored rebuilding in Brattle Square and used the power of his contribution to obtain that vote. This version became plausible after the Revolution when the two emerged as political rivals, but no evidence exists of a contest between them in 1772.[2]

Despite the additional expense, the old building would be demolished, the site enlarged, and a new meetinghouse erected on it. During construction the congregation was to worship at Dr. Chauncy's First Church, with both ministers sharing the preaching. The Sunday before demolition began in May, Cooper preached two sermons reviewing what had taken place within these walls dedicated to God by his grandfather Thomas Cooper and the other founders in 1699. In praising his predecessors in the Brattle Street pulpit, he gave thanks for their contributions to the "great Harmony and Peace" the society had enjoyed. "No uncomfortable Contentions have arisen among us. I esteem this one of the greatest Blessings of my Life."[3]

As strange as it seems by modern construction practices, the church's building committee called for bids on materials before settling on a plan for the new edifice. It would be built of stone and brick with a slate roof and an oak floor. In June the committee considered two plans using these materials. One had been drawn by John Singleton Copley, who already had painted more than thirty portraits of Brattle Street members. His proposal, though praised for its "Elegance and Grandure," was rejected in favor of a less ambitious one by Major Thomas Dawes, a local mason and an active Son of Liberty. It is unlikely that politics entered the choice. Dawes's plan would cost less to build, and as one of the masons on the job he was in a position to supervise the execution of his drawing. Copley, in contrast, had no practical building experience. So the student of eighteenth-century New England architecture is left to speculate whether a masterpiece may have been lost by the

church's failure to erect Copley's building on the choice location offered by Bowdoin.[4]

With a typical flourish, Hancock had reserved for himself the
privilege of selecting furnishings for the church with a portion of his
donation. He ordered crafted from fine mahogany a pulpit,
deacons' pew, and communion table. He equipped the pulpit with
the finest trimmings he could buy, including a curtain from
England of the "best silk Crimson Damask." In addition, he supplied pews for widows and other worthy poor who could not afford
their own. Over and above his £1,000, he paid for an English bell
weighing 3,220 pounds, the largest hung in any Boston church.
When Hancock's gifts were finally in place late in 1774, his bell
pealed the call to worship. Inside, the deacons sat in his pew, then
rose to serve communion from his table; and the preacher ex-
pounded the word of God from Hancock's pulpit while the poor
listened from his charity pews.[5]

As the building neared completion, Cooper requested Franklin
to recommend a "Machine" to "warm it in the cold and damp
Seasons of the Year." At the time, no Boston meetinghouse was
heated, and it seemed appropriate for Brattle Street to lead the way
toward more comfortable winter worship. "Your People, as they
are rich," Franklin replied, could perhaps afford to raise the inside
temperature by keeping a constant fire during the winter months in
one of the cast iron stoves now being tried in a few large buildings
in England. But he did not consider the expense and the consequent
dirt on the pews worth the meager results he had witnessed. Furthermore, Franklin was persuaded "from philosophic Considerations, that no one ever catches the Disorder we call a Cold from
cold Air, and therefore never at Meeting." As a result of Franklin's
advice, the new church remained unheated. Cooper thanked him
for the opinion that no one caught cold in church and quoted such
eminent authority "against some of our Physicians who seem to
think that all the Disorders of their Patients are caught there."[6]

By mid-summer 1773 the workmen had nearly finished. Bostonians described the structure in such terms as "superb" or "truly
magnificent." Measuring eighty feet long and sixty-five feet wide, it
was one-third larger than the demolished building. An exterior of
brick with stone quoins and trim and a square bell tower reaching
ninety feet above the ground presented more the appearance of a
fortress than of a typical New England Congregational meetinghouse. These formidable walls enclosed a lavish interior. Tall Co-

rinthian columns were topped by an entablature extending the full length of each side aisle to support an arched ceiling more than fifty feet high. At the front, matching pilasters of equal height created the same effect on the wall behind the ornately carved pulpit. Almost equally eye-catching were the rounded arches of the windows—whose glass Hancock had personally ordered from England—and the colored paneling on the aisle sides or ends of the box pews.[7]

At last the Brattle Street congregation had a sanctuary befitting its wealth and its minister's reputation for eloquence. As if to symbolize this alliance of the material and the spiritual, Cooper's name was inscribed on the cornerstone and Hancock's on a quoin above.[8]

A committee of frugal men accustomed to driving hard bargains had erected this impressive structure for £8,000. The sale of pews brought in nearly enough to complete payment. Choice pews sold for £50, with none on the main floor priced below £30. Since the socially prestigious families had generally contributed the most in the original subscription, there seems to have been little difficulty in deciding on the order in which members selected their pews. This potentially divisive business settled, the congregation first assembled for worship in its new meetinghouse on the last Sunday of July 1773.[9]

After the singing of an anthem, Cooper stood in a temporary pulpit (Hancock's was still being carved) and faced his people in their unfamiliar pews. He gave a sermon of thanksgiving for the "Smiles of Heaven" responsible for this happy day. In a period of intense political and religious controversy, his congregation had come through the ordeal of church building with remarkable outward harmony, and he emphasized the significance of its achievement: "A Spirit of Gentleness and Condescension, a Disposition mutually to oblige, has happily dwelt among us, and been superior to all the Trials of human Frailty which may naturally be expected upon such an Occasion; so that we can now come together, and have taken our Seats, in the House of Worship, with an uncommon Degree of Harmony and Complacency, becoming the Worshippers of the God of Peace."[10]

Samuel Cooper's self-image as a man of peace who conciliated rather than provoked is an important key to his personality and career. For a quarter century he had kept his pulpit free from public controversy and for a decade had ministered to the satisfaction of men and women who responded variously to the crisis in imperial relations. His own response to this crisis mirrored that of the leading Whigs who formed the nucleus of the Brattle Street congregation. They faced the imperial problem with every desire to preserve the social structure and local institutions they enjoyed. Men like Bowdoin and Hancock could never conceive of themselves as revolutionaries but were intellectually and emotionally prepared to defend the society in which their families had flourished, which meant a defense of the considerable freedom afforded by that society to most men, as well as of the positions of the elite at the top of it. Thus the "uncommon Degree of Harmony and Complacency" and the absence of "uncomfortable Contentions" which their pastor proclaimed as the distinguishing characteristic of the Brattle Street fellowship of worshippers assuaged their fears and renewed their confidence in serving society at large.

Nor was the power of this sense of solidarity unfelt by younger men of the congregation, for instance, Daniel Bell, in whom his pastor would later take a special interest. At present he could afford only a £15 pew in the gallery, but he aspired to emulate the successful merchants seated in the £50 pews below him. The War for Independence would provide the opportunity he sought.[11]

The appearance of harmony in the congregation may have reflected more Cooper's passion to avoid controversy than reality. But however contrived, the harmony offered a pleasant contrast to the incessant contention over questions of religion and public morality that showed no sign of abating in New England as the struggle with Britain intensified. Relatively successful in accommodating social strains, Bostonians had come to tolerate—and often, it seems, enjoy—the free venting of religious hostility. As Jonathan Mayhew had demonstrated, an entire career could be built on oral aggression in behalf of pious causes. Since the Great Awakening the weekly newspapers, whose editors welcomed controversial religious pieces as a way of increasing circulation, and the steady stream of polemical pamphlets sometimes gave the misleading impression that New Englanders might sooner make war with each other over theological, ecclesiastical, or moral issues than with England over her colonial policy.

The perennial question of what constituted acceptable standards of public morality took on added relevancy in the decade before 1776. Some patriots joined the battle against old England as a way of purging New England of irreligion and vice and returning to the pristine purity of the founders. Boston, with its dancing schools and balls, its conspicuous luxury, its plays (banned by law) disguised as concerts and operas, its whores, its lax Sabbath observance, and its freedom of speech displayed weekly in newspapers, appeared in many eyes to be a cesspool of iniquity. The *Boston Post-Boy* especially offended in quoting such language as "son of a bitch" and in reporting gossip concerning the amorous activities of the English nobility.[12]

Boston Whigs were particularly sensitive to questions of public morality. They charged that the conspiracy against American liberty represented an outcropping of English moral degeneracy, but they knew that rural Massachusetts, and even some Bostonians, believed that much the same decline had begun in the provincial capital. Consequently, the call for moral regeneration at home as the best defense against foreign tyranny became indispensable to union in a common cause of all who had any grievance against imperial rule. But Tories quickly pointed out that opulent merchants and irreligious politicians like the foulmouthed Otis hardly qualified as leaders of a crusade to redeem the country from its catalogue of sins. Conversely, the almost universal Tory persuasion that Samuel Adams masterminded the rebellion against England grew out of an exaggerated estimate of his ability to hide political ambition and cunning behind a "religious Mask."[13]

Tory accusations of cant seemed more convincing when it became noticeable that Adams and other Boston Whigs tolerated an avowed deist in their midst. Dr. Thomas Young had moved to town in 1766 from Albany, New York, and had entered Boston life with abandon.[14] He filled the newspapers with signed letters on medicine, politics, and religion. Even in the shadow of Boston's many churches, Dr. Young could not suppress his deistic zeal. His religious views shocked even some devout Whigs, particularly when in 1770 he publicly challenged George Whitefield's attack on deism. Whitefield's death seems to have silenced Young's advocacy of deism temporarily, but in the eyes of the most devout he had distressingly tainted the Whig cause, an embarrassment of which Hutchinson's supporters took full advantage.[15] Samuel Adams came to Young's defense. He dismissed attacks on the doctor's religion as the work of Tories who had cared nothing for creeds until they saw an opening to strike the cause of liberty in the name of religion. It was sufficient for Adams that Young had demonstrated "his political integrity" as an "unwearied assertor of the rights of his countrymen."[16] With pious Whigs joining the Tory

attack on Young, Dr. Cooper had good reason to hold himself
above controversy and to stress the harmony existing among his
congregation.

Like others of the Whig elite, Cooper had to bear radical
preachers as well as deistic revolutionaries. In nearby Salem the
Reverend Dr. Nathaniel Whitaker called for a Calvinistic crusade
against British tyranny. Handsome, physically and vocally powerful, vehemently Calvinistic, and boasting a Scottish D.D., the doctor stood ready to confront anybody, including King George III and
Parliament. His pulpit diatribes closed the door to all compromises.
With Whitaker and a few other radical preachers crying for English
blood, Cooper's public neutrality might seem by comparison
cowardly and ineffective to those who did not know of his private
stand at the center of the resistance movement.[17]

Another aggressive political parson appeared on the scene in
1771. William Gordon, an English dissenting clergyman, crossed
the ocean to guard his brethren in America against their two great
enemies: corrupt administration from without and moral decay
from within. He began preaching in a church at Roxbury across
Boston Neck. For the next fifteen years this self-assertive preacher
untiringly sought to thrust himself into the center of Massachusetts
public affairs. Cooper found him to be unavoidable, at times a
nuisance, but occasionally useful.[18]

Despite being meddlesome and gossipy, Gordon at times saw
issues clearly. Before sailing from England, he warned that reports
of New England's denial of religious freedom to its large Baptist
population were avidly accepted in London as evidence of the
hypocrisy of colonial leaders. Boston's churches of all denominations drew financial support from the voluntary contributions of
their parishioners. It was quite the reverse in the remainder of
Massachusetts where Congregational ministers were supported by
taxes, and as a result non-Congregationalists often encountered
severe restrictions upon their right to worship. Under pressure, the
legislature had finally permitted the issuance of certificates exempt-
ing Baptists, Anglicans, and Quakers from paying taxes to maintain the local Congregational minister. Still, in practice, particularly in isolated areas, the certificates proved difficult to obtain and
holders of them sometimes faced the harassment of Congregational
neighbors.[19]

Typically poorer and less educated than Congregationalists or
Anglicans, New England Baptists nevertheless produced some
skilled and militant leaders. Of these, Elder Isaac Backus, pastor at

Middleborough, Massachusetts, led the efforts to demonstrate the Whigs' inconsistency in denying religious freedom at home while fighting for political freedom within the empire. Winning a legal victory in 1771 through an appeal to the king in Council raised suspicions of Toryism against Baptists. Fortunately for the Whig cause, Hutchinson believed in the desirability of an established church and took Baptist complaints lightly. Continuing his struggle, in 1773 Backus persuaded most country Baptists simply to stop using the certificates of exemption. To his surprise, this "massive civil disobedience" did not overcrowd Massachusetts jails because the many violations were largely ignored by local magistrates preoccupied with the approach of rebellion against Britain. For the time being, pressures eased a little, though Backus never overlooked an opportunity to raise the fundamental question of religious liberty, as the Massachusetts delegates to the First Continental Congress would soon discover.[20]

A few years later when Massachusetts drafted its first constitution as a state, the Boston clergy would have to face squarely the issue of religious freedom. But in 1773, as he preached in the grandeur of his new sanctuary, Samuel Cooper was not inclined to worry lest some unknown Baptist farmer might have his cow seized and sold at half its value by a Congregational tax collector in order to compel payment of the local parish rates.

Of much greater consequence to Cooper and his colleagues at the moment seemed the renewed agitation over the possibility of the Church of England appointing a bishop for the American colonies. The issue had been contested, sometimes warmly, for the last half century. Without a resident bishop to ordain, confirm, and discipline, this episcopal church labored under a severe disadvantage. Southern Anglicans, nonetheless, had grown fond of their lax ecclesiastical pattern, typically established by law and controlled by a vestry system embedded in local society. But the northern episcopal clergy struggled to preserve and enlarge their parishes in a land where dissent had often become the establishment. An arm of the Anglican hierarchy, the Society for the Propagation of the Gospel in Foreign Parts, diverted some of the funds it raised for missions among Indians and slaves to supplement the meager salaries of its ministers in the populous northern towns. Thus supported, these clergymen looked to England for direction. They became strong advocates of an American bishopric and entreated the home government to establish one. Dependency in religion bred loyalty in politics. Beginning with the Stamp Act convulsion, it became easy for Whigs to tar advocates of an episcopate with the brush of Toryism by asserting that bishops and stamps both constituted chains with which to enslave colonials. Seeming to confirm this charge, the new Archbishop of Canterbury's campaign in the 1760s for an American bishopric coincided with passage of the revenue acts.[21]

Whig propagandists found episcopacy a near-perfect issue for their purposes. The majority of colonists north of Maryland came from a tradition of dissent which brought an emotional reaction to the specter of a powerful bishop. The issue strengthened ties between colonial and English dissenters, many of whom, as a result, gave more encouragement to the colonial fight for political freedom. From whatever source, attacks on the Church of England constituted oblique blows at king and Parliament, who were constitutionally bound to the hierarchy. Most important of all, in defending their "missionary" efforts in the colonies, Anglican prelates displayed an insulting ignorance of colonial geography, institutions, and culture that stimulated the awakening of an American nationalism.[22] Convinced that Governor Bernard was "deep in the plot" to impose a bishop on New England, Jonathan Mayhew had challenged the Society for the Propagation of the Gospel so effectively that he drew a reply from no less an antagonist than the Archbishop of Canterbury. In the five years after Mayhew's death, Charles Chauncy, though entering his sixties, published four antiepiscopal works. So it continued throughout the decade; hardly a Congregational or Presbyterian clergyman from Pennsylvania to New Hampshire who went on record failed to voice some degree of anxiety over the prospect of seeing a bishop's palace erected anywhere in North America.[23]

Assurances from the hierarchy that an American prelate would have only spiritual authority, and reliable intelligences from England that the government had no present plans to complicate American affairs with even the most modest proposal for an episcopate, only hardened clerical opposition to the "entering wedge" of a royal church. By 1770 American dissenters stood united on this point, if on no other. Few issues had received as much attention in the press, particularly of New York and Boston.[24]

Behind this verbal turbulence lay a seldom acknowledged reality: New England Congregationalists and Anglicans no longer differed on any religious principle that mattered to most laymen. The episcopate question in Boston had become largely a question of whether citizens would tolerate the preaching of unquestioning loyalty by Church of England clerics who called for royal authority and funds to prop up their altars. Three-quarters of a century after King's Chapel had been forcibly planted in the heart of the town, as many as a fifth of the inhabitants conformed to the royal church, yet no distinguishing marks separated laymen of the two communions. Foreign-born royal officeholders were nearly all Anglican, but each of the three congregations with which they worshiped contained numbers of Whigs. A half century of intermarriage between Anglicans and Congregationalists had left few elitist family circles unbroken by religion.[25]

More than most other Congregational leaders, Samuel Cooper was in a position to understand the significance of the episcopate struggle in Boston. Several leading Brattle Street families had Anglican branches. Cooper himself was the brother-in-law by marriage of East Apthorp, former Anglican rector at Cambridge and an opponent of Mayhew in the paper war over bishops. Thus Cooper could be certain of his ground when in 1768 he wrote to a New York foe of episcopacy that few of the "Laity of the Church of England among us, . . . wish to see a Bishop in America."[26]

Of course, Cooper stood with his brethren in the "Cause." In 1768, for example, he joined three other prestigious Boston ministers in an appeal to English dissenters for help in warding off the proposed episcopate. Though he had little regard for Chauncy's flurry of polemics, he prided himself on a cordial relationship with that venerable colleague. In ecclesiastical matters, as in politics, Cooper preferred to say little publicly, while privately exerting his influence where he thought it might be effective. At the close of the Revolution he would take a strong hand in weaning King's Chapel from the Church of England. Such moves by fiercely independent Anglican vestries were at least contemplated before the war. John Temple was suspected of having been the Boston Anglican who had written a newspaper letter opposing the American episcopate. Had a bishop ever set foot in pre-Revolutionary Boston, he might have encountered as much opposition from Episcopalians as from dissenters.[27]

Nevertheless, the episcopacy issue further reduced Hutchinson's capacity to govern the province. He had been brought up a Congregationalist, but as governor his duties required close association with various Anglicans, and he interpreted his commission as obligating him to give some measure of patronage to the royal church. Consequently, he occasionally attended services at

King's Chapel and had no scruples against taking communion there or standing at the baptismal font as godfather for children of Anglican friends. More significant, he came to perceive a relationship between dissension from the Anglican church and American political disturbances. He even considered formally conforming to the Church of England, but then thought better of it: "It is my opinion and I find it to be the opinion of the episcopal Clergy that I can do more good in the way I am at present than by wholly going over from the way of worship which is so universal through the Province and which always will be the prevailing way in America until the Inhabitants have other notions of civil government than they have at present." It followed naturally from this perspective that he approved the proposed American episcopate as a matter of plain justice and equality for members of the "national church."[28] Though unaware of Hutchinson's private opinion, the Whigs sensed his drift toward episcopacy. After his appointment as governor, they lost no opportunity to charge him first with "Occasional conformity" and later with "defection" to the royal church "meerly to qualify for or in order to hold places or pensions."[29]

Following the proclamation of Hutchinson's commission as governor in March 1771, he received the customary addresses from the various professions. The town's three episcopal ministers waited on him with an address stressing religion as "the best support of Government, and of . . . Loyalty to the King."[30] By contrast, the address of the Boston Congregational clergy, in Hutchinson's view, "was framed with great art" to avoid "the least appearance of their approbation of his appointment." They called for the new governor "to secure our invaluable Rights and Privileges" and to patronize the evangelical churches "of our Illustrious Ancestors the Founders of this Colony." In his response to addresses from the several non-Congregational bodies of clergy, Hutchinson stressed his devotion to the religious liberty denied them by the Congregational establishment in Massachusetts.[31]

Hutchinson's own pastor, the Reverend Dr. Ebenezer Pemberton of the New Brick Congregational society, was not yet ready to abandon the governor to King's Chapel. Their friendship appeared more than professional. Pemberton had been described the year before in the ballad on the Boston clergy as "puffing Pemb, who does contemn all Liberty's noble sons." A senior minister in his mid-sixties, he was a figure of some consequence. He presided over a sparsely attended session of the annual May convention of the province's Congregational ministers that voted a flattering address to the governor, calling on him to "employ every wise and prudent Method to restore that Harmony, which formerly subsisted between Great Britain and her Colonies, so much to their mutual advantage." A later effort to rescind the action failed. Hutchinson took advantage of this opening by returning his thanks for "so kind, so affectionate an Address from so respectable and venerable a Body of Men."[32] Throughout the summer Samuel Adams used the *Gazette* to cast on Pemberton the odium of having misrepresented the sentiments of the province's pastors.[33] Another *Gazette* writer commented that "It is a dark a threat'ning day,/When Priests had rather fawn, than pray."[34]

Confident of having further divided the opposition, Hutchinson issued in October 1771 the pre-Stamp Act form of the governor's proclamation for the annual Thanksgiving Day. It called for all citizens "to offer up their humble and hearty Thanks to Almighty God" because "He has been pleased"—among other blessings—"to continue to them their civil and religious Privileges" and "to enlarge and increase their Commerce." Hutchinson's choice of language seemed a rebuke to the House and Council of the year before, who had approved a resolution desiring the governor to substitute for the usual thanksgiving rite a "Day of solemn Humiliation and Prayer" on the ground that "this, in common with the other American Colonies, labours under many great and insupportable Grievances, and [that] there are others which we have Reason to fear, unless the Providence of God should graciously prevent their taking Place." Hutchinson, of course, had denied the request.[35]

Published as a broadside and in the newspapers the last week of October, the proclamation would by custom be read in the Congregational churches after service on Sunday, 10 November. But, in Cooper's opinion, reading such a proclamation in the churches would be "deemed by the People an open Insult upon them, and a prophane Mockery of Heaven. The general Cry was, we have lost our Most essential Rights, and shall be commanded to give Thanks for what does not exist."[36]

The *Gazette* listed the "civil and religious privileges" Massachusetts had lost, and stressed the "impious mockery . . . offered to the Supreme Being" by the governor's proclamation. Whig committees called on the pastors to demand that they refuse to read it to their congregations. Dr. Chauncy, so Hutchinson learned, was affronted that anyone could think him capable of reading such language from his pulpit. Only Dr. Pemberton refused to comply.

As he began to read the proclamation—perhaps with Hutchinson present—a number of Whigs rose from their pews and stalked out of the meetinghouse.[37]

Cooper reported this affair to Franklin and Pownall as evidence that there had been no lessening of hostility toward British measures: "nothing has of late occurred among us from which you may so well Judge of the Sentiments of the People." Indeed, "had the ministers inclined, it was not in their Power to read it, a Circumstance which never before took Place among us." Much later, Hutchinson explained that Pemberton's livelihood came from his estate instead of contributions from his congregation, and thus he did not have to bow to public pressure as did the other pastors. In Cooper's case, however, the governor thought that this preacher influenced his congregation "rather than being influenced by them."[38]

The controversy over the thanksgiving proclamation enlivened the winter of 1771–1772. Samuel Adams fumed that "He who can flatter a despot, or be flattered by him" has little "true religion," whatever his reputation for piety. One newspaper announced that "Pemberton stands very fair for an American bishop, or a handsome pension for life," while the *Gazette* reported the withdrawal of Whig members from his congregation, including one who had attended there for forty years. Directly or indirectly, this torrent of words pointed to the governor. Adams best explained what was at stake: "Should he [Hutchinson] once lose the Reputation which his friends have with the utmost pains been building for him among the Clergy for these thirty years past, as a consummate Saint, he must fall like Samson when his Locks were cut off." Late in 1771 a Whig printer of Boston published a political catechism, dedicated to Hutchinson and adopted from the familiar Westminster *Shorter Catechism*, to remind the governor that in the 1640s Parliament had waged war in the name of religion against an evil king and his ministers.[39]

Tory writers struck hard at such use of religion for political purposes. They pointed to the irreligion of Dr. Young and the hypocrisy of Samuel Adams and to the "natural tendency which their pressing the Clergy into service and engaging them in our political disputes has towards the subversion of the ecclesiastical constitution of the country." The answer came with varying degrees of fervor, but always in the familiar religious idiom: "Religion is the Bulwark of Liberty" because civil and religious liberty are inseparably intertwined; therefore, a vigilant clergy "may be instruments in the hand of God, to save all Americans, and consequently all Britons too, from abject slavery for many centuries."[40]

During the winter of 1771–1772, despite the "Pause in Politics," the emotional tensions of this society increased. Negroes petitioned for freedom, and an occasional white voice pleaded for an end to the abominable sin of slavery. The poor needed to vent their accumulated hostility. English corruption and irreligion formed the backdrop for assessing American virtue and piety. Yet some patriots expressed alarm at the growth of native vice, and Tories gloated over the knowledge that Whigs had taken an avowed deist into their ranks. Isaac Backus taught his Baptist brethren the necessity of civil disobedience to secure freedom of worship. The Anglican clergy preached loyalty to the king and declared their countrymen to be guilty of the sin of ingratitude by depreciating the benefits of British rule. In return, dissenters and even some members of the Church of England queried whether episcopacy could ever be compatible with American freedom. A few extremist preachers already urged colonists toward independence, and war if necessary, as a means of purging the land of manifold sins. And clergymen of all faiths faced accusations of dabbling too much or too little in politics.

In the center stood the dutiful, stolid figure of Thomas Hutchinson, convinced that most citizens had seen the error of their ways and that British power would finally coerce into surrender any unrepentant political radicals. He seemed oblivious to the mounting religious emotionalism underlying charges against him of venality and despotism and of an eagerness to sell the American birthright of political and religious liberty for British rank and gold.

Boston's social strain showed no sign of abating throughout 1772 and 1773. These years thus proved a propitious time for the construction of the new Brattle Street edifice. Unemployed artisans were set to work, and Hancock found one more occasion on which to display a public image so different from Hutchinson's. It was also the right hour for Samuel Cooper to accent the peace and brotherly love he wanted to preserve in his congregation.

11

That Old Serpent

J ohn Hancock's packet ship, the *Providence*, lifted anchor in Boston harbor on the morning of 6 August 1772 and sailed down East for what is now Maine but was then the eastern section of Massachusetts. On board for this combined "Party of Pleasure" and business trip were some of Hancock's favorite companions, including Thomas Brattle, whose father's position on the Council had never inhibited the son's steady pursuit of pleasure. Among others were Dr. Cooper, pastor to Brattle as well as Hancock, and Professor John Winthrop of Harvard College. They traveled in style with a barber and at least one servant. On Sunday Cooper preached at Portland. Then the party sailed to the mouth of the Kennebec River, where Hancock contributed handsomely toward the erection of a meetinghouse and the settlement of a minister in the infant town of Pownalborough.[1]

In many respects this party of one great merchant and shipowner, four smaller merchants, a college professor, and a Congregational preacher typified the Whig movement. All were moderates who had opposed British measures in some degree but now hesitated to face the alternatives of colonial independence or surrender to the doctrine of parliamentary supremacy. They had seen enough since 1765 to have some idea of what either course might mean. In the end they would choose independence in preference to loyalty—save Brattle, who dodged the issue by making the grand tour of Europe during the war. But for these and all except the most extreme Whigs, 1772 was a time for thought and reflection, for discovering whether one had the intellectual and emotional assurance needed to confront squarely the issue of imperial relations when and if it became inescapable. "Be prudent"— "particularly with regard to America," was the advice Hancock had given the man he sent to England on business in 1771.[2]

During the year preceding this summer of 1772, Hutchinson had gradually convinced himself that he was crippling the opposition by separating Hancock from Samuel Adams. "H[ancock] and A[dams] are at great variance," he wrote Bernard. "Some of my friends blow the coals and I hope to see a good effect." He rejoiced that Hancock's defection would cripple the radical Whigs by denying them access to this rich young man's purse. Nearly all testimony to a split between Adams and Hancock comes from Hutchinson's correspondence and contains a considerable measure of wishful thinking. At best, Hutchinson's hopes rested on nothing more substantial than differences over tactics among the Whig leaders. Only by accepting the time-hallowed myth that Boston resistance to Britain was largely the work of Samuel Adams and a handful of other radicals can one discover in 1772 a disabling split in Whig ranks.[3]

The Whig elite, who had formed the solid nucleus of opposition since passage of the Townshend Acts, naturally experienced occasional discomfort at the extreme language of the radicals and the increasing emotionalism of political and religious debate. A relaxation of tensions might facilitate some compromise short of the equally unwelcome alternatives of independence or parliamentary supremacy. In a calm moment even Samuel Adams could ponder the question, "Why should either side hasten on the alarming Crisis?"[4]

One ray of hope for a softening of the ministry's attitude reached Boston early in 1772 with the news that John Temple had been given a comfortable position in the English customs service. By a combination of family connections and threats to make public his case against Bernard, Temple had convinced the ministry that he must be provided for. Hutchinson was disgruntled: "You can't conceive how Molineux, Adams, [William?] Cooper and the rest of that clan triumphed when the news came of [Temple's] appointment and how dejected the friends of Government were in general." Dr. Chauncy circulated his own interpretation: the ministry deserved no credit for magnanimity; they had merely bribed Temple to prevent his publishing the journal he had kept of the reprehensible activities of the commissioners. Yet the Whigs could not completely discount what had happened. Instead of being summarily dismissed, the man symbolizing the demand of colonial merchants for sympathetic customs enforcement had been awarded a comfortable position. Perhaps, after all, there remained some hope of wringing further concessions from the North ministry.[5]

The differences existing among Whigs over how best to continue resistance surfaced at the March 1772 town meeting. John Hancock presided over four days of sessions in which the future of the Whig cause may well have been decided. In the end five of the seven selectmen had been replaced, leaving Hancock surrounded on the board of selectmen by six staunch Whigs fully responsive to the caucus.[6] (Beginning in 1773, when one change was made, five of the selectmen attended Brattle Street.) The last challenge to the Whig elite's hold on Boston came in the May 1772 election of representatives. An effort to oust Adams, who had been blamed for the "purge" of selectmen, failed when he was returned to the House on the coattails of a slate of moderate Whigs.[7]

A system of political caucuses, long in existence, hereafter functioned effectively to prepare in advance a slate of candidates to elect at town meetings. As a result, after 1772 no public contests among Whigs appear to have taken place. The Whig political organization stood on a broad base of power centering in elitist support but reaching into every rank of citizens. Even many of the so-called radicals owned substantial amounts of property or at least practiced a profession such as medicine or law. Important as were the political skills of Adams, Warren, William Cooper, and other activists, more than ever in 1772 John Hancock appeared to be the central figure. He personally symbolized the aims of the resistance movement. He helped to prevent a disintegration of the power base by keeping radical elements in check. And his very presence reassured conservative Whigs that they were not headed toward a social revolution.[8]

Samuel Cooper himself offers one of the most complete illustrations of the network of personal and political relationships forming the "Band of Brotherhood" among the town's Whigs. Pastor of Boston's most elitist church, he was completely at home in the finest mansions of his parishioners, whatever their political leaning. This preacher, nonetheless, kept a busy private hand in town and provincial politics. No other one man so enjoyed the confidence of the full range of opposition leaders: Otis, Bowdoin, Hancock, the two Adamses, Warren, Temple, Cushing, Phillips, and a score of others. He remained close to brother William, whose involvement was as total as it was routine. The son-in-law Dr. Cooper had acquired in 1766, when his daughter Judith married Gabriel Johonnot, appeared by 1771 in increasingly bold roles with the most aggressive Sons of Liberty. In the General Court, where personal links were more infrequent, the Whigs sometimes resembled a loosely organized political party; but in Boston Whiggism was embedded in a social structure of which John Hancock had emerged as the most effective symbol.

As selectman and representative Hancock had given much of his time to politics for several years, but in the spring of 1772 he seemed ready for the first time to exert leadership more in proportion to his influence. He negotiated a vague compromise under which Hutchinson hesitatingly returned the legislature to Boston without thinking he had yielded on that vital issue.[9] But even in its more comfortable quarters, the House proved intractable and the governor sent them home. In August, as Hancock's party sailed down East, Boston appeared uneasily quiet, except for the continued agitation in the newspapers. Most Whigs seemed willing to hold their ground, while testing the air to see if a new breeze blew from Whitehall. But from a governor born and bred among them, they had come to expect only a willing obedience to the orders of the ministry.

Whatever rift remained in Whig ranks was quickly healed by persistent reports that the judges of the province's highest court would, like the governor, also be freed from dependence on the legislature by salaries drawn from customs collections. In American eyes, any attempt to pay judges' salaries from a source controlled by the administration rather than the local assembly could be interpreted as one more denial to colonials of constitutional liberties enjoyed by Englishmen at home. The year before, Samuel Cooper had explained to Franklin that "the Civil List [of England] is the free Grant of a British Parliament, and is augmented from Time to Time at their Pleasure; but the American [customs] Revenue is not the Gift of the American Assemblies; it is extorted from them by mere Power, contrary to their just Remonstrances, and Humble Petitions."[10] If this process continued, in time the entire executive and judicial branches of colonial government would be filled by officials dependent on and thus responsible to the ministry. The likelihood of an independent judiciary particularly rankled American Whigs because eighteenth-century English judges enjoyed tenure during good behavior, while in the colonies after 1754 judicial commissions provided tenure at the pleasure of the crown. Governor

Hutchinson's judicial appointments had given every indication that he planned to fill the Massachusetts judiciary with men who shared his views of royal prerogative.[11]

Six months after the unsuccessful effort to unseat him from the assembly, Samuel Adams achieved the greatest political success of his career by calling into life the Boston Committee of Correspondence in response to reports that judges were to receive royal salaries. Judging by the lull in his writing during the summer, he had indeed been chastened by the May election and Hancock's June compromise to bring the General Court back to Boston. Cooper's opinion of Adams during these months may be inferred from his decision not to hand him a letter of reconciliation from Pownall, who had sent it to the preacher with firm instructions to deliver it to Adams only "if there be a temper and culture of mind to receive the good seed."[12] But by winter John Adams found his cousin "more cool, genteel and agreable than common" with his passions "concealed, and restrained." This tempered and moderated Samuel Adams began in the fall of 1772 to take a more responsible and consequently more effective part in Whig leadership because at last he had learned that he must not stray too far from the elitist center of the resistance movement.[13]

It struck Adams and Dr. Young that the familiar concept of a committee of correspondence might enable Boston to protest the innovation in the judiciary while discovering the depth of feeling on this issue in other Massachusetts communities. In October, after Hutchinson refused to advise the Boston town meeting, chaired by Hancock, whether he had received confirmation that "Stipends are affixed to the Offices of the Judges of the Superior Court," and after he turned down a subsequent petition to call the assembly into session to consider "a matter so important and alarming," Adams moved for the creation of a twenty-one member committee. The motion passed unanimously, despite the grave doubts of several leaders. Cooper later explained to Franklin that three of the four Boston representatives and "a Number of the most respectable Friends to Liberty in the Town" had opposed this step "from an Apprehension that many Towns, for various Reasons might not chuse to adopt it, and in that Case, the Attempt might greatly prejudice the Interest it was designed to promote." This lack of faith in the response of the towns apparently explains why Hancock, Cushing, Phillips, and two selectmen found their "private Business would not then admit" of their serving on the committee even after the unanimous vote to establish it. Thus the committee appeared to take on a radical coloration, but only by choice of moderate Whigs. Though divided over tactics, the Whig leaders had cautiously avoided public disagreement.[14]

Late in November another town meeting heard the committee's report, with Hancock again in the chair. After some minor changes it received unanimous approval and six hundred copies were ordered printed and distributed throughout Massachusetts. Thus came into being one of the most important pamphlets of the American Revolution, *The Votes and Proceedings of the Freeholders and other Inhabitants of the Town of Boston, In Town Meeting assembled*. Uniting in a single, plainly worded statement a summary of Whig political theory with a catalogue of the full range of specific grievances and an invitation for each town to judge the facts for itself, the several authors of *Votes and Proceedings* called on Massachusetts to determine its own future. They appealed not to king or Parliament but to the "collected wisdom of the whole People."[15]

Tories had generally absented themselves from the town meetings creating the Boston Committee of Correspondence and adopting *Votes and Proceedings*. Afterwards they charged that the entire proceedings had been highly irregular, with few citizens in attendance and negative votes not counted. Boston Whigs closed ranks against these charges. The selectmen issued an official statement concerning the number in attendance. Hancock's integrity as moderator was cited to refute the attack on voting procedures, and his name appeared conspicuously on page one of the printed pamphlet. Though not a member, Cushing frequently advised the Committee of Correspondence. The town instructed its clerk, William Cooper, to serve as secretary of the committee and take responsibility for distributing the pamphlets. Even James Otis, temporarily recovered from his mental and emotional problems, became the committee's first chairman. Outwardly united for the moment, the Whig leaders sent *Votes and Proceedings* to the selectmen of every town in the province, to all members of the General Court, and to influential friends both in and out of Massachusetts.[16]

No one, not even Samuel Adams, fully anticipated the response of the towns. The majority seriously accepted Boston's invitation to conduct their own inquiry into fundamental questions of government and to sit in judgment on the mother country's observance of the natural rights of colonists. As a result, during the winter and spring months citizens of more than one hundred towns began a constitutional debate that continued intermittently for eight years until they adopted a constitution for an independent Massachusetts.[17]

Belatedly recognizing the threat he faced, Hutchinson stimulated this debate immeasurably by convening the General Court early in January, so that he might confront directly the movement he saw beginning in the town meetings. He opened the session by challenging legislators either to refute his principles of government or to adhere to them. "I know of no line," he said in emphatic summary, "that can be drawn between the supreme Authority of Parliament and the total Independence of the Colonies." He urged representatives and councilors to lead the people to an understanding that everything "valuable to them depends upon their Connexion with their Parent State."[18]

Committees of the Council and House deliberately drafted full replies to the governor's message. Headed by Bowdoin, the Council committee concluded that representation can be deduced to be a natural right since it is necessary for the preservation of the natural rights of life, liberty, and property. The House committee, including Cushing, Adams, and Hancock, used Hutchinson's own *History of Massachusetts-Bay* and other authorities to demonstrate that the colonies had been established by their charters as "distinct States from the Mother Country." The two could, nevertheless, be "united in one Head and common Sovereign" and "live happily in that Connection and mutually support and protect each other." Contrary to Hutchinson's great hope, neither answer shied away from independence as a last resort.[19]

In March Cooper interpreted for Franklin the effect of the governor's message and the legislature's answers to it. "By the Replies of the two Houses, perfectly united in the main Principles, the Governor and his Friends received a Shock which they could not conceal; while the People are greatly confirmed in their Sentiments, and encouraged to support them." According to Cooper, as he informed Franklin in confidence, Hutchinson's strong personal effort to persuade the Council to alter its reply resulted in only two abstentions when the vote to reconsider was taken. This failure left the governor opposed "to both Houses, and the Body of the People, an undisguised and zealous advocate for every Thing we account a Grievance."[20]

Most responses from the towns came after the governor's message and thus constituted answers to it. As the *Gazette* printed them one after another, little doubt remained that Hutchinson's theory of imperial relations had been repudiated by the majority of politically active and articulate townsmen. Again in Cooper's words, "the public Acts of a great Majority of the Towns, whatever may be thought of the Manner of Expression in some of them, clearly demonstrates that it is not a small Faction, but the Body of the People, who deem themselves in a State of Oppression, and that their most essential Rights are violated."[21]

As much as he welcomed Hutchinson's discomfiture, Cooper's mood in March 1773 displayed a trace of apprehension. To Franklin he expressed an earnest wish "for some Pacification—some Lines to be drawn—some Bill of Rights for America," lest "Things . . . run into Confusion."[22] As he commented to Pownall, the future was uncertain: "I should have thought at the Time you left us, the Revolution I now see in the Sentiments and Hearts of the People next to impossible. You know what has been—I write what is, without pretending to predict what will be."[23]

Like many of his countrymen, the preacher's hopes for some compromise on the fundamental question of British power over the colonies had been buoyed in the fall of 1772 by news of Lord Dartmouth's having replaced the infamous Hillsborough as secretary of state for the colonies. His part in the repeal of the Stamp Act, together with his personal piety and patronage of evangelical religion, appeared in New England eyes to be the foundation of a sincere concern for the colonies. Such hopes proved largely illusory. Dartmouth's belief in the necessity of parliamentary supremacy and his dislike of political radicals constrained an otherwise genuine friendship for America. Cooper commented to Franklin that the "general Joy" with which Boston greeted the appointment was soon checked by Dartmouth's determined but unsuccessful attempt to punish the Rhode Islanders responsible for burning a schooner of the British navy. Nonetheless, some of those still praying for conciliation continued to give thanks for having "now a minister of state for the American department, in whom the talents of the statesman and the virtues of the christian are united."[24]

Hutchinson's battle with the General Court over constitutional theory and colonial disillusionment with Dartmouth seemed to strain Cooper's capacity to avoid public political involvement. At the beginning of 1773 the *News-Letter* contrived to identify him as a clergyman who preached one doctrine in religion and another in politics, but the publishers permitted an admirer to answer in verse:

> So Cooper speaks, enlight'ned from above,
> His teachings sure are right—for fill'd with love,
> He draws the Soul to Heav'n, as her abode,
> Her friends, the Angels, and her center, God.
> May we improve the truths his lips distill,
> Then shall we learn our heav'nly Father's will,
> And mount by Faith to the blest regions, where
> Pleasures perpetual flow, beyond compare.[25]

These lines pictured the Brattle Street pastor who held his people united while they awaited completion of their grand new house of worship. In the afternoon service of Sunday, 23 April 1773, John Adams detected another man—the politician—as he listened to Cooper preach on a text from Revelation: "And the great dragon was cast out, that old serpent, called the Devil, and Satan, which deceiveth the whole world: he was cast out into the earth, and his angels were cast out with him." Adams had reason to query in his diary, "Whether the Dr. had not some political Allusions in the Choice of this Text." Both were privy to a sensational secret, known also to Bowdoin, Hancock, and many other staunch Whigs in this congregation who like Adams would have listened understandingly. For all who knew the secret, the "old serpent, . . . which deceiveth the whole world" could be only Thomas Hutchinson.[26]

The previous December, Franklin in his capacity as agent had sent to Speaker Cushing a package of original letters. A covering letter explained that these formed "part of a Correspondence, that I have reason to believe laid the Foundation of most if not all our present grievances." Franklin stipulated that the letters were not to be printed or otherwise copied: they might be seen by Cushing, by the House committee corresponding with the agent, by councillors Bowdoin and Pitts, by Doctors Chauncy, Cooper, and Winthrop, and by a "few such other Gentlemen" whom Cushing might "think fit to show them to." After a few months the letters must be returned to Franklin, who was "not at Liberty" to disclose how he had obtained them.[27]

When Cushing opened Franklin's packet in March, he found that it contained six letters by Hutchinson, four by Andrew Oliver, one by Charles Paxton, and a few by others. Written from 1767 through 1769 to an English correspondent whose name had been erased, the letters contained no startling revelations. Those by

Hutchinson and Oliver, though, provided dramatic reiteration of the wholehearted sympathy of the present governor and lieutenant governor for the system of commercial regulation and taxation culminating in the Townshend Act and the American Board of Customs Commissioners.

Hutchinson had unequivocally reported that Hancock's *Liberty* had been seized "for a very notorious breach of the acts of trade." In two short sentences he stripped all ambiguity from the key issues separating him from the Whig elite of Boston: "I know of no burden brought upon the fair trader by the new establishment. The illicit trader finds the risque greater than it used to be, especially in the port where the board is constantly held." Pained for the plight of the commissioners, four of whom (excluding Temple) he held in "personal esteem," Hutchinson had nothing but contempt for the "ignorant" and lying Boston leaders who "very wickedly" deceived the populace into approving "highly criminal" measures that lead to increased "licentiousness." Most damaging of all, he had written that "there must be an abridgment of what are called English liberties." He doubted whether "a colony 3,000 miles distant from the parent state" could ever "enjoy all the liberty of the parent state."[28]

In his letters Oliver appeared self-seeking and eager for parliamentary intervention to force an alteration in the Massachusetts charter that would "weaken that levelling principle which is cherished by the present popular constitution." Paxton's letter had been written from the *Romney*, where the top customs officials had taken refuge after the *Liberty* riot. His plea was succinct: "Unless we have immediately two or three regiments, 'tis the opinion of all the friends to government, that Boston will be in open rebellion."[29]

The impression these documents made on those permitted to see them in the spring of 1773 can hardly be exaggerated. Read as a whole, the Hutchinson-Oliver letters brought even moderate Whig leaders to the realization that the heads of the present provincial administration, despite their nativity, had for the last several years completely identified their personal interests with the colonial policy of the British ministries and Parliament. Whereas the most successful of past English-born governors had seen the necessity of moderating between colonial and English positions, the native-born, Harvard-educated Thomas Hutchinson relied on troops and parliamentary sanctions to crush Boston into submission to changes in imperial relations dictated solely by the mother country's concerns. Such a governor obviously meant what he said when he declared the alternatives to be acknowledgment of parliamentary supremacy or independence. He could not be trusted to seek the compromise that most Whigs still preferred.

The day before he heard Cooper preach on "that old serpent," John Adams pondered in his diary the question of how long the "important Secret" could be kept from the public.[30] This question animated Whig preparation for the new General Court of May 1773. Boston returned its representatives with a "unanimity so conspicuous . . . at this important Juncture" and instructed them to consider seriously the question of joint action by American colonies against further British invasion of their rights.[31] In the customary election sermon before the governor and legislators, the Reverend Charles Turner of Duxbury bluntly epitomized Whig political philosophy and warned against "profound secrets" in government.[32] The traditional dinner following the sermon turned into a near riot when Hutchinson insisted on inviting the customs commissioners.[33] When, according to the charter, the new House and former Council had cast their votes for a new Council, two of Hutchinson's chief supporters had been dropped and eight strong Whigs elected. The governor negatived the election of the three new men he most disliked, including John Adams, but resignedly accepted the other five. Many years later Adams recalled that "My Friend Dr. Cooper attempted to console me" upon being negatived, "which he called a Check: but I told him I considered it not as a Check but as a Boost, a Word of John Bunyan which the Dr. understood." Whatever the language, Whig domination of the General Court at the opening of this 1773 term testified unmistakably to the failure of Hutchinson's appeal to the people of his province to accept the inevitability of parliamentary power over them.[34]

Massachusetts Whigs took heart at this juncture from news that they did not stand alone. Cooper informed Franklin, "I have seen high Eulogiums upon the Replies of our Council and Commons [to Hutchinson's speech on parliamentary supremacy], from Gentlemen of the most respectable Characters in other Colonies, where there evidently appears an increasing Regard for this Province, and an Inclination to unite for the common Safety." In one of its first acts of this session, the House passed a series of resolutions creating an intercolonial committee of correspondence in response to similar action by the Virginia House of Burgesses. Cooper was thrilled by the response: "All New England is now united with Virginia in this salutary Plan, and the Accession of most if not all the other Colonies is not doubted. This opens a most agreable Prospect to the Friends of our Common Rights."[35]

Confident of support from other colonies, the Whig-controlled legislature turned to the question of what public advantage could be taken of the Hutchinson-Oliver letters. By the opening of this session, so many representatives knew of the letters that a demand arose for full disclosure of their contents. On 2 June, after the galleries had been cleared, Samuel Adams announced that he stood ready to read the letters subject to the original restriction that they be "neither Printed nor Copied in Whole or in Part." After hearing them, that same day the representatives voted 101 to 5 to accept a report of a committee chaired by Hancock, which declared "that the Tendency and Design of the Letters . . . was to overthrow the Constitution of this Government, and to introduce arbitrary Power into the Province." The House then assigned to a committee the responsibility of recommending a further response to the letters. While they still could not be copied, "the substance of them was known everywhere, and the Alarm given," Cooper informed Franklin in explaining why the restrictions had to be violated in the public interest.[36]

After a week's delay, Hancock introduced the devious stratagem used to justify printing the letters. He announced to the House that he had discovered purported copies in circulation, and he moved that they be compared with the originals to determine their authenticity. The following day Adams reported that the man (Cushing) from whom he had received the original letters to read in the House now agreed that, since "copies of said Letters are already abroad," there no longer existed any reason why the representatives should not be "fully possessed of them to print, copy, or make what other Use of them they please." Accordingly, on 15 June the House approved publication. The publishers of the *Gazette* had already secretly printed the letters in a forty-page pamphlet which could now be released without delay. The Boston Committee of Correspondence sent the pamphlet, together with the House resolutions, to each Massachusetts town.[37]

In writing to Franklin, Cooper labored to put the best possible face on the publication of the letters contrary to explicit instructions. Despite the rumor that the copies reported by Hancock had

come from England by the last ships, many Members scrupled to act upon these Copies while they were

under such public Engagements to the unknown Pro-
prietor of the Originals. As the Matter was now so
public, and the Restrictions could answer no good
End, no View of the Sender, but on the contrary might
prevent in a great Measure a proper Improvement of
the Letters for the public Benefit, and for weakening
the Influence and Power of the Writers and their
Friends, it was judged most expedient, by the
Gentlemen to whom they were first shewn to allow
the House such an Use of the Originals, as they might
think necessary to found their Proceedings [upon] for
the common Safety.[38]

In other words, the advantage of publication to the Whig cause
must remain the one plea to excuse a violation of the confidence in
which the letters were sent to Boston. Consequently, Cooper
stressed results:

Nothing could have been more seasonable than the
Arrival of these Letters. They have had great Effect—
they make deep Impressions wherever they are
known. They strip the Mask from the Authors who
under the Profession of Friendship to their Country
have been endeavoring to build up themselves and
their Families upon its Ruins. They and their
Adherents are shocked and dismayed. The Confidence
reposed in them by many is annihilated; and Administration must soon see the Necessity of putting
the Provincial Power of the Crown into other Hands.
This is at present almost the universal Sentiment.[39]

Insisting that no copies of the letters could have been made in
England and sent to America, Franklin correctly surmised that the
report of copies circulating in Boston had been an "Expedient to
disengage the House." He nevertheless accepted the House's action
with good grace and a willingness to bear "any Inconveniences" he
might suffer as a result.[40]

Simultaneously with publication of the letters, the House overwhelmingly adopted a series of resolutions setting forth the Whig
view of their contents and concluding that the conduct of Hutchinson and Oliver necessitated a petition to the king for their removal
from office. On 23 June a petition to this effect was approved by a
vote of 80 to 11 and sent to Franklin for presentation to the king.

The Council followed suit with an equally bold set of resolutions passed by a two-thirds majority.[41]

Stunned and demoralized by the employment of his correspondence for partisan purposes, Governor Hutchinson concluded that the prospects of his "future usefulness" in the Massachusetts government had been so dimmed that he must now look to his personal financial security. He admitted to Bernard that after four years of "hard service" he doubted whether he could endure another political crisis. But he remained determined not to step down before being "honorably acquitted" and being rewarded with another position so that he would not be "left wholly without imployment and support in advanced life." By the end of June 1773 Hutchinson wanted nothing but an honorable escape from the burdens of office with assurance of an income equal to what he had received before elevation to the governor's chair. He appeared, wrote Samuel Adams, "totally disconcerted" but not humbled. Throughout the summer, newspaper writers wrung the last possible drop of utility from the letters by a method explained in the opening words of one attack: "The oftener we read Mr. Hutchinson's confidential Letters, lately detected and printed, the more virulence we discover in them against his native country."[42]

Although the name of the recipient had been removed from the Hutchinson-Oliver letters before Franklin acquired them, it quickly became known in Boston that they were all written to George Grenville's jack-of-all-trades, Thomas Whately, who had been a member of the House of Commons until his death in 1772. He and John Temple had been fast friends during the American's early years in England, but their friendship ended after Temple returned to Massachusetts and learned that Whately corresponded with Hutchinson and Oliver. Back in England at the beginning of 1771, Temple resumed his intimacy with Whately and was given access to his papers both before and after his death. Years later, when attempting to prove his loyalty to the American cause, Temple claimed a major share of the credit for obtaining the Hutchinson letters, even though at the time Franklin had publicly shouldered all the blame. Whatever the truth, both Franklin and Temple lost their positions under the crown as a result of this affair.[43] Temple's claim to the gratitude of Americans would become one of the most personally sensitive political issues confronting Samuel Cooper in the closing years of the War for Independence. But in 1773 the Boston preacher felt only relief that the governor's long suspected inner thoughts had finally been laid bare.

More convinced than ever that his administration was unimpeachable on any save emotional grounds, Hutchinson saw himself the victim of a conspiracy to raise against him a "popular clamor" sufficient to cause his dismissal for unpopularity alone. Massachusetts Whigs, he believed, had joined in a scheme to replace him by Franklin, Temple, or possibly Pownall. Thus he fought an effort from both sides of the Atlantic "to distress Government" in the province. At home he must deal not only with local demagogues but also with such respectable gentlemen as Bowdoin and Hancock, and with the hypocritical Dr. Cooper, whom he described as "one of the Clergy who is consulted in every affair and who though he prays for the Governor every Sunday yet wishes every other day in the week to have him removed."[44]

12

Next to Impossible

On 15 July 1773 John Adams took tea at Samuel Cooper's home with Samuel Adams, two other Boston Whigs, an unidentified "French Gentleman," and Thomas Mifflin of Philadelphia. An ardent Whig politician, Mifflin was vacationing at nearby Newport, Rhode Island, a popular summer resort for wealthy Philadelphians and southern planters. He typified those young men like Hancock and Josiah Quincy, Jr., whose travels in America before 1775 contributed significantly to a growing awareness that no colony stood alone in its opposition to Great Britain.[1]

Colonial Whigs were bound together by more than occasional acquaintanceship and their common status as colonials. Since the Stamp Act, they had consistently interpreted developments within the British Empire in the light of a remarkably uniform theory of how human freedom had developed and could be maintained. This ideology had been in part formed from and now drew confirmation from the heritage of the Protestant Reformation. In the colonial mind it was axiomatic that freedom flourished most in Protestant countries and languished in Catholic kingdoms. To the dissenter from the Church of England the most obnoxious trait of Anglicanism was the tendency of its prelates, following the example set by the infamous Archbishop Laud, to imitate their Roman counterparts in crushing the rights of free men.

The only sermon by Cooper in two decades that he consented to have published developed this familiar theme of the relationship of popery to liberty. In 1773 he gave Harvard's Dudleian Lecture, an endowed series founded to expose errors in religion. Contending that the "papal antichrist is ultimately intended" to be the "Man of Sin" mentioned in 2 Thess. 2:3, he reached the conclusion that "popery is incompatible with the safety of a free government. It sets up a sovereign head, superior to all civil rulers; a spiritual power that reaches to every thing upon earth, and can brook no control. Trampling upon the rights of conscience, and assuming an authority to absolve every sacred obligation, what pledge can it possibly leave us, for the security of civil freedom?"[2]

As this passage suggests, the unique American experience had reshaped Protestant ethical attitudes and English libertarian thought into a highly functional ideology on which to draw in the present imperial crisis. None of the "happy fruits of the reformation" had grown more abundantly in American soil than the ethic of work and frugality. Capital accumulation in the colonies had resulted largely from individual saving and not from British investment.[3] The Whig elite controlling Boston in 1773 were typically men who had either acquired fortunes through their own efforts or had inherited wealth from fathers who raised them while enlarging a small stock of goods in trade into a considerable estate. For these men human liberty centered on those individual and political freedoms which enabled one to acquire and protect private property. Likewise, throughout the colonies the widespread ownership of property had produced a society of transplanted Englishmen for whom the rights of man had become an inseparable amalgam of life, liberty, and property. When British legislation threatened existing American property or imposed new restrictions on the continued pursuit of wealth, colonists perceived more clearly "the logic of rebellion" in the many sources of political theory available to them. As one turns from the treatises on freedom widely used by American Whigs to their personal explanations for the need to employ such theory, the economic base of their ideology comes into sharp focus. As Cooper unabashedly phrased the point for his people, "Government was appointed for the Protection of Property."[4]

Those colonists most attuned to the economic freedoms inherent in Whig political theory were also those most influenced by the current state of trade. The apparent return of prosperity in the two years after the Massacre had stranded the resistance movement on a plateau of no rising demands. But by the fall of 1772 the bubble of credit expansion in England and Scotland had burst, leaving colonial merchants with a large excess of British goods which could not be sold at a profit but for which payment must eventually be made. The following year, commodities sold in Boston at the lowest wholesale prices of the last quarter century and brought even less in 1774. In response, Massachusetts merchants and ship-owners pushed harder to increase their exports to the West Indies, southern Europe, the wine islands, and Africa and to capture a larger share of the carrying trade of the empire. This heightened activity merely made the restrictions on American trade seem more galling, and all classes felt the pinch.[5]

Without such economic unrest Dartmouth might have succeeded in his attempt to bring about a détente in imperial relations. In the summer of 1773 he bypassed the governor and wrote confidentially to Speaker Cushing, promising to use his influence to restrain the exercise of Parliament's right to legislate for the colonies if the Massachusetts House would retract the "wild and extravagant Doctrines . . . contained in their Answer to the Speech of the Governor at the opening of the late Session of the General Court." In reply Cushing reiterated the unchanged Whig position that Parliament must return the colonies to the position they had enjoyed "at the conclusion of the late War."[6] Yet he appeared eager for any sign that the ministry had come to its senses. Instead, Parliament passed without division the Tea Act of 1773, a bill that in the eyes of American Whigs confirmed their essential case against Britain and required them to engage in open resistance once again.

Along with their English cousins, eighteenth-century Americans had become generally addicted to tea drinking. Colonists could legally import this product of China only from England through the East India Company, but the greater part of the tea consumed in America was smuggled in from Dutch sources. Britain's repeated efforts to curb smuggling had achieved only limited success. Then the repeal of all Townshend duties in 1770 except that on tea transformed this beverage into a symbol. Since the legal product was indistinguishable from the illegal, each sip of tea reminded an American of England's claimed right to tax its colonists. Franklin expressed to Cooper his hope that "in Drinking Tea, a true American, reflecting that by every Cup he contributed to the Salaries, Pension, and Rewards of the Enemies and Persecutors of his Country, would be half choaked at the Thought, and find no quantity of Sugar sufficient to make the nauseous Draught go down." Presumably a "true American" like Cooper would serve only Dutch tea in his parlor to such patriots as Mifflin;

but one cannot be certain, for even Hancock's ships carried some legal tea during 1771 and 1772. At best the occasional discouragement of tea drinking after 1770 remained a token defiance of Parliament. With his typical capacity for symbolism, John Hancock named one of his vessels, *Undutied Tea.* Meanwhile smuggling continued freely, particularly south of Boston.[7]

Seeking a solution to the acute and complex financial problems of the East India Company, Lord North in the spring of 1773 endorsed a plan by which the company could sell its surplus tea directly in America through its own agents instead of at public auction in London, as the law now stipulated. Furthermore, the rebate of all import duties on tea reshipped to America would make the company's tea more competitive in price with that smuggled from the Dutch. But North at the same time adamantly refused to approve repeal of the Townshend duty, even after being reminded in debate that a widespread objection to the principle of this duty, and not the price, prevented the company from enlarging its sales in the colonies. To North, the Tea Act constituted a domestic revenue bill designed to assist the company back on its feet. In sharp contrast, to American Whigs the Tea Act emerged clearly as a measure ingeniously constructed "to establish and confirm a tax on the colonists, which they complained of as unjust and unrighteous."[8]

The act contained another evil. By eliminating the middleman in its tea sales to America, the East India Company threatened private mercantile enterprise. If tea could be sold through royally appointed vendors, why not all imports? The specter of a few large chartered trading companies monopolizing all trade to the colonies, where obedient factors (or vendors) distributed goods at prices fixed in England, did not seem entirely farfetched to James Bowdoin. Even some London merchants warned their American customers that accepting tea would open the door to other monopolies. Thus mercantile fears contributed to the intensity of what Cooper identified as the "common Cause" of all Americans.[9]

In its choice of consignees for Boston, the East India Company destroyed whatever slight chance it may have had of successfully executing its tea monopoly in that town. Concerned for the financial future of his sons Thomas and Elisha, Governor Hutchinson welcomed the inclusion of their importing firm among the consignees. They were as obnoxious to Whigs for opposition to the late nonimportation movement as for their paternity. Another consignee, Richard Clarke, had less stubbornly resisted nonimportation but still lost no love on Whig politicians. Despite considerable social prestige and a pew at Brattle Street, he and his sons stood aloof from the controlling elite. Since the end of 1770, both the Clarke and Hutchinson firms had imported large quantities of dutied tea. The other two consignees were opportunistic merchants with no strong Whig connections.[10]

Boston's unofficial Whig political organizations appear to have been stung into action by the "current Talk of the Town" that these unpopular merchants would soon receive shipments of the East India Company's tea. Only the North End Caucus has left records. Its members voted on 23 October "that this body will oppose the vending of any Tea, sent by the East India Company to any part of the Continent, with our lives and fortunes." During the next month they evinced an eagerness to carry out this pledge, but none more so than Gabriel Johonnot, Samuel Cooper's son-in-law.[11]

The Sons of Liberty—the aggregate of Whig caucuses, clubs, and committees—summoned the consignees to appear at the Liberty Tree at noon on 3 November, and there, before the "People," to resign their offices and swear to ship back any tea they received. When they failed to appear, a committee including Molineux, Warren, and Johonnot carried these demands to Clarke's store, where the consignees had met to discuss their plight. "Their answer was rough and peremptory—no Resignation" (Cooper's words). As the committee withdrew, a rowdy segment of the accompanying crowd slightly damaged and dirtied the building before dispersing.[12]

The selectmen then issued a warrant for a town meeting to be held in two days. The meeting adopted a set of resolves calling on Americans to oppose the importation of tea by the East India Company and establishing a committee to seek the immediate resignation of the consignees. When the consignees gave only the most evasive answers to the demands of the committee, another session of the town meeting voted these replies to be "Daringly Affrontive to the Town" and instructed the Boston Committee of Correspondence to send the transactions of this two-day meeting to every Massachusetts town.[13]

For the next ten days the tea question continued to be agitated in the press and through rumors. In the middle of November one of Hancock's ships made port with the news that four vessels freighting the East India Company's tea were on their way to Boston. Responding to a new public outcry, the selectmen called a town meeting. That evening the Clarke family had to hold off a noisy mob that smashed the windows of their house and then hurled rubbish through the openings. Nevertheless, the next day the consignees once again resisted the town meeting's demand to resign.[14]

Frightened by what might now be in store for them, Clarke and the others petitioned the governor and Council to take temporary protective custody of the tea when it arrived. But the Council, united almost to a man behind Bowdoin's leadership, refused and made public its stand. Hourly expecting the tea ships, two members of the Clarke family then pleaded their case with the selectmen on Saturday evening, 27 November. They maintained that they had not sought this consignment and would do anything possible and just "to restore tranquillity to the Town." Though it was impracticable to ship back the tea, as the town insisted, they promised to do "nothing underhanded" and to consult the selectmen again once the tea arrived and they had seen the company's orders concerning it.[15]

Sunday morning the first tea ship anchored in the harbor. Its name, the *Dartmouth*, seemed to mock the high hopes for peace which only a year before had accompanied the appointment to the ministry of a reputed friend of America. After morning service, the selectmen disregarded the Sabbath by meeting on business; they expected to hear from the Clarkes, as agreed the evening before. Unable to locate Richard Clarke or his sons, they adjourned for the afternoon service. Five of the seven presumably worshiped at their accustomed places in the new Brattle Street Church. Regrettably, there is no record of what Samuel Cooper said as he preached on this sober occasion to Hancock and the other selectmen, to Joseph Warren and James Bowdoin, and to the empty Clarke pew. Following the service, the selectmen again sought Richard Clarke, only to be told that he was out of town. "The Meeting was then broke up," the record suggests, with an air of finality. Henceforth, the tea question would be resolved outside the constitution and the law.[16]

For all the Boston Whigs knew, they now had to deal with the first actual attempt to land the "weed of Slavery" in America. They compared the obstinate behavior of the local consignees with reports beginning to arrive of the "soothing Manner to the People" displayed by the consignees at New York and Philadelphia. They attributed this difference to Hutchinson's being the only governor willing—or perhaps eager—to enforce the Tea Act with military power if necessary. Cooper reported to Franklin his opinion that the consignees consulted the governor "in every Step." Who could believe otherwise when Hutchinson's own sons were among their number?[17]

In this state of mind, the "Body" of the people of Boston responded to a call for a mass meeting Monday morning, 29 November, at Faneuil Hall. The Boston Committee of Correspondence, increasingly exercising executive leadership, had also invited the committees of neighboring towns. When Hancock declined election as moderator so that he might attend a Council meeting, Jonathan Williams, a nephew of Franklin by marriage, took his place. William Cooper was named secretary. The "Body," as this assembly was called to distinguish it from a legal town meeting, moved to the Old South Church to accommodate better the overflow crowd that increased during the day until it reached 2,500, by conservative estimate. Resolutions that the tea must be returned "at all Events" and no duty paid on it passed without opposition. Still awaiting word from the consignees, the Body adjourned until afternoon. At that time it approved motions threatening the *Dartmouth*'s captain if his tea should be unloaded, and appointing a watch of twenty-five Sons of Liberty over the ship, now tied up at Griffin's Wharf.[18]

Hancock then warned the assembly of steps taken by Hutchinson to asperse all opposition to the tea scheme as riotous behavior justifying the intervention of troops to preserve order. He also reported the results of the morning's Council meeting, where once more the councillors had refused His Excellency's request that they jointly offer protection to the consignees and their tea. Hancock then moved the question, "Whether it be not the Sense of this Meeting, that the Governor's Conduct herein carries a designed Reflection upon the People here met; and is solely calculated to serve the Views of Administration." The motion carried unanimously in the affirmative, with Samuel Adams and Dr. Thomas Young seizing the occasion to blacken Hutchinson's character even further. Late in the afternoon, John Singleton Copley, the artist and son-in-law of Clarke, got word to Hancock that the consignees would respond to the town if given a little more time to study their orders from the East India Company, received only the evening before. Accordingly, the Body adjourned until morning.[19]

By Tuesday morning the consignees were all either secure at the Castle or were out of town, but they sent a written answer to the selectmen, which was read to the Body. Declaring it "utterly" out of their power to return the tea, they conceded only to store it until receiving further orders from England. The Body unanimously agreed to continue despite Hutchinson's order to disperse, and fruitless negotiations took up much of the day.[20]

Emotions ran high in Boston during this week. Hutchinson complained to Dartmouth that "it is in every body's mouth that H[ancock] said at the Close of the meeting he would be willing to spend his fortune and life itself in so good a cause." Another version reported that Hancock said, "My Fellow Countrymen, we have now put our Hands to the Plough and Wo be to him that shrinks or looks back." Perhaps such spirits explain why Hancock sent his chief clerk "Express" to New York and Philadelphia "to communicate the transactions of this town respecting the tea." Abigail Adams, now living in Boston, caught this mood in a letter: "The flame is kindled and like Lightning it catches from Soul to Soul." Another observer noted, " 'twould puzzle any person to purchase a pair of p[isto]ls in this town, as they are all bought up, with a full determination to repell force by force." Samuel Adams was reported to have informed the Body that he slept with arms at his bedside, "as every good Citizen ought."[21]

Would not salt water "make as good Tea as fresh?" Whig merchant John Rowe was heard to query before the Body on Wednesday, 30 November as he tried to remove from himself the odium of being part owner of a tea-carrying ship. And Dr. Young apparently proposed outright destruction of the tea. Yet, this extremist view found no support among most Whig leaders so long as there existed any hope of returning the tea untouched to the East India Company. But they refused even to consider permitting it to be landed at the Castle; for, once there and the duty paid, it could be smuggled ashore. Since in New England tea was currently in short supply and the price high, this large and inexpensive supply would prove an "almost invincible Temptation." Samuel Cooper, for one, had no faith that patriotism could overcome the common addiction to this brew.[22]

In seeking to force the *Dartmouth*'s owner to send his ship back to England with the tea intact, Boston Whigs ran afoul of the many acts regulating trade. Upon arriving in the harbor, a master must enter his manifest at the customhouse and pay required duties before unloading his cargo. If duties were not paid within twenty days of entry, the ship became liable to seizure by customs officers. Nor could the vessel be legally cleared for departure before the collector gave receipt for the duties. Thus the *Dartmouth* remained at Griffin's Wharf under guard by the Sons of Liberty while the leaders explored ways of accomplishing their purpose before 17

December, when the twenty days would expire. In the first two weeks of December two more tea ships reached Boston and eventually were tied up at Griffin's Wharf, where the same guard could serve for all three. Their owners apparently believed that cooperation with the Sons of Liberty in berthing the tea ships assured protection for their vessels and cargoes other than tea. All parties remained conscious of the 17 December deadline, for possibly on that day customs officers would attempt to seize the tea and sell it under protection of the military and naval forces stationed at the Castle. Hutchinson may have awaited such an outcome as he remained inactive at his home in Milton, a safe distance out of Boston. As in past crises, he sponsored no compromise.[23]

Assured of support within the province, Boston Whigs also took heart from news that in both Philadelphia and New York the consignees had refused to handle the tea. Responding to pressure, the owner of the *Dartmouth* agreed to ship the tea back to England if permitted to clear the harbor legally. As was to be expected, the collector and comptroller of customs refused to stretch the law to accommodate merchants with whom they had been at odds for a decade, and especially at a time when their superiors, the customs commissioners, had again fled to the Castle in fear for their lives. Without clearance from customs, the *Dartmouth* was denied a naval pass to leave the harbor.[24]

The Body convened again on Thursday morning, 16 December, with Samuel Cooper's close friend, Samuel P. Savage of Weston, in the chair. He had been elected moderator to dramatize the large representation of other eastern Massachusetts towns in this gathering of the "People." On this morning the largest crowd yet packed every square foot of space on the floor and in the galleries of the Old South Church. Upon learning of the failure of the *Dartmouth*'s owner to obtain a clearance from customs, the Body ordered him to make an immediate appeal to the governor at Milton for a pass to sail from Boston before the day ended.

At dusk word arrived of Hutchinson's refusal to issue a pass.[25] Cooper described and analyzed for Franklin what then occurred:

> As soon as the Governor's Refusal was known the
> Assembly was dissolved. Just before the Dissolution,
> two or three hundred Persons, in Dress and appearance
> like Indians, passed by the old South Meeting House
> where the Assembly was held, gave a War Hoop, and
> hastened to the Wharf where all the Tea Ships lay, and

demanding the Tea, which was given up to them without the least Resistance, they soon emptied all the Chests into the Harbor, to the Amount of about three hundred and fourty. This was done without Injury to any other Property, or to any Man's Person; An Interloper indeed, who had found Means to fill his Pockets with Tea, upon being discovered was stript of his Booty and his Cloaths together; and sent home naked. A remarkable Instance of Order and Justice among Savages. When they had done their Business, they silently departed, and the Town has been remarkably quiet ever since.

 . . . the Principle upon which they . . . acted, was, a thorough Detestation of the insidious Design of Administration, to establish and increase the American Revenue upon this Article, after fair and repeated Professions of an Intention to relieve us. In what Manner it will resent the Treatment we have given to this exasperating Measure is uncertain; but this much is certain, that the Country is united with the Town, and the Colonies with one another, in the common Cause, more firmly than ever. Should a greater military Power be sent among us, it can never alter the fixed Sentiments of the People, though [it] would increase the public Confusions, and tend to plunge both Countries into the most unhappy Circumstances.[26]

The destruction of ninety thousand pounds of tea, valued at nearly £10,000, was no sudden passion of a revolutionary mob. At the last hour, after all legal and extralegal means of persuasion had failed, a carefully prepared and tightly disciplined action achieved the Whig goal in the only way still possible. An observer of the final hours at the Old South noted that after the "Mohawks" passed the church, the Whig leaders quieted the remaining crowd to hear a "very merry" speech by Dr. Young on "the ill Effects of Tea on the Constitution." Moderator Savage then dissolved the meeting, but a small crowd remained gathered around the men who had guided events to this turn: Samuel Adams, Dr. Warren, John Hancock, William Cooper, Dr. Young, and others. They felt no need to hasten to Griffin's Wharf, for they understood what was underway there. They lingered in the ecstasy of this hour, best put into words by John Adams on the following day: "The die is cast. The people have passed the river and cut away the bridge. . . . This is the grandest event which has ever yet happened since the controversy with Britain opened. The sublimity of it charms me!"[27]

For Samuel Cooper the excitement of this week had been mixed with the deepest personal grief. On the day before the tea party, Hancock and Warren headed the pallbearers who carried Judith Cooper Johonnot to her grave. The "inflammatory fever" then prevailing in Boston deprived Cooper of a daughter, aged twenty-six.[28]

In the twenty-seven years since his marriage, the only evidence of Cooper's family life had been records of the birth of two daughters and the marriage in 1766 of Judith, the elder, to Gabriel Johonnot, of a prominent Boston Huguenot family. One of the most active of the younger Sons of Liberty, this son-in-law had been still another link between the preacher and the resistance movement. Judith left two sons, the first named after her father. Only five at his mother's death, Samuel Cooper Johonnot became the special object of his grandfather's affection and care. For the remainder of his life, Dr. Cooper seemed to look upon his grandson as a child of the American Revolution, as a living symbol of the "common Cause" that had manifested itself so perfectly in the week of his mother's death.[29]

In the months after the Boston Tea Party, Samuel Cooper no longer needed to be as careful in preserving the political neutrality of his pulpit. Over such issues as whether to pay the East India Company for the tea destroyed, Bostonians were beginning to divide along lines foreshadowing the final separation of 1776. But the Brattle Street pastor had little reason to fear that the impending struggle would hopelessly split his church. No evidence more dramatically illustrates Whig strength in Boston than the solidarity of the town's wealthiest religious society in the progression of events toward independence. With their fortunes, ships, trade, real estate, and perhaps their lives at stake, less than one-fifth of Cooper's parishioners showed any outward leaning toward loyalism.[30]

As far as the record shows, after the Tea Party twelve substantial men of the congregation never wavered in their support of Hutchinson and the king.[31] Six more were tied to the crown through employment, though not all later chose loyalism. And another dozen of Cooper's parishioners evidenced some degree of support for the royal government before eventually making their peace with the Whigs. Yet this opposition amounted to little when compared to the steady Whigs at Brattle Street, men like Isaac

Smith, Jonathan Williams, Oliver Wendell, Samuel Winthrop, John Pitts, Richard Dana, or Timothy Newell, to mention a few. Hoping to avoid a civil war, these men nevertheless stood their ground on the fundamental issues in the contest with Britain, even while they sometimes disputed with Whig politicians over tactics or maintained fellowship with their Tory relatives. But through all the turmoil to come, Cooper could remain confident of a movement grounded on the interests of such solid men as these and others like them in his church and throughout the town.

Had he entertained doubts concerning his congregation's ability to hold together in any coming storm, Cooper might have accepted the presidency of Harvard College when it was offered to him in February 1774. He quickly declined because of strong "Attachments to the Church and Congregation to which I minister." His parishioners returned the feeling by greeting his refusal to leave them, as one townsman noted, with "great Joy and Satisfaction."[32]

No one doubted that the British ministry would respond to the Tea Party with strong measures, but Bostonians would have to wait four months to learn the nature of that response. While a few timid souls urged immediate payment for the tea to avoid the wrath of Britain, most Boston Whigs confidently took steps to gird the resistance movement for whatever lay ahead. They set about informing the province, other colonies, and friends in the mother country that the Tea Party had resulted from the "obstinacy of consignees, their advisers and coadjutors." They launched a more vigorous crusade against the tea-drinking habit, calling on all patriotic citizens to "bravely sacrifice the obnoxious Drug at the Shrine of American Liberty," to "scorn to sip the draught that is tainted with the Blood of our Liberty." And the more zealous Whigs renewed their efforts to channel into the common cause the emotional energy generated by social and religious tensions. Hutchinson admitted to Dartmouth that his authority in Boston was at an end.[33]

The governor reluctantly convened the legislature in January. Whig leaders had determined to initiate impeachment proceedings against justices of the superior court who refused to spurn salaries from the crown. More than a quarter century afterwards, John Adams took full credit for having proposed impeachment to spare the judges a coat of tar and feathers. He recalled making this suggestion while dining at Samuel Winthrop's with Cooper and several members of the General Court. The idea caught on quickly, he explained, particularly since "Dr. Cooper and others were excellent hands to spread a rumor."[34] All judges except Chief Justice Peter Oliver succumbed to Whig pressure and declared that they would accept salaries only from the legislature. The House then petitioned for Oliver's removal. Hutchinson's refusal to grant this petition led an overwhelming majority of representatives to adopt "Articles of Impeachment of High Crimes and Misdemeanors against Peter Oliver." Soon afterwards, Hutchinson prorogued the legislature.[35]

The culmination of Whig preparation for Britain's response to the Tea Party—and a momentous hour in the American Revolution—came at noon on Saturday, 5 March 1774, when Hancock delivered the annual oration commemorating the Boston Massacre. Observances on this date in the last three years had firmly established the tradition that each March fifth Bostonians must learn anew the lessons of that fatal evening. This year the oration took on greater poignancy both because of the Tea Party and the orator.

"The Greatest Number of People that ever met on the Occasion" pressed into the Old South Church to hear the oration. Having served frequently as presiding officer of various assemblies, Hancock was no stranger to the public rostrum; and he had never been shy in expressing himself at town meetings or in the House of Representatives. But when this merchant prince turned political leader spoke, he commanded respect as much for who he was as for his emphatic, blunt speech. Now he mounted a pulpit which had held the most powerful clerical and political orators of the past, and Hancock's dramatic aura made him seem for the moment the equal of anyone who had ever climbed those pulpit stairs. Still a bachelor at thirty-seven, his health uncertain, his business virtually at a standstill, he must have understood that he had reached the point of no return in his long and gradual transition from trade to politics, from loyalty to rebellion. And the townsmen he faced sensed his personal crisis because they knew that his peril was also their own, even though they had less money and property to lose in an unsuccessful struggle with the might of England.[36]

The best evidence of how fully Hancock rose to the occasion is found in the diary of John Adams, a flatterer of no man: "1774 March 5th. Heard the oration pronounced by Coll. Hancock, in Commemoration of the Massacre—an elegant, a pathetic, a Spirited Performance. A vast Croud—rainy Eyes—&c. The Composition, the Pronunciation, the Action all exceeded the Expectations of every Body. They exceeded even mine, which were very considerable. Many of the Sentiments came with great Propriety from him. His Invective particularly against a Prefference of Riches to Virtue, came from him with a singular Dignity and Grace." That evening Adams dined with the family of his neighbor, Justice Edmund Quincy, where the talk was of possible political and military action against Massachusetts. Nevertheless, Adams wrote, "The Happiness of the Family where I dined, upon account of the Colls. justly applauded Oration, was complete."[37]

Such joy was understandable. In four thousand unmistakable words, Boston's wealthiest merchant had irrevocably committed himself to the Whig cause by pleading with his fellow citizens to fight and die, if necessary, in defense of their country. Hancock's bluntness left no room for doubt:

> The town of Boston, ever faithful to the British Crown, has been invested by a British fleet: The troops of George the Third have cross'd the wide atlantick, not to engage an enemy, but to assist a band of Traitors in trampling on the rights and liberties of his most loyal subjects in America, . . .
>
> But let not the miscreant host vainly imagine that we fear'd their arms. No, . . . we dread nothing but slavery. Death is the creature of a Poltroon's brains; 'tis immortality, to sacrifice ourselves for the salvation of our country. We fear not death. . . .
>
> We have all one common cause; let it therefore be our only contest, who shall most contribute to the security of the liberties of America. . . .
>
> Surely you never will tamely suffer this country to be a den of thieves. . . . I conjure you by all that is dear, by all that is honourable, by all that is sacred, not only that ye pray, but that you act; that, if necessary ye fight, and even die for the prosperity of our Jerusalem. Break in sunder, with noble disdain, the bonds with which the Philistines have bound you. . . .
>
> I have the most animating confidence that the present noble struggle for liberty, will terminate gloriously for America.[38]

The orator, the wealthiest and most active figure among the Whig elite, held up the improvident Samuel Adams and a "numerous host of Fellow-patriots" as "men who are superior to all temptation, whom nothing can divert from a steady pursuit of the interest of their country." By catching their "divine enthusiasm," Americans can know the joy of "delivering the oppressed from the iron grasp of tyranny"—a "tyranny" to be increasingly felt by the merchant. Had the Tea Act succeeded, "we soon should have found our trade in the hands of foreigners, and taxes imposed on every thing which we consumed; nor would it have been strange, if in a few years a company in London should have purchased an exclusive right of trading to America." This "plot" had been discovered and thwarted. "Yet while we rejoice that the adversary has not hitherto prevailed against us, let us by no means put off the harness. Restless malice, and disappointed ambition will still suggest new measures to our inveterate enemies.—Therefore let us also be ready to take the field whenever danger calls, let us be united and strengthen the hands of each other, by promoting a general union among us." Finally, Hancock proposed a congress of representatives from the colonial assemblies "as the most effectual method of establishing such an Union as the present posture of our affairs requires."[39]

Hancock's *Oration* had two editions in Boston by early April and was also published in Newport, New Haven, and Philadelphia. Isaiah Thomas's *Royal American Magazine* printed it with an engraving depicting Hancock's bust "supported by the goddess of liberty and an Antient Briton." In New York a Tory newspaper gave space to a lengthy refutation of the orator's interpretation of the Boston Massacre. And from England came word that the full text of the oration had been published in the *London Evening-Post*.[40]

Such success elevated Hancock to an even higher niche as the foremost New England patriot, but Tories attacked the oration as the effort of a "speechifying Fool" who had been duped into forming the "extravagant scheme of conquering England in the Pulpit of the Old South." They insisted that Hancock lacked the ability to prepare such an effective declamation. In England, John Mein announced in the press that it had been "composed for him by the joint efforts of the Reverend Divine Samuel Cooper, that Rose of Sharon, and by the very honest Samuel Adams, Clerk, Psalmsinger, Purloiner, and Curer of Bacon." Hancock's political detractors later took up the same theme, and in time the ghost-writer theory turned into hard fact. In his autobiography, written in the early 1800s, John Adams recalled hearing Samuel Adams tell that more than two-thirds of Hancock's "so celebrated" oration had been written by Drs. Warren and Church. Later, E. S. Thomas reminisced on the "electric effect" of the oration and declared that he had known for more than a half century that it "was written by the then celebrated, Rev. Dr. Cooper." But, Thomas added, "any man who ever heard Hancock address a public assembly, as I have, could not for a moment doubt his ability to write such an oration; the object was, to get him committed, beyond the hope of pardon, and that oration did it completely."[41]

Contemporary evidence throws only indirect light on the question of authorship. One member of the Brattle Street congregation wrote in April 1774 that the oration is "asserted to be" Hancock's "own production." Cooper, who must have known the truth, said nothing that has been preserved. Certainly Hancock, educated at Boston Latin School and Harvard College, could write effective, forceful prose, as his letters reveal; but he seldom wrote except when required by the duties of business or public office. His adjectival, ejaculatory oratorical style seems more imitative of Joseph Warren than of Adams or Cooper. The oration bears the marks of a dictated piece, much like the writer's business and political correspondence. One can speculate that Hancock, using available models of Whig polemics, dictated his thoughts for the oration to his business assistant and occasional amanuensis William Palfrey, who may have polished it with touches of his own. Palfrey's letters to John Wilkes display a similar spirit and a few of the stylistic characteristics of the oration. In addition, some trusted friend like Cooper may have been asked to read the manuscript before its delivery. But, speculation aside, we can be certain that Hancock's pride, the characteristic which his political foes emphasized most, would have prevented him from consenting to mouth an oration whose composition he had not directed.[42]

Much more to the point of authorship, the oration was a highly personal testimony of Hancock's political faith, in which he avowed *his* "sincere attachment" to the Whig cause, *his* readiness to sacrifice wealth and life for that faith, *his* trust in the other Whig leaders, and *his* "animating confidence" in final victory. No other man in New England, and likely in all the colonies, could have made a public declaration of equal weight at this critical hour.

March fifth had been a Saturday. Bostonians remained quiet on Sunday. At dark on Monday, the customary illuminated exhibits on King Street commemorating the Massacre were lighted for the first time. They had not been displayed Saturday evening, which was still the beginning of the Sabbath for some New Englanders. This year the exhibits included figures representing the trunks and severed heads of Henry VII's hated tax collectors, Empson and Dudley, lying in a pool of blood with the headsman's ax in view. Nearby portraits of the governor and chief justice gave the not-too-subtle suggestion that they deserved a similar fate. While most inhabitants pressed for a better view of this bloody scene, a band of "Indians" boarded the only tea ship to reach Boston since the Tea Party to again make this brew with salt water. On Tuesday, Lieutenant Governor Andrew Oliver, who stood second only to Hutchinson on the Whig list of local conspirators with the British ministry, was laid in this tomb while many Bostonians watched with undisguised joy. Chief Justice Peter Oliver lived in so much fear of the mob that he avoided his brother's deathbed and funeral.[43]

In this first week of March, Boston's unrepentance and Hutchinson's loss of actual power had been laid bare. On 10 May the town reelected its four representatives almost unanimously, with Hancock receiving every vote cast. Later that same day a ship arrived from London with news that the ministry had resolved to teach Boston a lesson in order and loyalty.[44]

Repeated representations by Hutchinson and other crown officers that disloyalty in Massachusetts stemmed solely from the ambitions of a handful of demagogues had ill-prepared the home government to deal realistically with a resistance movement widely supported in the province and throughout the colonies. New York and Philadelphia had prevented landing of the tea without destroying it; thus Boston alone stood guilty of a heinous crime against private property and public morality which few Englishmen in public life were willing to overlook. Even the gentle Lord Dartmouth now believed it imperative to apply whatever force might be necessary to separate the majority of law-abiding, "right-thinking" Bostonians from their radical leaders. Finding insufficient evidence to justify transporting ringleaders of the Tea Party to London for treason trials, the ministry turned to Parliament. At the end of March, George III gave his assent to the Boston Port Bill, which had made its way through Commons and Lords with surprisingly light opposition from the reputed friends of America. Beginning on 1 June, Boston harbor would be closed to all trade and its customhouse moved to another coastal town. The port would remain shut until satisfaction had been given for the lost tea and the sufferings of customs officials in recent disturbances, and until the town was peaceful and its merchants ready to pay customs duties.[45]

For reasons much like Dartmouth's, Thomas Pownall had voted for the Boston Port Bill. Two days after the bill became law, he rushed a letter to Cooper imploring the "Good and Prudent of the Province" to assert their authority so that "Good Sense" and "Good Principles" will "prevail over the Passions and Party of the Violent and Heedless, who have well nigh ruined the Town of Boston, and will ruin the Province." So far had Pownall lost touch with the Boston Whigs that he could now entreat them to avoid further "imprudence and Violence," though he admitted that "the stroke given is heavy and severe" and that "the Arm of Government raised threatens more."[46]

Perhaps his Boston correspondent could guess from the tone of this letter that Pownall would soon join the party of Lord North. Cooper's reply revealed how rapidly he was now moving away from the position he had shared with Pownall as late as two years before: "Your advice is sound and good to preserve a Moderate and pacific Spirit, but under our peculiar Circumstances and accumulated Grievances ha[r]d to be practised."[47]

Despite four months of steeling themselves, Boston Whigs still could not hide their shock as they read the Boston Port Bill over and over. They had apparently expected only a demand for payment by some deadline. But their shock produced action rather than panic. The Boston Committee of Correspondence, meeting with representatives of eight other towns on 12 May, quickly drafted a broadside calling on all Massachusetts towns and other colonies to counter Britain's divide-and-conquer policy with a firm union and a complete boycott of English goods.[48]

A town meeting to consider "what Measures are proper" in this emergency convened the next morning, Friday, 13 May, at Faneuil Hall. After Samuel Adams had been elected moderator, a prestigious committee went in search of Samuel Cooper with a request for him to open the meeting with a suitable prayer for this critical hour. While waiting, the citizens listened to Town Clerk Cooper read the entire text of the Port Bill. Then the committee reappeared with Dr. Cooper, who, "though he was just returned fatigued from a Journey," obliged the meeting with an "excellent Prayer." Before the day ended, committees had been appointed to consider all proposals for action and to communicate with other towns and colonies. By formal vote, townsmen emphasized their opinion that only a continental boycott of English manufactures could hope to force repeal of the Port Bill; Massachusetts should not be expected to make an unequal and ineffective sacrifice for the "Salvation of North America and her Liberties." As for Boston, the *Gazette* reported that "there was never more unanimity than appeared in Faneuil-Hall last Friday; . . . it was as perfect as human Society can admit of."[49]

That same day, General Thomas Gage sailed into the harbor after a year's leave in England. He returned not only as commander in chief but also as governor of Massachusetts. Gage took up the duties of office, while Hutchinson prepared to leave for England. The former governor expected to be reinstated with vindication after a military government of brief duration had brought people to their senses.[50]

Election day came on 26 May. General Gage received his first taste of the New England election sermon as he listened to a Whig clergyman preach from the text, "When the righteous are in authority, the people rejoice: but when the wicked beareth rule, the people mourn." Unimpressed, Gage negatived thirteen of the most Whiggish of the newly elected councillors, including Bowdoin and John Adams. He further refused the House's petition that he proclaim a fast to seek divine guidance in this dark hour. Such an observance would only "give an opportunity for Sedition to flow from the Pulpits," he explained to Dartmouth. Before the General Court could transact any essential business, Gage adjourned it to meet at Salem in ten days.[51]

Many Bostonians thought it fitting that the "damn'd arch traitor" Hutchinson sailed from Boston on 1 June, the very day when British warships closed that port to all trade. Before embarking, the displaced governor received the customary formal farewell addresses from only the episcopal clergy of Boston and neighboring towns, two dozen members of the provincial bar, and a collection of 123 men described as "Merchants and Traders of the Town of Boston, and Others." Some Massachusetts Whigs were dismayed at this tribute to Hutchinson by a sizable body of reputed merchants and traders who lamented the "Loss of so good a Governor." But this address carried no weight in Boston where the majority of signers were known to be men of little wealth and prestige. Samuel Adams correctly commented, "I verily believe I could point out half a score of Gentlemen in Town able to purchase the whole of them." On any Sunday, Cooper could have found in his congregation six firm Whigs with this financial capacity. Yet he must have had mixed feelings as he saw eleven of his parishioners on the list of addressors. The main danger of the address lay rather in the effect it might have on the attitude of other colonies toward Boston's plight and on the mother country's understanding of the strength of the resistance movement.[52]

Yet the merchants' and traders' address to Hutchinson did serve the Whig cause in a subtle way. It provided an opportunity for Samuel Adams, Charles Chauncy, and other patriots to rail against the mercenary merchants of both England and America who displayed a "readiness to become slaves themselves, as well as to be accessory to the slavery of others" in pursuit of "their own private separate interest." Conversely, such language also testified to the virtue of true Whig merchants who had risen above self-interest.

Of these, Hancock stood foremost. Much of his reputation throughout the American countryside had resulted from his perfect exemplification of the patriotic merchant who, despite great wealth, found public service personally more rewarding than trade. Devout, philanthropic, "a friend to righteous government," he appeared to stand ready to sacrifice everything he owned in defense of the political and religious freedom of American colonists. Even his chronically poor health, later a target of derision by political opponents, was publicly attributed in 1774 to an overexertion "against the enemies of Liberty." One admirer prayed that Hancock might be spared the fate of martyr "in the glorious cause of his country."[53]

In this wise, Boston Whigs looked for vindication not to English public opinion but to the citizenry of Massachusetts and the sister colonies. That vindication came quickly in response to the Port Bill. On 26 May courier Paul Revere returned from a trip southward with a report that "our Brethren in Rhode-Island, Connecticut, New-York and Philadelphia . . . universally declare their Resolution to stand by us to the last extremity."[54] In Virginia, the Anglican leaders of the House of Burgesses called for the first of June to be observed as an old Puritan "Day of Fasting, Humiliation, and Prayer." Thomas Jefferson long remembered that the "effect of the day, through the whole Colony, was like a shock of electricity, arousing every man, and placing him erect and solidly on his centre." A broadside from Virginia declared "that an attack, made on one of our sister colonies, to compel submission to arbitrary taxes, is an attack made on all British America, and threatens ruin to the rights of all, unless the united wisdom of the whole be applied."[55]

With the perspective of two years, Samuel Cooper in 1776 described the effects of the Boston Port Bill: "All Eyes were turned upon this Place; The Colonies saw our Distress, and the Violence and Injustice of the Hand that inflicted it; The Eye affected the

Heart; and the Severity of the British Government in this Instance effected what was before deemed by many next to impossible, Union of the Colonies."[56]

13

We Are the Frontier

Cooper did not have long to wait before learning the meaning of Pownall's warning that "the Arm of Government raised threatens more." During the first week in June, Boston received details of two additional bills being pushed through Parliament by the North government. Approved by the king on 20 May, these acts had been designed to correct the deficiencies of the provincial government that, in the opinion of Bernard and Hutchinson, made it impossible for any governor to suppress resistance to royal authority. The Massachusetts Government Act replaced the annually elected Council with one appointed by the king and serving during his pleasure. Town meetings for any purpose except elections would henceforth require permission from the governor, who also received the sole power to appoint and remove judges of the inferior courts, sheriffs, and other judicial officers. By the Administration of Justice Act, the governor, with "the advice and consent of the council," might decide in the interest of impartiality to send for trial to England or another colony anyone accused of committing a capital crime while lawfully engaged in the suppression of riots or enforcement of the revenue laws.[1]

Pownall thought the punishment too severe. "Americans will resist these measures," he told the House of Commons. But Lord North demanded of Parliament a stiffer course of action against a people who have "tarred and feathered your subjects, plundered your merchants, burnt your ships, denied all obedience to your laws and authority."[2]

Thus the mother country had decided on a policy of intimidating Boston, though in a way deemed in Whitehall to be fully legal. The harbor had been closed; political and military authority had been combined in a governor, who was to be given a council and judicial system sympathetic to the suppression of disorder and the upholding of royal authority; and orders had been issued to move an impressive array of naval and military forces to the Boston area. By late fall three thousand soldiers had arrived—one for each five inhabitants. Finally, Parliament passed a new quartering act to ensure the "lawful" stationing of these troops "where their presence may be necessary and required." All these moves rested on the assumption that Bostonians could be intimidated, that force would not have to be used, that the resistance movement had been a temporary delusion of people who could be brought to their senses by the firmness and legality of British policy. Yet neither Gage nor his ministerial masters had made contingency plans to be followed in case the policy of intimidation failed and consequently led to war.[3]

Most Whigs also feared war. But they believed their grievances to be genuine, and their ideology confronted them at every rhetorical turn with the likelihood that free men must eventually fight to preserve their liberties. The coercive acts had aligned behind Boston's Whigs those sections of the colonies most responsive to the ideological appeal, particularly in rural areas where distrust of the mercantile seaboard normally abounded. Thus it was that men like Hancock and Bowdoin found themselves taking steps that by the end of October 1774 would move Massachusetts into open rebellion, even while they hoped for an accommodation of their differences with Britain.

The new governor's attempt "to spirit up every Friend to Government" met with some initial success, as Cooper admitted to Franklin. On 8 June, 126 "merchants, traders of the town of Boston, and others" signed an address to Gage repudiating "lawless violence" and offering to pay their share of the cost of the destroyed tea and of damage done to the persons and properties of crown officials. Most signers had also been addressers of Hutchinson, but one notable addition appeared: the name of Timothy Fitch, a wealthy Brattle Street merchant. Since this was Fitch's only recorded lapse into Toryism, he seems to illustrate the momentary attraction of submission as the fastest method of reopening the port and restoring lost business. Cooper professed no surprise at such defections: "All Arts have been employed to terrify, cajole, divide, and mislead us—they have had some Effect, I wonder they have had no greater."[4]

The addressers of Hutchinson and Gage furiously opposed the Boston Committee of Correspondence's Solemn League and Covenant, which required signers to "suspend all commercial intercourse" with the mother country, to refuse to purchase or consume any English goods imported after 31 August, and "to break off all trade, commerce, and dealings whatever" with nonsigners. On this issue Tory merchants were joined by some Whigs and neutrals who insisted on the position taken by the town meeting in May that the province should not undertake a boycott of English goods until all colonies were ready to participate. Concluding that effective opposition to the coercive acts demanded an immediate nonimportation and nonconsumption pact, the committee had proceeded on its own authority. Its clerk, William Cooper, sent printed forms of the covenant for signature to all Massachusetts towns. His accompanying letter, it was charged, gave the false impression that Bostonians had generally subscribed to the covenant.[5]

Whig merchants dependent for a living on the importation of English goods responded angrily to the committee's action. They had hoped to import small stores through other ports while waiting for the organization of a universal boycott. One such importer, Brattle Streeter John Andrews, heatedly declared that he and other Whig merchants were as "well disposed in the cause of Freedom" as the committee members but "would equally oppose and detest Tyranny exercized either in England or America." That a zealous Whig such as William Palfrey, who was close to Hancock, condemned the Solemn League and Covenant reveals how far the committee had strayed from its supporting base.[6]

This issue came to a head in a two-day town meeting held in the Old South on 27–28 June. After spirited debate, a Tory motion to censure and disband the committee lost by a large majority. Many more Whigs would have supported a motion to suspend the boycott until the colonies took unified action, but Tories refused to sanction any form of resistance. The Whigs then closed ranks publicly with a resounding vote of confidence in the committee. At the same time, as if by tacit agreement, little further effort was made to bring townsmen into the Solemn League and Covenant— "that bane to harmony"—and most other towns followed the capital's example. Once more radical Whig politicians had been taught their dependence on the elite. A disgruntled Samuel Adams had wanted Massachusetts to be an example for other colonies. "For Shame!" he wrote in the *Gazette*; "Self Interested Mortals, cease to draw upon your worthy Fellow Citizens the just Resentment of Millions."[7]

Following this town meeting, Gage issued a proclamation against joining the Solemn League and Covenant, and Tories published a protest bearing 128 names, mostly addressers of Hutchinson and Gage. A second protest by eight Whig and neutral merchants spoke respectfully of the committee but warned of its "extensive Powers." Boston merchants had not come this far in their struggle for commercial freedom to commit now a patriotic but futile financial suicide while their rivals in Philadelphia and New York continued to trade at a profit. The desire of the town's mercantile Whigs for equality of sacrifice contributed to the growing expectations of a continental congress.[8]

Meanwhile at Salem, Gage found the General Court intractable. After a session of only ten days, on 17 June the governor dissolved the last legislature to meet in Massachusetts under royal authority. The House forced Secretary Flucker, Bowdoin's Tory brother-in-law, to read the proclamation of dissolution outside the locked door of the chamber, while inside the representatives debated and enacted the measures which Gage had sought to stop by sending them home, including a request for the clergy to observe the day of prayer the military governor had refused to proclaim.[9]

The Congregational preachers responded enthusiastically. As a result, on 14 July most work stopped in Massachusetts—and to a considerable extent elsewhere in New England—for the traditional Calvinist rite of distressed times, the day of fasting, humiliation, and prayer. Gage admitted that Boston kept the day as completely "as if it had been appointed by authority." Surprisingly few soldiers and sailors were seen on the nearly deserted streets. Perhaps they had taken seriously the warning of that irrepressible Tory jokester, the Reverend Dr. Mather Byles, who soberly informed some of the troops that on 14 July "forty thousand men would rise up in opposition to them with the clergy at their head."[10]

Cooper left no record of his preaching on this fast day, but we can be sure that he did not neglect his duty. Gage's subordinate in command, Lord Percy, seemed amazed at the widespread clerical support of resistance. During his first month in Boston he wrote home that "no body of men in this Province are so extremely injurious to the peace and tranquility of it as the clergy. They preach up sedition openly from their pulpits." He had heard that some country ministers denied communion to parishioners declining to sign the Solemn League and Covenant.[11] Calvinists did not expect the nobility of a corrupt and degenerate nation to understand or appreciate a people who publicly examined their sins to discover why God had permitted England to close their port, alter their charter, and fill their town once again with redcoats. Nor did Percy understand that such a people might emerge from the rite of confession with renewed confidence in the righteousness of their cause and with greater determination to continue resistance.

A preacher mouthing the formulistic language of the jeremiad did not always turn into a zealous revolutionary, as the next two years would demonstrate. Yet with few exceptions Boston's Congregational clergy sincerely preached the Whig political ideology in the religious idiom that for the majority of Americans remained meaningful and reinforcing of the personal, social, and economic forces behind resistance.[12] To no avail, the Tory of Calvinistic background vehemently denounced what he saw as a perversion of his religious tradition.

Despite his covert political activity, Cooper had no intention of employing his pulpit to precipitate an early crisis of loyalty among his parishioners. As late as November 1774, when the province was in open rebellion, he brought tears to many eyes in his congregation with a funeral sermon describing the exemplary life and deathbed piety of Thomas Gray, wealthy merchant and benefactor of the church. Gray's mercantile connections with the British army had seemingly been responsible for his recent atypical bitterness toward Whig politicians. He had joined in the Tory addresses to Hutchinson and Gage and had protested vigorously the Solemn League and Covenant. Yet his will included a bequest of £50 sterling for the pastor he loved, and "one of his last Requests was to be affectionately remembered to the Church where he had long been a Communicant."[13]

As Gray's case illustrates, one must deal with individuals, not generalities, in assessing the importance of the religious emotionalism generated against Hutchinson and now turned toward British rule altogether. But there can be little doubt that beginning at least in 1774 the common religious tradition of the majority of New Englanders provided a surrogate nationalism that helped to unify the region during the imperial crisis. No newspaper in America exceeded the *Boston Gazette* in appeals for Christian patriotism. The intermixture of piety and Whiggism in the *Gazette* became especially noticeable at the most critical stages of the resistance movement.[14]

Religion seemed to take on added fervor in Boston during the summer of 1774, in part because thousands of townsmen faced a daily struggle for survival. A warm-hearted outpouring of relief from Massachusetts and other colonies helped to feed the unemployed.[15] But a town accustomed to rely almost entirely on water transportation faced nearly insurmountable difficulties once its port had been shut down. Cooper complained to Pownall that the Boston Port Bill was being executed by the British army and navy "beyond the Rigor of the Act itself." Still, he could report that "the People endure all with an astonishing Calmness and Resolution."[16]

As a member of both governing boards of Harvard College, Cooper supported the decision not to hold the annual Commencement exercise in July 1774, "considering the present dark aspect of our public Affairs." This action avoided a public ceremony in which the governor would have been the highest-ranking dignitary. More important tasks demanded attention. With harmony restored after the heated debates over the Solemn League and Covenant, the town meeting and its numerous committees worked earnestly to meet essential needs and to encourage resistance to the coercive acts. Never had the Whig leaders stood more united or used their power more effectively. Demoralized and leaderless, Boston Tories had either to acquiesce in Whig control or to stake their future on the unlikely prospects of Gage's being able to govern the province by force.[17]

Gage enjoyed little success in carrying out the provisions of the Massachusetts Government Act. A variety of harassments made it nearly impossible to convene the Council. The Boston town meeting remained alive through repeated adjournments to avoid the requirement of obtaining the governor's permission before a warrant could be issued for a new meeting. By the beginning of September the judicial system of Massachusetts had largely ceased to function. Gage had to admit that "Civil Government is near its End."[18] After three months in Massachusetts, this general acknowledged the truth that Bernard and Hutchinson had never admitted: that resistance to British authority came not from the "Boston Rabble but the Freeholders and Farmers of the Country." He concentrated his army in Boston to provide a haven for loyal officials and to await the hostilities he now believed inevitable. "The first Stroke will decide a great deal," he warned Dartmouth.[19]

Their occasional rhetorical flourishes notwithstanding, Boston Whigs did not want war. They aimed at forcing Britain to adopt policies consonant with the continued development of economic and political freedom in her populous American colonies. Accordingly, they looked to the intercolonial congress, scheduled to open in Philadelphia early in September, as the best hope of victory through coercion short of war. "All Eyes are turned towards that important Assembly," Cooper informed Franklin in August.[20]

The call for a congress had come from several voices, none louder than Hancock's in his March fifth *Oration*. Finally the Virginia Committee of Correspondence took the lead in arranging for a September meeting in Philadelphia. Before permitting itself to be dissolved in June, the Massachusetts House had elected five delegates: Bowdoin, Cushing, John and Samuel Adams, and Robert Treat Paine, a Taunton lawyer and representative who spent much time in Boston. Unquestionably, Hancock would have been elected had he not been suffering one of his periodic spells of poor health. A few days before the delegation conspicuously set out for Philadelphia on 10 August, Bowdoin decided not to leave his seriously ill wife. With their past records of resistance, there is no evidence that the two most prestigious Whigs had grown timid and consciously or unconsciously sought excuses to remain home while lesser men put their necks in the noose. Both were already firmly behind the policy of economic coercion that the Massachusetts delegates would press Congress to adopt.[21]

John Adams and Paine were lawyers who had opposed each other in the Boston Massacre trials. More significant now, their associations in both Boston and outlying areas of the province gave them a solid understanding of the popular support for resistance. Cushing, Speaker of the House since 1766, was a merchant who had struggled with slight success to turn a profit under the acts of trade. He typified the passion of the Boston mercantile community for a commercial victory through economic pressure on Britain while maintaining as much order and stability as possible. Though sometimes seemingly embarrassed at the tactics of the most radical Whigs, Cushing remained close to his son-in-law, John Avery, an early leader of the Sons of Liberty.[22]

Samuel Adams reached his fifty-second birthday just after Congress opened. Radical only in resistance to Britain, he had achieved a position of leadership in the Whig movement after a long apprenticeship in the realities of power in a society where economic elitism and democratic politics were intertwined. In the summer before he left for Philadelphia, some friends rebuilt his barn, repaired his house, bought him a new wardrobe, and filled his purse with money. These friends remain unidentified, but they were obviously men of substance who did not want their representative to make a shabby appearance, especially at the intercolonial conference on which Whig hopes so largely rested. Again Adams had received a reminder of his dependence on those men who found his passion for liberty useful if at times excessive. He had long thought a congress to be "of absolute Necessity," though he had pushed hard for the province to adopt unilaterally the Solemn League and Covenant as an immediate response to the Boston Port Bill. Thwarted by the unwillingness of even Whig merchants and traders to stop importing and selling British goods while their rivals in other towns continued normal trade, Adams had no course but to transfer his remarkable political skills and energies to the advocacy of a continental policy of economic coercion.[23]

While Congress was in session, Samuel Cooper wrote letters to Cushing and the two Adamses. He signed at least some of them "Amicus," to avoid disclosure in case the mail should be intercepted. The two of these letters that have been preserved begin to lift the veil of secrecy hitherto hiding the preacher's relationship with the Whig leaders. Particularly revealing is the letter to Samuel Adams written on 5 September, the day Congress opened.

Cooper furnished Adams with a rapid and optimistic review of developments since the congressional delegation had left town: the resignations from the Council, the remaining councillors taking refuge with the army, and the breakdown of the court system. In addition, he described Gage's transfer to the Castle on 1 September of the province's powder stored near Cambridge. The resulting alarm brought an estimated three thousand militiamen to that town the following morning, by which time thousands more were on the way. More resignations followed this show of force. Even Thomas Oliver, newly appointed lieutenant governor, now feared to take his seat on the Council. Cooper had learned, correctly as it proved, of Gage's advising the ministry that he must remain on the defensive until given a much superior military force. As he wrote, Cooper's optimism soared: "Gage appears, it is said, embarrassed and sunk. Lord North and his Friends, either are, or probably soon must be, in the same Scituation."

He concluded with a strong plea for Congress to shape its action in the light of these favorable occurrences in the Boston area: ". . . should they act with a Spirit and Resolution, which the Times demand, as we doubt not they will, the Blow may be decisive. . . . If any should think we move too fast here, without waiting your Result, they must soon reflect, that we are the Frontier."[24]

In admonishing Samuel Adams to be firm, spirited, and resolute, to beware of caution and prudence, Cooper did not advocate radical political or military action. Rather, he meant to impress his zealous friend with the improved prospects for success of a policy of economic coercion if begun soon and steadfastly adhered to by all colonies until Britain felt the full effects on its trade. Five weeks later he was more explicit in writing to John Adams: "The struggle, as you justly observe, between fleets and armies and commercial regulations, must be very unequal: We hope, however, the congress will carry this mode of defence as far as it will go, and endeavor to render it as early effectual as it can be, since the operation of it must necessarily be slow."[25]

Their hope of bringing Britain to her knees by measures short of war left Cooper and other Boston Whigs wholly dependent on Congress. If sufficient economic pressure could not be brought to bear on England, the mercantile community must either give up its struggle for commercial freedom and attempt to make the most of trade under a more rigorous British rule or abandon the town and join those rural patriots who had already expressed a readiness to fight. The "country people," explained John Andrews, are "vastly more vigilant and spirited than the town." Cooper pointed out that when the "people" rushed to Cambridge on 2 September, ready to march on Boston, "the Select men and Committee of Correspondence for this Town went from hence to confer with them, and prevent Things from coming to Extremities." But in either case, acquiescence or war, Boston's trade would suffer heavy blows. "Therefore, Gentlemen [of Congress], wrote "A Distressed Bostonian" in the *Evening-Post*, "our eyes are unto you, and, under God, we expect deliverance from your joint counsels and wise determination."[26]

"The People say their all is at Stake; they act only on the Defensive: Should they allow the new Regulations to take place, Property and Life are at the Mercy of Men incensed against them; and they should soon be incapable of making any opposition even a Commercial one."[27] Cooper wrote these words to Franklin on 9 September, the day when a convention of Suffolk County adopted nineteen resolutions that provided a platform for a united Whig stand. One of nine similar county meetings, the Suffolk convention brought together representatives of the towns forming the county in which Boston was situated. Joseph Warren, more and more the best Whig tactician, skillfully harmonized differences of opinion and interests between Boston and the outlying towns. The result was unanimous agreement on the Suffolk Resolves, which called for the county to prepare for a defensive war and even be ready to take offensive action in response to further provocation from Britain.[28] Paul Revere rode posthaste to Philadelphia with the Resolves, and Congress endorsed them unanimously. Once so committed, Congress proceeded to meet handsomely the major expectations of Boston Whigs. Few delegates failed to accept the necessity of a declaration of economic war against Britain to add muscle to whatever petition for a redress of grievances they might draft. After compromising questions of the self-interest of individual colonies, Congress adopted a plan of economic coercion, in the drafting and passage of which Cushing had taken a major part.[29]

By the terms of the Association, on 1 December all imports would cease from Great Britain and Ireland. No tea or slaves would be imported from any source. The ban also applied to the main imports from the English West Indies and the wine islands of Europe. Beginning on 10 September 1775, all exports to Great Britain, Ireland, or the West Indies, "except rice to Europe," would stop. Most significant of all, the Association was not to be voluntary; it included enforcement provisions applying to everyone involved in trade. On the positive side, this pervasive economic plan called for the encouragement of American manufactures, agriculture, and stock raising, and it implied that price controls must be established "so that no undue advantage be taken of a future scarcity of goods." In a genuinely revolutionary step, the fifty-three delegates who signed the Association on 20 October solemnly bound themselves and their constituents to adhere to this agreement until all the objectionable acts had been repealed.[30]

Congress also issued an address to the people of Great Britain, a memorial to colonists justifying the actions of Congress, an address to the inhabitants of Quebec, and a petition to the king. This amazingly productive session of seven weeks was motivated throughout by the plight of Boston. In more explicit resolutions than those endorsing the Suffolk Resolves, Congress approved in October the opposition of the people of Massachusetts to the coercive acts and declared that if an attempt be made to execute these acts by force, "all America ought to support them in their opposition." Congress also gave its blessing to "a suspension of the administration of Justice" in Massachusetts and recommended that should it prove necessary for Whigs to evacuate Boston, other colonies ought to "contribute towards recompensing them for the injury they may thereby sustain." At the same time, Congress called on both Gage and the Bostonians to avoid provocative acts. American resistance should be firm but defensive while there remained any hope of achieving a reconciliation with the mother country on terms acceptable to the colonies.[31]

The notable successes of the Massachusetts delegates had been achieved under considerable pressure. They had felt the necessity of living down New England's reputation for religious fanaticism. They had faced penetrating questions concerning the adherence of Boston merchants, particularly John Hancock, to earlier nonimportation agreements. They had been pursued to Philadelphia by a party of Baptist leaders, headed by the persistent Isaac Backus, who hoped to enlist the support of Congress in their fight to lift the restrictions that the Congregational establishment of Massachusetts placed on their sect. Still, in the opinion of one delegate—likely Paine—a spirit of "almost universal Unanimity" had animated Congress.[32]

All but Paine made a triumphal return to Boston early in the evening of 9 November. For the remainder of that evening the church bells pealed a welcome. Loudest of all was Hancock's huge bell, which had finally arrived and had been installed in the Brattle Street Church tower two weeks before. The resounding metallic chorus proclaimed the hope of Boston Whigs as it was expressed a few days later by one of Cooper's parishioners, Nathaniel Appleton, a small·merchant or trader and an active member of the Boston Committee of Correspondence: "It is the universal voice of this people, that they will sacredly observe the injunctions and recommendations of the grand congress."[33]

The delegates returned to a province in open rebellion. Transforming itself into the Provincial Congress, the legislature had elected Hancock its president and assumed most of the powers of a sovereign government, though ostensibly only in an advisory capacity. Gage informed the ministry that the end had been reached: Britain must either surrender to colonial demands or fight with sufficient force to overwhelm the rebels quickly.[34]

Whatever his inner fears, Cooper remained outwardly calm and confident. He sincerely hoped that the firm stand of Americans would eventually bring conciliatory gestures from the mother country. In November a Harvard student heard Dr. Cooper in a sermon mention "that he was well informed the minds of people were more favourable towards us on the other side the Atlantic." This hopeful report had come from Franklin.[35] Cooper as well as Gage now realized that colonial intransigence left the issue of war or reconciliation up to the ministry. The Boston preacher was not the only Whig who nursed some lingering hopes that Britain's libertarian soul would finally master her lust for imperial power. Still he and his colleagues in resistance understood the stakes of the struggle they had begun. They did not need the reminder given them in September 1774 by a newspaper letter that urged the redcoats, once the war began, immediately to plunder and put to the sword the estates of the "authors" of the province's miseries, among them the two Coopers, Chauncy, Bowdoin, Hancock, Cushing, Samuel Adams, and the publishers of the *Gazette* and the *Spy*.[36]

The burden of responsibility for the consequences of a war lay heavily on the consciousness of the Whig leaders in the five months preceding the outbreak of hostilities in April 1775. They cooperated with Gage "to secure the Peace and good order of the Town."[37] They sent their brilliant young advocate, Josiah Quincy, Jr., to England to gather intelligence. Racked with tuberculosis, Quincy sacrificed his life for a mission that ended in frustration; he died at the moment he stepped on American soil again, one week after the first shot of the war.[38] Franklin returned to America two weeks after Quincy. During the past winter he had engaged in fruitless and exasperating secret negotiations with the ministry.[39] As Quincy and Franklin left London, another Bostonian arrived. Hancock had sent William Palfrey on a ship to Charleston and thence to England. For two months Palfrey renewed friendships with Wilkes and with English merchants who had served the Hancock firm. But neither did he discover any reason to think that the present government might back down.[40]

Most distressing to Quincy, Franklin, and Palfrey had been the deafness of the ministry to all bids for conciliation, even by members of Parliament. The secret orders sent to Gage reveal that as early as January 1775 the ministry had decided to resort to war if necessary to force recognition of parliamentary supremacy by the colonies. But Massachusetts would have to wait until April to be certain that the appeals of the Continental Congress had been rejected.[41]

During the fall of 1774 and the following winter, most Boston Whigs remained quiet but resolute. A few emulated the timid and hesitant John Rowe, who seemed to take unusual pleasure in socializing with the top military and naval officers on occasions, such as the queen's birthday, when he could evidence his personal loyalty to the throne. More typical was the grand display of solidarity by all classes supporting resistance in October at the funeral of William Molineux, who had been the most important link between the Whig elite and the town's laboring men. A "Great Concourse of People" turned out to see his remains laid in the grave by, among other pallbearers, four of Boston's wealthiest men.[42]

At the end of November the Boston Congregational pastors voted not to read Gage's thanksgiving proclamation. Instead, they joined the country clergy in observing 15 December, set by the Provincial Congress as a day of humiliation, prayer, and thanksgiving that "God may be pleased to continue to us the blessings we enjoy, and remove the tokens of his displeasure, by causing harmony and union to be restored between Great Britain and these colonies." The jeremiad had never worked better. Congregation after congregation heard its minister review the scriptural basis for Whig ideology; clothe the Continental Congress with righteousness; deplore the establishment of Catholicism in Quebec by recent parliamentary act; and detail a religious justification for a war of last resort in defense of spiritual and civil liberty, even against the parent state. These "Presbyterian priests are the most dangerous of all beings," commented General Frederick Haldimand, then second in command to Gage. Unwilling to recognize the authority of the Provincial Congress, Boston's Anglican clergy declined to observe the fast of 15 December, thus accenting the connection between episcopacy and loyalty.[43]

The Provincial Congress had appealed for support of the resolutions of the Continental Congress, especially the Association. To carry out the Association, towns were urged to create at once committees of inspection charged to prevent all further imports of proscribed goods and to enforce, beginning on 10 October 1775, an absolute prohibition on the sale or purchase of such imports. In granting a grace period of nine months in which to sell present stocks of English goods the Provincial Congress made a unifying concession to the mercantile sections of the colony. With its port closed, Boston had little immediate need for machinery to enforce the Association; nevertheless, the town meeting promptly approved the appointment of a sixty-three-member committee of inspection, one quarter of whom attended Cooper's church. This committee represented the entire network of commercial, familial, and social relationships forming the structure of the Whig movement in Boston. In most American ports the terms of the Association received strict attention. The first united attempt to win concessions from Britain by coercion, the Association demonstrated the reality behind the oft-repeated slogan that Boston suffered in the common cause of all America.[44]

For many years to come Boston patriots would look back on the glorious period of 1775–1776, when, in their view, a widespread American love of freedom had motivated the creation of a new nation in which Christian patriotism temporarily overcame man's innate selfishness. Above all, the solidarity of Massachusetts towns, both agricultural and commercial, in the face of British military power convinced Boston Whigs that they fought in the cause of human freedom rather than self-interest. To the first entreaties of the Boston Committee of Correspondence the majority of towns had responded in chorus, denying Parliament's right to tax the colonies and Hutchinson's dogma of parliamentary supremacy. With the concentration of British troops in Boston and the organization of the first Provincial Congress, the resistance movement had become truly provincial. Now throughout the winter and spring, in town after town, militia companies drilled, local Whigs dominated the town meetings, and preachers justified rebellion.[45]

No one has yet provided a complete explanation of the "Spirit of '76" which began to manifest itself throughout Massachusetts late in 1774. The shared political beliefs, the development of a consciousness of political power through participation in town meeting and assembly, the common heritage of Calvinistic theology and congregational polity, the psychological reactions of a colonial people toward their imperial master, and the economic distress in rural areas fully as grievous (if less articulated) as the restrictions on commerce: these themes must all be included in any analysis.[46]

But any such analysis must give due weight to the leadership and example of Boston. The struggle since 1760 against what the merchants considered to be an unfair regulation of their trade in favor of rival interests had called forth a score of effective politicians, spokesmen, and opinion leaders. While defending Boston, these men—Otis, Hancock, Bowdoin, the Adamses, the Coopers, Cushing, Chauncy, Warren, Quincy, Young, and more—had encouraged the remainder of the province, and to a major extent the other twelve colonies, to satisfy a long-felt hunger for self-determination. The process reached culmination when leadership was assumed by the Provincial and Continental congresses and Boston's struggle was thus enlarged into a national battle for American rights.

Preparation for war, not further debate, was the order of the day when the second Provincial Congress opened at Cambridge on 1 February. The unanimous election of Hancock as president evidenced the resolute mood of the delegates. Gage called the actions of Congress "Rebellious," and Admiral Samuel Graves wanted to burn Boston in retaliation; but Gage restrained him and awaited the ministry's decision. The strength of his army had peaked at approximately thirty-five hundred men in December— still too small, he believed, to subdue the entire province.[47]

The winter of 1774–1775 alternated between bitter and unseasonably mild weather. Crowded into hastily prepared barracks, often idle distilleries, the British enlisted soldiers frequently deserted despite the certainty of being shot if caught. Dozens died of various contagions and were buried "at the bottom of the common." Many sought escape in Boston's cheap liquor, which made it possible for a man to get drunk "for a Copper or two."[48]

Gage's officers developed a passionate dislike of Boston Whigs, a hostility that climaxed late one evening in January in a "general battle" between the Boston night watch and a party of officers leaving a tavern. Both sides suffered wounds before sober officers intervened.[49] In this atmosphere, violence was feared if the Whigs attempted to hold their annual commemoration of the Boston Massacre. Nonetheless, Joseph Warren agreed to give the oration. Some forty British officers crowded their way into the Old South Church to hear the orator proclaim that "the American beholds the Briton as the russian, ready *first* to take away his property, and *next* what is dearer to every virtuous man, the liberty of his country."

Emitting only a few hisses, the British officers "behaved tollerably well." But afterwards they voiced some objections to the customary votes appointing committees to thank the orator, publish the oration, and select an orator for the coming year. Someone mistook an officer's cry of "Oh! Fie!" for "Fire!" And at that moment drums and fifes could be heard as a regiment of redcoats passed the Old South on its way back from drilling. An anxious minute or two ensued while hundreds fled to avoid what they imagined to be either a burning building or the mass arrest of Whigs by troops now surrounding the church. Refusing to panic, the leaders stood their ground, restored order, and concluded the meeting with dignity.[50]

Warren's *Oration* was rushed through the press and offered for sale on 15 March. That day, Dr. Thomas Bolton delivered an oration at a mock town meeting staged by royal officers. Its significance was manifold. Bolton (or Boulton), a Tory who had practiced medicine at Salem before joining the British army, did what no one had ventured since John Mein. From the balcony of the British Coffee House in the heart of Boston, he launched a vile personal attack on the prominent men of the resistance movement whom he deemed most vulnerable. It is likely that Bolton's *Oration* was published by James Rivington in New York, for no Boston printer, despite the presence of the army, would have dared so to provoke the Sons of Liberty. This mock oration offered no solace to neutrals or moderate Whigs. By picturing "the absurdity of Rowe," who stupidly attempted to fraternize with the top British officers after he had invented the "new method of making Tea," Bolton drew a sharp line between loyalty and rebellion that left no middle ground for those like Rowe still hoping to find a compromise solution.[51]

Reserving his longest blast for Cooper, Bolton stripped off the preacher's gown of clerical immunity and held him up to public view as being hand in glove with the Whig chiefs, a hypocrite who prostituted his religion for political gain. Bolton advised the Doctor to "make sermons against fornication" and to "enforce the seventh command." Apparently Cooper's reputation as a ladies' man had grown too tempting for Tories to ignore. More puzzling was the advice to "give curtain lectures against stealing." This might be presumed to refer only to smuggling and the destruction of the East India Company's tea were it not for the annotation by an eighteenth-century hand in a copy of the *Oration* now in the John Carter Brown Library: "Dr. Cooper's wife is a Noted Thief." So little is known of Judith Bulfinch Cooper that it is impossible to dismiss this comment as only another Tory attempt at defamation of Whig character. Certainly the extant fragments of her husband's diary give no hint of any such problem. Yet Bolton urged the preacher to "Reform the Rebel, Thief and W[hore]," and John Andrews, a Brattle Street parishioner, admitted that this *Oration* exposed the "Domestic troubles of some very worthy characters among us," though "with so false a gloss."[52]

Thursday, 16 March, had been proclaimed by the Provincial Congress as the day for the customary spring fast. Though the

Anglican clergy refused to keep a fast not appointed by the governor, in Boston "all the Shops were shut up, and all business suspended."[53] On this day Cooper preached an old fast sermon he had first delivered during the disastrous smallpox epidemic of 1752. He had adapted it to the French war in 1755 and had repeated it again in 1769 following the first occupation by British soldiers. Now he found the same sermon suitable for another threatening hour of Boston's history. The text contained his entire message: "O Israel, trust thou in the Lord: he is their help and their shield" (Ps. 115:9).[54]

It may have been easier for Bostonians to trust in the Lord after reading *Calculations on American Population*, published a few weeks before by Edward Wigglesworth, the divinity professor at Harvard College. He calculated that the American population would continue to double every twenty-five years, thus surpassing England's in half a century and reaching the astonishing figure of more than one billion by the end of the twentieth century. Obviously Parliament could not for long continue to suppress a people increasing at a rate unequalled "since the patriarchal ages."[55] By March 1775 Bostonians were also reading the latest chapter of *The first Book of the American Chronicles of the Times*, a scriptural parody in which the men of Boston refused to sell their "birthright for a dish of Tea."[56] In April appeared *The Group*, a metrical satire on the Mandamus Council written by Mercy Otis Warren, sister of James Otis and wife of James Warren, the leading Whig of Plymouth.[57] By contrast the collected edition of John Mein's *Sagittarius's Letters* also circulated in Boston at this time. Written the year before to a London newspaper, these letters denigrating the characters of the Boston "Saints" appeared in a volume "Humbly Inscribed To the very Loyal and truly Pious Doctor Samuel Cooper, Pastor of the Congregational Church in Brattle Street."[58]

In literature, then, as well as in politics, the Whig cause by April 1775 had matured to the point where all risks could be consciously accepted in a military confrontation with the ministry. At the beginning of the month Cooper wrote to Franklin, "The Union and Firmness of this and the other Colonies have rather grown than diminished; and they seem prepared for all Events."[59]

The Provincial Congress reconvened at Concord on 22 March and moved quickly to complete the organization of a Massachusetts army that would be Cromwellian, at least on paper. Gage's new orders from England, though decided on in late January, had not been dispatched until the middle of March. By the time these orders reached him on 14 April, Massachusetts Whigs had already received various reports of Parliament's refusal to consider the appeal of the Continental Congress and of its overwhelming support for the ministry's decision to use coercion in America.[60] According to Gage, the rebel chiefs had fled from his clutches before his new orders arrived:

> . . . on the arrival of two vessels at Marblehead, on the 8th of April, 1775, an unusual hurry and commotion was perceived among the disaffected. It being on a Sunday morning [the next day, 9 April], Doctor Cooper, a notorious rebel, was officiating in his meeting-house, and on notice given him, pretended sudden sickness, went home and sent to another clergyman to do his duty in the evening [afternoon service]. He with every other chief of the faction left Boston before night, and never returned to it. The cause, at the time unknown, was discovered on the 14th of said month, when a vessel arrived with government despatches, which contained directions to seize the persons of certain notorious rebels. It was too late. They had received timely notice of their danger, and were fled.[61]

This account lacks precision in details that can be checked. Adams and Hancock were living in Lexington during the session of the Provincial Congress at nearby Concord. From there James Warren wrote on 7 April, "The Inhabitants of Boston are on the move. H[ancock] and A[dams] go no more into that Garrison, the female Connections of the first come out early this morning and measures are taken relative to those of the last." Joseph Warren was also at Concord, but he returned to the capital after Congress adjourned. Bowdoin lay on a sickbed in his Boston mansion.[62]

Gage's report concerning Cooper appears no closer to the truth. According to the preacher's diary, he had left Boston by Monday, 10 April, but only for a short rest: "The Troubles in Boston increasing and having received Several Menaces and Insults, particularly at Mrs. Davis having a scurrilous Song offered me by an Officer, I left Boston, and came with my Wife to Mr. Savages at Weston, designing to ride in the country for the Recruiting my Health; and to return to Boston where I left my dear Child, all my Plate, Books and Furniture."[63]

The town of Weston, where his friend Samuel P. Savage lived, lay about twelve miles due west of Boston. During the next four days Cooper visited Roxbury and Milton to the south and returned on Friday to Weston, with a stop in Waltham. He rode for his health and doubtless took the political pulse of those he met on this segment of Boston's periphery. Saturday he and Mrs. Cooper traveled north to Lexington, where they dined with John Hancock's Aunt Lydia at the parsonage of the Reverend Mr. Jonas Clark. Here, so Cooper recorded in his diary, he "found by accounts from England that Administration were determined on coercive Measures." On Sunday he preached at nearby Sudbury in a three-way exchange of pulpits that provided a preacher for the Brattle Street Church. Whether by now he believed himself a marked man is uncertain; but on Monday his wife went to Boston as if to arrange for a longer absence. She returned to Weston that evening without their daughter Nabby (Abigail), who would remain in town with the two Negro servants to look after the house and personal property as long as possible. At twenty, Nabby was an adult, but her father naturally feared for the safety of his only surviving child.[64]

Dartmouth's secret orders left little doubt in Gage's mind that he was now expected to make a show of force with the troops at his command. Some reinforcements were on the way, but the ministry had no plans to raise the twenty thousand men Gage had thought necessary to subdue New England. As a start, Dartmouth advised him to arrest the leaders of the Provincial Congress, though questions of tactics were left to the general's discretion. That the pious Lord Dartmouth, noted friend of the colonies, should draft the military orders that began the War for Independence, constitutes one of the supreme ironies of American history.[65]

With the Provincial Congress adjourned on 15 April, Gage decided for the moment not to arrest its leaders. Instead, on the night of 18 April he sent more than seven hundred grenadiers and light infantry to destroy the military stores hidden by the rebels in Concord. Shortly after dawn the next morning, the first shots were exchanged on Lexington Green. The British column pressed on to Concord and attempted to carry out its mission. By now hundreds of militia and minutemen moved toward that town in answer to the alarm spread throughout the countryside by couriers, musketfire, and church bells. Sleeping at Weston, Cooper was awakened at three o'clock in the morning to hear the news. He and his wife dressed and rode off through the dark to confer with brother William, who had also left Boston and had taken lodgings in or near Weston.[66]

Any doubt that Americans could stand and face British regulars ended with an attack on the redcoats guarding the North Bridge at Concord. The column had to fight its way back to Lexington under steady fire. There it was momentarily saved by the arrival of a larger relief party under Lord Percy. Both sides expressed amazement at the zeal with which some colonials threw themselves against the redcoats. English officers wrote home of the "spirit of enthusiasm" and the rage "of a true Cromwellian" they had encountered.[67] Massachusetts men recounted instances of heroism. These Cooper relished vicariously. He rejoiced in his diary over a lad of sixteen who borrowed an antiquated musket and rushed out to kill a redcoat, and over a physician who thrust his bayonet through a British grenadier and escaped to tell the tale.[68] A decade of resistance, both rhetorical and conspiratorial, had prepared this minister of the gospel to accept war against the mother country as a regrettable necessity.

14

O People Saved
of the Lord

*I*n the view of Cooper and other Boston Whigs, the British action of 19 April had begun a civil war, not a rebellion. After six years of bloodshed they would boast with Tom Paine of having accomplished the "greatest and completest revolution the world ever knew." But in April 1775 they took pride in their long-suffering and patience in the face of repeated British provocations. Despite contradictory evidence on who fired the first shot at Lexington, it was at once fixed as an article of Whig faith that the redcoats, as agents of "ministerial Vengeance," had wantonly slaughtered "loyal and dutiful Subjects" who refused to abandon their rights and submit to slavery. Once hostilities commenced, the war itself became a transforming experience that confirmed the ideology of resistance, justified all countermeasures, and transferred to the emerging nation-state a legitimacy and sacredness hitherto reserved for divinely anointed monarchs.[1]

For Cooper personally, the war proved a transforming experience. Fifty when the shooting started, he had begun to show the physical marks of recurrent spells of poor health and increasing nervous tension. But the war brought an exhilarating freedom from the painful necessity of public neutrality on resistance to Britain. For the remaining eight years of his life he obviously relished his ministerial role of high priest to the new Israel whose spiritual capital was Boston. And the years of fighting would present even more opportunities for the clandestine political ventures that had so animated his existence in the past. Yet like most exiled Bostonians in the last week of April 1775, his immediate concern had to be the question of how to survive while Boston underwent a siege.

Gage decided against marching his men out of Boston again until reinforcements arrived. This delay presented the Massachusetts Committee of Safety the opportunity of ringing the town with a provincial army enlisted for the remainder of 1775. With the troops contributed by other New England colonies, the loosely organized besiegers at times outnumbered Gage's army nearly three to one. Discouraged by his situation, the general half-heartedly set about improving Boston's defenses.[2]

Cooper had no way of knowing when, if ever, he would stand again in the Brattle Street pulpit. Nor could he be certain that his daughter would be permitted to join the family in exile. After lengthy negotiations, Gage agreed that, when all citizens had surrendered their arms, Bostonians desiring to leave might do so and take their "effects." When he saw that the majority planned to leave, the general then stated that "effects" meant only whatever necessities could be easily removed in a single trip. Nevertheless, the exodus proceeded so rapidly that nearly half had left by the first week in May and another quarter sought permission to follow.[3]

Abigail (Nabby) Cooper received a pass to leave Boston on 30 April, and was with her parents at Weston that evening. She left their house in the care of the two servants, who chose to remain even though Cooper had offered to provide for them in the country. Four days later, the family received some trunks of clothing and other necessities brought out by brother William's children. Though his furniture and library had to be abandoned, the Doctor had made certain not to be separated from his file of old sermons, the tools of his trade with which he hoped to earn a living while in exile.[4]

But he had left in Boston his letters from Franklin and Pownall, together with draft copies of his letters to them. In 1779 this entire collection was presented to George III by Benjamin Thompson, a Massachusetts loyalist then serving as undersecretary to Colonial Secretary Lord George Germain. Thompson explained in writing to the king that Cooper had entrusted the letters to David Jeffries, the town treasurer, who in turn soon fled Boston, leaving most of his possessions with a loyalist son, Dr. John Jeffries. When preparing to leave town with the army in March 1776, Dr. Jeffries discovered the correspondence and carried it with him to Halifax, and then in 1779 to London, where he "made a present of them to Mr. Thompson."[5]

Dr. Jeffries's part as described in this account seems generally correct, for after reaching London he showed the letters to Hutchinson. Later, the former governor suspected that Thompson had obtained them by another of his many intrigues rather than as a gift. Whatever the truth, Thompson, later to win scientific fame as Count Rumford, paid a remarkable tribute to the Boston preacher so often castigated by loyalists. Thompson presumed to lay at "His Majesty's feet" the correspondence of the "Reverend Doctor Cooper, . . . a Man of great weight and influence among the people, who admired him as much for his Abilities, as they respected him on account of his Holy profession, and his exemplary life and conversation."[6]

In Weston, Cooper lived within riding distance of the two headquarters of the provincial army at Cambridge and Roxbury, and even closer to Watertown where the Provincial Congress met. After 19 April he traveled almost daily to visit these locations and to confer with the military and civilian leaders. He declined the chaplaincy of the Provincial Congress because the state of his affairs prevented his regular attendance. To put his affairs in order he needed a regular preaching assignment that offered some prospect of remuneration. Early in May the Groton church invited him to supply its vacant pulpit. Though this town lay too far from the center of activity for Cooper's liking, for the next two months he was usually able to persuade nearby ministers to travel to Groton while he preached in their churches. Such were the fruits of his prestige as one of the leading men of Massachusetts, both in and out of the pulpit.[7]

At Watertown on 12 May, Cooper heard the congressional debate on whether to assume the full powers of civil government. Such a step appeared mandatory if the army was to be both provided for and held subservient to civil authority, but it was decided to refer this momentous question to the Continental Congress. While awaiting word from Philadelphia, Massachusetts Whigs observed the regular election day at the end of May by convening the newly elected Provincial Congress and as usual holding simultaneously the annual convention of the Congregational pastors. Cooper took heart to see as many clergymen in attendance as in the past. For his part, he drafted an address of the clergy to the Provincial Congress that combined an offer to supply chaplains for the army with an expression of the clergy's "entire confidence" in the leadership of Congress.[8]

Gage had received reinforcements slowly, including Major Generals William Howe, Henry Clinton, and John Burgoyne, sent to spur him to action. Following his new orders from home, on 12 June Gage issued a proclamation drafted by the jocund and grandiloquent Burgoyne. This ineffectual document declared martial law, while offering a pardon to all rebels who would lay down their arms except Samuel Adams and John Hancock, whose offenses were "of too flagitious a nature to admit of any other consideration than that of condign punishment." Burgoyne prefaced these terms with a review of how "infatuated multitudes" had been led to rebellion by "incendiaries and traitors," including those clergymen who used the name of God "to excite and justify devastation and massacre."[9]

Gage had neglected to occupy and fortify the hills overlooking Boston from Dorchester on the south and Charlestown on the north, but the New England army had not yet taken advantage of his inaction. Now at last the British generals laid plans to seize both of these strategic locations. With several thousand Whigs still living among the troops in Boston, the news spread quickly across the Charles River, where the Massachusetts Committee of Safety and the military commanders responded by deciding to fortify Bunker Hill on the Charlestown peninsula. On the night of 16 June, a detachment of about one thousand men worked feverishly under the cover of darkness to erect a small redoubt, though by some unexplained error of judgment they had been ordered to Breed's Hill, closer to Boston than the higher and more defensible Bunker Hill. With daylight, they continued to improve their earthworks under the terrifying but ineffective fire from ships of the Royal Navy. That afternoon, 17 June, General Howe blundered as badly as his enemy had done in fortifying the wrong hill. He sent twenty-three hundred of his best soldiers in a frontal attack against more than three thousand New Englanders who had taken positions in the redoubt or nearby. In a pitched battle lasting three to four hours the redcoats finally cleared the peninsula of Americans, whose disorganization and shortage of powder had prevented their inflicting a major defeat on Gage's army.[10]

A year later Cooper criticized in a sermon the weaknesses of the New England army and its generals in the Battle of Bunker Hill: "Had they been properly supported by some who were sent for that Purpose, the American War would perhaps have been closed at once."[11] Still, New Englanders appreciated that the British had paid for their victory with over one thousand casualties. The psychological costs may have been higher, for the lingering hope that American patriotic zeal would cool in the face of a charge by picked regulars had been erased from the British military mind. Less aggressive than ever, Gage satisfied himself with holding Charlestown while abandoning plans to seize Dorchester heights. The burning of Charlestown during the battle to deny Americans the cover of the town's buildings made Whigs even more eager to credit and spread any story of British atrocities.[12]

Among the 450 New England casualties had been Dr. Joseph Warren. Appointed a major general three days before, he had not yet been commissioned. Against the advice of those who thought it foolish to risk the life of such an important leader, he insisted on fighting as a volunteer at the front line. One of the last to retreat, he took a bullet in the skull as he left the redoubt. Warren's accomplishments as a physician and politician, in a lifetime of only thirty-four years, justified Cooper's public tribute to his slain parishioner: "Our loss in Numbers was small; but we lost much in a single Life."[13]

The loss of Warren placed even greater importance on the decisions made before 17 June by the Continental Congress concerning the Massachusetts government and army. When his health had improved, Hancock was added to the Massachusetts delegation to the Second Congress. He and Samuel Adams slipped away from the fighting on 19 April to join the other delegates for the slow trip to Philadelphia. News of Lexington and Concord turned their journey into a conspicuous procession, especially through New York and into Philadelphia. Congress, as scheduled, organized on 10 May under the gavel of Peyton Randolph, president of the first Congress. When Randolph returned home after two weeks, the vote for his successor was unanimous. John Adams informed his wife, "Our amiable Friend Hancock, . . . is our President."[14]

In the Congress at Philadelphia, as well as in the Provincial Congress at Watertown, the bloodshed of 19 April had silenced doubts concerning the necessity of fighting a defensive war. But in both bodies there were those who feared that steps toward political independence would close the door to reconciliation. As a result, the Continental Congress rather timidly resolved that Massachusetts should continue under its charter with the governor and lieutenant governor considered absent, their offices vacant, and the

Council nonexistent. Under these conditions, the province should elect its assembly as formerly, and the new assembly should choose a Council. Then the two houses "should exercise the powers of Government, until a Governor, of his Majesty's appointment, will consent to govern the colony according to its charter."[15]

Except for the bare outline of the official record, the momentous events of the next ten days in Philadelphia remain heavily shrouded. Congress agreed to assume control and support of the New England army, to reinforce it with companies of riflemen raised in the middle and southern colonies, and to place it under the command of George Washington, a forty-three-year-old Virginian who had held a colonel's commission in the French and Indian War.[16]

A quarter of a century later, after Washington's death had completed his transformation into a demigod, John Adams in his autobiography assigned himself the major share of credit for the Virginian's selection. By the time he wrote his autobiography, Adams believed that Hancock had harbored "an Ambition to be appointed Commander in Chief," though perhaps only to have the honor of declining. Adams acknowledged that Hancock might have had some pretensions to this compliment, because until that time his "Exertions, Sacrifices and general Merit in the Cause of his Country, had been incomparably greater than those of Colonel Washington." Yet, by describing the "mortification and resentment" he saw on Hancock's face when Washington was nominated, Adams painted his colleague's vanity in indelible colors.[17]

As it turned out, Adams provided the only account of the selection of Washington. Consequently his version has been accepted by most historians and biographers as the literal truth instead of the reflections of a retired statesman who sought to assign a single cause and time to the beginning of the gradual break between him and Hancock. Adams wrote long after it had become the fashion for Hancock's political opponents to belittle his ability, character, and contributions by comparison with those of Washington. No contemporary evidence that Hancock expected or coveted the post of commander in chief has ever come to light. Adams remembered that "Dr. Cooper told me, he [Hancock] was so offended, that Washington was appointed instead of himself, that his friends had the utmost difficulty to appease him." Cooper, of course, was in no position to have known Hancock's reaction at Philadelphia. If this remark referred to some later jealousy of Washington, it would not confirm Adams's classic account of what happened on 14 June, 1775.[18]

As far as the record shows, once the choice was made, all of the Massachusetts delegates, none more warmly than Hancock, recommended the new commanding general to the citizens of their province. In his selection, they achieved the main goal of Hancock and most Boston Whigs since the Boston Port Bill: full nationalization of resistance to Britain. Among other tributes, in 1778 Hancock presented to Samuel Cooper for baptism his new-born son, to be named John George Washington Hancock.[19]

Washington reached Watertown on Sunday, 2 July, assumed command the next day, and set about the herculean task of transforming the mass of volunteers into a regular army, while simultaneously standing in readiness for the expected attack from Boston. Cooper called at headquarters on Wednesday morning. He met the commander in chief and renewed acquaintance with General Charles Lee and Thomas Mifflin, Washington's aide. At noon the preacher dined with the generals and their staffs. In the afternoon he and some of them visited the fortifications on Prospect Hill, from which they could observe the British troops in Charlestown. Joseph Reed, Washington's secretary, had brought Cooper letters from the Adamses and Cushing.[20]

Throughout the remainder of the siege Cooper would be a frequent visitor at Washington's headquarters, where he always received the deference due one of the most influential men of the province. His moderate and conciliatory spirit lifted him above the inevitable rivalries for preference among army officers and for spoils among politicians. Enjoying the confidence of both military and political leaders, he continued to travel widely throughout eastern Massachusetts, contributing to the war effort in sermon and in conversation his buoyant faith that Americans were fighting in a righteous and just cause that must prevail.[21]

Shortly after Washington's arrival, the Committee of Safety appointed three clergymen to prepare a "fair, honest and impartial account of the late battle of Charlestown" as an antidote to "general Gage's misrepresentations." Though named first on the committee of three, Cooper turned the drafting of this document over to the Reverend Peter Thacher of Malden, a gifted young minister who had observed the battle from a distance. Cooper and the third member, the Reverend William Gordon, seem only to have edited Thacher's account and added a few partisan remarks. It was then sent to England at the end of July to become in effect the only official American report of the battle.[22]

Following the recommendation from Philadelphia, the Provincial Congress requested the towns to elect representatives for a General Court to open on 19 July. Approximately two hundred Boston voters in exile chose representatives at Concord the day before. With the avowed Tories absent, the new House took on an even more Whiggish appearance. After a day's delay and a lively division over candidates, the House selected a Council of staunch Whigs to assume the executive powers of the governor declared absent. Though little noticed today, the Council election of 1775 stands as a landmark of American Revolutionary history. For the first time in the Revolution, the authority hitherto exercised by a royal governor passed to a body responsible to the elected representatives of the people. In its initial act, the new General Court legitimized all actions of the provincial congresses.[23]

Massachusetts's resumption of its charter coincided with the first nationalistic rite of the colonies united in rebellion. The Continental Congress resolved that Thursday, 20 July, "be observed, by the inhabitants of all the English colonies on this continent, as a day of public humiliation, fasting and prayer." This attempt to fuse the Calvinistic heritage of the majority with a budding American nationalism brought a widespread response. In Massachusetts men marveled at the thought of all true patriots from Maine to Georgia being "on their knees at once, supplicating the Aid of Heaven." Like so many of his countrymen on this continental fast day, Cooper heard two sermons in a country church, for he was visiting friends in central Massachusetts.[24]

At the end of July Cooper became the interim minister of the Watertown Church, a position he held for the remaining eight months of his exile from Boston. In October he found lodgings for the family at Waltham within easy riding or even walking distance of his new charge. At Watertown he was more than ever in the center of political and military affairs. Here the General Court met, and during its sessions Cooper preached to the legislators on Sunday in the same meetinghouse in which the representatives deliberated throughout the week. Speaker James Warren and his wife, Mercy Otis Warren, joined the admirers of his pulpit eloquence. At Watertown, too, the *Boston Gazette* had resumed publication. Brother William, who had also moved to Watertown, was elected to the House in September. Quickly becoming one of the most active representatives, at the end of the month he was chosen speaker *pro tempore*. In addition he received appointments as register of probate and justice of the peace for Suffolk County.[25]

Watertown was also nearer to Gabriel Johonnot's quarters with the army at Cambridge. Though he had remarried after Judith's death, he remained close to his former parents-in-law. He had been commissioned a lieutenant colonel in Colonel John Glover's regiment of Marblehead mariners, one of the best-disciplined and most colorful units under Washington's command. While Johonnot served throughout the war, Cooper took full responsibility for the care of his grandson, Samuel Cooper Johonnot.[26]

The Continental Congress took a month's recess in August, and the Massachusetts delegates hurried home for the short recess. Cooper saw them on 17 August at Watertown, where they met for a report to the leaders of the General Court and a quick inspection of the military lines.[27]

Hancock rushed south again to Fairfield, Connecticut, where his Aunt Lydia was spending the siege. She had with her there Dorothy Quincy, who became Mrs. John Hancock on 28 August and accompanied her husband back to Philadelphia. Much at home in the lively company of her family, Cooper had watched Dolly Quincy grow to attractive womanhood ever since that Sunday in 1747 when Dr. Colman had baptized her at the Brattle Street Church. Now the war denied him the opportunity of performing the most important wedding ceremony of his career. All he could do was to send his blessings in a letter to Aunt Lydia.[28]

As the siege continued into the fall with no more than rumors of future attempts to lift it, Massachusetts Whigs reeled with shock at the news that Dr. Benjamin Church had been arrested on suspicion of corresponding secretly with Gage. Cooper likely heard, on 29 September when he was eating supper with General Ward, that a letter in code from Church to the British commander had been intercepted. A writer and politician as well as a physician, Church had delivered the March fifth oration in 1773. Since then he had stood high in Whig counsels and had been given some of the most sensitive tasks. When arrested at the end of September, he was a member of the Massachusetts House and surgeon general of Washington's army. Without additional evidence Church's guilt could not be conclusively proved, and it turned out that there was no existing statute under which he could be tried. The House, nevertheless, expelled him, thus removing his claim to legislative immunity. Still maintaining that he had acted only in the American interest, Church was held in protective custody in the Norwich, Connecticut, jail, according to the recommendation of the Continental Congress. Popular feeling against him rose to the point where he could never again hope to practice medicine in New England.[29]

In May 1776 Church appealed the harsh conditions of his confinement to the Continental Congress, which instructed the Massachusetts Council to set him at liberty under sufficient bond. Cooper protested privately to Samuel Adams that such "an unprincipled, wicked Man" should be set free. But out of regard for Church's relatives, the preacher did not want to make a public protest. Church was returned to Massachusetts, where the authorities protected him against attempts on his life for more than a year until he finally disappeared into exile under mysterious circumstances. The discovery of his duplicity raised continuing questions of loyalty and of the moral basis for true patriotism. For example, in October 1775 the General Court recommended to the Harvard Corporation and Overseers that only those "whose political Principles they can confide in" be permitted to hold positions at the college. As a member of both boards, Cooper lent his support to this requirement. A written declaration of political principles was eventually required from each tutor and professor.[30]

Gage sailed for England on 11 October, leaving General Howe in command. Four days later at Watertown, Cooper greeted Benjamin Franklin, whom he had not seen since they became regular correspondents. The Philadelphia Congress had sent Franklin and two other members to confer with Washington on the future of the Continental army. With winter approaching, the American commander saw his situation as desperate, particularly since many enlistments would expire before the first of the year. But the committee brought instructions from Congress politely suggesting that Washington either attack Boston with the troops he now had or maintain the siege throughout the winter with fewer and less well-paid men. Once on the scene, the committee saw that the army must be strengthened, not weakened. After two weeks they returned to Congress and persuaded that body to adopt measures more in line with Washington's actual needs.[31]

Cooper seemed much involved with the congressional committee's visit to the war zone and the resulting council of war. On 17 October he dined with Washington, members of the committee, and Bowdoin, whose health had temporarily improved. Two days later Cooper attended the dinner meeting of the General Court with the committee, the general officers of the army, and representatives of the other New England colonies.[32]

Then on Thursday afternoon, 26 October, Cooper called at Washington's headquarters to begin a three-day send-off for Franklin by his closest friends. Bowdoin, Professor and Mrs. Winthrop, and Cooper escorted their distinguished guest southward. Mrs. Cooper joined the party before they reached Colonel Josiah Quincy's home in Braintree (now the Wollaston section of Quincy), where they dined and spent the night. Abigail Adams, a dinner guest at Quincy's, met Franklin for the first time and formed temporarily favorable impressions of the famous natural philosopher she and her husband would come to distrust later on European diplomatic missions. The next day the party moved on to Middleborough, where Bowdoin lived in Peter Oliver's former residence. Saturday was given to fellowship, mingled with serious discussion of military and political affairs, before Franklin set out on his return journey Sunday morning.[33]

Cooper's prestige was not limited to Whig circles. General Burgoyne provided diversion for his officers by turning Faneuil Hall into a theater where they could stage plays. Their first performance came early in December when they presented *Zara*, with a special prologue written by the general himself. Washington, his generals, and Dr. Cooper received invitations sent through the lines at Roxbury under a flag of truce.[34]

The preacher's intimacy with generals and statesmen, however personally satisfying, did not ease the economic strain of being cut off from his normal source of livelihood. Though his total financial resources remain obscure, his diary reveals a daily concern for subsistence. He gratefully recorded the occasional cash contributions he received from scattered Brattle Street parishioners, a free shoeing for his horse, the gift of a pair of shoes for Nabby, a present of "two fine Chickens," a new wig, and other items of benevolence. His income from preaching was uncertain and slow. After being engaged at Watertown his financial outlook did not brighten; he merely had a more convenient and influential preaching assignment. The House of Representatives elected him its chaplain at the end of November, but he again declined because "the Doctor's Health, Situation and other Engagements, would not admit of his attending the House as a Chaplain." In writing to John Adams concerning arrangements for the reorganized army in December 1775, Speaker Warren exclaimed, "What shall be done for our good friend Doctor

Cooper? He is a staunch friend to the cause, a great sufferer, and no income to support him. Must he not be provided for in the civil list? Do devise something."[35] Numerous other Massachusetts politicians found paid civil or military positions related to the war effort. But the "Divine Politician" had to "devise" for himself.

As Abigail Adams was doing in Braintree, Mrs. Cooper tried to assist the family's finances by dabbling in the drygoods business. In January her husband ordered from New York "Goods" worth £72. These arrived in time for him to note that his wife sold twenty silk handkerchiefs on the last day of that month. Thereafter she was often away "on Business" with the Doctor's horse and chaise, while he remained at home or walked to his Watertown parish. She also sold ribbons. Perhaps she lost a sale in February by not being at home when Mrs. Washington and the wives of General Gates and aide-de-camp Mifflin made a social call on the Coopers.[36]

By the beginning of 1776 Bostonians had endured more than eight months of war. Despite the hardships of being uprooted, those Whigs who had left town suffered far less than those who remained. John Adams wanted the "Distresses of Boston painted by Dr. Cooper's Pencil," but only sporadic and inaccurate reports of conditions behind the British lines reached Watertown.[37]

Boston's civilian population had dropped to around thirty-five hundred. Of these, some twenty-five hundred were women and children mostly belonging to loyal families, for the Whig men who remained had usually sent their wives and children into the country. Some Whigs had chosen to stay in the hope of being able to guard their property. Others, like the four selectmen still in town, were denied permission to leave. Surrounded by plundering redcoats and worried Tories, and distressed by the difficulty of procuring food and fuel, the Whigs remaining in Boston faced an uncertain daily existence. Though hardly military tyrants, the British generals threw a few Whigs into jail for short terms and threatened others with similar treatment. But even those arrested usually received more verbal than physical abuse.[38]

Only three Congregational ministers continued in town throughout the siege. The Tory Mather Byles would budge for no man, even after his congregation had mostly gone. Samuel Mather and Andrew Eliot endeavored to carry on the Boston Thursday Lecture until poor attendance and their other burdens led them in December to suspend this weekly service for the first time in nearly a century and a half. After sending his family away, Eliot planned to remain only temporarily to serve his parishioners who had not yet been able to leave. When in the fall he decided to go, he was denied a pass. He accepted his fate as the will of God, and during the severe winter months gave himself unstintingly to the care of the prisoners and the sick. Though their priests had not fled, Boston's Anglican congregations were nearly as diminished as the Congregational. Dr. Henry Caner complained that the "wealthier part" of his parish had "provided for themselves by removing to England or elsewhere," leaving only a few poor parishioners to pay his salary at a time when the scarce fresh provisions brought exorbitant prices.[39]

The Congregational meetinghouses dominated Boston's skyline too much to escape the military eye for long. In September Gage ordered Timothy Newell, selectman and Brattle Street deacon, to surrender the key to Cooper's church so that a group of Scotsmen and other Presbyterians could hold services in it. On the seventeenth, and apparently for a few Sundays thereafter, a defrocked minister named Morrison, a deserter from the American army, preached Tory doctrine from the pulpit donated by Hancock. According to a Whig prisoner taken to hear the first sermon, it "reflected grossly on the ministers of the town as preachers of sedition, and on the people, saying they were ungrateful in being the destroyers and murderers of those very people who protected them from the French and Indians of Canada." Morrison became equally well known among Whigs for his skill in enriching himself through his weekday job as "searcher of those people who were permitted to leave the town."[40]

With the approach of winter the meetinghouses were put to more utilitarian uses. The Brattle Street building became a barracks after an inspection revealed that its heavy columns made it unsuitable to be used as an indoor riding ring. Instead, the pews were removed from the Old South and its floor covered with tanbark and manure so the Lighthorse Dragoons could school their mounts in cold weather. The West Church, where Mayhew had preached his radical political and religious doctrines, was converted into a barracks and its steeple taken down because it was well situated for sending messages to the American camps at Cambridge. Even Dr. Byles's Hollis Street meetinghouse housed soldiers. Only the Anglican buildings were spared from military use. In the most serious desecration of all, Howe ordered the Old North building— the church of the Mathers—razed and the wood given to Tories for fuel. Some smaller properties were also officially appropriated under the military doctrine that "the King must have wood."[41]

Benjamin Franklin by Joseph Siffred Duplessis

Courtesy of the New York Public Library

Elizabeth Bowdoin Temple
by John S. Copley
*Courtesy
of Dr. Irving Levitt*

John Temple
by John S. Copley
*Courtesy
of Dr. Irving Levitt*

Count d'Estaing
Courtesy
of National Archives

Chevalier de La Luzerne
by Charles Willson Peale
Courtesy of Independence
National Historical Park

John Adams by Charles Willson Peale

Thomas Pownall by Daniel Gardner
(present location unknown)

A

SERMON

PREACHED BEFORE HIS EXCELLENCY

JOHN HANCOCK, Esq;

GOVERNOUR,

THE HONOURABLE THE

SENATE,

AND

HOUSE of REPRESENTATIVES

OF THE

COMMONWEALTH

OF

MASSACHUSETTS,

OCTOBER 25, 1780.

BEING THE DAY OF THE
COMMENCEMENT OF THE CONSTITUTION,
AND
INAUGURATION OF THE NEW GOVERNMENT.

BY SAMUEL COOPER, D.D.

COMMONWEALTH OF MASSACHUSETTS:
PRINTED BY T. AND J. FLEET, AND J. GILL.

Title page of Samuel Cooper's Sermon
at the inauguration of the new Massachusetts government,
1780

Since in effect uprooted Whigs and Tories had exchanged homes for the duration of the siege, the threat of retaliation checked the wholesale destruction of property in Boston. Among other examples, General Burgoyne lived in the mansion of Bowdoin, who held the lieutenant governor's home, as it were, for security. Frequently the better houses of Whigs in exile were rented to army officers. Cooper's "was let to a Capt. Cochran of the British Army upon written Engagement," likely between the officer and Dr. Bulfinch, who remained in town. Hancock's mansion was thought by Whigs to be the one building in Boston most certainly marked for destruction. On the contrary, General Clinton lived there for most of the siege and prided himself on its care. Notwithstanding the pressures of war, the British generals, if not always their men, displayed a surprisingly large measure of that respect for private property which characterized eighteenth-century English society.[42]

The Whigs, in turn, at first had little desire to inflict damage on the town to which they expected to return after the expulsion of the British army. But as the siege dragged on, there developed more willingness to attack Boston whatever the consequences. In December the Continental Congress granted Washington permission to attack Boston, regardless of the resulting destruction, a plan to which Hancock agreed, though he stood to lose the most in property. But even after passing the reenlistment crisis at the end of 1775, Washington's army still lacked the powder and artillery to launch a conventional attack on a besieged town.[43]

Washington's impatience to take the offensive was increased by discouraging news from other quarters. In October the burning of Falmouth (now Portland, Maine) by a British naval force had spread fear along the entire New England coast. Then in January word came that the two small expeditions sent to conquer Canada had been disastrously repulsed in their joint attempt to storm the fortress at Quebec during a snowstorm on the night of 30 December. Meanwhile, any hope of a change of British policy had been dashed with the news that George III and his Parliament had called for crushing the American rebellion. Washington knew that the American cause rested on his striking a blow at Boston while he retained the advantage of numbers.[44]

Henry Knox, a Boston bookseller turned colonel of artillery, provided the spark needed by the Continental army. More than two hundred miles away at Ticonderoga the captured British fort contained a good assortment of artillery. In December and January the stout Knox directed the incredible feat of conveying to the American lines by boat and sledge fifty-nine of these pieces weighing perhaps sixty tons. Some were placed in new fortifications close enough to threaten Boston.[45]

South and east of Boston lay the Dorchester peninsula, whose hills both camps had often considered seizing and fortifying. Artillery on these heights could reach much of the town and the Castle in the harbor, but the marshy approaches and rough terrain made the job seem hardly possible. Finally Washington and his generals developed a broad plan of action to begin by fortifying in one night the two more distant Dorchester hills. As Cooper tried to sleep on the second and third nights of March, he heard the American batteries cannonade Boston for the first time since the war began. At nightfall on Monday, 4 March, Boston began to receive its heaviest artillery fire yet, while two thousand or more men with 280 wagons and carts moved through the marshes toward the hills. Unlike the similar nighttime fortifying of Breed's Hill, this action was carefully planned and meticulously prepared. At daybreak the king's army awoke to the sight of six fortified works on the two hills. If Howe cared to attack the new American position, thirty-five hundred fresh men and a considerable array of artillery awaited his assault troops.[46]

It was 5 March, the sixth anniversary of the Boston Massacre. On the morning of this day that might decide the fate of their town, many Bostonians not in the army held a town meeting in the Watertown meetinghouse. After a prayer by Cooper, the Reverend Peter Thacher delivered the annual oration "to perpetuate the Memory of the horrid Massacre." At twenty-four, this son of the deceased Whig politician Oxenbridge Thacher had already been marked as one of New England's most eloquent speakers. He concluded by contrasting the moral, political, and military decay of England with the "free and extensive empire" being formed and defended by American statesmen and generals possessed of an abundance of the qualities that once made Britons great. After hearing young Thacher, Cooper dined with his townsmen at Coolidge's Tavern, where "there appeared an affectionate regard for each other."[47]

Upon discovering that his cannon could not be elevated to fire upon the Dorchester fortifications, Howe prepared for a nighttime attack before a storm of near hurricane force foreclosed that possibility. Perhaps seeking only an excuse to escape a bloody defeat, a British council of war on the sixth decided to evacuate Boston.[48]

Before anyone outside Boston knew the enemy's intention, the province observed a fast on 7 March. Washington's general orders called for his soldiers "to pay all due reverance, and attention on that day, to the sacred duties due to the Lord of hosts." As if the war had been suspended for the fast, artillery from both sides remained quiet on the seventh. Cooper preached twice at Watertown, using for one service a fast day sermon first given during the last war with France. The language of 1758 was perfectly appropriate for 1776: "We seem now to be called to make our utmost and perhaps last Effort, to remove the Encroachments, and defend ourselves from the Oppressions of an inveterate and merciless Enemy."[49]

Through the Boston selectmen Howe sent word that in evacuating the town he would not destroy it if his forces could take their departure unmolested by the American army. Though he took precautions against a trick, Washington seemed content to let Howe escape with his army intact.[50] Boston Tories were not abandoned to Whig revenge. Given only a few hours to decide, over nine hundred chose to leave with the troops, and on 10 March boarded the five transports provided by Howe. They had room and time to take along only their compact valuables and sufficient sea stores for the voyage to Halifax. The Whigs in town lived through ten days of terror as they guarded against plundering and fire during the frantic preparations for evacuation. After several delays and elaborate precautions against a rearguard attack, the troops embarked on 17 March and their transports anchored in the harbor.[51]

Boston's deliverance came on a Sunday. Six days before, Cooper had conferred with Generals Gates and Washington concerning "the Manner of our taking Possession of Boston should the Enemy leave it." The commander in chief feared that the British had "laid several Schemes" in the town they were evacuating for infecting the Continental army with smallpox. On Sunday morning after the fleet had gone to its anchorage, the selectmen rode through the lines at Roxbury to inform the commander. Washington greeted them warmly and sent them to Watertown "to acquaint the Council of this happy event," while one thousand continentals, all recovered from smallpox, marched into the liberated town. At Watertown following the afternoon service, Cooper met his deacon, the Boston selectman Timothy Newell, who brought both wonderful and discouraging news which the minister recorded in his diary: "He gave us an Account from Boston that the British Army had left it, of the great Plunder on the House Furniture and Goods of the Inhabitants; and of my own in particular."[52]

General Washington made his entry into Boston on Monday and went at once to the Hancock mansion to ascertain its condition. Finding the interior and contents in good order, he posted two sentries as an appropriate guard for the home of the president of the Continental Congress. Hancock's other Boston properties had not fared as well, leaving him with less incentive than ever to rebuild his uncle's commercial empire. In an act of symbolic spite, someone had chipped Hancock's name from the cornerstone of the Brattle Street Church.[53] Generally, though, except for the consumption of numerous small wooden buildings and fences for fuel, the town was less damaged than had been feared.

Mrs. Cooper and Nabby went to Boston on Tuesday with food for their relatives and servants. They found, as reported by Newell, most of the furniture and household equipment missing from their house. Though in the meantime his wife and daughter made several trips, for some reason the Doctor did not return to town until a week later. Even then, he was shocked at the "melancholy Scene" of "many Houses pulled down by the British Soldiery, the shops all shut. Marks of Rapine and Plunder every where."[54]

Cooper petitioned the General Court for permission "to supply my desolated empty House with Furniture from Dwellings left by the Enemies to our Country." But before the court acted officially, the committee in charge of abandoned dwellings, on which brother William served, let him begin to take his pick of household goods. The first items came from the residence of Charles Paxton, the archenemy of Whig merchants. In the beginning only loaned, all of Paxton's sequestered furniture was sold to the preacher two months later at a favorable price, paid in the inflated Massachusetts paper currency. Their exile ended, on 6 April the family returned to their Boston home, refurbished with Tory finery.[55]

Two days before, Washington had left for New York where he expected the next British thrust. Bostonians had made the most of the two weeks after the evacuation, during which the commander remained in the area to make certain the enemy fleet sailed for another port. With all his generals Washington heard a sermon at the reopening of the Boston Thursday Lecture on 28 March. Afterwards the General Court feted the officers at a dinner which concluded with "many very proper and pertinent Toasts." It was an hour of triumph. "Joy and Gratitude," reported the *Gazette*, "sat on every Countenance and smiled in every Eye." In the afternoon the generals, Cooper, and other gentlemen attending the dinner walked to Fort Hill where they inspected and discussed Boston's defenses. Local leaders worried lest the town be left with insufficient forces to repel a surprise attack.[56]

Amid other forms of congratulations, Washington received a doctor of laws degree from Harvard, voted by the Corporation on 3 April. A day later Cooper signed the diploma, with the other fellows of the Corporation, and went to headquarters for the presentation ceremony, only to discover that the commander had already departed for New York.[57]

While the Brattle Street building underwent repairs and the scattered congregation slowly returned, union services were held at the First Church, whose sanctuary had escaped damage. Here on 7 April Cooper preached in Boston for the first time in a year. At the afternoon service he delivered an "occasional" sermon to a "large Assembly." Freed from all restrictions of the past, he confidently and clearly reviewed the events and ideas that had led to this day and infused this history with the emotions of Boston Whigs as they contemplated their triumph in the light of the price paid for the preservation of their liberties. No other short document balances so accurately the economic, political, and religious forces that had led the vast majority of Boston's elite to espouse the ideology of rebellion.[58]

By his text Cooper prophesied what proved to be fact, that Boston had seen its last redcoat: "Moreover I will appoint a place for my people Israel, and will plant them, that they may dwell in a place of their own, and move no more; neither shall the Children of Wickedness afflict them any more, as aforetime" (2 Sam. 7:10).

After a quick nod to ancient Israel and to New England's pious, liberty-loving ancestors, Cooper assigned full responsibility for the American rebellion to the ministry and its colonial underlings. "The Core of the present Controversy" had been the willingness of a legislature "three thousand Miles distant from us, unelected by us, without the Sphere of our Influence, and unknown to us," to employ the sword in support of an unconstitutional claim "to make Laws binding upon us in all Cases whatsoever, and to dispose of our Persons and Properties at their own Pleasure." Americans had been slow to resist their mother country, but Parliament's "despotic" acts and the ministry's repeated abuse of royal power had at last produced an undreamed-of union of the colonies.

Singled out to be made an example of the folly of resisting British might, Bostonians had bravely and unselfishly "referred their Cause, which they knew was a publick one, to the whole American Continent." Still, both Massachusetts and the Continental Congress acted on a "purely Defensive" plan; war had begun by act of Britain. Since 19 April Americans had fought bravely but humanely, a style of combat befitting those "contending for the Right of human Nature" and contrasting sharply with the actions of armies "employing their utmost Efforts to establish Despotism."

And now, the ideals and solidarity of the American union had found personification in a new leader. Already in April 1776, Cooper could outline much of the Washington legend that would take final shape in the nineteenth century: a young man of unusual "military Sagacity" had been saved from the massacre of General Braddock's army in order that the new American nation might benefit from his virtues: self-denial, disinterested virtue, consummate prudence, singular magnanimity, wisdom, and vigor.

Thanks to the brilliantly planned and executed occupation of Dorchester heights assisted by interpositions of divine providence, Boston had been recovered without the expected bloodshed and devastation. The British "Indignities" to the houses of God, however, were a "Disgrace to any civilized Nation: but of a Piece with their Barbarity in burning so many Towns." Yet, there was cause for weeping as well as rejoicing. "Many whose Lives have been graciously preserved are irreparably damaged in their Estates." And some familiar faces were missing, none more notable than Joseph Warren.

Finally, Cooper looked to the future:

> America is now in Pangs; Like the church represented to St. John she is in Pain to be delivered—God grant that the Birth may be glorious; and more than repay the Agonies with which it is introduced. To have our Rights as Men and Christians established upon a solid and permanent [base?] will infinitely more than compensate for all this struggle. Our burnt Towns may be rebuilt; our stagnated Commerce may soon flow again with a superior Tide, in the old, or in other Channels. . . . Boston has been so distinguished a Mark of the Rage of the Enemy, and so remarkably preserved that it seems reserved by Providence for some important Purposes, and held up this Day as a Pledg of future Security and

Happiness to all America: May God in his Providence
realize these pleasing Expectations, and render the
sublime Language addressed to his People of old, in
every Sense applicable to us: Happy art Thou, O Israel,
who is like unto Thee, O People saved of the Lord, who
is the Shield of thy Help and the Sword of thine Excellency.

God's promise to His People had not changed. He wanted for
them "a Land that should be made their own Property by the best
Title; where they should possess the Fruits of their own Industry
not at the Will of another; and should enjoy the Soil and its Produce, secure from Tyrannic oppression, and unmolested by those
that hated them." Though the "Gift of Heaven," this New World
"Land of Canaan" must be acquired and maintained at the "Price of
much Toil and Blood." Bostonians better understood the meaning
of this paradox as they tried to put their lives together again after
eleven months of siege and exile.

As Cooper preached this sermon, Joseph Warren's body lay in
the Boston State House. It had been identified and removed from its
Bunker Hill grave on Saturday. Monday afternoon, a single rite
honored the fallen hero and purged King's Chapel of its royalist
gospel. Before reinterment the casket was borne to the Chapel for a
memorial service attended by everyone who could crowd into the
official church of the royal governors. Cooper prayed, then a young
Whig orator made a spirited plea for American independence from
Great Britain.[59]

15

The Last Step

*I*n the eighteen months after the British evacuation of their town, Bostonians faced difficulties that more than ever tested Samuel Cooper's ability to preserve their confidence in the American cause. For many, the final break with the king was an emotional trauma. Factions appeared among the Whig leaders. The British renewed the war by invading New York. Meanwhile, Boston was left nearly defenseless against a possible attack from the sea, rumors of which circulated freely. Smallpox, inflation, and food shortages brought widespread suffering and misery, especially to ordinary citizens. The political awakening of rural Massachusetts was changing the balance of power in the legislature. The disposition of the property of loyalist exiles and the treatment to be accorded those supporters of the king who had not fled raised the fundamental question of allegiance to the new state. But once back in his pulpit, Cooper was ready for whatever the times might demand of him.

After being cleaned, repaired, and furnished with new pews, the Brattle Street meetinghouse opened again for Sunday services on 19 May 1776. Cooper preached to a reduced congregation. Some eighteen loyalist families had fled, either with General Howe during the evacuation or earlier by private means. Other parishioners remained temporarily in the country for fear of a food shortage in Boston or of the smallpox that was beginning to spread through the town. Some were absent on various military or political assignments, and a few had died during the siege.[1]

Of the dead, no one was so missed as Lydia Hancock, who passed away unexpectedly in April at the Connecticut home where she had been waiting out the siege. She died unattended by her beloved nephew, whom she had planned to visit soon in Philadelphia to enjoy vicariously his prestige as "President of the American Congress." A pillar of the Brattle Street Church for forty years, she was nearly as close to her pastor as to her nephew. In a final benevolence, she bequeathed her mansion on Queen Street to the church as a parsonage. When Dr. Cooper moved into it in 1778, he lived in a style befitting the importance of his leadership and the wealth of his congregation.[2]

Aunt Lydia died a few months before her nephew became the first to affix his striking signature on the engrossed copy of the Declaration of Independence, thereby tendering the final pledge of his life and fortune to the success of the American union. Despite the fame of this autograph, his importance has been diminished because historians have tended to concentrate on the inevitable personal rivalries that were beginning to develop among Boston's Whig leaders, rather than on the intensity and near unanimity of their quest for independence. Here, as on so many other points, a study from Cooper's perspective provides a valuable corrective to centrifugal accounts.

During the developing imperial crisis of the preceding decade, the men around Cooper had seldom acknowledged the possibility of independence from the mother country. Still, however uncomfortable the thought, they obviously perceived, as Bowdoin admitted in 1772, that a "foundation" had been laid for the "separation of the Colonies from Britain." Six months of civil war quashed most hopes that stubborn American military resistance would bring Britain to her senses. Private reports from Europe convinced the Boston leaders that there no longer existed a middle ground between submission and independence. In December 1775 Bowdoin and William Cooper both urged Congress to move toward independence. During January the Massachusetts legislature issued a proclamation that came near to asserting the colony's independence. The rhetorical power of Thomas Paine's *Common Sense*, published that month, intensified a conviction already reached in Massachusetts. After Howe had been forced out of Boston, the issue of independence no longer seemed in doubt among the town's leading Whigs. Four days following the evacuation, Samuel Cooper wrote to Franklin, then serving in Congress, to inquire sarcastically, "Must we return to the mild and gracious Government of Britain?" He added that *Common Sense* "is eagerly read and greatly admired here," and that the "Inability of our Enemies to subdue us by Force is more and more apparent."[3]

By April, Samuel Adams—who, contrary to the legend, had not been an early advocate of independence—was ready to take his stand. He summarized his view for the Brattle Street preacher in two terse questions: "Is not America already independent? Why then not declare it?" Cooper replied, "People here almost universally agree with you. . . . They say that . . . the Moment we determined to defend ourselves by Arms against the most injurious Violence of Britain we declared for Independence; i.e. that like any free People attacqued, we would either be totally subdued, or be at Liberty to make our own Terms."[4]

A few days later, in commenting to John Adams on the action of Congress on 6 April in throwing open American trade to all nations except England, Cooper pressed for independence as an aid to trade and the best plan for a successful end to the war: "This, they say here, would have great Effect upon the Colonies but especially on Foreigners. Their Merchants would more readily trust their Effects here, and their Governments have a clearer ground for protecting the Trade; as well as our own Merchants enter with greater Spirit into new channels of Trade, which, if you do not mean speedily to recur to the old ones, are now become absolutely necessary for the Supply of the Continent. . . . The most likely Way to bring the War to a speedy and happy Issue is to take the last Step, not with an apparent Caution and Timidity, as if we distrusted ourselves, but with an air of Confidence and unshaken Resolution."[5]

The readiness of Cooper and other New England leaders for independence was the psychological result of their having tasted first the bitter cup of war. Not all colonial Whigs could dissolve their loyalty to the crown so easily. Even among those favoring independence, in New England as in other sections, questions of the proper timing for a declaration and whether Congress or the colonial assemblies should take the lead in moving toward formal separation delayed action. As a result, the Massachusetts delegates to Congress waited restlessly for the union of minds required before an effective declaration could be issued. As Samuel Adams explained to Cooper, "We cannot make Events. Our Business is wisely to improve them."[6]

In the months before independence, Cooper's political role can be described somewhat more precisely from the evidence found in his frequent correspondence with the two Adamses in Philadelphia.

Just as he had preserved peace in his congregation during pre-Revolutionary days by maintaining a public stance of neutrality and by holding his pulpit above partisan strife, so now he seemed determined to serve as a mediating agent among the Whig leaders who were forming factions in a contest for power and patronage.

The trouble began in the Massachusetts delegation to the Second Continental Congress, perhaps in part from the strain of living together at the same boardinghouse. Resentful of the attention given in Philadelphia to Hancock, who because of illness had missed the First Congress, the Adamses uneasily watched his elevation to the presidency. Since the resolutions and proclamations of Congress were published widely in the press over the president's signature, Hancock quickly became more celebrated than ever throughout the colonies. There had never been the slightest suggestion that his election was as president pro tem, yet John Adams fumed privately when Hancock did not offer to relinquish the gavel upon the first president's return. Meanwhile, Adams convinced himself that Hancock had coveted the post of commander in chief of the Continental army and would never forgive the nomination of the Virginian by a fellow Massachusetts delegate. More important, the Adamses pushed through, over the mild opposition of Hancock and Cushing, the appointment of their friend and political ally, James Warren, as paymaster of Washington's army. Warren was happy to have the office with its salary and to see the first break in Hancock's control of army patronage in the province. In the remote atmosphere of Philadelphia it was easy to lose sight of the realities of political power in Boston. The Adamses sprinkled their letters home with strictures on pretended patriots and on the evil of voting "for any man to fill a public office, merely because he is rich." Meanwhile, Cushing and Paine, the other Massachusetts delegates, drew closer to Hancock.[7]

When the province resumed its charter government in July 1775, a rump Boston town meeting failed to elect Cushing to the House of Representatives, of which he had been speaker for many years. This move was regarded as a slap at Cushing, even though afterwards he was, as Samuel Adams put it, "kicked up Stairs" to the Council. Warren became speaker and loomed for a while as the leading political figure remaining in the province. At the end of the year, Elbridge Gerry of Marblehead, more acceptable to Warren and the Adamses, was given Cushing's place in the congressional delegation. The circumstances surrounding this change remained clouded. Cushing had expressed some interest in returning to take

up his necessary and remunerative duties as judge of probate for
Suffolk County, and the selection may have been complicated by a
protracted contest between the House and Council over their
respective authority in choosing military officers. Whatever the
details, by the beginning of 1776 Hancock, Cushing, and Paine saw
themselves opposed by a "Junto" of a few men resolved to "settle a
Test of Political Rectitude and destroy every one that will not comply with their mode of Conduct." Paine charged the speaker with
shattering the union of Whigs responsible for Boston's successful
opposition to Britain. At the same time, Hancock assured Cushing
of his support and friendship. Tories, of course, did all they could
to fan such flames of dissension among members of Congress.[8] The
emergence of these two factions had more to do with personalities
and patronage than with substantive issues such as independence or
the war effort. While they sometimes disagreed over details of im-
plementation, all Massachusetts delegates favored independence.
Cushing appeared cautious and moderate when compared with the
most zealous Whigs, and Hancock held great political power while
exercising leadership only in such areas as patronage; but both
were as firm on the main issue as their chief ally in the House,
William Cooper, who had spoken out early and passionately for
separation from Britain.[9]

   In gradually alienating himself from Hancock, Samuel Adams
limited his political future. Essentially a local politician, he proved
too old and too unsuited by temperament or talents to become a national statesman of the republic in the making. Thus his unwillingness to remain in harness with the enigmatic man who would
continue for many years to hold the key to political power in
Massachusetts weakened the home base required for Adams to exercise as large an influence as he craved in American affairs. The
younger John Adams, on the other hand, possessed the talents to
rise above local politics and would emerge as a major American
statesman. Yet ironically, his jealousy and harping criticism of
Hancock spurred an opposition that would eventually reduce his
cousin to political impotence.

   For the moment, this factionalism remained sporadic and
relatively insignificant. Of the major leaders, Bowdoin held himself
the most aloof from partisanship and retained the friendship of
both sides, though poor health curtailed his political activities.
Samuel Cooper—the pastor of Bowdoin, Hancock, and sometimes John Adams, the confidant of Samuel Adams, the preacher
best liked by James and Mercy Warren, the brother and intimate of

William Cooper, and for many years a covert Whig politician of major importance—began to find himself thrust perhaps even more than he wished into the role of "Divine Politician." His skills in human relations, with which he had built one of the foremost ministerial careers of colonial America, were to be severely taxed in his old age; but one measure of his success is the absence from his correspondence of the partisan temper that marked the letters written by the men around him.

With Cushing home and sitting in the Council, that body stiffened its resistance against efforts of the House to share the executive power formerly exercised by the royal governor. In order to raise the necessary militia units, the Council agreed for this time only to a joint election of officers. At the end of January the House chose Hancock the first major general and Warren the second. The Council then refused to accept Warren because of a technicality, which he believed had not been enforced in other cases. Here the question rested until May, when Warren withdrew. In the interval Hancock grew impatient to receive his commission. He had solicited the appointment, promising when he returned from Congress "to put the militia upon a Respectable footing." With that fondness for ostentation that so irritated John Adams, General Hancock planned to "Appear in Character"—to wear his uniform in Philadelphia, as was the practice with some other militia officers among the delegates.[10]

The Council also proved less ready than the House to move quickly in confiscating estates of loyalist exiles and in continuing the suspension of civil actions in the courts pending agreement on a permanent form of government. Likewise, the Council refused to concur in a House resolution recommending that each town advise its representatives to be elected in May on the question of instructing the Massachusetts congressional delegates to press for a declaration of independence. Disappointed with the Council's action, Cooper nevertheless emphasized to Samuel Adams that it had resulted from strategic reasoning rather than opposition to independence itself.[11]

Refusing to be blocked by a veto of the Council on a matter involving the election of its own members, the House ordered William Cooper to have printed in the newspapers a new resolution asking each town to instruct its representatives "whether that if the honorable Congress should, for the Safety of the said Colonies, declare them Independent of the Kingdom of Great-Britain, they the said inhabitants will solemnly engage with their Lives and Fortunes to Support the Congress in the Measure." By this step the House intended to turn the spring election of 1776 into a referendum of independence, but the request came too late for all towns to consider it, and the issue was blurred by a simultaneous discussion of the proper basis for representation in the legislature.[12]

For eighty-five years the Massachusetts House had represented towns rather than population or property. Each town, depending on its size, could send one or two representatives, except that Boston was permitted four. The greatest population growth had taken place in the east, leaving the larger coastal towns underrepresented. These towns now faced the unwelcome prospect of a new government being established by a General Court dominated by the less populous agrarian sections, traditionally hostile to commercial and maritime interests. The danger loomed greater since the strongest Whig leaders, who had constructed the sectional alliance against royal government, were now dead, ill, or absent in Philadelphia. Boston appeared less concerned than the towns of Essex County, north of the capital, which in April 1776 petitioned the General Court for a more equitable system of representation. In response, on 3 May the House rushed through an "Act . . . for a more equal Representation." A Council dominated by easterners readily concurred. Whether this act passed at a time when many western representatives had already gone home, or whether as the result of a legislative compromise, has never been determined. In either case, the spring election of 1776 raised to a high level of consciousness the consequences of independence: its effect on the war effort, the necessity of determining the theoretical basis of political authority in an independent province and nation, and the seemingly unavoidable scramble for patronage, individual power, and sectional dominance.[13]

Under the new law, the town meeting of 23 May elected twelve solid Whigs to the legislature and unanimously adopted instructions for its representatives that put the town unmistakingly on record in favor of independence but left the time and manner of the formal declaration as a strategic question for the national legislature to decide. Likewise, in May and June most Massachusetts towns instructed their representatives to support a declaration of independence by Congress. Though some of these decisions came too late to influence the deliberations in Philadelphia, in all their mail from home, the Massachusetts delegates read one persistent theme: Congress must act soon and when it does it can be assured of support from the colony that felt first the iron rod of

British tyranny. So persistent became the demand from Boston Whigs that Congress take the lead that both John and Samuel Adams eventually felt the need to defend the deliberate pace of that body.[14]

From their local perspective, Cooper and other Boston rebels, with their necks in the noose, saw an actual declaration as indispensable to force moderate and undecided citizens off the fence, to provide a legal basis for punishing treason to the new state, and to prosecute the war with all possible foreign assistance. Writing to Samuel Adams on 30 June, the Boston preacher queried, "ought not some Constitutions to be formed and vigorously executed, that shall render it equally hazardous and penal to act against the Rights of America, as Britain has made it to defend them?" He added, "We may deceive ourselves and greatly injure if not ruin our Cause, by relying too much on its intrinsic Goodness, and the Generosity of human Nature. Our Safety is that a vast Majority are engaged in this Cause, and that this Majority have it in their Power, to form such Alliances, and such Political Coercions as well as Encouragements as are sufficient to its own Preservation, and to secure the grand Point."[15]

By the time Adams received this letter, Congress had taken the action for which Cooper pleaded. Richard Henry Lee of Virginia introduced his famous motion for independence on 7 June, and John Adams rose to second it. On 2 July Congress approved Lee's motion and, two days later, the text of the Declaration of Independence.[16]

The post carried the Declaration to Boston on Saturday, 13 July. Cooper left no record of his preaching on Sunday, but on Monday he rushed off letters of congratulations to the Adamses. His words contained a medley of hope and anxiety: "The Declaration must give a new Spring to all our Affairs. Britain cannot exert herself more vigorously nor cruelly against us than she had done before and the Boldness and Decisiveness of the Measure may appall her, especially if it be followed with speedy and earnest Applications to foreign Powers to make a Diversion in our Favor: Some of them I am persuaded stand ready for this. Were she once embroiled with France and Spain America has Nothing to fear. If we can defend ourselves this Campaign, the Work will grow lighter by the next. We must use the Pickaxe and Spade—we must burrough in the Earth—Our soil will both defend and feed us."[17]

Independence was officially proclaimed in Boston at 1:00 P.M. on Thursday, 18 July, when the county sheriff read the Declaration from the State House balcony to the crowd below in King Street. A cacophony of guns, bells, and cheers expressed the ecstasy of the day. Inside the Council chamber, legislators, army officers, selectmen, and clergy enjoyed a "proper Collation," while outside men and boys ranged through the streets stripping royal insignia from buildings.[18]

In the morning, before this celebration, Abigail Adams heard a "very Good Sermon" at the Thursday Lecture, where she listened to Cooper repeat his election sermon of 1756, with a hastily revised conclusion incorporating the Declaration of Independence into his original theme of Moses "choosing rather to suffer Affliction with the People of God, than to enjoy the Pleasures of Sin for a Season." With only the substitution of four manuscript pages, this pragmatic preacher leaped the twenty years from the Anglo-French war, when colonials clung desperately for protection to the skirts of mother Britain, to the glorious day of independence when he could appeal to heaven the justice and righteousness of repudiating that same mother country:

> We contend only for the Rights that belong to human Nature; that all Men are entitled to, by an higher Charter, than any written one; the great Charter of Reason, and the eternal Laws of Nature's God, . . . Rights which no Man, or Body of Men can with the le[a]st Shadow of Justice demand us to renounce; Rights which it is not in our Power to resign, inasmuch as they are made by God inseperable from our Nature; so that had we, instead of claiming and insisting upon them, been so foolish and mad as to have formally renounced them, the Renunciation would have been intirely null and void—we had no Right to make it, and no Man or Body of Men could ever have a Right to receive it: Reason and Revelation both reclaim against it; They absolve us from such an unrighteous Obligation; or rather they at once shew us that it is no obligation at all; and oblige us instantly to resume what we had impiously attempted to alienate from ourselves.[19]

Hardly a religious document in origin or phraseology, the Declaration nevertheless quickly took on a sacred aura as pastors and congregations incorporated it into their system of belief and defended it with the same emotivity as divine truth. The Massachusetts Council ordered it read in all churches at the conclusion of the first afternoon service after the minister had received the official printed copy. In Boston, on 11 August, every pastor complied, including the assistant rector of the one Anglican church still open after the other royal clergy had fled. James Warren, present that afternoon at Brattle Street, observed that Cooper's reading was "attended to by the Auditory with great solemnity and satisfaction." It was a major source of strength of the Revolution in Boston that in the transfer of allegiance from royal to republican government the religious component of legitimacy and loyalty intensified rather than lessened.[20]

Little was known in Boston concerning the authorship of the Declaration. Cooper seems to have thought for a while that John Adams deserved the credit. A member of the drafting committee, Adams apparently sent his wife an early copy in his own handwriting which Cooper was permitted to read. Yet the question held little significance in 1776, for the important news was that Congress had declared independence, not that Jefferson's rhetoric had announced the action to the world.[21]

Because Hancock had presided over the Congress that adopted the Declaration, and because that ineluctable document had been issued over his signature as president, his fame reached its peak in this summer of American independence, as the newspapers attest. By contrast, John Adams wrote from Philadelphia that he had seen there "but a little of that pure flame of Patriotism" that burned in the breast of a James Warren. In another letter that he decided not to mail, he spoke of the "sordid Meanness" of the souls of his fellow delegates, one of whom—likely Hancock—"covers as much of it, as ever disgraced a mortal, under the most splendid Affectation of Generosity, Liberality, and Patriotism." If he knew the thoughts of the Adamses concerning him, Hancock remained openly unfazed. He rejoiced that he had been offered the use of the "most Airy Elegant house" in Philadelphia; that James Warren's unwillingness to leave New England with the army had opened the way for his replacement as paymaster general by William Palfrey, the trusted associate of prewar days; and that his brother, Ebenezer Hancock, had been provided for as deputy paymaster general for the New England area.[22]

In the summer of 1776, Samuel Cooper had hardly an inkling of the price yet to be exacted for the successful completion of the Revolution now begun. Since Bunker Hill, he had hoped each battle would be the last, the one that would finally bring Britain to the realization that she could neither conquer the colonies nor dictate peace terms to them. Yet, for him the Declaration of Independence had cast the die, and he was mentally prepared to see the struggle through. But he could not have fully anticipated the five years of warfare, suffering, and societal disruption that lay ahead.

Cooper responded to "the times that try men's souls" as he had to the crisis of the last French war. His soothing ministry of reassurance was in more demand than ever. In the years 1776–1778 he preached ten times in churches of the Boston area a sermon he had written in 1754 when France launched its drive for domination of North America. Entirely spiritual and containing no reference to public affairs, this sermon concluded with words of therapeutic force: "Let then our Perswasion of this most comfortable Truth, that our Times are in God's Hand, chear and refresh our Minds; and banish every inordinate Fear or Sorrow. We are not left to the Disposal of blind Chance or inexorable Fate; We are not left to our own Weakness and Folly to choose and provide for Ourselves; We are not left to the Will of our Enemies; But the Lord reigneth."[23]

During all his career the Divine Politician remained Boston's leading prophet of a deity whose goodness is so great that "if we resign Ourselves to Him, unworthy as we are, we cannot fail of becoming the Objects of his special Care." After Abigail Adams had attended the Brattle Street Church during the summer of 1776, she wrote to her husband, "I rejoice in a preacher who has some warmth, some energy, some feeling." This vitality in Cooper's ministry emanated from his whole being in these years when the former colonists fused their material and spiritual concerns into an embryonic nationalism capable of sustaining a prolonged war effort.[24]

For months after the evacuation, Cooper fretted constantly over Boston's "almost totally defenceless" condition. British shipping still used the outer harbor, Washington had left too few troops to guard against a surprise attack, and the area commander, General Artemas Ward, who was "always sick, and seldom to be seen," appeared incapable of "quick Decision" or "great activity." In his frequent letters to the Adamses, the minister pleaded that Nathanael Green or some other general "of the best Qualities be sent to this Department immediately." Little encouragement came either from Philadelphia or from Washington's headquarters in New York, though Ward soon submitted his resignation.[25] Boston's vulnerability became more frightening to Cooper after he learned of the complete failure of American endeavors to capture

Philad.ᵃ 20 July 1776

Dear Sir

My constant attention to the Business of my Department, both Day & Night prevents one the pleasing Satisfaction of duly attending to my Friends, & under these circumstances I trust I shall stand Excus'd for not writing often, they however are very near my heart, & to whom I wish every good.

I have only Time to Inclose you this morning's papers, to which Refer you for every thing stirring here. I most sincerely Congratulate you on the Success of our Arms in South Carolina, may the same Almighty Being who has so interpos'd hitherto in our favr. still protect & Defend us, & may our future Conduct be such as to see his farther Salvation.

I Beg my Respects yr. good Lady & Family, in wch. Mrs. Hancock Joins me, & to yr. Brother & Lady & Family, & indeed to all Friends.

I am in great haste, with every wish in your favr. Dr Sir

Yours very hum.

John Hancock

Revd. Dor Cooper

John Hancock to Samuel Cooper, 20 July 1776

"I can most chearfully trust the important Affairs
of America at this critical Season in such Hands"

Samuel Cooper to Benjamin Franklin, 17 September 1776

and hold Canada against British arms and to win the support of French Canadians. He urged Congress to punish any officers who had failed in their duties in that theater of war, for as long as Canada remained a base of British operations New England would never feel secure.[26]

Meanwhile, Bostonians set to work repairing and improving the fortifications of the town and harbor, which they considered sufficiently strong by June to risk an undertaking that Cooper and many others had urged since the evacuation: a joint action by militia and Continental forces to plant artillery on the islands of the outer harbor. During the night of the thirteenth, enough batteries were erected to drive from Nantasket Road the next morning a man-of-war and the eight transports it guarded. Cooper jubilantly reported the action and its results to John Adams: "We have now not a British Ship of War in any Harbor, not a British Soldier un-captivated in all N. England. It is remarkable that the Port of Boston was thus opened on the very day it was shut up two Years ago; for you remember that from 1 June 14 Days of Grace as they were called, were allowed." The "first Fruits" of opening the harbor were enjoyed at once as several privateers tied up at Boston docks with their prizes.[27]

In July, along with independence, came encouraging military news. A combined British naval and military force had failed in an attempt to take Charleston, South Carolina. Furthermore, North Carolina loyalists had been so decisively defeated by colonial militia in February that they were now unable to assist royal forces sent to the South. "Carolina has made a noble beginning," exclaimed Cooper. "May the same Success attend us in every Quarter."[28]

By now Cooper was generally aware of British plans for the campaign of 1776. The cabinet had been reorganized to move Dartmouth to a less active post and replace him with Lord George Germain as secretary of state for the colonies. Fortunately for Americans, the new secretary proved as unsuccessful in making and executing grand strategy as his predecessor had been in convincing the colonists of the ministry's good intentions. But Germain did not lack energy. He worked tirelessly to recruit and transport the more than fifty thousand soldiers, including German mercenaries, who had been authorized for the American war. One army was to proceed south from Canada along the Lake Champlain water route. Another, commanded by General Sir William Howe, would land at New York and Newport, with the assistance of naval forces under the direction of his brother, Lord Richard Howe. The two armies would crush the rebellion in New England before turning south.[29]

In keeping with their reputation at home as English Whigs friendly to America, the Howe brothers were also designated as peace commissioners with broad though vague powers to pardon and restore the lawful government, on the basis of Lord North's earlier proposals for conciliation, to political units accepting such a pardon. Long delays while the cabinet compromised disputes over their instructions prevented the peace commissioners from acting before Congress declared independence; but reports of the coming effort at reconciliation spurred the final Whig movement for formal separation.[30] Cooper had been one of the strongest advocates of negotiation with England from only a position of strength as an independent nation. His comment after the Howes reached New York was typical of his attitude: "The Court of Britain is truly magnanimous—it would delude us and the Nation with a seeming Desire of Pacification, while it makes every Effort to destroy us; and depends upon conquering America this Campaign. The military Commanders are its Peacemakers."[31]

Upon reaching American waters, Lord Howe issued a declaration explaining "his Majesty's most gracious intentions." He also dispatched friendly letters to various individuals, among them Franklin, whom he had known in England. Though Congress refused to take official notice of the peace commission, it permitted Franklin in a private capacity to answer Howe. He chided his lordship for coming "so far on so hopeless a Business" and eloquently rebuffed his pretensions of offering a realistic basis for reconciliation. It was too late to negotiate, Franklin made plain, except as independent states at war. At once Franklin sent copies of this correspondence with Howe to Cooper, who circulated it to good effect in Boston.[32]

While the Howes made awkward and fruitless peace overtures, they readied an overwhelming force for an assault against New York. Landing on 22 August, the British army drove Washington slowly and deliberately into New Jersey. After several narrow escapes from destruction, the Continental army crossed into Pennsylvania early in December, leaving the British in control of most of New Jersey as well as of New York and Long Island. That same month a force of six thousand under General Clinton easily took Newport, though General Howe postponed his other plans for New England and went into winter quarters. In the north, American forces had been concentrated at Fort Ticonderoga to make a stand against the invading army from Canada when Benedict Arnold's inspired delaying action on Lake Champlain won a postponement in that arena also.[33]

Of the five prewar newspapers, only the *Gazette* resumed publication in Boston after the siege. By fall, however, two new Whig papers were being published, and the three kept Bostonians fully informed concerning the worsening situation on the fighting fronts.[34] Nevertheless, Cooper outwardly remained confident and relaxed, predicting that France would soon make a move in America's favor and expressing complete confidence in the leadership of Congress and Washington.[35]

Boston had ready for public display in September 1776 its newly organized Independent Company, consisting of some eighty gentlemen of various ages and occupations from the first families. It became the smartest military company in New England, but the presence of such an elegant home guard, armed with weapons diverted from the Continental army, only increased the suspicion in rural areas that the capital had not contributed its share of available manpower to the Continental forces.[36]

Beyond the Independent Company, the town did all it could to organize home defense with the slim resources available. In September the population still did not exceed eight thousand—half the prewar figure—and of these, nine hundred were in military or naval service. General Gage had so thoroughly appropriated firearms that now, excluding the weapons of the Independent Company, only 197 muskets could be counted in the hands of citizens. A plan was approved by which it was hoped every adult male could be supplied with a musket and ammunition, but both were so scarce that the following May the town in desperation petitioned the General Court to arm the Boston militia. Officially, at least, Boston Whigs seemed determined to fight to the last man if the enemy ever again menaced the town.[37]

Independence and warfare notwithstanding, smallpox must be accounted the "reigning Subject" in Boston during the summer and early fall of 1776. Spreading quickly and widely, this disease became in the opinion of John Adams "the King of Terrors to America this year." Among other consequences, it helped to defeat the Continental army in Canada. By July James Warren could report that the "Small Pox prevails. . . . In Boston they have given up all thoughts of stopping it, and everybody is inoculating." A week later he noted that Boston "is now become a Great Hospital for Inoculation. . . . I can't describe the alteration and the gloomy appearance of This Town. No Business, no Busy Faces but those of the Physicians. Ruins of buildings, wharfs, etc., wherever you go, and the streets covered with grass." On 5 July alone, several hundred underwent inoculation. A firm believer in mass inoculation, Cooper labored to establish hospitals and urged stern measures for preventing the contagion from spreading through the army.[38]

By mid-September, when only six houses in Boston still flew the red smallpox flag, of the 4,988 individuals who had been inoculated, only 28 had died; whereas 29 had perished of the 304 who had contracted the disease in the natural way. Decisive and speedy medical action had spared Revolutionary Boston from a plague more devastating than British taxation.[39]

War and smallpox had virtually ended Boston's trade. According to Cooper in September, "our own Navigation is almost wholly turned into Privateering." Each prize brought in encouraged other owners to fit out their faster vessels as privateers to prey on English shipping that supplied the royal army and traded with the West Indies. In time the war would bring profitable trading opportunities for the most enterprising merchants and shipowners; but after the harbor had been closed for two years the outlying ports held the initiative in the new trade outside the empire. So Boston mercantile and shipping interests, seeking to regain their economic leadership, looked to privateering, army contracts, building and supplying the proposed American navy, and increased commercial relations with France. It was a risky and more demanding economic climate in which younger men often outdid the great merchants of the prewar era. Possessing a fortune more than ample to support his political career, Hancock made no effort to revive his business.[40]

Whatever their current economic activity, by the end of 1776 Boston's Whig elite could no longer ignore the threat of wartime finance to their accumulations of capital. During the first two years of war, the Massachusetts legislature had cautiously issued a little over £1,000,000 of paper currency, more than half of it in interest-bearing treasury notes. In the same period, Congress and the other states had flooded the country with their emissions. Given the hesitancy of the new state governments to assume and use the power of taxation, currency finance became the only possible means of meeting the expenses of war. Massachusetts passed laws requiring both its bills and those issued by Congress to be accepted as legal tender and providing penalties for depreciating this currency. Nevertheless, when the increased quantity of money in circulation and the greater demand for goods brought a sharp rise in prices after evacuation, a rapid and devastating depreciation seemed inevitable to Cooper. Such a prospect particularly threatened the clergy, who lived on a fixed salary. Identifying as always with the interests of his congregation, Cooper seemed equally concerned for those like Hancock and Bowdoin who had large sums lent out at interest. These debts might opportunely be repaid in depreciated currency at a fraction of their face value in specie.[41]

Cooper's advocacy of the national currency first became apparent in December 1775 when he persuaded James Warren to exchange his Massachusetts bills into Continental notes.[42] The solution for impending depreciation advanced by Cooper and a "Number of the most sensible" Boston Whigs represented an early form of the economic nationalism, designed to tie men of property to the central government, which later became associated with the financial policies of Alexander Hamilton. Prompted by their mutual friend, Colonel Josiah Quincy, the preacher offered a proposal to John Adams in July 1776:

> Would it be expedient, That no Currency should be allowed in any of the Colonies but Continental—that every Colony should call in its own outstanding Notes, exchanging them for continental, borrowed for its own internal Use? Would not this prevent indiscreet Emissions in the smaller ones, and a thousand Altercations respecting their Credit? Would not the pledged Faith of an whole Continent better support the Value of all the Notes now extant, than it can be supported in their present various Forms? Would this not cement us more together, and be attended with other Advantages? And might not the Congress, should it find its Notes abroad in too great a Quantity, borrow them of the Possessors at an Interest, which would lessen their Quantity and enhance their Value.[43]

Adams replied in full agreement. Though they did not explicitly say so in detail, Cooper's circle of Whigs seemed to want Congress to finance the war with an expanding national currency controlled by loan certificates, purchasable with depreciated paper money but paying interest fixed in the value of specie, and secured and eventually redeemed through heavy taxation. In May 1777 the Boston town meeting endorsed most features of this plan. Cooper possessed an immense faith in the ability of the continent to support the war at any price once independence was militarily assured.

Thus the more American capital was staked on independence, the more irreversible became the step taken at Philadelphia in July 1776.[44]

This position naively assumed that Congress could persuade the states to tax uniformly, that prices could be held in line, and that agrarian interests would support a program chiefly beneficial to commercial classes. Yet had all the states followed the Massachusetts example after 1776 in limiting emissions of its own paper currency and in taxing heavily to retire what was in circulation, the United States would have come much closer to checking the price inflation and currency depreciation that nearly swamped the new nation in 1779 and 1780. An emphasis on the suffering produced by this unfortunate outcome has obscured the indispensable contribution of currency finance to the American cause.[45] Franklin understood precisely, as he explained in a letter to Cooper written from France in 1779: "This Effect of Paper Currency [depreciation as a form of hidden taxation] is not understood on this Side [of] the Water. And indeed the whole is a Mystery even to the Politicians, how we have been able to continue a War four years without Money, and how we could pay with Paper, that had no previously fixed Fund appropriated specifically to redeem it. This Currency, as we manage it, is a wonderful Machine. It performs its Office when we issue it; it pays and clothes Troops, and provides Victuals and Ammunition; and when we are obliged to issue a Quantity excessive, it pays itself off by Depreciation."[46]

Still, the process was painful. In the fall of 1776 Boston began to feel the increasing weight of inflation on its unstable economy. Firewood and foodstuffs increased in price to the point where schoolmasters had to be voted an 80 percent salary supplement in order for them to subsist. The plight of the poor, some of whom were just now returning to town after the siege, and of the families of soldiers became desperate with the approach of winter. Though the town meeting authorized the borrowing of funds for poor relief, issued warnings against forestalling the market, and endeavored to revive the fishery, there was little more that a town largely dependent on supplies shipped or hauled in could do to resist national economic pressures.[47]

Accepting the recommendations of a conference of New England states, the General Court in January passed a comprehensive regulating act for prices and wages designed to check "avaricious Conduct." Additional acts forbade the exportation of scarce commodities. At first Boston made a concerted effort to enforce this system of economic controls with but partial success at best. For all their efforts townsmen suffered a severe food shortage during most of 1777. July saw housewives forcibly opening the stores of merchants who refused to sell such scarce items as coffee and sugar at the listed prices. Thomas Boylston, one of Cooper's most prominent parishioners, was physically abused by a hundred or more women until he surrendered the keys to his warehouse. Charges and countercharges between town and country grew more heated. In May the town meeting, using language reminiscent of its late attacks on British tyranny, called for repeal of the regulating acts. Modifications introduced by the General Court that same month kept the system in effect through the summer, while a nationwide debate took place on the theory and merits of economic controls. In September, again following the lead of a convention of New England states, Massachusetts repealed its regulating acts, leaving towns and voluntary associations to do what they could to check inflation.[48]

The inflationary peak would not be reached for another three years, but already Cooper showed the effects of his personal struggle for subsistence. In June 1777 he privately railed against engrossing merchants who "are the same in general every Where. Gain is their Point. Things are risen to a most exorbitant Price; and I suspect there are secret Agents to depreciate the Currency." The only record of his income begins in 1779, at which time the Brattle Street Church regularly augmented his salary to compensate for inflation. No clergyman in New England had a wealthier congregation. In addition, he received grants for serving as chaplain of the General Court and for attending meetings of the Harvard Corporation. He lived in apparent style in Lydia Hancock's mansion. Nonetheless, price inflation and currency depreciation threatened him as well as the body of the clergy with impoverishment.[49]

In these difficult times the fortunes of war supplied a husband for Abigail Cooper in the person of Joseph Hixon, a West Indian planter, whose family estate lay on Montserrat, one of the Leeward Islands. Sailing on business to London, his ship fell prey to an American privateer and was brought into Boston in October 1776. Three months later he quietly married the minister's only surviving child, now twenty-two. Her father insisted that he had consented to this "Alliance" only after discovering "good Reason to esteem him a Gentleman of Probity and Worth." Part of the evidence seems to have been an inventory showing slaves valued at £7,595 on the plantation that Hixon and his brother had inherited.[50]

Abigail Adams reported to her husband in April a different version of this sudden marriage, notice of which was kept out of the newspapers and even the church records:

> The present Subject of discourse is the unfortunate Daughter of Dr. C[oope]r, who having indiscreetly and foolishly married a Stranger, after finding him a Sot, has the additional misery of finding herself the wife of a married Man and the Father of 5 children who are all living. About 3 weeks after he saild for the West Indias a Letter came to Town directed to him which was delivered to her, and proved to be from his wife, who after condoling with his misfortune in being taken prisoner, Lets him know that she with her 5 children are well, and to add to mortification tis said her complexion is not so fair as the American Laidies.
>
> I most sincerely pitty her unfortunate Father, who having but two children has found himself unhappy in both. This last Stroke is worse than death [a reference to the death of the older daughter, Judith, in 1773].[51]

This account seems to mix truth and gossip in proportions inseparable today. In any case, the Coopers did not abandon Hixon, and in time the marriage gained respectability. After completing his business in England, Hixon returned to Boston in 1782, when he and Nabby settled down in Boston to raise a family. They baptized their first child, born in the year after his grandfather's death, with the name Samuel Cooper Hixon.[52]

Hixon's feat of winning Nabby's hand in three months, and then being permitted to continue on his voyage to London in the middle of the war, was all the more remarkable in that he was a British subject about whom questions of allegiance would naturally arise. Yet, characteristically, the pragmatic preacher did not let theoretical questions of this sort interfere with self-interest—in this case an apparently valuable marriage alliance. Too, Cooper seldom showed any trace of bitterness toward the Englishmen or even the Tories he had known and respected personally.

Boston was spared a bloodbath following the evacuation because almost every vehement and dangerous loyalist had fled. A few mild Tories decided not to leave with Gage but to take their chances with the Whig regime. Typical of these was a notable merchant of the Brattle Street congregation, Thomas Amory, whose leanings toward Anglicanism had never seemed to disturb his pastor. Naturally, the Reverend Dr. Mather Byles remained in town to irritate Whigs with his scorn and puns. But in April 1776 only eighty-seven "inimical" persons could be listed as living in Boston, and the list included some who had already departed. Though the General Court gave the justices of the peace authority to jail these or take bond for their good behavior, not many seemed to have been confined. By July the Boston Committee of Correspondence, Inspection and Safety could find only thirteen Tory names to present to a special court of enquiry. Of these, Amory and a few others were temporarily exiled to nearby Massachusetts towns. Not until May 1777 did the General Court enact the statutes necessary to deal with the various levels of disloyalty to the new state and nation.[53]

In April, before the General Court passed the new legislation, "five Tory villains" were carted out of town and warned not to return. Other Tories were publicly promised the same treatment if they continued their alleged conspiratorial activities. A statute added in May permitted town meetings to act as a grand jury, presenting by majority vote inhabitants of "inimical Dispositions" to stand trial on charges less than treason but nevertheless punishable by banishment. At a stormy town meeting on 17 May, Boston voters pushed aside the suggestion that they ignore this new act and continue to extirpate Tories by extralegal means. After another session, one which reminded an observer of the "affair of the witches at Salem," twenty-nine names were voted onto the list of "inimical" persons required to stand trial. Thomas Amory and a number of the men on this list seem never to have been tried, and several others won acquittals. For some inexplicable reason the first Tory brought to trial, and one of the few to be convicted, was a harmless seventy-year-old Congregational preacher, no less a person than a grandson of Increase Mather.[54]

Mather Byles had ministered to the Hollis Street Church for almost forty-five years when its congregation summarily dismissed him in August 1776 for having joined the enemy "against the Liberties of our Country." Meanwhile the Tory doctor defiantly walked the streets with the usual self-assurance of the Mather clan compounded by the flippancy of the punster. One of the several choice stories told of him in this period describes his rejoinder to Cooper's repeatedly passing his house without calling. Finally confronting his fellow minister, he remarked, "Dr. Cooper, you treat me just like a baby." "I hardly take you, Sir," responded a startled Cooper. "Sir," said Byles, "you go by, by, by."[55]

In June 1777 a jury convicted Byles under the new statute as a person "so inimically disposed towards this and the other United States of America that his further residence in this State is dangerous to the public peace and safety." Perhaps no one had intended to prosecute him to this extent, for the sentence of banishment was never executed; his only punishment consisted of a brief period of house arrest. Never ceasing to poke fun at the Whigs and conscious of being a hero among exiled loyalists, Dr. Byles lived out another decade in Boston as a loyal subject of George III. His two spinster daughters continued to play this charade in their father's house for a half-century after his death.[56]

The food shortage and exorbitant prices of 1777 thoroughly confused charges of political disloyalty with those of profiteering and currency manipulation. Increasingly the term "Tory" was used more to condemn fellow citizens displaying the usual human frailties than to identify those favoring a return to the British Empire. In the summer of 1777 the movable effects left by the exiles were put on the auction block, the absentees were banished permanently in 1778, and the following year their real estate was confiscated and sold. During this lengthy process of political purification, Cooper avoided public vindictiveness. He felt little personal need to utilize the atrocity stories which some of his ministerial colleagues spread and authenticated.[57]

As the burden of the war became heavier in 1777, among the vast majority of Bostonians bred on covenant theology many puzzled over the spiritual meaning of their situation, as almost any issue of a newspaper will document. They easily catalogued the conspicuous sins which deterred the Almighty from accomplishing his grand purpose for this people. Most authors of these newspaper jeremiads, nonetheless, could not hide an enduring confidence that American righteousness would eventually prevail. One writer in the *Gazette* called attention to the significance of the number seven in biblical prophecy and suggested that when three sevens came together in one year there must be a great event in the offing. He prophesied "that this very Year 1777 will be the grand Jubilee of American Freedom and Independency."[58]

In his pulpit Cooper distilled the essence of this tribal quest for motivation through the traditional rite of purification. His God had proclaimed, "Come, my People; You to whom I have revealed myself—you who stand in a peculiar Relation to me, and account me to be your God; you who desire to be under my Care and Protection; who would lay hold on my Strength, and make Peace with me—I am ready to conduct you as my peculiar Charge to a Retreat of Safety and Peace. Come then to me—Remember your Relation to me, and act up to it."[59]

16

Like the Israelites

The winter of 1777–1778 brought two changes that were to complete Samuel Cooper's transformation from preacher-politician to statesman. John Hancock came home and renewed his strong dependence on his pastor. Equally important, Cooper's early advocacy of an alliance between the United States and France extended his sphere of influence across the Atlantic.

For the first time since the beginning of the war, Samuel Cooper's most famous parishioner entered Boston on 19 November 1777. Hancock had traveled from Pennsylvania with an escort of Continental light horse. Church bells and artillery salvos announced the homecoming of the president of the Continental Congress and first major general of the Massachusetts militia, while "Gentlemen of all Orders" rushed to pay their respects. In marked contrast, Samuel and John Adams returned to their homes eight days later with a complete absence of fanfare.[1]

During the nearly two and a half years that Hancock had presided over Congress, he had used the presidency as a stage on which to become a personal symbol of national unity and determination to win independence.[2] By the end of 1777, only Washington had outdone him in embodying the cause of American nationhood. But Hancock's pretentious exemplification of democratic elitism was little understood or appreciated by his Massachusetts colleagues in Congress. For nearly a year before Hancock's return, the Adamses had suspected his desire to become the first governor of independent Massachusetts. John Adams threatened to retire rather than worship "An Idol in the Chair," and Samuel Adams fretted that a "Fool" for a governor would corrupt "the Morals and Manners of the People."[3] But Massachusetts needed a prince, and Hancock at age forty was ready to play the part. Once home, he set out to regain his mastery of town and state politics. A few days after returning, he donated 150 cords of firewood to the poor, and in February he advertised in all Boston newspapers his willingness to accept payment of debts in Continental bills "in preference to Gold or Silver."[4]

Hancock was the one Whig politician who could bring a measure of stability to Revolutionary politics in Boston and in the state legislature. Preferring the charms of his wife to the claims of statesmanship, James Warren at best had provided only sporadic leadership. For all of his activity, William Cooper had no following. Joseph Hawley had emerged as a major leader from western Massachusetts but now suffered from physical and mental infirmities. Samuel Adams, who had never won the full confidence of Boston's Whig elite, wisely remained in Congress. Though still active, Cushing enjoyed little popular support. John Adams prepared to leave for a diplomatic mission in Europe. Had James Bowdoin been able to take a vigorous part since the outbreak of the war, he could have remained a center of power; but his poor health and distaste for mass politics had kept him on the sidelines, and in 1777 he temporarily dropped out of public life altogether. Hancock alone possessed those assets—prestige as a Revolutionary statesman, confidence of the Boston elite and of the commercial classes elsewhere, widespread popularity in the agrarian sections, and ambition for power and popularity—necessary to create a commanding political personage. Moreover, he had always been willing (in sharp contrast to Bowdoin) to spend his inherited fortune on a political career. It is impossible to calculate what the American Revolution cost John Hancock in money, but any estimate must be high.[5]

After the evacuation, Boston's Whig elite remained as much in control of town affairs as ever. The lowest class of men were now usually in the army or at sea. Those eligible artisans who bothered to vote in town meetings continued to elect gentlemen of trade and law residing in the better sections. Wards one, two, and three of the crowded North End, where mostly workingmen lived, produced no selectmen nor sent any representatives to the General Court.[6] Hancock had little trouble reassuming nominal leadership of the surviving Whig elite who had been the backbone of prewar resistance to

Britain. Some of these were moderate men like John Rowe, who, whatever their past hesitation and reservations, now accepted independence and wanted to get on with business in the republic.[7]

Rising young men also clustered around Hancock. Conspicuous among these was John Lowell, a Newburyport lawyer who moved to Boston in 1776, joined the Brattle Street Church, and took his pastor as a political mentor. Likewise, another young lawyer, James Sullivan of Maine, found an association with Hancock the most rapid route to political power. He too would come under Cooper's influence.[8]

The leading men of Boston and other commercial towns saw in Hancock's prestige and popularity throughout the state a hope of lessening the influence in the General Court of the country towns, which could sometimes control the assembly by unexpectedly sending their full quotas of representatives. Far more astute politically than his opponents usually conceded, Hancock sensed in this sectional conflict and in the general uncertainties and tensions of the day an opportunity for him to rise above partisanship and to emerge as the leader who transcended sectional and class differences. After his return to Massachusetts, he exerted himself to become a "very active and popular Member in the House," as his archenemy James Warren fearfully observed.[9] Though Hancock had been reelected to Congress, he remained home to carry on his political labors until after the May elections of 1778, at which time the measure of his success became evident in the composition of the new House. Warren was eliminated from the legislature by a humiliating defeat in his own Plymouth town meeting, and a Hancock henchman replaced him as speaker. An embittered Warren attributed his defeat to the "Cunning of a party here, who have set up an Idol they are determined to worship with or without reason." He warned Samuel Adams that "the plan is to Sacrifise you and me to the Shrine of their Idol." Equally significant, the representatives elected to the Council five Bostonians and a clear majority of councillors sympathetic to eastern interests.[10]

Hancock had become the most dominant political personality Massachusetts had seen in high position. While the Adamses called for (though did not always practice) unselfish statesmanship directed toward high national purposes, their rival regarded himself as the personification of the American cause and judged the patriotism of men according to their willingness to serve that cause in an obeisant relationship to him. This self-image was perfectly appropriate to a man on horseback or to a modern political boss; but

Hancock was neither. Though he could and did provide significant leadership upon occasion, he lacked the qualities of sustained command. Always notable as a presence, a symbol, a princely figure, he usually depended on others to make and execute policy but without relinquishing his power to them. Accordingly, historical judgments of him rested on whether one stressed his many contributions to the Revolution and his remarkable ability to win political support from the masses or his failures, foibles, and vanity. Political opponents naturally emphasized and exaggerated his weaknesses, but their inability to dent his popularity or reduce his political power remains the foremost testimony to his achievements. One of the greatest of these has been largely unheralded. His ambition to be governor and the desire of his followers, Dr. Cooper among them, to exercise through Hancock the executive power of the new state contributed significantly to the process by which Massachusetts overcame severe conflicts of interest to adopt a new constitution.

Boston, like most Massachusetts towns, quickly accepted the Articles of Confederation as a basis for a permanent union of the American states.[11] Adoption of a state constitution proved to be an infinitely more difficult process because of fundamental differences between the commercial and agrarian sections. The Boston town meeting proposed a convention called for the single purpose of framing a government. But a General Court, temporarily dominated by western members, turned itself into a constitutional convention after holding an inconclusive referendum on its authority to do so. Representatives and councillors close to Hancock labored behind the scenes to draft a constitution that made major concessions to agrarian interests. The Constitution of 1778 offered the Massachusetts countryside more power than it would ever again have in its grasp during the Revolutionary generation. Yet it satisfied few and was rejected by a vote of five to one.[12]

Boston and many other towns offered a variety of reasons to explain their refusal to ratify. But Cooper succinctly went to the heart of the matter when he wrote Franklin that "we must go on as we are, and wait for more settled Times to compleat our Government." Caught up in the prosecution of the war and the inextricable questions of monetary policy, taxation, control of the militia, and constitutional theory, the main interests of the state had to test their strengths further before settling on a new form of government.[13]

John Hancock emerged as the political victor in the defeat of the Constitution of 1778. Though he took no public part in its creation nor made any effort to secure its ratification, he "very diligently" attended sessions of the House during the winter and spring of 1778 while his supporters in the convention demonstrated their readiness to compromise differing views and interests. The reputation he gained as a friend of the rural areas lay behind his sweeping victory in the May elections. He would have to wait two years, as it turned out, to be governor, but there remained little question that when the time came he would be the only candidate with sufficient statewide prestige and popularity to win that office.[14]

Hancock's enemies saw in these proceedings a stroke of "State legerdemain" by which the convention had produced a document so defective as to ensure its nonratification while enhancing the popularity of the "Idol." When the Reverend William Gordon made such a charge in the press, the General Court publicly dismissed him from his post as its chaplain and gave the position to Cooper when the new legislature convened the last of May.[15]

On 3 June after it had become apparent that there would be no gubernatorial office to fill this year, Hancock left Boston to return to Congress, where he hoped to take part in the ratification of the Articles of Confederation. He set out at 1:00 P.M., accompanied by a large party of gentlemen. Hancock and Cooper rode in the same carriage. At Watertown the party sat down to "an elegant dinner" followed by toasts and a "salute of Cannon." A sizable crowd gathered outside the tavern to send Hancock on his way with three cheers. James Warren offered his own interpretation of this departure: "The Great Man Tarried here till after Election, and then went off with the Pomp and retinue of an Eastern Prince."[16]

It is regrettable that during their close association of some forty years Samuel Cooper never once recorded his private opinion of Hancock, but at least he did not make the common and often costly mistake of judging him to be a weak man. Hardly blind to the vanity, capriciousness, and pomposity of his famous parishioner, Cooper still recognized and valued in him those qualities of political leadership that contributed so significantly to the Revolutionary movement and to the emergence of a republican state and nation. Unlike Warren and the Adamses, he saw that much more could be accomplished in league with Hancock than in opposition to him. As a leading power behind the throne of this republican prince, Cooper could exert in the final years of the Revolution a political power normally impossible for a man of the cloth.

The preacher's influence on Hancock was nowhere stronger than in foreign policy. Cooper became the chief New England advocate of a close military and diplomatic relationship with France and of Franklin's diplomatic efforts to establish and maintain such a tie. Hancock held no firm views on foreign policy, but with Cooper as his mentor, he moved in the same direction.

In September 1776 Congress had elected Benjamin Franklin one of three commissioners to the court of France. That October he sailed to join Silas Deane and Arthur Lee, the other commissioners, who were already in Europe. Franklin wrote an "affectionate" farewell to Cooper on the day of embarkation and long cherished the reply: "When I informed . . . Dr. Cooper, that I was ordered to France, being then seventy years old, and observed, that the public, having as it were eaten my flesh, seemed now resolved to pick my bones, he replied that he approved their taste, for that the nearer the bone the sweeter the meat."[17]

The French people received the venerable sage of Philadelphia so enthusiastically that four months after his arrival he could write the Boston preacher that "All Europe is on our Side of the Question, as far as Applause and good Wishes can carry them." Even before receiving this cheering letter, Cooper had taken it upon himself to keep Franklin informed of developments in America. Sensing that Franklin would use his letters in France as evidence of the situation in America, he expressed gratitude for the indispensable French secret aid to the colonies, yet incessantly reiterated the necessity of that court's taking a more open part in the war, for its own advantage as well as America's.[18]

The British were well aware that France might change its course from secret to open support of the American cause. General Howe proposed to Lord Germain a massive military offensive for the summer of 1777 as the surest method of discouraging direct French intervention. With little hope of raising the large reinforcements that Howe wanted, Germain combined the various recommendations of his generals in America into a less ambitious but still promising plan. Howe was granted his desire to make an early push overland toward Philadelphia. He would occupy the new republic's capital while preventing Washington from detaching troops to oppose General Burgoyne. This colorful officer had been given command of the force that was to march south from Canada to take Fort Ticonderoga and Albany. Then Burgoyne would join Howe's command for the final extinction of colonial resistance.[19]

Fueled by reports from Franklin and Arthur Lee, rumors of impending blows by Britain spread rapidly through Massachusetts during the spring and early summer. By the middle of June Bosto-

nians knew the truth that Burgoyne had reached Quebec in May
without any sizable addition to the forces already stationed there.
Still the alarms continued. In July Cooper wrote a special sermon
—a rare exertion for him—with which to comfort his congregation
after an "Alarm of the Enemies Fleet on our Coasts." General
Howe changed his plans by deciding to sail rather than march to
Philadelphia. After his transports lifted anchor at New York late in
July, they were reported off Cape Ann and bound for Boston. During the resulting panic every available team was pressed into service
to cart families and their effects into the country.[20]

The real danger came from Canada. Burgoyne had collected a
host of more than eight thousand, mostly regulars, and in June
headed for Ticonderoga, where thirty-five hundred Americans
hoped to stall the invasion until more militiamen responded to the
alarm. Cooper agonized over the failure of the eastern states to
reinforce and supply this vital post. He blamed the deficiency on
the officers and quartermaster but even more on the New England
culture: "Property is more equally divided among the People of N.
England than almost any where else—they know the Endearments
of a Family. Such a People may assemble and do great Things on a
Push: but it is difficult, even in a Cause in which their Hearts are
engaged, to persuade them to become Soldiers under a strict
Discipline, for Years. . . . We have indeed fewer at Ticonderoga
than I imagined."[21]

While Boston observed the first anniversary of the Declaration
of Independence, Burgoyne's artillerists dragged cannon up a hill
overlooking the fortifications at Ticonderoga and forced the
American commander to save most of his men by the sudden nighttime evacuation of the Fort. "No Event since the Commencement
of the War has excited such Indignation and Astonishment as the
Evacuation of Tyconderoga in so disgraceful a Manner!" This
widely shared reaction of Cooper represented as much fear as indignation, for the doors to New England and New York now
seemed wide open to Burgoyne's army. Cooper's voice mingled
with those crying for an investigation and "exemplary Punishment
to the Delinquents." But he soon became aware that the apparently
disastrous loss of Ticonderoga had aroused the "substantial Men"
of New England and New York to their greatest effort. "Indignation rises, Fear does not depress us," he assured the Massachusetts
delegates to Congress. "Some spirited officers to lead our Men at
the Northward may yet waste and ruin the Enemy—I hope every
Nerve will be exerted."[22]

Burgoyne did not press his advantage during July when the American forces opposing him were demoralized and scattered. He moved slowly through the wilderness with all his artillery, baggage, and entourage. While Howe's army remained at sea, Washington felt free to send north two of his best generals with as many Continentals as could be spared. To defend their homes and families, New England militia companies surged toward the Hudson. When Burgoyne moved his main force south again in September, he discovered that (in Cooper's words) "he had ventured too far into a Country where all men were Soldiers." Refusing to hold a safe position, he lost heavily in engagements on 19 September and 7 October and consequently found himself surrounded by overwhelming numbers of Continentals and militiamen. At Saratoga on 17 October a still undaunted Burgoyne surrendered according to the generous terms of a "Convention" that permitted his entire army, once disarmed, to return home bound in honor never to fight again on American soil during the present war. Uncertain of how strong a British force was marching up the Hudson toward Albany, General Horatio Gates had not held out for an unconditional surrender.[23]

After repeated rumors of a capitulation, the terms of the "Convention" reached Boston late on Wednesday, 22 October. Cooper's joy was at first dampened by Gates's "unaccountable" concessions to "an enemy totally in our Power." But the jubilation produced by this "most important and Glorious Event" quickly overcame his doubts. As a feature of Thursday's celebration, he "made an excellent Prayer of Praise and Thanksgiving" before the House of Representatives. On Sunday he stood assuredly in his pulpit to explain the meaning of Saratoga to a happy and relieved congregation: "There is no People whose Circumstances of Settlement in the common Course of Divine Providence more nearly resemble those of the Israelites when they were conducted by a divine hand to Canaan, than these States, and particularly, the N. England ones. . . . This has been verified in that compleat Victory in which we this day rejoyce. . . . What an Effect on the Enemy; on our own Forces; on the British Nation; and on the Courts in Europe. What a Change to have that whole Army, that threatened such Devastation, surrendered into our Hands. It is the Lord's Doing, and it is marvellous in our Eyes."[24]

One paragraph of this sermon would have shocked the congregation a few years before. Now, two and a half years of war had prepared them to hear a Congregational preacher pronounce his holy blessing on the Catholic sovereign of France. Freely acknowl-

edging that the timely arrival of large quantities of arms and supplies from Europe had made possible the defeat of Burgoyne,
Cooper concluded, "The Joy of this Conquest becomes enlarged by
the Share which our Allies take in the Merit and in the Joy. . . .
May Heaven bless the Monarch of France, and his Dominions; and
still honor him as a Defender of the Rights of Mankind."

There must have been some Brattle Street worshipers on this
Sunday who were not too overcome with emotion to recall that in a
sermon of 1759 Cooper had described the French as an "inveterate
and implacable Enemy to our Religion and Liberties; inflamed with
Romish Bigotry; perfidious, restless, politic, and enterprizing: An
Enemy that has ever made War against us in a Manner shocking to
Humanity." Or that as late as 1773 he had denounced popery as at
best the "extremest despotism," a religion "incompatible with the
safety of a free government." But who could take exception to his
current doctrine that heaven "saves us in its own Way"?[25]

The Saturday before, Cooper had written a long letter to
Franklin, which would prove to be the most significant and revealing of their fifteen-year correspondence. Massachusetts was preparing a fast "running Vessell" (a brigantine) to rush the news of
Saratoga to the American commissioners in France. Jonathan Loring Austin, a young man from one of Boston's most prominent
Whig families, had been selected to carry letters from Cooper and
others, as well as copies of recent newspapers and the public
documents relating to the termination of Burgoyne's campaign.[26]

Cooper composed his letter with an obvious sense of destiny.
First, he reviewed the military news in considerable detail, stressing
the "Firmness and Resolution" shown after the loss of Ticonderoga
by the people and their leaders, who considered no other course of
action than "turning out the Militia to make a Stand." Though
"Vagrants and the meaner Sort had been before enlisted into the
Continental Levies," the militia who crushed Burgoyne were the
"substantial Men" of New England. Their complete victory had
opened the way for some troops from the northern army to recapture the Hudson River and to reinforce Washington in Pennsylvania. Cooper put the best possible light on American defeats
elsewhere. Whatever might happen in other quarters, the "Total
Ruin of the Army from Canada must in the end be fatal" to
Howe.[27]

After reporting the news, Cooper reached the grand question
of his letter: How will the European powers respond to Saratoga?

Will the British ministry send another army? Or will they rather acknowledge American independence and liberties while seeking an alliance to secure commercial advantages in the former colonies? If such an offer should be made while France and Spain continue to delay proffering open recognition and alliance, it would find powerful adherents in America, even among some of those "who have been extremely averse to her arbitrary and despotic Claims." "You know," he reminded Franklin, "the Force of old Connections and long Habits; and that the worst Treatment does not always wholly efface them; and that our Liberties once secured, many would deem an Alliance with Britain the most natural. I will only add: that though we are indebted to France and Spain for their secret and important Aid, yet their openly keeping aloof from us for so long a Time has made such a Plan on the Part of Britain the more practicable." Cooper maintained that he knew from intercepted letters that, if the mother country failed to crush colonial resistance in the present campaign, English merchants would favor granting independence "for the Sake of Commercial Advantages."[28]

With many others in Europe and America, he saw that the War for Independence had reached a major turning point:

> Now then is the Time for France to take an open and determined Part, which without Hazard to her, must at once secure our Independence, disappoint the Friends of Britain, and strengthen the Hands of her own here, and give them firm and the most popular Ground to exert themselves in her Favor; for we know that Governments in all Countries, and especially in this, cannot without such Ground proceed as they wish. I am well informed that Letters will go by this very Opportunity to influential Persons in Britain proposing an immediate Calling of a new Parliament, a Change of Ministry, and a Ceding Independence to us as the Basis of a thorough Reconciliation, and a Means of securing to her the trade of these States, and of avoiding what she must now above all dread, a War with France and Spain in Conjunction with them: and she must be more than ever infatuated if she does not without Delay adopt such a Measure. I write freely and in confidence to you as a Friend, but no more upon this Point, except that the Letters I speak of as going to Britain, are from private

Persons, and from one in particular of no small Influence here.

We are ready to hope that the Account of our Successes will confound the British Ministry, divide the Nation at least, raise a Clamor against the Promoters of the
War that cannot be stilled easily, and prevent any large
Force coming over in the Room of Burgoyne's Army,
which you will observe is not prevented by the Convention from serving in Europe: But should Howe end the
Campaign more favorably to himself than we expect,
and should Britain, determined to carry on the War,
take such a Step, is it possible that France and Spain
should not exert themselves in the most efficacious
Manner to prevent it?[29]

Cooper held no illusions that France and Spain would enter the
war for any reasons except their own self-interest. His advocacy of
an alliance so motivated stemmed from the complete course of
resistance and war that had opened with Governor Bernard's administration. After seventeen years of conflict, the ideological and
psychological alienation from England of most Whig leaders was
total, and they had developed a strong sense of personal identification with the new nation. At this juncture they feared that a war-
weary mother country might offer her rebellious colonies an accommodation sufficiently attractive to secure its acceptance
through enervation of the war effort. Such a settlement would leave
the colonies politically autonomous or even independent, but
weak, divided, with compromising leadership by nominal Whigs or
Tories, and economically dependent again on Britain. In this even-
tuality, there could be little hope that New England's commercial
interests would be any better able to flourish in competition with
English rivals than before the war. In Boston, at least, the quest for
economic autonomy had been a major spring of the Revolution.
Among the younger and most enterprising men of the commercial
community, the desire remained strong to seek a revival of their
prosperity free from the shackles of British trade regulations. The
lure of French gold and trade overcame much of the natural aversion to an alliance with the hated enemy of the past generation.

Furthermore, any accommodation with the mother country
seemed certain to hazard the financial stake of Americans in the
war. During 1777 Congress made strenuous efforts to obtain more
money through loans and thus reduce the need for currency emis-

sions. The commissioners in France arranged for an annual secret grant from that government which could be used to pay the interest on loan certificates. Though the results proved disappointing, the total of current and past loan certificates constituted a sizable investment, mostly by the commercial classes, in the creation of a national government sufficiently strong and successful to pay its obligations.[30] This economic question lay heavily on Cooper's mind as he urged Franklin to press France for recognition and open assistance.[31]

Now that in the fall of 1777 the possibility of a British military victory seemed remote, Cooper feared most a compromise settlement that, however conciliatory, limited American freedom of action in either the economic or political sphere. The psychological and ideological elements of incipient American nationalism were undergirded by powerful economic ambitions. In New England these included not only the aspirations of the Whig elite but also the desire of the farmer to maintain the unusual prosperity brought to agrarian areas by the increased demand for and the higher prices of agricultural products. Though the commercial centers had suffered heavily thus far in the war, their leaders had reason to be thankful that the bulk of the population in the countryside enjoyed a higher standard of living.[32] Even while the Whig farmer and Whig merchant clashed over domestic political issues, in most cases neither saw after Saratoga any marked advantage to be gained by a return to the British Empire.

There remained, however, as Cooper had indicated to Franklin, notable exceptions. General Gates was among the few prominent Americans who pleaded for the ministry to withdraw from the war immediately and endeavor to revive England's cultural and commercial ties with America.[33] To prevent such a movement from gaining momentum, Cooper staked all his hopes on an alliance with France.

Austin crossed the Atlantic in four weeks and delivered his dispatches to the American commissioners on 4 December. Heartened by confirmation of earlier reports concerning the entrapment of Burgoyne, they quickly renewed their application to the French government for an alliance. Franklin wrote to Cooper that among the supporting documents communicated to the ministry was "your excellent letter of October 25." He added, "I am sure it had a good effect." As evidence that Franklin had done so, a partial translation of this letter can be found today in the archives of the ministry of foreign affairs at both Paris and Madrid.[34]

The French foreign minister, Charles Gravier de Vergennes, needed no urging. He aimed to revive the European prestige and leadership France had lost by the Peace of 1763. Though the cornerstone of his policy became the family alliance of the thrones of France and Spain, he saw the revolt of the American colonies as the most promising opportunity for these two Bourbon powers to strike a damaging blow at Great Britain. After solidifying his position at court, in 1776 he succeeded in persuading both monarchs to advance funds with which to supply arms for the colonies. Popular though the rebels' cause was with the French people, powerful elements in the ministry opposed Vergennes's American policy, and the court at Madrid showed no trace of enthusiasm for the prospect of an independent republic adjacent to Spain's restless colonies in the New World. Nevertheless, in the summer of 1777 Vergennes proposed an open alliance with the United States. When Spain still remained reluctant at the beginning of December, he concluded that, if necessary, his country must take this step alone in order to prevent the colonies from accepting the conciliatory overtures expected from Britain. The news of Saratoga, arriving just after Vergennes reached this decision, quickened the pace of negotiations. On 6 February 1778 the three American commissioners and a representative of Louis XVI affixed their signatures to a treaty of amity and commerce and to a separate treaty of defensive alliance.[35]

Congress had originally authorized the commissioners to negotiate only a commercial treaty, but the military setbacks at the end of 1776 led to secret instructions giving them a virtual blank check with which to bring France and Spain into the war against Britain.[36] Yet after the signing, Franklin emphasized to Cooper how little the major power had demanded from the infant republic as a price for the two treaties: "Their great Principle declared in the Preamble, is perfect Equality and Reciprocity of Conditions, the advantages mutual, Commerce free &c. France guarantees the Independence, Sovereignty and Liberty, with all the possessions of the United States, and they [the United States] guarantee to the most Christian King his possessions in the West Indies.—No monopoly of our Trade was desired, it is left open to all we chuse to trade with.—In short, the King has acted a noble and magnanimous part, as well as a wise one; For it is undoubtedly the interest of France that this Treaty should be durable; which was not so likely if advantage had been taken of our present difficulties to exact hard terms."[37]

Across the English Channel the first reports of Burgoyne's fate produced general consternation and brought on a major debate in the House of Commons. Among the speakers, Governor Pownall advocated what Cooper had expected Britain to propose: the recognition of American independence within a federal union designed to preserve the commercial and cultural ties of the English-speaking peoples against French influence. But Pownall failed to reduce the intransigency of the king, the ministry, and most of Parliament against independence. After hinting in December at conciliatory measures short of independence, North waited until the middle of February to introduce bills repealing most of the acts to which colonists objected, including the tax on tea and the Massachusetts Government Act. He further proposed to abandon the right of taxation except for the regulation of trade and to establish a commission with broad powers to make whatever additional concessions might be necessary to restore peace in America. The prime minister offered the exact settlement American Whigs had hoped and prayed for only three years before. Even before Parliament passed the bills in March, news of their contents was rushed to Philadelphia, where Howe made certain that Congress, now forced to meet at York, Pennsylvania, learned of their provisions.[38]

The American commissioners endeavored to give Congress the earliest possible notice of France's decision to enter an alliance. As soon as a preliminary agreement had been reached in December, they dispatched Simeon Deane, brother of the commissioner, as a messenger to Congress. Storms disabled his ship and forced a return to Brest after six weeks, thus preventing Americans in the winter of Valley Forge from learning the heartening news from Europe. Not until 8 March did he embark on another French frigate, which touched the Maine coast on 14 April and made its way to Boston five days later.[39]

April 19 came on a Sunday, the third anniversary of the opening battle of the American Revolution. Just before Cooper began to conduct the afternoon service at Brattle Street, he was handed a letter that Deane had brought from Franklin. He hurriedly read the opening paragraph, then stepped into Hancock's finely carved mahogany pulpit to make the first public announcement in America of the French alliance.[40].

"For this," he wrote to Franklin, "I gave public Thanks, and implored the Blessing of Heaven on the King of France and his Dominions. It was a new Thing in more Senses than one, and struck the whole Congregation with an agreable Surprize, who most cordially joyned in that Act of Devotion. Your agreable Dispatches came at a most seasonable Time. After having done great Things we needed something to give us a new Spring." Franklin somehow managed to have this extract from Cooper's joyful letter published in a London newspaper.[41]

Monday evening the American Coffeehouse (the British Coffeehouse renamed) was illuminated as Boston's first citizens gathered to celebrate the alliance and to anticipate "with Pleasure, the rising Glory of America." A toast rang out to Louis XVI of France, and another proposed, "May the Free and Independent States of America prove an Assylum for the Sons of Oppression in all Quarters of the Globe." "You cannot conceive," Cooper exclaimed, "what Joy the Treaties with France have diffused among all true Americans, nor the Chagrine they have given to the few interested and slavish Partizans of Britain among us. They had great Hopes, had France continued unallied to us, to have deceived us, and brought us to a shabby Accommodation. These Hopes are now dead."

On Tuesday, Deane left overland for Congress. Cooper advised his congressional friends "to publish the Treaties soon, with pertinent Remarks, particularly on the Magnanimity of the King of France, and the Fidelity of that Court to their Treaties with other States." Deane reached York just after Congress adjourned on Saturday 2 May. A special session was convened to receive his dispatches. On Monday the delegates unanimously ratified both treaties and passed a resolution praising the "magnanimity and wisdom of his most Christian majesty." For Cooper, the telltale event of these proceedings had been the spirited rejection by Congress of Lord North's bills ten days before, at a time when the members had "heard nothing of this decisive Step in France."[42]

With the French alliance a new chapter opened in the history of the United States and in the life of Samuel Cooper.

17

Mon Cher Docteur

$H$is enthusiasm for the French alliance did not blind Cooper to the practical difficulty of turning this marriage of convenience into a working relationship of more than psychological advantage to the American cause. In his letter announcing the signing, Franklin had stressed both the importance and the difficulty of warm relations with the new ally. This warning was not lost on Cooper, who saw clearly that Franco-American harmony was necessary not only to bring the war to a victorious conclusion but also to "promote those Mercantile Connections which are one Object of the Alliance."[1]

The task would be as difficult as Franklin anticipated. Already some of the French officers recruited for service in America under the generous terms agreed to by Silas Deane gathered in Boston to sail home to register complaints of ill-usage and unfulfilled contracts.[2] British commissioners were crossing the Atlantic to preach reconciliation with the mother country instead of an unnatural alliance with the inveterate enemy of the common culture and freedom of the English-speaking peoples. Coming in the wake of the commissioners, John Temple had secretly staked his political future on the prospects of this proposed reconciliation. Silas Deane was also on his way home, recalled by Congress to answer questions concerning his service in France. He sailed to the United States on the same ship as Conrad Alexandre Gérard, the first minister of France, who had instructions to defend Deane against his congressional enemies. No American knew at the time that, while enjoying the confidence of Vergennes and Franklin, Deane had also been a willing participant in a complex maze of private trade, currency speculation, and international intrigue. Prior to returning he seemingly had agreed with a British master spy on a plan of reconciliation through inducements of finance and patronage. Incredible as it seems, the recalled American commissioner carried with him on his return voyage some of the hopes of both the French and the English monarchs. Whichever course events took, Deane expected to come out on top.[3]

Unaware of this assorted duplicity, Cooper saw only the necessity of cooperation with France. In the spring of 1778, shortly after news of the alliance, a number of French ships tied up at the Boston docks. On one of these came John Holker, a man in his early thirties who had been informally commissioned to report to Vergennes on conditions in America. Holker's father, outlawed for his part in the Jacobite uprising of 1745, had fled his native England and settled in France, where the crown utilized his industrial knowledge. The two Holkers had taken a major part in the procurement of supplies in Europe for the Continental army, and the son was among those who thought that a war between France and England would revive American credit in Europe and open the possibility of making large fortunes in currency speculation and trade. Holker remained in Boston during May. Bilingual, affable, and interested in trade, he quickly became a popular figure who eased the natural awkwardness of the several private and public entertainments given for the French officers in port. He left for Congress with a warm recommendation from Cooper to Samuel Adams.[4]

From the beginning, Cooper and Franklin mutually understood the importance of favorable publicity to the promotion of Franco-American friendship. On 1 June 1778 the preacher informed his friend, "As two young Printers of my Parish propose to publish a new Paper, and to encourage their Attention, I have promised them occasional Communications from my Correspondence, I should be much obliged to you for such public Papers &c as may tend to enlighten and entertain our Country, and particularly give it the most agreable Vision of the late Alliance and strengthen the Friendship between France and America."[5]

Thus appeared on 15 June the first number of the *Independent Ledger*, a clear new voice of American nationalism and for the next year the one newspaper on the continent most dedicated to the French alliance. Cooper's identifiable contributions to this journal make all the more regrettable the impossibility of identifying the large amount of material that it is reasonably certain he had contributed to the Boston press of the past quarter-century.⁶

Franklin valued Cooper's support of the alliance as an example that a leading American clergyman could rise above the traditional long-existing Protestant enmity toward Catholic France. He continued to make good use of the preacher's letters, sending some to Vergennes and contributing two to *Affaires de l'Angleterre et de l'Amérique.*⁷ Published ostensibly at Antwerp, but actually at Paris from 1776 to 1779, this journal was Vergennes's secret effort to counter the hostile view of the American Revolution that colored the reports reaching Europe through English sources. Franklin, and later John Adams, communicated often with the editor, Edmé-Jacques Genêt, chief interpreter of the foreign office. As a result, *Affaires* became a major medium for the dissemination of favorable news from America.⁸ Through Franklin's efforts, the "Pasteur de la principale Église de Boston," as *Affaires* described Cooper, became known in France during 1778 as a particular and notable friend of the alliance.⁹

His early and sustained support of France did not escape critical notice in America. In July 1778 the main loyalist newspaper, the *Royal Gazette* of New York, printed a letter containing excerpts from Cooper's sermon on the fall of Quebec in which he had stressed the obligation of the colonies to Britain for saving them from an "implacable enemy" to their liberties and religion. Now, commented the writer, "this same Dr. Cooper, in his public prayers every Sunday, calls for God's vengeance upon the whole English nation, and for the best of his blessings upon their 'most potent and magnanimous new ally Lewis 16th, King of France.' " The conclusion of this letter struck a familiar note in the increasing number of attacks on the alliance: "If there is as much stability in the Doctor's religion as there is in his politics, and as ardent a desire for independence with regard to the former as the latter, we may expect to see him, in less than twenty years, embrace the scarlet whore, and adorn the first Papal chair in America."¹⁰

As a pledge of its faithfulness to the alliance, in April France sent a powerful fleet across the Atlantic under the command of Comte d'Estaing. Unfavorable winds delayed the comte's arrival until July, a month after the British Peace Commission had landed in America.

After passage of his conciliatory bills, Lord North indifferently carried through the organization of a peace commission charged with the task of thwarting the French alliance and retaining the trade of Britain's American colonies. Its nominal head was Lord Carlisle, a young nobleman of no great weight, noted chiefly in the past for his gambling and his foppish dress. William Eden, an ambitious undersecretary of state, provided the actual leadership for the commission. A third member, George Johnstone, had served briefly as governor of Florida and had acquired a reputation in parliamentary debate as a friend of the colonies.[11]

Hardly an impressive delegation, the commissioners nonetheless came with extensive powers to effect a reconciliation on the basis of an explicit acknowledgment that the British colonial system was indeed what the colonists had conceived it to be before 1763. Their instructions authorized almost any concession short of independence and free trade, but made it clear that "upon the subject of Commercial Regulations, the prevailing Principle has always been [and must continue to be] to secure a Monopoly of American Commerce." Enjoined to preserve this principle and to guard the property rights of English merchants, the commissioners had little to offer the Boston mercantile community, now more relaxed after Saratoga and attracted by the prospects of trading with France and exploring other hitherto forbidden commercial channels. Cooper was particularly incensed over Commissioner Johnstone's use of the American mails to send private letters from English merchants urging their former commercial associates in the colonies to receive the commission with open minds.[12]

Before the commissioners left for America, Paul Wentworth, the chief British secret agent, prepared for their guidance "Minutes respecting political Parties in America and Sketches of the leading Persons in each Province." Freely mixing hearsay and Tory bias with common knowledge, the "Minutes" were of little practical value to the commissioners, but they did reveal plainly Cooper's reputation as a behind-the-scenes director of Boston politics. After recounting the standard view of Hancock and the Adamses, Wentworth turned to the preacher: "The Rev. Dr. Cooper—an useful Man to move others—of great Talents and equal discretion—supervises and plans every Measure of Consequence—a great writer, and very ingenious argumentator. Has great influence over the first Movers, but especially guides—James Bowdoin." Accepting Wentworth's advice at face value, Lord Carlisle placed Cooper's name fourth on his personal list of "Leading Men" in Massachusetts.[13]

Wentworth's idea of Cooper's influence on Bowdoin likely came from John Temple. Since his dismissal from the English customs service in 1774, Temple had been living on the largess of friends and relatives while awaiting an opportunity to reenter governmental service, the only gainful employment he had ever known. He fancied himself serving as a mediator between the colonies and the mother country, but came to the realization in 1777 that the growing interest of France in the American rebellion would eventually destroy any hope of reconciliation and, as a result, end whatever bargaining power he retained with the ministry. Discouraged at this prospect, he appealed to Franklin for assistance in removing himself, his wife, and his two sons to Boston by way of France.[14]

North's decision to organize a peace commission gave a sudden turn to Temple's fortunes. While in Paris seeking to intrigue with the American commissioners before they finished negotiating a treaty with France, the trusted Wentworth saw on Franklin's desk a letter from Temple addressed to John Adams. The spy's subsequent report seemed to confirm that Bowdoin's son-in-law did indeed still have important connections in the colonies and could be a force for reconciliation.[15] As a result, Temple concluded a most favorable bargain with the ministry. In return for present and future financial rewards and the promise of a baronetcy, he agreed to return to America and "faithfully exert his utmost influence" in support of the commissioners' efforts to achieve a reconciliation.[16]

The generous terms of Temple's employment meant that he was being returned to America with an apparent vindication of his pattern of considerate customs enforcement. But in so doing, Britain attempted to face the reality of 1778 with a solution to the problems of 1775. Temple delayed his passage while insisting on accommodations appropriate to his assumed status. When he finally stepped ashore in New York in August, the commissioners had already been at work for two months without achieving any important success.[17]

To the commissioners' overwhelming chagrin, they reached Philadelphia in June without being informed that General Clinton had been ordered to evacuate that town, retreat to New York, and detach part of his army for an expedition against French possessions in the West Indies. Not knowing of Temple's involvement with the peace commissioners, Cooper saw only that they had come "upon a Fool's Errand." On 1 July, as Clinton's army reached the safety of New York harbor after suffering heavy losses and getting no better than a draw at the Battle of Monmouth, Cooper could reassure Franklin that the "Enemy by leaving Philadelphia, are unravelling all they did last Year." Seemingly certain of the failure of the Peace Commission and anticipating the arrival of d'Estaing, the preacher grew almost ecstatic: "Our Harbor looks alive with French Vessels, and a Number of late Prizes. The Hopes of the Tories, and British Partizans, are now as the giving up of the Ghosts." Everywhere Cooper thought he could hear the cry, "Independence; and Fidelity to our Treaties."[18]

The commissioners continued to insist that the French alliance was unnatural and consequently inwardly offensive to the majority of the people. They failed to appreciate the counterbalancing psychological function of the treaties in bolstering American assertions of nationality. Speaking the mind of the commercial classes, the Philadelphia merchant prince Robert Morris sought to impress upon the commissioners that independence would make possible a mutually advantageous commercial alliance between the two countries that could never be achieved while Britain continued its efforts to dominate its former colonies. In Boston, as in Philadelphia, economic maturity contributed to the quest for political sovereignty. Cooper's zeal for the French alliance resulted largely from his position of leadership in a commercial community. Yet that zeal may also have cloaked a private fear that the alliance was too artificial a union to hold together under the strain of a protracted war effort. The arrival of a French fleet would provide the first test.[19]

France's entry into the war forced the British cabinet to look to home defense. While the ministers debated, the Comte d'Estaing sailed unmolested from Toulon past Gibraltar and headed for the North American coast with twelve ships of the line, four frigates, and four thousand marines. Belatedly, Admiral John Byron put to sea in pursuit, but the delay meant that for a few weeks the French would enjoy naval superiority in American waters. Only d'Estaing's bad luck prevented the decisive victory and early termination of the war for which Cooper fervently hoped. Light winds so slowed the comte's crossing that he missed by ten days the opportunity of overtaking Lord Howe's inferior fleet on its way to New York following the evacuation of Philadelphia. D'Estaing then set a course for New York, where he planned to destroy Howe and bottle up Clinton's men between the sea and Washington's army. From the scattered reports reaching Boston, Cooper learned enough of the military and naval operations to encourage him to relish the thought that "our country . . . will soon be compleatly delivered." But d'Estaing's ill fortune continued at New York, where he discovered that the largest French men-of-war could not navigate the channel at low tide. Leaving Howe's fleet safe inside the harbor, he agreed with Washington to undertake a joint attack against the British garrison at Newport, Rhode Island.[20]

New England patriots had been vexed by the unopposed British occupation of Newport at the end of 1776 and the resulting establishment within sixty miles of Boston of an enemy naval base guarded by three thousand or more soldiers. A "secret" but expensive attempt by Massachusetts and Connecticut troops to drive the British from Rhode Island in the days following Burgoyne's defeat miscarried before a single blow was struck, and Congress was left to pay the bill for a "sham Expedition" that had to be hushed up in the interest of morale.[21]

After d'Estaing anchored near Newport on 29 July, citizens of all ranks responded enthusiastically to the proposal that they join the French in the destruction of the only British stronghold in New England. Major General John Sullivan of New Hampshire commanded the American forces in Rhode Island. Washington granted the request of his quartermaster general, the brilliant Nathanael Greene, to return to his native state to serve under Sullivan during this campaign. To Rhode Island also came the Marquis de Lafayette, a French volunteer just entering his twenties, who during the past year had proved himself worthy of his major general's commission in the Continental army. Lafayette's excitement rose at the prospect of holding a command in the first joint operation of the allies. As if to make this enterprise even more appealing to New Englanders, Washington also ordered to Rhode Island the brigade commanded by the popular Marblehead general, John Glover, regarded by Cooper and many others as the ablest general officer from Massachusetts.[22]

D'Estaing waited impatiently while Sullivan supplemented his Continentals with militiamen to raise an army estimated at ten thousand. Back from Congress at the end of July, Major General Hancock left to take his place at the head of the Massachusetts militia. The citizen soldiers who rushed toward Newport, as the *Independent Ledger* observed, were often "men of character and property." One Salem company of one hundred men was said to have in its ranks thirty worth an average of £10,000 sterling each. Not to be outdone, Bostonians boasted that their Independent Company had not a single soldier worth less than this figure. "You have the flower of all New England in your Army," General Greene pointed out to General Sullivan.[23]

By invitation of the Council, Cooper preached the Thursday Lecture on 6 August before Hancock and the Boston militia left for Rhode Island. Always at his best on such occasions, on this day he exceeded his past performances with an inspired and masterful religious interpretation of all that had led to this eventful hour in the history of the American people when they neared victory in a "Contest . . . for those Rights that are the Foundation and Security of all Civil Happiness." After reviewing other remarkable sustaining providences, Cooper emphasized the significance of God's latest work in their behalf, the intervention of France "at a most seasonable Time."[24]

While Cooper preached, d'Estaing and Sullivan were discovering the difficulties of battlefield cooperation between allies. Expecting an easy victory, each wanted to capture the garrison while the other merely lent support. Lafayette added to the tension with his plan to symbolize the alliance by leading an American force under the French admiral's direction. The two commanders eventually set Monday, 10 August, for a joint attack against the island on which Newport is situated, the French from the harbor and the Americans from the mainland. Accordingly, on Saturday d'Estaing forced his way past the British batteries and landed his marines on a nearby harbor island where they would be in position for the planned assault. The resulting tightening of British lines led the rash Sullivan to begin the invasion on Sunday without consulting his ally. A disgruntled d'Estaing was preparing, nevertheless, to aid the Americans when Lord Howe's fleet appeared off Newport harbor. Reloading his marines, the comte sailed out the next morning to engage Howe, whose squadron had been reinforced by some of Byron's ships. As the fleets moved into battle positions on the following day, both were scattered and damaged by a three-day storm which swept from the mainland after playing havoc with Sullivan's army. The British ships straggled back to New York, while the crippled French fleet regrouped slowly off Newport. After d'Estaing's captains surveyed their battered vessels, they persuaded the comte to abandon the siege and head for the shelter of Boston harbor to refit.[25]

Following the storm, the American army had continued to press the enemy while waiting for the French to return. Thus d'Estaing's decision to go to Boston left Sullivan in what he described as an exceedingly "delicate" situation. He pleaded with the comte to send his marines and men-of-war into action for at least two days. When this entreaty failed, Sullivan and his general officers sent after the departing admiral an angry protest that described the desertion of Newport as "derogatory to the honor of France, contrary to the intentions of His Most Christian Majesty and the interest of his nation, and destructive in the highest degree to the welfare of the United States of America, and highly injurious to the alliance formed between the two nations."[26]

This undiplomatic protest reached d'Estaing as his fleet entered Boston harbor on 28 August. That evening Sullivan began a retreat to the northern end of the island, a move that climaxed in a stiff engagement on the following day. Their forces weakened by the desertion of disheartened militia, and knowing that Clinton neared Newport with sizable reinforcements, the American generals advised a move to the mainland to avoid a disaster. During the night of 30 August Sullivan cleverly evacuated his men and equipment without knowledge of the enemy, only a few hours before Clinton arrived with four thousand fresh troops. Meanwhile, Howe gathered more of Byron's ships and sailed again to strike at d'Estaing, only to find the French fleet anchored under the cover of Boston's harbor batteries. The campaign of 1778 had ended, except for British raids on New Bedford and Martha's Vineyard.[27]

So too ended Cooper's hopes for a crushing victory to celebrate the alliance and perhaps end the war. Instead, the connection with France had turned sour in many mouths. If the alliance was to be preserved, Bostonians would have to see to it while the French fleet refitted in their harbor.

At the time of the Newport venture, nearly all of Boston's Whig leaders still agreed with John Adams that the French alliance is a "Rock upon which we may safely build" and that loyalty to the treaties with France is "our American Glory." Thus for a brief moment in the fall of 1778 they pulled together again as they had done so effectively during pre-Revolutionary crises. The result of their exertions demonstrated anew the strength of Whig leadership in the town. Not a word of public criticism escaped. Boston newspapers faithfully praised the ally and extracted as much glory as possible from the repulse at Newport. And with all the collective effort, John Hancock and Samuel Cooper received the lion's share of credit for saving the alliance during d'Estaing's stay in Boston.[28]

Hancock had not covered himself with glory as a general in the Newport campaign. His presence had inspirational value, but he was ill suited by experience and health for the rigors of a battlefield command. Political opponents ridiculed his conduct in the field and passed on to posterity unfounded stories concerning what James Warren mocked as a "noble Example of Heroism," deserving of celebration by "a Homer or a Virgil." On the contrary, Hancock seems to have conducted himself at Newport with dignity and to have contributed whatever he could to the siege. The *Independent Ledger* reported that "General Hancock's arrival on the Island, and appearance before the army, visibly heightened the good spirits of the troops, and particularly of those from Massachusetts." Lafayette, nonetheless, may have hit on the partial truth when he suggested that the former president of Congress had little fondness for English bullets and gladly seized the opportunity of returning to Boston on 26 August to be on hand when the fleet arrived.[29]

Samuel Adams and James Warren had spread the report that Hancock was cool to the alliance, and they now expected him to oppose it publicly "if he can thereby establish his Popularity."[30] D'Estaing, well aware that Hancock had signed the protest of the American generals, could not be certain of the reception he would receive in Boston.[31] Resentful of Sullivan's slur on France's honor and fearful that d'Estaing faced more of the same, Lafayette hurriedly left his command and followed Hancock to Boston. He found the comte "much displeased" at the protest and with "many other circumstances" but still professing a "warm desire of serving America."[32]

On 29 August, while the American army at Newport came under heavy British fire, d'Estaing and his chief officers came ashore in Boston to all the military honors the town could muster on short notice. Then, with Lafayette and a group of Americans, they dined at Hancock's mansion where the marquis had been invited to lodge. With his typical flair, Hancock delighted the comte by presenting him a portrait of Washington to hang in the wardroom of his flagship. The genial host also promised Lafayette a copy as soon as an artist could be employed to paint one. That afternoon d'Estaing explained his departure from Newport to the satisfaction of a committee of the Massachusetts Council. The results of this day gratified and relieved Lafayette, who noted to Washington that Hancock "did much distinguish himself by his zeal on the occasion."[33]

D'Estaing sought to relieve Hancock of the "embarrassment in which he found himself for having signed the protest" by assuring Washington that the statesman-general had softened Sullivan's letter before signing it as a military duty. The comte added, "I have named the honorable general John Hancock a patron of the French: he has become one, and he has fulfilled this function during our sojourn in Boston."[34]

D'Estaing impressed Bostonians with his sincerity by offering to march overland to Rhode Island with the few hundred infantrymen he could muster from his crippled fleet. Sullivan's retreat from the island obviated the need to put the comte to the test, but his gesture received publicity through the newspapers.[35] Lord Howe's appearance off Boston on 1 September ended any lingering doubts as to the value of the French presence. D'Estaing erected additional batteries on some harbor islands and drew his ships into a defensive alignment. As a result, Howe sailed away, leaving relieved townsmen to praise the French admiral and General Hancock, whose "spirited exertions on this occasion," the newspapers emphasized, "did him great honor."[36]

Cooper undoubtedly played a major role in Boston's warm welcome to the fleet of Louis XVI, though his activities are at first difficult to pinpoint. Lafayette described him as "extremely useful" but gave no details.[37] By now the preacher read French and was attempting to speak it. How he learned the language is unknown. It had been taught for years in Boston and at Harvard College by a variety of native speakers, all duly certified to be Protestant. In 1774 Franklin had sent Cooper the French edition of his scientific papers with the expectation that he would read this work before depositing it in the Harvard library.[38] Four years later, a visiting French nobleman conversed with him and recorded that, "although he expresses himself with difficulty in French, he understands it perfectly well" and "knows all our best authors."[39] The oft-told story of the Brattle Street pastor's speaking Latin to the French visitors rests upon a questionable source. Likely, though, Latin proved useful in conversation with such a noted scholar as the Chevalier de Borda, one of d'Estaing's captains. Cooper's zeal for the alliance and his natural facility for language proved equal to the task of communicating with the officers of the allied squadron. He was pleased to see that for the remainder of the war the study of French enjoyed great popularity among the Whig elite, some of whom, particularly a number of the wives, quickly became conversant in what one of the several new teachers advertised as "the polite French Language."[40]

As Franklin had warned, upper-class citizens of the two countries could overcome their past antagonism for each other more easily than "common people and sailors." The French commoners manning the fortifications at Hull on the South Shore so pillaged that tiny town as to provoke an official protest to the General Court. In Boston "certain monopolizers" supplying the fleet were accused of raising the price of provisions for townsmen. Of several brawls involving Frenchmen, the most serious took place on 8 September. A nondescript gang of sailors demanded bread from the onshore bakery of d'Estaing's fleet. When refused, they attacked the bakers with clubs. Two French officers attempting to stop the melee were beaten; and one, the Chevalier de Saint-Sauveur, died a week later from his wounds. A Boston waterfront mob had killed a young nobleman, who happened to be "the first Chamberlain to his Royal Highness, Count d'Artois, brother of his Majesty the King of France." Once again the alliance seemed to totter.[41]

D'Estaing remained calm and accepted the assurances of local leaders that the rioters had not been Americans but captured Englishmen permitted to enlist on privateers. The Massachusetts Council offered a reward for their apprehension, while the newspapers praised the "prudence and moderation" of "this great man" commanding the ally's fleet. When the French declined the General Court's offer of an elaborate state funeral for Saint-Sauveur, Cooper arranged for the remains to be quietly interred in a crypt of King's Chapel—another purification rite for this architectural symbol of royal power. The General Court also voted to provide a "monumental stone" bearing an inscription to be supplied by d'Estaing. He welcomed this opportunity to perpetuate the memory of his dead lieutenant "as a mark of friendship between the two peoples." His inscription included the hope that all efforts to separate France and America would continue to be unfruitful. Somehow, perhaps because of what the comte vaguely referred to as "deliberations in Boston," the erection of a monument was sidetracked and eventually forgotten until 1917, when again France and the United States were allied. Only then was the stone displaying d'Estaing's inscription raised at the entrance to King's Chapel and dedicated by officials of Massachusetts and France.[42]

Cooper contributed to the Boston newspapers several short pieces defending and praising d'Estaing's conduct.[43] These cannot always be positively identified, but it seems certain that he was the correspondent to the *Independent Ledger* who compared the restraint of the French military following the attack on their bakery to the "wanton and butcherly" attack on civilians by British soldiers in the Boston Massacre.[44]

The preacher's attitude toward d'Estaing was widely shared by Massachusetts officialdom. On the morning of 22 September the comte and his captains made a ceremonial entry into Boston. After a reception by the General Court, they breakfasted at Hancock's. According to the newspapers, "a universal joy and satisfaction was visible in the countenances of all who were present upon this happy auspicious occasion." That same week the general officers returned for an elegant dinner given at Faneuil Hall by both houses of the legislature. And the following day d'Estaing, Lafayette, and a "number of other officers and gentlemen" dined with the local American commander. But the junior officers excluded from this official fraternizing may have taken a different view of their assignment. A German officer interned at Cambridge with Burgoyne's army reported that the Frenchmen visiting him expressed their dislike of Americans "in no very light terms."[45]

Appointed French consul at Philadelphia and naval agent for the French in all American ports, John Holker returned to Boston to assist in refitting the fleet. Remaining over two months this time, he became even more popular in Whig circles than before. Mercy Otis Warren could hardly restrain herself in writing to John Adams of Holker's "many accomplishments," and Cooper described him as a "man of Sense and a Man of Business," a prime example of "how happy it is for us that the Interest of France is so closely combined with our's in the glorious Revolution."[46]

With Holker was Joseph de Valnais, a Frenchman who had served briefly as a cavalry captain in the American army. Leaving military service, he sought to turn his excellent command of English to personal advantage through a connection with Holker. D'Estaing found de Valnais able and useful and joined Holker's recommendation that he be appointed consul in Boston. Even before the commission was issued at the beginning of 1779, he functioned unofficially in the office. Intimacy with these two ambitious men opened for Cooper new lower-level channels of communication to French interests, and their opinion of him helped to confirm the impression that Vergennes and Gérard had already formed of his usefulness to the alliance.[47]

But as long as the fleet remained in Boston, the preacher had easy access to d'Estaing. Lafayette had become a strong advocate of a new plan to conquer Canada, a scheme to which Cooper and

Hancock gave their blessing. Toward this end, late in October d'Estaing issued a proclamation, entitled in English, *Declaration Addressed in the Name of the King to All Former French Subjects in North America*. This document reminded French Canadians that they would always be French and urged them not "to raise a parricidal hand" against their motherland but instead to ally themselves with the United States and thus be assured of the protection and support of their rightful sovereign, Louis XVI.[48]

At Hancock's suggestion, Cooper arranged for a translation of the *Déclaration* into English. Apparently he had help, for two of the three draft copies of the translation now among his personal papers are in another hand. Published in the newspapers at the beginning of December, the English version was in the long run more significant than the French original. It served to educate Americans that one price of the alliance was the granting of religious freedom to Catholicism in neighboring Canada, a concession they had vehemently opposed when Britain granted it in the Quebec Act of 1774. Lest anyone escape its meaning, the English version of *Déclaration* appeared in the Boston newspapers with a preface reminding readers that Congress had promised Canadians an "absolute freedom respecting religion." By translating and disseminating this document, even before Congress had released it for circulation in Canada, Cooper took the lead in affirming a readiness to accept the full implications of alliance with a Catholic power.[49]

As d'Estaing prepared to sail at the end of October, Cooper offered in the *Independent Ledger* a generous evaluation of the comte's contributions thus far to the American cause and urged continued fidelity to the alliance, because France "is our ally, not our master." He was confident that it was in France's own interest to support American independence.[50]

D'Estaing's last days in Boston were given to a climactic round of socializing. He entertained large parties on his flagship, where tables were set before the full-length portrait of Washington given him by Hancock; and, on one occasion at least, "music and dancing for the young folks closed the day." Abigail Adams, thrilled at the attention paid by the French officers to the wife of an American commissioner to their country, complained that few Boston families reciprocated the comte's hospitality; so she and Colonel Quincy did all they could to entertain in Braintree.[51] Yet again, one man made up for any neglect by others. On 29 October as the *In-*

dependent Chronicle reported, "a superb Ball was given at Concert-Hall, by General Hancock, at which were present His Excellency Count D'Estaing, and a Number of Officers belonging to the French Fleet.—There were upwards of a Hundred of the principal Ladies of the Town present, who being richly and elegantly dressed, added a most inchanting Brilliancy to the Evening, and in the Eyes of their Countrymen, at least, gave no bad Specimen of *American* female Grace and Beauty!"[52]

Hancock's detractors expressed disgust at the lavishness of his farewell ball and held it up as the major example of an "Unbounded Licentiousness in dress, Equipage and Liveing" which already had gone far toward decaying the moral fiber of true Whiggism in the province. Their fear of "Idolatry" had been confirmed for them earlier this month when the House of Representatives voted to bestow on Hancock a marquee and other "Appendages suitable to his Rank," as if he were a major general in a European army. Fortunately, the Council had refused to concur in such an "iniquitous" measure. Now the "Idol" had spent a small fortune—£1500 on the ball alone, they speculated—entertaining d'Estaing from a motive of making himself popular rather than out of a sincere desire to serve the Revolutionary cause. Equally incriminating, a week after the General Court had passed the act banishing Tory refugees for life, Hancock's ball had indiscriminately mixed some fifty lukewarm Whigs and outright Tories with such worthies as Dr. Cooper, the Council, and the visiting Frenchmen. From Philadelphia, Samuel Adams gloomily prophesied that "when ambitious Men aim at establishing a Popularity by confounding the Distinction between Virtue and Vice and through the Degeneracy of Times they can effect it, the People will tamely submit to a Master."[53]

The leading Whigs, nevertheless, had nothing but praise for the conduct of the forces under d'Estaing. As James Warren observed them, "the French Officers and Seamen in this Squadron behave themselves Extreemly well; they are indeed the most peaceable, quiet and orderly set of men in their profession I ever saw." "Chastity, temperance, industry, sobriety and purity of morals—added to politeness and complasance" was Abigail Adams's characterization of d'Estaing's men. Someone, likely Cooper, offered in the *Independent Ledger* a partial explanation of why French and Americans were more civilized and humane than Englishmen: "Whatever cause may be assigned for it, it has long been remarked that those who dwell on a Continent, other circumstances being equal, are less rough and boisterous than those who inhabit islands. . . . [Britons] are frequently called throughout Europe 'haughty Islanders.' "[54]

With sadness the Whigs watched the fleet sail on 4 November. A storm had scattered Admiral Byron's waiting men-of-war long enough for the French vessels to clear the harbor and set a course for the West Indies. One day before sailing, d'Estaing wrote an affectionate farewell note in which he promised to retain a "most tender attachment" to and "lively recognition" of "Mon cher Docteur." The note began: "The real auspices are those of friendship; I leave with new testimonies of yours. I accept them and cherish their augury. This moment I steal from my duties is well employed, for it comforts my heart; like me a little, my dear Doctor, for I like you very much; be good enough sometimes to tell your compatriots that they will always have in me someone who is devoted to them, I swear to this."[55]

By the time of d'Estaing's departure, the frustration of the British Peace Commission was complete. After experiencing the American nationalism that viewed observance of the treaties with France as the "first solemn sacred Faith" of the new nation, the commissioners hardened their position. They concluded their mission with a *Manifesto and Proclamation* appealing to the people to repudiate Congress and its alliance by renewing their allegiance to the mother country. This document further insulted American nationality by insisting that independence would be "calamitous to the Colonies," which must then become merely "an accession to France." In that case, Britain, directed by the "laws of self-preservation," would be forced "to render that accession of as little avail as possible to her enemy." Congress answered with its own *Manifesto*, promising that "if our enemies presume to execute their threats, or persist in their present career of barbarity, we will take such exemplary vengeance as shall deter others from a like conduct." Still thinking from mercantilistic premises, the commissioners could not understand that for most American leaders and many of their people the French alliance had become the emblem of an intensifying American nationalism.[56]

Cooper's newspaper defense of the alliance had been conducted with the pronouncements of the commissioners in mind. The *Manifesto and Proclamation* had appealed to the American clergy to compare France's record of oppression of Protestantism with Britain's guardianship of religious liberty. Against this background the Boston preacher's partisanship for France took on a new public significance, while privately John Temple's return to town accentuated the difficulties of the role Cooper had chosen for himself.

When Temple arrived in New York during August 1778, he seems to have expected that his prestige and reputation would gain him immediate access to Congress. But he had foolishly persuaded the ministry to send over with him Dr. John Berkenhout, a physician who made his "secret" mission so obvious that he was soon arrested and sent behind British lines. Temple proceeded more cautiously to solicit Congress for permission to visit Philadelphia, and he counted on the good offices of Samuel Adams to further this request. In addition, he hoped that his father-in-law would join him in the capital. Apparently he envisioned himself being gratefully received in Philadelphia as a hero of the prewar resistance movement, and consequently able with Bowdoin's support to persuade Congress to abandon France and make peace with Britain on the most favorable terms contained in the commissioners' instructions.[57]

Suspecting the circumstances of his return, Congress respectfully denied Temple's request and advised him to apply to one of the state governments if he intended to reside in the country. Bowdoin, while defensive of his son-in-law's intentions, had no desire to risk his health by a trip to Philadelphia. So Temple had little choice but to move his family to Boston, where he could be certain of a warm welcome. He arrived on 28 September and was promptly cleared of suspicion by the Massachusetts Council.[58]

Of Huguenot origin and weary of a war during which he had known little but illness and separation from close relatives, Bowdoin had accepted the French alliance with limited enthusiasm as a temporary expedient to balance the might of Britain. His main concern was to end the struggle as quickly as independence could be assured. He looked on the return of his son-in-law as a possible sign that the ministry inclined toward granting independence and signing a "treaty which might end in a solid peace, founded on the independence of America, and the mutual interests of both countries." As John Temple measured the American climate of opinion, he concealed his arrangement with the ministry even from

Bowdoin, who soon became convinced that his son-in-law was the proper person to persuade the coming session of Parliament of the futility of continuing the war.[59]

Temple required only six weeks in Boston to remove any doubts in the minds of his Whig friends that "he has all along been, and now is, a hearty friend to America." As a result, in November he could leave for Philadelphia carrying a most impressive set of recommendations from the Councils of Massachusetts and New Hampshire, Chauncy, Cooper, Bowdoin, Winthrop, Warren, and General Sullivan. He traveled by way of Washington's headquarters, where he added to these credentials a bland endorsement from the commander in chief; and also on his journey he acquired recommendations from the governors of Connecticut and New Jersey. Temple told no one the precise nature of his business with Congress but broadcast hints that he was privy to useful information concerning the views and plans of the parliamentary opposition to the North Government. Cooper, accepting Bowdoin's judgment, appeared convinced as he wrote to Samuel Adams that Temple has, since his return, "given every evidence of the same Attachment to his native Country and its Liberties that he ever expressed, and in a Manner nobly negligent of his own private Interest."[60]

Hardly had Temple left town before Cooper weakened his testimonial by advising Adams to use his own judgment because in Philadelphia he would have "more and better Intelligence respecting Men and Things." Moreover, Cooper confessed, the recommendations had not been spontaneous but had been solicited by Temple and "his particular Friends here." The preacher very likely had heard a word of caution from Holker or de Valnais. As early as July, Gérard knew that Temple had been granted permission by the British commanders to pass through their lines on his mission to Congress. In a letter carried by and praising Holker, who returned to Philadelphia in December, Cooper encouraged Adams to question Temple to determine "what his particular Views are in going to Congress, or how far it may be proper to comply with them."[61]

When Temple reached Philadelphia on 1 December, the delegates were beginning to form blocs over the charges of Arthur Lee against Silas Deane, and the French minister had come to regard Lee's supporters as distrustful of the alliance. In this atmosphere Temple's credentials made him even more suspect in the eyes of some, who pointed out that the esteem in which he was held in New England only increased his usefulness to the ministry. Since many of the recommendations were addressed to him, Samuel Adams felt obliged to escort the visitor to the home of the president of Congress for an introduction. A week later a newspaper writer warned an unnamed Massachusetts delegate against fraternizing with Temple. Adams then sought to reassure Gérard of his absolute loyalty to the alliance, and they agreed at least that delegates should avoid any suspicion of dealing with a "secret Emissary from the Enemy," even though such distrust of him might be without foundation. Increasingly embarrassed by Temple's presence, Adams flatly refused as "improper" his request for a copy of the treaties with France. Four days afterwards, Temple left for New England, much to the relief of the Massachusetts delegates. They had no way of understanding that Temple, with his skill in playing both sides, endeavored to create the impression in Whitehall of having earned his passage to America. His success was relatively significant. As the peace commissioners sailed home after having failed to set foot outside the British lines in New York, Temple spent three weeks in Philadelphia probing the views of congressional delegates. And he conversed with a variety of Americans as he traveled from New York to Boston, then to Philadelphia and back to Boston.[62]

While Temple returned to Massachusetts, Cooper enjoyed the opportunity of deepening his acquaintance with Lafayette. Beginning on 11 December the young marquis spent a month in Boston waiting to sail for France. Soon the preacher's letters began singing the Frenchman's praises.[63] Lafayette had worked for months to win American approval of his plan to conquer Canada. He hoped to return soon with the backing of his government for a joint expedition. Not until reaching France would he learn that Congress had reluctantly yielded to Washington's counsel against a Canadian invasion or that such a conquest had no place in the thinking of Vergennes on how to end the war. For now, Lafayette appeared confident of Hancock's approval; but Cooper, at least, endorsed the Canadian expedition only on certain conditions, as he made clear to Franklin: "I fear our Inability to do this, unless we have Assistance and can procure Loans from abroad. If such a Plan of Operation is adopted, France must give the most unequivocal Assurances, that she means not to resume the Government of Canada, but to incorporate it with the united States."[64]

Crossing the Atlantic in less than a month on an American ship appropriately named the *Alliance*, Lafayette carried this letter to Franklin, now the sole American minister plenipotentiary to

France. On 16 February Franklin forwarded to Vergennes a long extract from Cooper's letter praising d'Estaing's conduct and the "superior order and civility prevailing in the French forces," but including the passage stating conditions for the Canadian venture. If Vergennes read this extract carefully, he could have been under no illusion that the Boston preacher's zeal for the connection with France sprang from any motive except his assessment of where American interests lay.[65]

18

Even at This Price

*A*t the beginning of 1779, a young Bostonian noted in his diary: "Spent the evening at a Club that is formed and held by a number of sensible and reputable young gentlemen for the improvement of the social faculties. This club consists of young lawyers, physicians, preachers and merchants and the time is spent without set rules or ceremonies."[1]

A member of the Harvard Class of 1769, this diarist belonged to the generation of Americans who had come to maturity during the height of the imperial crisis. Some members of this age group, Alexander Hamilton and Gouverneur Morris for example, were finding brilliant and satisfying careers in the service of the new republic; but in Boston, trade and the professions remained more appealing than politics or the military. Four years of war had greatly diminished the normal range of opportunities. Yet the war also held out the tempting prospect of inordinate profits in such risky enterprises as privateering, currency speculation, profiteering, and military contracting. These prospects lured the younger Holker to America, heightened the anticipation of many native-born youths, and even prompted a few older merchants to stake their capital on daring new ventures. By and large, however, Boston's Whig elite merely tried to ride out the war in such a way as to protect what they owned. The evidence bears out Samuel Adams's observation of 1778 that "the old substantial Merchants have generally laid aside trade and left it to Strangers or those who from nothing have raised fortunes by privateering."[2] Many an older Boston merchant must have mused on the irony of a struggle for commercial interests that had culminated in the devastation of normal trade ever since Parliament closed the port in 1774.

Cooper had espoused an alliance with France in part out of an expectation that trade with the ally would help to compensate for the loss of British commerce. This hope began to fade in 1779 as American traders learned in how few cases French goods could match in quality, quantity, or price the former imports from the mother country. At the same time French merchants complained of heavy losses incurred through the depreciation of American money and the capture of their vessels by the enemy.[3] Still, younger Bostonians continued to leave for Europe in search of profitable mercantile connections. Others sought to get a hand in the profits to be made from contracting to supply the French forces in America. In both cases, they usually utilized Cooper's connections with Franklin or Holker to further their purposes.[4]

The Brattle Street pastor pulled every string he held in behalf of Daniel Bell, an ambitious young member of his congregation, who became Holker's commercial agent in Boston; and it is possible that Cooper shared in Bell's profits. In his twenties during the Revolution, Bell typified those among this war-bred generation who had learned well the lesson that many of New England's great fortunes had been acquired by shrewd young merchants during past wars in which many other young men died for their country.[5]

Cooper's pragmatic religion and Hancock's gaudy politics suited the Daniel Bells far better than the moralistic patriotism preached by Samuel Adams. If one discounts by 90 percent the lamentations in the press, Boston's urban community still witnessed a remarkable wartime increase in gambling, high fashion, dancing, and social intermingling of the sexes. "Such a total Change of Manners in so short a period I believe was never known in the History of Man," Mercy Otis Warren concluded in 1778. Samuel Adams worried lest his "dear native Town" had "exchanged her manly Virtues, for Lenity and Luxury and a train of ridiculous Vices which will speedily sink her in Contempt." Even Franklin complained to Cooper that his countrymen in the midst of a war exported "solid provision of all kinds" in exchange for imports of "fashions, luxuries, and trifles."[6]

While Adams, Warren, and others anguished over what they perceived as the moral crisis of American patriotism, most Bostonians concerned themselves with the more elementary problem of survival. During the winter of 1778–1779 the difficulty of a depreciating currency was compounded by a severe shortage of flour, brought on by interstate rivalry and the disruption of normal trade. So serious did the food crisis become that a cry for bread could be heard in Boston streets in March, when a few hundred of the most destitute went with little or no food for several days. "If we are not allowed Flour from the Southern States, we shall soon starve," wrote Cooper, his usual optimism gone for the moment. When in April he preached a "most beautiful discourse upon the parable of the loaves and fishes," the message had more than spiritual meaning. Town officials worked hard to feed the poor, but the ability of the wealthier to pay ever higher prices for available foodstuffs made the task next to impossible. And famine accelerated the increase in crime so conspicuous during the last two years.[7]

A pervasive war-weariness settled on Boston during the hard winter months of 1778–1779. Though the fighting had now shifted to the Caribbean and southern theaters, four years of struggle had failed to expel the British from the states. D'Estaing's fleet had so far succeeded only in changing the enemy's strategy without winning any victories. The British peace commissioners had gone home with reports of colonial intransigence that strengthened the hands of those English leaders who refused even to contemplate the possibility of American independence. No one could be certain of the outcome of the world war now on the horizon, as Spain and Holland in addition to France sought to take advantage of England's discomfiture. Notwithstanding the new nation's need for a settled central government, ratification of the Articles of Confederation had been stalled by a dispute over western lands. Massachusetts still faced the divisive question of its state constitution. More discouraging than the political and military outlook, the depreciation of the Continental currency, after being briefly reversed by news of the French alliance, worsened in 1779 until by April its ratio to specie stood at 16 to 1 with no halt in sight.[8]

Writing to Samuel Adams in March 1779, Cooper summarized his view of the country's prospects: "Peace is the general Wish. The Events of War are uncertain; the State of our Currency though it has benefited some, has distressed many; should we carry the War beyond the Spirit of the People and the Army to accompany it, our Enemies might greatly avail themselves of such a Circumstance. And yet, as we have gloriously gone so far, I think we may rely that the Body of the People would still endure, and make every Exertion, rather than stop short of a safe and honourable Closure."[9]

By the time he wrote these words, Cooper had become the leading New England promoter of the view that France's commitment to American independence remained the one sure hope of preserving all thus far accomplished toward the creation of a free republic. He had consistently maintained this position for the last two years and saw no reason to change his mind now. If anything, the spiritual and material exhaustion of the American people in a long war and Britain's renewed hostility toward independence had confirmed his judgment that his country's self-interest lay in cultivating the alliance. It was a pro-American rather than a pro-French position, one most succinctly summarized by Franklin in a letter to his Boston friend the following year: "We certainly owe much to this nation; and we shall obtain much more, if the same prudent conduct toward them continues, for they really and strongly wish our prosperity, and will promote it by every means in their power."[10]

Neither Franklin nor Cooper was blind to the reality that Vergennes aided the revolting colonies only to further France's interests. Yet they also understood well what some others wanted to forget: American soldiers had fought the Redcoats with arms and ammunition largely obtained through French sources. The republic's staggering economy had been kept alive through French grants, loans, and trade. And in 1778, for the first time since hostilities began, French sea power had deprived Britain of her absolute control of North American waters.[11]

There can be little doubt that Cooper's devotion to France resulted from a combination of his independent judgment with a profound respect for Franklin's assessment of the European situation. No one would likely have questioned the sincerity of his advocacy of the alliance had he not in 1779 begun to accept a stipend from Louis XVI as compensation for his services in promoting American friendship for France.

Near the beginning of 1779, Joseph de Valnais approached Cooper with some overtures in behalf of Gérard, France's minister to the United States. De Valnais found the preacher very interested, particularly when it became clear that compensation was involved.[12] On 17 January Gérard wrote to inform Vergennes of the arrangement he had concluded with the Brattle Street pastor:

Dr. Cooper, an intimate friend of Dr. Franklin [and] the best orator of Massachusetts, has been one of the principal instigators of independence in New England. To his political talents he adds the religious influence that a leading clergyman must have on a people who maintain a strong tinge of fanaticism and religious enthusiasm. Such is the man, Your Excellency, who I believe should be bound to the King's interests. Several of the articles he published justifying the conduct of M. le Comte Estaing at the time when General Sullivan had aroused the entire East against this Vice Admiral and the French led me to thank him for them and to make known my desire to see him use his talents and influence for the same cause. His response was so filled with good will and seemed so significant to me that I engaged a friend of the Doctor to settle the details with him. The proposition has been very well received. He asked for an annual salary of 200 pounds sterling as compensation for what he lost and suffered for the common cause and to pay a vicar in order to free himself completely for the work he undertakes.

It seemed to me, Your Excellency, that such an eminent man deserved to be bought even at this price, and I have accepted the terms he requested. . . .

Dr. Cooper particularly proposes to inspire the American people with the respect and admiration due the King, esteem for the nation, and confidence in the principles and inclinations of His Majesty by using all the appropriate materials to accomplish this important objective; he strongly desires that I furnish them to him and that I request you to have sent to me everything that could further this end. By attacking the unbelievable prejudices to which the British cling to keep the Americans turned against us, he hopes to encourage union and personal trust between the two nations and to destroy the individual aversion to us that the American people continue only too often to display.[13]

Though he remained on the French payroll until his death, Cooper nowhere recorded his understanding of the services he had contracted to perform in this highly secret agreement. It is certain, nevertheless, that he would have objected to Gerard's use of the term "bought" (*acheté*). Judging by other French sources and by his letters to the French ministers to the United States, he never believed himself to be sacrificing his integrity by accepting money from a foreign government. His country was formally allied with and considerably dependent upon that government; British policy aimed at weakening the American war effort by breaking up the alliance; thus, as de Valnais informed Gérard, Cooper was "firmly persuaded that in favoring France he is at the same time favoring the cause of the United States."[14] As he may have reasoned with himself, why should he refuse financial support that enabled him to continue and enlarge the advocacy of a cause undertaken many months ago with no hope of reward except the advancement of his country's interest?[15]

During the American economic morass of 1779–1781, any offer of an income fixed in specie would have severely tested the holiest saint or the most self-abnegating patriot; and Cooper was neither. De Valnais, who would prove to be a scheming adventurer himself, professed to detect a "penchant for gold" in this minister of the gospel who obviously welcomed the opportunity of achieving a measure of financial stability for his family while he carried on his wide range of religious and political activities.[16]

With their fixed salaries, the clergy were among the greatest sufferers from inflation. The Brattle Street pastor again fared better than most of his colleagues, for this wealthy congregation regularly voted him special grants in a generous effort to keep his income abreast of rising prices. As a result, during 1779 his salary was maintained at approximately two-thirds of its intended value. In that year he was paid £1,400 in the inflated currency to supplement a stated salary of £4 per week (exclusive of parsonage and firewood), a total of £1,608 in cash, which had a specie value of around £100, one-half of the annual payment he had been promised by Gérard.[17] He received his first year's stipend—4,800 livres in the French unit—at the end of 1779, and was paid quarterly thereafter at the same rate.[18] Even after inflation had been checked at the end of 1781, more than half of his total salary still came from Versailles.

No inventory of Cooper's estate was ever filed. Perhaps brother William, clerk of probate as well as town clerk, stretched the law in the hope of letting the secret of this extra income go to the grave with the Divine Politician. There is only the word of Jonathan Williams, Franklin's grandnephew, that Cooper "left a good Estate for one of his Cloth." If so, his heirs owed some thanks to Vergennes, who willingly approved and continued the arrangement made by Gérard.[19]

As will be seen, John Temple eventually suspected Cooper to be a French pensioner but never became sufficiently certain to make the charge openly. In England the Hutchinson-Oliver circle of loyalists spread the same rumor, likely originating from those in the government who had access to some intercepted letters of the French minister. Yet Cooper was seldom mentioned by name in these letters, for the few French officials privy to the secret endeavored to protect his anonymity. They and he were so successful that no scandal hampered the remainder of his career. Had the evidence been available, political opponents would surely have used it, his cloth notwithstanding.[20]

In subsidizing the Boston preacher, Gérard and Vergennes recognized what the British ministry also knew, but what historians failed to discover for two centuries: by the end of 1778 Samuel Cooper had become the central figure of Boston politics. The more or less unknown selectmen still administered town affairs in the interest of the Whig elite, while the conspicuous prewar leaders were often absent or inactive. Samuel Adams served in Philadelphia at a distance largely isolating him from town politics. William Phillips had not resumed his vigorous leadership after the siege. Bowdoin was only slowly and reluctantly stepping forth as a rival to Hancock, whose strength sustained the unpopular though diligent Cushing. Hancock's periods of aloofness from public concerns now increased in frequency and duration, correlating apparently with more intensified bouts of the gout and other ailments.[21] Still the reality of Massachusetts politics was unchanged: Hancock's popularity and resulting political power, however capriciously he employed it, remained the base of major action.

Cooper's relationship to Hancock from 1779 on is seldom explicitly documented, but two conclusions seem clear. In no sense did the preacher control the statesman, who never played the puppet for anyone. On the contrary, Cooper with all of his skills in human relations found difficult the slightest manipulation of this man whose actions regularly baffled those closest to him. Nonetheless, Hancock's pastor maintained an intimacy with him that, though somewhat restrained and deferential, made possible an effective collaboration. Increasingly, Hancock relied for information, advice, and defense on Cooper, who consequently found new openings to influence him. This role was later distorted by wags and critics into that of "Prime Minister" to the "King." But by such shorthand Bostonians indicated only that the fastest route to Hancock's mansion lay through the study of the Brattle Street pastor. Visiting Frenchmen often discovered that path as quickly as local young men with political ambitions.

Both an interpreter and a molder of public opinion, Cooper now stood at the center of Boston's political life, from which vantage he continued his efforts to discover and promote policies favorable to his mercantile community and to reconcile dissenters to these policies. In 1779 he was the only major Boston Whig still on good terms with all the surviving prewar leaders; and he struggled to preserve these relationships as long as possible. As Franklin's main New England correspondent and confidant, he enjoyed a reflected international prestige, the most recent fruit of which was a rewarding covert connection with the French government. Yet, in his mind, he remained above all the minister of the town's most affluent and influential church, whose congregation he could now serve on a broader scale than ever before. If he used some of his stipend from France to relieve himself of pastoral duties ("to pay a vicar"), it was only to hire an occasional substitute in the pulpit. It was characteristic of him that he saw the importance of the material as well as the spiritual needs of his people. While Bowdoin and Hancock drew on their accumulated capital to live comfortably in the midst of economic distress, their pastor assisted younger and less prosperous parishioners to take advantage of wartime opportunities for profit making.

But how can the pursuit of self-interest be compatible with the claims of patriotic service to one's country during a war for survival? Arthur Lee and his brother, Richard Henry Lee, had raised this question before the nation, charging Silas Deane with misuse of his position in France to enrich himself.[22] In an age when government procurement depended on the skills and confidential connections of merchants who naturally mixed public business with their private concerns, Deane was far guiltier, we know today, than most American agents; nevertheless, the Lees could not muster sufficient evidence to prove their suspicions.[23] After recalling Deane, Congress postponed a settlement of his case for many months; finally, at the end of 1778 he attempted to clear himself in the press. During the last days of 1778 and the first two months of 1779, Boston newspapers filled their pages with little but reprints of the charges and countercharges hurled in this controversy that shook Congress and much of the new nation.[24]

Samuel Adams, who had come to respect and work closely in Congress with Richard Henry Lee, found himself irresistibly drawn to Arthur Lee's side in this contest, particularly after John Adams replaced Deane and reported seeming irregularities in the conduct of business by the commissioners.[25] Neither of the Adamses shared the commercial values of the elite upon whose support their careers had thus far rested. Similarly, the Lee brothers had often been at odds with the Virginia aristocracy. In Congress the Adamses and Lees had established close ties with men they could esteem as disinterested patriots who had early stepped forth against Britain. These "old Whigs" had come by the beginning of 1779 to regard themselves as the saviors of the Revolution against interested men who, whatever their professions of patriotism, put position and wealth above the nation's welfare.[26] Their bête noire was Robert Morris, the Philadelphia merchant prince whose mercantile empire proved indispensable to the war effort, but with whom Deane had been connected in business before going to France.[27] The Lee-Adams Junto, as they came to be called, saw in the Deane affair the test case of whether the republic could stand against a "Combination of political and Commercial Men, who may be aiming to get the Trade, the Wealth, and Power and the Government of America into their own Hands."[28]

With some help from his cousin, Samuel Adams made a determined effort to turn Samuel Cooper against Deane. In several letters early in 1779 he compared Deane's "commercial and interested" views with Arthur Lee's "long and unremitted Attachment to the Interests of America and of Mankind." Adams stressed his "fixed Opinion, founded on particular observations, that there is a joynt Combination of political and commercial Men to exclude all vigilant Patriots from publick Councils and Employments knowing that Vigilance and unimpeached, unsuspected Fidelity will be an effectual Bar to the carrying such politico commercial Plans into Execution." Thinking from this conspiratorial premise, Adams rejected Deane's claim to priority over Lee in negotiating French aid and his contention—the factual nub of the dispute—that some of that aid had been given in the form of loans to be repaid rather than as outright grants. America, he feared, is "too unsuspecting long to continue free."[29]

In response, Cooper only subtly revealed his opinion. While assuring Adams of his concern for vigilance against "Tory and Commercial Plans," he explained that Deane's original publication had been impressive in Boston, at first because of "the close Connection and Confidence he appeared to have with Dr. Franklin, and the Court of France, who are vigilant, inquisitive, and well acquainted with the Characters of Men, and whose Interest it is to preserve our new Republic, and counter work the Designs of Britain against it." Still, Cooper expressed his respect for the Lee family and his hope that Congress could decide the issues wisely despite the heat of the controversy.[30]

In Philadelphia, Gérard found himself drawn into the politics of the Lee-Deane affair, not so much in defense of Deane as in opposition to the threat which in his mind Arthur Lee posed to the alliance. The French minister spoke good English and dealt with the delegates socially and informally as well as through official channels. Insensitive to the variety of sectional and personal contests for position and power among the shifting representation in Congress, Gérard saw the delegates as either friendly or hostile to his view that America's only hope of defeating British power was in following French leadership. In the debates over the proposed attack on Canada and over Silas Deane's integrity, he identified an anti-French faction in Congress, headed by Samuel Adams and Richard Henry Lee, determined to exact as much as possible from the alliance while remaining highly suspicious of France's intentions toward the United States. He even believed such men capable of conspiring with Temple or other British agents to betray France in return for the recognition of American independence. In response, Gérard enmeshed himself more deeply in congressional politics and set out to enlist writers, Cooper among them, who could influence public opinion on the vital questions related to the alliance.[31]

The main subject of Gérard's concern was Article VIII of the treaty of alliance, which read: "Neither of the two parties shall conclude either truce or peace with Great Britain, without the formal consent of the other first obtained; and they mutually engage not to lay down their arms until the independence of the United States shall have been formally, or tacitly, assured by the treaty or treaties, that shall terminate the war." This treaty did not take effect until the outbreak of war between France and Britain. Since there had been no declaration of war from Whitehall, Gérard's instructions called for him to secure a formal recognition of the binding force of Article VIII. Seemingly satisfied with polite but vague assurances at first, he waited until December 1778 to demand a formal acknowledgment for the purpose of quelling the rumor that in the absence of a declaration of war the United States could negotiate separately with Britain. Gérard made this demand the week after the arrival in Philadelphia of John Temple, whom he believed to be the chief source of such a rumor.[32]

Congress delayed five weeks while it continued debates on Deane. During this debate, Thomas Paine, at Gérard's insistence, was discharged from his position as secretary to the Committee on Foreign Affairs for indiscreetly disclosing, in a published attack on Deane, the existence of French secret aid before the alliance. Finally, on 14 January, Gérard got his wish: a unanimous resolution declaring the treaty with Article VIII to be in effect.[33] But in debate over this resolution the view had been expressed that public disclosure of the treaty would give Britain an advantage in peace making; for she would realize that once France was disposed toward peace the war could be ended with no concession to the United States except independence.[34] Gérard, seeing in this a determined stand against him by Adams and Lee, increased his efforts in opposition to them. Among other actions, he attempted to add the jobless Paine to his staff of writers, but had to look elsewhere when "Common Sense" quickly proved too unreliable to be worth the French gold he was offered.[35]

Cooper congratulated Samuel Adams on what Congress had done respecting Article VIII. Unlike Gérard, he knew the mind and spirit of this Boston politician too well to think him capable of intriguing with Temple to bring about a reconciliation with Britain. Back in Boston after his visit to Congress, Temple continued to advise anyone who would listen that a victorious France would prolong the war by making exorbitant demands on an exhausted Britain, which, if finally exacted, would totally destroy the balance of power established at such a high price in the Seven Years' War. Temple apparently found some support among those who, in Cooper's words, "are for putting Britain on the compassionate List, and for inducing America from meer Pity to save her from becoming a Province to France."[36] To counter such opinion, Cooper wrote an unsigned newspaper article in defense of Article VIII. Had there been no such provision in the treaty, he argued, a sense of obligation would still have prevented Congress from negotiating a separate peace. Beyond obligation lay American self-interest:

> This Article is moreover a great Security to us, against our internal and external Enemies. For our Independence is evidently as much the Interest of France, that we may depend upon her Vigilance to guard us not only against the Power, but the Wiles and Gold of Brit-

ain, and against her secret Emissaries and Friends, who will employ every Art to divide us, and delude us back to such a Dependence upon her, as must soon produce a new War, or end in our total Enslavement. Nor is there any ground to suppose that France would wish to carry on the War after Britain had offered reasonable Terms to her and the States upon the basis of our Independence. The securing this Point is evidently the great Object of the Treaty; Britain has never offered to concede it. And the more closely we are united with France, the more we act in conjunction and mutual Confidence, the sooner it is likely to be established. France was long in deliberating, before she took the Part that she expected would bring her into a War; and from the noble and pacific Disposition of her young Monarch, we may be satisfied she will take the first fair Opportunity that Britain shall give, for closing it.[37]

Temple had no inkling that this direct attack on him had been written by Cooper, nor did he yet suspect the preacher's relationship to the French government. In February Temple announced his intention of returning to Europe by the first convenient opportunity. His credibility had suffered further when his brother Robert, whose loyalty, in Cooper's judgment, was at best "equivocal," went to Philadelphia in February to press a claim for damages done to the family farm at Charlestown by the Continental army during the siege of Boston. Congress partially paid the claim, but the case raised again old questions concerning the Temples. De Valnais warned Holker that the real purpose of Robert Temple's trip was to continue the work of his brother toward repudiation of the alliance and a reconciliation with the mother country.[38]

John Temple remained in Boston until 23 May, when he sailed for Holland. Consul de Valnais filled his reports to Holker with tales of Temple's intrigues, particularly with General Horatio Gates, who commanded the Continental forces around Boston during the winter of 1778–1779. Temple knew that after Burgoyne's surrender, Gates, a native-born Englishman, had written to an English nobleman a plea for peace which was read in the House of Lords. He also sought to take advantage of Hancock's hostility toward Gates. De Valnais maintained that Temple allied himself closely with the general, that both were "inveterate enemies of Silas Deane," and that Temple had access to Gates's correspondence. He did not entirely exaggerate, for, before leaving, Temple wrote the general concerning the purpose of his trip, which was to persuade influential Englishmen of the "total impracticability of Great Britain's effecting anything more than her own further distress, if not ruin, by continuing the war against this country." He urged Gates to assist this effort: "Your sentiments, if I judge right, are nearly the same as these, and I doubt not your letters . . . will freely express these sentiments, and may contribute much to induce that infatuated country to put an immediate end to so ruinous a war."[39]

Temple carried to Europe a letter to Pownall in which Bowdoin reiterated the essential Whig case against Britain and expressed his doubt that the mother country could ever recapture the colonies, especially now when she must also contend with France. Therefore, the longer the war "is continued, the less valuable will peace be to her whenever it shall take place; particularly in this instance, among others, that use will habituate us to foreign commodities and manufactures, to the exclusion, in a great degree, of British, which from custom, if time does not efface it, would be preferred on equal terms." Bowdoin's longing for peace had not weakened his resolution to achieve independence and free trade, a stand "from which America cannot and will not now recede." If Britain makes peace soon on these terms she can regain most of her American trade. He assured Pownall that Temple's stay in America had left him "abundantly convinced" of these facts.[40]

Bowdoin likely did not know of—or at least all the terms of—his son-in-law's employment by the ministry, nor could he have known of his pastor's arrangement with the French. He artlessly spoke the voice of the mercantile community, largely convinced that independence was now the only way to achieve free trade, the goal which had animated the prewar resistance movement in Boston. Prodded by Temple, Bowdoin had come to rest his hopes on an awakened England reviving trading relations with her former colonies, while Cooper looked to free America's profitable association with France. Yet both saw commerce as the chief instrument with which their country must build a glorious future. Bowdoin recognized the value of the French contribution, just as Cooper understood that French commerce could never fully displace the English. In any discussion of Boston's Revolutionary politics, it is vital to note that those leaders who remained at home during the peacemaking kept their feet on the solid ground of commercialism better than those who served mainly in Congress or in diplomatic missions.

Notwithstanding the warnings he received through French sources, Cooper was not ready to abandon Temple. In April he wrote to Samuel Adams to inquire if Temple could not be "honoured with some public Message to the Minority in England, that when Times change, may give him some Weight with the Friends to Liberty." He asked Adams whether nothing can "be done of this Kind for a Gentleman, whose Attachment to the Interest of America seems to prevail under much Discouragement." When no response came from Congress, the following August Cooper joined Bowdoin, Cushing, Chauncy, and Samuel Adams—with the conspicuous omission of Hancock—in signing a "Certificate" attesting to Temple's services to his country, particularly in procuring the Hutchinson letters.[41]

Meanwhile Gérard persisted in his fantasy that Temple conspired with the Lee-Adams Junto to bring about a reconciliation with England, even believing him to be carrying to Europe the Junto's secret instructions for Arthur Lee. He urged Vergennes to order his arrest if he should set foot in France. But Temple remained only briefly in Holland before returning to England, where he walked the streets of London boasting that he had recently dined with General Washington. Thomas Hutchinson ventured to George III the opinion that Temple "was willing to secure both sides." The king dismissed the subject calmly, remarking only, "That's bad."[42]

19

Even in the Tenderest Cases

No chapter of Samuel Cooper's complex and often contradictory career seems more incongruous than his relationship with Joseph de Valnais. Nearly twenty-five years younger than "the sweet Reverend," as he once referred to Cooper, this French soldier of fortune had enjoyed little success until making a connection with Holker and consequently being appointed to the Boston consulate. Now he dreamed of further improving his situation by combining "love and fortune." He observed to Holker that "Twenty thousand pounds sterling . . . and a sufficiently pretty little woman merit respect." But in love, as in much else, his heart overcame his head. He eventually married an attractive young lady from a respectable but poor branch of the Quincy family.[1]

His commission as consul in Massachusetts ports reached de Valnais in February 1779. He observed the occasion by hoisting the French flag at the Whig tavern in Congress Street, where he gave a dinner party for local notables. Toasts were heard to John Holker, to the immortalization of the negotiators of the Franco-American alliance, and to "Perpetual Union" between the two countries. As consul, de Valnais faced in the next few months an abundance of problems with trade and resident French nationals; but he appeared to take genuine delight in an association with Cooper marked by an interesting mixture of warmth and deviousness.[2]

Under Gérard, whom he never met, Cooper's usual line of communication to the French minister in Philadelphia was through the local consul to Holker. Although in June 1779 he began to file regular consular reports with the minister of marine and colonies, de Valnais considered himself primarily responsible to his patron Holker, with whom he corresponded regularly. These letters reveal the consul's growing intimacy with and dependence on the preacher. In March he wrote, "I have everywhere been persuaded that our reverend friend is sincere in his attachment to France by the manner in which he has spoken to me even of his best friends, joined with the impartiality he has shown toward them in several conferences that we have had; all this proves to me that he acts with frankness. He becomes more and more necessary to our interests. . . . He renders me in particular the greatest service by his counsels." A few weeks later de Valnais added, "He is really completely essential to us; as for myself, I derive the greatest advantage. I dare to assert that he merits our confidence in all respects."[3]

Lest Holker and Gérard should think him completely under Cooper's influence, de Valnais offered frequent assurances of being "not blinded" and "always on guard." To put "our reverend friend" on his toes, he wrote—or took credit for writing—a piece by "A Liberal Patriot" published in a Boston newspaper on 1 May. This article warned Bostonians not to heed the plea of Thomas Apthorp, a Tory who had returned and petitioned to have his name removed from the act of banishment. Apthorp had been close to Temple and was related to Cooper's wife; so the "Liberal Patriot" accused "one of the celebrated Ministers of the Gospel" of lobbying with the General Court in Apthorp's behalf at the prompting of a "geometrical politician among us"—unmistakable references to Cooper and Temple. De Valnais described with relish to Holker the effects of this article on Cooper:

> If you had seen him running about the streets of Boston on the day this piece appeared you would have laughed heartily. He came to me to confide his uneasiness on the subject, telling me there was not a word of truth in it. I reassured him. When he saw that I was undisturbed on this count, he was satisfied and we laughed over it afterwards. It never occurred to him that I was the author and I was careful not to tell him. As you may well believe, it is nevertheless a good idea that he be aware that he is being watched, because then he will not dare start anything he imagines might come to my knowledge.[4]

The consul's attempt to discipline Cooper may only have in effect strengthened the public image the preacher attempted to maintain as a moderate who wanted to conciliate all factions among Whigs. His skill in playing this role was again demonstrated in June 1779, when he took the lead in moving Harvard College to bestow in a single ceremony doctor of law degrees on General Gates and Consul de Valnais. *Doctor* de Valnais hastened to inform Gérard of this "striking proof of the esteem and respect they wish to show my nation as well as me personally."[5]

Behind this facade of harmony, Cooper faced the severest test of his belief that French and American interests fell nearly together in the struggle against Britain. Vergennes had become convinced that Spain's involvement was essential to the successful conclusion of the war. But that colonial power had no desire to contribute toward the creation of a free American republic likely to rival her ambitions in the New World and to incite her restless colonies there to rebellion. After delaying by proposing mediation to Great Britain, Spain signed a secret convention with France in April 1779. By this agreement Vergennes paid a high price for Spain's entry, including a promise to continue fighting until Britain returned the former Spanish possession of Gibraltar. This provision increased the difficulty of fulfilling Article VIII of the Franco-American alliance. In addition, France agreed to support Spanish plans in Florida and the lower Mississippi Valley and to grant her a share of the Newfoundland fishery, should that British territory be taken. With all these concessions, Vergennes could not secure a commitment to American independence from the court of Madrid.[6]

In February, while these negotiations were under way, Gérard informed Congress that Spain's anticipated actions, through either mediation or war, made peace more imminent; consequently, he advised the appointment of a peace plenipotentiary and the drafting of instructions setting forth proposed terms for a settlement of the war. Expecting Congress to act speedily, he urged the delegates to be moderate in their demands in order to calm Spanish fears concerning American ambitions and to keep the question of independence unencumbered by desires for territorial aggrandizement. To the surprise and chagrin of Gérard, his communication touched off six months of lively congressional debate during which the objectives of the alliance underwent a close scrutiny.[7]

Congress stood united in insisting on the formal recognition of American independence as the one indispensable condition of any settlement, and there was a surprisingly easy agreement on the boundaries to be claimed. In contrast, the questions of the navigation of the Mississippi and participation in the North Atlantic fisheries dragged on into the summer. Still unaware of Spain's hostility toward the new republic, the delegates treated the Mississippi issue cautiously to avoid offense to the Spanish ministry; instead, the complex issue of the fishery became the main focus of congressional debate and partisanship.

For the past century France had struggled with Britain over the Newfoundland fishery, only to find her position there eroding rapidly after the peace of 1763. A major objective of Vergennes in allying his nation with the revolting colonies had been to gain the exclusive right to a desirable location on the Newfoundland coast where French fishermen, far from home, could base their labors on the large banks nearby.[8] Deane and Franklin, impatient for an alliance in the spring of 1777, had gone so far as to propose to Vergennes the joint conquest of all British possessions in North America with France to receive, among other gains, "half the Fishery of Newfoundland."[9] The treaties signed a year later accepted the French view of their fishing rights but left a settlement of the fishery until after the fortunes of war had been revealed.[10] But in 1779 Newfoundland and Nova Scotia remained firmly under British control, and neither ally appeared willing or able to wrest these territorial bases of the fishery from the common enemy. By declaring their independence Americans had forfeited all claim as Englishmen to fish offshore and to dry their catches on the coasts of these British colonies. Any American demand at the peace table for the establishment of these rights by treaty would weaken France's effort to improve its own position and might deny it the only likely return from this side of the Atlantic on a heavy investment in American independence. Naturally Vergennes and Gérard detected ingratitude in congressional delegates who advocated making demands on Britain likely to be met only at France's expense.[11]

No Massachusetts politician could view the fishery question with indifference. Dried fish had been the colony's most valuable commodity for export, representing from 1768 to 1772, according to one set of figures, more than half the value of all exports, two-thirds of those to the West Indies, and 90 percent of those to southern Europe and the Wine Islands.[12] By the exportation of dried fish, whale oil, and a few other commodities, together with earnings from shipping services, Massachusetts capitalists had managed to pay for English imports. The war had virtually ended deep-sea fishing for all participants, but obviously the hoped-for commercial prosperity in the peacetime years ahead required the rebuilding of a flourishing fishing industry.

Yet the most desirable settlement of the fishery question took on a baffling complexity in astute mercantile minds. If the allies failed to conquer Nova Scotia and Newfoundland by force, France expected Congress to relinquish all claim to inshore fishing and drying on the Newfoundland coast so that she could better press her case there under prior treaty rights. Americans, of course, could fish the Grand Banks off Newfoundland, which lay outside the territorial limits, but the problem of where to dry the catch remained. Gérard was willing for the United States to contend with Britain for shore rights in Nova Scotia, but he warned that his monarch would not prolong the war to obtain that concession.[13]

Underlying all questions concerning the fishery was the uncertainty of the American commercial situation at the war's end. Only the establishment of favorable trading relations with France and Great Britain, especially with access to the West Indian markets of both, could maximize the value of the fishery to Massachusetts. Also significant would be the new relationship of the Boston-centered economy to the fishing industry carried on by resident Newfoundlanders, whose exports of fish to Europe had begun to surpass those of Massachusetts on the eve of conflict. Above all loomed the need to regain a competitive position in the carrying trade. In this equation of interrelated economic factors, it was possible to make gains on one side while losing more on the other. As they viewed the indecisive military and diplomatic situation in 1779, Boston's mercantile leaders were hard put to envision the most favorable commercial balance they might expect to achieve in the peacemaking that seemed near.[14]

But for Samuel Adams the fishery issue presented a clear and simple challenge to the fulfillment of the American Revolution. Judging the North ministry not yet prepared to make a sincere peace offer, he saw more danger in "an Accommodation with Great Britain than in any Stage of the War." What security, he inquired of Cooper, would the United States have if Canada, Nova Scotia, and Florida are left in the enemy's hands? The fishery is vital as the nursery of seamen for an American navy as well as the basis of an extensive trade. None "reach the Pinnacle of Eminence and Glory but the virtuous and brave." Let the struggle continue until a decisive triumph eliminates all danger of inexperienced American diplomats being duped by European courts into signing a treaty that provided nominal independence but no genuine security for the new nation.[15]

Richard Henry Lee eagerly joined Adams to lead a fight against yielding to French wishes on the fishery. One year before signing the alliance, Arthur Lee had warned Congress of the danger of making concessions to France "of which we might sorely repent hereafter." Such alertness to American interests had made him persona non grata to Vergennes and Gérard, so his brother now believed.[16] It was thus time for the old revolutionaries to step forth again with the boldness of 1775 lest weaker and self-interested men win the day. James Lovell of Boston, secretary of the Committee on Foreign Affairs, threw his energy behind Adams and Lee. Despite his talents and his intimacy in youth with Hancock and other sons of the elite, Lovell had never risen above his schoolmaster status until the Revolution thrust him into Congress and awakened an ambition for diplomatic service. Like Adams, he had served Boston's mercantile community without becoming part of it.[17] The fishery question provided them both with an opportunity to continue and enlarge the moral and nationalistic criticism of commercialism begun in the attack on Deane. Because of the regional importance of the fishery, they could count on the nearly solid support of the New England delegates, and they received considerable if uncertain assistance from members representing the middle states. With the notable exceptions of Lee of Virginia and Henry Laurens of South Carolina, the southern delegates refused to countenance any continuation of the war to procure fishing rights.[18] Lee, Adams, and Lovell, nevertheless, mustered the strength to prevent a resolution of this section of the instructions until late in July. All the while Gérard's impatience mounted.[19]

In their private correspondence Cooper emphasized to Samuel Adams the difficulties of extending the war in the hope of obtaining a territorial right to the fishery:

> The Fishery is agreed on all Hands here, to be indispensable. We cannot do without it. Nova Scotia and Canada ceded to us with it, would be a great and permanent Protection to it, would prevent any Views of Britain to disturb our Peace in [the] future, and cut off a Source of corrupt British Influence, which issuing from those Places might diffuse Mischief and Poison through the States. On the other hand it is said by many—The War has greatly exhausted us—Our Spirit of Enterprise

is not high. An Attempt upon Canada and Nova Scotia must be secured by a superior Fleet of our Allies. The Calls in Europe and the W. Indies render this at least doubtful. Such an Attempt must certainly involve us in a vast additional Expense, while our Finances labour so much with the present. Provisions, especially Grain of all Kinds are scarce, and threaten a Famine in the Eastern States: An unsuccessful Attempt would bring us into a most disagreeable Situation. Should we have Peace on the Cession of Independence and the Fishery, Canada, Nova Scotia, and Florida would in time naturally unite with us: or should another War ensue upon their Account, the united States having restored their Currency, enlarged their Commerce and their People, and in every View fresh and vigorous, might easily wrest these Provinces from the distant Power of Britain. From the best Observation I can make the last seems to be the prevailing Opinion here.[20]

As if to show a different climate of opinion, two Boston newspapers on 22 April published pseudonymous warnings against acquiescence in an unfavorable treaty for which "insidious tories, as well as timid and indolent whigs" were preparing the public. "An Inquirer" wrote, "We have suffered enough in this war, to purchase a permanent and advantageous peace," and he added Newfoundland to the list of areas which must be seized from Britain. "Confederatio" demanded the ratification of any peace treaty by the state legislatures to guard against undesirable cessions to the enemy. Gérard hastened these articles to Vergennes as evidence of the rise in the United States of an anti-Gallican party insisting on the conquest of all North America and hinting that only the politics and ill will of France stood in the way of such "brilliant acquisitions."[21]

A week later a "correspondent" (almost certainly Cooper) in the *Independent Chronicle* set forth the essential position on the fishery taken by the leading spokesmen for American commercialism:

Nothing, says a correspondent, can be of greater moment to the new-born nation of America in the negotiations for peace, than a proper care of the fishery. It is particularly the life of the New-England States; and we can no more do without it, than our brethren at the

southward can without rice, indigo, tobacco and flour.
But the importance of the fishery is not confined and
partial; it is general, and extends to all the States: For
what is this nation without a navy? What are ships without men? And what nursery of seamen is comparable to
an extended fishery? It may therefore be relied on, that a
branch of traffic so absolutely necessary to some States,
and so essential to the grandeur and security of all, will
be particularly attended to by those who have hitherto
so gloriously conducted us through the war. Even those
among us who are most disposed to peace, scruple not
to say, we had better continue the war indefinitely, and
to the last extremity, than not to secure the fishery to the
extent we have always enjoyed it. France, and all the
European powers who mean to trade with us, are deeply
interested in this point. For the means of remittance is
the means of trade, and without the fishery, our commerce with Europe will be much confined. In this view,
even Britain herself must wish, for the sake of her own
advantage, and the vent of her own manufactures
among us, to see us in the full possession of such a
branch of commerce.[22]

This position evidenced not so much faith in France's good intentions toward the United States as in a competition between that
country and England for the postwar American market. In the
opinion of Gouverneur Morris, who led the fight in Congress
against the Lee-Adams position, to demand a share of the fishery
from Great Britain as an ultimatum for a peace treaty was "the certain way of losing the thing when if proper measures be taken it
must certainly be gained." These "proper measures," as Congress
finally agreed, were to let France and Britain enjoy equal trading
privileges with the United States, but only after Britain had entered
into a commercial treaty which continued to Americans their "common right to fish," and with equal resolution to impress upon
France the commercial importance of backing American fishing
claims. By pursuing this method, Cooper emphasized to Adams,
"should we establish our Independence upon tolerable Terms,
though not such as we could wish, and [consequently] be free from
the enormous Expenses of the War, our increasing Vigor and
Numbers would be a sure Pledge of our attaining in [the] future not
only what may be absolutely necessary, but highly convenient." For
Cooper the leading national issue of 1779 had become clear: "Shall

we secure our Independence upon the Offers or Prospects we now have, or shall we under all our Difficulties trust to the Hazards of War, and risque all that we have obtained." In Boston those who had much to lose or who hoped to gain much more looked to an era of peace and free trade as their chief security.[23]

Cooper seemed to fear most the plea made in Congress by Elbridge Gerry from the Massachusetts fishing town of Marblehead. Gerry declared the readiness of the people of New England to "stand alone again without allies or friends, before they would barter away their rights." The commercial argument is so powerful, he concluded, that Britain will concede the fishery whenever she is ready to acknowledge independence. Thus the issue must be settled before any peace treaty is acceptable. This view received strong support throughout New England, particularly from Boston's satellite towns. For example, William Vernon of Providence, now serving on the Boston Naval Board, wrote to John Adams in the spring of 1779, "I hope no dishonorable Peace will take place, we had rather linger out this distructive War, for Years, than leave our Enemies incircled about us, from Nova Scotia to the Floridas, with perhaps the Loss of the Fishery, while we are left only to Possess the skirts of the Shores."[24]

The Boston preacher had long been partial to France, and his views on peacemaking resembled those held by some leading commercial spokesmen and by many members of Congress; thus it is difficult to evaluate the influence of French gold on his position. In April 1779 even Consul de Valnais seemed persuaded that Bostonians, though war weary and eager for peace, would never purchase it at the price of abandoning their claim to the fishery. But at about this time Gérard endeavored to strengthen American loyalty to the alliance and to French views on the peace by employing more hired writers, including Hugh Henry Brackenridge, who had been put on the payroll after Thomas Paine proved unmanageable. As "The Honest Politician," this future American literary figure contributed during the next year a long series of pro-French articles to a Philadelphia newspaper, some of which were reprinted in New England. The writings of "Americanus," an unidentified French hireling from the middle states, drew more attention in Boston, especially his analysis of the fishery question, which was reprinted in August and explained at length the argument for not jeopardizing a speedy end to the war by demanding from Britain an explicit recognition of the American right to fish as before the Revolution.[25]

The fishery was too delicate a question for Cooper to rely on a public discussion to win his case. Instead, he worked privately to influence important men. This effort went undocumented except for de Valnais's reports to Holker, which were composed more to put the consul's services in a favorable light than to appraise accurately the accomplishments of his reverend friend. The report of 3 June, written partially in code, stated Cooper's objective bluntly:

> Dr. Cooper is working to destroy the influence of Mr. S. Adams in this state. He has already succeeded in ruining him in the opinion of several important men who are even his best friends and sole supporters. These men believe that the Americans ought to be moderate in their peace terms, and that they ought above all to fear the loss of France's friendship by such extravagant demands as sole fishing rights. These two persons [two of these?] swear that America will be forever lost without France's support. Dr. Cooper has the greatest hope of succeeding in his efforts against Mr. Samuel Adams. Since he was fortunate enough to persuade these two people, I have no doubt that he will succeed in destroying the influence of a certain person [Adams]; but in my opinion he will not succeed in eliminating the prejudice [against the French] that I have mentioned in preceding [letters].[26]

The activity described in this report had apparently been stimulated during May when Gérard sent his nephew and secretary, identified only by the last name of Meyer, to Boston in response to the desire of "one of the most esteemed leaders of Massachusetts Bay" to be informed concerning the coming pacification.[27] In June this "esteemed" leader wrote two letters to Gérard which so delighted him that he had them transmitted in code to Vergennes. Since only the coded copies survive, it is impossible to identify the author from the handwriting. He may have been Thomas Cushing, who a month later went on record as actively opposing the Lee-Adams position.[28] More likely, judging by the style and contents, Cooper was this leader. Whoever wrote them, the two letters gave Gérard all the reassurance he could have asked: "In my opinion, the States cannot adopt a better policy than to bind themselves closely to the alliance and to observe in all cases the wise moderation for which it sets the example. The opponents [of France in Congress] are playing an unwise and hazardous role both for themselves and for their country." Americans have no claim to the fishery beyond their own shores but can obtain a share through "Soft and fair means" and commercial pressure after the peace. The writer maintained that in private conversations he had persuaded several "persons of influence in Government and Trade," among them Francis Dana, of the correctness of these views. And he pledged himself to oppose attempts "to create jealousies here against the Southern States or our Ally upon these points," while managing "all things cautiously and so as to keep as many friendships and as broad a bottom as may be for our common cause." But he warned the French minister that "the present moment is not the time" for a public discussion of these issues. Even though an open and fair hearing would bring the truth to light, the enemy might take advantage of such a procedure.[29]

Samuel Adams left Philadelphia and returned to Boston at the end of June. A weary and frustrated Richard Henry Lee resigned from Congress earlier the same month. Thus they were both absent when their colleagues finally agreed not to make a share of the fishery an ultimatum for peace but to require such a concession in any commercial treaty with Britain. The delegates then turned to the choice of a peace negotiator. Glorying in their self-ascribed roles as the "most decided friends to the Liberties of America," Lee and Adams left the younger Lovell to uphold the cause of true virtue in Congress. Busier than ever, this former Boston schoolmaster still found time to daydream of living as a farmer in a Nova Scotia liberated and governed by that paragon of republican excellence, General Horatio Gates—and no doubt freed of the "low Arts" of political and commercial men.[30]

Ill and hoping to return soon to France, Gérard jumped to the conclusion that his masterful diplomacy had preserved the alliance from the personal excesses of Lee and Adams. In mid-June he informed Vergennes that "Mr. Lee has been accused before the whole Virginia Assembly of having sacrificed the interests of America and the Alliance, and the storm raised against Mr. Samuel Adams in Boston is about to force him to return to that city. These two champions find themselves compelled by the public uproar to change their tunes. They are now eagerly doing all they can to establish their pretensions for peace and to throw the blame for delays on their antagonists."[31]

Adams had hardly come home in disgrace, for he was elected moderator of the first town meeting after his return.[32] Still he had to face again the political reality so easily forgotten in Philadelphia. Though relatively inactive, his adversary Hancock had been elected

Speaker of the House of Representatives, a position in which he would be conspicuous until a new constitution created the office of governor.[33] Hancock had taken no public part in the recent controversies and had broken off his correspondence with Deane.[34] Yet there existed no question but that he stood behind Cooper and Cushing in their loyalty to the alliance. Apparently de Valnais expected Adams to launch a public drive to gain support for his views on pacification: instead, he worked privately. When the conversation turned to the subject of peacemaking at the home of "one of the most influential Boston merchants," where he had chanced to encounter Samuel Adams, de Valnais withdrew, feeling that he was "de trop" in such company. In July the consul assured Holker that he and the preacher had not let down their guard: "Mr. S.A. . . . has not yet set forth his projects. Our respectable friend [Cooper] and I watch him closely. But he still says nothing since his arrival which might indicate his feelings to the people of this town." A week later de Valnais wrote that Cooper "has formulated a plan against the stubborn supporters of the fishing interests which before long will give you as well as His Excellency [Gérard] all the satisfaction you promised yourselves as to the zeal and attachment of this worthy friend. This plan ought to destroy or at least diminish much of the influence of Mr. S.A."[35]

Here matters stood on 3 August 1779, when Gérard's replacement, the Chevalier de La Luzerne, landed in Boston. He came recommended by Franklin as one who bears a "most amiable character, has great connections, and is a hearty friend to the American cause." John Adams, returning home on the French frigate that carried La Luzerne to America, noted him to be a "large, and a strong Man" who "has a singular Look with his Eyes" and the habit of closing his eyelids while conversing. During the voyage Adams found occasion to warn the outgoing minister concerning the danger of connecting himself with "Individuals or Parties, in America, so as to endanger our Union." He also educated him on the contributions of Samuel Adams to the Revolution. La Luzerne in turn advised his traveling companion not to judge the potential of Franco-American commerce by the trickle of trade so far, carried on in France by a "Parcell of little Rascals, petits Coquins, and Adventurers who have sold the worst Merchandises for great Prices" while the "great and able Merchants had not yet traded to America." The diary kept by Adams on this voyage provides the first evidence of those quiet but consummate diplomatic talents that were to make La Luzerne one of the most effective representatives ever sent to the United States by a foreign country.[36]

The chevalier and his party came ashore to cries of "Long live the King!" and "Long live the protector of our liberties!" During a stay of one month in Boston he was overwhelmed by personal honors and expressions of respect for Louis XVI and of attachment to the alliance. These included a public reception by the Massachusetts Council and a convocation at Harvard. House guests of Thomas Cushing, La Luzerne and his staff were also given a dinner in the Hancock mansion, whose owner had to scour the countryside to find choice food in a season when farmers had little desire to market their produce in town for the increasingly worthless paper money. For his part, the minister entertained Hancock and other notables on board the *Sensible*, the French frigate which had brought him to America. Though speaking little English, he still conveyed through interpreters a spirit of sincerity, modesty, and amiability that even Samuel Adams found temporarily disarming.[37]

Privately, La Luzerne faced demands from Samuel Adams and others to send the *Sensible* in support of a strike by Massachusetts militia against a small English garrison recently established at the mouth of the Penobscot River in Maine. Reluctant to refuse the first request made of him in this country, the chevalier agreed in principle while using treaty technicalities to delay sending the frigate. After this expedition collapsed from inept leadership, Adams, backed by Gates, pressed La Luzerne to commit his country to a joint attack on Canada. Again expressing interest and understanding, the minister indicated his willingness to give every consideration to this "delicate" proposal when it came officially from Congress. These discussions, as well as all of his experience in Boston, left strong impressions on the envoy's mind, which he summarized for Vergennes: "I believe the State of Massachusetts to be firmly set on the principles of independence and on the Alliance; however, in spite of this I have reason to believe that we will find her more demanding and obstinate than suits us concerning the interests and system of pacification which is taking form."[38]

Still, the outlook was not entirely discouraging, for La Luzerne could report that "most of the French whose commercial interests have led them to Boston are pleased with their treatment by the government and by individuals." He appeared to share the view expressed by another French chevalier at this time that Bostonians "treat state affairs like commercial operations" and thus "judge us to be like pedlers, very honest thieves" who are liked more than esteemed. This French noble took comfort in the realization of Samuel Adams's worst fear; he believed that the "mercantile spirit and luxury are gradually stifling the love of independence" in Bostonians.[39]

La Luzerne's month in Boston afforded him the opportunity of reappraising his government's employment of Cooper. He seems to have been well satisfied, for they reached an understanding concerning their future relationship, and shortly afterwards the preacher was paid his first year's salary. In writing to thank La Luzerne for a gift of wine and for other kindnesses, Cooper began, "Nothing could have [made?] a stronger Impression upon my Mind than the kind Regard with which you were pleased to honour me during your Residence in this Place." And he concluded, "It will be the pleasure of my Life in every way within the small Compass of my Abilities to promote this Object [the alliance], and to fulfill every Direction respecting this or any other Matter, with which you shall please to favour me." A month later he received La Luzerne's general suggestions for preparing favorable publicity concerning the present French naval operations in American waters. Until his death, the pastor of the Brattle Street Church would remain in direct and frequent communication with the minister of France to the United States. "Your views and your friendship are well known to me," La Luzerne wrote Cooper, "and I believe you are equally convinced of mine."[40]

Only two months after his return from France, John Adams learned that he must sail back as the American "minister plenipotentiary for negotiating a treaty of peace and a treaty of commerce with Great Britain." His election had come at the end of an intense struggle in Congress between factions and sectional interests, a contest rendered incredibly complex by a maze of strategic moves and by the personal ambitions of some delegates for diplomatic posts. When the voting ended, Franklin was kept in Paris by a narrow vote, John Jay was sent to negotiate a treaty with Spain, and John Adams was to go to Paris to be on hand for the anticipated negotiations with Britain. Though Arthur Lee had been left without portfolio, the Lee-Adams faction took heart in the appointment as peace plenipotentiary of a New England man they considered to be one of them.[41]

Congress selected another Bostonian, Francis Dana, as secretary of the mission. Adams also took with him his sons aged twelve and nine, and he granted the request of a doting grandfather to let

Samuel Cooper Johonnot accompany them as a companion. On 14 November this eleven-year-old lad said his farewells and joined John Quincy and Charles Adams on the *Sensible*. As the ship passed the Castle while falling down to Nantasket Road, Hancock had himself rowed out to drink a toast to the success of the voyage.[42]

"My little Grandson," Cooper informed Franklin, "goes to France with a View to acquire the Purity of the French Language in Speaking and Writing. . . . He already loves his Country and its Rights, and in Consequence has a particular Respect for France, which I wish to increase. I send him partly, as a dear Pledge of my own Esteem and Gratitude for a Nation to whom my Country is so much indebted, and of my sincere Inclination to act, even in the tenderest Cases, in the true Spirit of the Alliance."[43]

In the "true Spirit of the Alliance," the Americans on board the *Sensible* included a Boston merchant who was going to Europe on a "Plan of Business" and carrying a recommendation from Cooper to Franklin. After a small leak forced the *Sensible*'s captain to put into a northwestern Spanish port on 8 December, Adams and his party set out through the Spanish mud, braved the Pyrenees in winter, and covered more than one thousand miles before reaching Paris early in February 1780. By Lafayette, now returning to America, Adams informed Cooper that little Sammy was "well and very contented" after this arduous journey. He also cast the observations he had made since his arrival into a succinct lecture to the preacher: "Instead of wishing and hoping for Peace, my dear Countrymen must qualify themselves for War, and learn the value of Liberty by the Dearness of its Purchess. The Foundations of lasting Prosperity are laid in great military Talents and Virtues. Every sigh for Peace, untill it can be obtained with Honour, is unmanly."[44]

20

Nobles Freely Chosen by Ourselves

*T*oward the end of a severe winter that had brought much suffering from hunger and cold, the tenth anniversary of the Boston Massacre fell on a Sunday in 1780. Cooper adapted to the occasion an old sermon from the text, "The kingdom of God is not meat and drink; but righteousness and peace, and joy in the Holy Ghost." The climax came in these words: ". . . these States have been like the Vision of Moses, a Bush that burned and was not consumed."[1]

The simile of the burning bush aptly expressed the concern of Boston's leaders. A decade after the first bloodshed of 1770, it seemed questionable whether the nation would persevere to bring the war to a successful conclusion. The fervent hope for peace in 1779 had proved illusory, yet few wanted to face the demands of another campaign. After the food crisis of March 1779, some Bostonians could not erase the fear of starvation from their minds. The winter of 1779–1780 brought a near-record snowfall and extreme cold to Boston at a time when British activities in Maine had interrupted a major source of inexpensive firewood by sea.[2] As compared to the middle and southern states, where the army now was forced to expropriate large quantities of supplies, rural Massachusetts still fared well. But the farmer had little incentive to send his produce to market in the commercial towns. At the same time, both the rural and urban poor believed the merchants to be enriching themselves by speculation in the scarce foodstuffs. Such a report spread in the fall of 1779 concerning Cooper's protégé, Daniel Bell, who purchased provisions for the French navy.[3]

During 1779 and the first half of 1780, the Boston town meeting, the Massachusetts legislature, and voluntary associations of merchants and towns engaged in renewed attempts to establish effective economic controls.[4] All the while, nonetheless, prices continued to climb in Boston. In 1779 Congress doubled the quantity of its currency in circulation. By the time Cooper delivered his 5 March sermon the following spring, it required approximately sixty continental dollars to purchase goods worth one dollar in specie. In this depressing spring of 1780, the possibility of a national collapse could not be ruled out.[5] Peace at any price held a strong attraction for the town's laboring men, who bore the brunt of hard times.[6]

In March 1780 Congress made a final effort to save its currency by revaluating it at forty to one of specie, then asking the states to collect it in taxes at this rate and exchange it for a new limited Continental emission. The plan failed within a year, but in the meantime the burden of Revolutionary finance passed back to the states, thus depriving Congress of a major source of power. Yet through all this economic chaos Congress kept faith with the commercial classes by guarding the value of its loan certificates. Similarly, Massachusetts in its wartime financial measures and in the confiscation of loyalist estates was careful to protect the interest of creditors. Though currency depreciation and eventual repudiation constituted a heavy tax to pay for the war, Boston's elite still gave thanks that the reins of government were held by such "responsible" men. But the failure of the state to settle its government threatened the continuation of these sound policies.[7]

Along with other leaders in 1780, Cooper exhorted his countrymen to persist in the struggle and worked to bring into being a new Massachusetts government. No one, however, seemed more fearful of the collapse of the American cause than La Luzerne. He had to be dissuaded from circumventing Congress in a direct personal appeal urging the states to a total exertion against the common enemy.[8] But through Cooper the French minister was able to fill the Boston newspapers with such appeals. He went so far as to instruct the preacher to promote a plan which called on the ladies to raise a bounty to supply Washington's soldiers with luxury items beyond the essentials of government issue. Dutifully, Cooper obeyed, though he saw little chance of the scheme's success.[9]

There was much else for which he could take credit in his reports to La Luzerne. Under such pseudonyms as "A Soldier," "A

Republican," "Hambden," and "A Farmer," he pleaded for citizens to make "united and most vigorous exertions in the noble cause of our country," all the while holding fast to the alliance and supporting the new French forces being sent to America. From the pieces that can be positively identified and from the abundance of other writings over the same pseudonyms, Cooper emerges as one of the leading propagandists at work this year in Boston. Yet his pseudonymous exhortations rang true with those delivered from the Brattle Street pulpit. With the issues of peacemaking temporarily thrust into the background by renewed fighting and domestic crises, he could more sincerely than ever believe that in serving France he also served America.[10]

Words alone could not preserve the Revolution. After the evident weakening of Congress, the states had to turn their eyes from Philadelphia and look to themselves for salvation. As in critical periods of the past, the Whig leaders put aside their differences and united in the common cause, this time to create a constitution that would revitalize republican Massachusetts while embodying the objectives of those principally responsible for the break with Britain.

Last of the major states to settle its government, Massachusetts still moved slowly after rejecting the Constitution of 1778. In February 1779 the General Court asked the towns if they were now ready to form a government and whether a convention should be organized for that unique purpose. The response led to the call for a constitutional convention to meet at Cambridge on 1 September. That proved to be a propitious date, for by then Bowdoin and Hancock were in better health, Samuel Adams was home from Congress, and John Adams was able to attend the first sessions before returning to Europe.[11]

The Boston town meeting had insisted that membership in the convention be truly proportional, but the General Court avoided that troublesome issue by simply permitting each town to send the number of its representatives in the House and decreeing every freeman twenty-one or over eligible to vote in this organic function, regardless of his property qualifications.[12] In a sparsely attended meeting, Boston elected twelve delegates, the representation to which it was entitled, even though in recent years the town had economized by sending only seven representatives to the House. There were no surprises. In addition to Hancock, Bowdoin, and Samuel Adams, the delegates included six merchants, one lawyer, an architect-builder, and a physician. All had been active to some extent in town politics. Adams had the dual distinction of being the oldest and the only poor delegate. Seven of the twelve attended Cooper's church, and all but two had Harvard degrees. By selecting such men to draft a constitution, Boston's Whig elite gave evidence of its pertinacity in maintaining political control through successive generations and in holding to those economic and political objectives that had motivated resistance to Britain.[13]

Of some three hundred delegates attending the opening session in September, Boston men provided the most significant leadership. The convention elected James Bowdoin president and for secretary chose Samuel "Bishop" Barrett, a forty-year-old merchant politician with literary pretensions. His service proved less valuable than that of John Lowell, Cooper's parishioner and political protégé, who distinguished himself throughout the convention. Lowell, along with Bowdoin and the two Adamses, was elected to the drafting committee of thirty-one. In order to prepare the proposed constitution as quickly as possible, this committee turned the initial task over to John Adams, who, though Boston's adopted son, represented his native Braintree. By the end of October Adams had a draft constitution, modified by the committee, ready for the convention's consideration. He then set sail for France before learning the fate of his work.[14]

The convention took up the draft constitution in sessions lasting from 28 October to 12 November, and 5 January to 2 March. Despite vigorous debate, few appreciable changes resulted before the document was approved and submitted to the towns for ratification. Each town was advised to consider it article by article and to offer amendments that would correct any part deemed unacceptable by a majority of voters.[15]

Had he been retained by them to put their constitutional desires in writing, John Adams could hardly have written a document more in line with the views of Boston's Whig elite. It began by declaring the "natural, essential, and unalienable" rights of man to include the "right of acquiring, possessing, and protecting property." Society is to protect each individual "in the enjoyment of his life, liberty and property, according to standing laws." The thirty articles of the "Declaration of . . . Rights" clearly and forcefully summarized the maxims of Whig ideology that had shaped the response of colonial leaders to Britain's efforts after 1760 to alter imperial relationships.[16]

The "free, sovereign, and independent" state established by the constitution was to be governed through a political structure resembling the old charter government stripped of its colonial inferiority and bolstered by explicit safeguards for property and other rights. Each spring, freemen of twenty-one or over who met modest property requirements were to elect the governor, senators, and representatives. To be eligible for these offices, one must be "of the Christian Religion" and possessed of the specified property—a moderately limiting requirement for representatives, more so for senators, and severely so for governor. The forty seats in the Senate were apportioned among counties according to the "proportion of the public taxes paid," while the House roughly represented population under an elaborate scheme designed to allay the suspicions of the smaller towns.

Memories of Bernard and Hutchinson notwithstanding, the executive branch received a large grant of power. The governor was given a veto over acts of the legislature (subject to being overridden by a two-thirds vote of both houses), the power to appoint judicial officers, and the authority to pardon most offenses. He also became commander in chief of the state's armed forces. In a startling reversal of pre-Revolutionary Whig strategy, the constitution required the legislature to provide the governor with an "honorable stated salary, of a fixed and permanent value." Though he carried out many of his functions with the advice and consent of the Council (consisting of nine senators chosen by joint vote of both houses), the governor received power to preserve the independence of the executive and judicial branches. As a further step in this direction, judges were to hold office during good behavior and the justices of the Superior Court were to have "permanent and honorable salaries." Now that sovereignty had passed from the king in council to "We . . . the People of Massachusetts," a strong, balanced government could be advocated as the servant rather than the enemy of human liberty.[17]

Along with the proposed constitution, the towns received *An Address of the Convention* justifying its main features. Carefully prepared by a committee of five—including three Bostonians and another soon to move to that town—the *Address* also came in for close attention on the convention floor in an effort to render it consensual. This revealing document plainly acknowledged that the Senate had been designed to represent property. Furthermore, the property qualification for voting was defended as a means of keeping from power men "who will pay less regard to the Rights of Property because they have nothing to lose." A justification of the strong gubernatorial office received equal attention. When one man or body of men "enact, interpret and execute the Laws, property becomes too precarious to be valuable." Therefore, the governor, who under the proposed constitution is "emphatically the Representative of the whole People," is given those powers necessary "that a due balance may be preserved in the three capital powers of Government." If Samuel Adams drafted the *Address*, as has been maintained on the basis of insufficient evidence, he had learned well the minds of the Whig elite.[18]

Boston took up the constitution in a town meeting that continued by adjournments through the first two weeks of May. After agreeing to propose some inconsequential amendments, the 887 voters present gave their unanimous consent to all of the document except Article III of the "Declaration of . . . Rights," which dealt with the religious establishment. This article had been the main point of contention in the convention, whose debates had overflowed into the newspapers. As so often happened throughout Massachusetts history, the intertwining of political and religious freedoms occupied center stage.[19]

Article II guaranteed the right of the individual to worship God "in the manner and season most agreeable to the dictates of his own conscience." But the next article appeared to take away this right by investing the legislature with the authority to require a citizen to attend and support some Protestant teacher "of piety, religion and morality." A few Bostonians thought Article III provided an insufficient legality for the town's unique system of voluntary church attendance and maintenance. Quickly overcome with a proposed amendment, this objection caused little concern. Rather the Baptists, who had become the most numerous and significant American foes of religious establishment, led the battle against what they saw as a step backwards to the intolerance of an earlier day.[20]

In this contest, Isaac Backus and the country Baptists were joined by Samuel Stillman, the college-educated and gifted, though folksy, pastor of Boston's First Baptist Church and one of the town's most popular preachers.[21] He struck at Boston supporters of Article III, particularly the local clergy, not only on general principles of religious liberty but on the inconsistency of the capital's enjoying a voluntary system of support for the clergy, while its spokesmen advocated compulsion for the other towns. At the final sessions of the town meeting, with only Article III left on the agenda, Cooper and Stillman clashed in a lengthy debate. According to one observer, Dr. Cooper "in his elegant and smooth way cut him up, and brought his comments down to nothing."[22]

At the conclusion of this debate, the town meeting tried to placate Stillman by including him on a committee with Cooper, Lowell, and two others, to propose changes in Article III. The committee brought in a revision which retained a system of mandatory church support while providing additional options for religious dissenters. This amendment passed, as did by a smaller majority a motion instructing Boston's delegates not to delay ratification of the constitution if such a revision could not be obtained. It came as no surprise that more voters were interested in "some Form . . . to give Stability and force to Government" than in a protracted struggle for religious freedom. Thus Boston returned the constitution to the convention with recommended changes but also with a clearly expressed desire to have that body complete whatever work proved necessary to institute the new government without again consulting the people.[23]

The convention reassembled in the Brattle Street Church on 7 June. Returns from the towns were so ambiguous that the votes could be tallied in such a way as to indicate acceptance of most sections of the constitution by the required two-thirds majority. Despairing of finding a consensus among the various amendments proposed to Article III and the other articles drawing heaviest criticism, the delegates after a week declared the entire constitution ratified as it stood. By a strict count, Article III at least had not been approved; yet the delegates correctly sensed the desire of the large majority on the entire question. Even those strongly advocating a more democratic form of government usually acquiesced, with the hope that experience would prove them right by 1795 when the constitution could be amended in another convention.[24]

In the Constitution of 1780 the commercial centers of eastern Massachusetts regained whatever dominance they had lost during the upheaval since 1775: that is to say that control of the Revolution had been returned to the hands of the men who had begun it.[25] Their resurgence resulted from no class conspiracy but from a brief reunion of that effective leadership that had won the day against Bernard and Hutchinson. As in past crises, the Whig chiefs grounded their efforts on the political ideology, the profound respect for property values, and the religious system common to the great majority. Differences of policy notwithstanding, these foundations of Massachusetts culture had been authenticated and strengthened by five years of war experience. Samuel Adams himself seemed reluctant to move from the "good Humour" with which "this great Business was carried through," to the hard questions of war, diplomacy, politics, and economics on which this culture provided no certain basis of agreement.[26] However one judges their performance in these divisive areas, the statesmen of Revolutionary Massachusetts had in both process and result created the model for constitutions in the American republic.[27]

Obviously pleased when for some unexplained reason he received more votes than Hancock in the May 1780 election of representatives under the old government, Samuel Adams resigned his seat and returned to Congress that July. Hancock's relatively minor role in the convention and his finishing fifth in this election, together with Bowdoin's return to political life, led Adams to cherish a brief hope that the outcome of the first gubernatorial election was not a foregone conclusion. Yet, as he later admitted to his wife, he understood why the choice of Hancock appeared a political necessity to most citizens. Who else enjoyed the prestige and popularity to bind the state's diverse interests to the new government in these difficult times? While William Gordon, James Warren, and a few other Hancock depreciators sought some way to keep "one of the most egregious triflers" out of the governor's chair, designing young politicians like James Sullivan prepared to ride Hancock's coattails to position and power.[28]

The election came on the first Monday of September. In Boston the results surprised even Hancock's warmest supporters: he had 858 votes to only 64 for Bowdoin and 1 for Samuel Adams. Similarly, throughout the state Hancock received more than 90 percent of the votes cast.[29] When writing the news to Franklin and John Adams, Cooper could only explain that "the Popular Interest of Mr. Hancock appears from this Choice to be much greater in the State than even his Friends imagined."[30] Cooper spoke plainly the truth that was to be later obscured by the snowballing myth of Samuel Adams's primacy in the Boston resistance movement. Historians of the Revolution would lose sight of Hancock's decisive role from 1765 to 1776, but Massachusetts voters did not. For the remainder of his lifetime the vast majority gave him their votes out of a deep sense of gratitude and because they saw in him a personification of republican ideals. It could hardly have been a secret that Hancock's wealth had steadily declined as a result of a war in which some other well-placed men made fortunes. With their protracted and exaggerated emphasis on his executive weaknesses and personal vanities, political opponents failed to tarnish his image among the masses of citizens whose transfer of loyalty from a monarchy to a republic required effective symbolization.

Hancock's personal appeal to voters not ordinarily concerned with politics had been vividly illustrated in the Boston election, when 923 turned out to vote for governor but nearly two-thirds left without casting a ballot for lieutenant governor. Though the point is difficult to document, it seems no less true that across the entire state one persuasive argument in favor of the constitution had been the near certainty of having a popular governor.[31]

Boston's church bells and artillery batteries announced the beginning of the new government on Wednesday, 25 October. After the General Court organized and officially counted the gubernatorial ballots, a committee of both houses waited on the governor-elect in his mansion and escorted him to the State House where he made a short, modest accceptance speech. He then took the oath of office and was proclaimed "Governor of the Commonwealth of Massachusetts."[32] (In England Thomas Hutchinson had died suddenly a few months before and was thus spared the agony of reading the news of this day that for him would have marked the ultimate disgrace of his native land.)[33]

Having concluded their political duties by the middle of the afternoon, the governor and legislators marched through throngs of noisy celebrants from the State House to the First Church to hear Hancock's pastor deliver the first election sermon under the constitution. The honor came as close as propriety permitted to a public acknowledgment of this preacher's political contributions to the Revolution and to the creation of a republican Massachusetts.

Cooper's text celebrated the democratic elitism that had characterized much of Massachusetts history and had now transformed Hancock into a republican prince. He condensed two verses from Jeremiah (30:20, 21) to read: "Their Congregation shall be established before me: and their Nobles shall be of themselves, and their Governor shall proceed from the midst of them." After justifying revolt and independence, Cooper extolled the constitution, framed by a free and happy people enjoying the fruits of their own labors. Under this excellent frame of government, he continued, voters naturally give their suffrages to "men who have steadily acted upon the noble principles" on which it rests: brave, unselfish, public-spirited men who are "Nobles freely chosen by ourselves." Foremost among these stood Governor Hancock, whose "name as President of Congress, authenticates that immortal act," the Declaration of Independence; "who had taken too early and decided a part, and done too much for the liberties of America, to be forgiven by its enemies"; and who has become the cornerstone "in our political building." "Behold the man" chosen by his fellow citizens to be the "first Magistrate of this free commonwealth!" Lest he appear to fawn, Cooper abruptly switched to a brief, casual exhortation on the typical election sermon dictum that public office is a public trust and the consequent obligation of citizens to "keep an eye of care upon those who govern."[34]

Without mentioning the Baptists by name, he pleaded for "mutual candour and love, and an happy union of all denominations in support of a government, which though human, and therefore not absolutely perfect, is yet certainly founded on the broadest basis of liberty, and affords equal protection to all. Warm parties upon civil or religious matters, or from personal considerations, are greatly injurious to a free state, and particularly so to one newly formed." These words were to draw a vigorous printed rejoinder from Isaac Backus.[35]

In the spirit of the constitution, Cooper called upon those in authority to preserve inviolate the credit of Massachusetts. "An established honour and fidelity in all public engagements and promises, form a branch of righteousness that is wealth, is power, and security to a State." Here, Americans could learn from Britain, whose power has rested chiefly "upon the long and nice preservation of her faith in all monied matters" and upon maintaining a "fair character with her creditors." Such care is overwhelmingly important in the American states, which, being a new nation, "have a national character to establish, upon which their very existence may depend. Shall we not then rely that the present government will employ every measure in their power, to maintain in this commonwealth a clear justice, an untainted honour in all public engagements; in all laws respecting property; in all regulations of taxes; in all our conduct towards our sister states, and towards our allies abroad."[36]

With this transition, the election preacher proceeded to praise the French alliance as "natural and likely to be lasting." French generosity toward America became more understandable when one studied how that monarchy "has been the nurse and protectress of free republics," a truth to which Switzerland bears witness. "The personal and royal accomplishments of Louis the Sixteenth are known and admired far beyond his own extended dominions, and afford the brightest prospect to his subjects and allies." Spain also has "evidently engaged in our cause" by joining her arms to France's. Cooper implored God to bless these princes, yet his praise for the Bourbons could be interpreted as mild in comparison to his past eulogies. This was an hour for nationalistic self-reliance rather than overdependence on foreign aid.[37]

It had been a pleasant fall day, but the sunshine coming through the windows of the First Church was turning to twilight. A banquet awaited at Faneuil Hall.[38] Yet Cooper took time to impress upon those before him that the grand purpose of this day's solemnity was to launch a government capable of energizing the war effort. He held out no hopeful promise of an early or easy peace; but however difficult the remaining struggle, the rewards justify the effort: "We seem called by heaven to make a large portion of this globe a seat of knowledge and liberty, of agriculture, commerce, and arts, and what is more important than all, of christian piety and virtue."[39]

Whatever his intentions, Cooper's consummate performance at Hancock's inauguration established him more clearly in many eyes as the power behind the throne, the "Prime Minister" in the new government. When the governor delivered a short address to the legislature a week later, it was rumored to have been written by his pastor. Compare the sermon and the address "and behold the man," parodied one of Hancock's detractors.[40]

While Massachusetts was adopting its constitution and electing its first republican governor, the military balance on the continent remained indecisive. Cooper longed for total victory and saw only defeat in the prospect of protracted stalemate. His European correspondents had little to report except a growing obstinacy at the British court, sparked by an increased hatred of the former colonists. As a result, his posture noticeably stiffened. Though continuing to take orders from La Luzerne and to praise the alliance at every opportunity, Cooper utilized his connections with the French to impress on the ally his views, especially the necessity of naval support for the American cause. The opportunist in the preacher welcomed foreign gold, but livres could not quench his primary concern for the success of the Revolution.

The gloom produced by the hard winter of 1779–1780 had been temporarily dispelled when the *Hermione* put into Boston harbor on 28 April. This French frigate carried back to America the Marquis de Lafayette, who had spent the past year in France pleading for more aid from his sovereign. After a series of delays, his importunity prevailed. He returned with orders to inform Washington that an army of six thousand, supported by six ships of the line, was on the way. During Lafayette's four days in Boston he was overwhelmed by the warmth of his reception. He made no public announcement of his good news and privately seems only to have vaguely intimated it to a very few important people. Yet Cooper informed La Luzerne on the day of Lafayette's departure, "It is the common Talk here that the Return of the Marquis has something more in it than merely his joining the Army."[41]

The marquis renewed his acquaintance with Cooper and delivered mail from Franklin and Adams. During this visit Lafayette put his seal on the preacher's contributions to the alliance by writing a letter of introduction to Vergennes for Gabriel Johonnot, who was anticipating a business trip to France. In addition to his great personal merit, the letter read, "he is the son-in-law of my intimate friend Doctor Cooper, whose reputation is known to you. Amongst all the Americans most ardently attached to the French alliance, and most fitted to establish it on a lasting basis, we must especially put Doctor Cooper at the head of the list of our friends."[42]

Cooper also cultivated the friendship of two men arriving with Lafayette: Louis de Corny, the advance commissary agent of the French army, and Captain Latouche of the *Hermione*. While Lafayette and de Corny hastened away to fulfill their duties, the captain remained in port and placed his frigate temporarily at the service of the state. Among a round of hospitality, he gave a dinner on the *Hermione* for the Massachusetts Council. Consul de Valnais's inexplicable behavior on this occasion provided public evidence of why the French ministry had come to regard him as unfit for his position.[43]

De Valnais appears to have enjoyed better relations with Bostonians than with French nationals in the town, and no one in his government had found him reliable. His successor had been appointed by February 1780 but for some reason did not arrive for more than a year. De Valnais may have caught wind of the intended change. At Latouche's dinner his behavior was generally disrespectful, and he singled out for insult one of the officers who had accompanied Lafayette to Boston. A resulting duel on the next day left the consul wounded; his antagonist died the following month, though possibly from other causes. As a result, de Valnais acquired the reputation of a "manslayer." In the words of a Frenchman who visited Boston soon afterwards and was overturned in a coach driven recklessly by the consul, he "was a good fellow, but not very well adapted for the post which he filled."[44]

The consul's deficiencies rendered Cooper's services all the more valuable. Visiting French notables invariably called on him and sometimes were received by Hancock through a personal introduction from the preacher. Typically they found Cooper to be a "man of intelligence, eloquent and enthusiastic," perceived vaguely his relationship to Hancock, and noted his importance in town politics. He was called on as well to deal with a variety of problems arising from the alliance. For example, at the beginning of 1781, sailors from French and American naval vessels in Boston harbor engaged in a bloody brawl. A grand jury indicted seven Frenchmen for being accessories in the death of an American. Eventually a pacifying compromise was arranged, for which La Luzerne gave much of the credit to the "prudence and influence of Dr. Cooper."[45]

Membership for a few French gentlemen in the American Academy of Arts and Sciences proved a useful if minor way of strengthening the alliance. This learned society, the second in the United States, was chartered by the legislature and organized in mid-1780, with Bowdoin as president and his pastor as vice-president. In later years John Adams took full credit for proposing such a society and persuading Cooper to undertake its organization.[46] That incurable gossip, William Gordon, reported that Hancock threatened to leave the Brattle Street Church because Cooper listed Samuel Adams before him on the first bill of incorporation. Gordon did not seem to realize that he destroyed the force of this jibe at his adversary by implying that Hancock acquiesced in a second bill listing all names in alphabetical order. If Cooper's skill in navigating between Scylla and Charybdis failed him in this instance, as Gordon maintained, no outward sign appeared.[47] Despite the war, the American academy got off to an impressive beginning. A delighted Commissary de Corny accepted Cooper's offer of membership as an "honor" and "another link attaching me to you."[48]

Cooper was not too busy entertaining visiting Frenchmen to welcome Arthur Lee, who arrived in August 1780 and remained several weeks in Boston. After giving La Luzerne advance notice of Lee's coming, Cooper went out of his way to develop an acquaintance with this controversial diplomat. He escorted him to Cambridge for an inspection of Harvard College and applauded the General Court's grant of land to Lee in recognition of his services. Finally, he sent him on his way to Philadelphia with glowing letters of introduction to three Connecticut clergymen. Perhaps he sought to quiet talk of his subservience to French interests and to appease Samuel Adams while still privately giving the French minister the impression of having Lee under surveillance.[49]

In this same spirit, even those Whigs most suspicious of the ally's intentions at the peace table greeted enthusiastically the news that a French army and fleet were crossing the Atlantic. When the French forces actually landed at Newport in July 1780, that nation's honor had never appeared brighter in New England.[50]

The Comte de Rochambeau, a veteran campaigner, had been given command of the expeditionary force in preference to Lafayette, who was only a junior officer in the French military establishment. A shortage of transports forced Rochambeau to sail with only five thousand men, leaving the other one thousand—and more, it was hoped—to come soon in a second division, bringing not only reinforcements but more adequate supplies and munitions. While at sea he learned that Charleston, South Carolina, had fallen to a British siege with the heaviest American losses of the war. Rochambeau then set his course for Newport, which the enemy had evacuated the previous October. His men came ashore weakened by illness and in no condition to fight. Within a few days of the landing, a British fleet appeared off Newport, and Clinton's army from New York was reported moving toward Rhode Island. The New England militia turned out but found no enemy, for once again British military and naval commanders proved incapable of agreeing on a plan of attack.

Preserved from an immediate battle, the French army quickly revived its men and strengthened its position. But summer turned to fall without the arrival of the second division. In September Admiral Rodney's fleet from the West Indies reached New York, giving the British overpowering naval superiority on the American coast. In an effort to find a promising plan for a joint operation, Washington and Rochambeau conferred at Hartford that same month. The two generals repressed Lafayette's impatience for action and agreed to await further French aid. Their decision spread pessimism, particularly after Washington, on the way back to his New Jersey headquarters, stumbled onto Arnold's treason at West Point.[51] At the suggestion of Captain Latouche, Cooper published in a Boston newspaper a favorable account of French naval engagements in the West Indies, where the fleet under the Comte de Guichen cruised during the spring and summer.[52] It had been expected that de Guichen would follow Rodney north. Instead he headed for home, leaving the fleet at Newport virtually blockaded. Thus as Massachusetts prepared to launch its new government, the military scene darkened again.[53]

Cooper made the most of French inaction. He offered his services to Rochambeau and endeavored to involve son-in-law Johonnot in the business of supplying the army and fleet at Newport. Rochambeau may have known of the preacher's secret connections with his government, for late in September he sent his treasurer general to Boston for a clarification of matters of common concern. Cooper was entrusted to assist this officer and particularly to make him acquainted with Hancock and Bowdoin.[54] Rochambeau himself did not come to town until the middle of December, when he and his party spent a week as Hancock's house guests, with the Brattle Street pastor often in their company. Meanwhile, La Luzerne had quietly visited Boston for a few days in October during a tour to assess the military and political situation in the northern colonies.[55]

As another hard winter settled in, the nature of the new American crisis was as plain to the French officials in the United States as it was to the Americans with whom they dealt at all levels. After visiting Boston, La Luzerne reported to Vergennes that he had found the people loyal to the alliance but uncertain whether they were equal to the task of organizing and sustaining a final push against Britain.[56] Congress called on the state for quotas of soldiers enlisted for the duration and for large quantities of supplies and money. Yet by its actions Congress revealed its dependence on Louis XVI. It sent William Palfrey, Hancock's former associate and now Washington's paymaster, to France as consul general and commercial agent in the hope of expediting the flow of supplies. And Congress dispatched John Laurens as a special envoy to entreat further loans and aid from the French court.[57] No one analyzed the situation more closely than La Luzerne, who suggested to Vergennes that, though the American cause rested on a better foundation than its leaders now understood or admitted, the psychological stimulus of another loan was essential to a vigorous exertion.[58]

Cooper, like others, sniffed the wind for a scent of the hoped-for aid. Toward the close of the year he learned that the Marquis de Castries had become French minister of marine and colonies. De Castries's son, attached to the army at Newport, solicited from the preacher a letter of introduction to Samuel Adams before visiting Philadelphia. In complying with this request, Cooper expressed the hope that the father's appointment would bring an increase in military aid from France. But soon afterward he received a letter from John Adams containing a stern lecture on overreliance on foreign assistance. The war, Adams feared, might rage on for twenty years during which Americans would have to rely mostly on themselves.[59]

Cooper appears to have had this gloomy admonition in hand when he wrote a letter to Adams on 9 February 1781, which he sent by the ship on which Laurens sailed that day from Boston on his mission of supplication. Though regretting the slowness of filling army quotas for the coming campaign, Cooper could more optimistically announce that the new legislature had put the state on a hard money basis and taken other steps "to restore public credit." Still, foreign loans remained vital: "We cannot pay the Charges of the War in the Year, and are sensible of the Necessity of Loans. . . . Without which I am afraid we shall not be able to act in the common Cause as our Friends expect and we wish."[60]

John Adams's petulant independence would prove useful in coming peace negotiations, but, as Cooper gently implied to him, it appeared entirely inappropriate at a time when Vergennes was flooded with appeals for aid from Rochambeau, La Luzerne, and Lafayette, as well as from Congress and Washington. With the immediate fate of the United States in his hands, the foreign minister ordered La Luzerne to warn Congress against an overreliance on foreign credits and to emphasize that his court's confidence in Franklin remained a major reason for French largesse. Before Laurens reached Paris, Franklin informed Congress of an outright gift of six million livres, to be drawn on directly by Washington.[61]

American financial and commercial affairs in France were not to benefit from William Palfrey's business talents. Late in December 1780 he sailed from Philadelphia in a "new Ship of 16 Guns" which soon disappeared without a trace. Before embarking, Palfrey wrote an affectionate farewell to his patron thanking him for continued favors "through a long connection and acquaintance" and offering to perform any service in France. A member of Hancock's intimate "Sunday Evening Circle," Palfrey knew him as well as any man. It was Hancock's fate to be deprived in later life of those associates on whom he had most depended.[62]

During the early months of 1781 the Boston town meeting gave its main attention to filling its quotas for a permanent Continental army and for supplies and money to support that army. It was easier to collect taxes than recruits in a town where among the poorer classes nearly all men of military age were already in service or at sea trying their fortune on a privateer. Even sailors proved hard to find in New England's largest port. The departure of Laurens had been delayed for days until a partial crew for his frigate could be rounded up with the aid of Governor Hancock, some prominent merchants, the lure of a "tempting bounty," and a "volunteer draft from the Continental troops." Gabriel Johonnot sailed with Laurens as a gentleman passenger who agreed to serve "on the quarter deck in case of an encounter" or to help the officers suppress a mutiny by the motley crew. He has resigned his colonel's commission in one of the best Continental regiments to go into private business—with the full approval of his father-in-law. For all of his patriotic exhortations, Cooper approved of the voluntary bounty system of recruiting which protected local militia companies and left gentlemen free to decide for themselves how best to contribute to the national cause.[63]

To fill its quota of 181 men, assigned by the legislature at the close of 1780, Boston had to draw largely on the wealthier wards. The town meeting approved an ingenious plan that came closer to a draft than ever before, but by May only 121 men had been recruited. Some eligible Bostonians, many complained, had enlisted in other towns that offered higher bounties.[64]

To meet its quotas of beef and clothing for the Continental army during the first half of 1781, Boston resorted to short-term borrowing when tax collections could not be made in time. "Gentlemen of Property" were induced to serve their country by a premium of 10 percent for terms as short as three months. During this final drive to support the war, the town meeting tried but failed to reform the inefficient and often mysterious system of tax collection that had once ensnared Samuel Adams; but the effort did at least confirm the principle that the assessors' methods and books must be open to inspection by citizens.[65]

But by far the heaviest war tax was the depreciation of the Continental currency. With the repeal of the legal tender laws in the spring of 1781, it soon became worthless and passed from circulation in July. Congress abandoned attempts at currency reform and went on a specie basis, as did Massachusetts. Boston's trade suffered from the resulting confusion, yet merchants generally welcomed the transition. Cooper's salary from his congregation provides one clear illustration of the readjustment to specie. In the first half of 1781 he received £288 per week in the old currency. In a desperate effort to calculate what was due, as paper money lost its last bit of value, the church treasurer handed him £4,320 on 16 July. Two weeks later his salary was set at £4 "hard money" and remained constant thereafter.[66]

Though prices were high, this summer in Boston saw goods and foodstuffs more plentiful than at any time since 1775. Charges of importing merchandise from England and of unloading worthless currency upon unsuspecting people could not hide the economic upswing stimulated by the return to specie, the gold spent to supply the French army, a bountiful harvest on nearby farms, and a rich haul of enemy shipping by scores of privateers. Even before this year's campaign proved to be the last, Boston's Whig elite began to view the Revolution with a new sense of satisfaction.[67]

Cooper welcomed the ratification of the Articles of Confederation on 1 March 1781. For three years ratification had been delayed by a deadlock over the question of state claims to western lands. The final break came in January when La Luzerne moved Maryland to ratify by hinting that French naval protection for that state's coasts depended upon its accession to the Confederation. Thus at long last, thanks to the French minister, the United States had a federal constitution. Congress set about creating executive departments, most noticeably elevating Robert Morris, Hancock's friend and Holker's business ally, to the position of superintendent of finance. Enjoying the confidence of La Luzerne, Morris worked with him to find emergency support for the campaign of 1781 while at the same time reorganizing the finances of the new nation. Cooper expressed to the French minister his opinion that these internal improvements might be as important as victories in the field.[68]

Material favorable to France—much of it surely from Cooper's pen—continued to appear in the newspapers. For instance, the dying words of Louis XVI's father were purported to be, "It is enough for France to be just, and not to suffer other princes to be usurpers, or to oppress her Allies!" These "sacred words," commented the *Independent Chronicle*, had been well "attended to by this wise and beloved monarch." The *Chronicle* also informed its readers that "the three most celebrated Directors of the Finances in France (Sully, Colbert, and Necker) have all been protestants." Little did anyone in Boston know that Necker was a stubborn opponent of Vergennes's intervention in the American rebellion.[69]

When Colonel Johonnot sailed to France with John Laurens, he carried to Franklin a pamphlet his father-in-law had prepared two years before in defense of the Comte d'Estaing's American campaign of 1778. For fear of offending General Sullivan, Cooper had suppressed this writing except to insert a paragraph or two in the newspapers. Now Sullivan was out of the army and in Congress, where he followed La Luzerne's lead. Furthermore, word had reached Boston of the controversy aroused in France by the failure of d'Estaing to capture Newport (1778) and Savannah (1779) in joint operations with American land forces. So the Boston preacher retitled his pamphlet "A Letter from an American Gentleman to his Friend in France" and asked Franklin to have it published anonymously in Europe. Cooper explained in a letter to d'Estaing that this effort was a "small Acknowledgment of your Kindness and Friendship to me which is among the greatest Honours of my Life and indelibly engraven on my Heart." Obligingly, Franklin turned the "Letter" over to a close friend, the Abbé Morellet, for translating and editing. In May he informed Cooper that it had been privately printed and distributed where it "may serve the Interests of that excellent Officer, and great Friend of America."[70]

Cooper expected d'Estaing to return to American waters with a new fleet. Instead, Boston learned late in April 1781 that "M. de Grasse is appointed to the command of a squadron to consist of 25 ships of the line, which is said will sail this spring for America and the West Indies; and Count d'Estaing will remain with the command of the grand European fleet."[71] In anticipation of de Grasse's assistance, Washington and Rochambeau agreed to move their armies into position for an attack on New York, to where in June Rochambeau marched his troops. Meanwhile in the South, the surge of local militiamen and the appointment to that theater of the ablest Continental officers turned back the British conquest of the interior. Still General Cornwallis kept his army intact and finally established a fortified base at Yorktown. For the time being, all Washington could do was to order Lafayette to dog Cornwallis without risking an encounter.

Rochambeau and La Luzerne saw the opportunity and urged de Grasse to sail from the Caribbean directly to the Chesapeake. A man of precise moves, this French admiral replied that he would risk leaving the French West Indies helpless and put his fleet at their service from the end of August until 15 October. Consequently, Washington abandoned his preference for a blow at Clinton and joined Rochambeau in forced marches toward Yorktown. De Grasse arrived as he had promised. With twenty-four ships of the line, including the most powerful man-of-war afloat, he drove off a smaller British fleet from New York on 5 September in a little-heralded but key engagement of the War for Independence. Joined now by the squadron which had slipped out of Newport, the French fleet held a temporary command of the sea. Cooper's prayer had been answered.

With a hostile fleet at his back, at the end of September Cornwallis discovered himself besieged on land by an overwhelming number of American and French troops, including additional men landed from de Grasse's vessels. A combination of mismanagement and indecisiveness rendered futile the belated British rescue efforts. After a prolonged bombardment and some brief skirmishes, in which Lafayette distinguished himself for the last time in an American uniform, Cornwallis surrendered on 19 October.[72]

A week later Lafayette found time to write to his preacher friend in Boston of the "Glorious, and important success, we have obtained."[73] But Cooper had already heard an unofficial report of the stunning victory at Yorktown. He hastened to congratulate Franklin on the "happy Success" made possible by "additional Proofs of the Fidelity and Generosity of our great and good Ally."[74]

Boston set aside 5 November—its prewar "Pope's Day"—to celebrate the fruits of its alliance with Catholic France. From dawn until late evening "demonstrations of gratitude and joy" filled the streets, public buildings, taverns, and private parlors. Hancock exceeded the best of his past performances in such celebrations. That afternoon he gave an "elegant dinner at the Bunch of Grapes tavern" for distinguished townsmen and the highest French officers, most of whom then moved to the Hancock mansion, "where they found a brilliant assembly of ladies, and preparations for a ball in the most beautiful economy." While the elite and their guests danced inside, the governor provided fireworks for the townspeople outside.[75]

At Boston's American Coffeehouse, Continental officers raised their glasses to thirteen toasts. The first struck a keynote to this joyous day: "Perpetuity to the alliance between America and France."[76]

21

Prime Minister

*F*renchmen of distinction who visited Boston during the last years of the war often displayed an intense curiosity concerning the prime movers of the Revolution, and especially the preacher, as one described Cooper, "celebrated by the part he has had in the Revolution of this Country."[1] Of all these Frenchmen who recorded their observations, the Vicomte de Rochambeau, son of the French general, may have exhibited the keenest perception. Returning to Boston late in 1782 with the French units embarking from that port, he took the time to appease his inquisitiveness on the origins of the American rebellion. After visiting Hancock and Samuel Adams, he made his way to the Brattle Street parsonage: "I next saw Dr. Cooper, Mr. Hancock's counselor and the friend of Samuel Adams. He is learned, eloquent, but at the same time flattering and quite willing to suit his speech to the tone of those with whom he is speaking, and particularly to the immediate conditions, which gives him great popularity. I do not wish to say that he is a hypocrite, but that he shows the shrewdness of a man who says only what he wishes to say."[2]

This chameleonic quality, which the younger Rochambeau saw as Cooper's distinguishing personal trait, received its severest test in the two years after Yorktown. United in ideology, Boston's Whig leaders had prosecuted the war with no fundamental differences of primary objectives; but they had disagreed over the specifics of strategy and policy and above all over the merits of fellow Whigs. With a measure of victory assured but its extent yet to be determined at a European peace table, with a state constitution giving permanence to the realization of their domestic war aims, and with their renewed dominance in Massachusetts politics, the Boston leaders had no intention of encouraging the rise of an opposition by fragmenting their power. As a result, town politics took on a paradoxical appearance after 1781. While various Whig cliques vilified each other in the newspapers over personal issues, they displayed a high degree of unanimity and mutual respect in town meetings and elections.

In the center remained John Hancock. The combination of his personal popularity and constitutional prerogative made him the most powerful elected official in North America. Hardly a firm or diligent executive, he nonetheless jealously guarded the power and prestige of his office. During the summer of 1781, he avoided giving direct answers to Washington's requests for men and supplies, seemingly out of pique at the commander in chief's conferring with Rochambeau at Newport without coming on to Boston to pay his respects, or perhaps because he considered inadequate Washington's response to the request of the legislature for an accounting of Massachusetts arms in the Continental service. However his psyche functioned in this instance, Hancock lost no popular support by taking up the cause of state sovereignty.[3]

No one received a majority of votes for lieutenant governor in the election of 1780, thus leaving the decision to the legislature, which chose Bowdoin. He promptly declined because of a "precarious" state of health and because the election returns had not convinced him that he enjoyed the confidence of the "good people of the State." Next the legislature elected James Warren, but he also turned down the office in a public letter in which he felt compelled to deny that a personal dislike of the governor was at the base of his refusal to service. Finally, Thomas Cushing was chosen. The declensions of Bowdoin and Warren cleared the way for a Hancock henchman to hold the lieutenant governorship for many years to come.[4]

Belying his public statement, Warren continued privately to scorn the governor. A month after his inauguration, Hancock gave the largest ball the town had ever seen. Warren protested to John Adams that "our New Government has been Ushered in with Great Splendor, Balls, Assemblies, Entertainments and Feasts equal to any thing you can tell of in Europe." After Cushing's son-in-law had been given Samuel Adams's former position as secretary of the commonwealth, Warren fumed that Hancock "has already effected here what Hutchinson was never able to do," the removal of Adams from all share in the government. In Philadelphia Adams learned from Warren that he had been personally abused by William Cooper, as the town clerk was wont to do with everyone who "will not worship the Great Image." Professing unconcern for himself, Adams replied that "there is no Absurdity into which Idolatry will not lead Men." He reluctantly prepared to abandon his hope that Boston would become the "Christian Sparta." Mercy Otis Warren summarized her disdain for the governor in words that helped to fix his posthumous reputation: "the Guilded puppet placed on the public Theatre a few years ago (for certain purposses) is Become the Idol to whom the supple Homage of Adulation is paid, by a people once Disinterested, Firm, Discerning, and Tenatious of Their Rights." She thought herself incapable of describing fully the "Rapid Growth of Idolatry, the Worship of the pageant, the Mimic Greatness of Monarchy in Embrio." A newspaper writer estimated that "our gentry" had spent sufficient funds on entertainments to maintain an entire regiment throughout the war.[5]

As the mails brought him such reports, Samuel Adams thought he understood why Cooper's correspondence with him had nearly ceased. At the beginning of 1781 he observed to his wife, "Our new Era of Government, I fancy, has occasioned a Revolution in political Circles and a Change of Connections. I cannot otherwise account for the long Silence of my Friend Doctor Cooper. I used to correspond with him very confidentially. We indeed thought aloud together. . . . I have written several Times to him, and once desired particular Information, which he might have given me without offending any Man, but he has not done it." Admitting now that this letter to Mrs. Adams was indirectly addressed to the preacher, Adams went on to defend his stated preference for a governor more "endowed with those great Qualities which should characterize the first Magistrate of so respectable a Commonwealth." And he concluded by lecturing Cooper on "sober republican Principles."[6]

At her husband's request, Mrs. Adams let the Brattle Street minister read this letter. He hastened an apologetic reply, professing that his inattention to someone for whom he had the "most cordial Esteem and Affection" resulted from the press of duties and "meer Laziness." It certainly "did not arise from the Fear of offending any Man; nor from a Revolution in political Circles, or a Change of Connections produced by our new Era of Government."

Cooper concluded by promising "to explain all Points" when he could speak with Adams again.[7] Seemingly nostalgic for the glorious days of 1775–1776, Adams acknowledged this reply as "very obliging and satisfactory to me." With some apparent pride, he called Cooper's attention to the publication of Jonathan Odell's Tory verse, *The American Times*, in which the "quadruple allies" —Hancock, Cooper and the two Adamses—were pointed out as the rebel leaders of Massachusetts.[8]

By the time Adams left Congress permanently in the summer of 1781, Hancock's hold on the governorship had tightened. Despite a newspaper appeal by Adams from Philadelphia for a large turnout of voters not blinded by a "false Glare of Virtues held before their Eyes," in the election of April 1781 Hancock and Cushing encountered virtually no opposition in Boston and throughout the state. But in this same political climate—aptly characterized by historian Van Beck Hall as "Politics without Parties"—Adams received a strong vote in his native town for the Senate. When that body met it elected him its president.[9] Though he would not have admitted it, the presidency of a Senate dominated by the commercial towns made a fitting reward for a politician who had served the Whig elite for the last two decades. Returned to this familiar dependency, he gradually grew less restive with that relationship. "I glory in being what the World calls, a poor Man," he wrote, but he never made the mistake of thinking his political talents equal to advocacy in Boston of any form of radicalism except that of opposition to British tyranny.[10]

In the first elections under the constitution, Boston continued to choose for the House of Representatives men from the circle of active Whigs, among them even John Rowe, now purged of the stigma of his earlier timidity.[11] Younger men making their way in business or the professions were usually too busy to enter politics— except for an occasional ambitious newcomer such as lawyer James Sullivan. It mattered little who from this elite represented Boston in the House during 1781–1783 while the legislature adopted a financial program highly favorable to the interests of the commercial towns. The most important of these measures provided for payment of the interest and principal of the state debt in such a way as to keep faith with those moneyed men who had backed the Revolution.[12] There was so much satisfaction with the state government that in 1781 and 1782 the town meeting saw no need to continue the practice of instructing its representatives on domestic matters. And the instructions of the following year made only one chief point (seemingly out of a fear that agrarian interests were about to reassert themselves): "You will always remember that you represent a Trading Town."[13]

This harmony on essential issues could never fully disguise the personal tensions among Whigs, especially at the time of the annual gubernatorial elections. For example, in 1781 it was publicly said in Hancock's defense that "there is a junto, who from a spirit of envy to the Governor, and the stings of disappointment in their own bosoms, are determined to censure all, but what comes from their own little neglected party."[14] Yet the pressure of these tensions did not become fully apparent until John Temple arrived in Boston in October 1781. His return sparked a controversy that dominated the Boston newspapers for the next two years and fully vented those passions typical of American politics, but still without a formal break in Whig solidarity.

Since Temple had left for England in the summer of 1779, rumors persisted in Philadelphia that he would soon return to Congress with a compromise peace proposal from the British ministry.[15] Much to the contrary, his advice on American affairs was pushed aside by Lord North, and he found himself sharing in the odium of the Carlisle commission's failure.[16] Temple's position in American eyes was further compromised when his brother's family conspicuously sailed from Boston to England during 1780. Then at the beginning of 1781, the loyalist newspaper of New York scoffed at the gullibility over Temple of leading Americans, including Washington.[17]

Crossing to Holland in July 1781, Temple pleaded for a testimony from Franklin acknowledging that they shared equally the credit for obtaining the Hutchinson letters. Franklin did not reply, apparently for fear of offending Vergennes. Temple did better with John Adams, who wrote on his behalf to the president of Congress. Without presuming to judge the case, Adams expressed disbelief in the most damaging rumors concerning Temple and recalled that the former customs commissioner had communicated "intelligence of very great importance" to the leaders of resistance in the prewar period.[18] Not knowing the equivocation of this letter, Temple may have counted on it to dispel the cloud of suspicion above his head. But in Philadelphia, La Luzerne and his secretary continued to inform Vergennes that Bowdoin's son-in-law was "l'Emissaire des Anglois" who influenced John Adams to take a hard line toward France. Undoubtedly Cooper had also received similar reports from La Luzerne, though no such letters have come to light.[19]

Temple landed in Boston on 22 October, but before he could join in celebration of the Yorktown victory he received a summons to appear before the governor and Council. He defended his activities in England as being in the interest of America, and he even went so far as to avow (so he later maintained) that he now believed the French alliance to have been the salvation of the United States. The Council, nevertheless, voted to refer to the legislature the question of whether he had forfeited his American citizenship by an unauthorized return to England in 1779. That body passed the question back to the governor, who then directed his attorney general and political ally, Robert Treat Paine, to seek a judicial decision. Meanwhile, the Council required Temple to post a large bond to ensure that he neither communicated with the enemy nor opposed the policies of state or nation. Father-in-law Bowdoin and cousin John Pitts went surety on the bond, under which Temple lived in Boston for nearly two years while his case was tried over and over in the newspapers.[20]

Samuel Adams understood at once the political significance of Temple's return: "Those who hope for a Change of Person in our first Magistrate next Spring will be much embarrassed by this Circumstance." Normally imperturbable, Bowdoin was known to be sensitive and defensive on whatever concerned his daughter's husband; furthermore, James Warren had courted Temple's friendship in recent years. By merely doing their "patriotic" duty to conduct a thorough inquiry into the loyalty of this well-placed man, of whom there were genuine grounds for suspicion, Hancock's partisans could take the offensive against both his only rival for office and his most outspoken personal detractor.[21]

La Luzerne promptly learned, probably from Cooper, of Temple's reception in Boston, and he sent a complete report to Vergennes.[22] Temple and his supporters held Cooper particularly responsible for the storm raised against him. Apparently they expected the preacher to stand forth in his behalf. Instead, Cooper's connections with Hancock and La Luzerne necessitated his taking a position of public neutrality which was tantamount to an admission of a suspicion of disloyalty. There is no record of an open break between Cooper and Bowdoin over Temple, even after Bowdoin's son-in-law had become known—in the words of a visiting Frenchman—as a "famous opponent of Dr. Cooper."[23] Yet Bowdoin seemed to countenance through silence the series of newspaper attacks on Cooper by Temple or his friends that began in January 1782. The first of these laid bare the inconsistencies of a career combining divinity and politics:

> Is it the business of a clergyman, to devote the greater part of his time to the study of politicks, which should be employed in the more important business of his profession, viz. In exhorting and improving the virtue of his parishoners?
>
> Is not a levity of manners and behaviour inconsistent with the profession of a clergyman?
>
> Is not a disregard to the Sabbath, in this way of receiving and paying visits, setting an example which ought to be reprobated by the virtuous part of every community, and derogatory to the character of a clergyman?
>
> Is it not derogatory to the profession of a clergyman, to spend that time, which ought to be appropriated to the study of religion, to the ignoble business of gazette scribbling; and might it not be more pleasing and improving to his parishioners, to have a part of his time employed in making sermons; instead of scarcely allowing himself time to new-vamp old ones?
>
> Is not the craft and subtility of a politician inconsistent with the open and honest sentiments which ought to inspire the mind and influence the conduct of a clergyman? and ought not every clergyman (even if grown tired of his profession) to take advice from the sixth chap. of *Matthew* and 24th ver. No man can serve two masters, for either he will hate the one or love the other, or else he will hold to the one and despise the other, ye cannot serve God and Mammon.[24]

In this style the newspaper war raged furiously throughout the winter and spring of 1782. Hancock was compared to Richard Cromwell, described in Sir Henry Vane's diatribe as a man who wore a sword but had never drawn it, "a man without birth, without courage and without conduct." He drew fresh attacks for his lavish entertainments, his treatment of Samuel Adams, and his political machinations. A query directed at Cooper accused him of acting in the capacity of "Prime Minister" and recommending "impolitic or injudicious measures" to the "Great Man." Another newspaper writer used an extract from a sermon to suggest that the Brattle Street pastor neglected one part of his flock (Bowdoin) while ministering to another (Hancock).[25]

Hancock's defenders reminded Bostonians that he had entertained French officers not for display but to cement the alliance and that Samuel Adams himself had been a member of the committee of Congress arranging for the elegant reception given Gérard in Philadelphia. "It is a folly to keep a public table? Why does the President of Congress, General Washington, &c. do it? Is it a vice to dance?—why have assemblies and balls upon the surrender of Cornwallis been countenanced by the good men and patriots of each great town in America?" Is it better for a public figure to spend inherited wealth in the public interest and be called an "extravagant fellow" or to hoard it and be called a "miser"? (Bowdoin had carefully preserved his wealth during the war.) Who had sacrificed a greater fortune in his country's cause than Hancock? Who had been earlier and more persevering in opposing British tyranny? And who had been more faithful in the several public trusts given him by a grateful citizenry? Attempts to raise suspicion in the public mind against such a governor can only be the work of a "disappointed and ambitious mind, governed by an insidious and rancorous heart."[26]

Surely, exclaimed one Hancock partisan, none of these undeserved charges could have come from the pen of Samuel Adams, who was popularly suspected of being the "Consistent Republican," the pseudonymous author of several letters against the governor. "It is possible that the man who has been so intimately connected with the Governor through the various stages of our political disputes; who has had so many instances of his steady virtue, and unbiased patriotism, should now be the first to raise the jealousy of the people, and endeavour to blast a character which he cannot but revere?"[27] But another writer answered this question with a biblical parody:

> And it came to pass in process of time, that the people said with one voice, let John reign over us, and be the first amongst our princes, and let Samuel be next unto him, to assist him in going out and coming in aright before us.
>
> But Samuel spake not unto John either good or bad. Now this Samuel had often cried in the gate of the city, saying, the voice of the people is the voice of God;

but lo when the voice of the people had made John their
Governor, he said that this is the voice of an evil spirit,
for he was angry. . . .
    And the people all cried, and said Samuel shall not
slay John, for he hath done no evil.[28]

None of this strong verbiage affected the outcome of the
Boston election of 1 April 1782. Hancock received all but 9 of the
607 votes cast for governor, and Adams went back to the Senate
with nearly as strong a vote from Boston. After the election the censure of the governor halted temporarily; but the question of Temple's loyalty would not subside, for he determined to clear his name
in such a way as to vindicate his family and the others who trusted
him. Counting on the letter of John Adams, he appealed to Congress to release its contents in his behalf. Instead, pressured by La
Luzerne, the delegates referred Temple's case to the Massachusetts
executive in a resolution that came close to incrimination. On the
heels of this blow, the *Boston Gazette* published the memorial of
the customs commissioners of 1768 appealing for British troops to
be sent to prevent an "open revolt of this town." At the bottom
stood the signature of Temple along with those of the four obnoxious commissioners.[29]

Learning that this memorial had been reprinted in newspapers
as far south as Philadelphia, Temple published a long review of his
conduct as a commissioner which emphasized his dissent from the
actions of the other commissioners and his communicating their
secret proceedings to the Whig leaders. Indeed, he had carried this
very memorial as soon as it was written to Dr. Cooper's house,
where Hancock, Adams, and Otis were called to inspect it. On that
occasion these gentlemen had profusely thanked Temple for his
"fidelity and attachment to the just rights and welfare of his
country."[30]

After a grand jury found no cause for an indictment and after
the governor had transmitted the congressional resolution to the
legislature, Temple appealed to that body to take cognizance of his
case. Accordingly, a joint committee conducted an investigation.
As could be expected, it discovered no evidence either to prove or
disprove his major contention of having been instrumental in obtaining the Hutchinson letters. On the question of whether he had
gone to England in 1779 with the knowledge and approval of
Boston leaders, only Bowdoin and Chauncy testified to such an
understanding. Cooper emphatically denied before the committee
that he had known of Temple's plan to return to England by way of

Holland in order to correct inaccuracies in the reports of the Carlisle commissioners. Temple had to admit under oath that the cagey Doctor had not "in express words" approved of this plan, though neither had he disapproved of it.[31] The case dragged over into the next session, but finally a resolution releasing Temple from his bond and declaring him friendly to the United States narrowly passed both houses. Hancock pocket-vetoed the resolution and prorogued the legislature.[32]

Someone in the Temple party struck back quickly by advertising for a copy of Cooper's 1759 printed sermon on the fall of Quebec in which he had denounced the French nation as an "inveterate and implacable Enemy to our Religion and Liberties." Temple seems to have hit on the truth that Cooper was a French pensioner without ever being sufficiently certain of his ground to do more than drop such vague hints.[33]

James Sullivan now stepped forth as the chief defender of Hancock and Cooper. At thirty-eight, this younger brother of General John Sullivan had already enjoyed a full career as a lawyer, judge, and Massachusetts politician. He moved permanently to Boston in 1782 and took a pew at Brattle Street. His unremitting industry compensated for Hancock's increasing lethargy, with the result that Sullivan rapidly became the actual "prime minister" in a public role that the preacher could never assume.[34]

Sullivan had possibly written some of the earlier newspaper pieces in this controversy. Now he and Temple blasted at each other under their own names, and the newspaper battle intensified during the fall of 1782 and the ensuing winter months.[35] When Sullivan announced his intention of stating the case against Temple before the fall session of the legislature, the newspapers printed every scrap of evidence or gesture of support the powerful Bowdoin family could elicit. In addition, Temple demanded that Cooper publicly declare his views, rather than seeking in private to appease both sides.[36] But the Doctor believed himself ill-used and resolved to keep silent while Temple injured himself by the uncalled-for virulence of his outbursts.[37] Denying that he had been employed by anyone, Sullivan presented a deposition to the legislature which attempted to demonstrate that "it would raise a Jealousy in the mind of our Allies" to acquit one against whom there was so much evidence of collaboration with the enemy. On his manuscript copy of this deposition, Temple noted, "here is the burthen of the Song! . . . Pensions are not to be continued, but as they shall be industriously earned." In another comment on this document, Temple wrote of Sullivan, "What a Wonderful Politician! he has not been Cooper's pupil to no purpose."[38]

Still, knowing that there was only one man in Massachusetts who could clear him of Sullivan's assertions that he was hostile to Franklin and the alliance, Temple in October addressed an open letter to Cooper. With a deference too sarcastic to be effective, he appealed to the Doctor "not only as a Gentleman and a profound Politician, but in the more eligible and exalted character of a Preacher of the Gospel of Truth (than which, with you, all other considerations must be as nothing . . .)."[39]

Using Cooper's continued public silence as evidence of his duplicity, Temple's friends took aim again at the "Prime Minister." Sullivan was pictured as a "cooper's adze." But most of all they railed at the "Divine Politician," who "had a very convenient memory" of his past associations with Temple and who employed the services of that "dirty pettyfogger" Sullivan to destroy a deserving man who had suffered in the service of his native America.[40]

The controversy appeared to climax in December with a brief exchange in the *Gazette* over whether Bowdoin's connection with Temple rendered him unfit to be governor or whether the attack on his son-in-law had been motivated by a desire to support the "sinking Cause" of Hancock. Likely the principals had not intended to go this far, for the newspaper vituperation now slackened abruptly. Both sides had stabbed in the dark: Sullivan at Temple's bargain with the ministry in 1778, and Temple at Cooper's special relationship with France. But Boston Whigs had too much at stake to permit a profuse bloodletting. As if all of the overheated rhetoric had been an innocent amusement, in the April election of 1783 Boston voted for Hancock over Bowdoin, 747 to 60, and gave Adams his best vote yet for the Senate.[41]

Temple remained under bond until after the final peace with Britain. When the legislature referred the case again to Attorney General Paine, he delayed as long as possible, then ruled Temple's citizenship to be a "political question beyond the extent of his office." The legislature failed to agree on further action until the fall of 1783, at which time it passed a resolution releasing Temple from his bond but without exoneration; and Hancock's signature ended the long affair. Having lost his chances of suitable employment in the United States, Temple took his family back to Europe. Thus ended Revolutionary Boston's most sensational controversy.[42] The

British ministry fulfilled part of its commitment to him in 1778. Created a baronet and appointed British consul general at New York, *Sir* John Temple settled on American soil again in 1785. Here he and the still-beautiful Elizabeth (Bowdoin) enjoyed the prestige and genteel style of living they had so long sought.[43]

Over the protests of Hancock's opponents, Boston elected James Sullivan to the House of Representatives in 1783 despite some doubt that he met the one-year residency requirement. But for the most part Bostonians remained well satisfied with their town and state governments. As one townsman observed late in 1783, the recent attacks on Hancock had only proved "that if the arch-angel Gabriel had been appointed our Governor, we soon should have raised a clamor against him." Cooper, as the reputed "Prime Minister," had a share of that clamor directed at him. Yet even John Temple's desperate taunts had failed to do more than slightly tarnish his carefully cultivated image as a faithful minister of the gospel.[44]

John Temple's failure to win acceptance in Boston coincided with Great Britain's last efforts to separate the rebellious colonists from their powerful ally before settling down to serious peacemaking. Like Franklin, Cooper had always recognized that the alliance was an artificial liaison motivated solely by mutual self-interest. His unremitting labors to preserve the alliance stemmed more from a private recognition of its fragile structure than from personal financial gain. Convinced that the chief hope of his country's independence lay in cooperation with France, he had been willing to go to almost any length to accommodate the ally.

In the months before Yorktown, the impoverished Continental Congress came under the nearly complete domination of the French minister. La Luzerne, described by one member as the "eagle eyed Politician of our great Ally," made effective use of his political talents and of his king's money.[45] In the dark financial and military situation of 1780–1781, the majority of the congressmen saw nowhere to turn except toward France. But Vergennes was also weary of fighting a long war which his rivals at court opposed. He stood ready to make peace on whatever terms would offer an acceptable balance of gains for France's varied and complex interests. After his many contributions to their cause, he hoped that the Americans would follow his lead in peacemaking. For a while in 1781, he entertained the possibility of ending the war by a truce leaving Britain in possession of some sections of her colonies, with nominal independence for the remainder. In any case, he wanted no American aspirations encumbering his negotiations.[46]

Following instructions from Vergennes, La Luzerne in Philadelphia prepared the delegates for the dismal possibility of a truce, and worked to curb the independence of John Adams. During June 1781, Congress revised its instructions to Adams by reducing American ultimata to independence for all of the colonies and the maintenance of the treaties with France. In all other matters he was to seek his country's interests with the knowledge, advice, and consent of the "generous ally" on whom reliance is placed "for effectual support in every thing that may be necessary to the present security, or future prosperity, of the United States of America." That same month Congress surrounded Adams with four other peace commissioners, including Franklin and John Jay (then in Spain).[47]

Elated at this result, La Luzerne reported to Vergennes that he regarded the negotiations as now being in the hands of Louis XVI, "except for independence and the treaties." He assigned the principal credit for this success to two of his paid supporters: Cooper, whose influence he believed had removed Samuel Adams from Congress; and General John Sullivan, whose activity had broken the solidarity of New England congressmen on peace objectives.[48]

La Luzerne might have been less generous in his praise of the Boston preacher's contribution had he read Cooper's letter to Franklin written in October 1781, after the first report of Yorktown. While lauding French aid in bagging Cornwallis, Cooper expressed his hope that the fishery question "may be settled as far in our Favor as Circumstances will possibly admit."[49] With peace in the offing, Cooper appeared uneasy in following the lead of Vergennes on the fishery. His uneasiness arose in part from the fear of the coastal towns that other sections of the republic would not support a claim to the fishery lest they give a "dangerous Superiority of Strength to the Eastern States."[50]

Samuel Adams and James Lovell saw these sectional differences as weakening the American position at the peace table and insisted that Congress even continue the war if necessary to obtain its share of the fishery and other American desiderata. For men so minded, the fishery was first a point of national honor and only second a commercial question. Unlike them, Cooper supported the efforts of Robert Morris to bring order out of the country's financial chaos, and he trusted Franklin to extract the maximum advantage from the alliance. Both Morris and Franklin were well regarded in Paris, where the Adamses were as much distrusted as they were in London. Thus from Cooper's perspective in Boston, loyalty to France and the advancement of American commercial interests remained compatible. Still, at the end of 1781 he could not hide his anxiety over the peacemaking. Being so close to La Luzerne, he could hardly have failed to perceive, at least dimly, that Vergennes preferred an independent American nation to be confined within limits ensuring its continued dependence on France.

For more than a year Lovell worked feverishly to persuade Congress to strengthen the instructions of 1781. His efforts produced no ultimatum, but only a resolution that the commissioners should contend with "earnestness" for a share in the fishery and for the boundaries described in the instructions given John Adams in 1779. Now representing Virginia in Congress, where he seconded Lovell, Arthur Lee wrote gloomy letters to his Massachusetts friends in which he predicted that Franklin, "both a dishonest and incapable man," would be the instrument of France's excluding Americans from the fishery. "God forgive" Congress for trusting him! "The Yoke is riveted upon us."[51]

While awaiting news of Britain's reaction to Yorktown and of the hoped-for first steps toward peace, Cooper more than ever devoted his time to making the alliance function smoothly in Boston. In the relations of Massachusetts with France he came closer to filling the role of "Prime Minister" than he did in domestic affairs.

De Valnais's replacement as consul, Philippe-Andre-Joseph de Létombe, finally arrived in October 1781. Unlike his predecessor, Létombe was no adventurer, but a civil servant of good reputation. He found the consulate in wretched condition, its records in disorder, and its funds unaccounted for and devalued by inflation. Most of the Frenchmen living in Boston, he decided, were rogues or bankrupts who, with de Valnais's encouragement, opposed the new consul's assumption of authority. At once he became entangled in a web of mixed jurisdictions as he attempted to carry out his duties. In apprehending deserters from French vessels, he had to face—as had English captains before the war—the wrath of Boston's waterfront mobs.[52]

Létombe never enjoyed as close a relationship to Cooper as had de Valnais, but he nevertheless found the preacher's services indispensable in dealing with the Massachusetts government. It was left to Cooper to satisfy La Luzerne as to why one of the consul's cases dragged on without settlement. At the same time Cooper made certain that local authorities understood that cases in law involving Frenchmen were public rather than merely personal and that their consequences "must affect the important Connection between the two Nations."[53]

The new consul's reports revealed the failure to achieve one important objective of the alliance: France had not found in America an outlet for its products. The shoddy French trading goods so far sold in Boston were no competition for English wares, and the losses incurred through depreciation had cooled the ardor for American trade of the best French firms. The consul took the promotion of trade to be one of his main functions, but he discovered no effective method of doing so. As it became evident following Yorktown that English goods under various guises were increasingly offered for sale in Boston, he decided to postpone until after the war a commercial memoir he had promised his government. Létombe stands out as one of the few realists who perceived an American taste for English goods, acquired from long habit, to be more powerful than Britain's army and navy.[54]

French naval commanders in Boston went out of their way to oblige local merchants, who responded with entertainments and addresses expressing their appreciation. What prosperity the town enjoyed in wartime depended on supplying the ally's forces and on the harvest from privateering. Boston's post-Yorktown mood could be read unmistakably. The final test of the alliance would be its peacetime commercial benefits.[55]

Cooper took particular delight in the new republic's observances of the birth of a first son to the French queen. Boston celebrated on 12 June 1782. After a day of bell ringing, cannon firing, feasting, and toasting, at night the common was crowded with spectators—so Cooper boasted to the French minister—viewing the fireworks provided by the governor, and the illumination of the Hancock, Bowdoin, and other mansions bordering the common. "In this Town, I can say with Truth," Cooper wrote to Franklin and La Luzerne, "the public Tokens of Joy far exceeded any Thing ever known here upon the Birth of a Prince of Wales or the Birth Day of any British King."[56] Boston's festivities were hardly outdone a month later in Philadelphia, where La Luzerne freely spent the royal gold to encourage thousands to demonstrate their attachment to the alliance.

Festivities for the dauphin's birth helped to soften the news from the West Indies in June that de Grasse had been defeated and captured by Rodney in a major naval engagement. Cooper took credit for some newspaper "Reflexions" on this "unfortunate" battle, attributing de Grasse's defeat to the "mere casualties of calms and currents." He emphasized that only "weak people judge of the final issue of a war by some detached and accidental events while the wise keep their eye upon the respective resources of the belligerent powers and the general course and balance of affairs." Let no one be deceived; "the more France bleeds in a war occasioned solely by her connection with these States, the more endeared must she be to every honest and generous American."[57]

The apparent loss of most of his correspondence with La Luzerne makes it impossible to determine what else of the steady stream of pro-French writing came from his pen in the last two years of the war. Much of it, obviously, was his.

In August part of de Grasse's fleet, under the command of the Marquis de Vaudreuil, put into Boston to refit in preparation for transporting Rochambeau's army home. From then until the army arrived and the fleet sailed in December, the town swarmed with more French noblemen than at any time in its history. Hancock bestirred himself to provide a royal welcome for Vaudreuil, but the gout soon laid up the governor again. The burden of entertainment fell to Cooper and Lieutenant Governor Cushing. They did well, according to the Baron von Closen, who concluded that "the residents of Boston are, perhaps, the French army's most cordial friends."[58]

No single tableau better illustrates Boston's determination to honor the alliance than the funeral procession in November 1782 for a French ensign. Behind a priest holding a silver crucifix, the body was borne "in a Sling by four Marines, and the Pall supported by six Officers, each with a lighted Taper." Then followed two priests, "one of them in his white Robes reading the Burial Service, and both with Tapers burning." Behind them solemnly marched Vaudreuil and Cushing, followed by the Council, the clergy in a body, the selectmen, and "many of the most respectable Gentlemen of the Town."

At least one of the French Catholic chaplains fraternized freely with the Boston clergy, not only in the exchange of visits to their respective religious rites, but also at private social gatherings. During this period a young Boston clergyman wrote to a friend, "If you was here, you would be compleatly Frenchified."[59]

The French visitors who recorded their observations of Boston in these months seldom neglected to take the measure of the con-

spicuous Brattle Street minister. Their descriptions collectively confirm his place in the town's life and candidly delineate his
distinguishing personal traits. Rochambeau's chief engineer, Colonel Jean-Nicolas Désandroins, found easily accessible "the famous
Dr. Cooper who has contributed so much to the Revolution, and
who is alleged by some to have been the prompter behind President
Hancock. . . . He is a secretive man who seems very subtle at first
glance, and a man who always weighs his words, thereby arousing
mistrust. He has much wit, learning and eloquence."[60]

Among those French nobles rushing to America after
Yorktown, lest they miss the glory of conquest, came the Prince de
Broglie with a letter of introduction from Franklin to Cooper. His
journal offers another candid appraisal:

> The Rev. Dr. Cooper, famous for his bold ser-
> mons, his discourses purely political, . . . his supple, in-
> sinuating and crafty spirit, and also his extensive and
> varied knowledge, is one of the men whose character
> and deportment struck me the most forcibly at Boston.
> His conversation is interesting, and although he ex-
> presses himself with difficulty in French, he understands
> it perfectly well, knows all our best authors, and has
> sometimes cited, even in the pulpit, passages from
> Voltaire and Jean Jacques Rousseau. . . . He writes
> sprightly verses, and carries certainly much cleverness
> under the immense wig of a clergyman, which he wears
> bigger and more heavily powdered than any of his
> brethren. He has enemies among the clergy as well as
> the laity, and he is generally accused of a ductility quite
> machiavellian.[61]

The Comte de Ségur, son of the French minister of war and intimate of the best Parisian literary and artistic circles, accompanied
de Broglie to America. He quickly caught the preacher's fancy.
When writing his memoirs half a century later, the Comte still
recalled that this Boston divine's "great talents procured him
zealous partisans and ardent enemies."[62] Among those most impressed with Cooper was Major General Chastellux, who met him
at a dinner given by the consul, where he "found upwards of twenty
persons assembled, both French officers and Americans; among the
latter was Doctor [Samuel] Cooper, a man justly celebrated, and no

less distinguished by the graces of his mind and the amenity of his character, than by his uncommon eloquence and patriotic zeal. . . . Among the Americans attached by political interest to France none has displayed a more marked attention to the French, and none has received from Nature a character more analogous to theirs."[63] For the remainder of his long life, lived through the travail of the French Revolution and the Napoleonic era, Comte Mathieu de Dumas recalled Cooper's warning that to plant free government in Europe's unfriendly soil would cost much more blood than the victory of liberty in America's virgin soil.[64]

It is refreshing to read the journal of Rochambeau's chief commissary. When Cooper explained the mild December that greeted the soldiers encamped in Boston awaiting embarkation by saying, "Heaven smiles upon the troops of France," Claude Blanchard noted the remark as coming from this "pompous protestant clergyman."[65] Nor did Bostonians appeal to the Comte de Clermont-Crèvecoeur, who concluded that they were all cold, inscrutable merchants.[66] On the whole, though, the noble officers recorded more positive views of Boston society, even on the subject of feminine comeliness.

As the fleet sailed on 24 December, Cooper sensed that an epoch ended for him and for the town. Only to Franklin could he confide his feelings: "What must I feel at this Moment when I am called to part with . . . so many Noblemen and Gentlemen of the King's Army and Fleet, who allow me to call them my Friends, whose great and good Qualities have seized my heart and from whom I have received the most obliging Attentions. I know not which is the greatest, either the Honor and Pleasure they have given me in their Acquaintance or the Regret I feel at parting with them."[67] The captain of a man-of-war, the Chevalier de Puget du Bras, presented Cooper with portraits of Henry IV and "his great Minister" Sully as a parting gift. These artistic reminders of the Protestant elements in France's history proved to be poor symbols of the permanency of the alliance. But death would spare Cooper this knowledge.[68]

Nor would he live to witness the result of his arranging for Albert Gallatin, a young Swiss immigrant, to teach French during the school year 1782–1783 at Harvard College. After a year, Gallatin moved southward, carrying letters of recommendation from Cooper and others, to seek a wider outlet for his obvious talents. As a Jeffersonian politician, secretary of the treasury, and diplomat, for the next sixty years he pursued one of the fullest careers in American public life.[69]

In his last years of life, Cooper's prestige, his clerical garb, the continued need for essential Whig solidarity, and the importance of the alliance combined to spare him from most public criticism. Yet in 1782 and 1783 those Whigs who regularly struck at Hancock and Franklin grew noticeably silent concerning him. The unquenchable William Gordon saw his duty to warn John Adams against continuing a confidence with the "French Dr." who was both "Franklified and Frenchified." He wrote in September 1782, "Silver-tongue Sam is the pink of complaisance to the French Admirals, Generals and Officers. You would never have believed him to have been the author of a Sermon upon the Conquest of Canada, . . . The French [in Cooper's view] are the most disinterested people in the world. They are everything, but Protestants; and their being otherwise is a matter of no great importance."[70]

By the time Adams received this warning, he, Franklin, and Jay—the only commissioners who had reached France—were close to signing a preliminary treaty of peace with Great Britain. Meanwhile, the Massachusetts General Court resolved to spurn "every idea of deviating from the treaty of the United States with his Most Christian Majesty in the smallest article, or of listening to proposals of accommodation with the Court of Great Britain in a partial and separate capacity." This resolution was appropriately passed on 4 July 1782, and appeared in the newspapers over the signatures of both Hancock and Samuel Adams, in their respective offices. "I never was more pleased with the Spirit of my Country," commented Cooper to Franklin.[71]

But toward the end of summer a letter from Franklin arrived with the discouraging news that the British king and ministers seemed less willing to grant independence after their naval victory in the West Indies. Then in September Washington advised Cooper that "in the present Situation it is our Duty to be preparing in the best manner possible for a Continuance of the War." No further word arrived for the remainder of the year; but as Cooper watched the ally's fleet sail away in December, he could hardly believe that his prayers for an end to the long war would be unanswered.[72]

He sensed correctly, for on 26 December Franklin wrote to him summarizing the preliminary treaty with England signed a month before: "We have taken some good steps here towards a peace. Our Independence is acknowledged; our boundaries as good and extensive as we demanded; and our fishing more so than Congress expected."[73]

John Jay had reached Paris in June 1782 to find that Franklin had already conducted a series of discussions with representatives of the English ministry. The venerable doctor kept Vergennes just well enough informed of these conversations to make it plain that England sought to divide the allies before entering negotiations. The French foreign minister appeared not to object to separate negotiations conducted with his knowledge and subject to his final approval of agreements reached. In the ensuing maze of intrigue, secret peace feelers, and duplicity, Franklin and Jay nicely complemented each other's efforts. As the younger commissioner grew increasingly distrustful of France's and Spain's intentions for America, his older colleague supported him as much as possible without sacrificing the complete confidence of Vergennes.[74]

The French foreign minister now leaned toward the view that France's interest in the fishery required the exclusion of Americans from it. La Luzerne's reports of the insistence of Samuel Adams and other New England men on the priority of American over French claims had hardened Vergennes's position.[75] With Franklin weakened by illness, Jay now took the lead in independent negotiations with England. Generally agreeing on the need for such a course, Franklin still relied on the power struggle between France and England, rather than on a naive confidence in the ally's benevolence, to advance the cause of his country. Without clinging to the French alliance, he maintained, the United States could not profit from the European balance of power. Thus, to abandon it now would be folly, as he explained to Cooper: "It is our firm connection with France that Gives us weight with England, and respect throughout Europe."[76]

John Adams joined the two commissioners in Paris on 26 October after concluding a commercial treaty with Holland. He discovered that Jay and Franklin had already reached substantial agreement with the British negotiator, though the fishery and two other critical issues remained unsettled. Once over the high hurdle of independence, Britain had rather easily conceded most of Congress's boundary claims in order to counter the ambitions of Spain and to cool American passion for the conquest of Canada.

Hostile toward Vergennes and distrustful of Franklin, Adams bolstered Jay's independence of the French court. Yet the three negotiated realistically and flexibly, constantly playing on England's need to weaken the Bourbon powers. In a month of intensive discussions, both sides made sufficient concessions to permit the signing of a preliminary treaty on 30 November that granted the new nation the fishery and made generous concessions on other contested points. The commissioners had magnificently concluded the War for Independence by obeying their own understanding of the realities of European power politics rather than the instructions of Congress.[77]

It was left for Franklin to justify the commissioners' conduct to Vergennes, who until the last had worked tacitly to discourage Britain from making such broad concessions to her former colonists. Though dismayed that England had bought rather than made a peace, the comte was not ready to abandon the alliance. The ship carrying the preliminary articles of peace to Philadelphia also had on board the first installment of the new French loan.[78]

It would have been appropriate for the war to have ended in Boston on 19 April 1783, but the official congressional declaration of a cessation of arms did not reach Hancock until four days later. At one o'clock on the twenty-third, the Suffolk County sheriff read the proclamation from the State House balcony. News of peace had been arriving too gradually over past weeks for this day to touch off more than a mild celebration; and concern for the future chilled the ecstasy that might have been expected on the occasion. Governor Hancock proclaimed 15 May a day of fasting and prayer to beseech the Almighty "to continue his gracious providence over us; especially," among other blessings, "That he would be pleased to bless our husbandry, to revive and prosper our trade, navigation, and fishery."[79]

Cooper's joy over the tidings from Europe was tempered by the maliciousness of gossip concerning Franklin's stand during the negotiations. John Adams's letters to America exaggerated his own contributions to the peace and seemed to confirm, at least in the mind of one so disposed as James Warren, Arthur Lee's fanatical belief in Franklin's warped and evil nature.[80] In advising Cooper of the preliminary articles and cautioning him that the United States must still preserve the alliance, Franklin had warned against permitting the "private resentments of particular persons to enter into our public counsels."[81] On 5 May the Boston preacher responded in the most candid letter of their long correspondence:

> There is a Party among us, disposed to avail themselves of every Incident, and of all personal Resentments to weaken and divide our public councils and injure the Alliance. Regard to the general Good, as well as

Private, and the most constant Friendship, oblige me to state Things as they are. It is, then, confidently whispered among us that Letters have been received from Paris, both in this State and in Philadelphia, which mention, that the Court of France was at Bottom against our obtaining the Fishery and Territory in that great Extent in which both are secured to us by the Treaty. That our Minister at that Court [Franklin] favoured, or did not oppose, this Design against us; and that it was owing to the Firmness, Sagacity, and Disinterestedness of Mr. Adams, with whom Mr. Jay united, that we have obtained those important advantages. I have not seen any of these Letters, and am considered, I suppose, as too much attached to the Alliance with France and that American Minister who so happily negociated it, to be trusted with such a Communication: they are said, however, to come from some of our Plenipotentiaries at Paris, and particularly from Mr. Adams, a Gentleman against whom I never was prejudiced, having had a long Friendship and Respect for him. It is certain some of his particular friends have believed and propagated these Reports, as they say, upon the best Authority. It has also been said from the same Quarter that the Court of France secretly traversed Mr. A.'s views in Holland, for obtaining of the United Provinces an acknowledgement of our Independence, and that the same Part had been acted in Spain and Russia. All these Things are incredible to me, and though they make some Impression at present, Truth is great and will prevail. Care I hope will be taken, both at Congress and in Europe, as far as public Prudence will permit, to state as soon as may be these Matters in a just Light, and to prevent the public Mischiefs, as well as private Injuries that may arise from Misrepresentations in Matters of such Moment. For myself, I stand and speak and act upon my old Ground, our Independence supported and defended by the Friendship of France; and they who take the fairest and most effectual Measures to cultivate this Friendship are most my Friends as being friendly to my country. If through Ingratitude, Folly, Personal Pique or Treachery, we lose so generous, so powerful, so faithful, and in our present

Situation, so natural a Friend as the King of France, we
fall, and deservedly, into Contempt and Ruin. But I am
persuaded there is good Sense and Virtue enough in the
Government and People of America to prevent so
shameful a Fall.[82]

For perhaps the only time in his later years, Franklin appeared
deeply concerned for his reputation. He sent this section of
Cooper's letter—anonymously "from a very respectable person in
America"—to Jay and Adams with a demand for satisfaction. Jay
replied with a warm testimony to his venerable colleague's "strong"
and "steady attachment" to the causes of the fishery and full boundaries. Adams only grudgingly acknowledged that Franklin had
agreed to the independent negotiations and had been "able and
useful" throughout them.[83]

Franklin also sent this extract from Cooper's letter to Vergennes. The comte held no illusions of enjoying the undying
gratitude of Americans for his incalculable contributions to their independence. He cautioned La Luzerne to answer the charges of
Adams and other anti-Gallicans only if necessary to preserve the
alliance. At times Vergennes seemed to admire the ability of
diplomats from an infant republic to master so quickly the intricate
game of European realpolitik.[84]

Cooper received a copy of Adams's and Jay's acknowledgment
of Franklin's contribution to the negotiations, but died before he
could make much use of these documents.[85] In poor health, and appreciative of his stipend from La Luzerne, he likely never
understood fully the limitations of French self-interest in advocacy
of American objectives at the peace table. Yet his overall view of
the importance of the total French share in the achievement of independence must be judged more correct than the narrow perspective of Samuel Adams, who now suggested that he and other
leaders of the Revolution had done Louis XVI a favor by providing
him with an opportunity to cripple Britain.[86] How little Vergennes
had gained for his king by sending money, supplies, fleets, and
soldiers to America did not become fully apparent until the storm
of revolution broke in France six years later.

22

States-man

*T*he definitive treaty ending the war for all belligerents was not signed until 3 September 1783, and it required another eight months to exchange ratifications. Still, the departure of the French and news of the preliminary treaty with Britain turned 1783 into the year of peace for Bostonians. For them, two occurrences of that year—one an act of God and the other carefully staged—effectively symbolized the end of the long contest whose outcome they could not foresee when it opened two decades before.

In May lightning struck James Otis dead. Frequently deranged during the war years, he had at times been an embarrassing nuisance to the Whigs. But with one bolt from heaven, Otis could be celebrated in Boston as the "first in patriot fame" who earliest "To list'ning crowds resistance dar'd proclaim."[1] A few weeks before his instantaneous death, Otis had been sufficiently calm to have the honor of moderating the ceremonial town meeting held annually on 5 March. This occasion saw both his last public act and the final Massacre oration. When the orator had finished, William Cooper moved to merge the 5 March anniversary with the celebration of Independence Day. The voters agreed. Accordingly, on 4 July 1783, Boston acknowledged the completion of the Revolution by fusing the local commemorative rite with the national observance, "the foundation of which will last," they predicted, "as long as time endures."[2]

Members of the General Court, then meeting in town, joined with the Bostonians who gathered at the Brattle Street Church the morning of the fourth. "The Rev. Dr. Cooper, after a polite and elegant Address to the auditory, returned Thanks to Almighty God for his goodness to these American States, and the glory and success with which he had crowned their exertions." Following an anthem, Dr. John Warren, the martyred Joseph Warren's younger brother, delivered an oration that proclaimed "commercial intercourse and connection" to be a more important security of freedom "than all the obligations of morality and religion, in their usual state of debility." But he went on to warn against the corrupting power of "immense wealth" that had driven even the House of Commons, once the "palladium of Liberty," to adopt a system of mercantile regulation of the colonies designed "to enrich some crouching favorites at home." Despite its modern secular dress, that lesson was essentially the one Grandfather Sewall had struggled to master: How does an individual or a nation pursue wealth while remaining virtuous, free, and patriotic?[3]

Samuel Cooper's answer to this question—his doctrine that there existed no unavoidable conflict between self-interest and true virtue—had survived the Revolution with hardly a scar. It had enabled him confidently to embrace Catholic France, to accept a stipend from court, to seek commercial opportunities for his friends, and to devote an ever larger portion of his time to politics. In marked contrast to Samuel Adams, he taught that God approved rather than condemned the prevailing ethos, though, of course, he cautioned against abuses and excesses. For him and the most enterprising of his fellow townsmen, religion functioned to confirm and guide their quest for happiness instead of denying the inherent validity of that pursuit.

His undemanding and unexamined Calvinism remained unshaken to his dying day. Arminianism, less conspicuous since Mayhew's death, had silently invaded a number of pulpits in the Boston area, though preoccupation with the war had shelved most serious theological controversy. An itinerant preacher, John Murray, had since 1772 gained a slight following in town for his teaching that Christ's atonement afforded salvation for all men. Murray's preaching finally brought into the open Dr. Charles Chauncy's long-suppressed manuscript advocating a more sophisticated doctrine of universalism. Defenders of orthodoxy lost no time in counterattacking. Theological controversy in the Boston press quickly resumed its normal intensity in the years after Yorktown.[4]

As always, Cooper would have none of it. At the beginning of 1782, he took part in a council of ministers and lay delegates called to ordain Oliver Everett as pastor of the New South Church. When some of the ultraorthodox members pressed Everett closely concerning his views on the Trinity, Chauncy lost his temper and insulted the two laymen who were questioning most. The council appeared on the point of breaking up without ordaining Everett, when in the words of one member, "Dr. Aquinas Cooper with a very mellifluous tone begged to ask one question: 'Do you believe, Mr. Everett, that there are 3 persons, &c., and that these 3 are one?' 'Yes, Sir.' " This nominal orthodoxy satisfied Cooper and a majority of the council, who then ordained Everett without further inquiry.[5]

While indifferent to theological speculation, Cooper saw clearly the political significance of ecclesiastical issues such as the future of King's Chapel. This church of the royal governors had been used during most of the war by the Old South congregation. With repairs to the Old South building nearly completed in the fall of 1782, the wardens of the Chapel resumed holding episcopal services there and began to search for a settled rector to replace the now infamous Henry Caner. Dr. Thomas Bulfinch, senior warden and Cooper's brother-in-law, took the lead in these arrangements. But behind the scenes the Brattle Street pastor, who was also close to other important members of the Chapel, played a leading role in preventing the restoration of this symbolic church to the regular Anglican communion.[6]

Partially as a result of Cooper's efforts, the wardens engaged young James Freeman, trained at Harvard for the Congregational ministry, to read services during a six months' trial. A patriot, Freeman received permission to Americanize the liturgy and to follow his own discretion in using the Athanasian Creed, unpopular for its unintelligibility, especially on the Trinity. In April 1783 Freeman was chosen pastor but remained out of episcopal orders. He scoffed at the dogma of apostolic succession and considered a trip to England for ordination too "base and servile for a free republican." The Chapel was weaned from Anglicanism, and Freeman's people gradually followed his theological progression

towards Unitarianism. Cooper had demonstrated once again that
more could be accomplished by private influence than by public
noise.[7]

Pleas of neo-Puritans such as Samuel Adams and the shocked
outcries of the orthodox against heresy were nothing new in
Boston. Yet at the coming of peace, the town could no longer
disguise the extent to which seven years of war had widened the
cultural differences between it and the country towns. Early in
1783 the Boston town meeting lodged a strong constitutional protest against a sweeping Sabbath observance act passed by the
Massachusetts legislature in October. This resolution reiterated the
ideology so recently utilized against Britain, and it anticipated the
constitutional doctrine of the major nineteenth-century American
protests against actions of the federal government. It served notice
that Sabbatarian laws could no longer be enforced in Boston, not
only because of the presence of numerous citizens of foreign states,
but also because freemen quietly walking the public streets on a
Sunday were unwilling to acknowledge the jurisdiction of a Sabbath warden, appointed under this act, who "like Paul in the time
of his Infidelity," might fancy that "in persecuting Christians, he is
doing God's service."[8]

Having taken its stand on the primacy of the natural right to
move from place to place on the Sabbath over the biblical injunc-
tion, the town meeting postponed the appointment of Sabbath
wardens for a year and got down to more vital business. Surprisingly few citizens continued to rail against the profaning influence of
"foreign papists" or the growing use of Sundays for leisure. As
Bostonians looked to their uncertain future in the postwar period of
readjustment, they naturally placed economic concerns first. "You
will always remember that you represent a Trading Town," the
newly elected representatives were instructed in 1783. If Boston
was to fulfill its economic goals in the Revolution, a complex of
shipping, trade, fishing, private credit, and public fiscal policy must
be restored and maintained in a healthy and expanding state.[9]

Cooper had been a strong supporter of Congress from the
beginning and had rejoiced at the ratification of the Articles of Confederation in 1781. Furthermore, he acknowledged that the "States
have a good Financier in Mr. Morris." Yet he well understood that
the attitude of the Boston elite toward the federal government in
peacetime would reflect their current assessment of Congress's
economic policies.[10]

The nationalists controlling Congress in 1781 proposed to
strengthen the Articles of Confederation with an amendment giving

Congress its first taxing power in the form of a 5 percent impost (or excise) on imports. Whatever the impost might do for the efforts of Robert Morris to buttress the federal government by funding the Revolutionary debt, it was difficult for Boston's economic leaders to accept it at a time when the state struggled to put its own financial affairs in order. The General Court postponed consideration of the amendment while protesting to Congress that the burden of the impost fell unfairly on the commercial states and that local merchants already were forced to sell some imports below cost. Congress rejected these complaints and urged ratification. At the end of the session in March 1782, a bill to ratify passed both houses despite widespread opposition from leading commercial towns. Representatives from the country towns had generally supported the measure in a vague hope of reducing their heavy property taxes.[11]

Seeking a compromise that would allow him to straddle the issue, Hancock pocket-vetoed the ratification act, while professing his willingness to accept an amended version. Such a bill passed in the next session, but he again vetoed it. The General Court, however, declared the act approved on a technicality and forwarded notice of ratification to Congress. In the end, the controversy proved pointless, for Rhode Island first and Virginia later prevented the impost amendment from receiving the required unanimous approval of the states.[12]

In the spring of 1783, Congress offered a more complex substitute for the defeated amendment. It granted the national legislature for twenty-five years a varied impost supplemented by grants from the states to be raised by direct taxation. Some in Massachusetts viewed this as a scheme to finance the "five years' full pay" that Congress had voted for Continental army officers in lieu of the customary half pay for life promised earlier. The rural areas were less enthusiastic about this financial package, while the commercial towns had begun to look more favorably on the plans of Robert Morris. But opposition was so generally strong that in July the legislature approved a letter to Congress threatening dissolution of the union over the issue of retirement pay for officers. In reply Congress defended its action and warned Massachusetts of the consequences of refusing to support the federal government.[13]

Cooper gave Hancock the major credit for the General Court's passage of the impost section of the congressional proposal in October after a protracted and complex debate. The governor's address to a joint session, the preacher informed Franklin, had carried the vote by impressing the legislators with the "Importance of supporting public credit."[14] In the letter to Franklin, written in his last months of life, Cooper appears like a "prime minister" ascribing the credit for a ministerial measure to the "monarch." If the governor's address had carried the impost to passage, it was a significant victory for which he owed much of the success to Morris, who had sent him extracts from a letter in which John Adams pleaded for the states to "consider themselves as one body animated by one soul" in discharging the debts of Congress.[15] But Hancock's friendship with Morris had been based on their personal affinity while together in Pennsylvania, rather than on an appreciation of the financier's plans to vitalize the central government under the Articles.

Cooper's death was to deprive Boston of its major spokesman for the nationalists who resisted the efforts of localists to prevent the slightest transfer of state sovereignty to Congress.[16] It was a serious loss in a town where one localist filled half a newspaper page denouncing the clergy who prayed "for Congress as the Supreme Council of the States" and declaring that the "moment the idea of Congress being a supreme legislature takes place, that moment we lose our sovereignty and independence." Although his political leadership was circumscribed by a clerical role, the Brattle Street pastor again in this instance far better represented the views of the commercial elite than leaders such as Samuel Adams or James Warren. Hancock needed him, of course, but so did Franklin and Morris. The 1783 impost eventually failed to obtain unanimous approval by the states. Before then, Morris laid down the burden taken up a few years later by Alexander Hamilton. Dying when he did, Cooper was spared any disillusionment with the fruits of independence.[17]

He was also spared most of the controversy over the efforts of refugees to regain their citizenship and property. Boston's commercial families seldom joined in the hue and cry against Tories and loyalists who had not actively supported Britain's cause. A few of the most prominent families had members who had gone to England during the war, either as outright loyalists or in an effort to avoid a definite commitment to either side. Thomas Boylston, one of the wealthiest of Cooper's parishioners, received permission from the General Court in 1778 to sail for England on "business," provided he post a $10,000 bond to "do nothing to the prejudice" of his state or country, to return within four years, and then to pay his share of war taxes. He lost his fortune through bad investments in England and never set foot in the United States again.[18]

Another member of the Brattle Street Church, Hancock's amiable companion Thomas Brattle, left for Europe soon after the shooting began in 1775. He spent time in England, where he both fraternized with loyalists and rendered notable services to American prisoners of war. By the time he came home in 1779, his loyalty had become a political issue. As late as 1783, a petition for his removal from the act of banishment failed by one vote to clear the House of Representatives. The following year he established his loyalty and recovered his property through the courts.[19] Less fortunate was Bowdoin's brother-in-law, George Erving, who, though likely as much a Whig as Boylston and Brattle, recoiled from violence to the extent that he became a reluctant refugee and went into permanent exile.[20]

Cooper's attitude toward the loyalists at the war's end found expression in 1782 when he recommended to Franklin, "Mr. Jonathan Amory, formerly a noted Merchant of this Town, and who left us at the Opening of the War, and went to England, and afterward at Newport took an Oath of Allegiance to the British King, but has long wished and applied for Leave to return to his native Country, from which he is now excluded by Law. He is a Gentleman of an amiable private Character, and has never taken an active part against his Country." Amory's two brothers, Thomas and John, had raised their families in the Brattle Street communion. John too had gone to England, while Thomas remained to take his chances in Boston and look after family affairs. The two absent brothers longed to settle again in Boston. Cooper found it impossible to resist the "Importunity" of Amory's friends and relatives that he do what he could to speed the return of John and Jonathan.[21]

However willing he might be to welcome the return of previously uncommitted members of elite families, Cooper's unwitting involvement in the protracted campaign against the restoration of John Temple's citizenship had helped to arouse fears, particularly in outlying areas, against the peril of postwar leniency toward the refugees, and made more difficult the homecoming of men such as Brattle and Amory. Perhaps for this reason, John Adams cautioned the preacher in September 1783 that the treaty provisions concerning loyalists "ought to be sacredly fulfilled, and the Recommendations at least decently treated and calmly considered. Errors on the side of forgiveness and Indulgence will be of the safest kind." Eventually absentees like the Amorys, who protested that their loyalty to their native land had been compromised by accident rather than intent, were usually able to resume their places in

Boston society. The restoration of the property of returnees proved to be a more difficult task, the outcome often depending on how successful their Whig relatives had been in delaying or avoiding confiscation proceedings.[22]

Thomas Pownall was among those who dreamed of returning to Massachusetts. By 1780 he had joined the opposition. Any possibility of his receiving a cabinet post or serving as a peace negotiator had vanished with the presentation to George III of his correspondence with Cooper. He lost his seat in Commons in the election of 1780 and bowed out of public life after publishing a widely read pamphlet, *A Memorial Most Humbly Addressed to the Sovereigns of Europe*, in which he urged Europeans to recognize the significance of the American Revolution.[23]

As a private citizen, Pownall reopened his correspondence with Cooper and Bowdoin in 1783. "I consider this wonderfull Revolution," he wrote, "as the interposition of Divine Providence, superceeding the ordinary course of human affairs." He deeded his five hundred acres of Maine land to Harvard College for the establishment of "Lectures on the Science of Polity and Law" designed "to form the minds of the students to become efficient and good members of a free state." In addition, he asked Bowdoin to search for a suitable estate on which he could settle in Massachusetts and to promote his appointment as a general of militia. Typical of Governor Pownall's career, all of these proposals—including the Harvard lectures—failed to be implemented. Employing his considerable talents and energy in a wide variety of research and writing, he lived quietly in England until his death in 1805.[24]

If the present governor of Massachusetts recalled his trip to England in 1760 under Pownall's care, he gave no indication. In those twenty-three years between the end of Pownall's governorship and the celebration of peace, few American careers had taken such an unpredictable course as Hancock's. He seemed in an appreciative mood in October 1783 as he wrote to congratulate Washington upon his retirement after "services, which consecrate your name to all posterity." Hancock enjoyed another decade of life and unparalleled popularity among the masses of his state, and thus caught a glimpse of the "increasing splendor and prosperity of a rising nation" that he had predicted to Washington.[25]

So too, most of Cooper's colleagues in revolution had years remaining, but his life ended quickly after the final peace. On 20 November he attempted to write a short note to Franklin: "I never in all my Life wrote a letter with half the Difficulty of this—Sick in my Chamber, attended by two Physicians." He promised to write more "as soon as my Health is restored," but this proved to be his last letter to the close friend he had seen so seldom. His illness was described as a "disorder of the lethargic kind," apparently a viral infection of the nervous system, some variety of encephalomyelitis. No contemporary evidence confirms the posthumous rumor that he had "sacrificed his life to the inordinate use of Scotch snuff."[26]

By the beginning of December his condition had so worsened that the clergy called a special service at Brattle Street to pray for his recovery. The "Prime Minister now lies sick of a fever," wrote one of Temple's friends; if he recovers, "it will give him an opportunity to be more of a spiritual man and less of a politician." Despite a few lucid intervals, he deteriorated until on 23 December he was "given over" to the care of his Maker. Death came on 29 December, after an illness of six weeks. He seemed to welcome the end, for "fear of living as the shadow of himself," and he died—so his friends believed—with the consolation of faith in "those evangelical truths which he had preached to others."[27]

His elaborate funeral on 2 January contrasted sharply with the simple death rites of his Puritan forebears. A funeral anthem, especially composed and printed for this occasion, was "performed." It began with the line, "Samuel the Priest gave up the Ghost, and all Israel mourned."[28] Then John Clarke, Dr. Chauncy's junior colleague, preached a sermon that honestly characterized Cooper as both a "states-man" and a "minister of religion."[29]

A remarkably perceptive obituary written for the newspapers by James Sullivan constituted the best biography of Cooper until the twentieth century. How fortunate it had been for the United States, Sullivan emphasized, that "this reverend patriot" understood politics as well as divinity, that he had been "among the first" to take an "early and decided part in the policies of his country," that "he did much to obtain foreign alliances," and that his talents and personality seemed "peculiarly formed by heaven" for the "happy purpose" of subduing prejudices against the French and conciliating the "habits and manners of the two nations."[30] Writing to his cousin John in France, Samuel Adams merely noticed the "Death of our good Friend Dr. Cooper." With greater apparent sorrow, a young Boston clergyman observed, "Dr. Cooper's death is felt by none more than the clergy in this town. We have lost the life of our association and the *goût* of our literary entertainment."[31]

From Philadelphia La Luzerne informed Vergennes: "The pension we made to an individual in Boston ceased as of 1 January. He did not leave this life without sending me an expression of his gratitude for the favors he had received from the King. He was an excellent citizen, a man of much merit and skill; in serving his country well, he never ceased to give proof of his attachment to [our] King and nation." With no hope of securing another correspondent of Cooper's ability and influence, the French minister did not make a replacement, though there was at least one anonymous applicant.[32]

Cooper had died without seeing again his last hope for an heir worthy of the Cooper heritage, the grandson he had sent to Europe four years before. From his deathbed he recommended his "petit-fils" to La Luzerne. Despite Franklin's admonition to return quickly, Sammy Johonnot could not tear himself away from the pleasures of Paris in time to board the last ship of the season bound for New England. As a result, he sailed to a southern port and did not reach home until two weeks after Cooper's death, despite the efforts of Sullivan to rush him to Boston at any expense.[33] At the last Commencement Harvard College had granted Sammy an A.B. in absentia.[34] He received in trust one-third of his grandfather's estate, which though never inventoried, was reputed to be unusually substantial for a clergyman.[35] With all the care and affection lavished on him, he failed to fulfill the expectations of his grandfather, who regarded him as a living symbol of the Revolution. While still young, Johonnot established himself as a lawyer in Portland, Maine, where tradition holds that he "kept the town in a uproar for two or three years by his satirical talent, and was finally mobbed out of town." He died young and in obscurity as vice-consul in British Guiana.[36]

In the January of Cooper's funeral, newspaper advertisements offered for sale a large variety of freshly imported goods, mostly from England, and invited subscriptions to the stock of the town's first bank. Thus, as it had begun twenty years before, the American Revolution in Boston ended with new hopes for an expanding commerce.

By experience, talents, and position, Samuel Cooper was perfectly prepared to integrate the values of commercial Boston into the mainstream of the town's religious and political culture. He served primarily the Whig elite, but he understood well the wide appeal of a religious legitimization of the self-interests of all men. He never forgot why Bostonians had committed those first acts of resistance that led to war and independence. The investigation of local leaders like Cooper often brings better into focus the goals of the Revolutionary movement than the study of the most conspicuous leaders who, caught up in greater glory of the national cause, sometimes lost touch with the fundamental needs of their constituents.

If the founding fathers are not required to move over to make room for Dr. Cooper, he at least deserves to stand alongside Samuel Adams in the pantheon of the American Revolutionary great. But wherever one judges this preacher to rank among the leaders of the Revolution, the significance of his life transcends a personal narrative. His career provides a fresh perspective on the time-hallowed story of Boston's progression from resistance to rebellion.

The Revolution that began in Cooper's Boston was not a radical plot hatched and nursed to maturity by a master revolutionary. Rather it emerged as the unexpected and at first unwelcome climax of a course of action initiated by the socio-economic elite in response to British measures and supported by a large cross section of all citizens. In many respects, John Hancock had a more decisive leadership role than Samuel Adams, but group rather than individual action characterized the resistance of Boston Whigs. More important than any of the few famous leaders was the large extent to which Boston's wealth was pitted against Britain. The town's strength through two decades of turmoil and war lay in its cohesive society, bound together by culture, religion, and economic interdependence. Cooper's involvement with France, his personal gain aside, highlights the French contribution to American independence that has been so seldom gratefully acknowledged.

These conclusions, suggested by the study of Cooper's life, cannot be fully tested in a biography. Nonetheless, making the acquaintance of the "Divine Politician" creates a dissatisfaction with past accounts of Revolutionary Boston and suggests the direction a revision might take. The manifold associations of this intriguing preacher challenge historians to probe more deeply into what has seemed an all too familiar chapter of American history. After two centuries, much remains to be discovered.

Short Titles
and Abbreviations

AASP	*Proceedings of the American Antiquarian Society*
A&R	*The Acts and Resolves, . . . of the Province of the Massachusetts Bay.* Vols. 18–21. Boston, 1912–1922.
AFC	L. H. Butterfield, ed. *Adams Family Correspondence.* Vols. 1–2, 1963; 3–4, 1973. Cambridge, Mass.: Harvard University Press.
AHR	*American Historical Review*
Akers, *Mayhew*	Charles W. Akers. *Called Unto Liberty, A Life of Jonathan Mayhew, 1720–1766.* Cambridge, Mass.: Harvard University Press, 1964.
AL MSS	Arthur Lee Manuscripts. Harvard University Library.
AM	Microfilms of the Adams Papers. Massachusetts Historical Society.
Andrews, *Boston Merchants*	Charles McLean Andrews. *The Boston Merchants and the Non-Importation Movement.* In *Publications of the Colonial Society of Massachusetts.* Vol. 19. 1917. Reprint. New York: Russell & Russell, 1968.
Andrews, "Letters"	Winthrop Sargent, ed. "Letters of John Andrews, Esq. of Boston, 1772–1776." *Proceedings of the Massachusetts Historical Society,* 8(1864–1865):316–412.

APS   American Philosophical Society.

BAC Records   Transcripts of British-American Customs Records, 1750–1777. Massachusetts Historical Society.

Bailyn, *Ordeal*   Bernard Bailyn. *The Ordeal of Thomas Hutchinson.* Cambridge, Mass.: Harvard University Press, 1974.

Barrow, *Trade and Empire*   Thomas C. Barrow. *Trade and Empire.* Cambridge, Mass.: Harvard University Press, 1967.

Baxter, *Hancock*   W. T. Baxter. *The House of Hancock.* 1945. Reprint. New York: Russell & Russell, 1965.

BBC   Edward Channing and Archibald C. Coolidge, eds. *The Barrington-Bernard Correspondence.* Cambridge, Mass.: Harvard University Press, 1912.

BC   *Boston Chronicle*

BF   Benjamin Franklin

BEP   *Boston Evening Post*

BG   *Boston Gazette*

Bigelow, *WBF*   John Bigelow, ed. *The Works of Benjamin Franklin.* 12 vols. New York, 1904.

BM   British Museum

BNL   *Boston News-Letter*

"Boyle"   "Boyle's Journal of Occurences in Boston, 1759–1778." *New England Historical and Genealogical Register*, 84(1930):143–171, 248–272, 357–382; 85(1931):5–28, 117–133.

BPB   *Boston Post-Boy*

Bradford, *S&A*   [Alden Bradford, ed.] *Speeches of the Governors of Massachusetts, from 1765 to 1775; and the Answers of the House of Representatives, to the Same . . .* Boston, 1818.

Brennan, *Office-Holding*   Ellen E. Brennan, *Plural Office-Holding in Massachusetts, 1760–1780.* Chapel Hill, N.C.: University of North Carolina Press, 1945.

Brown, *Hancock*	Abram English Brown. *John Hancock, His Book.* Boston, 1898.
Brown, *Revolutionary Politics*	Richard D. Brown. *Revolutionary Politics in Massachusetts: The Boston Committee of Correspondence and the Towns, 1772–1774.* Cambridge, Mass.: Harvard University Press, 1970.
BSM, 1764–1768	*A Report of the Record Commissioners of the City of Boston, containing the Selectmen's Minutes from 1764 Through 1768.* Boston, 1889.
BSM, 1769–1775	*A Report of the Record Commissioners of the City of Boston, containing the Selectmen's Minutes from 1769 Through April, 1775.* Boston, 1893.
BSM, 1776–1786	*A Report of the Record Commissioners of the City of Boston, containing the Selectmen's Minutes from 1776 Through 1786.* Boston, 1894.
BSR	*Records of the Church in Brattle Square.* Boston, 1902.
BT MSS	Bowdoin-Temple Manuscripts. Massachusetts Historical Society.
BTP	*Bowdoin-Temple Papers.* 2 vols. *Collections of the Massachusetts Historical Society.* 1:54 (1897); 2:61(1907).
BTR, 1758–1769	*A Report of the Record Commissioners of the City of Boston, Containing the Boston Town Records, 1758 to 1769.* Boston, 1886.
BTR, 1770–1777	*A Report of the Record Commissioners of the City of Boston, Containing the Boston Town Records, 1770 Through 1777.* Boston, 1887.
BTR, 1778–1783	*A Report of the Record Commissioners of the City of Boston, Containing the Boston Town Records, 1778 to 1783.* Boston, 1895.
Burnett, *Letters*	Edmund C. Burnett, ed. *Letters of Members of the Continental Congress.* 8 vols. 1921–1936. Reprint. Gloucester, Mass.: Peter Smith, 1963.
Carter, *Gage*	Clarence E. Carter, ed. *The Correspondence of General Thomas Gage with the Secretaries of*

Carter, *Gage* (continued)

State, and with the *War Office and the Treasury, 1763–1775.* 2 vols. New Haven, Conn.: Yale University Press, 1931, 1933.

Cary, *Warren*

John Cary. *Joseph Warren: Physician, Politician, Patriot.* Urbana, Ill.: University of Illinois Press, 1964.

Cobbett, *PH*

William Cobbett, ed. *The Parliamentary History of England from the Earliest Period to the Year 1803.* 36 vols. London, 1806–1820.

CJ

Continental Journal (Boston)

CP

Papers of William and Samuel Cooper. Henry E. Huntington Library, San Marino, Calif.

CPEU

Correspondance politique, Etats-Unis, Archives du Ministère des Affaires étrangères, Paris. Library of Congress transcripts and microfilm.

CPEUS

Correspondance politique, Etats-Unis, Supplément, Archives du Ministère des Affaires étrangères, Paris. Library of Congress transcripts and microfilm.

CSMP

Publications of the Colonial Society of Massachusetts

Dickerson, *BMR*

Oliver M. Dickerson, ed. *Boston under Military Rule (1768–1769) as Revealed in a Journal of the Times.* Boston: Mount Vernon Press, 1936.

DJR

Anne Rowe Cunningham, ed. *Letters and Diary of John Rowe, Boston Merchant, 1759–1762, 1764–1779.* Boston, 1903.

Doniol, *Histoire*

Henri Doniol. *Histoire de la participation de la France à l'établissement des Etats-Unis d'Amérique, Correspondance diplomatique et documents.* 5 vols. Paris, 1886–1892.

Dorr

Harbottle Dorr newspaper collection. 4 vols. Massachusetts Historical Society microfilm.

DT, *Diary*

William Tudor, ed. *Deacon Tudor's Diary.* Boston, 1896.

EP, "Diary"

"Diary of Ezekiel Price, 1775–6." *Proceedings of the Massachusetts Historical Society,* 7(1863–1864):185–262.

Ferguson, *Power*

E. James Ferguson. *The Power of the Purse.* Chapel Hill, N.C.: University of North Carolina Press, 1961.

Fitzpatrick, *WGW*

John C. Fitzpatrick, ed. *The Writings of George Washington.* 39 vols. Washington, D.C.: U.S. Government Printing Office, 1931–1944.

Fowler, *Hancock*

William M. Fowler, Jr. *The Baron of Beacon Hill: A Biography of John Hancock.* Boston: Houghton Mifflin, 1980.

French, *First Year*

Allen French. *The First Year of the American Revolution.* 1934. Reprint. New York: Octagon Books, 1968.

Gardiner, *WGC*

C. Harvey Gardiner, ed. *A Study in Dissent: The Warren-Gerry Correspondence, 1776–1792.* Carbondale, Ill.: Southern Illinois University Press, 1968.

Gipson, *British Empire*

Lawrence H. Gipson. *The British Empire Before the American Revolution.* 15 vols. (1–3 rev. ed.). New York: Alfred A. Knopf, 1958–1970.

Griffin

Frederick Griffin. *Junius Discovered.* Boston, 1854.

"Gordon"

"Letters of the Reverend William Gordon, Historian of the American Revolution, 1770–1799." *Proceedings of the Massachusetts Historical Society,* 63(1929–1930):303–613.

Hancock MSS

Papers of Thomas and John Hancock. New England Historic and Genealogical Society, Boston.

Handlin, *Sources*

Oscar Handlin and Mary Handlin, eds. *The Popular Sources of Political Authority, Documents on the Massachusetts Constitution of 1780.* Cambridge, Mass.: Harvard University Press, 1966.

HC	Henry Caner
HC, Letterbook	Letterbook of Henry Caner. University of Bristol Library, England.
Holker, Papers	Papers of John Holker. 40 vols. Library of Congress.
Hulton, Account	[Henry Hulton]. Some Account of the Proceedings of the People of New England from the Establishment of a Board of Customs in America to the breaking out of the Rebellion in 1775. Princeton University Library.
Hulton, "Letters"	Wallace Brown. "An Englishman Views the American Revolution: The Letters of Henry Hulton, 1769–1776." *Huntington Library Quarterly*, 36(1972–1973):1–26, 139–151.
IC	*Independent Chronicle* (Boston)
IL	*Independent Ledger* (Boston)
JA	John Adams
JA, *Diary*	L. H. Butterfield, ed. *Diary and Autobiography of John Adams.* 4 vols. Cambridge, Mass.: Harvard University Press, 1961.
JA, *Papers*	Robert J. Taylor, ed. *Papers of John Adams.* 4 vols. Cambridge, Mass.: Harvard University Press, 1977–1979.
JA, *Legal Papers*	L. Kinvin Wroth and Hiller B. Zobel, eds. *Legal Papers of John Adams.* 3 vols. Cambridge, Mass.: Harvard University Press, 1965.
JA, *Works*	Charles Francis Adams, ed. *The Works of John Adams.* 10 vols. Boston, 1850–1856.
JB	James Bowdoin
JCC	Worthington C. Ford, ed. *Journals of the Continental Congress, 1774–1789.* 34 vols. 1904–1937. Reprint. New York: Johnson Reprint Corp., 1968.

Jensen, *Founding*

Merrill Jensen. *The Founding of a Nation: A History of the American Revolution, 1763–1776.* New York: Oxford University Press, 1968.

JH

John Hancock

JHRM

Journal of the . . . House of Representatives, of . . . Massachusetts-Bay. Cited by year or session dates as originally published.

JPC

William Lincoln, ed. *The Journals of Each Provincial Congress of Massachusetts in 1774 and 1775.* Boston, 1838.

JT

John Temple

KM

King's Manuscripts. British Museum.

Labaree, *Tea Party*

Benjamin Woods Labaree. *The Boston Tea Party.* New York: Oxford University Press, 1964.

LC

Library of Congress

LCP

"Letters of Samuel Cooper to Thomas Pownall, 1769–1777." *American Historical Review,* 8(1903):301–330.

LL

La Luzerne

LL, Letterbooks

Letterbooks of the Chevalier de la Luzerne, deposited in Archives des Affaires étrangères (Paris) by the estate of Anita de Kergorlay.

Mayo, *Additions*

Catherine B. Mayo, ed. *Addition to Thomas Hutchinson's "History of Massachusetts Bay."* Worcester, Mass.: American Antiquarian Society, 1949.

Meng, *Gérard*

John J. Meng, ed. *Despatches and Instructions of Conrad Alexandre Gérard, 1778–1780.* Baltimore, 1939.

Meredith, *Amory*

Gertrude Euphemia Meredith. *The Descendants of Hugh Amory, 1605–1805.* London, 1901.

MHS   Massachusetts Historical Society

MHSC   *Collections of the Massachusetts Historical Society*

MHSP   *Proceedings of the Massachusetts Historical Society*

Morris, *Peacemakers*   Richard B. Morris. *The Peacemakers*. New York: Harper & Row, 1965.

Nasatir and Monell, *FC*   Abraham P. Nasatir and Gary Elwyn Monell. *French Consuls in the United States: A Calendar of Their Correspondence in the Archives Nationales*. Washington, D.C.: Library of Congress, 1967.

Nash, *Crucible*   Gary B. Nash. *The Urban Crucible: Social Change, Political Consciousness, and the Origins of the American Revolution*. Cambridge, Mass.: Harvard University Press, 1979.

NEQ   *New England Quarterly*

NEHGR   *New England Historical and Genealogical Register*

NYPL   New York Public Library

O'Donnell, *La Luzerne*   William Emmett O'Donnell. *The Chevalier De La Luzerne, French Minister to the United States, 1779–1784*. Bruges, 1938.

Oliver, *AR*   Douglass Adair and John A. Schutz, eds. *Peter Oliver's Origin and Progress of the American Rebellion, A Tory View*. San Marino, Calif.: Huntington Library, 1961.

Patterson, *Political Parties* Stephen E. Patterson. *Political Parties in Revolutionary Massachusetts*. Madison, Wis.: University of Wisconsin Press, 1973.

PBF   Leonard W. Labaree (vols. 1–14) and William B. Willcox (vols. 15–21), eds. *The Papers of Benjamin Franklin*. 21 vols. New Haven, Conn.: Yale University Press, 1959–1978.

Quincy, *Reports*   Josiah Quincy, Jr. *Reports of Cases . . . in the Superior Court of . . . Massachusetts Bay, Between 1761 and 1772*. Boston, 1865.

SA

Samuel Adams

SAP

Samuel Adams Papers. New York Public Library.

SC

Samuel Cooper

SC Diary

Diary of Samuel Cooper. 1: 7 Jan. 1753–13 Jan. 1754, *N.E. Historical and Genealogical Register* 41(1887):388–391. 2: 1 Jan. 1764–2 Feb. 1765; 22 Oct.–31 Dec. 1769, *N.E. Historical and Genealogical Register* 55(1901):145–149. 3: 19 April, 1775–17 May 1776, *American Historical Review* 6(Jan. 1901):301–341. 4: 10–18 April 1775, Massachusetts Historical Society. 5: 10, 27, 30 April 1775, Massachusetts Historical Society.

Schlesinger, *Merchants*

Arthur Meir Schlesinger. *The Colonial Merchants and the American Revolution.* 1918. Reprint. New York: Atheneum Press, 1957.

Sewall, *Diary*

M. Halsey Thomas, ed. *The Diary of Samuel Sewall, 1674–1729.* 2 vols. New York: Farrar, Strauss and Geroux, 1973.

Seybolt, *Officials*

Robert Francis Seybolt. *The Town Officials of Colonial Boston, 1634–1775.* Cambridge, Mass.: Harvard University Press, 1939.

Shepherd and Walton, *Shipping*

James F. Shepherd and Gary M. Walton. *Shipping, Maritime Trade, and the Economic Development of Colonial North America.* Cambridge, (Cambridge University Press), 1972.

SHG

Clifford K. Shipton. *Sibley's Harvard Graduates, Biographical Sketches of Those Who Attended Harvard College.* Vols. 4–16. Cambridge, Mass.: Harvard University Press, 1932–1972.

SM Letters

Samuel Mather's Letters to His Son. Massachusetts Historical Society.

Smyth, *WBF*

Albert Henry Smyth, ed. *The Writings of Benjamin Franklin.* 10 vols. New York, 1907.

Sparks MSS

Sparks Manuscripts. Harvard University Library.

Spy	*Massachusetts Spy.* (Boston 1770–1775; Worcester, 1775–).
Stevens	B. F. Stevens, ed. *Facsimiles of Manuscripts in European Archives Relating to America, 1773–1783.* 25 vols. London, 1889–1898.
Stinchcombe, *American Revolution*	William C. Stinchcombe. *The American Revolution and the French Alliance.* Syracuse, N.Y.: Syracuse University Press, 1969.
TC	Thomas Cushing
Temple-Whately	Copies of Letters that passed between Mr. Whately, secretary to the Treasury, and Mr. Temple, Surveyor General of the Customs in North America—principally on Public affairs, and written by direction of the Rt. Hon. Mr. Grenville. Henry E. Huntington Library.
TH	Thomas Hutchinson
TH, Corr.	Correspondence of Thomas Hutchinson in the Massachusetts Archives, Massachusetts Historical Society typescripts.
TH, *D&L*	Peter Orlando Hutchinson, ed. *The Diary and Letters of His Excellency Thomas Hutchinson.* 2 Vols. Boston, 1884, 1886.
TH, *History*	Lawrence Shaw Mayo, ed. *The History of the Colony and Province of Massachusetts Bay by Thomas Hutchinson.* 3 vols. Cambridge, Mass.: Harvard University Press, 1936.
Thomas, "Partisan Politics"	Leslie J. Thomas. "Partisan Politics in Massachusetts During Governor Bernard's Administration, 1760–1770." Ph.D. dissertation, University of Wisconsin, 1960.
TP	Thomas Pownall
WAL	*Warren-Adams Letters.* 2 vols. *Collections of the Massachusetts Historical Society.* 1:72(1917); 2:73(1925).
Warden, *Boston*	G. B. Warden. *Boston, 1689–1776.* Boston: Little, Brown & Co., 1970.

Waters, *Otis Family*	John J. Waters, Jr. *The Otis Family in Provincial and Revolutionary Massachusetts.* Chapel Hill, N.C.: University of North Carolina Press, 1968.
WC1	William Cooper, father of Samuel Cooper
WC2	William Cooper, brother of Samuel Cooper
Wharton, *DC*	Francis Wharton, ed. *The Revolutionary Diplomatic Correspondence of the United States.* 6 vols. Washington, 1889.
WMQ	*William and Mary Quarterly*, 3rd series.
WP	William Palfrey
WP MSS	Papers of William Palfrey. Harvard University Library.
WSA	Harry A. Cushing, ed. *The Writings of Samuel Adams.* 4 vols. New York, 1904–1908.

Notes

Prologue

1. [Jonathan Odell], *The American Times: A Satire. In Three Parts. In which are Delineated the Characters of the Leaders of the American Rebellion . . .* (London, 1780), pp. 7–9.

2. Stevens 1:71.

3. Meng, *Gérard*, pp. 480–482.

Chapter 1

1. Sewall, *Diary*, 1:459–460; 2:948–949, 1028, 1034; and passim.

2. In addition to Sewall, *Diary*, see *Letter-Book of Samuel Sewall, MHSC* 51, 52 (1886, 1888); Ola Elizabeth Winslow, *Samuel Sewall of Boston* (New York, 1964); and T. B. Strandness, *Samuel Sewall: A Puritan Portrait* (East Lansing, Mich., 1967).

3. *BNL*, 6, 27 Aug. 1705. Frederick Tuckerman, "Thomas Cooper of Boston and His Descendants," *NEHGR* 44(1890):53–54. Sewall, *Diary*, 1:307, 324–325. Seybolt, *Officials*, p. 86. *First Report of the Record Commissioners of the City of Boston*, 2nd. (Boston, 1881), pp. 23, 68, 106, 139, 152, 160. Suffolk County, Mass., Probate Records 16:169–170.

4. Benjamin Colman, *Jesus weeping over his dead Friend. A Sermon Preached the Lords-Day after the Funeral of the Reverend Mr. William Cooper* (Boston, 1744), pp. 27–28. *BSR*, pp. 13–14, 96. "Memoranda from the Rev. William Cooper's Interleaved Almanacs," *NEHGR* 30(1876):435, 436. *BNL*, 28 May 1716. WC1 to [Stephen] Williams, 17 Nov. 1716, NYPL. *SHG* 5:599, 625. Sewall, *Diary*, 2:693.

5. The vast literature on the founding of the church is summarized in Perry Miller, *The New England Mind, From Colony to Province* (Cambridge, Mass., 1953), chs. 15, 16.

6. Ebenezer Turell, *The Life and Character of the Reverend Benjamin Colman . . .* (Boston, 1749). Anthony Gregg Roeber, " 'Her Merchandize . . . Shall Be Holiness to the Lord': The Progress and Decline of Puritan Gentility at the Brattle Street Church, Boston, 1715–1745," *NEHGR* 131(July 1977):175–195.

7. A sketch of WC1 is in *SHG* 5:624–634, but there exists no adequate account of his influence, which in many ways exceeded that of his better known colleague.

8. Sewall, *Diary*, 1:935, 939, 941, 942, 948–949, 954–955. Sewall, *Letter-Book*, 2:310–312. *BSR*, p. 15. "William Cooper's . . . Almanacs," 30:435.

9. *BNL*, 25 Dec. 1740. Sermon preached 28 Dec. 1740, "the Sabbath after my Dear Wife's Decease," CP. *BSR*, pp. 106, 143, 144, 146, 149, 151, 155. "William Cooper's . . . Almanacs," *NEHGR* 31(1877):52,54. Tuckerman, "Thomas Cooper," pp. 55–58.

10. Henry F. Jenks, *Catalogue of the Boston Latin School* (Boston, 1886), pp. 45–47. *The Common School Journal* 12(1850):311. *SHG* 8:441–446.

11. *SHG* 11:176–177, 237, 290.

12. Waters, *Otis Family*, pp. 110–111.

13. *SHG* 10:420–422.

14. Sketches of each are in *SHG* 10.

15. *SHG* 10–12, passim.

16. Samuel Eliot Morison, *Three Centuries of Harvard, 1636–1936* (Cambridge, Mass., 1936), pp. 67–68. "Sketch of the Life of Rev. Jacob Green, A.M.," *Christian Advocate* 9(1831):634–637.

17. Faculty Records, 1, 21 Sept. 1742, Harvard University Archives.

18. 5 Dec. 1743, Jonathan Mayhew MSS, Boston University.

19. CP. This verse is in SC's hand, but there is no other identification of authorship.

20. Among the vast evidence of the participation of the Brattle Street pastors in the Great Awakening, the following are particularly revealing: Colman's account of Whitefield's visit in Colman MSS, MHS. WC1's published sermons and sermon MSS (CP) for 1740–1743. Isaac Chanler, *New Converts exhorted to Cleave to the Lord* (Boston, 1740), p. iii. Colman, *Souls flying to Jesus Christ* (Boston, 1740). WC1 to_____, Boston, 4 Mar. 1741, American Antiquarian Society, Worcester, Mass. Jonathan Edwards, *The Distinguishing Marks of a Work of the Spirit of God* (Boston, 1741), pp. v, vii, xv. WC1 to his son, *BG* 23 April 1742. Clayton Harding Chapman, "Life and Influence of the Rev. Benjamin Colman, D.D., 1673–1747" (Ph.D. diss., Boston University School of Theology, 1947), ch. 7, provides a detailed study of the Brattle Street Church in the revival. For general background see Edwin Scott Gaustad, *The Great Awakening in New England* (New York, 1957). On Chauncy see Edward Michael Griffin, "A Biography of Charles Chauncy (1705–1787)" (Ph.D. diss., Stanford University, 1966), chs. 2–3.

21. *The Government and Improvement of Mirth* (Boston, 1707).

22. Colman, *Jesus weeping*, p. 33. Edwards, *Distinguishing Marks*, p. ix.

23. *A Continuation of the Reverend Mr. Whitefield's Journal From Savannah June 25, 1740* (Boston, 1741), p. 56. Diary of Henry Flynt, Dec. 1740–Jan. 1741, Harvard University Archives. "Sketch of . . . Jacob Green," p. 523. Akers, *Mayhew*, pp. 32–34. *SHG* 11 has many examples of student participation in the revival. *BG*, 20 Apr. 1741. *MHSP* 53(1919–1920):198.

24. Akers, *Mayhew*, p. 32, *SHG* 11:247. *BSR*, p. 101.

25. See note 19.

26. Flynt Diary, Dec. 1740–Jan. 1741. *SHG* 11:148.

27. Nothing is known of his activities in this period except that the college records indicate his continuation in residence after graduation.

28. *BSR*, pp. 28–30. The Boston newspapers report fully his illness and death.

29. Colman, *Jesus weeping*, p. 34. John M. Merriam, "Historic Burial-Places of Boston and Vicinity," *AASP* 7(1890–1891):391–392.

30. Colman, *Jesus weeping*, p. 37.

Chapter 2

1. Anthony Gregg Roeber, " 'Her Merchandize . . . Shall Be Holiness to the Lord': The Progress and Decline of Puritan Gentility at the Brattle Street Church, Boston, 1715–1745," *NEHGR* 131(July 1977):175–194.

2. *One shall be taken and another left* (Boston, 1741). *The Sin and Danger of quenching the Spirit* (Boston, 1741). See also WC1's sermons for 1740–1743 in CP.

3. Nash, *Urban Crucible*, pt. 1, passim.

4. *BSR*, pp. 30–31. Ebenezer Turell, *The Life and Character of the Reverend Benjamin Colman* . . . (Boston, 1749), pp. 51n, 220. *SHG* 9:450–453; 10:412–413, 508.

5. CP. See also *BG*, 5 June 1744.

6. *BG*, 4 Dec. 1744. *BEP*, 19 Nov., 10, 24 Dec. 1744.

7. *BSR*, pp. 31–34. *BG*, 1 Jan. 1745. *BNL*, 3 Jan. 1745.

8. *The Testimony* . . . *of Harvard College* . . . *against* . . . *George White-field* . . . (Boston, 1744). George Whitefield, *A Letter to* . . . *Harvard College* . . . (Boston, 1745). This controversy can be followed in the Boston newspapers during 1745–1746. *SHG* 10–11 contain many examples of ordination disputes.

9. Benjamin Colman, *One chosen of God* . . . *A Sermon Preached at the Ordination of the Reverend Mr. Samuel Cooper* . . . *May 21, 1746* (Boston, 1746), p. 20. *The Diary of William Bentley*, 4 vols. (1905–1914; reprint ed., Gloucester, Mass., 1962), 1:355–356. *BG*, 19 Jan. 1784. *BSR*, pp. 35–36.

10. *BSR*, p. 37. The MS sermon, CP, without pagination, is from 1 Tim. 1:10–11.

11. His statement on predestination was a deemphasized summary of the view of WC1: "And as God acts from Counsel and Design: and known to Him are all his Works from the Beginning: So we learn from his Word, that all who in Time repent and obey the Gospel were chosen and appointed by Him unto Eternal life, before the World began. He then determined to give them, those Means of Knowledge and Grace, which should be effectual through his Sacrifice to their Salvation."

12. *One chosen of God*, passim. *BSR*, pp. 35–37. *BNL*, 22 May 1746. *BG*, 27 May 1746.

13. *SHG* 11:176–336. *BEP*, 7 July 1746. Diary of Robert Treat Paine, 2 July 1746, MHS.

14. CP has the list of contributors. See also *BSR*, p. 37.

15. *Diary of William Bentley*, 3:87. The library was appraised for £374. Suffolk County, Mass., Probate Records 28:448–449; 36:491; 45:343–350. It is possible that some of WC1's many small debts were connected with the Land Bank, in which Benjamin Colman's brother was a partner.

16. *BSR*, pp. 108–111, 128, 146, 240, 246. Ellen Susan Bulfinch, *The Life and Letters of Charles Bulfinch, Architect, with Other Family Papers* (Boston, 1846), pp. 11–19. *SHG*, 6:233; 12:16–23. Suffolk County, Mass., Probate Records 37:250–251; 58:246–249. *BG*, 12 Dec. 1757.

17. *BSR*, p. 170.

18. Turell, *Colman*, pp. 174n–175n, 226n, 228. *BEP*, 31 Aug. 1747. *BNL*, 3 Sept. 1747. *BG*, 22 Sept. 1747.

19. SC and two fellow ministers wrote the preface for Turell's *Colman*.

20. *BSR*, pp. xii, 37–39.

21. SC Diary 1–2, passim.

22. The Henry E. Huntington Library has 146 of SC's sermons, and NYPL has 32 plus some fragments.

23. *A Sermon Preach'd April 9, 1760. At the Ordination of the Reverend Mr. Joseph Jackson* . . . (Boston, 1760), pp. 23–24, 33–35.

24. SC exchanged frequently with the liberal Charles Chauncy and less often with the arch heretic, Jonathan Mayhew. Another liberal minister published a sermon he preached at Brattle Street: Robert Breck, *The Duty of Ministers* . . . (Boston, 1748).

25. Sermons: Heb. 3:12, 24 Sept. 1758, CP; 1 John 5:4, Jan. 1768, NYPL.

26. Sermons: Matt. 11:30, Feb. 1746, CP; Rev. 14:13, Apr. 1749, CP.

27. Sermon: Ps. 18:46, Feb. 1750, CP.

28. Sermons: Matt. 26:42, 22 Jan. 1764, CP; Ps. 26:3, 29 Jan. 1749, CP.

29. Undated sermon fragment, NYPL.

30. Sermon: 2 Peter 1:10, Oct. 1765, CP.

31. E.g., sermon: Oct. 1755, CP.

32. Sermon: Col. 1:21–22, n.d., CP.

33. Sermon: Ps. 40:8, 22 Mar. 1759, CP. Edwards's *True Virtue* was one of his *Two Dissertations* published posthumously (Boston, 1765).

34. SC, *A Sermon Preached to the Ancient and Honourable Artillery Company . . . June 3, 1751* (Boston, 1751), p. 28.

35. Commonplace-Book of Ephraim Eliot, as quoted in *SHG* 11:194.

36. Phillis [Wheatley] Peters, *An Elegy Sacred to the Memory of that Great Divine, the Reverend and Learned Dr. Samuel Cooper* (Boston, 1784), p. 4.

37. Carl Van Doren, ed., *The Letters of Benjamin Franklin and Jane Mecom* (Princeton, N.J., 1950), pp. 3–33, 83–84.

38. JA, *Diary* 2:71. *AFC*, 1:156, 231; 2:79.

39. Despite his reputation for eloquence, there has been no study of SC as a speaker except Elaine Lynch Jones, "The Published Sermons of Samuel Cooper: A Study in Invention" (M.A. thesis, University of Wisconsin, 1967).

40. James Sullivan in *BG*, 19 Jan. 1784. E.g. see his sacramental sermon, July 1747, CP.

41. *BSR*, pp. 27–28, 37–38. Benjamin Colman, *A Letter . . . to the Reverend Mr. Williams of Lebanon* (Boston, 1744), p. 8. *Diary of William Bentley*, 2:379; 4:496. In 1751 SC wrote a recommendation for John Barnard's "A new Version of the Psalms of David . . ." (MS, MHS).

42. John Andrews described a sermon by SC that "drew tears from most of the audience" (Andrews, "Letters," p. 386). A long list of European visitors made a point to hear SC while they visited Boston.

43. John Clarke, *A Sermon Delivered at the Interment of . . . Samuel Cooper* (Boston, 1784), p. 26. William Sullivan, *The Public Men of the Revolution* (Philadelphia, 1847), p. 66.

44. JA, *Diary* 2:13.

45. *BG*, 19 Jan. 1784.

Chapter 3

1. The major views of colonial Boston are reproduced and described in Justin Winsor, *The Memorial History of Boston*, 4 vols. (Boston, 1880–1881), 2:530n–532n and passim.

2. *BSR*, pp. 28–30, 35–37. List of contributors to SC's "now going to house keeping," CP.

3. Franklin Bowditch Dexter, ed., *Extracts from the Itineraries and Other Miscellanies of Ezra Stiles, D.D., LL.D., 1755–1794. With A Selection from his*

Correspondence (New Haven, Conn., 1916), pp. 100–101, 120. *BNL*, 12, 19 Feb. 1741. William Pencak, "The Social Structure of Revolutionary Boston: Evidence from the Great Fire of 1760," *Journal of Interdisciplinary History* 10(Autumn 1979):267–268.

4. Jules Davis Prown, *John Singleton Copley in America, 1734–1774* (Cambridge, Mass., 1966), pp. 130–131, and passim.

5. Toward the end of the war Boston merchants formed "The Society for encouraging Trade and Commerce." Of the 147 signatures on the original articles of organization, 46 (24 percent) can be identified as Brattle Street worshipers, and this list does not include a few of the wealthiest merchants of the congregation. The undated articles and list of subscribers are in Ezekiel Price MSS, MHS.

6. Massachusetts Archives, 132, State House, Boston. Approximately 20 percent of the individual assessments are missing, but these are from wards at a distance from the church. Thus, though a few conspicuous Brattle Street names are among the missing, their inclusion would not appear to make a significant difference in these estimates of the congregation's relative wealth. Identification of members of the congregation is based primarily upon activity (baptism, marriage, owning the covenant, renting a pew, etc.) revealed in *BSR* from 1760 to 1783. Because of the confusion of names, uncertain dates of death, and changes in church affiliation, the list contains an inevitable margin of error. It is likely, however, that more names are omitted, particularly of older families who no longer had children to baptize, than are mistakenly included. I have identified 274 families, a figure close to Andrew Eliot's estimate of 280 families attending Brattle Street in 1761 (see n. 13).

7. JA, *Papers* 2:114.

8. For recent discussions of Boston's economic and social problems see Nash, *Urban Crucible*, passim; G. B. Warden, "The Distribution of Property in Boston, 1692–1775," in *Perspectives in American History* 10(1976):81–113; Pencak, "Social Structure"; and Bruce C. Daniels, "Long Range Trends of Wealth Distribution in Eighteenth Century New England," *Explorations of Economic History* 11(1973–1974):123–135.

9. Sermon: Ps. 40:8, Mar. 1759, CP. For Edwards, see Perry Miller, *Jonathan Edwards* (New York, 1949), pp. 285–297; and Patterson, *Political Parties*, p. 12.

10. Robert V. Wells, *The Population of the British Colonies in America before 1776: A Survey of Census Data* (Princeton, N.J., 1975), pp. 82–85. Nash, *Urban Crucible*, pp. 407–408.

11. *A Sermon Preached in Boston, New-England, Before the Society for Encouraging·Industry, and Employing the Poor; August 8, 1753* (Boston, 1753), pp. 3–8. Nash, *Urban Crucible*, pp. 188–193, discusses the background of this sermon.

12. Sermon: Matt. 11:5, Mar. 1754, CP.

13. Sketches of all the preachers mentioned here are in *SHG*. For recent studies of Mayhew and Eliot, see Bernard Bailyn, "Religion and Revolution: Three Biographical Studies," *Perspectives in American History* 4(1970):83–124. An example of Stillman's appeal is found in Alice Morse Earle, ed., *Diary of Anna Green Winslow, a Boston School Girl of 1771* (Boston, 1894), p. 69. It is impossible to make an accurate estimate of the size of Boston congregations without doing more work than the results would justify. In 1761 Andrew Eliot estimated that his church ministered to 300 families; Cooper's, 280; Trinity (Anglican), 250; Old South, 200; First and West, 150 (Dexter, *Extracts from . . . Ezra Stiles*, pp. 100–101.) My detailed studies of the West and Brattle Street congregations indicate that Eliot's figures were fairly accurate.

14. Benjamin Gale, _The Present State of the Colony of Connecticut Considered_ ([New London] 1755), p. 6. Thomas Clap, _The Answer of the Friend in the West_ (New Haven, 1755), p. 6. _SHG_ 7:194; 11:194, 367, 377, 516; 12:208. Jonathan Belcher Letter-book, 12 Sept. 1750, MHS. _PBF_ 3:116–117, 271; 4:64–65, 68–69.

15. _A Discourse concerning Unlimited Submission and Non-Resistance to the Higher Powers_ (Boston, 1750), preface.
A Sermon Preached . . . in Boston, . . . June 3, 1751 (Boston, 1751), pp. 39–40.

16. _SC Diary_, 1:390. _JHRM_, 1753, pp. 8, 64, 68, 76, 89, 90, 96. _A Conference Held at St. George's in the County of York_ [20 Sept. 1753] (Boston, 1753), passim. _BEP_, 24 Sept., 8 Oct. 1753. _PBF_ 5:112.

17. E.g., SC's sermon 11 Aug. 1763, CP.

18. _BNL_, 30 Nov. 1755.

19. _BNL_, 21 Mar. 1760.

20. For discussions of the social covenant theory and the jeremiad see Perry Miller, _The New England Mind, the Seventeenth Century_ (New York, 1939), _From Colony to Province_ (Cambridge, Mass., 1953); Alan Heimert, _Religion and the American Mind_ (Cambridge, Mass., 1966), pp. 62–63, 324–332, 423–435; and Sacvan Bercovitch, _The American Jeremiad_ (Madison, Wisconsin, 1979).

21. Baxter, _Hancock_, 113–114, 141–142.

22. Sermon: Deut. 5:29, 4 Apr. 1754, CP.

23. Ibid.

24. _A Sermon Preached in the Audience of his Honour Spencer Phips, Esq; . . . May 26th. 1756_ (Boston, 1756), p. 11.

25. Sermon: 2 Chron. 20:3–4, 3 July 1755, CP.

26. Sermon: Jer. 2:14–17, 28 Aug. 1755, CP.

27. Sermon: Ps. 60:12, 21 Sept. 1755, CP.

28. _A Sermon . . . October 16th, 1759. Upon Occasion of the Success of His Majesty's Arms in the Reduction of Quebec_ (Boston [1759]), pp. 28–29, 36, 40.

29. Sermons: Luke 13:1–5, 18 Dec. 1755, CP; Ps. 20:7, 22 July 1756, CP; Jer. 6:8, 21 Apr. 1757, NYPL; Ps. 90:11, Sept. 1757, CP.

30. Sermon: Ps. 2:11, 17 Nov. 1757, CP.

31. J. Clarence Webster, ed., _The Journal of Jeffrey Amherst_ (Toronto, 1931), p. 86.

32. _A Sermon . . . October 16th, 1759_, pp. 39, 52–53.

33. Sermon: Amos 3:6, Mar. 1760, CP.

34. Sermon: James 1:23–24, Apr. 1762, CP.

35. Sermon: Ps. 29:10–11, 11 Aug. 1763, CP.

36. Cf. Heimert, _Religion and the American Mind_, ch. 3; and Perry Miller, "From the Covenant to the Revival," in James Ward Smith and A. Leland Jamison, eds., _The Shaping of American Religion_ (Princeton, N.J., 1961), pp. 343–349.

37. Sermon: Jer. 2:14–17, 28 Aug. 1755, CP.

38. Undated sermon fragment, NYPL.

39. _A Sermon upon Occasion of the Death of . . . George the Second_ (Boston, 1761), pp. 29, 39.

40. _Pietas et Gratulatio Collegii Cantabrigiensis apud Novanglos_ (Boston, 1761). Ode 13, which begins "As, on her white-clift, sea-girt shore, . . ." is attributed to SC in all but one of the copies marked by contemporaries in a position to have knowledge of authorship. Ode 28, which begins "Some Seraph touch the sacred lyre!" is undisputably attributed to SC. See Justin Winsor, "Pietas et

Gratulatio. An Inquiry into the Authorship of the Several Pieces," Harvard University Library *Bulletin*, 1(1879):305–308.

41. *Pietas et Gratulatio*, p. 51.

42. Ibid., pp. v–viii.

43. Ibid., pp. 7–26.

44. *A Sermon . . . October 16th, 1759*, p. 31.

45. Sermon: Ps. 20:7, 22 July 1756, CP.

46. Sermon: 2 Chron. 20:3–4, 3 July 1755, CP.

47. For examples of other important sermons preached during the French war and repeated during the Revolution, see in CP those first delivered on the following dates: 13 July 1755; 22 July 1756; 20 Mar. 1757; 17 Nov. 1757; 6 Apr. 1758; July 1758.

48. For a summary of recent interpretations of the Old Testament fathers, see Jacob M. Myers, "The Way of the Fathers," *Interpretation: A Journal of Bible and Theology* (1975):121–140.

Chapter 4

1. Particularly helpful here is John A. Schutz, "Succession Politics in Massachusetts, 1730–1741," *WMQ* 15(Oct. 1958):508–520.

2. John A. Schutz, *William Shirley* (Chapel Hill, N.C., 1961).

3. The first adequate account of the excise controversy is Paul S. Boyer, "Borrowed Rhetoric: The Massachusetts Excise Controversy of 1754," *WMQ* 21(July 1964):328–351. See also Schutz, *Shirley*, pp. 179–180.

4. As far as can be determined, the attribution of *The Crisis* ([Boston] 1754) to SC is based on the two copies at the Boston Athenaeum that have "Dr. Samuel Cooper" written on their title pages in what appears to be an eighteenth-century hand. Since SC was awarded his honorary doctorate in 1767, his name was obviously added long after publication. Isaiah Thomas, the chief authority on the authorship of anonymous publications in this period, lists no author for the *Crisis* of 1754 but assigns to SC another anonymous *Crisis* written later during the Stamp Act controversy. (Isaiah Thomas, *The History of Printing in America* [1874; reprint ed., New York, 1964], 2:520.) In view of such confusion and uncertainty, and without additional evidence, one cannot positively attribute *The Crisis* to SC.

5. *Crisis*, p. 10. To sample the other arguments in the controversy, see the following newspapers for 1754: *BG*: 16 July, 13, 20 Aug.; *BEP*: 5 Aug., 23 Sept., 7, 21 Oct. The House was so incensed at one of the anonymous pamphlets published in opposition to the excise that it threw the supposed printer into jail for a short time (Thomas, *History of Printing*, 1:129–134).

6. Schutz, *Shirley*, passim.

7. John A. Schutz, *Thomas Pownall* (Glendale, Calif., 1951), pp. 15–84.

8. Caroline Robbins, *The Eighteenth-Century Commonwealthman* (Cambridge, Mass., 1959), pp. 311–319.

9. Schutz, *Pownall*, pp. 85–180. Gipson, *British Empire* 7:160–163, 316–325.

10. Bailyn, *Ordeal*, pp. 39–45. Malcolm Freiberg, "Thomas Hutchinson: The First Fifty Years (1711–1761)," *WMQ* 15(Jan. 1958):53–55. Schutz, *Pownall*, pp. 93, 136–137, 155–156, 178. Waters, *Otis Family* pp. 116–117. Baxter, *Hancock*, pp. 136, 141–142, 247–248. TH, *History*, 3:41–42. *BEP*, 5 June 1758.

11. SM Letters, 19 April 1760.

12. *WSA* 4:238.

13. Schutz, *Pownall*, p. 48. HC to Rev. Dr. Nichols, 6 Oct. 1760, HC, Letter-book.

14. *WSA* 3:172. *BG*, 6 Jan. 1766.

15. [Boston] 1760. For authorship see *BG*, 6 Jan. 1766, Dorr. Samuel and Hannah Waterhouse had children baptized at Brattle Street in 1757 and 1759 (*BSR*, pp. 177, 178).

16. P. 7.

17. TH, Corr. 26:194. SC served as chaplain 1753–1754; Pemberton, 1755–1757; then SC again, 1758–1762 (*JHRM* for these years). The chaplain was chosen at the beginning of each annual session.

18. P. 16.

19. See "colonelling" in *OED*.

20. *BEP*, 7, 14, 21 Apr., 12 May 1760. *BPB*, 14 Apr. 1760. SM Letters, 31 Mar., 19 Apr., 1760. *SHG* 10:232–233.

21. *BEP*, 9 June 1760.

22. SM Letters, 7 June 1760.

23. With all due allowance for the traditional verbiage, the several farewell addresses to TP reflect the quality of his administration. See particularly the addresses of the Council and House (*BPB*, 31 Mar. and other newspapers for this week), of the Boston merchants (*BG*, 19 May and other newspapers), and of the town of Boston (*BTR*, 1758–1769. pp. 31–32).

24. *BNL*, 29 May 1760.

25. Baxter, *Hancock*, p. 147. Fowler, *Hancock*, pp. 38–41. Schutz, *Pownall*, pp. 194–290. George H. Guttredge, "Thomas Pownall's *The Administration of the Colonies*: the Six Editions," *WMQ* 26(Jan. 1969):31–46.

26. *BG*, 19 May 1760.

27. Gertrude S. Kimball, ed., *Correspondence of William Pitt*, 2 vols. (1906; reprint ed., New York, 1969), 1:214.

28. Nash, *Urban Crucible*, ch. 9, summarizes the drastic effects of the war on Boston.

29. For an example of the exaggerated rhetoric of the peace celebrations see Jonathan Mayhew, *Two Discourses Delivered October 25th, 1759* (Boston, 1759), pp. 39, 60–61.

30. Nash, *Urban Crucible*, chs. 1–9, passim. Warden, *Boston*, ch. 7.

31. For general background see Oliver Dickerson, *The Navigation Acts and the American Revolution* (Philadelphia, 1951), ch. 5 and pp. 294–295. For Lechmere see *BNL*, 3 Jan. 1771; "Boyle" 84:168; Barrow, *Trade and Empire*, p. 141.

32. *BPB*, 14 Apr. 1760.

33. George Louis Beer, *British Colonial Policy, 1754–1765* (reprint ed., Gloucester, Mass., 1958), chs. 5–7. Richard Pares, *War and Trade in the West Indies, 1739–1763* (1936; reprint ed., London, 1963), chs. 8–11.

34. Kimball, *Correspondence of William Pitt*, 2:320–321, 357–358.

35. Beer, *British Colonial Policy*, pp. 105–113. Dickerson, *Navigation Acts*, pp. 168–170.

36. For a short summary statement see Andrews, *Boston Merchants*, pp. 23–33.

37. This conclusion is based on a comparison of the members of the Boston merchants club organized in 1763 (Ezekiel Price MSS, MHS) with a file of heads of families in the Brattle Street congregation, compiled from *BSR* and other sources. Ownership of ships is estimated from the 1771 Boston tax list (see ch. 3, n6).

Chapter 5

1. See the index references to WC2 in Seybolt, *Officials*. John T. Hassam, "Registers of Probate for the County of Suffolk, Massachusetts, 1639–1799," *MHSP* 36(1902):92–104.

2. *SHG* 9:365–366. *BSR*, p. 246. *BG*, 14 Sept. 1761.

3. Hassam, "Registers," pp. 102–103. Frederick Tuckerman, "Thomas Cooper, of Boston, and His Descendants," *NEHGR* 44(1890):56.

4. SAP, 24 June 1769(?).

5. *BSR*, pp. 176–178. Diary of William Cooper, 1764–1766, MHS.

6. JA, *Works* 10:284.

7. JT is in neither *Dictionary of American Biography* nor *Dictionary of National Biography*.

8. Prime Temple, *Some Account of the Temple Family* (New York, 1887), pp. 26–61. HC to Dr. Burton, 1 July 1766, HC, Letterbook. JA, *Diary* 2:41. Samuel G. Drake, *The History and Antiquities of Boston* (Boston, 1856), pp. 567, 628n, 685. Lewis M. Wiggin, *The Faction of Cousins, A Political Account of the Grenvilles, 1733–1763* (New Haven, 1958), pp. 129–130, 130n. JT to Barlow Trecothick, 21 Apr. 1768, BAC Records.

9. *BG*, 2, 23 Nov. 1761. JT to Commissioners, 1 Jan. 1762, BAC Records. Gertrude S. Kimball, *Correspondence of William Pitt*, 2 vols. (1906; reprint ed., New York, 1969) 2:429. *BBC*, pp. 30–32, 35–37, 39, 45–49. George Louis Beer, *British Colonial Policy, 1739–1763* (reprint ed., Gloucester, Mass., 1958), pp. 118–121. Barrow, *Trade and Empire*, pp. 169–172. Carl Ubbelohde, *The Vice-Admiralty Courts and the American Revolution* (Chapel Hill, N.C., 1960), pp. 33–36. Thomas, "Partisan Politics," ch. 2.

10. JT's correspondence in BAC Records, box 2, pp. 4–7, 22–23, 28–31, 63–64, 69–71, 90–93. "A Fair Trader," *BG*, 7 Dec. 1761. Ubbelohde, *Vice-Admiralty Courts*, pp. 38–39. Barrow, *Trade and Empire*, pp. 176–177.

11. Waters, *Otis Family*, pp. 110–116. *SHG* 11:248–250.

12. *BBC*, p. 53. Waters, *Otis Family*, pp. 117–120. Brennan, *Office-Holding*, pp. 29–34. Bailyn, *Ordeal*, 47–50.

13. Waters, *Otis Family*, pp. 120–124. TH, *History*, pp. 62–69. JA, *Legal Papers* 2:106–147. Quincy, *Reports*, p. 416.

14. TH, *History*, p. 69. Waters, *Otis Family*, pp. 136–138.

15. This conclusion is based on my study of the advertisers in the two newspapers.

16. [Samuel Waterhouse], *Proposals for printing by Subscription the History of Adjutant Trowel and Bluster* [Boston, 1763]. (Evans suggests 1766 as a likely date because on 28 June there is a reference in *BEP* to Otis as "Bluster," but this was a common nickname for him even among friends earlier in the 1760s. From internal evidence I conclude that *Proposals* was printed no later than 1763.) JA, *Diary* 1:238.

17. Waters, *Otis Family*, pp. 136, 181.

18. Peter Oliver credits Otis with using the name "black Regiment" for the clergy he sought to enlist for his party (Oliver, *AR*, p. 29). Samuel Mather to his son, 15 Mar., SM Letters. *SHG* 10:140. Akers, *Mayhew*, 153–161. Mayhew to Thomas Hollis, 6 Apr. 1762, Hollis Papers, MHS.

19. *BEP*, 25 Apr. 1763. JA, *Diary* 1:283. JA, *Papers* 1:177.

20. Waters, *Otis Family*, pp. 139–149. Brennan, *Office-Holding*, pp. 41–67. *JMHR*, 1763, pp. 3–8. *BG*, 16 May 1763. Bernard to Richard Jackson, 8 June 1763, Sparks MSS. Thomas, "Partisan Politics," pp. 107–124.

21. Sermon: Ps. 24:10–11, 11 Aug. 1763, CP.

22. Normal E. Saul, "The Beginnings of American-Russian Trade," *WMQ* (Oct. 1769):596–600.

23. The original articles of organization (undated) and subscribers thereto are in Ezekiel Price MSS, MHS. See also Andrews, *Boston Merchants*, pp. 3–7.

24. Thomas C. Barrow, "Background to the Grenville Program, 1757–1763," *WMQ* 22(Jan. 1965):93–104. Barrow, *Trade and Empire*, chs. 6–8. Allen S. Johnson, "The Passage of the Sugar Act," *WMQ* 16(Oct. 1959):507–510.

25. *BG*, 2 Jan., 6 Feb. 1764. BAC Records, box 2, pp. 28–29. Barrow, *Trade and Empire*, pp. 176–181. Gipson, *British Empire*, 10:202–207.

26. Gilman M. Ostrander, "The Colonial Molasses Trade," *Agricultural History* 30(1956):177–184. BAC Records, box 2, p. 7.

27. " 'State of Trade,' 1763," *CSMP* 19 (Boston, 1918), pp. 379–390. Bernhard Knollenberg, *Origin of the American Revolution: 1759–1766* (New York, 1960), pp. 176–180. Barrow, *Trade and Empire*, pp. 181–185. Ubbelohde, *Vice-Admiralty Courts*, pp. 44–54.

28. Thomas, "Partisan Politics," has a good account of this affair, pp. 125–133.

29. *BTR*, 1758–1769, pp. 116, 119–122. *WSA* 1:1–7.

30. Oxenbridge Thacher, *The Sentiments of a British American* (Boston, 1764), reprint in Bernard Bailyn, ed., *Pamphlets of the American Revolution, 1750–1776* (Cambridge, Mass., 1965), pp. 483–498.

31. The four pamphlets were: *The Rights of the British Colonies Asserted and Proved* (Boston, 1764); *A Vindication of the British Colonies* (Boston, 1765); *Brief Remarks on the Defence of the Halifax Libel on the British American Colonies* (Boston, 1765); and *Considerations on Behalf of the Colonists in a Letter to a Noble Lord* (London, 1765).

32. Bailyn, *Pamphlets*, pp. 409–417, 546–552. Ellen Elizabeth Brennan, "James Otis: Recreant and Patriot," *NEQ* 12(Dec. 1969): 691–725. Waters, *Otis Family*, pp. 132–133, 151–156.

33. *BG*, 12 Aug. 1765. Bailyn, *Pamphlets*, pp. 460, 464–465, 571–572.

34. Barrow, *Trade and Empire*, pp. 186–197. *BG*, 6 Aug. 1764.

35. *DJR*, pp. 64–65. *BG*, 6 Aug. 1764.

36. BAC Records, box 2, pp. 63–64, 69–71, 90–93, 153–154. *BBC*, pp. 88–90, 92–93. Jordan D. Fiore, "The Temple-Bernard Affair, A Royal Custom House Scandal in Essex County," *Essex Institute Historical Collections*, 90(Jan. 1954):58–83. *BG*, 9 Oct. 1769.

37. SC Diary 2:146. *BG*, 6, 13 Aug. 1764.

38. Brown, *Hancock*, p. 28. Diary of William Cooper, 12 Aug. 1764, MHS. BT MSS 1:11.

39. Fowler, *Hancock*, pp. 1–49.

40. SC Diary 2:147. *BSR*, pp. 184, 185, 188. *BPB*, 10 Sept. 1764. Cary, *Warren*, pp. 12, 23–24.

Chapter 6

1. These figures are reasonably accurate estimates, based on existing records, except for the number of deaths, which is a projection made from the ratio of deaths to baptisms for all of Boston, 1745–1765. See the table in *BPB*, 11 Jan. 1773.

2. Franklin B. Dexter, ed., *Extracts from the Itineraries and Other Miscellanies of Ezra Stiles* (New Haven, Conn., 1916), pp. 438–439. Akers, *Mayhew*, pp. 77–78. *PBF* 12:199–200.

3. Ellen Susan Bulfinch, *Life and Letters of Charles Bulfinch* (Boston, 1896), p. 28. Pomeroys and Hodgkin to BF, 18 Mar. 1767; BF to Pomeroys, 1 Aug. 1767, APS. Smyth, *WBF* 5:36–37, 196–197. *PBF* 10:278; 11:254–255. *BG*, 16 Nov. 1767; 15, 29 (supplement) Feb., 18 Apr. 1768.

4. Alice Morse Earle, ed., *Diary of Anna Green Winslow, A Boston School Girl of 1771* (Boston, 1894), pp. 14–15.

5. *BPB*, 30 Jan. 1769.

6. Brown, *Hancock*, pp. 61–62.

7. *BPB*, 3 June 1765.

8. Murray G. Lawson, "The Route of Boston's Trade, 1752–1765," *CSMP* 38(1947–1951):81–120. *Historical Statistics of the United States* (Washington, D.C., 1960), p. 757. Baxter, *Hancock*, p. 158. Arthur Harrison Cole, *Wholesale Commodity Prices in the United States, 1700–1861* (Cambridge, Mass., 1938), pp. 3–8, 117–118. *BPB*, 1, 8 Oct. 1764. *BEP*, 21 Jan. 1765. Nash, *Urban Crucible*, 244–246, 253–254.

9. The best general account is Edmund S. and Helen M. Morgan, *The Stamp Act Crisis* (Chapel Hill, N.C., 1953). For the importance of the admiralty court issue, see David S. Lovejoy, "Rights Imply Equality: The Case Against Admiralty Jurisdiction in America, 1764–1776," *WMQ* 16(Oct. 1959):459–484.

10. "Boyle," 84:168. Word that the Stamp Act had been passed does not seem to have reached Boston until the middle of May (*BG*, 20 May 1765), although the newspapers reported debates on the bill and various rumors concerning it all during this month.

11. *BG*, 13 May 1765, Dorr. Waters, *Otis Family*, pp. 153–154. Thomas, "Partisan Politics," pp. 155–162.

12. *BEP*, 13 May 1765.

13. *DJR*, p. 82. *BG*, 24 Nov. 1774. *BNL*, 24 Nov. 1774. JA, *Diary*, 1:271. *CSMP* 19(Boston, 1918):379–380.

14. *A Sermon Preached before His Excellency Francis Bernard, Esq; . . . May 29th* (Boston, 1765), pp. 43, 44, 47–48, 52, 53.

15. *BEP*, 3 June 1765 (supplement).

16. *BPB*, 1, 8 Oct. 1764; 1 July 1765. *BEP*, 21 Jan. 1765.

17. *BG*, 19 Aug. 1765 (supplement). Malcolm Freiberg, "An Unknown Stamp Act Letter," *MHSP* 78(1966):138–142. Samuel Mather to his son, 17 Aug. 1765, SM Letters. DT, *Diary*, pp. 17–18. *DJR*, pp. 88–89. Jonathan Mayhew to Thomas Hollis, 19 Aug. 1765, *MHSP* 69(1947–1950):174–176.

18. *BG*, 16 Sept. 1765 (supplement). "Boyle," 84:169. *BEP*, 21 Aug. 1769.

19. Morgans, *Stamp Act Crisis*, pp. 119–123. Avery is quoted in *SHG* 14:384.

20. *BG*, 2 Sept. 1765. *BPB*, 2 Sept. 1765. Morgans, *Stamp Act Crisis*, pp. 126–129. DT, *Diary*, pp. 18–20.

21. Mayhew's memorandum on what he said in this sermon, Jonathan Mayhew MSS, Boston University. *NEGHR* 46(1892):16–20.

22. Clarke's name appears on the 1773 pew list of the Brattle Street Church (*BSR*, between pp. 40–41). On the wedding see SC Diary 3:149 and *BG*, 30 Nov. 1769. Jonathan Mayhew to TH, 27 Aug. 1765. Jonathan Mayhew MSS, Boston University.

23. Cf. Bernard Friedman, "The Shaping of the Radical Consciousness in Pro-

vincial New York," *Journal of American History* 56(Mar., 1970):781–801.

24. Alfred F. Young, "The Crowd and the Coming of the American Revolution: From Ritual to Rebellion in Boston" (Paper prepared for the Davis Center Seminar, 23 Jan. 1976).

25. TH, Corr. 26:158. *BBC*, pp. 227–229. Carter, *Gage*, 1:68.

26. Morgans, *Stamp Act Crisis*, pp. 129–143. Young, "Crowd," passim. *BG*, 16 Dec. 1765. Baxter, *Hancock*. pp. 236–239. Meredith, *Amory*, pp. 129–136.

27. Sermon: 2 Sam. 7:10 [1776], CP.

28. Waters, *Otis Family*, pp. 154–157. *SHG* 11:265–266.

29. JA, *Diary* 1:271. Diary of William Cooper, 1 Sept. 1765, MHS.

30. *BEP*, 4 Sept. 1782.

31. JT's position in Boston is revealed by his being included in 1765 among the legislators, clergy, and other leading citizens making the annual visitation of schools (*BTR*, 1758–1769, pp. 180–181).

32. Petition of Boston merchants to JT, Ezekiel Price MSS, MHS. Morgans, *Stamp Act Crisis*, pp. 135–139. Gipson, *British Empire*, 10:343–346.

33. *BTR*, 1758–1769, p. 177. *BNL*, 8 May 1766. Thomas, "Partisan Politics," ch. 8.

34. *BBC*, p. 110.

35. *BTR*, 1758–1769, pp. 180, 182–184.

36. *BG*, 31 Mar., 3 Apr. 1766. *BEP*, 28 Apr. 1766 (supplement).

37. *BG*, 19 May 1766. *DJR*, p. 95. *BPB*, 26 May 1766. Diary of William Cooper, 18 May 1766, MHS.

38. *BG*, 16 June, 8 Sept. 1766. *BEP*, 16 June 1766. Jensen, *Founding*, pp. 174–185. Brown, *Hancock*, pp. 123–124.

39. *JHRM*, 1766, pp. 3–146, passim. Bernard to TP, 26 Oct. 1765, Sparks MSS. *BC*, p. 110. Bernard to Board of Trade, 7 July 1766, Sparks MSS.

40. Akers, *Mayhew*, pp. 211–222. Alden Bradford first recorded the story of SC's deathbed interview with Mayhew in *Memoir of the Life and Writings of Rev. Jonathan Mayhew, D.D.* (Boston, 1838), p. 431. The story seems to have come from friends of the two ministers from whom in their old age Bradford drew information.

41. For a discussion of the importance of family connections in government, see Robert M. Zemsky, "Power, Influence, and Status: Leadership Patterns in the Massachusetts Assembly, 1740–1755," *WMQ* 26(Oct. 1969):502–520.

42. *BG*, 12 Jan. 1767. *BSR*, p. 252. *SHG* 12:152; 13:323; 14:151. SC Diary 2:147. Oscar Zeichner, *Connecticut's Years of Controversy* (Chapel Hill, N.C., 1949), p. 60. *BTP* 1:248, 427–428.

43. *BG*, 26 Jan. 1767. *BSR*, p. 252. *SHG*, 9:76–81. Prime Temple, *Some Account of the Temple Family* (New York, 1887), p. 58.

44. Francis G. Walett, "James Bowdoin and the Massachusetts Council," (Ph.D. diss., Boston University, 1948), pp. 100–101. *DJR*, p. 121. Lewis M. Wiggin, *The Faction of Cousins* (New Haven, Conn., 1958), p. 130n. JT's sister was married to Edmund Quincy, Jr., thus linking him to another family of merchants (*BEP*, 31 Mar. 1766).

Chapter 7

1. *PBF* 18:4.

2. Jensen, *Founding*, pp. 207–214. Carter, *Gage*, 1:135–137.

3. *DJR*, p. 146. *BTP* 1:84. P.D.G. Thomas, "Charles Townshend and the American Taxation in 1767," *English Historical Review* 83(1968):33–51. Robert J. Chaffin, "The Townshend Acts of 1767," *WMQ* 27(Jan. 1970):90–121. Gipson, *British Empire*, 11:ch. 3. Barrow, *Trade and Empire*, ch. 10.

4. Chaffin, pp. 95–96, 111n. Dora Mae Clark, "The American Board of Customs, 1767–1783," *AHR* 45(1940):777–778. *BG*, 26. Oct., 9 Nov. 1767. Barrow, *Trade and Empire*, pp. 221–222. *BTP* 1:78–84, 287. BAC Records, box 2, pp. 188–189.

5. *BG*, 21 Sept., 9, 23 Nov. 1767. *BEP*, 7 Sept., 26 Oct., 2 Nov. 1767. *BNL*, 26 Nov. 1767. "Boyle," p. 253. *Letters of a Loyalist Lady* (Cambridge, Mass., 1927). TH, Corr. 25:183–185, 205–208.

6. *BTR*, 1758–1769, pp. 220–225. *BPB*, 2 Nov. 1767. Andrew Eliot to Thomas Hollis, 10 Dec. 1767, Hollis MSS, MHS.

7. *BEP*, 31 Mar., 19 May, 16 June 1766; 15 June 1767.

8. 30 Nov. 1767. Waterhouse is identified as the author in *BG*, 11 Jan. 1768, Dorr.

9. "Jemmicumjunto," *BEP*, 11 Jan. 1768.

10. *BG*, 23 Nov. 1767. *BEP*, 23, 30 Nov. 1767. *BTR*, 1758–1769, p. 225. *BNL*, 26 Nov. 1767. Thomas Cushing to Dennis De Berdt, 15 Oct. 1767, AL MSS 1:39.

11. *WAL* 1:3–6. *BNL*, 26 Nov. 1767. *LCP*, p. 306. The "Farmer's Letters" began in *BEP* and *BG* 21 Dec. 1767 and ran through Feb. *BTR*, 1758–1769, pp. 243–244.

12. *BBC*, p. 146. *JHRM*, 1767–1768, pp. 148, 164, and Appendix.

13. *BBC*, pp. 147–148.

14. Warren's letter, signed "A True Patriot," is in *BG*, 29 Feb. 1768 (supplement). For a full account see Cary, *Warren*, pp. 66–68, and Thomas, "Partisan Politics," pp. 439–446. Particularly interesting is Andrew Eliot's comment on this affair in a letter to Thomas Hollis, 18 Apr. 1768, Hollis MSS, MHS.

15. *BBC*, pp. 147–150.

16. JT to Barlow Trecothick, 21 Apr. 1768, BAC Records, box 2, p. 189. JT to Thomas Whately, 21 Jan. 1771, Temple-Whately. *BTP* 1:287–288. *BG*, 25 Mar. 1782. *BEP*, 14 Sept. 1782. Copies of the memorials are in BAC Records, box 2, beginning with 12 Feb. 1768.

17. *DJR*, pp. 150, 153, 157. *Letters of a Loyalist Lady*, p. 10. Andrew Eliot to Thomas Hollis, 18 Apr. 1768, Hollis MSS, MHS. *BBC*, pp. 148–149. Commissioners to Treasury, 28 Mar. 1768, BAC Records, box 2. Bernard to Shelburne, 19 Mar. 1768, Sparks MSS. *BG*, 9, 23 May 1768. *BEP*, 23 May 1768. *BTR*, 1758–1769, pp. 250, 253. HC to Nathaniel Rogers, 5 May 1768, HC, Letterbook. TH, Corr., 10 Aug. 1768, 26:318–320.

18. *BTR*, 1758–1769, p. 245. TH to TP, 7 June 1768, TH, Corr. 25:262. TH, *History*, 3:140–141. Francis G. Walett, "The Massachusetts Council, 1766–1774: The Transformation of a Conservative Institution," *WMQ* 6(Oct. 1949):605–627. Brennan, *Office-Holding*, pp. 93–94.

19. Baxter, *Hancock*, 259–261. Commissioners to Treasury, 12 May 1768, BAC Records, box 2. TH to Richard Jackson, 17 Apr. 1768, TH, Corr. 26:299.

20. D. H. Watson, "Joseph Harrison and the *Liberty* Incident," *WMQ* 20(Oct. 1963):585–595. TH to Richard Jackson, 16–18 June 1768, TH, Corr. 26:310–312. *BEP*, 20 June 1768. *BPB*, 26 June 1768. "Letter from Joshua Henshaw, Jr.," *NEHGR* 22(1868):402–403. William James Smith, ed., *The Grenville Papers*, 4(London, 1853):306–307. George G. Wolkins, "The Seizure of John Han-

cock's Sloop *Liberty*," *MHSP* 55(1921–1922):239–284. JA, *Legal Papers* 2:173–193. Barrow, *Trade and Empire*, pp. 230–234. O. M. Dickerson, "John Hancock: Notorious Smuggler or Near Victim of British Revenue Racketeers?" *Mississippi Valley Historical Review* 32(Mar. 1946):517–540.

21. *BEP*, 6 June 1768. *BG*, 13 June 1768. *MHSP* 47(1913–1914):191–192. Watson, "Harrison," p. 589. An excellent example of the solidarity between merchants and radicals brought on by the *Liberty* incident is the composition of the committee of twenty-one that called on Bernard at Roxbury on June 14 (*DJR*, pp. 165–166.).

22. JA, *Legal Papers* 2:177–184. Carl Ubbelohde, *The Vice-Admiralty Courts and the American Revolution* (Chapel Hill, N.C., 1960), pp. 124–127. *BTR*, 1758–1769, pp. 257–258. Cary, *Warren*, pp. 77–78. *DJR*, pp. 165–166. *BEP*, 20 June 1768.

23. *BTP* 1:288. *Letters of a Loyalist Lady*, p. 15.

24. *BG*, 11, 25 Mar. 1782. I assume that JT wrote this defense of himself because he was in Boston at the time attempting to prove his loyalty, and because he wrote many such statements in the third person. It is possible that another wrote this letter from information supplied by JT. Since the memorial of 16 June and supporting documents were published by the Whigs the following year, JT's account appears reliable (*BEP*, 18 Sept. 1769).

25. Hulton, *Account*, pp. 122–123.

26. *JHRM*, 1768, pp. 68–98, appendix 1–14. *BG*, 27 June; 4, 11, 18 July; 8 Aug. 1768. Andrew Eliot to Thomas Hollis, 7 July 1768, Hollis MSS, MHS. TH to William Bollan, 14 July 1768, TH, Corr. 26:314–315. Thomas, "Partisan Politics," pp. 454–477.

27. *BNL*, 25 Aug. 1768, postscript. *BEP*, 22 Aug. 1768.

28. *BTR*, 1758–1769, pp. 259–264.

29. *BEP*, 19, 26 Sept. 1768. *BG*, 25 July; 1, 15 Aug.; 5 Sept. 1768.

30. Sermon: Deut. 5:29, 4 Apr. 1754, CP. Note how close SC's position here is to that privately expressed by the Amory brothers, merchants of his congregation (Meredith, *Amory*, pp. 151–152).

31. Sermon: Ps. 2:11, 17 Nov. 1757, CP. The quoted passage was added for delivery in 1768.

32. The first extant letter of their correspondence is TP to SC, 30 Jan.1769, which acknowledged SC's letters of the previous 5 Oct. and 26 Nov. (Griffin, pp. 204–209). John A. Schutz, *Thomas Pownall* (Glendale, Calif., 1951), pp. 195–214. *BEP*, 20 Apr. 1767, supplement.

33. Schultz, *Pownall*, pp. 195–214. TP's election to the House of Commons was announced in Boston on 20 Apr. 1767, *BEP* supplement.

34. *BEP*, 5 Dec. 1768. G. H. Guttridge, "Thomas Pownall's *The Administration of the Colonies*: the Six Editions," *WMQ* 26(Jan. 1969):31–46. John Shy, "Thomas Pownall, Henry Ellis, and the Spectrum of Possibilities, 1763–1775," in Allison Gilbert Olson and Richard Maxwell Brown, eds., *Anglo-American Political Relations, 1675–1775* (New Brunswick, N.J., 1970), pp. 155–186.

35. TP's influence in Boston is made evident by the town's newspapers from 1766 to 1775, as well as by the large volume of his correspondence with the Whig leaders. I have profited from reading in manuscript a close study of TP's parliamen-

tary career: Robert E. Sullivan, " 'A Prophetic Voice about America': Thomas Pownall in Parliament, 1767–1780."

36. LCP, pp. 303–304.

37. *BPB*, 19 Sept. 1768. *BG*, 26 Sept., 3 Oct. 1768. *BEP*, 3 Oct. 1768. Richard D. Brown, "The Massachusetts Convention of Towns, 1768," *WMQ* 26(Jan. 1969), 94–104.

38. *BBC*, pp. 254–258. The resolves and address are in Merrill Jensen, ed., *English Historical Documents* 9(New York, 1962):720–722. See also John C. Miller, "The Massachusetts Convention, 1768," *NEQ* 11(1934):468–471.

39. LCP, p. 304.

40. TP to WC2, 30 Jan. 1769, SAP. TP spoke on 26 Jan. and 8 Feb. The first is not recorded in detail in Cobbett, *PH*. Both speeches were printed in Boston in a composite work under the title *The Speech of Th-m-s P-wn-ll, Esq; Late G-v-rn-r of this Province, in the H--se of C-m--ns, in Favor of America* [Boston, 1769]. The speech of 8 Feb. is given fully in Cobbett, *PH*, 16: cols. 494–507. TP discusses these speeches in his letters to SC of 30 Jan. and 13 Feb. (Griffin, pp. 204–213). The ms. copy of the 30 Jan. letter (KM 202) contains a summary of the 26 Jan. speech. TP also sent SC a copy of his 8 Feb. speech, but the Boston edition was printed from copies arriving earlier (LCP, p. 306). It is likely that TP's speeches used material from SC's letters to him of 5 Oct. and 26 Nov. that are now missing (Griffin, p. 204). See also Gipson, *British Empire*, 11:234–238.

41. *Virginia Gazette* (Rind), 15 June 1768. *BC*, 20, 24 Apr. 1769. According to Evans, there may have been four separate American editions of this pamphlet.

42. LCP, p. 306.

43. Cobbett, *PH*, 16: cols. 610–622. Gipson, *British Empire*, 11:242–244. *MHSC* 49(1885): 334–341.

44. Griffin, pp. 223, 231.

45. *BTP* 1:142–143. LCP, p. 309. Andrew Eliot to Thomas Hollis, 29 Jan. 1769, Hollis MSS, MHS. Dickerson, *BMR*, p. 110.

46. *BG*, 26 Sept. 1768. *BEP*, 3 Oct. 1768. TH to Richard Jackson, n.d., TH, Corr. 26:337–338. Carter, *Gage*, 1:206. *DJR*, pp. 175–176.

47. *BPB*, 26 May 1766. On Byles see *SHG* 7:464–493, and Arthur W. H. Eaton, *The Famous Mather Byles* (Boston, 1914).

48. *DJR*, p. 177. Bernard Bailyn, *The Ideological Origins of the American Revolution* (Cambridge, Mass., 1967), pp. 61–63, 112–115. David L. Jacobson, ed., *The English Libertarian Heritage* (Indianapolis, Ind., 1965), pp. 226–227.

49. Dickerson, *BMR*, p. viii. Arthur Schlesinger lists the newspapers printing the "Journal" in *Prelude to Independence, The Newspaper War on Britain, 1764–1776* (New York, 1957), p. 313.

50. To Israel Mauduit, 5 Dec. 1768, TH, Corr. 26:332. Among other evidence for group authorship, part of the entry for 6 Feb. (Dickerson, *BMR*, pp. 61–62) is taken from an earlier piece in *BG* (30 Jan. 1769) attributed to SC by Dorr (2:382).

51. Marginal note in *BEP*, 12 Dec. 1768, Dorr. See also Dorr 2:421, 524, 745. "Vigilator" in *BG*, 5 Dec. 1768, refers to the "authors of the Journal," but another writer also sympathetic to the Whig cause mentioned a single author (*BG*, 6 Mar. 1769).

52. 24 July 1769, SAP.

53. *BEP*, 18 Jan. 1768.

54. *MHSP*, 40(1906–1907):536. Bernard to TH, 29 July 1769, TH, Corr. 25:321–322. Schlesinger, *Prelude*, p. 100.

55. Dickerson, *BRM*, pp. 64–65.

56. Ibid., pp. 16, 35, 39, 43, 47, 51, 71, 86, 94, 99, 108–109, 118–119.

57. Ibid., pp. 13, 19, 21, 22, 36, 38–39, 46–47, 54, 57, 63, 67, 68, 72, 76, 85, 124–125.

58. Ibid., pp. 78, 83–84, 123–124, 125.

59. Dorr 2:781

60. LCP, p. 311.

61. *PBF* 16:182–184.

Chapter 8

1. For discussions of this topic see Michael Kammen, *Empire and Interest: The American Colonies and the Politics of Mercantilism* (Philadelphia, 1970); and Marc Egnal and Joseph A. Ernst, "An Economic Interpretation of the American Revolution," *WMQ* 29(Jan. 1972):3–32.

2. LCP, pp. 312–313.

3. *BTP* 1:142.

4. LCP, pp. 308–316.

5. TH, Corr. 26:333. TH, *History*, 3:163–165. Francis G. Walett, "Governor Bernard's Undoing: An Earlier Hutchinson Letters Affair," *NEQ* 38(June 1965):217–226; and "James Bowdoin, Patriot Propagandist," *NEQ* 23(Sept. 1950):322–327. Six letters of Bernard to Hillsborough and one from Gage to Hillsborough were first published in a four-page supplement to *BEP*, 10 Aug. 1769.

6. *BEP*, 26 June 1769. *BG*, 26 June 1769.

7. *BG*, 21 Aug. 1769. LCP, p. 307. Dickerson, *BMR*, pp. 108–109. Mayo, *Additions*, p. 16

8. *BEP*, 21 Aug. 1769. *DJR*, p. 191. JA, *Diary* 1:341. *MHSP* 11(1869–1870):140–142.

9. SC Diary 2:148. George H. Nash, III, "From Radicalism to Revolution: The Political Career of Josiah Quincy, Jr.," *AASP* 79(Apr. 1969):253–290.

10. TH, Corr. 26:328–329, 387. LCP, p. 311. Bailyn, *Ordeal*, pp. 165–170.

11. *PBF* 16:117–120.

12. *BEP*, 13 June 1769; also *BG*, 12 June and *BNL*, 15 June. The same piece was republished in Verner W. Crane, ed., *Benjamin Franklin's Letters to the Press, 1758–1775* (Chapel Hill, N.C., 1950), pp. 161–162.

13. Griffin, pp. 246–254.

14. LCP, pp. 303, 313.

15. Andrews, *Boston Merchants*, pp. 46–63. Jensen, *Founding*, pp. 283–287. Schlesinger, *Merchants*, pp. 105–131.

16. *PBF* 16:182–184. LCP, pp. 302–308.

17. The linking of the two newspapers in the Whig cause was acknowledged by the "Journal of the Times" in 1769 with the notice that henceforth both would be denied the advertisements that maritime law required admiralty courts to publish (Dickerson, *BMR*, p. 90).

18. O. M. Dickerson, "British Control of American Newspapers on the Eve of the Revolution," *NEQ* 24(1951):455–459.

19. E.g., *BNL*, 28 July, 4 Aug. 1768; 7 Sept. 1769.

20. TH, Corr. 26:417–419, *BG*, 24 Oct. 1768; 15 May 1769. "The Proceedings of a Town Meeting held . . . the 4th October, 1769," Sparks MSS, 3:37. *MHSP* 47(1913–1914):25–26.

21. Among others in Nov. 1768 the commissioners dismissed John Fisher, brother-in-law of Governor Wentworth of New Hampshire and collector at Salem and Marblehead. The *BG* lamented that an officer who was "rather strict" but "punctual and impartial" should meet this fate (7 Nov. 1768). Also the Whigs believed that Samuel Venner, secretary to the commissioners, had been removed because of his friendship with JT (*BG*, 6 Nov. 1769; 14 May 1770). For examples of renewed efforts at enforcement see *BNL*, 4 May 1769; *BG*, 17 Oct. 1768; and *DJR*, p. 193.

22. In addition to the *BC* itself, see the following: John E. Alden, "John Mein: Scourge of Patriots," *CSMP* 34(1943):571–599; Dickerson, "British Control of American Newspapers," pp. 460–467; Andrews, *Boston Merchants*, 69–71; JA, *Legal Papers* 1:151–154; Schlesinger, *Merchants*, pp. 159–162.

23. *WSA* 1:378–380. Meredith, *Amory*, p. 160.

24. Boston newspapers for 4–21 Sept. 1769. TH, Corr. 26:372–373, 376. JA, *Diary* 1:343. *MHSP* 47(1913–1914):209–210. Waters, *Otis Family*, pp 176–177.

25. *BC*, 26 Oct. 1769. [John Mein], "Key to the Characters published in the Boston Chronicle of October 26, 1769," Sparks MSS 10. Alden, "John Mein," pp. 568–569. TH, Corr. 26:400, 403. TH, *History* 3:187.

26. LCP, pp. 313–314. Broadside, "The Merchants and Traders in this Town," Boston, 6 Dec. 1769. *BTP* 1:158. Schlesinger, *Merchants*. pp. 131–134. *Observations* was published in Boston, 1769.

27. Broadside, 6 Dec. 1769. Andrew Eliot to Thomas Hollis, 25 Dec. 1769, Hollis MSS, MHS. Broadside, "The merchants, and all others, . . . " Boston, 16 Jan. 1770. *SHG* 14:289–291.

28. LCP, pp. 314–316. For another account, see George Mason to_____, 24 Jan. 1770, Sparks MSS, 10:3.

29. LCP, pp. 315–316. TH, *History* 3:192. Mayo, *Additions*, p. 17. TH, Corr. 26:436. Broadside, "At a Meeting of Merchants and Traders, at Faneuil-Hall, on the 23d January 1770." Martha Curtis to WC2, 30 Jan. 1770, SAP. Boston newspapers for Jan. and Feb. 1770.

30. *BEP*, 26 Feb. 1770. *DJR*, p. 197. JA, *Diary* 1:349–350. JA, *Legal Papers* 2:396–411. Hiller B. Zobel, *The Boston Massacre* (New York, 1970), pp. 173–179.

31. LCP, p. 316. *BNL*, 8 Mar. 1770. *BG*, 12 Mar. 1770. TH, *History*, 3:194–196. Zobel, *Massacre*, pp. 180–205.

32. *BTR*, 1770–1777, pp. 1–3. TH, *History*, 3:197–198. Zobel, *Massacre*, pp. 206–209.

33. LCP, p. 317. *BTR*, 1770–1777, pp. 3–4.

34. LCP, p. 317.

35. HC, Letterbook, 22 May 1770.

36. JA, *Legal Papers* 3:6–7. Zobel, *Massacre*, pp. 219–221.

37. LCP, p. 318. *BTR*, 1770–1777, pp. 10, 13, 15, 17–19, 20. *JHRM*, 1770, p. 170. The *Narrative* (Boston, 1770) is discussed in Francis G. Walett, "James Bowdoin, Patriot Propagandist," *NEQ* 23(Sept. 1950):213–214. The committee's letter to John Wilkes illustrates its work (*MHSP* 47:213–214). On Robinson's motives in going to England, see his letter to TH, 1 Nov. 1769, TH, Corr. 25:335–336.

38. (Boston, 1770), pp. 5–6, 8, 9–12.

39. Oliver, *AR*, pp. 91–92. *MHSP* 61(1927–1928):282–283. Cf. Zobel, *Massacre*, pp. 221–222.

40. TH, Corr. 26:471–473; 27:112–113. Oliver, *AR*, pp. 87–88. The meeting at JT's house is also mentioned in Hulton, Account, p. 163.

41. LCP, p. 320.

42. Mayo, *Additions*, p. 31. Zobel, *Massacre*, chs. 8–9.

43. *PBF* 18:3–4.

44. Donald C. Lord and Robert M. Calhoon, "The Removal of the Massachusetts General Court from Boston, 1769–1772," *Journal of American History* 55(Mar. 1969):735–738. Bradford, *S&A*, pp. 194–195. TH, *History*, 3:201–202. TH, Corr. 25:391–394; 26:460–461, 471–472.

45. Overseers Records, 3:30, 32. Harvard University Archives. Mayo, *Additions*, pp. 21–22. TH, Corr. 25:401; 26:427, 476–477.

46. Corporation Records, 2:329–332, Harvard University Archives. BG, 26 Jan. 1767. TH, Corr. 26:478–479.

47. *BG*, 2 Apr. 1770. Mayo, *Additions*, p. 23. Griffin, p. 275.

48. *BTR*, 1770–1777, pp. 21, 22, 26–32, 33. TH, Corr. 26:491–492. Waters, *Otis Family*, pp. 177–178. *DJR*, p. 201. Mayo, *Additions*, pp. 23–25.

49. *BG*, 4 June 1770. Charles Chauncy, *Trust in God . . .* (Boston, 1770), pp. 22–38.

50. A. W. Plumstead, ed., *The Wall and the Garden: Selected Massachusetts Election Sermons 1670–1775* (Minneapolis, 1968), pp. 326–346.

51. TH, Corr. 26:531–532; 27:6–8.

52. Griffin, pp. 255, 263. Jensen, *Founding*, pp. 325–326. Labaree, *Tea Party*, pp. 42–43. Cobbett, *PH*, 26: cols. 856–874, 928–929. LCP, p. 319. For the Boston reprint of this speech see Early American Imprints, no. 42, 157.

53. TH, Corr. 25:391–394, 401; 26:481, 485. Brown, *Hancock*, p. 169. *BG*, 17 Sept. 1770. Andrews, *Boston Merchants*, pp. 83–94. LCP, pp. 319–320. *DJR*, pp. 204–205.

54. *Spy*, 14, 18 Aug. 1770. *BG*, 20 Aug., 3 Sept., 15 Oct. 1770. *BNL*, 6 Sept. 1770. TH, Corr. 26:540–542. Jensen, *Founding*, pp. 364–372. Andrews, *Boston Merchants*, pp. 86–101. WSA 2:58. LCP, pp. 321–322.

55. *BG*, 17 Sept. 1770. BTP 1:215. TH, Corr. 27:9–10, 112–113. TH, *History*, 3:221–223. LCP, p. 322.

56. Griffin, pp. 258–259, 265–273, 277–286. Cobbett, *PH*, 16: cols. 979–995. *BG*, 24 Sept., 1 Oct. 1770. BTP 1:199–202, 212–218. TH, Corr. 27:37–38. Carter, *Gage*, 1:273–274.

57. TH, *History*, 3:223–225. TH, Corr. 27:9–10. *JHRM*, 1770, p. 92. Bradford, *S&A*, pp. 255–262, 273–278, 286–290. *BEP*, 15, 29 Oct. 1770. *Proceedings of His Majesty's Council . . . Relative to the Deposition of Andrew Oliver* (Boston, 1770).

58. Griffin, pp. 219–224, 225, 229, 243–245. LCP, p. 321. Andrew Eliot to Thomas Hollis, 28 June 1770, Hollis MSS, MHS.

59. Crane, *Franklin's Letters*, pp. xlii–xlvi. *PBF* 17:160–165.

60. *PBF* 16:233–235, 243–249.

61. *PBF* 17:274–275, 285–287.

62. *JHRM*, 1770, pp. 113, 123, 124. TH, Corr. 27:51. TH, *History*, 3:227–229. LCP, p. 324.

63. Bradford, *S&A*, pp. 246–247, 278–279, 290–292. TH, *History*, 3:224–227.

64. TH, Corr. 27:60–62. *PBF* 18:3–4.

Chapter 9

1. *PBF* 18:3.

2. "Boyle," 84:267. Hulton, Account, pp. 171, 179–184. *BTP* 1:113–116, 151–153, 236, 247. TH, Corr. 26:405, 408, 409–410, 422, 429; 27:55. *BNL*, 22 Nov. 1770. *BG*, 27 Nov. 1769. Dora Mae Clark, "The American Board of Customs, 1767–1783," *AHR* 45(1940):790–791. LCP, p. 323. *CSMP* 34(1943): 422.

3. *DJR*, pp. 205–206, 207. Carter, *Gage*, 1:274. Whitefield's visit and posthumous influence can be followed at great length in the Boston newspapers from Aug. 1770 through the following three years. No evidence has turned up to verify Luke Tyerman's statement that SC preached a funeral sermon for Whitefield to a capacity crowd in the Brattle Street Church (*Life of the Rev. George Whitefield*, 2 vols. [New York, 1877], 2:620n).

4. *BTP* 1:160–161; 170–172, 208–212, 218, 294–295. *BG*, 15 Oct. 1770. Griffin, pp. 286–287. LCP, pp. 320–324. *PBF* 18:211–213; 19:15. *BPB*, 26 Aug. 1771. TH, Corr. 27:214.

5. Richard B. Sheridan, "The British Credit Crisis of 1772 and the American Colonies," *Journal of Economic History* 20(June 1960):161–186. James F. Shepherd and Gary M. Walton, "Estimates of 'Invisible' Earnings in the Balance of Payments of the British North American Colonies, 1768–1772," *Journal of Economic History* 19(June 1969):231–232. JA, *Diary* 2:20. Baxter, *Hancock*, pp. 279–280.

6. An estimate based on the Massachusetts tax valuation list of 1771, Massachusetts Archives, 132:92–147.

7. Ibid.

8. Shepherd and Walton, "Estimates of 'Invisible' Earnings," pp. 235–251.

9. JA, *Works* 10:260.

10. All of these men stand high in one or more categories on the 1771 tax valuation list.

11. Samuel Eliot Morison, "The Commerce of Boston on the Eve of the Revolution," *AASP* 32(Apr. 1922):50.

12. *PBF* 17:285–287; 18:3–4.

13. The 1771 tax valuation list shows a total of £14,839 in "Factorage, or the Value of Commissions or Merchandize," and the incomplete listing of individuals contains thirty-one names in this category. The only prominent Whig listed here was William Molineaux, evidence that opens the possibility that his Whig political activities constituted a means of striking at others engaged in the same business activity, such opponents of nonimportation as Thomas Hutchinson, Jr., and Colburn Barrell.

14. The ballad is printed in James Spear Loring, *The Hundred Boston Orators* (Boston, 1854), p. 10.

15. LCP, p. 319.

16. Among the many Tory descriptions of SA, see Oliver, *AR*, pp. 39–41.

17. *BTR*, 1758–1769, pp. 202–203, 241, 242, 271–272. *BTR*, 1770–1777, pp. 69, 162. *BSM*, 1764–1768, pp. 261, 287. *BSM*, 1769–1775, pp. 10, 56. *BG*, 19 Mar. 1770. *BNL*, 8 Mar. 1770. *DJR*, p. 183. *WSA* 1:200.

18. *BEP*, 23 Nov. 1767. The culmination of the disparagement of JH came in [Stephen Higginson], *The Writings of Laco* (Boston, 1789), reprinted as *Ten Chapters in the Life of John Hancock* (New York, 1857).

19. The Brattle Street Samuel Adams became a communicant in 1742, was mar-

ried in 1763 to Mary Willings, and in 1789 was transferred to the Old South Church
after having attended the New South Church "for many years past" (*BSR*, pp. 42,
101, 252). The famous Samuel Adams lived on Purchase Street near the New South
Church, a considerable distance from Brattle Street. TH confirms that SA was attending the New South in 1772 (Mayo, *Additions*, p. 44).

20. LCP, p. 324. *PBF* 20:481.

21. *DJR*, pp. 211–212, 215, 216. *BG*, 14 Jan., 10 June 1771. *Spy*, 28 Jan.
1771. *BPB*, 22 Apr. 1771. JA, *Diary* 2:10–11.

22. *BG*, 25 Feb. 1771.

23. Baxter, *Hancock*, pp. 281–282. Seybolt, *Officials*, pp. 311–312, and
passim. All but three of the nineteen selectmen are on the 1771 tax valuation list,
and these three can be placed from other sources among the elite.

24. *BG*, 21 Aug. 1769.

25. *BEP*, 28 Aug. 1769. *BG*, 26 Mar., 23 Apr., 28 May, 4 June 1770.

26. TH, Corr. 26:460–461; 27:72–74, 46–47, 60–62, 74–76, 77, 98–101,
107–108, 112–113, 128–129, 143–144, 149–150, 193, 199. *JHRM*, 1770,
pp. 185–253.

27. *PBF* 18:172–175.

28. LCP, p. 325.

29. The 1771 tax valuation list gives a total of 407 slaves between fourteen and
forty-five years of age. Adding 20 percent for taxpayers missing and guessing at 100
slave children and slaves over forty-five, produces an estimate of 600. The Negro
population of Boston fluctuated from year to year, but it seems safe to assume that
there were nearly 1,000 on the eve of the Revolution. Thus one can speak roughly of
the town's population as from 6 percent to 8 percent Negro, with the number of free
and slave nearly equal. The 1765 Boston census listed 811 "Negroes and
Molattoes," a figure that may not have included numerous transients and other
unsettled black workers (*BSM*, 1764–1768, p. 170). See also the appendices to
Lorenzo Johnston Greene, *The Negro in Colonial New England* (1942; reprint ed.,
New York, 1968).

30. Boston tax valuation list, 1771.

31. Suffolk County, Mass., Probate Records, 38:128–132. JA, *Diary* 2:13–14.

32. *BSR*, p. 187.

33. *BSR*, pp. 184, 185, 187, 189. Herbert S. Allan, *John Hancock* (New York,
1953), p. 80.

34. E.g., *BG*, 2 Apr. 1770.

35. Samuel Sewall wrote and published *The Selling of Joseph* (Boston, 1700).

36. Dickerson, *BMR*, pp. 3, 6, 16, 17, 18, 21. *BSM*, 1769–1775, p. 45.

37. For a general discussion of the role of sailors, see Jesse Lemisch, "Jack Tar
in the Streets: Merchant Seamen in the Politics of Revolutionary America," *WMQ*
25(July 1968):371–407.

38. The best description of Boston's social strains is Nash, *Urban Crucible*.

39. TH, Corr. 27:171–173. For a discussion of what little is known concerning
the Boston caucus, see G. B. Warden, "The Caucus and Democracy in Colonial
Boston," *NEQ* 43(Mar. 1970):19–45; and Alan and Katherine Day, "Another Look
at the Boston 'Caucus,' " *Journal of American Studies* 5(Apr. 1971):19–42.
Although he does not deal with the larger and more complex Boston town meeting,
Michael Zuckerman describes a process of consensus formation through town
government that with certain differences applies to Boston as well as the smaller
- towns he studied: *Peaceable Kingdoms: New England Towns in the Eighteenth Cen-*

tury (New York, 1970); and "The Social Context of Democracy in Massachusetts," *WMQ* 25(Oct. 1968):523–544.

40. *BTR*, 1758–1769; 1770–1777.

41. E.g., "Manlius" in *BEP*, 23 Dec. 1771.

42. Sermon: 2 Sam. 7:10, CP. Though undated, this sermon was preached in 1776. But I think I am justified in quoting it here because it was a summary sermon detailing SC's views on the entire Revolutionary movement.

Chapter 10

1. *BG*, 17, 24 Feb. 1772. *BNL*, 20 Feb. 1772. Andrews, "Letters," p. 322. Samuel Kirkland Lothrop, *A History of the Church in Brattle Street, Boston* (Boston, 1851), pp. 94–96. Lothrop's account is based in part on documents since lost. Some additional details are given in John Gorham Palfrey, *A Sermon Preached to the Church in Brattle Square, July 18, 1824* (Boston, 1825), pp. 64–65.

2. *BG*, 9 Mar. 1772. Lothrop, *History*, pp. 96–99.

3. *BG*, 18 May 1772. Sermon: Ps. 102:14, 10 May 1772, NYPL. There appears to be no direct evidence that additional land was acquired. Illustrations made much later reveal the church building so crowded by other structures as to leave doubt that the site was enlarged. For the arrangements to worship with First Church, see *CSMP* 39(1961):254, 255–256.

4. *BG*, 2 Mar. 1772. *MHSC* 71:185–187. Jules David Prown, *John Singleton Copley in America, 1738–1774* (Cambridge, Mass., 1966), pp. 82, 102–116, 123–124. Lothrop, *History*, pp. 99–100. JA, *Diary* 1:238.

5. Lothrop, *History*, p. 101. Correspondence concerning the new church from the Hancock MSS is reprinted in Brown, *Hancock*, pp. 172–173, 177–178. *BNL*, 20 Oct. 1774. JH's letter ordering the bell is not in his letterbook.

6. *PBF* 20:114–115, 269–270, 480.

7. *Spy*, 22, 29 July 1773. Franklin Bowditch Dexter, ed., *Extracts from the Itineraries and Other Miscellanies of Ezra Stiles* (New Haven, Conn., 1916), p. 97. *PBF* 20:114–115. Brown, *Hancock*. pp. 172–173. Exterior and interior views of the church are reproduced in *BSR*. The Bostonian Society has the model of the church formerly at MHS. For another description see *MHSP* 47(1913–1914):229. A number of additions and changes over the next century make it difficult to describe accurately the building as it existed in SC's day.

8. Lothrop, *History*, p. 100.

9. The original pew list is reproduced in *BSR* between pp. 40–41. *Spy*, 22 July 1773. Lothrop, *History*, p. 101.

10. *Spy*, 29 July 1773. *BSR*, p. 38. Sermon: Gen. 28:17, CP.

11. Bell's pew is indicated on the pew list, *BSR*, 40–41.

12. E.g., *BPB*, 16, 30 Mar. 1772.

13. The Tory view is well set forth in Oliver, *AR*, p. 41; but similar statements can be found in most Tory comments on the Whigs.

14. For biographical details see Henry H. Edes, "Memoir of Dr. Thomas Young, 1731–1777," *CSMP* 11(1906–1907):2–54; David Freeman Hawke, "Dr. Thomas Young—'Eternal Fisher in Troubled Waters,' " *New-York Historical Society Quarterly* 55(Jan. 1970):7–29; and Pauline Maier, "Reason and Revolution: The Radicalism of Dr. Thomas Young," *American Quarterly* 28(Summer 1976): 229–249.

15. *Spy*, 18, 28, 30 Aug.; 4 Sept. 1770. *BEP*, 27 Aug. 1770. *BSM*, 1769–1775, p. 97.

16. *WSA* 2:374–379.

17. *BG*, 11, 18 Mar. 1771. *BNL*, 3 Aug. 1769. Leon Burr Richardson, *History of Dartmouth College* (Hanover, N.H., 1932), 1:51–67. Alan Heimert, *Religion and the American Mind* (Cambridge, Mass., 1966), pp. 500–501.

18. "Gordon," pp. 309–312. *SHG* 13:60–85.

19. "Gordon," p. 311. William G. McLoughlin, *New England Dissent, 1630–1833*, 2 vols. (Cambridge, Mass., 1971), 1: passim. For a shorter summary of the general problem, see McLoughlin's "Massive Civil Disobedience as a Baptist Tactic in 1773," *American Quarterly* 21(Winter 1969):710–727.

20. William G. McLoughlin, *Isaac Backus and the American Pietistic Tradition* (Boston, 1967). *BEP*, 6 Aug., 29 Oct. 1770. McLoughlin, "Massive Civil Disobedience." TH, Corr. 27:103–105. McLoughlin, *New England Dissent*, I, 531–546.

21. For general accounts, see Carl Bridenbaugh, *Mitre and Sceptre* (New York, 1962); and Arthur Lyon Cross, *The Anglican Episcopate and the American Colonies* (New York, 1902).

22. For a good example of the role of Anglican missionaries in the development of American nationalism, see the controversy in the Boston newspapers in Feb. and Mar. 1763, following the death of an S.P.G.–supported missionary at Braintree. The most frequently cited excuse for colonial attacks on the S.P.G. was to respond to slighting remarks concerning the colonies made in the annual sermon given before that society by one of the Anglican bishops.

23. Akers, *Mayhew*, pp. 166–197. Chauncy's publications were *A Letter to a Friend* (Boston, 1767), *The Appeal* (Boston, 1768), *A Reply to Dr. Chandler's 'Appeal Defended'* (Boston, 1770), and *A Compleat View of Episcopacy* (Boston, 1771).

24. Griffin, pp. 234–235. Bridenbaugh, *Mitre and Sceptre*, pp. 260–313. Edmund S. Morgan, *The Gentle Puritan, A Life of Ezra Stiles* (New Haven, Conn., 1962), pp. 210–225, 237–254, provides a revealing study of "Anglicophobia."

25. William Stevens Perry, ed., *Historical Collections Relating to the American Colonial Church* 3(Hartford, 1873):544–545. The estimate of the proportion of Anglicans in Boston is a rough calculation based on the figures given by Ezra Stiles (Dexter, *Extracts*, pp. 100–101). Evidence of intermarriage is widespread, but *SHG* and the marriage notices in the Boston newspapers are the best sources.

26. SC to William Livingston, 18 Apr. 1768, Livingston Letterbook A, MHS. Dr. Thomas Bulfinch, brother of Mrs. SC, married Susan Apthorp in King's Chapel on 13 Sept. 1759 (*BNL*, 17 Sept. 1759). See also Ellen Susan Bulfinch, *The Life and Letters of Charles Bulfinch* (Boston, 1896), pp. 32ff.

27. *MHSC* 54(1891):23–25. SC to William Livingston, 18 Apr. 1768, Livingston Letterbook A, MHS. *BSR*, p. 38. Franklin Bowditch Dexter, ed., *The Literary Diary of Ezra Stiles*, 1(New York, 1901):134. The letter by "B.W." appeared in the *New York Gazette*, 29 Aug. 1768, and was reprinted in *BG*, 23 Jan. 1769. For the controversy over it, see *BG*, 23, 30 Jan.; 6 Feb.; 13 Mar. 1769. Attribution to JT was by Chauncy (Dexter, *Extracts*, pp. 447–448).

28. TH, Corr. 27:265, 377–380.

29. *BG*, 1 Jan., 16 Apr. 1770; 11, 25 Mar., 20 May 1771. *Spy*, 28 Jan., 25 Apr. 1771. TH, Corr. 27:109. SM Letters, 1771, passim.

30. *BNL*, 21 Mar. 1771.

31. TH, *History*, 3:240. *BNL*, 21, 28 Mar., 29 Apr. 1771. *BEP*, 1 July 1771. *BG*, 29 Apr. 1771.

32. James Spear Loring, *The Hundred Boston Orators* (Boston, 1854), p. 10. *BNL*, 3 June 1771. Dexter, *Diary of Ezra Stiles*, 1:110–111.

33. *WSA* 2:172–177, 186–188, 193–204. *BNL*, 27 June, 18 July 1771.

34. *BG*, 8 July 1771.

35. *JHRM*, 1770, pp. 98, 101. *BEP*, 5 Nov. 1770.

36. *LCP*, pp. 325–326.

37. *BG*, 4 Nov. 1774. *Spy*, 7 Nov. 1771. *LCP*, pp. 325–326. Mayo, *Additions*, p. 44. TH, *History*, 3:249–250.

38. *LCP*, pp. 325–326. Mayo, *Additions*, p. 44. Smyth, *WBF* 5:357–358.

39. *WSA* 2:273, 276. *BG*, 11, 18 Nov. 1771. *Spy*, 14 Nov. 1771. *A Ministerial Catechise, Suitable to be Learned by all Modern Provincial Governors, Pensioners, Placemen, &c. Dedicated to T--H-- Esq.* (Boston, 1771).

40. *Boston Censor*, 4 Jan., 8 Feb., 7 Mar. 1772. *BNL*, 16 Apr. 1772. *BG*, 18, 25 May, 26 Oct. 1772. *BEP*, 7 Sept., 5 Oct. 1772.

Chapter 11

1. *DJR*, pp. 232–233. William Willis, ed., *Journals of the Rev. Thomas Smith, and the Rev. Samuel Deane* (Portland, 1849), pp. 221, 332. *BEP*, 31 Aug. 1772. *AFC* 1:252. *SHG* 14:568–572.

2. Others making this cruise were Tuthill Hubbard and Samuel Calef, small merchants and fishing companions of John Rowe; Nicholas Bowes, JH's cousin who kept a shop; and Captain Hood, who appears in the JH records by no other name. For the advice to William Palfrey, see JH to Palfrey, 1 Jan. 1771, WP MSS.

3. TH, Corr. 27:258, 260–261, 284–285, 286–287. TH, *History*, 3:248–249. Mayo, *Additions*, p. 43. *WSA* 2:296–297; 3:23–24.

4. *WSA* 2:309.

5. *BEP*, 9 Mar. 1772, and other Boston newspapers for this week. Charles R. Ritcheson, *British Politics and the American Revolution* (Norman, Okla., 1954), pp. 136–141. *BTP* 1:111–113, 247–249, 265–266, 278–284, 287–290. JT to Whately, 21 Jan. 1771, Temple-Whately. William Palfrey to JH, 26 Feb. 1771, WP MSS. *BG*, 11 May 1772. TH, Corr. 27:340–341, 384–385. JA, *Diary* 2:70–71.

6. *BTR*, 1770–1777, pp. 52, 62–77, 110. *BSM*, 1769–1775, p. 110. *DJR*, p. 225. *BEP*, 23 Mar. 1772. *BG*, 9, 23 Mar. 1772. *BNL*, 19 Mar. 1772.

7. *Boston Censor*, 25 Apr., 2 May 1772. *BNL*, 9 Apr. 1772. *BEP*, 23 Mar., 13, 27 Apr. 1772. *WSA* 2:329–331. *BTR*, 1770–1777, p. 78. Mayo, *Additions*, p. 47.

8. The taxable assets of the six new selectmen may be found in the 1771 tax valuation list. "Proceedings of the North End Caucus," 23 Mar. 1772 to 9 May 1774 are in the appendix to Elbridge Henry Goss, *The Life of Colonel Paul Revere*, 2 vols. (Boston 1891), 2:635–644.

9. For summaries of JH's role, see Fowler, *Hancock*, pp. 140–142; and Donald C. Lord and Robert M. Calhoon, "The Removal of the Massachusetts General Court from Boston, 1769–1772," *Journal of American History* 55(Mar. 1969):735–755.

10. *PBF* 18:173.

11. Bernard Bailyn, ed., *Pamphlets of the American Revolution, 1750–1776*, (Cambridge, Mass., 1965), pp. 34–35. *BG*, 27 July 1772. *MHSP* 37(1903):34–35.

12. Griffin, pp. 294–299. Since the original of TP's letter to SA (10 Apr. 1772) is with SC's correspondence in the British Museum rather than with any of the collections of SA letters, I assume that it was retained by SC and not delivered to SA.

SC's reply, if any, to TP's letter with the enclosure for SA (5 Apr. 1772) has not been found. TP invited SA to review his conduct and to judge him by the "fruits" he had borne, rather than remembering past animosities.

13. JA, *Diary* 2:74.

14. *BG*, 26 Oct., 9 Nov. 1772. *BTR*, 1770-1777, pp. 83-93. TH, *History*, 3:259-262. Brown, *Revolutionary Politics*, pp. 44-57. *PBF* 20:110-115. *BNL*, 9 Nov. 1772. *WAL* 1:15.

15. *BTR*, 1770-1777, pp. 93-108. Brown, *Revolutionary Politics*, pp. 58-80.

16. *BNL*, 4, 10 Dec. 1772. *BG*, 7, 14 Dec. 1772. *WAL* 1:15. *WSA* 2:379-380, 382-389. Brown, *Revolutionary Politics*, pp. 66-68.

17. Brown, *Revolutionary Politics*, pp. 92-121.

18. *JHRM*, 1772, pp. 138-143. TH, Corr. 27:448-449, 461-462.

19. *JHRM*, 1772, pp. 178-190. Bradford, *S&A*, pp. 342-351. *The Speeches of . . . Governor Hutchinson, . . . With the Answers of his Majesty's Council and the House of Representatives* (Boston, 1773).

20. *PBF* 20:110-113.

21. Ibid. Brown, *Revolutionary Politics*, pp. 89-92.

22. *PBF* 20:114.

23. LCP, p. 328.

24. B. D. Bargar, *Lord Dartmouth and the American Revolution* (Columbia, S.C., 1965). *BNL*, 5 Nov. 1772. *PBF* 20:110-111. Franklin Bowditch Dexter, ed., *The Literary Diary of Ezra Stiles*, 1(New York, 1901):345-351, 382-385. *WSA* 3:59. Gordon, pp. 586-600. *BG*, 27 Sept. 1773.

25. "I. H.," 26 Nov. 1772. "Orestes," 7 Jan. 1773. "Phylander," 14 Jan. 1773.

26. JA, *Diary* 2:79-80, 81. The text was Rev. 12:9.

27. *PBF* 19:411-413.

28. *Copy of Letters Sent to Great-Britain, by his Excellency Thomas Hutchinson, the Hon. Andrew Oliver, and several other Persons, born and educated among us* (Boston, 1773), pp. 3-18.

29. Ibid., pp. 18-37.

30. JA, *Diary* 2:81.

31. *BTR*, 1770-1777, pp. 131-134.

32. *A Sermon Preached before his Excellency Thomas Hutchinson, Esq; . . . May 26th. 1773* (Boston, 1773), pp. 18-25, 29-31, 32-33, 37-41.

33. *BG*, 31 May 1773. Hulton, Account, p. 379. *Spy*, 3 June 1773. *DJR*, p. 245. "Boyle" 84:364. "Diary . . . of Mr. Thomas Newell," *MHSP* 15 (1876-1877):338-339.

34. *BPB*, 31 May 1773. JA, *Diary* 2:83; 3:325. *JHRM*. 1773, pp. 6-7. TH, *History*, 3:284-285.

35. *PBF* 20:232-233.

36. Ibid., 20:232. *JHRM*, 1773, pp. 26-27, 28.

37. *JHRM*, 1773, pp. 41, 44, 56, 57. *Spy*, 17 June 1773. Brown, *Revolutionary Politics*, pp. 145-146.

38. *PBF* 20:133-134.

39. Ibid.

40. Ibid., 20:321-322, 323.

41. *JHRM*, 1773, pp. 58-61, 75, 76, 88. *WSA* 3:45-48. *PBF* 20:243-244. *BG*, 21, 28 June 1773. TH, *History*, 3:288-297.

42. TH, Corr. 27:495-496, 500-501, 502-503, 506. *WSA* 3:49. *BG*, 26 July 1773. Bailyn, *Ordeal*, pp. 250-254.

43. Charles W. Akers, "New Hampshire's 'Honorary' Lieutenant Governor: John Temple and the American Revolution," *Historical New Hampshire* 30(Summer 1975):88–90.

44. TH, Corr. 27:546.

Chapter 12

1. JA, *Diary* 2:83–84. Kenneth R. Rossman, *Thomas Mifflin and the Politics of the American Revolution* (Chapel Hill, N.C., 1952), pp. 13–14.

2. *A Discourse on the Man of Sin; Delivered in the Chapel of Harvard College, in Cambridge, New-England, September 1, 1773* (Boston, 1774), pp. 30, 65–66.

3. James F. Shepherd and Gary M. Walton, "Estimates of 'Invisible' Earnings in the Balance of Payments of the British North American Colonies, 1768–1770," *Journal of Economic History* 29(June 1969):261–262.

4. Sermon: 2 Sam. 7:10, CP. For a general discussion of Whig ideology, see Bernard Bailyn, *The Ideological Origins of the American Revolution* (Cambridge, Mass., 1967). Gordon Wood is more explicit on the question of property in *The Creation of the American Republic, 1776–1787* (Chapel Hill, N. C., 1969), pp. 214–222.

5. JH to William Jones, 4 Nov. 1772, Hancock MSS. Richard B. Sheridan, "The British Credit Crisis of 1772 and the American Colonies," *Journal of Economic History* 20(June 1960):161–186. Ruth Crandall, "Wholesale Commodity Prices in Boston during the Eighteenth Century," *Review of Economic Statistics* 16(1934):126–128. James F. Shepherd, "Commodity Exports from the British North American Colonies to Overseas Areas, 1769–1772: Magnitudes and Patterns of Trade," *Explorations in Economic History* 8(1970):5–76, passim. Shepherd and Walton, "Estimates of 'Invisible' Earnings," pp. 231–232, 236–237, 240–241, 250, 256, 257. See also the tables of imports and exports in Merrill Jensen, ed., *English Historical Documents*, 9(New York, 1962):392–411.

6. Dartmouth to Cushing, 19 June 1773, Stevens 2025. Cushing to Dartmouth, 22 Aug. 1773, Stevens 2028.

7. Labaree, *Tea Party*, pp. 3–57. PBF 17:313. Joseph A. Goldenberg, *Shipbuilding in Colonial America* (Charlottesville, Va., 1976), p. 92.

8. Labaree, *Tea Party*, pp. 58–79.

9. Labaree, *Tea Party*, 1:327–330. PBF 20:494–497, 500–505.

10. Labaree, *Tea Party*, pp. 87–88, 104–106. SHG 8:550–562; 15:264–268. TH, Corr. 27:529.

11. BG, 18 Oct. 1773. Elbridge H. Goss, *The Life of Colonel Paul Revere*, 2 vols. (Boston, 1891), 2:635–644.

12. PBF 20:501. DJR, pp. 252–254. MHSC 52(1914):202. Labaree, *Tea Party*, pp. 109–110.

13. BTR, 1770–1777, pp. 141–146.

14. Labaree, *Tea Party*, pp. 112–114. TH, *History* 3:304–306. Mayo, *Additions*, p. 66. DJR, p. 254. BG, 22 Nov. 1773. BSM, 1769–1775, p. 202. BTR, 1770–1777, pp. 147–148.

15. TH, *History*, 3:306–308. Mayo, *Additions*, pp. 66–69. BG, 22 Nov. 1773. Francis G. Walett, "James Bowdoin and the Massachusetts Council," (Ph.D. diss., Boston University, 1948), pp. 195–198. Brown, *Revolutionary Politics*, pp. 158–161. BSM, 1769–1775, pp. 195–198.

16. *BG*, 29 Nov. 1773. *BSM*, 1769–1775, p. 203. "Diary . . . of Mr. Thomas Newell," *MHSP* 15(1876–1877):345.

17. *AFC* 1:89. *PBF* 20:501. *BG*, 22, 29 Nov. 1773. *BEP*, 29 Nov. 1773.

18. "Diary . . . of Mr. Thomas Newell," p. 345. *BG*, 6 Dec. 1773. *DJR*, pp. 255–256. Brown, *Revolutionary Politics*, p. 161.

19. L. F. S. Upton, ed., "Proceedings of Ye Body Respecting Tea," *WMQ* 22(Apr. 1965):289–292. *BG*, 6 Dec. 1773.

20. *BG*, 6 Dec. 1773. *DJR*, p. 256. TH, *History*, 3:309–310. *MHSC* 52(1914):211–213. Labaree, *Tea Party*, pp. 120–125.

21. TH, Corr. 27:581–582. Upton, "Proceedings," pp. 294–296. Andrews, "Letters," pp. 324–325. *AFC* 1:88–89

22. Upton, "Proceedings," pp. 294–295, 299. *PBF* 20:502.

23. Labaree, *Tea Party*, pp. 126–132, 141–142. On this and other points of the tea crisis, the detailed account by Richard Frothingham in the *Life and Times of Joseph Warren* (Boston, 1865), pp. 233–286, is still useful. TH, Corr. 27:581–582.

24. *BG*, 27 Dec. 1773, supplement. Labaree, *Tea Party*, pp. 134–138. Upton, "Proceedings," pp. 296–297. Hulton, Account, p. 380.

25. *BG*, 27 Dec. 1773, supplement. Andrews, "Letters," pp. 325–326. Upton, "Proceedings," pp. 297–298. SC to Savage, 29 May 1769, Lemuel Shaw MSS, MHS, box 1.

26. *PBF* 20:500–505.

27. Labaree, *Tea Party*, p. 141. Upton, "Proceedings," p. 298. JA, *Works* 9:333.

28. *BG*, 13 Dec. 1773. Andrews, "Letters," p. 327. A list of pallbearers and mourners is in CP.

29. *BEP*, 22 Dec. 1766. *BSR*, pp. 170, 183, 252. Andrew Johonnot, "The Johonnot Family," *NEHGR* 7(1853):141–142.

30. It is impossible to identify all of the families attending the Brattle Street Church at any one time, for many left no record of attendance. But from lists compiled of all known members of the congregation and of all Bostonians who gave any public indication of support for royal government or later loyalism, I conclude that the Tory element at Brattle Street did not exceed 20 percent. For example, of 101 legible names on the 1773 list of pewholders in the new church building, 18 evidenced some degree of Toryism, but only 10 of these were hard-line Tories who did not eventually acquiesce in separation from Britain.

31. William Bowes, Alexander Brimer, William Burton, Richard Clarke, Archibald Cunningham, Martin Gay, John Gore, Lewis Gray, Francis Green, William Jackson, John Lovell, Joseph Scott.

32. Corporation Records, 2:396; Overseers Records, 3:69; Harvard University Archives. A draft of SC's letter declining the presidency is in CP. *DJR*, pp. 262–263. *BG*, 14 Feb. 1774.

33. *BEP*, 10 Jan. 1774. *BG*, 27 Dec. 1773; 3, 17 Jan., 11 Apr. 1774. Brown, *Revolutionary Politics*, pp. 167–177. Frank W. C. Hersey, "Tar and Feathers: The Adventures of Captain John Malcom," *CSMP* 34(1934):429–473. *Letters of a Loyalist Lady* (Cambridge, Mass., 1927), pp. 70–72. TH, *D&L* 1:115.

34. JA, *Diary* 3:298–302. JA, *Works* 20:236–241.

35. *JHRM*, 1773, pp. 113–243 passim. *DJR*, pp. 262–263. TH, *History*, 3:315–326.

36. *BG*, 31 Jan. 1774. *BTR*, 1770–1777, pp. 109–110, 148, 149. *DJR*, p. 264.

37. JA, *Diary* 2:89–90.

38. JH, *An Oration delivered March 5, 1774* (Boston, 1774), pp. 6–7, 10, 15, 18, 20.

39. Ibid., pp. 16–19.

40. *BG*, 11 Apr. 1774. *BNL*, 21 Apr. 1774. *MHSP* 61(1927–1928):281–285. *BPB*. 15 Aug. 1774.

41. *BEP*, 2 May 1774. Thomas Bolton, *An Oration delivered March Fifteenth, 1775* ([Boston?], 1775), p. 5. [John Mein], *Sagittarius's Letters* (Boston, 1775), pp. 103–107. JA, *Diary* 3:384. E. S. Thomas, *Reminiscences of the Last Sixty-Five Years*, 2 vols. (Hartford, Conn., 1840), 1:245, 2:168–169.

42. Andrews "Letters," p. 327. Palfrey's letters to John Wilkes are in *MHSP* 47(1913–1914):196–197, 198, 200–201, 204–206, 208. See also the examples of Palfrey's writing quoted by John Gorham Palfrey, "Life of William Palfrey," in Jared Sparks, ed., *Library of American Biography*, 2nd. ser. (Boston, 1845), 7:337–448. John Gorham Palfrey noted that there had once been among William Palfrey's papers "an oration, now lost, commemorating the Boston Massacre, of March, 1770" (p. 407). In the winter and spring of 1774 Palfrey seems to have been more intimately connected with JH than at any other time in their association. (See the WP MSS, for these months.)

43. *BG*, 7, 14 Mar. 1774. JA, *Diary* 2:90, 91. *DJR*, pp. 264–265. Labaree, *Tea Party*, pp. 164–167. TH, *History*, 3:326, 326–327n. Oliver, *AR*, pp. 111–112. *SHG* 7:383–413.

44. *BTR*, 1770–1777, p. 166. *DJR*, p. 269.

45. Labaree, *Tea Party*, pp. 170–193. Gipson, *British Empire*, 12:107–116. Jack M. Sosin, "The Massachusetts Acts of 1774: Coercive or Preventive?" *Huntington Library Quarterly* 26(May 1963):235–246. Franklin B. Wickwire, *British Subministers and Colonial America, 1763–1783* (Princeton, 1966), pp. 146–147. *BG*, 16 May 1774. *Spy*, 12 May 1774, supplement.

46. Cobbett, *PH*, 17:cols 1159–1163, 1186. *BTP* 1:360–361. Griffin, pp. 299–300.

47. *LCP*, pp. 328–329. In the parliamentary election of 1774, TP accepted a seat arranged for him by Lord North, thus beginning a period of four years during which he generally supported the ministry as the best way of securing peace and restoring the colonies to their rightful place in the British Empire. Boston newspapers did not report TP's part in debates on the Port Bill (among others, *BG*, 16 May 1774).

48. *BG*, 16 May 1774. Brown, *Revolutionary Politics*, pp. 185–187.

49. *BTR*, 1770–1777, pp. 172–174. *BG*, 16 May 1774.

50. Carter, *Gage*, 1:355. John Richard Alden, *General Gage in America* (Baton Rouge, La., 1948), pp. 197–206. *DJR*, pp. 270–271. Andrews, "Letters," p. 328. *BG*, 23 May 1774. TH, *History*, 3:329.

51. Gad Hitchcock, *A Sermon Preached before His Excellency, Thomas Gage, . . . May 25th, 1774* (Boston, 1774), pp. 46–49. *JHRM*, 1774, pp. 6–7, 15. Carter, *Gage*, 1:355–356. Robert E. Brown, *Middle-Class Democracy and the Revolution in Massachusetts, 1691–1780* (Ithaca, N.Y., 1955), pp. 333–334.

52. *DJR*, pp. 272–273. Andrews, "Letters," p. 328. The addresses were printed in *BNL*, 26 May, 2 June 1774, and other newspapers. "Boyle", 84:375. *BG*, 30 May 1774. *BPB*, 30 May 1774. *BEP*, 30 May 1774. *WSA* 3:121, 124–125. Carter, *Gage*, 1:356. Addressers of TH identified as Brattle Street members are William Burton, Martin Gay, John Gore, Thomas Gray, Francis Green, William Jackson,

Archibald NcNeil, Samuel Minott, Joseph Scott, Joseph Turell, and William Bowes.

53. *WSA* 3:122–125. *MHSP* 37(1903): 266–268. [Charles Chauncy], *A Letter to a Friend* (Boston, 1774), pp. 28–34. Josiah Quincy, Jr., *Observations on the Act of Parliament Commonly Called the Boston Port Bill* (Boston, 1774). *BEP*, 2 May, 18 July 1774. JH suffered long illnesses, apparently complications of gout, during the summer of 1771 and the first half of 1774. See his letterbook for these periods, Hancock MSS.

54. *BG*, 30 May 1774.

55. *BG*, 13, 27 June 1774. John Pendleton Kennedy, ed., *The Journals of the House of Burgesses of Virginia, 1773–1776* (Richmond, Va., 1905), pp. 124, 132. Bernard Mayo, ed., *Jefferson Himself: The Personal Narrative of a Many-Sided American* (Charlottesville, Va., 1970), pp. 49–50. "An Association, signed by 89 members of the late House of Burgesses," in Julian P. Boyd, ed., *The Papers of Thomas Jefferson*, vol. 1 (Princeton, N.J., 1950):107–109.

56. Sermon: 2 Sam. 7:10, CP.

Chapter 13

1. News of these two bills reached Boston late on 2 June (*DJR*, pp. 273–274) and were published in a broadside the following day.

2. *BG* and *BPB* gave the front page of 13 June 1774 to a report of the debate in Commons on the second reading of the Massachusetts Government Act.

3. John Shy, *Toward Lexington, the Role of the British Army in the Coming of the American Revolution* (Princeton, N.J., 1965), pp. 407–413.

4. Carter, *Gage*, 1:359. *PBF* 21:273–276. The address to Gage is in *BEP*, 13 June 1774. Of the 126 names, 113 had also been addressers of TH.

5. Andrews, "Letters," p. 330. Albert Matthews, "The Solemn League and Covenant, 1774," *CSMP* 17(1915):103–122. Brown, *Revolutionary Politics*, pp. 191–194.

6. Andrews, "Letters," pp. 331–332. Brown, *Revolutionary Politics*, pp. 198–199.

7. *BTR*, 1770–1777, pp. 176–178. *DJR*, pp. 276–277. *WSA* 3:130–133. Andrews, "Letters," p. 336. Brown, *Revolutionary Politics*, pp. 199–203.

8. *BG*, 4 July 1774. *BEP*, 4 July 1774. Carter, *Gage*, 1:358–359. Andrews, "Letters," pp. 332, 343. John Cary emphasizes the contributions of the Solemn League and Covenant to the Association adopted by the First Continental Congress in his *Warren*, pp. 139–146.

9. Carter, *Gage*, 1:357. *JHRM*, 1774, pp. 17–18, 20–21, 44–47.

10. *BG*, 11 July 1774. Charles Warren, *Jacobin and Junto* (Cambridge, Mass., 1931), p. 37. Dorr 4:533. Carter, *Gage*, 1:361. *BNL*, 21 July 1777. Andrews, "Letters," p. 333.

11. Charles Knowles Bolton, ed., *Letters of Hugh Earl Percy from Boston and New York, 1774–1776* (Boston, 1902), pp. 29, 31.

12. *BG*, 25 July, 1 Aug. 1774. Oliver, *AR*, is especially vehement against the "Clergy sounding the Trumpet of Rebellion."

13. *AFC* 1:128. Andrews, "Letters," p. 386. *BPB*, 21 Nov. 1774. *BNL*, 24 Nov. 1774.

14. E.g., 25 July 1774.

15. *MHSC* 19(1822):158–166.

16. *LCP*, pp. 328–329.

17. Overseers Records 3:73, Harvard University Archives. *DJR*, p. 280. *BG*, 25 July 1774. *BTR*, 1770–1777, pp. 178–190. Carter, *Gage*, 1:363–364.

18. Albert Matthews, "Documents Relating to the Last Meetings of the Massachusetts Royal Council, 1774–1776," *CSMP* 32(1933–1937):460–504. Andrews, "Letters," pp. 338–339, 341, 343, 346, 349, 351. *PBF* 21:298–302. *BTR*, 1770–1777, pp. 183–193. *BSM*, 1769–1775, pp. 224–225. Carter, *Gage*, 1:365–368.

19. *PBF* 21:276. *BEP*, 29 Aug. 1774. Andrews, "Letters," pp. 342, 343. Carter, *Gage*, 1:371–372; 2:652.

20. *PBF* 21:275. Charles Chauncy to Richard Price, 18 July 1774, *MHSP* 37(1903):268–270.

21. John Pendleton Kennedy, ed., *Journals of the House of Burgesses of Virginia, 1773–1776* (Richmond, Va., 1905), pp. 136, 147, 152–159. *JHRM*, 1774, pp. 45–46. *BEP*, 18 July 1774. *BG*, 15 Aug. 1774. Francis G. Walett, "James Bowdoin and the Massachusetts Council," (Ph.D. diss., Boston University, 1948), p. 219.

22. *WAL* 1:26–32. Burnett, *Letters*, 1:50. *SHG* 12:462–482; 11:377–395; 14:384–389.

23. Andrews, "Letters," pp. 340–341. *WSA* 3:115, 122–124, 143–144.

24. This letter is in SAP. At the end, SC notes that he has also written to Cushing and JA, and that Cushing "will explain my Signature." The handwriting is unquestionably SC's. His other letters to members of the Massachusetts delegation have been lost except the one to JA, 16 Oct. 1774, JA, *Papers* 2:189–192.

25. JA, *Papers* 2:189–190.

26. Andrews, "Letters," p. 351. *PBF* 21:299. *BEP*, 5 Sept. 1774, supplement.

27. *PBF*, 21:299.

28. Cary, *Warren*, pp. 153–158. Harry A. Cushing, *History of the Transition from Provincial to Commonwealth Government in Massachusetts* (New York, 1896), pp. 101–111. *JPC*, pp. 601–605. *BEP*, 19 Sept. 1774.

29. *WSA* 3:156. *JCC* 1:31–41, 43, 51–53, 57, 62–63, 74–81, 100–101. JA, *Diary* 2:134–135, 137–140. *AFC* 1:157. H. James Henderson, *Party Politics in the Continental Congress* (New York, 1974), pp. 42–44. Cf. Schlesinger, *Merchants*, pp. 413–419.

30. *JCC* 1:75–81.

31. Ibid., pp. 57–62.

32. JA, *Diary* 2:131–132, 135, 150, 152, 152–154n, 156. *WSA* 3:158. *AFC* 1:156–157, 166–167. Burnett, *Letters*, 1:26–27. William G. McLoughlin, *New England Dissent, 1630–1833*, 2 vols. (Cambridge, Mass., 1971), 1:556–568. Franklin Bowditch Dexter, ed., *The Literary Diary of Ezra Stiles* (New York, 1901), 1:470–471.

33. *BG*, 14 Nov. 1774. "Diary . . . of Mr. Thomas Newell," *MHSP* 15(1876–1877):361. Josiah Quincy, *Memoir of the Life of Josiah Quincy Jun. of Massachusetts* (Boston, 1825), p. 203.

34. Carter, *Gage*, 1:375–382; 2:656, 658–659. *BTR*, 1770–1777, pp. 190–192. *JPC* 1–74.

35. *MHSC* 54(1891):62. *PBF* 21:306–307.

36. This letter appeared in *Rivington's New York Gazetteer*, 8 Sept. 1775, and in *BEP*, 19 Sept. 1774. I attribute it to a Tory author for two reasons. No friend to the Whig cause would have embarrassed SC and Chauncy by publicly associating these clergymen with rebellion. James Rivington, who first published the letter,

would soon turn his paper into a Tory organ. Though it may have been written by a wag with no political leanings, I doubt that this letter was a hoax, as some writers have suggested.

37. *BTR*, 1770–1777, pp. 194–195.

38. Quincy, *Memoir*. *SHG* 15:479–491. George H. Nash, III, "From Radicalism to Revolution: The Political Career of Josiah Quincy, Jr.," *AASP* 79 (Apr. 1969):253–290. Mark Antony DeWolfe Howe, ed., "Journal of Josiah Quincy, Jun., During his Voyage and Residence in England from September 28th, 1775, to March 3d, 1775," *MHSP* 50(1916–1917):433–471.

39. *PBF* 21:540–599.

40. The journal of Palfrey's trip is in WP MSS. John Gorham Palfrey, "Life of William Palfrey," in Jared Sparks, ed., *Library of American Biography*, 2nd ser. (Boston, 1845), 7:395–400. *JPC*, pp. 419, 420.

41. John R. Alden, *General Gage in America* (Baton Rouge, La., 1948), pp. 233–241. Allan J. McCurry, "The North Government and the Outbreak of the American Revolution," *Huntington Library Quarterly* 34(Feb. 1971):141–157. Richard W. Van Alstyne, "Parliamentary Supremacy versus Independence: Notes and Documents," *Huntington Library Quarterly* 26(May 1963):201–233. Bernard Donoughue, *British Politics and the American Revolution, the Path to War, 1773–75* (London, 1964), chs. 6–12.

42. *DJR*, pp. 285–291. *BG*, 24 Oct. 1774. *MHSC* 54(1891):61.

43. The vote of the Boston pastors, 28 Nov. 1774, is in the Washburn MSS, MHS. *JPC*, pp. 27–28. *BG*, 19 Dec. 1774. Of the many sermons preached on this occasion, those by William Gordon, Joseph Lyman, Samuel Williams, and John Lathrop were published in Boston. Haldimand is quoted in Allen French, "General Haldimand in Boston, 1774–1775," *MHSP* 66(1974):91. On Anglicans see Henry Caner to TH, 22 Dec. 1774, HC, Letterbook.

44. *JPC*, pp. 56–60, 69–72. *BG*, 20 Mar. 1775. *BTR*, 1770–1777, pp. 205–207. *BEP*, 12 Dec. 1774. Andrews, "Letters," p. 389. *MHSP* 32(1897–1899):139–142. Schlesinger, *Merchants*, chs. 11–13.

45. Brown, *Revolutionary Politics*, pp. 58–247.

46. Brown, *Revolutionary Politics*, and many other recent studies of Massachusetts throw light on the response of the towns to Boston's appeal.

47. *JPC*, pp. 75, 83–84, 86–97, 89–90, 91–93. *BTR*, 1770–1777, p. 211. Carter, *Gage*, 1:391–393. Alden, *General Gage in America*, pp. 221, 224–232. John Barker, *The British in Boston* (Cambridge, Mass., 1924), p. 24. French, *First Year*, pp. 19–20.

48. Barker, pp. 14, 18. Andrews, "Letters," pp. 388, 390, 391, 392, 393, 397.

49. *BEP*, 23 Jan., 13 Mar. 1775. Charles Knowles Bolton, ed., *Letters of Hugh Earl Percy from Boston and New York, 1774–1776* (Boston, 1902), p. 44. Barker, pp. 19–28. *DJR*, p. 289. Andrews, "Letters," pp. 395–396.

50. *WSA* 3:196, 206–207. *BTR*, 1770–1777, pp. 214–216. *Diary of Frederick Mackenzie*, 2 vols. (Cambridge, Mass., 1930), 1:9–10. Joseph Warren, *An Oration Delivered March Sixth, 1775* (Boston, 1775), pp. 11–12, 13–14, 21–22. Barker, pp. 25–26. *New York Gazetteer*, 16 Mar. 1775. TH, *D&L* 1:528–529.

51. *BG*, 13 Mar. 1775. Thomas Bolton, *An Oration Delivered March Fifteenth, 1775, at the Request of a Number of the Inhabitants of the Town of Boston* (n.p., 1775), pp. 3, 5. E. Alfred Jones, *The Loyalists of Massachusetts* (London, 1930), pp. 43–44. Andrews, "Letters," p. 400.

52. Bolton, *Oration*, pp. 3, 7–8. Andrews, "Letters," pp. 402–403.

53. *JPC*, pp. 107–108. DT, *Diary*, p. 50. *Diary of Frederick Mackenzie*, p. 12. *DJR*, p. 290. Andrews, "Letters," p. 400.

54. CP, box 2.

55. (Boston, 1775), pp. 5, 6–7, 22–24.

56. J. R. Bowman, "A Bibliography of *The First Book of the American Chronicles of the Times, 1774–1775*," *American Literature* 1(1929–1930):69–73. *BG*, 13 Mar. 1755, ff.

57. *The Group* (Boston, 1775). *AFC* 1:196, n.5. *MHSP* 63(1928–1929): 15–22.

58. More likely published in London or New York, the colophon of *Sagittarius's Letters* reads, "Boston. Printed: By Order of the Select Men, and sold at Donation Hall, for the Benefit of the distressed Patriots. MDCCLXXV." For the attribution to Mein see John R. Alden, "John Mein: Scourge of Patriots," *CSMP* 34(1943):571–599.

59. *MHSP* 7(1863–1864):124.

60. *JPC*, pp. 110, 114, 120–129. *MHSP* 37(1903):285. Alden, *General Gage in America*, pp. 233–240. *MHSC* 50(1888):283–284; 34(1858):371–372. Cary, *Warren*, pp. 180–181. *WAL* 1:44. Bolton, *Percy*, p. 48. Andrews, "Letters," p. 402. WP to JH, 19 May 1776, WP MSS.

61. *MHSC* 34(1858):371–372. The intercepted letter from someone at Bristol to Cooper has not been found; but WP wrote to JH the following year of having a letter from a "particular friend of mine at Bristol" (19 May 1776, WP MSS).

62. *WAL* 1:45. Cary, *Warren*, pp. 181–185.

63. SC Diary 5. It is uncertain when this entry dated 10 April was written, for it goes on to include events through 19 April. Samuel Kirkland Lothrop in *A History of the Church in Brattle Street, Boston* (Boston, 1851) quotes this passage from a little-known segment of SC's diary, but mistakenly gives the date as 16 April. His error has created much of the confusion over when SC left Boston.

64. SC Diary 4, 5.

65. Carter, *Gage*, 2:179–183. John R. Alden, "Why the March to Concord?" *AHR* 49(1944):450–452.

66. Alden, *General Gage in America*, pp. 242–243. Allen French, *General Gage's Informers* (1932; reprint ed., New York, 1968), pp. 3–69. SC Diary 3:303.

67. French, *Informers*, pp. 70–114. Harold Murdock, *The Nineteenth of April 1775* (Boston, 1925). Bolton, *Percy*, pp. 52–53. J. E. Tyler, "An Account of Lexington in the Rockingham Mss. at Sheffield," *WMQ* 10(Jan. 1953):99–107.

68. SC Diary 5.

Chapter 14

1. *JCC* 2:24–44.

2. French, *First Year*, chs. 4–9.

3. "Boyle" 85:12–13. Andrews, "Letters," pp. 405–406. SC Diary 5. *MHSP* 16(1879):281, 287. *DJR*, pp. 292–294. Diary of Benjamin Guild, 26 Apr. 1775, MHS. John Barker, *The British in Boston* (Cambridge, Mass., 1924), p. 38.

4. SC Diary 3:304, 305, 306; 5:30 Apr.

5. Thompson's account of how this correspondence came into his hands is given at the beginning of a ms. volume of letters from this collection copied in a clerk's hand for the benefit of the monarch (KM 204).

6. Ibid. TH, *D&L* 2:337–338. W. J. Sparrow, *Count Rumford of Woburn, Mass.* (New York, 1965). Allen French, *General Gage's Informers* (1932; reprint ed., N.Y., 1968), pp. 115–146. *SHG* 15:419–427.

7. *JPC*, pp. 184, 187, 189. SC Diary 3:303–312.

8. SC Diary 3:309–310. *JPC*, pp. 219–220, 229–231, 273, 280, 281, 283–284, 290.

9. French, *First Year*, chs. 11, 13, 14. *JPC*, pp. 330–331n.

10. Carter, *Gage*, 1:404–405. French, *First Year*, chs. 15–16.

11. Sermon: 2 Sam. 7:10, CP.

12. French, *First Year*, pp. 256–264. Carter, *Gage*, 2:686–687. *WAL* 1:59.

13. Sermon: 2 Sam. 7:10, CP. Cary, *Warren*, pp. 217–223.

14. *JPC*, p. 55. *AFC* 1:195, 207. Barker, p. 45. *The Journal and Letters of Samuel Curwen* (Boston, 1864), p. 29. *JCC* 2:58–59.

15. *JCC* 2:81–82. *WAL* 1:56–57, 67. Burnett, *Letters*, pp. 116–117, 118–119.

16. *JCC* 2:84–101.

17. JA, *Diary* 3:321–323.

18. Ibid., 3:324–325. For a summary of interpretations of JH by Tories and political foes see James Truslow Adams, "Portrait of an Empty Barrel," *Harper's Magazine* 161(1930):425–434.

19. Burnett, *Letters*, pp. 130–131, 134–135, 135–137. *BTP* 1:384–385. Fitzpatrick, *WGW*, 3:353, 353n. *BSR*, p. 190.

20. Douglas Southhall Freeman, *George Washington*, 3(New York, 1951):475–509. SC Diary 3:313. These letters and SC's answers to them have not been found.

21. SC Diary 3 passim.

22. *JPC*, pp. 589, 594. Harold Murdock, "Rev. Peter Thacher's Report on Bunker Hill," *MHSP* 59(1925–1926):36–45. Thacher's report in *AASP* 19(1908–1909):438–442; and the committee's official report in *Richard Frothingham, History of the Siege of Boston*, 5th ed., (Boston, 1890), pp. 381–384. SC does not refer to this assignment in his diary, though it no doubt occasioned his meeting with the committee on 12 July (Diary 3:314).

23. *JPC*, pp. 359–360, 450–451, 757–758. John Pitts to SA, 20 July 1775, SAP. *WAL* 1:56–57. SC Diary 3:314–315. *JHRM*, 1775, pp. 3–4, 6–7. *BG*, 24 July 1775. Harry A. Cushing, *History of the Transition from Provincial to Commonwealth Government in Massachusetts* (New York, 1896), pp. 170–184. The Council's assumption of executive power was conspicuously illustrated by its judicial appointments reported in *BG*, 2, 9 Oct. 1775.

24. *JCC* 2:87–88. *WAL* 2:416. *AFC* 1:216, 254. DT, *Diary*, p. 59. SC Diary 3:315.

25. SC Diary 3, passim. *AFC* 1:324n. *BG* published its last number in Boston on 17 April and resumed publication at Watertown on 5 June 1775. *JHRM*, 1775, p. 107. *BG*, 28 Aug., 11 Sept. 1775.

26. SC Diary 3 passim. George A. Billias, *General Glover and His Marblehead Mariners* (New York, 1960), p. 66.

27. *JCC* 2:239. *Essex Gazette*, 17 Aug. 1775.

28. *BG*, 11 Sept. 1775. *WAL* 1:110. *BSR*, p. 170. SC Diary 3:317.

29. SC Diary 3:320–321. *WAL* 1:121–123, 137–138. *JHRM*, 1775, pp. 162, 171, 186, 198, 201–206. French, *Informers*, pp. 147–201. *JCC* 3:334.

30. *JCC* 4:352. SC to SA, 6 June 1776, SAP. French, *Informers*, pp. 197–201. *A&R* 19:103. Overseers Records, 3:85–87, 90, 91, Harvard University Archives. SC Diary 3:340–341.

31. John R. Alden, *General Gage in America* (Baton Rouge, La., 1948), pp. 233–241. *WAL* 1:125, 149, 169–170. SC Diary 3:322. *JCC* 3:266–267, 270–271, 318, 321–325, 328ff. Fitzpatrick, *WGW* 3:505–513; 4:22–23, 41, 55. JA, *Works* 9:362–364.

32. SC Diary 3:322.

33. SC Diary 3:323. *AFC* 1:313, 320–321.

34. SC Diary 3:327. Barker, p. 68. *MHSP* 56(1922–1923):260–263.

35. SC Diary 3 passim. *JHRM*, 29 Nov. 1775–20 Feb. 1776, pp. 2, 13. *WAL* 1:192–194.

36. SC Diary 3:329, 332–335.

37. *WAL* 1:144.

38. *CSMP* 32(1937):501–502. *MHSP* 16(1878):289–291. "A Journal Kept by John Leach during his Confinement by the British, in Boston Gaol, in 1775," *NEHGR* 19(1865):255–263. Samuel Lane Boardman, *Peter Edes, Pioneer Printer in Maine* (Bangor, 1901), pp. 93–109.

39. Records of the Hollis Street Church in Boston, 1732–1788, 27 Aug., 22 Oct., 19 Nov. 1775, MHS. *MHSP* 16(1878):182–183, 280–306. Henry Wilder Foote, *Annals of King's Chapel*, vol. 2(Boston, 1896):293. Andrew Eliot to Jeremy Belknap, 5 June, 19 Nov. 1775, Belknap MSS 7, MHS. William Stevens Perry, ed., *Historical Collections Relating to the American Colonial Church*, 3(Hartford, Conn., 1873):584. HC to Bishop of London, 22 July 1775, HC, Letterbook.

40. Timothy Newell, "A Journal Kept During the Time that Boston was Shut Up in 1775–6," *MHSC* 31(1852):263, 266–268, 270. Frothingham, *Siege*, p. 239. *Virginia Gazette* (Dixon), 28 Oct. 1775; 13 Jan. 1776. *Virginia Gazette* (Pinkney), 10 Jan. 1776. Leach, "Journal," p. 262. Boardman, *Edes*, pp. 107–108. *MHSP* 59(1925–1926):133.

41. Newell, "Journal," pp. 268–269, 270, 271. TH, *D&L* 2:9–10. James Thacher, *A Military Journal During the American Revolutionary War* (Boston, 1827), p. 44. EP, "Diary," p. 239. *MHSC* 71(1914):368. *NEHGR* 19(1865):313–315. Andrew Eliot to Isaac Smith, 9 Apr. 1776, Smith-Carter MSS, MHS. Benjamin Franklin Stevens, ed., *General William Howe's Orderly Book* (reprint ed., Port Washington, N.Y., 1970), p. 160.

42. *MHSP* 16(1878):299. SC to BF, 21 Mar. 1776, APS. Isaac Cazneau to JH, 4 Apr. 1776, Hancock MSS.

43. *JCC* 3:444–445. Burnett, *Letters* 1:286. *MHSP* 14(1875–1876):275–279. William Abbatt, ed., *Memoirs of Major-General William Heath* (New York, 1901), pp. 27–28. Freeman, *Washington*, 3:567–586; 4:1–22.

44. Fitzpatrick, *WGW* 4:133–134, 208–210, 244, 254–257, 278–280, 348. French, *First Year*, 539–545, 376–422, 595–620. Gipson, *British Empire*, 12:339–343.

45. North Callahan, *Henry Knox* (New York, 1958), pp. 33–55. Abbatt, *Heath*, pp. 30, 31, 32. Thomas Williams Baldwin, ed., *The Revolutionary Journal of Col. Jeduthan Baldwin* (Bangor, Me., 1906), pp. 17–28.

46. Freeman, *Washington*, 4:22–31. Charles Martyn, *The Life of Artemas Ward* (New York, 1921), pp. 190–200. Fitzpatrick, *WGW*, 4:349–358, 363–365, 373–374. Abbatt, *Heath*, pp. 30–31. SC Diary 3:335. Barker, pp. 69–70. *BG*, 11 Mar. 1776.

47. *BTR*, 1770–1777, pp. 225–227. SC Diary 3:336. Peter Thacher, *An Oration Delivered at Watertown, March 5, 1776* (Watertown, Mass., 1776), pp. 13–15. *BG*, 11 Mar. 1776. SC Diary 3:336. EP, "Diary," p. 240.

48. SC Diary 3:336. *DJR*, p. 300. Barker, p. 70. Fitzpatrick, *WGW* 4:373–374. Stevens, *Orderly Book*, pp. 225–226, 229. Freeman, *Washington* 4:36–39.

49. Fitzpatrick, *WGW* 4:369. DT, *Diary*, p. 61. SC Diary 3:336. Sermon: Josh. 5:13–14, 6 Apr. 1758, CP.

50. Newell, "Journal," pp. 274–275. Barker, pp. 70–71. SC Diary 3:336. *Baldwin*, pp. 29–30. Fitzpatrick, *WGW* 4:385–386, 390–392. *MHSP* 47(1913–1914):109–110.

51. *MHSP* 18(1880–1881):266–268. *CSMP* 22(1937):502–504. TH, *D&L* 2:46–47. Stevens, *Orderly Book*, pp. 230, 237. *DJR*, pp. 301–303. Newell, "Journal," pp. 274–275. Andrews, "Letters," pp. 409–410. *AFC* 1:358–359, 369.

52. SC Diary 3:336–337. Fitzpatrick, *WGW* 4:389–390, 394–395, 404. Newell, "Journal," p. 276.

53. *MHSP* 14(1875–1876):284. Isaac Cazneau to JH, 4 Apr. 1776, Hancock MSS. Fitzpatrick, *WGW* 4:403–404.

54. SC Diary 3:337, 338. SC to BF, 21 Mar. 1776, APS.

55. SC Diary 3:338, 339. *A&R* 19:314–315; 21:49–50. *JHRM*, 13 Mar.–10 May 1776, pp. 40–41, 84, 85.

56. SC Diary 3:338–339. *New-England Chronicle*, 4 Apr. 1776. *BG*, 1 Apr. 1776. *DJR*, pp. 305–306.

57. SC Diary 3:339. *New-England Chronicle*, 25 Apr. 1776. *SHG* 12:501–506.

58. SC Diary 3:340. *BG*, 8 Apr. 1776. *AFC* 1:373. The manuscript of this un-dated sermon is in CP. For the full text and evidence on dating see Charles W. Akers, ed., "A Place for My People Israel': Samuel Cooper's Sermon of 7 April 1776," *NEHGR* 132(Apr. 1978):123–139.

59. SC Diary 3:340. Andrew Eliot to Isaac Smith, 9 Apr. 1776, Smith-Carter MSS, MHS. *AFC* 1:374–375. Perez Morton, *An Oration; Delivered at the King's Chapel In Boston, April 8, 1776* (Boston, 1776).

Chapter 15

1. Samuel Kirkland Lothrop, *A History of the Church in Brattle Street, Boston* (Boston, 1851), pp. 108–109. SC Diary 3:341. According to my lists, seven Brattle Street families left with Howe, seven had gone into exile earlier, and another three or four loyalist families from the church had been scattered under circumstances not entirely clear.

2. *BG*, 6, 20 May 1776. JH to William Palfrey, 20 Apr., WP MSS., Suffolk County, Mass., Probate Records, 76:512–516, 585. Lothrop, *History*, pp. 110–113. William Bant to JH, 6 Aug. 1776, Hancock MSS.

3. *BTP* 1:301. JB to SA, 9 Dec. 1775, SAP. JA, *Papers* 3:357–358. *A&R* 19:947–949. SC to BF, 21 Mar. 1776 (date supplied from SC Diary 3:338), APS.

4. *WSA* 3:273–277. SC to SA, 18 Apr. 1776, SAP.

5. JA, *Papers* 4:138–139.

6. *WSA* 3:281–285.

7. *WAL* 1:87, 91, 93, 94, 112, 151–152, 161–162, 180–181, 201–203. *WSA* 3:230–232, 247–248.

8. James Pitts to SA, 20 July 1775, SAP. *WAL* 1:93–94, 173, 177–178, 179, 183, 190, 191–192. *JHRM*, 29 Nov. 1775–20 Feb. 1776, pp. 44–165; 20 Sept.–11

Nov. 1775, pp. 269–270. *JCC* 4:122. TC to Paine, 29 Feb. 1776; Paine to Joseph Palmer, 1 Jan. 1776; Paine to James Warren, 1 Jan. 1776; TC to Paine, 13, 29 Feb. 1776; R. T. Paine MSS, MHS. Gardiner, *WGC*, pp. 3–4. *WSA* 3:268–269. JH to TC, 17 Jan. 1776, *MHSP* 60(1926–1927):98–99. TC to WC2, 23 Oct. 1775, *MHSP* 36(1902):97–99.

9. A better indication of TC's position than the personal slurs on his attachment to the American cause is his urging Paine to work in Congress for the passage of the "test act" to separate loyalists from true Americans. (TC to Paine, 29 Feb. 1776, R. T. Paine MSS, MHS.) As much as JA scrutinized JH's behavior, he could report no weakness on the issue of independence except that the president was "courted" by one of the "cold party." (JA, *Diary* 3:367–368.)

10. *JHRM*, 29 Nov. 1775–20 Feb. 1776, pp. 225–226, 262, 263, 306; 13 Mar.–10 May 1776, p. 260. James Warren to SA, 14 Feb. 1776, *MHSP* 14:280–281. JH to TC, 17 Jan., 7 Mar., *MHSP* 60(1926–1927):100, 107.

11. *JHRM*, 29 Nov. 1775–20 Feb. 1776, pp. 293, 309, 310, 312; 13 Mar.–10 May 1776, passim. SC to JA, 6 May 1776, AM 346. SC to SA, 13 May 1776, SAP.

12. *JHRM*, 13 Mar.–10 May 1776, pp. 269, 274, 276. *BG*, 13 May 1776. SC to SA, 13 May 1776, SAP.

13. *JHRM*, 13 Mar.–10 May 1776, pp. 235, 242, 277. *A&R* 5:502–503. Handlin, *Sources*, pp. 73–78. *WAL* 1:240–241. SC to JA, 6, 13 May 1776. AM 346.

14. *BTR*, 1770–1777, pp. 234–235, 236–238. JA, *Works* 9:401–402. *WSA* 3:303–305.

15. SC to SA, 30 June 1776, SAP.

16. *JCC* 5:425–426, 427, 428–429, 431, 506–507, 509, 510–516.

17. SC to SA, 15 July 1776, SAP. JA, *Papers* 4:383–384.

18. *New-England Chronicle*, 25 July 1776. *CJ*, 25 July 1776. Edward Oliver Fitch, ed., *The Diary of William Pynchon of Salem* (Boston, 1890), p. 12. *AFC* 2:56.

19. *AFC* 2:56. The undated ms. of his election sermon, from Heb. 11:24–26, is in CP. The four pages added are at the end.

20. *New-England Chronicle*, 15 Aug. 1776. *WAL* 1:268. *DJR*, p. 316. Charles Mampoteng, "The New England Clergy in the American Revolution," *Historical Magazine of the Protestant Episcopal Church* 9(Dec. 1940):270–275.

21. JA, *Papers* 4:457–458. *AFC* 2:48n–49n.

22. *AFC* 2:51, 60, 70, 99–100, 112. JH to TP, 19 Oct. 1777, Palfrey MSS. *MHSP* 60(1926–1927):104–105.

23. Sermon: Ps. 31:15, Apr. 1754, CP.

24. Ibid. *AFC* 2:79.

25. SC to SA, 18 Apr., 30 June, SAP. JA, *Papers* 4:137–139, 197–199, 355–356, 357–358.

26. SC to JA, 6 May 1776, AM 346. JA, *Papers* 4:215–216, 355–356. SC to SA, 30 June 1776, SAP.

27. *AFC* 1:405; 2:9–11, 17–19. *CJ*, 6 June 1776. *DJR*, p. 311. SC to JA, 6 May, 27 May, 1 July 1776, AM 346. SC to SA, 29 Apr. 1776, SAP. William Bell Clark, *George Washington's Navy* (Baton Rouge, La., 1960), pp. 159–160.

28. SC to SA, 29 July 1776, SAP.

29. Gerald Saxon Brown, *The American Secretary: The Colonial Policy of Lord George Germain, 1775–1778* (Ann Arbor, Mich., 1963), pp. 37–62.

30. Ibid., pp. 63–73. Ira D. Gruber, "Lord Howe and Lord George Germain:

British Politics and the Winning of American Independence," *WMQ* 22(Apr. 1965):225–243. Charles R. Ritcheson, *British Politics and the American Revolution* (Norman, Okla., 1954), pp. 200–207. Weldon A. Brown, *Empire or Independence* (Baton Rouge, La., 1941), ch. 5.

31. JA, *Papers* 4:137–139. SC to SA, 29 July 1776, SAP.

32. *New England Chronicle*, 2 Aug. 1776. *JCC* 5:597. *BTP* 1:400–401. SC to BF, 17 Sept., APS. JA, *Papers* 4:457–458. SC's copy of BF's letter to Howe, 20 July 1776, is in CP. Upon receiving this correspondence, SC replied to BF at once, but his letter has not been found. Howe's answer to BF is in Wharton, *DC*, 2:111–112. See also WP to JH, 31 July 1776, Palfrey MSS.

33. John R. Alden, *A History of the American Revolution* (New York, 1969), ch. 18.

34. Discontinued were the *Post-Boy, Evening-Post,* and *News-Letter.* The *Massachusetts Spy* had moved to Worcester. New papers were the *New-England Chronicle* (soon to become the *Independent Chronicle*) and the *Continental Journal.*

35. SC to BF, 17 Sept. 1776, APS.

36. *AFC* 2:73. "Boyle" 85:124–125, 127, 129. *IC,* 19 Sept. 1776. Clark, *Washington's Navy,* pp. 170–171. "Gordon," pp. 331, 332, 334.

37. *BTR,* 1770–1777, pp. 245, 246, 278–280. The figure of 8,000 is an approximation based on the 1,566 families reported in *BTR.*

38. *WAL* 1:257n–258n, 260, 261, 262, 263. EP, "Diary," pp. 259–261. *AFC* 2:65–67, 70, 72, 79, 81–82, 93, 94–95, 98, 101, 143. JA, *Papers* 4:384. See also the newspapers and *BSM* for the period of the epidemic.

39. *BSM,* 1776–1786, p. 10. *BTR,* 1770–1777, p. 246.

40. JA, *Papers* 4:457–458. SC to BF, 17 Sept. 1776, APS. Baxter, *Hancock,* pp. 287–288. Robert A. East, *Business Enterprise in the American Revolutionary Era* (New York, 1938), pp. 49–71.

41. JA, *Papers* 4:355–356. Ferguson, *Power,* pp. 25–47. William B. Norton, "Paper Currency in Massachusetts during the Revolution," *NEQ* 7(1934):45–52. Oscar and Mary F. Handlin, "Revolutionary Economic Policy in Massachusetts," *WMQ* 4(1947):7–11. Ralph V. Harlow, "Economic Conditions in Massachusetts during the American Revolution," *CSMP* 20(1918):164–167.

42. SC Diary 3:329.

43. JA, *Papers* 4:355–356, 457–458.

44. Ibid., 4:375–376. SC to BF, 25 Oct. 1777, APS. *BTR,* 1770–1777, pp. 285–286. Ferguson, *Power,* pp. 35–39.

45. Norton, "Paper Currency," pp. 57, 69. Ferguson, *Power,* pp. 42–44. The tax bills are scattered through *A&R* 5.

46. Smyth, *WBF* 7:294.

47. *BTR,* 1770–1777, pp. 249–262.

48. Ibid., pp. 259–265, 276, 283, 284–285. *A&R* 5:583–589, 642–647, 733–734. Gardiner, *WGC,* pp. 60, 66. SC to SA, 12 June 1777, SAP. *AFC* 2:172, 182–183, 212, 295, 296n. *WSA* 3:365. Fitch, *Pynchon,* p. 33. Richard B. Morris, "Labor and Mercantilism in the Revolutionary Era," in Richard B. Morris, ed., *The Era of the American Revolution* (New York, 1939), pp. 93–116. Handlin, "Revolutionary Economic Policy," pp. 13–16.

49. SC to SA, 12 June 1777, SAP. *A&R* 19:945; 20:386. *IC,* 16 Oct., 13 Nov. 1777. Receipts of SC's salary from 1779 to 1783 are in Smith-Carter MSS, MHS.

50. LCP, pp. 329–330. SC to BF, 28 Mar. 1777, Henry E. Huntington Library. SC to Isaac Smith, Jr., 5 Feb. 1777, Smith-Carter MSS, MHS. William

Gordon to BF, 26 Feb. 1777, Historical Society of Pennsylvania. The inventory of Hixon's slaves is in CP, box 1.

51. *AFC* 2:202.

52. SC to BF, 25 Oct. 1777, APS. *BSR*, p. 191.

53. *MHSP* 18(1880–1881):266–268. Isaac Cazneau to JH, 4 Apr., Hancock MSS. *A&R* 19:315–316. "Record of the Boston Committee of Correspondence, Inspection and Safety, May to November, 1776," *NEHGR* 30(1876):382–383, 385–386, 442–443. *DJR*, pp. 308–309, 315. Miles Whitworth to Andrew Eliot, 25 May 1776, Andrews-Eliot MSS, MHS. On Thomas Amory, see *SHG* 11:6–7, and the references to him in *BSR*.

54. *BG*, 21 Apr., 9 June 1777. *AFC* 2:223. *IC*, 8 May 1777. *MHSC* 54(1891):110–111, 115–116. *A&R* 5:647. *BTR*, 1770–1777, pp. 280–282.

55. Records of the Hollis Street Church, 9 Aug. 1776, MHS. *MHSC* 54(1891):104, 106–107, 123–124. *NEHGR* 34(1880):17. *MHSC* 34(1858):106.

56. *BG*, 9 June 1777; 7 Feb. 1780. Arthur Wentworth Eaton, *The Famous Mather Byles* (Boston, 1914), pp. 161–223. *MHSC* 54(1891):122.

57. *WAL* 1:368–369. *A&R* 5:912–918, 966–971.

58. *BG*, 10 Mar. 1777.

59. Sermon: Is. 26:20–21, CP.

Chapter 16

1. *CJ*, 21 Nov., 4 Dec. 1777. *WSA* 3:416–417.

2. Edmund C. Burnett, "Perquisites of the President of the Continental Congress," *AHR* 35(1929–1930):69–71. *JCC* 12:1222–1223. William Gordon, *The History of the Rise, Progress, and Establishment of the Independence of the United States*, 3 vols. (New York, 1789), 2:298. JH's view of his presidency is set forth in a letter to WP, 19 Oct. 1777, Palfrey MSS.

3. JA, *Diary* 2:259–260. *WAL* 1:340, 376–377.

4. *BTR*, 1770–1777, p. 294. *BG*, 2 Feb. 1778. *CJ* and *IC*, 5 Feb. 1778. *BG*, 9 June 1777.

5. No inventory of Thomas Hancock's estate was ever filed, and JH's estate required a century to be settled. What can be learned from the probate records, however, suggests a considerable drop in JH's total worth. But the fluctuating value of money and the lack of records as to how JH spent his money make accurate estimates impossible. JB, on the other hand, emerged from the Revolution with an enlarged estate. See the Suffolk County probate records for these men and Fowler, *Hancock*, p. 281.

6. Occupations of Boston taxpayers are given for most wards in "Assessors' 'Taking Books' of the Town of Boston, 1780," Bostonian Society *Publications* 9(Boston, 1912):8–59. The ward residence of selectmen and representatives can be established from this source and from the Boston tax valuation list of 1771.

7. Rowe was elected to the House in 1780 and seems to have remained an active supporter of JH (*BTR*, 1778–1783, pp. 138, 152).

8. *SHG* 14:650–661; 15:299–322.

9. Gardiner, *WGC*, p. 110.

10. *JHRM*, 1778, pp. 3–6. *WAL* 2:13, 20, 24–25, 42.

11. *BTR*, 1770–1777, pp. 297, 298. *JCC* 11:663. *IC*, 15 Jan. 1778.

12. Handlin, *Sources*, pp. 95–379. Patterson, *Political Parties*, pp. 153–196.

13. Handlin, *Sources*, pp. 202–379. SC to BF, 1 June 1778, APS.

14. Gardiner, *WGC*, p. 114. Patterson, *Political Parties*, pp. 187–188.

15. *IC*, 2, 9, 16, 30 Apr. 1778. *A&R* 20:345. "Gordon," pp. 307, 401. *JHRM*, 1778, p. 7.

16. Essex Institute Historical *Collections* 55(1919):163. "Gordon," p. 394. Burnett, *Letters*, 3:319. *WAL* 3:20–21.

17. *JCC* 5:827; 6:897. Carl Van Doren, ed., *The Letters of Benjamin Franklin and Jane Mecom* (Princeton, N.J., 1950), p. 300. BF's letter to SC, 25 Oct. 1776, has been lost, but an extract is in the Massachusetts Archives. SC's comment was made in a letter to BF, 17 May 1778, University of Pennsylvania Library. His immediate reply has not been found, but see SC to BF, 27 Feb. 1777, APS.

18. Smyth, *WBF* 7:55–56. SC to BF, 27 Feb., 30 Mar. 1777, APS. SC speaks of a number of other letters in this period that have not been found.

19. Gerald Saxon Brown, *The American Secretary: The Colonial Policy of Lord George Germain* (Ann Arbor, Mich., 1963), pp. 81–106.

20. Wharton, *DC*, 2:272–273. Bigelow, *WBF* 5:213–214. SC to SA, 12 June 1777, SAP. Sermon: Is. 26:20–21, July 1777, CP. *AFC* 2:300--301. "Boyle" 85:1.

21. SC to SA, 12 June 1777, SAP.

22. John R. Alden, *A History of The American Revolution* (New York, 1969), pp. 313–315. SC to JA, 24 July 1777, AM 347. SC to BF, 25 Oct. 1777, APS. *WSA* 3:388–389.

23. Alden, *American Revolution*, ch. 20. SC to BF, 25 Oct. 1777, APS.

24. SC to JA, 22, 24 Oct. 1777, AM 348. *A&R* 20:184–185. *CJ*, 23 Oct. 1777. *IC*, 23 Oct. 1777. Fragment of a sermon preached "Sabbath after Burgoyne's Surrender," CP, box 3.

25. *A Sermon . . . Upon Occasion of the Reduction of Quebec* (Boston, [1759]), pp. 45–48. *A Discourse on the Man of Sin* (Boston, 1774), pp. 57–58. SC to JA, 24 July 1777, AM 347.

26. SC to BF, 25 Oct. 1777, APS.

27. Ibid.

28. Ibid.

29. Ibid.

30. Ferguson, *Power*, pp. 35–40. SC to JA, 1 July 1778, AM 349.

31. SC to BF, 25 Oct. 1777, APS.

32. Ralph V. Harlow, "Economic Conditions in Massachusetts during the American Revolution," *CSMP* 20(1918):176–178.

33. *MHSC* 62(1902):175–176.

34. Wharton, *DC* 1:630–632; 2:444–445. Jonathan Williams to the Commissioners, 4 Dec. 1777. University of Virginia Library. Edward E. Hale and Edward E. Hale, Jr., *Franklin in France*, 2 vols. (Boston, 1887–1888), 1:154–158. The original of SC to BF, 25 Oct. 1777 (APS) has a small section marked to be omitted from the translation. See also BF to SC, 27 Feb. 1778, Bancroft Library, University of California, Berkeley. The files of the Papers of Benjamin Franklin at Yale University contain information on the French translations now located in Paris and Madrid. These were misdated 24 Oct.

35. John J. Meng, *The Comte de Vergennes: European Phases of His American Diplomacy (1774–1780)* (Washington, D.C., 1932), pp. 11–69. Samuel Flagg Bemis, *The Diplomacy of the American Revolution*, 2nd ed., (Bloomington, Ind., 1957), pp. 16–61.

36. *JCC* 5:813–817. Wharton, *DC* 2:240–241. *Secret Journals of the Acts and Proceedings of Congress* (1821; reprint ed., New York, 1967), 2:38–41.

37. BF to SC, 27 Feb. 1778, Bancroft Library, University of California, Berkeley.

38. Solomon Lutnick, *The American Revolution and the British Press, 1775–1793* (Columbia, Mo., 1967), pp. 100–124. Cobbett, *PH*, 19:cols. 525–528, 530. Brown, *The American Secretary*, pp. 131–147. Weldon A. Brown, *Empire or Independence* (Baton Rouge, La., 1941), pp. 205–234. Burnett, *Letters* 3:178–179.

39. Wharton, *DC* 2:506–512. *BG*, 20 Apr. 1778.

40. SC to BF, 13 May 1778, University of Pennsylvania Library.

41. Ibid. *London Daily Advertiser*, 10 July 1778.

42. *CJ*, 23 Apr. 1778. SC to BF, 13, 14 May 1778, University of Pennsylvania Library. *JCC* 10:374–380; 11:417–455, 457–458.

Chapter 17

1. BF to SC, 27 Feb. 1778, Bancroft Library, University of California, Berkeley. SC to BF, 21 Nov. 1778, APS.

2. Among much other evidence, see Richard Henry Lee to SA, 15 Nov. 1777, SAP.

3. Julian P. Boyd, "Silas Deane: Death by a Kindly Teacher of Treason?" *WMQ* 16(1959):165–187, 319–342, 515–550, esp. 329–334.

4. William Abbatt, ed., *Memoirs of Major-General William Heath* (New York, 1901), p. 150. *WAL* 2:8–10. SC to BF, 13 May 1778, University of Pennsylvania Library; 1 June 1778, APS. SC to SA, 27 May 1778, SAP. Stevens, 760, 839. On the Holkers, see André Rémond, *John Holker, manufacturier et grand fonctionnaire en France au XVIIIme siècle, 1719–1786* (Paris, 1946); and Howard C. Rice, Jr., ed., *Travels in North America in the Years 1780, 1781, and 1782 by the Marquis de Chastellux*, 2 vols. (Chapel Hill, N.C., 1963), 1:330–332. Some of the son's prealliance activities can be traced in *The Deane Papers*, 1–3, *Collections of the New-York Historical Society*, 19–21(1886–1888); see particularly 2:185, 293, 465, and 3:36–41. The major source for the younger Holker's American activities is the forty volumes of his manuscripts in the Library of Congress, which will be used extensively in following chapters.

5. SC to BF, 1 June 1778, APS.

6. The *Independent Ledger* was published by Edward Draper and John W. Folsom. *BSR* contain considerable references to Draper but nothing on Folsom. They continued to publish the paper in partnership until the end of 1783, after which Folsom continued it until Oct. 1786.

7. On 25 July BF wrote to Vergennes, "I send enclosed a Letter from Dr. Cooper to me" (Smyth, *WBF* 7:184). This was likely the letter of 1 June, later published in *Affaires* (see n. 8). Translations of SC's letters to BF of 13 and 14 May are now in the Archives des Affaires étrangères (Paris) as intercepted letters (Stevens 826, 838); but it seems certain that these came from BF rather than being intercepted. BF also sent Vergennes a copy of most of SC's letter to him of 4 Jan. 1779 (CPEU 7:31–32).

8. Largely ignored by historians, *Affaires de l'Angleterre et de l'Amérique* offers an expression of Vergennes's changing outlook on the American rebellion, as Gilbert Chinard has indicated in the *Newberry Library Bulletin*, 2nd Ser., 8(Mar. 1952)225–236. Though the one study of Genêt and his more famous son (Meade Minnigerode, *Jefferson, Friend of France* [New York, 1928]) only mentions *Affaires*, it does establish the importance of the elder Genêt as a propagandist

(pp. 34–37). Genêt's letters to BF of 26 July, 16 Aug. 1778 (APS), acknowledge receipt of his letters from SC. See also Genêt's letters to JA from June to Oct. 1778 (AM 349), and Genêt to JA, 24 Oct. 1778 in Wharton, *DC* 2:806. Useful too is the long note in JA, *Diary* 2:354–355. Translations of SC's letters to BF of 1 June, 1 July 1778, were published in *Affaires* 12:cxlix–clii, ccx–ccxiii. SC to JA, 4 Jan. 1779, appeared in 15:clxxvii–clxxix. These volume and page numbers are to the complete set in MHS, which though imperfect is the best available set of this confusing publication. For a collation of sets in American libraries, see Paul Leicester Ford, "Affaires de l'Angleterre," *Pennsylvania Magazine of History and Biography* 13(July 1889):222–226.

9. *Affaires* 15:clxxvii; 17:cxi.

10. 1 July 1778.

11. The fullest account of the Carlisle Peace Commission is Carl Van Doren, *Secret History of the American Revolution* (1941; reprint ed., New York, 1968), pp. 59–116. Also useful are Charles R. Ritcheson, *British Politics and the American Revolution* (Norman, Okla., 1954), pp. 258–286; and Weldon A. Brown, *Empire or Independence* (Baton Rouge, La., 1941), pp. 244–292.

12. "Orders and Instructions" to the commissioners, Stevens 440. Petition to the king of London merchants trading with America, 10 March 1778, Stevens 1063. SC to SA, 6 July 1778, SAP.

13. "Minutes," Stevens 487; see also 3, 71. On Wentworth, see Michael G. Kammen, *A Rope of Sand* (Ithaca, N.Y., 1968), pp. 282–283; and Sir Lewis Namier and John Brooke, *The House of Commons, 1754–1790*, 2(London, 1964):623–624.

14. *BTP* 1:377–379. TH, *D&L* 1:349. JT to Captain Dowse, 10 July 1777, SAP. JT to BF, 11, 29 July 1777, APS.

15. Wentworth to [William Eden], 7 Jan. 1778, Stevens 489.

16. Stevens 424–434. *The Carlisle Papers, Royal Historical Manuscripts Commission 15th Report, Appendix, Part IV* (London, 1897), p. 359. *BTP* 1:418–419.

17. TH, *D&L* 2:238. The fullest account of JT's mission of 1778–1779 is Lewis Einstein, *Divided Loyalties, Americans in England during the War of Independence* (London, 1933), pp. 87–101.

18. SC to BF, 1 July 1778, APS. On the relation of military strategy to the work of the peace commission, see William B. Willcox, *Portrait of a General, Sir Henry Clinton in the War of Independence* (New York, 1964), pp. 211–237.

19. Stevens 1115, 1180. Burnett, *Letters*, 3:294.

20. Gerald S. Brown, "The Anglo-French Naval Crisis, 1778: A Study of Conflict in the North Cabinet," *WMQ* 13(Jan. 1956):3–25. Willcox, *Portrait of a General*, pp. 211–219, 237–238. Ira D. Gruber, *The Howe Brothers and the American Revolution* (New York, 1972), pp. 303–318. Jonathan R. Dull, *The French Navy and American Independence* (Princeton, N.J., 1975), pp. 122–123. SC to BF, 1 July 1778, APS. Useful to balance accounts from the English point of view is "Précis de la Campagne de 1778," CP, box 1. This was apparently prepared for SC at the order of d'Estaing. Though laudatory of d'Estaing, it contains some details not found elsewhere, and was the basis for SC's "A Letter from a Gentleman in America to his Friend in France" (Edward E. Hale and Edward E. Hale, Jr., *Franklin in France*, 2 vols. [Boston, 1887–1888], 1:183–193) written at the end of 1778 but not sent to BF until three years later (SC to BF, Feb. 1781, APS). Doniol, *Histoire*, 3:367–374, 447–450. Fitzpatrick, *WGW* 12:178–180, 183–187, 188, 201–203, 208–214. *JCC* 11:684.

21. *AFC* 2:211. The abortive Newport expedition aroused great interest throughout New England: "Boyle" 85:131. Gardiner, *WGC*, p. 95. *AFC* 2:351–352, 367, 369. Burnett, *Letters*, 3:2, 12, 38, 103, 367. *A&R* 20:197, 230, 232–233. *JCC* 9:1027; 11:761.

22. Fitzpatrick, *WGW* 12:201–203, 218–219, 232–233, 263–268. Theodore Thayer, *Nathanael Greene* (New York, 1960), pp. 251–253. Henri Doniol, ed., "Correspondance inédite de La Fayette: lettres écrites au Comte d'Estaing," *Revue d'Histoire diplomatique* 6(1892): 395–448. Louis Gottschalk, *Lafayette Joins the American Army*, 2nd imp. (Chicago, 1965), pp. 236–248. George A. Billias, *General John Glover and His Marblehead Mariners* (New York, 1960), pp. 163–165. Stinchcombe, *American Revolution*, pp. 48–50.

23. EP, "Diary," p. 334. *CJ*, 6 Aug. 1778. Carl Van Doren, ed., *The Letters of Benjamin Franklin & Jane Mecom* (Princeton, N.J., 1950), p. 183. *IL*, 10 Aug. 1778. Otis G. Hammond, ed., *Letters and Papers of Major-General John Sullivan*. 3 vols. (Concord, N.H., 1930–1939), 2:251.

24. *CJ*, 6 Aug. 1778. The manuscript of this sermon (CP, box 3) is incomplete. It begins with point 4, but from the contents I have identified it as the sermon SC preached at the Boston Thursday lecture on 6 Aug. 1778.

25. Doniol, *Histoire*, 3:374–382, 384–392, 450–457. Hammond, *Sullivan* 2:169–242. "Précis de la Campagne de 1778." Letter of the Comte de Breugnon, 10 Oct. 1778, Stevens 1974. Gottschalk, *Lafayette Joins the American Army*, pp. 245–250. Gruber, *Howe Brothers*, pp. 310–318. Billias, *Glover*, pp. 165–168. Stinchcombe, *American Revolution*, 50–51.

26. Hammond, *Sullivan* 2:243–246.

27. Ibid. 2:248–263, 266–276, 280–288. Billias, *Glover*, pp. 168–173. Thayer, *Greene*, pp. 254–258. Gruber, *Howe Brothers*, pp. 318–320. Willcox, *Portrait*, pp. 249–251. Gottschalk, *Lafayette Joins the American Army*, 265–266. Stinchcombe, *American Revolution*, pp. 55–57.

28. *WSA* 4:79–80. *WAL* 2:39–40. TC to JA, 21 Oct. 1778, AM 349.

29. *WAL* 2:42–43, 44. Gottschalk, *Lafayette Joins the American Army*, pp. 256–257. Gardiner, *WGC*, p. 126. *IC*, 24 Aug. 1778. Hammond, *Sullivan* 2:346. Doniol, "Correspondance," pp. 422–423, 425.

30. *WAL* 2:9–10. *WSA* 4:60–61.

31. D'Estaing to Gérard, 29 Aug. 1778, CPEUS 1.

32. Louis Gottschalk, ed., *The Letters of Lafayette to Washington, 1777–1779* (New York, 1944), p. 62. Doniol, "Correspondance," pp. 420–425.

33. *CJ*, 3 Sept. 1778. Gottschalk, *Lafayette to Washington*, pp. 62–63. TC to JA, 21 Oct. 1778, AM 349. Fitzpatrick, *WGW* 12:501.

34. Doniol, *Histoire* 3:361–365, prints the French text of this letter.

35. Hammond, *Sullivan* 2:278–280, 293–294. *IL*, 31 Aug. 1778, and other Boston papers for this week. D'Estaing to Gérard, 29 Aug. 1778, CPEUS 1.

36. *CJ*, 3 Sept. 1778. *DJR*, pp. 321, 322. Abbatt, *Heath*, 117–178. EP, "Diary," p. 337. Meng, *Gérard*, p. 284n. Gruber, *Howe Brothers*, pp. 319–320. Hammond, *Sullivan* 2:298–290, 299–301, 346–347. Fitz-Henry Smith, Jr., *The French at Boston during the Revolution*, Bostonian Society *Publications*, 10(1923):23–38.

37. [William A. Duer, trans.], *Memoirs, Correspondence and Manuscripts of General Lafayette Published by His Family*, 1(London, 1837):58–59, 82.

38. Smyth, *WBF* 4:203–204. H. M. Jones discusses the colonial study of French in *America and French Culture, 1750–1848* (Chapel Hill, N.C., 1927),

pp. 183–190 and passim. Occasional advertisements by teachers of French appeared in the Boston newspapers.

39. E. W. Balch, trans., "Narrative of the Prince de Broglie," *Magazine of American History* 1(1977):378–379.

40. *IC*, 24 Dec. 1778. Samuel Breck, who was seven in 1778, wrote in later life that "the early intercourse with the French was through the medium of Latin, and the celebrated Doctor Cooper was a useful and general interpreter." Breck's knowledge or memory may be questioned and also the meaning of this sentence. It can be interpreted to read that those who knew Latin attempted to converse with Frenchmen in that tongue, while they depended on SC when they needed an interpreter who spoke French. (H. E. Scudder, ed., *Recollections of Samuel Breck with Passages from his Note-Books* [Philadelphia, 1887], pp. 46–47.) For the typical use of this source, see Esther Forbes, *Paul Revere and the World He Lived In* (Boston, 1942), p. 328. In all of SC's correspondence with visiting Frenchmen, there is only one letter in Latin (from La Touche, 25 Aug. 1780, CP).

41. Smith, *French at Boston*, pp. 36–37. *CJ*, 27 Aug. 1778. *IL*, 14 Sept. 1778. Stevens 1974. *Diary of Frederick Mackenzie*, 2 vols. (Cambridge, Mass. 1930), 1:405. *A&R* 20:497.

42. *IL*, 14 Sept. 1778. *A&R* 20:476. Vicomte de Noailles, *Marins et Soldats Francais en Amérique pendant la Guerre de l'Indépendance des Etats-Unis* (Paris, 1903), pp. 46–48. D'Estaing to Gérard, 30 Oct. 1778, CPEUS 1. Allan Forbes and Paul F. Cadman, *France and New England*, 2(Boston, 1927):20–29.

43. On 17 Jan. 1779 Gérard wrote to Vergennes concerning SC; "Plusieurs Ecrits qu'il publia pour justifier la conduite de M. le Cte d'Estaing lorsque le gal Sullivan avoit excité tout l'Est contre ce vice-Amiral et contre ce francois m'engagèrent à l'en remercier . . ." (Meng, *Gérard*, p. 481).

44. *IL*, 14 Sept. 1778. SC's known relationship to this newspaper, the style and contents of the writing, and the lack of other articles more likely to be his defense of d'Estaing, lead me to conclude that this and the other pieces in *IL* from a "correspondent" are by SC. See the additional evidence for this attribution in note 50.

45. *IC*, 24 Sept., 1 Oct. 1778. *DJR*, p. 322. *WAL* 2:48–49. *JHRM*, 1778, pp. 49, 51. *A&R* 20:486. Abbatt, *Heath*, p. 179. William L. Stone, trans., *Letters of Brunswick and Hessian Officers during the American Revolution* (Albany, 1891), p. 175.

46. *JCC* 11:713. *WAL* 2:56. *DJR*, p. 322. *IL*, 14 Dec. 1778. SC to SA, 1 Dec. 1778, SAP.

47. *AFC* 2:267–268. André Lasseray, *Les Francais sous les Treize Etoiles (1775–1783)*, 2 vols. (Paris, 1935), 2:462–463. *A&R* 20:636. *JCC* 8:539; 13:97. D'Estaing to Gérard, 30 Oct. 1778, CPEUS 1.

48. D'Estaing to Gérard, 30 Oct. 1778, CPEUS 1. Doniol, "Correspondance," pp. 446–447. Gustave Lanctot, *Canada and the American Revolution*, trans., Margaret M. Cameron (Cambridge, Mass., 1967), pp. 179–185, 273–276. A copy of the original *Déclaration* is in Doniol, *Histoire* 3:464–466.

49. Doniol, "Correspondance," p. 446.

50. *IL*, 26 Oct. 1778. The language in this piece is very similar to the last paragraph of SC's "A Letter from a Gentleman in America to his Friend in France" (Hale, *Franklin in France*, 1:183–193). This was a pamphlet-sized defense of d'Estaing, based on a "Précis de la Campagne de 1778," obtained from an unknown French source, likely d'Estaing's secretary. But SC deferred publication of this pamphlet for fear of antagonizing General Sullivan. He did, however, use parts of it in

newspaper articles, of which this is an example. See SC to BF, 1 Feb. 1781, APS; and SC to d'Estaing [Feb. 1781?], CP. An incomplete draft copy of the "Letter" is in CP.

51. *DJR*, p. 323. *IL*, 26 Oct. 1778. Isaac Smith to JA, 9 Nov. 1778, AM 349. *AFC* 3:109–110. SC to JA, 4 Jan. 1779, AM 350. *WAL* 2:54–55.

52. *IC*, 5 Nov. 1778.

53. Gardiner, *WGC*, pp. 129–130. *WAL* 2:51–55, 57–60, 65, 66–68. "S" to _____, beginning "My Dear. Secret and Confidential," Boston, 28 Oct. 1778, MHS Miscellaneous Papers 15. *WSA* 4:92–93. Diary of Benjamin Guild, 28 Oct. 1778, MHS. *JHRM*, 1778, pp. 69, 71. *A&R* 5:912–918.

54. *WAL* 2:51. Abigail Adams to JA, 23 Nov. 1778, AM 349. *IL*, 2 Nov. 1778. I attribute this piece from a "Correspondent" to SC because of his identification as the "Correspondent" in other cases.

55. EP "Diary," p. 338. D'Estaing to SC, 3 Nov. 1778, CP.

56. *WAL* 2:37. Meng, *Gérard*, pp. 571–757. Stevens, 529, 1177, 1199. *The Carlisle Papers*, pp. 367–368.

57. *WSA* 4:54–56. JT to BF, 11 July 1777, APS. Berkenhout's journal of his trip to Philadelphia, with a useful introduction by Howard Peckham, was published in the *Pennsylvania Magazine of History and Biography* 4(1941):54–56.

58. *JCC* 11:858–860. *WSA* 4:54–56. *BTP* 1:425–427. *IC*, 1 Oct. 1778. WP to JT, 8 Oct. 1778, WP MSS.

60. SC to SA, 7 Nov. 1778, SAP. Charles Chauncy to SA, 7 Nov. 1778, SAP. John Winthrop to SA, 9 Nov. 1778, SAP. *WAL* 2:63. *BTP* 1:427–431. Hammond, *Sullivan* 2:418. *JCC* 12:1186, 1201. Fitzpatrick, *WGW* 13:309. Burnett, *Letters* 3:533–534. *The Deane Papers*, 3, *Collections* of the New York Historical Society, 21(1888):79.

61. SC to SA, 20 Nov., 1 Dec. 1778, SAP. Meng, *Gérard*, p. 251.

62. *WSA* 4:95–111. Meng, *Gérard*, p. 423. Burnett, *Letters* 3:516, 519, 533, 536. *Deane Papers* 3:79. JT to SA [16 Dec. 1778], SAP. SA to JT [16? Dec. 1778], SAP. Doniol, *Histoire* 4:28–31, 50–56. SA's refusal to furnish JT copies of the treaties represented more annoyance than a desire to keep them secret. A week before this request both had been printed in *IC* (10 Dec. 1778).

63. Smyth, *WBF* 7:291–292. SC to JA, 4 Jan. 1779, AM 350.

64. SC to BF, 4 Jan. 1779, APS. See also Gottschalk, *Lafayette Joins the American Army*, pp. 304–320.

65. This extract was enclosed in BF's letter to Vergennes, 16 Feb. 1779, CPEUS 7.

Chapter 18

1. Diary of Benjamin Guild, 12 Jan. 1779, MHS.

2. *WSA* 4:19.

3. JA, *Diary* 2:357–358, 360–361, 388.

4. E.g., SC to BF, 21 Nov. 1778; 4 Jan., 13 Nov. 1779, APS. Joseph de Valnais to Holker, 20 Jan. 1779, Holker 2.

5. *BSR*, pp. 174, 190, 191, 193, 194, 195, 196. SC to SA, 19 Jan. 1779, SAP. Holker 2–8 passim.

6. *WAL* 2:54. SA to S. P. Savage, *MHSP* 43(1909–1910):332–333. Bigelow, *WBF* 8:152–153. Among dozens of examples in the Boston newspapers, see the

following: *BG*, 20 Apr., 14 May, 15 June 1778; *CJ*, 29 Oct. 1778; *BEP*, 7 Nov. 1778.

7. *BTR*, 1778–1783, pp. 36–47. *DJR*, pp. 325–326. Diary of John Eliot, Mar. and Apr. 1779, MHS. DT, *Diary*, pp. 74–77. Gardiner, *WGC*, pp. 135–136. SC to SA, 14 Mar. 1779, SAP. The newspapers amply document the increase in crime, which was often blamed on soldiers or sailors from other countries or regions.

8. Ferguson, *Power*, p. 32.

9. SC to SA, 14 Mar. 1779, SAP.

10. Bigelow, *WBF* 7:205–206.

11. For a different perspective, see Richard B. Morris, *The American Revolution Reconsidered* (New York, 1967), ch. 3.

12. De Valnais to Holker, 11 Jan. 1779, Holker 2.

13. Gérard to Vergennes, 17 Jan. 1779, Meng, *Gérard*, pp. 480–482.

14. De Valnais to Gérard, 5 Feb. 1779, Holker 2.

15. La Luzerne to Vergennes, 30 Mar. 1784, LL, Letterbooks.

16. De Valnais to Holker, 11 Jan. 1779, Holker 2.

17. The record of payments to SC from his congregation during 1779–1783 are in the Smith-Carter MSS, MHS. See also the comment concerning one of the special payments to him in a letter of 28 Oct. 1778, beginning "My dear. Secret and Confidential," MHS Miscellaneous Papers 15. The specie value of £1,608 is calculated on the basis of an average ratio for 1779 of Continental currency to specie of 16 to 1, which may be too low. But a conservative estimate seems desirable in view of the impossibility of calculating the exact value of each sum paid SC at the time he received it. By Oct. the ratio had reached 30 to 1 (Ferguson, *Power*, p. 32). In addition, SC was paid £75 in Feb. 1779 for his services as chaplain to the General Court for one year (*A&R* 20:598). This sum represented perhaps £7 in specie value if it was paid promptly.

18. La Luzerne to Vergennes, 4 Jan., 30 Mar. 1784, LL, Letterbooks. See also the other finance letters scattered through the letterbooks. SC was not mentioned by name when entering the amounts paid him, but the letter of 30 Mar. 1784 makes it clear that he was the recipient. For a discussion of these finance letters, see O'Donnell, *La Luzerne*, p. 58n and passim.

19. Suffolk County, Mass., Probate Records, 83:8–10; 96–673; 605:127–128; 610:318. Jonathan Williams to BF, 29 Dec. 1783, APS. Vergennes to La Luzerne, 25 Sept. 1779, CPEUS 10.

20. TH, *D&L* 2:404. LL to Vergennes, 30 Mar. 1784, LL, Letterbooks.

21. *BTR*, 1778–1783, pp. 58, 83, 105. De Valnais to Holker, 11 Jan. 1779, Holker 2. Brown, *Hancock*, p. 228.

22. *WAL* 1:379–382.

23. E. James Ferguson, "Business, Government, and Congressional Investigation in the Revolution," *WMQ* 16(July 1959):293–318. Julian P. Boyd, "Silas Deane: Death by a Kindly Teacher of Treason?" *WMQ* 16(1959):165–187, 319–342, 515–550.

24. The chief writings in this controversy may be conveniently read in the *Deane Papers*, 3, *Collections* of the New-York Historical Society for the Year 1888 (New York, 1889).

25. *WAL* 2:67–71.

26. Burnett, *Letters*, 3:530–531. Edmund S. Morgan, "The Puritan Ethic and the American Revolution," *WMQ* 24(Jan. 1967):25–33.

27. Ferguson, "Business, Government, and Congressional Investigation," pp. 297–303, 316–317. H. James Henderson, *Party Politics in the Continental Congress* (New York, 1974), pp. 187–213.

28. *WSA* 4:115.

29. *WSA* 4:104–108, 111, 113, 115–120, 126–128. JA, *Works* 9:478–480.

30. SC to SA, 5, 19 Jan. 1779, SAP. SC to JA, 4 Jan. 1779, AM 350.

31. Meng, *Gérard*, pp. 347–570 passim. Meng's introduction is helpful in understanding Gérard's attitude toward his American assignment.

32. Meng, *Gérard*, pp. 98–99, and the dispatches cited here. *JCC* 11:448–455, 574–575; 12:1197–1198.

33. *JCC* 13:30–38, 48–49, 54–55, 61–63.

34. James Lovell to SA, 13 July 1779, SAP.

35. Meng, *Gérard*, pp. 500, 689.

36. SC to SA, 5 Jan. 1779, SAP. SC apparently misdated this letter by writing Jan. for Feb., for it was written after he had received word of the congressional action of 14 Jan. See also de Valnais to Holker, 16 Mar. 1779, Holker 3.

37. *BG*, 15 Feb. 1779. This article is attributed to SC by de Valnais in a letter to Holker, 16 Mar. 1779, Holker 3.

38. SC to SA, 5 Jan. (5 Feb.?), SAP. *JCC* 13:260, 288–289. De Valnais to Holker, 5 Feb. 1779, Holker 2. Burnett, *Letters* 6:81n. Whigs divided over the loyalty of Robert Temple, who had gone to England at the outbreak of hostilities but returned to his family in Massachusetts in 1776. The Hancock faction tended to oppose him, while the Adams-Warren faction was favorable. His influence resulted from his wife being the daughter of former Governor William Shirley and from JT's connection with the Bowdoins.

39. *IL*, 24 May 1779. De Valnais to Holker, 16 Mar., 3 Apr., 22 Apr., 6 May, 14 May, Holker 3. *BTP* 1:432–434.

40. *MHSP* 5(1862):241–244.

41. SC to SA, 15 Apr. 1779, SAP. "Certificate of James Bowdoin and Others," *BTP* 1:434–436. This "Certificate" was originally dated Aug. 1779, but a later hand wrote 21 May 1779. Since SA was not in Boston during May but was in Aug., I assume the original date to be correct. One can also assume that the space left under JB's initial signature was left in the hope that JH could be persuaded to sign. See the editor's note on p. 434. JT carried with him to England a forceful letter from Charles Chauncy to Richard Price declaring the colonies to be stronger and more determined than ever to hold fast to their independence (*MHSP* 38[1903]:319–321).

42. Meng, *Gérard*, pp. 617–618, 732. Richard B. Lloyd to W. T. Franklin, 15, 20 July 1779, APS. TH, *D&L* 2:269, 270–271, 272, 293.

Chapter 19

1. De Valnais to Holker, 22 Apr. 1779, Holker 3. He married Eunice Quincy in 1781; see Edward Elbridge Salisbury, *Family Memorials*, 2 vols. (New Haven, Conn., 1885), 1:319–323.

2. *JCC* 13:97. *A&R* 20:636. *CJ*, 4 Mar. 1779. *DJR*, p. 326.

3. Nasatir and Monell, *FC*, pp. 9–12. De Valnais to Holker, 16 Mar., 6 May 1779, Holker 3.

4. De Valnais to Holker, 16 Mar., 29 Apr., 6 May 1779, Holker 3.

5. Overseers Records 3:161, Harvard University Archives. Gordon, p. 417. *SHG* 12:377–378. *IL*, 21, 28 June 1779. De Valnais to Gérard and Holker, 25 June 1779, Holker 4.

6. Doniol, *Histoire* 3:803–810. Morris, *Peacemakers*, pp. 14–16. John J. Meng, *The Comte de Vergennes: European Phases of His American Diplomacy (1774–1780)* (Washington, D.C., 1932), pp. 41–84.

7. Meng, *Gérard*, pp. 101–104. Burnett, *Letters* 4:69–71, 373–374.

8. For background on the fishery, see Harold A. Innis, *The Cod Fisheries:The History of an International Econcomy,* rev, ed., (Toronto, 1954), chs. 1–7. The importance of the fishery in Vergennes's thinking is discussed in Dallas D. Irvine, "The Newfoundland Fishery: A French Objective in the War of American Independence," *Canadian Historical Review* 13(1932):268–284; and Orville T. Murphy, "The Comte de Vergennes, the Newfoundland Fisheries, and the Peace Negotiations of 1783: A Reconsideration," *Canadian Historical Review* 47(1965):32–46.

9. Silas Deane to Vergennes, 18 Mar. 1777, *The Deane Papers, 3, Collections* of the New-York Historical Society (New York, 1888), pp. 25–27.

10. *JCC* 11:419–455.

11. Meng, *Gérard*, pp. 359, 546–547, 593–595, 606, 651, 655–656, 666–675, 804–814.

12. James F. Shepherd, "Commodity Exports from the British North American Colonies to Overseas Areas, 1768–1772: Magnitudes and Patterns of Trade," *Explorations in Economic History* 8(Fall 1970):5–76.

13. See n. 11 above.

14. Innis, *Cod Fisheries*, pp. 199–312. James F. Shepherd and Gary M. Walton, "Estimates of 'Invisible' Earnings in the Balance of Payments of the British North American Colonies, 1768–1772," *Journal of Economic History* 29(June 1969), 230–263.

15. *WSA* 4:126–128, 148–150.

16. Wharton, *DC* 2:292. Burnett, *Letters* 4:227–228.

17. Lovell's career is sketched in *SHG* 14:31–48.

18. H. James Henderson, *Party Politics in the Continental Congress* (New York, 1974), ch. 7.

19. Wharton, *DC* 3:175–178.

20. SC to SA, 14 Mar. 1779, SAP.

21. *CJ*, 22 Apr. 1779. *IC*, 22 Apr. 1779. Meng, *Gérard*, pp. 615–620, 626–630.

22. *IC*, 29 Apr. 1779.

23. Burnett, *Letters* 4:334. *JCC* 14:960–966. SC to SA, 13 May 1779, SAP.

24. Burnett, *Letters* 4:275n. *Secret Journals of the Acts and Proceedings of Congress* (1821, reprint. ed., New York, 1967), 2:173–189, 201–216. William Vernon to JA, 10 Apr. 1779, AM 350.

25. De Valnais to Holker, 22 Apr. 1779, Holker 3. Meng, *Gérard*, pp. 689–691. Burnett, *Letters* 4:276n–278n. Stinchcombe, *American Revolution*, pp. 68–69. *IL*, 21 June, 2 Aug., 20 Sept., 1 Nov. 1779. *BEP*, 11, 25 Sept. 1779.

26. De Valnais to Holker, 3 June 1779, Holker 4.

27. John J. Meng, "Secretary of Legation Meyer," *Records* of the American Catholic Historical Society of Philadelphia 46(1935):26–28.

28. TC to Samuel Holten, 28 July 1779, Boston Public Library.

29. Written 2 and 25 June, 1779, the letters are printed in Meng, *Gérard*, pp. 734, 787–788. The first, translated into French before being coded, begins by

referring to an earlier letter to Gérard that the writer had sent by Meyer. It is known that Meyer had carried a letter from SC to Holker; so he may also have carried one to Gérard. (De Valnais to Holker, 14 May 1779, Holker 3.) This letter mentions "our friend here," a natural way for SC to refer to de Valnais. The letter of 25 June, coded in English, seems to present a more detailed account of SC's activities described briefly by de Valnais in his report to Holker on 3 June. The private conversations and concern to make as few enemies as possible are very typical of SC. Thus it seems reasonable to make a tentative attribution to SC.

30. *IC*, 1 July 1779. Burnett, *Letters* 4:254–255, 227–228. *WAL* 2:117–119.

31. Meng, *Gérard*, p. 718.

32. *BTR*, 1778–1783, pp. 69–70.

33. *JHRM*, 1778, p. 5.

34. Wharton, *DC* 2:716–717.

35. De Valnais to Holker, 8, 15, 23 July 1779, Holker 4; 12 Aug. 1779, Holker 5.

36. Bigelow, *WBF*, 8:89–90. JA, *Diary* 2:380–400. Eugene Parker Chase, trans. and ed., *Our Revolutionary Forefathers: The Letters of Francois, Marquis de Barbé-Marbois* (New York, 1929), pp. 39–64, passim.

37. LL to Vergennes, 4 Aug. 1779, CPEU 9. *BG*, 30 Aug. 1779. *IL*, 30 Aug. 1779. Chase, *Revolutionary Forefathers*, pp. 65–66, 78–82. Brown, *Hancock*, p. 228. *WSA* 4:165.

38. LL to Vergennes, 18 Aug. 1779, CPEU 9; 3 Sept., CPEU 10.

39. LL to Vergennes, 3 Sept. 1779, CPEU 10. "Summary of the political and military Condition of America, 16 November 1779, in the hand of the Chevalier de Fleury," Stevens 1616.

40. SC to LL, 6 Oct. 1779; LL to SC, 25 Oct., 1 Nov. 1779, CP.

41. *JCC* 15:1107–1114. H. James Henderson, "Congressional Factionalism and the Attempt to Recall Benjamin Franklin," *WMQ* 27(Apr. 1970):246–247. Burnett, *Letters* 4:365, 381, 437–439, 443–448.

42. *JCC* 15:1115, 1127–1128. JA, *Diary* 2:400. SC to JA, 14 Nov. 1779, AM 350. Samuel Cooper Johonnot's journal of this voyage, entitled "A Journal by G.B.," is in AM 330.

43. SC to BF, 12 Nov. 1779, APS. Claude-Anne Lopez provides a full account of the career of SC's grandson in "A Story of Grandfathers, Fathers, and Sons," Yale University Library *Gazette*, 53(Apr. 1979):177–195.

44. SC to BF, 13 Nov. 1779, APS. JA, *Diary* 2:400–434. JA to SC, 23, 28 Feb. 1780, AM 96. JA to Gabriel Johonnot, 23 Feb. 1779, AM 96.

Chapter 20

1. Sermon: Rom. 14:17, 10 June 1764, CP.

2. John Clarke to Timothy Pickering, 21 Oct. 1779, Pickering MSS, MHS. LL to Vergennes, 18 Aug. 1779, CPEU 9. DT, *Diary*, pp. 79–82. SC to JA, 23 May 1780, AM 351.

3. Ferguson, *Power*, ch. 4. Ralph V. Harlow, "Economic Conditions in Massachusetts during the American Revolution," *CSMP* 20(1918):176–180. De Valnais to Holker and Daniel Bell to Holker, 25 Nov. 1779, Holker 6.

4. These efforts can be followed in *A&R* 5, 21; *BTR* 1778–1783; and the town's newspapers. For general discussions see Richard B. Morris, "Labor and Mer-

cantilism in the Revolutionary Era," in Richard B. Morris, ed., *The Era of the American Revolution* (1939; reprint ed., New York, 1965), pp. 110–112, 116–119; and Harlow, "Economic Conditions," pp. 180–182.

5. Ferguson, *Power*, pp. 30, 32.

6. *MHSC* 54(1891):171–178.

7. Ferguson, *Power*, 46–52, 65–69. Richard D. Brown, "The Confiscation and Disposition of Loyalists' Estates in Suffolk County, Massachusetts," *WMQ* 21(Oct. 1964):534–550. Oscar and Mary F. Handlin, "Revolutionary Economic Policy in Massachusetts," *WMQ* 4(1947):23–26.

8. Burnett, *Letters* 5:79. Wharton, *DC* 3:483–486.

9. LL to Vergennes, 14 Aug. 1780, CPEU 13. SC to LL, 13 July, 3 Aug. 1780, CP. *CJ*, 13 July 1780. *IC* 13 July, 10 Aug. 1780.

10. SC to LL, 15, 21 June; 13 July; 3, 17 Aug. 1780, CP. SC attributed to himself the following: "A Republican," *CJ*, 15 June 1780; "A Soldier," *CJ*, 15 June 1780; "A Soldier," *IC*, 15 June 1780; "Verus," *IC*, 22 June 1780; "Hambden," *IC*, 13 July 1780; "A Farmer," *IC*, 3 Aug. 1780. Judging by style and contents, he was also the writer of many more pieces appearing under these and other pseudonyms during this period. E.g.: "A Soldier," *BG*, 8 May 1780; "A Soldier," *BG*, 5 June 1780; "Sydney," *IC*, 8 June 1780; "A Soldier," *IC*, 6 July 1780; "A Soldier," *CJ*, 13 July 1780; "A Soldier," *IC*, 13 July 1780; "A Republican," *IC*, 17 Aug. 1780.

11. *A&R* 20:626; 21:70–71.

12. *BTR*, 1778–1783, p. 66. *A&R* 21:70–71. Handlin, *Sources*, pp. 404–431.

13. *BTR*, 1778–1783, pp. 83–84. Sketches of five of the seven lesser-known members are in *SHG*: Oliver Wendell, 12:367–374; Nathaniel Appleton, 12:355–359; John Lowell, 14:650–661; Samuel A. Otis, 14:471–480; Charles Jarvis, 16:376–383; and Samuel Barrett, 14:135–142. Ellis Gray was a Boston merchant who had served as representative, and Thomas Dawes was an architect-builder and currently a representative.

14. *Journal of the Convention for Framing a Constitution of Government for the State of Massachusetts Bay* (Boston, 1832), pp. 7–36. JA, *Diary* 2:401n. SC to LL, 15 June 1780, CP. SC to JA, 23 May 1780, AM 351. *SHG* 14:135–143.

15. *Journal of the Convention*, pp. 34–169.

16. Ibid., pp. 221–222.

17. Ibid., 228–249.

18. Ibid., pp. 130, 152, 154–155, 156, 159, 216–221. The committee to prepare the *Address* consisted of James Sullivan, a Groton lawyer soon to move to Boston to join forces with JH; three Boston delegates: Samuel Adams, John Lowell, and Ellis Gray; and the Reverend Samuel West, a popular Whig preacher of Dartmouth. It was assumed by Wells that SA was the principal author (William Wells, *The Life and Public Services of Samuel Adams*, 3 vols. [Boston, 1865], 3:89–96).

19. *BTR*, 1778–1783, pp. 125–129. The progress of Article III through the convention can be traced in the *Journal of the Convention*. The newspaper controversy began with the 1778 proposed constitution and continued through the next two years.

20. *Journal of the Convention*, p. 223. *BTR*, 1778–1783, pp. 129–130.

21. For Stillman see *SHG* 14:216–227.

22. John Eliot to Jeremy Belknap, 23 May 1780, *MHSC* 14(1891):187–189.

23. Ibid. *BTR*, 1778-1783, pp. 129–135.

24. *Journal of the Convention*, pp. 170–187. Handlin, *Sources*, pp. 475–930. Samuel Eliot Morison, "The Struggle Over the Adoption of the Constitution of Massachusetts, 1780," *MHSP* 50(1916–1917):358–401.

25. Van Beck Hall, *Politics Without Parties, Massachusetts, 1780–1791* (Pittsburgh, 1972), pp. 63–93, 347–348. Patterson, *Political Parties*, 247.

26. *WSA* 4:199–200.

27. For background, see Gordon Wood, *The Creation of the American Republic, 1776–1787* (Chapel Hill, N.C., 1969), parts 2, 3 passim.

28. *BTR, 1778–1783*, pp. 136–137. *WSA* 4:199–200, 205–206, 210, 211–212. *WAL* 2:135, 138–139. "Gordon," pp. 436–437.

29. *BTR, 1778–1783*, p. 150.

30. SC to JA, 8 Sept. 1780, AM 352. See also SC to BF, 8 Sept. 1780, APS.

31. *BTR, 1778–1783*, pp. 150–151.

32. *IL*, 30 Oct. 1780. DT, *Diary*, p. 85.

33. TH, *D&L* 2:353–355.

34. *A Sermon Preached before His Excellency John Hancock . . . October 25, 1780 . . .* [Boston, 1780], pp. 1–36.

35. Ibid., pp. 37–38. William G. McLoughlin, *New England Dissent, 1630–1833*, 2 vols. (Cambridge, Mass., 1971), 1:633.

36. *Sermon . . . October 25, 1780*, pp. 40–42.

37. Ibid., pp. 42–44. This section of the sermon praising France found its way into the French archives: "Extrait d'un Sermon prêché à Boston par le Dr. Cooper le 25 octobre 1780 pour le commencement de la nouvelle Constitution et l'inauguration du nouveau Gouvernement," CPEU 14.

38. Edward Oliver Fitch, ed., *The Diary of William Pynchon of Salem* (Boston, 1890), p. 77. *IC*, 2 Nov. 1780.

39. *Sermon . . . October 25, 1780*, pp. 45–47, 52.

40. *Diary of William Pynchon*, p. 78. *CJ*, 2 Nov. 1780.

41. Louis Gottschalk, *Lafayette and the Close of the American Revolution*, 2nd imp. (Chicago, 1965), pp. 1–80. Lafayette to Vergennes, 2 May 1780, Stevens 1623. SC to LL, 2 May 1780, CP. *IC*, 4 May 1780, and the other Boston newspapers for this week.

42. SC to LL, 2 May 1780, CP. Lafayette to Vergennes, 1 May 1780, Stevens 1622.

43. SC to JA, 23 May 1780, AM 351. *IC*, 18 May 1780. Lafayette to LL, 24 May 1780, *AHR* 20(Jan. 1915):348–349.

44. JA to Abigail Adams, 27 Feb. 1780, AM 351. Evelyn M. Acomb, ed. and trans., *The Revolutionary Journal of Baron Ludwig von Closen, 1780–1783* (Chapel Hill, N.C., 1958), pp. 65n, 72–73. LL to Sartine, 2 Dec. 1780, CPEU 14. Lafayette to LL, 24 May 1780, *AHR* 20(Jan. 1915):348–349. André Lasseray, *Les Français sous les Treize Etoiles*, 2 vols. (Paris, 1935), 1:202–206. Thomas Balch, ed., *The Journal of Claude Blanchard* (Albany, N.Y., 1876), pp. 51–52. De Valnais appears to have submitted no consular reports for the year 1780 (Nasatir and Monell, *FC*, pp. 11–12).

45. Acomb, *von Closen*, pp. 65–66. Balch, *Blanchard*, pp. 49–50, 85. *IC*, 4 Jan. 1781. LL to de Castries, 21 Mar. 1781, CPEU 16. JH Letterbook, 4 Jan. 1781, MHS. LL to Vergennes, 26 Jan. 1781, CPEU 15.

46. *A&R*, 5:1194–1196, 1369–1370. *Correspondence of the Late President Adams, Originally Published in the Boston Patriot* (Boston, 1809), pp. 159–165. Worthington Chauncey Ford, ed., *Statesman and Friend, Correspondence of John Adams with Benjamin Waterhouse, 1784–1822* (Boston, 1927), pp. 26–27.

47. "Gordon," pp. 445–446.

48. De Corny to SC, 27 Sept. 1780, CP. See also the loose sheet in CP that begins, "Si Mr. le Docteur pense . . ."

49. SC to LL, 2 May 1780, and [17 Aug. 1780], CP. SC to BF, 8 Sept. 1780, APS. SC to JA, 8 Sept. 1780, AM 352. SC to SA, 21 Sept. 1780, SAP. SC to Elliot, Stiles, and Huntington, 19 Sept. 1780, in Richard Henry Lee, *Life of Arthur Lee*, 2 vols. (Boston, 1829), 1:165–167. SA to SC, 7 Nov. 1780, *WSA* 4:216–218. BF to SC, 2 Dec. 1780, in Smyth, *WBF* 8:182–183. Arthur Lee to SC, 18 Jan. 1781, CP.

50. *WSA* 4:197. *MHSC* 54(1891):199. SC to LL, 13 July 1780, CP.

51. Claude C. Sturgill, ed., "Rochambeau's Mémoire de la Guerre en Amérique," *Virginia Magazine of History and Biography* 78(Jan. 1970):34–40. SC to JA, 8 Sept. 1780, AM 352. Arnold Whitridge, *Rochambeau* (New York, 1965), pp. 67–104. William Abbatt, ed., *Memoirs of Major-General William Heath* (New York, 1901), pp. 225–233. Gottschalk, *Lafayette and the Close*, pp. 94–141. William B. Willcox, *Portrait of a General* (New York, 1964), pp. 324–339.

52. Latouche to SC, 25 Aug. 1780, CP. SC to Latouche, 22 Sept. 1780, CP. *IC*, 14 Sept. 1780.

53. Abbatt, *Heath*, p. 234. Gottschalk, *Lafayette and the Close*, pp. 110–112.

54. SC to Latouche, 22 Sept. 1780, CP. De Corny to SC, 27 Sept. 1780, CP.

55. *IC*, 19 Oct., 14, 21 Dec. 1780. SC to LL, 14 Dec. 1780, CP. Wharton, *DC* 4:59. *WAL* 2:141.

56. 3 Nov. 1780, CPEU 14.

57. *JCC*, 18 passim. SA to SC, 7 Nov. 1780, *WSA* 4:216–218. Burnett, *Letters* 5:488–489.

58. LL to Vergennes, 3 Nov. 1780, CPEU 14.

59. SC to SA, 31 Dec. 1780, SAP. "Dans l'Armée de La Fayette; Souvenirs inédits du Comte de Charlus," *La Revue de Paris*, 64ᵉ annee (July 1957):94–110. JA to SC, 9 Dec. 1780, AM 102. Morris, *Peacemakers*, pp. 196–198.

60. AM 354.

61. Wharton, *DC* 4:254–256, 277, 278–279, 281–282, 317–318, 327–330.

62. TP to JH, 18 Dec. 1780, Palfrey MSS.

63. Wharton, *DC* 4:249–250, 252. SC to BF, 1 Feb. 1781, APS. SC to JA, 9 Feb. 1781, AM 351.

64. *BTR*, 1778–1783, pp. 161–164, 194–195, 204, 206.

65. Ibid., 1778–1783, pp. 165–170, 179–183, 185–186, 198–199, 201–202, 205–209, 210–211. *IC*, 18 Jan., 15 Mar. 1781.

66. Ferguson, *Power*, pp. 65–67. Fitch, *Pynchon*, p. 89. Jonathan Amory to his brother, 2 Mar. 1781, in Meredith, *Amory*, pp. 225–226. Receipts for SC's salary are in Smith-Carter MSS, MHS.

67. *BTR*, 1778–1783, pp. 177, 187, 205, 210. Burnett, *Letters* 5:502. DT, *Diary*, p. 89. *MHSC* 54(1891):211.

68. SC to LL, 1 Mar. 1781, CP. *JCC* 19:138–140, 208–224. St. George L. Sioussat, "The Chevalier de la Luzerne and the Ratification of the Articles of Confederation by Maryland, 1780–1781," *Pennsylvania Magazine of History and Biography* 60(Oct. 1936):391–418. Burnett, *Letters*, 5:548. Clarence L. Ver Steeg, *Robert Morris, Revolutionary Financier* (Philadelphia, 1954), pp. 72–77.

69. *IC*, 28 June, 12 July 1781. Morris, *Peacemakers*, ch. 5.

70. SC to BF, 1 Feb. 1781, APS. SC to d'Estaing [Feb. 1781], CP. An incomplete draft copy of the "letter" is in CP, box 1, and the whole was published in Edward E. Hale and Edward E. Hale, Jr., *Franklin in France*, 2 vols. (Boston, 1887–1888), 1:183–193. It seems to follow closely "Précis de la Campagne de 1778" (CP, box 1), which may have been prepared for SC by someone on d'Estaing's staff. For the controversy over d'Estaing's conduct, see Howard C. Rice, Jr., and

Anne S. K. Brown, trans. and eds., *The American Campaigns of Rochambeau's Army, 1780, 1781, 1782, 1783*, 2 vols. (New Haven, Conn. and Providence, R.I., 1972), 1:303–307. BF to SC, 15 May 1781, APS. On Franklin and the Abbé Morellet, see Claude-Anne Lopez, *Mon Cher Papa, Franklin and the Ladies of Paris* (New Haven, Conn., 1966), pp. 284–290. BF also informed SC that his "letter" would be published in the *Gazette de Leyde*; but the staff of the Papers of Benjamin Franklin at Yale University reports that no such item appeared in that periodical.

71. *IC*, 26 Apr. 1781.

72. This sketch is indebted to the following: Sturgill, "Rochambeau's Mémoire," pp. 50–63. Rice and Brown, *American Campaigns*, 1 passim. Gottschalk, *Lafayette and the Close*, chs. 9–13. Willcox, *Portrait of a General*, chs. 9–10. Whitridge, *Rochambeau*, chs. 9–13. Douglas S. Freeman, *George Washington*, 5(New York, 1952), chs. 17–23.

73. 26 Oct. 1781, *AHR* 8(1902):89–91.

74. SC to BF, 27 Oct. 1781, APS.

75. *IL*, 12 Nov. 1781.

76. Ibid.

Chapter 21

1. "Diary of a French Officer, 1781," *Magazine of American History* 4(1880):208.

2. Jean-Edmond Weelen, *Rochambeau, Father and Son*, trans. Lawrence Lee (New York, 1936), pp. 266–268.

3. Fitzpatrick, *WGW* 21:78–79, 339–340; 22:220–222, 337–338, 340–341, 436–437, 446–447, 454–455, 468–469.

4. *BTP* 1:444–445. *CJ*, 16 Nov. 1780.

5. *IL*, 27 Nov. 1780. J. Scollay to SA, 7 Jan. 1781, SAP. *WAL* 2:144–151, 157–158, 159–161. *WSA* 4:236–239. *CJ*, 21 Dec. 1780. Samuel A. Otis to SA, 10 Nov. 1780, SAP.

6. *WSA* 4:244–248. If SA had written "several Times" to SC, some of these letters were likely never delivered. Only one letter from this interval has survived, and SC denied knowledge of a request for information from SA.

7. 3 Apr. 1781, SAP.

8. *WSA* 4:258–260. [Jonathan Odell], *The American Times: A Satire in Three Parts. In which are Delineated the Characters of the Leaders of the American Rebellion* (London, 1780), pp. 7–8.

9. *WSA* 4:250–253, 255–258. *BTR*, 1778–1783, p. 193. Van Beck Hall, *Politics Without Parties, Massachusetts, 1780–1791* (Pittsburgh, 1972).

10. "Gordon," p. 471. *WSA* 4:226.

11. *BTR*, 1778–1783, pp. 152, 196, 247, 309, 312, 319–320.

12. Hall, *Politics*, pp. 104–114.

13. *BTR*, 1778–1783, pp. 197, 248, 312–314.

14. *CJ*, 1 May 1781.

15. Burnett, *Letters* 5:79–80, 96; 6:206.

16. *London Courant and Westminster Chronicle*, 6 Dec. 1780.

17. George Atkinson Ward, ed., *The Journal and Letters of Samuel Curwen* (Boston, 1864), pp. 298–299. *Royal Gazette*, 17 Feb. 1781.

18. Theodore Sizer, *The Autobiography of Colonel John Trumbull* (New Haven, Conn., 1953), pp. 72–75. *BTP* 1:455–463. JA, *Works* 7:457–459.

19. Marbois to Vergennes, 16 Oct. 1780, CPEU 14. LL to Vergennes, 1 June 1781, CPEU 17.

20. BT MSS, 26 Oct.–24 Dec. 1781, passim. *A&R*, 1780–1781, pp. 805–806. *CJ*, 5 Dec. 1782. *BTP* 1:464–469. JH to Robert Treat Paine, 23 Nov. 1781, John Hancock Letterbook, MHS. For the beginning of the newspaper controversy, see *BG*, 19 Nov., 3 Dec. 1781; and *IL*, 10 Dec. 1781.

21. *WSA* 4:267–268. *BTP* 1:454–455. *WAL* 2:250.

22. LL to Vergennes, 24 Nov. 1781, CPEU 19. Lafayette to LL, 22 Dec. 1781, *AHR* 20(Apr. 1915):611–612.

23. E. W. Balch, trans., "Narrative of the Prince de Broglie," *Magazine of American History*, 1(1877):379.

24. *CJ*, 3 Jan. 1782.

25. Nearly every issue of a Boston newspaper from Jan. through Mar. could be cited here, but see particularly the following: *CJ*, 17 Jan. 1782; *IL*, 11 Feb. 1782; *BEP*, 2 Feb. 1782.

26. *CJ*, 31 Jan., 14 Feb. 1782. *IL*, 18 Feb. 1782.

27. *IL*, 18 Feb. 1782.

28. *CJ*, 28 Feb. 1782.

29. *BTR*, 1778–1783, p. 245. *BG*, 6 May 1782. *JCC* 22:101–102. Samuel Osgood to James Lovell, 2 Mar. 1782, SAP. Arthur Lee to JB, 8 Mar. 1782, BT MSS. JH to Robert Treat Paine, 21 Mar. 1782, R. T. Paine MSS, MHS. *BG*, 11 Mar. 1782.

30. *BG*, 25 Mar. 1782.

31. SC to BF, 22 July 1782, APS. *CJ*, 5 Dec. 1782. JH to Senate and House, 24 Apr. 1782, BT MSS. JT's deposition that he had discussed his trip to England with SC, dated 10 May 1782, is in BT MSS. See also SC to SA, 15 Apr. 1779, SAP.

32. BT MSS, passim for June 1782. SC to BF, 22 July 1782. *CJ*, 5 Dec. 1782.

33. *CJ*, 11 July 1782. SC to BF, 6 Sept. 1782, APS. *A Sermon . . . Upon Occasion of the Reduction of Quebec* (Boston [1759]), pp. 47–48.

34. Thomas C. Amory, *Life of James Sullivan with Selections from His Writings*, 2 vols. (Boston, 1859). *SHG* 15:299–322.

35. SC to BF, 6 Sept. 1782, APS. *CJ*, 18, 25 July; 1, 8, 15, 22 Aug.; 5 Sept. 1782. *BG*, 5 Aug. 1782. *BEP*, 25 July, 17 Aug. 1782. *IC*, 22 Aug. 1782. The full controversy can be followed in each issue of the Boston newspapers.

36. *BEP*, 14 Sept. 1782.

37. SC to BF, 6 Sept. 1782, APS.

38. *BG*, 30 Sept. 1782. The annotated copy of Sullivan's deposition is in BT MSS.

39. *CJ*, 3 Oct. 1782.

40. *BEP*, 2, 16, 30 Nov.; 7, 14, 21 Dec. 1782. Samuel Dexter to JT, 16 Oct. 1782, and another letter, undated but near this date in BT MSS.

41. *BG*, 9, 16 Dec. 1782. *BTR*, 1778–1783, pp. 307–308.

42. *BTP* 2:12–21. James Sullivan to Benjamin Lincoln, 18 Nov. 1782, James Sullivan MSS, MHS. JB to TP, 20 Nov. 1783, *MHSP* 5(1860–1862):245–246. Jonathan Trumbull to Dartmouth, 1 Oct. 1783, Stevens, 2107. *WAL* 2:233–234. TH, *D&L* 2:399. Guy Carleton to JT, 15 Aug. 1783, BT MSS.

43. *WAL* 2:250–251, 263, 265.

44. *BTR*, 1778–1783, p. 309. "Gordon," pp. 493–494. *WAL* 2:219. *BEP*, 9 Aug., 29 Nov. 1783. *CJ*, 28 Aug. 1783. [SC] to [LL], 21 Nov. 1782, CP.

45. Stinchcombe, *American Revolution*, pp. 166–167. Burnett, *Letters* 7:115–117, 379.

46. Morris, *Peacemakers*, pp. 169–209.

47. *JCC* 20:605–619, 625–628, 638–640, 651–654. *Secret Journals of the Acts and Proceedings of Congress* (1821; reprint ed., New York, 1967), 2:408–449. O'Donnell, *La Luzerne*, pp. 122–138.

48. LL to Vergennes, 11 June 1781, CPEU 17.

49. SC to BF, 27 Oct. 1781, APS.

50. *Resolves of the General Court of . . . Massachusetts* [Boston, 1781], p. 80. *JCC* 21:1122n–1123n. *BTR*, 1778–1783, pp. 211, 212, 213–217, 218–219.

51. *JCC* 22:44–45. O'Donnell, *La Luzerne*, pp. 139–145. *WAL* 2:171–174.

52. Wharton, *DC* 4:702. JA to SC, 2 Mar. 1782, AM 102. *CJ*, 4 Oct. 1781. *IL*, 21 Jan. 1782. Létombe's consular reports are available in the United States on a Library of Congress microfilm: Archives Nationales, Affaires Étrangères, series B I, 209, Correspondance Consulaire, Boston, vol. I, 1779–1785. These reports are calendared in Nasatir and Monell, *FC*, pp. 12–27. For Létombe's taking up his duties, see fols. 54–144.

53. Lafayette to LL, 22 Dec. 1781, *AHR* 20(Apr. 1915):611–612. SC to LL, 1 Jan. 1782, CP; there is a translation of an extract of this letter in CPEU 20. LL to de Castries, 20 Jan. 1782, CPEU 20.

54. See Létombe's consular reports, fols. 127–128, 250–251, 252–254, 255, 260–263, 302–303; and particularly, Létombe to Castries, 18 July 1782, fol. 179 and the attachment, fol. 180. The advertisement by "M. M. Coulougnac, and Com'y. Merchants in Lyone, a City in France," ran in *IL*; e.g., 18 Mar. 1782.

55. SC to BF, 27 Oct. 1781, APS. William Phillips to Vaudreuil, 20 Aug. 1782; JH to Isaac Smith, et al., 14 Oct. 1781, E. Price MSS, MHS. Létombe's consular reports, fols. 57, 184. *MHSC* 54(1891):233. *IL*, 8 Oct. 1781.

56. SC to [LL], 13 June 1783, CP. SC to BF, 15 June 1782, APS. O'Donnell, *La Luzerne*, pp. 218–219. *CJ*, 20 June 1782. *IC*, 12 Dec. 1782. Letombe's consular reports, fols. 190–191. SA to LL, June 1782 [?], SAP.

57. SC to [LL], 13 June 1782, CP. *IC*, 13 June 1782. *BG*, 10 June 1782.

58. SC to BF, 6 Sept. 1782, APS. SC to [LL], 21 Nov. 1782, CP. The welcome for Vaudreuil is detailed in the Boston newspapers beginning 12 Aug. Evelyn M. Acomb, ed. and trans., *The Revolutionary Journal of Baron Ludwig von Closen, 1780–1783* (Chapel, Hill, N.C., 1958), p. 273.

59. *CJ*, 7 Nov. 1782. Howard C. Rice, Jr., ed., *Travels in North America in the Years 1780, 1781 and 1782 by the Marquis de Chastellux*, 2 vols. (Chapel Hill, N.C., 1963), 2:637, n. 53. John Eliot to Jeremy Belknap, 7 Dec. 1782, Eliot MSS, MHS. *MHSC* 54(1891):224–225.

60. L'Abbé Charles Nicolas Gabriel, *Le Maréchal de Camp Desandroüins, 1729–1792* (Verdun, 1887), p. 363. Notices of the writers and bibliographical details of this and other journals by French officers serving in the American War of Independence are conveniently provided by Howard C. Rice, Jr., and Anne S. K. Brown in *The American Campaigns of Rochambeau's Army*, 2 vols. (Princeton, N.J. and Providence, R.I., 1972), 1:285–345.

61. BF to SC, 8 Apr. 1782, BF Letterbook, L.C. Balch, "Narrative of the Prince de Broglie," pp. 378–379.

62. BF to SC, 7 Apr. 1782, BF Letterbook, LC. SC to BF, 21 Dec. 1782, CP. Eveline Cruickshanks, ed., *Memoirs of Louis Philippe, Comte de Ségur* (London, 1960), p. 161 and introduction.

63. Rice, *Chastellux*, 2:505–506. SC to [LL], 21 Nov. 1782, CP.

64. Mathieu Dumas, *Memoirs of His Own Time*, 2 vols. (London, 1839), 1:83–84.

65. Thomas Balch, ed., and William Duane, trans., *The Journal of Claude Blanchard* (Albany, 1876), p. 182.

66. Rice and Brown, *American Campaigns* 1:82.

67. SC to BF, 21 Dec. 1782, CP.

68. SC to du Bras, 23 Dec. 1782, CP.

69. Henry Adams, *The Life of Albert Gallatin* (1879; reprint ed., New York, 1943), pp. 10–44. Raymond Walters, Jr., *Albert Gallatin* (New York, 1957), pp. 11–15. Bigelow, *WBF* 8:227–228. G. L. de Marignac to BF, 9 Feb. 1782, APS. JA, *Works* 7:479. *Diary of William Bentley*, 4 vols. (1905–1914; reprint ed., Gloucester, Mass., 1962), 2:12.

70. "Gordon," pp. 470, 471, 476, 495.

71. Morris, *Peacemakers*, pp. 257–269. *BG*, 17 June 1782. James Lovell to SA, May 1782 [?], SAP. *Resolves of the General Court of . . . Massachusetts* (Boston, 1782), p. 40. *CJ*, 11 July 1782. SC to BF, 15 June, 22 July 1782, APS.

72. SC to JA, 22 July 1782, AM 357. Bigelow, *WBF* 9:366–370. Fitzpatrick, *WGW* 25:200–201.

73. Smyth, *WBF* 8:648.

74. Morris, *Peacemakers*, pp. 248–310.

75. Stinchcombe, *American Revolution*, pp. 190–193. Morris, *Peacemakers*, pp. 318–319, 324–326, 329–330. O'Donnell, *La Luzerne*, pp. 202–203. Wharton, *DC* 5:238–241.

76. Morris, *Peacemakers*, pp. 323–346. Smyth, *WBF* 8:638–649. Gerald Stourzh, *Benjamin Franklin and American Foreign Policy* (Chicago, 1954), pp. 163–185.

77. JA, *Diary* 3:37–85. Wharton, *DC* 6:11–49, 96–100. Morris, *Peacemakers*, pp. 355–384.

78. Wharton, *DC* 6:107–108, 150–153. Morris, *Peacemakers*, pp. 383–385.

79. *CJ*, 10, 17, 24 Apr. 1 May 1783.

80. E.g., *WAL* 2:184–187, 190–194; and JA, *Works* 7:652–654, 9:514–517.

81. Smyth, *WBF* 8:648–649.

82. This extract of SC to BF, 5 May 1783, is given here from Edward E. Hale and Edward E. Hale, Jr., *Franklin in France*, 2 vols. (Boston, 1887–1888), 2:202–204. The original has not been found, but a copy of this extract in an eighteenth-century hand is in APS. Both an English copy and a French translation of the extract are in CPEU 24.

83. Wharton, *DC* 6:686, 692–693, 696–697. BF made the same request of Henry Laurens, who had arrived only in time to sign the preliminary articles; see BF to Laurens, 10 Sept. 1783, South Carolina Historical Society.

84. O'Donnell, *La Luzerne*, pp. 236–237.

85. (Copy) JA to BF, 13 Sept. 1783, CP. Smyth, *WBF* 9:487. Richard Balche to BF, 21 June 1784, APS.

86. *WSA* 4:287–291.

Chapter 22

1. *CJ*, 23 May 1783. The classic account of Otis's last two years is William Tudor, *The Life of James Otis* (Boston, 1823), pp. 481–488.

2. *BTR*, 1778–1783, pp. 289–291, 294–295, 304–305. *IC*, 6 Mar. 1783.

3. *Acts and Laws of Massachusetts, 1782–1783* (Boston, 1783), pp. 707–708. *CJ*, 10 July 1783. *BTR*, 1778–1783, pp. 321–323. John Warren, *An Oration Delivered July 4th, 1783* (Boston, [1783]), pp. 10–20, 28, 30.

4. Conrad Wright, *The Beginnings of Unitarianism in America* (Boston, 1955), ch. 7 and passim. *CJ*, 27 May 1779. *BEP*, 29 May 1779. *IL*, 7 June 1779.

5. *MHSC* 54:225–226. Moses Everett, *A Sermon Preached at the Ordination of the Reverend Oliver Everett* (Boston, 1782).

6. *Diary of William Bentley*, 4 vols. (1905–1914; reprint ed., Gloucester, Mass., 1962), 1:ix–x; 2:418; 4:141–142. DT, *Diary*, pp. 95–96. Henry W. Foote, *James Freeman and King's Chapel, 1782–87* (Boston, 1873), pp. 3–8. Hamilton Andrews Hill, *History of the Old South Church*, 2 vols. (Boston, 1890), 2:211–212, 215–218, 224.

7. Foote, *Freeman*, pp. 9–29. Wright, *Beginnings*, pp. 210–212.

8. *Laws and Resolves of Massachusetts, 1782–83*, pp. 63–70. *BTR*, 1778–1783, pp. 280–285.

9. *BTR*, 1778–1783, pp. 294, 312–315. *BEP*, 19 Apr., 31 May 1783.

10. SC to JA, 22 July 1782, AM 257.

11. *JCC* 19:110–113, 421–427. Jackson Turner Main, *The Antifederalists* (Chapel Hill, N.C., 1961), pp. 72–84. Merrill Jensen, *The New Nation* (1959; reprint ed., New York, 1965), pp. 57–58. E. James Ferguson, "The Nationalists of 1781–1783 and the Economic Interpretation of the Constitution," *Journal of American History* 56(Sept. 1969):241–261. Van Beck Hall, *Politics Without Parties* (Pittsburgh, Pa., 1972), pp. 147–151.

12. *WSA* 4:272–275. John Lowell to SA, 8 July 1782, SAP. *JCC* 22:361. Hall, *Politics*, pp. 148–152. Burnett, *Letters* 7:123–124, 166–167. SC to [LL?], 13 June 1782, CP.

13. *JCC* 24:207–210, 256–262; 25:607–613. Main, *Antifederalists*, pp. 86–87. Hall, *Politics*, pp. 147–149, 153–157. Jensen, *New Nation*, pp. 74–76. Ferguson, *Power*, pp. 210–212.

14. SC to BF, 16 Oct. 1783, APS. *Acts and Laws . . . of Massachusetts . . . 1783* (Boston, 1783), pp. 40–42.

15. Wharton, *DC* 6:536–537, 703. Burnett, *Letters* 7:333–335.

16. *CJ*, 27 Feb. 1783. Jackson Turner Main, in *Political Parties before the Constitution* (Chapel Hill, N.C., 1973), demonstrates the tendency from 1783 to 1789 for legislators to align themselves into cosmopolitan or localist blocs and view the main issues accordingly. In May 1783 a committee appointed by the town meeting and chaired by SA had instructed the Boston representatives to guard against delegating further power to Congress (*BTR*, 1778–1783, pp. 310, 313). For other examples of growing localism, see *CJ*, 6 Nov. 1783; *WAL* 2:229–232; and Burnett, *Letters* 7:414–416.

17. For background, see Ferguson, "Nationalists of 1781–1783."

18. *A&R* 20:433–434. Lorenzo Sabine, *Biographical Sketches of Loyalists of the American Revolution*, 2 vols. (Boston, 1864), 1:248–249.

19. *SHG* 14:568–572. Hall, *Politics*, 138–140. Main, *Parties before the Constitution*, pp. 90–92.

20. *SHG* 14:151–157. *BTP* 1:472–479.

21. SC to BF, 6 Sept. 1782, APS. Meredith, *Amory*, pp. 209–245.

22. JA to SC, 10 Sept. 1783, AM 106. Hall, *Politics*, pp. 138–142. Richard D. Brown, "The Confiscation and Disposition of Loyalists' Estates in Suffolk County, Massachusetts," *WMQ* 21(Oct. 1964):538–540. David Edward Maas, "The

Return of the Massachusetts Loyalists," (Ph.D., diss., University of Wisconsin, 1972), passim.

23. John Fortescue, ed., *The Correspondence of King George the Third: from 1760 to December 1783* (new imp.; London, 1967), 4:353. Edward E. Hale and Edward E. Hale, Jr., *Franklin in France*, 2 vols. (Boston, 1887–1888), 2:22. John A. Schutz, *Thomas Pownall* (Glendale, Calif., 1951), pp. 256–262.

24. *MHSP* 5(1860–1862):244–248. *MHSP* 16(1878):178–179. *BTP* 2:3, 5–6, 23.

25. Jared Sparks, ed., *Correspondence of the American Revolution*, 4(Boston, 1853):49–50.

26. SC to BF, 20 Nov. 1783, APS. *BEP*, 3 Jan. 1784. William Sullivan, *The Public Men of the Revolution* (Philadelphia, 1847), p. 66.

27. *BTP* 2:29. "Gordon," p. 502. *MHSC* 54(1891):269. *BG*, 19 Jan. 1784.

28. Printed as a broadside, the funeral anthem was also published with Phillis [Wheatley] Peters, *An Elegy Sacred to the Memory of that Great Divine, the Reverend and Learned Dr. Samuel Cooper* (Boston, 1784).

29. John Clarke, *A Sermon Delivered . . . at the Interment of the Rev. Samuel Cooper* (Boston, 1784), p. 25.

30. *BG*, 19 Jan. 1784, and the other Boston newspapers for this week. Sullivan's manuscript of this obituary is among his MSS at MHS.

31. *WSA* 4:291. *MHSC* 54(1891):269.

32. LL to Vergennes, 30 Mar. 1784, LL, Letterbooks. Barbé-Marbois to Vergennes, 1 Apr. 1785, CPEU 29.

33. Smyth, *WBF* 9:144–146. James Sullivan to Henry Knox, 17 Dec. 1783, James Sullivan MSS, MHS. LL to Vergennes, 30 Mar. 1784, LL, Letterbooks. Claude-Anne Lopez, "A Story of Grandfathers, Fathers, and Sons," Yale University Library *Gazette* 53(Apr. 1979):187–194. SC to Samuel Cooper Johonnot, 26 Dec. 1782, 23 June 1783, Yale University Library.

34. Overseers Records 3:268–269, Harvard University Archives. The degree was in recognition of his study at the Academy of Geneva. He also received the customary M.A. three years later.

35. Suffolk County, Mass., Probate Records 83:8–10; 96:672; 605:127–128; 610:318. Jonathan Williams to BF, 29 Dec. 1783, APS. One-third of the estate went to the widow and another one-third to Abigail Cooper Hixon, whose share was protected from her husband by a trust. A draft copy of the will is in CP. The estate was still unsettled in 1888, when the probate court ordered an inventory within three months; but none was filed. It is possible that WC2, clerk of probate, and his brother-in-law, Oliver Wendell, judge of probate, connived to prevent a revelation of SC's income from France by postponing a settlement of the estate. If so, they were completely successful.

36. William Willis, ed., *Journals of the Rev. Thomas Smith, and the Rev. Samuel Deane* (Portland, Maine, 1849), p. 355n.

A Note on the Manuscripts of Samuel Cooper

Twentieth-century historians have had easy access to the extant manuscripts of Samuel Cooper and have used them sporadically in countless studies. But because his papers were widely scattered and his importance concealed by his profession, until now no one has studied the entire body of manuscripts in an effort to determine his place in Revolutionary Boston.

The Henry E. Huntington Library of San Marino, California, has the largest collection of Cooper's personal papers. These include a number of family documents and some correspondence, of which the most important items concern his connection with France. The bulk of the collection consists of 146 of Cooper's manuscript sermons and 45 of his father's. Thirty-two sermons, plus a few fragments, are in the New York Public Library. Hardly exciting or easy reading, these sermons are nonetheless the essential documentation for the nature of Cooper's ministry and the relationship of his preaching to the American Revolution.

Letters to Cooper from Pownall and Franklin, together with drafts of his to them, were carried to England during the American Revolution by a Boston loyalist. This collection, now in the British Museum (King's MSS 202–204), has been largely published. "Letters of Samuel Cooper to Thomas Pownall, 1769–1777," ed. Frederick Tuckerman, appeared in the *American Historical Review*, 6 (January 1930):301–330. Pownall's letters to Cooper were included with general completeness and accuracy in Frederick Griffin's *Junius Discovered* (Boston, 1854), a mistaken attempt to prove that Pownall was the mysterious Junius. The Franklin–Cooper correspondence for 1769 to 1774, which is at the British Museum and the American Philosophical Society, has received definitive publication in volumes 16–21 of *The Papers of Benjamin Franklin*, ed. William B. Willcox (New Haven: Yale University Press, 1972–1978). But only one-fourth of the letters from 1775 to 1783 appear in the older editions of Franklin's works: *The Works of Benjamin Franklin*, ed. John Bigelow, 12 vols. (New York, 1904); and *The Writings of Benjamin Franklin*, ed. Henry Albert Smyth, 10 vols. (New York, 1907). The majority of the letters for this period are in the possession of the American Philosophical Society, and the remainder are dispersed among several institutions.

The correspondence of Cooper with John Adams, nearly all unpublished, is available in the microfilms of the Adams Papers, Massachusetts Historical Society, reels 89, 91, 93, 96, 102, 106, 345-352, 357. The Samuel Adams Manuscripts, New York Public Library, contain Cooper's letters to Samuel Adams and drafts of Adams's to Cooper. Only a few of these appear in *The Writings of Samuel Adams*, ed. Harry A. Cushing, 4 vols. (New York, 1904-1908).

After Cooper's death the almanacs in which he kept his diaries were scattered by some unknown process, and the majority were lost. The diary for 7 January 1753–13 January 1754, now in the New-York Historical Society, was published in *The New England Historical and Genealogical Register*, 41 (1887): 338-391. Among the Cooper Papers in the Huntington Library are the diaries for 1 January 1764–2 February 1765, 22 October–31 December 1769 (published in the *Register*, 55 [1901]: 145-149); and 19 April 1775–17 May 1776 (published in the *American Historical Review*, 6 [1901]:301-341). The Massachusetts Historical Society has a diary fragment for 10 April–18 April 1775, and what seems to be a separate diary with longer entries for 10, 27, 30 April 1775.

The Published Works of Samuel Cooper

A Sermon Preached to the Ancient and Honourable Artillery Company, in Boston, New-England, June 3. 1751. Being the Anniversary of their Election of Officers. Boston, 1751.

A Sermon Preached in Boston, New-England, Before the Society for Encouraging Industry, and Employing the Poor; August 8. 1753. Boston, 1753.

[attribution uncertain] *The Crisis.* Boston, 1754.

A Sermon Preached in the Audience of His Honour Spencer Phips, Esq; Lieutenant Governor and Commander in Chief; the Honourable His Majesty's Council; and the Honourable House of Representatives, of the Province of the Massachusetts-Bay in New-England, May 26th. 1756. Being the Anniversary for the Election of His Majesty's Council for the said Province. Boston, 1756.

A Sermon Preached before His Excellency Thomas Pownall, Esq; Captain-General and Governor in Chief, The Honourable His Majesty's Council and the House of Representatives, of the Province of the Massachusetts-Bay in New-England, October 16th, 1759. Upon Occasion of the Success of His Majesty's Arms in the Reduction of Quebec. Boston, [1759].

A Sermon Preach'd April 9. 1760. At the Ordination of the Reverend Mr. Joseph Jackson, to the Pastoral Care of the Church in Brooklin. Boston, 1760.

A Sermon upon Occasion of the Death of Our late Sovereign, George the Second. Preach'd before His Excellency Francis Bernard, Esq; Captain-General and Governor in Chief, the Honourable His Majesty's Council, and House of Representatives, of the Province of the Massachusetts-Bay in New-England, January 1. 1761. At the Appointment of the Governor and Council. Boston, 1761.

A Discourse on the Man of Sin; Delivered in the Chapel of Harvard College, in Cambridge, New-England, September 1, 1773: At the Lecture, Founded by the Honorable Paul Dudley, Esq. Boston, 1774. Second edition, corrected, Boston, 1774.

A Sermon Preached before His Excellency John Hancock, Esq; Governour, the Honourable the Senate, and House of Representatives of the Commonwealth of Massachusetts, October 25, 1780. Being the Day of the Commencement of the Constitution, and Inauguration of the New Government. [Boston, 1780.]

Index